SIDNEY RIGDON

Sidney Rigdon

date unknown (courtesy Archives, Church of Jesus Christ of Latter-day Saints).

SIDNEY RIGDON

A Portrait of Religious Excess

BY

Richard S. Van Wagoner

SIGNATURE BOOKS ❦ SALT LAKE CITY
1994

Jacket design: Randall Smith Associates

❧

Drawing on jacket: Sidney Rigdon, in A. W. Cowles,
"The Mormons: Pen and Pencil Sketches, Illustrating their Early History,"
Moore's Rural New Yorker, 23 January 1869, 61.

❧

Sidney Rigdon: A Portrait of Religious Excess
was printed on acid-free paper and meets the permanence
of paper requirements of the American National Standard for
Information Sciences. This book was composed,
printed, and bound in the United States.

98   97   96   95   94   6   5   4   3   2   1

Library of Congress Cataloging-in-Publication Data
Van Wagoner, Richard S.
Sidney Rigdon : a portrait of religious excess /
Richard S. Van Wagoner.
p.   cm.
Includes bibliographical references and index
ISBN 1-56085-030-2
1. Rigdon, Sidney, 1793 - 1896.
2. Mormon converts—United States—Biography.   I. Title.
BX8695.R56V36 1993
289.3'092—dc20
[B]   92-17137
CIP

To Mary,

the center of my universe

Contents

Acknowledgements

I appreciate the assistance of archives, special collections, and library staffs at the historical department, Church of Jesus Christ of Latter-day Saints (Salt Lake City, Utah); the Marriott Library, University of Utah (Salt Lake City); the Lee Library, Brigham Young University, (Provo, Utah); the Utah State Historical Society (Salt Lake City); and the Cuba (New York), Friendship (New York), and Lehi (Utah) public libraries. Special assistance was provided by Stan Larson (Marriott Library); Research Publications (Woodbridge, Connecticut); Vaughn Chapman (Finleyville, Pennsylvania); Myrtle S. Hyde (Ogden, Utah); H. Michael Marquardt (Sandy, Utah); the Reverend Stanley Smith (Salt Lake City); and my three daughters, Lisa Mortensen, Amanda Gray, and Jennifer Van Wagoner.

In addition, I wish to thank the editors and staff of Signature Books for their consideration and friendship as well as professionalism in bringing this biography to publication. Gary James Bergera first suggested the idea of a Rigdon biography many years ago. I thank him for his persistence in bringing Sidney and me together. I am indebted to a number of other people for inspiration and suggestions at various stages of this work. Mary C. Van Wagoner and Trea West in particular profoundly shaped my thinking, writing, and organization. Aside from their valuable contributions, however, I am entirely responsible for the final outcome of this book.

Introduction

History is always written wrong; that is why it is necessary to rewrite it.

—George Santayana

Among the many American millennialist groups of the nineteenth century, the Latter-day Saints boast a particularly interesting past. Thriving on the spectacular, the faith counts heroic martyrs, epic treks, supernatural manifestations, and valiant struggles against hostile powers. An attraction to prophetic posturing and swagger resides deep in the Mormon psyche, which seems inordinately susceptible to legend and exaggeration. Joseph Smith, Jr., and Brigham Young, figures of mythic scale, live on in the souls of millions of modern followers. But long before Young entered the stage through a side door after the drama had already started, Sidney Rigdon, a fiery ex-Baptist preacher, emerged as Smith's foremost adviser, strategist, and divinely-appointed spokesman, a role the Book of Mormon had predicted thousands of years earlier.

Together Rigdon and Smith, in a theological partnership, led a nineteenth-century religious revolution that is still on-going in many respects. Rigdon's role in the birth of Mormonism was substantial, yet the lion's share of his contribution has been obscured by official alteration of original records. Once the hierarchy began to tidy up Mormon history, Rigdon was swept out the back door.

Born in 1793 in the rolling hill country near Pittsburgh, Pennsylvania, Rigdon seemed propelled from an early age to avoid the sweat, dirt, and menial labor of the farmstead. His lengthy quest for self-validation, like a compass needle in search of True North, led him into the Baptist ministry.

Well suited for preaching, Rigdon was blessed with a powerful and mellifluous voice, enthusiasm, and a prodigious memory for scripture. His listeners gulped his words in like a gush of cool water. An avatar of eloquence who carried the flame of the visionary tradition, he could sway by the sheer force of his faith, passion, and ideological fervor.

But Rigdon did not ease through mortality on silver wings. His eighty-three years transcend everyday tragedy. He simply cannot be measured by an ordinary yardstick. Episodically his existence was overshadowed by melancholia, a metaphysical sadness best known today as Bipolar Affective Disorder or Manic-Depressive Illness. Rigdon's debilitation, possibly precipitated by a childhood head injury, often plunged him into the blackest despair or spiraled him into unrealistic ecstasy or religious compulsiveness.

Although Rigdon led as tragic a life as his God would allow, he was fed by the well-springs of Baptist origin and was a preeminent seeker of truth. Prior to converting to Mormonism he was a leading figure in the Reformed Baptist Movement, led by Alexander Campbell, a spiritual descendant of early Christian reformers of the sixteenth and seventeenth centuries. His prospects in that association, however, were eventually punctured by theological swordplay with Campbell.

While licking his wounds at his Mentor, Ohio, home, Rigdon was visited by Mormon missionaries en route to the western frontier. Presented a copy of the Book of Mormon, Rigdon quickly assessed that it affirmed his own beliefs in a literal gathering of Israel and an imminent millennium. Baptized into the new movement, the former minister was forever bound to Joseph Smith.

Serving as Smith's chief aide and collaborator, Rigdon participated in virtually every major Mormon endeavor, except polygamy, and helped to shape many of the distinctive practices and teachings of the 1830s. Few Latter-day Saints cast a larger shadow on the church's history. But a combination of health problems and ultimate loss of faith in Smith resulted in the diminishment of Rigdon's position of eminence.

After Smith's 1844 murder, Rigdon and Brigham Young engaged in an ecclesiastical dogfight for primacy. Young, a masterful strategist with a political adroitness Rigdon lacked, won the mantle. Rigdon was excommunicated and consigned to outer darkness.

Some think the central drama of Rigdon's life played out in Nauvoo, Illinois, but he lived for another thirty-two eventful years in Pennsylvania and New York. Never losing faith in himself, he refused to let his religious talent be buried in dotage. Though imposing a mysterious sentence of self-exile, he began accumulating a mass of theological information, insights, ideas, and questions for which there was no outlet, no opportunity to expound or express.

Just as Rigdon found himself paddling in the doldrums, a group of former Mormons approached him by mail and provided the impetus for his continued involvement in religious controversy. His personal poverty, curmudgeonly qualities, and malevolent temperament prevented him from governing in person. So Rigdon presided over his distant followers through hundreds of written communications and a spokesman named Stephen Post.

Rigdon's life-long orientation left him passionately preoccupied with religion. This was the enticing mistress that filled the empty spaces in his psyche. His son Wickliffe wrote that his father "was from his youth a [very] religious man who believed that religion was the greatest subject for man[']s contemplation in the world and his whole life was devoted to that cause."[1] Like other addicts he was not satisfied with the cruel, ruthless realities of mortal existence. He lived his entire adult life in the pursuit of Zion, longing for the blessed hope of the Second Advent. In the process, he lost the natural, slow rhythm of life. His constant rushing towards the ideal left him haunted to his death by the specter of greatness unachieved.

The contradictions of religious fanaticism are fascinating. There is something powerful and compelling about the manner in which intense ardor can imprison the human soul. One of the striking facts in the lives of many of the world's religious leaders is their apparent abnormality, an eccentric nature sometimes erupting into psychosis. Prominent Mormon psychiatrist Louis A. Moench has written that "the line between religious thought or behavior and mental disorder is sometimes thin."[2] Adding insight to this theory, Lillian H. Robinson, professor of psychiatry at Tulane University School of Medicine, wrote that religion, although "not a disease, like compulsive defenses it can become pathological when it is excessive, maladaptive, and totally preoccupying."[3]

"Zealot" describes all that Sidney Rigdon was—a masterpiece of tortured ambivalence and religious fanaticism. A man of vast eccentricity, he is a biographer's dream. As both a fifth-generation Mormon and a rock-ribbed skeptic, I have a spiritual thirst for wholeness: a union with God. I do not apologize for exposing the warts and double chins of religious leaders. Fallible men and women are all God has on earth. Perhaps through the observations and interpretations I attempt here, others will feel more at ease with their own wrinkles.

Notes

1. J. Wickliffe Rigdon, "Life Story of Sidney Rigdon," archives, Historical Department, Church of Jesus Christ of Latter-day Saints, Salt Lake City, Utah.

2. Louis A. Moench, "Mormon Forms of Psychopathology," *AMCAP Journal*, Mar. 1985, 64.

3. Lillian H. Robinson, ed., *Psychiatry and Religion: Overlapping Concerns* (Washington, D.C.: American Psychiatric Press, Inc., 1986), 76.

Section 1.

The Baptist Years

CHAPTER 1.

Peters Creek

The Ohio, one of North America's great rivers, originates in the Appalachian Plateau of Western Pennsylvania at the junction of the Allegheny and the Monongahela. From the 1600s on, the Ohio Valley, claimed by both France and England, has played a strategic role in the development of the continent.

Major George Washington, dispatched on a surveying mission to the valley by Governor Dinwiddie of Virginia, established a British fort at the fork of the Ohio in 1754. Before its completion, it was captured by the French, who named it Fort Duquesne. After years of conflict, British general John Forbes moved on the fort in 1758, finding it in flames and the French in flight.

To assure their dominance at the source of the Ohio, the British in 1761 constructed a five-sided stronghold, Fort Pitt, named in honor of the British statesman William Pitt the Elder. After defeating Pontiac's native forces in 1763 and resolving a boundary dispute between Pennsylvania and Virginia, the influx of settlers in the Pittsburgh area rose dramatically. The American Revolution's conclusion raised the floodgates.

Typical of immigrants to the Allegheny frontier was Sidney Rigdon's father William, a prominent Harford County, Maryland, resident prior to his removal west.[1] William and thirty-four others, duly elected by the citizenry, signed the Bush Declaration of 22 March 1775, believed to be the first Declaration of Independence issued by a representative body in America. "We the Committee of Harford County," began the resolution:

> having most seriously and maturely considered the Resolves and Association of the Continental Congress, and the Resolves of the Provincial Convention, do most heartily approve of the same and as we esteem ourselves in a more particular manner intrusted by our constituents to see them carried into execution, we do most solemnly pledge ourselves to each other, and to our Country, and engage ourselves by every tie held sacred among mankind to perform the same at the risque of lives and fortunes.[2]

In 1776 William Rigdon put his name to the "Declaration of the Association of Freemen of Maryland," drawn up by delegates to the state convention at Annapolis. Copies of the declaration had been sent for signing to war committees in various counties. Those refusing to sign were fined or imprisoned. Rigdon and others pledged, in part, as follows:

> We, inhabitants of Maryland, firmly persuaded that it is necessary and justifiable to repel force by force, do approve of the opposition of arms to the British Troops.

We do unite and associate, as one band, and firmly and solemnly engage and pledge ourselves to each other that we will, to the utmost of our power, promote and support the present opposition.

We do in like manner, unite, associate, and solemnly engage in the maintenance of good order and the public peace to support the civil power in the due execution of the laws, so far as may be consistent with the present plan of opposition.[3]

During the Revolutionary War William served as a private in Company No. 12, commanded by his older brother Alexander Rigdon. After the war, William, who owned a large plantation and a number of slaves, decided that "from conscientious scruples in regard to the lawfulness of slavery," he should free his slaves. He did so, sold his property, and moved to the southwest corner of Pennsylvania with his older brother Thomas.[4]

The Rigdon brothers settled in Washington County, later to become Allegheny County, about fifteen miles from Pittsburgh. On 10 February 1785, 150 acres of land were granted Thomas Rigdon. Eight months later William received 358 and 3/8 acres situated nearby along the Piney Fork branch of Peters Creek in St. Clair Township.[5]

The township—today comprising more than a dozen communities, including Library, the city closest to the Rigdon homesite—was bounded by the Ohio River, the Monongahela River, and Chartiers Creek. An 1805 description claimed the township was a "full fifteen miles in length ranging in breadth from six to ten miles."[6]

Past forty, William Rigdon married Nancy Gallaher, eldest daughter of Bryant and his second wife Elizabeth Reid Gallaher. The Gallaher family had moved to Pennsylvania from New Jersey and apparently lived in St. Clair Township also. William and Nancy Rigdon became the parents of four children. Carvel was born in 1790; Sidney S.[7] entered the world on 19 February 1793, followed by Loammi (also spelled Loami and Loamie) in 1796 and by Lacy (the only daughter), who arrived in 1799.

Although the family had neighbors—the Larimers, Wallaces, Riggses, and Murrays—the region was still wild and unstable when the Rigdon brothers first settled. Only three years before, a nearby Indian attack massacred seven members of a Baptist minister's family. The minister, his wife, and their ten children had set out on foot for religious services a half-a-mile away. Absorbed in thought, the father had lingered behind, and he was soon aroused by shrieks. Rushing ahead, he saw his family being attacked. His wife screamed for him to escape, which he succeeded in doing. His family, all tomahawked and scalped, were left for dead although two daughters survived.[8]

Aside from the dangers of newly settled areas, daily hardship was taxing. Children were expected to work alongside their parents, with little time for play or self-improvement. William Rigdon, a stern man with rigid ways, viewed idleness as wicked. Book learning, aside from common school education obtained at the nearby log school during the winter, was deemed unacceptable.

Young Sidney, introverted and melancholy, held a contrary opinion about learning. Possessing a restless mind that revealed itself early, he began borrowing books from whomever would lend them and spent time alone, pondering and reading. A son, Wickliffe, later wrote that Sidney "was never known to play with the boys; reading books was the greatest pleasure he could get."[9] Rigdon himself recalled that in his youth he had "an insatiable thirst for reading."[10]

History, literature, English grammar, and the Bible were Sidney's passions. Wickliffe, who eventually became an attorney, noted that his father "was as familiar with the Bible as a child is with his spelling book." Sidney enjoyed an impressive memory and could recall "everything he read and in this way he laid up a fund of Knowledge that was of great value to him in later years. . . . [H]e was regarded as a well informed young man in the community in which he lived."[11]

But William Rigdon did not support his son's passion for books, particularly when reading interfered with chores. He refused the boy's request for candles to read by after dark. Undaunted, Sidney gathered a supply of hickory bark. At nightfall, after his parents had retired, he would burn the bark in the fireplace and read by the hearth.

Upon completing his common school education, Rigdon wanted more, but the opportunity for further education fell instead to his younger brother Loammi, who, because of an unspecified medical condition, was less suited for strenuous work. Wickliffe explained that "It was the rule in the country, that when a boy was too feeble to work on a farm they would send him to school [higher education]. . . . Sidney Rigdon wanted to go to school and pleaded with his father and mother to let him . . . but they would not consent . . . saying to him that he was able to work on the farm and he could not go."[12]

When Sidney was seventeen, his sixty-two-year-old father became incapacitated by illness and dictated his will on 22 May 1810. Nancy was bequeathed the home, outbuildings, timber rights, and one third of the farmstead. To Carvel was given "one hundred acres of land on the Southeast end of my plantation." Sidney, still underage, was nevertheless willed "one hundred acres of land on the North side," while Loammi, also underage, was given the remainder of the land. The elder Rigdon also "designed my son Loammi to be a Physician. I wish him to be conducted through the learning and studies at the expense of the monies that I have appropriated for that purpose and under the care and discretion of my executors."

William insisted that all the farm profits go to his wife because "My son Carvel is now an apprentice. My son Loammi is in learning and have not got through his studies, and my son Sidney under age. Therefore, I give and bequeath all the profits of my Plantation to my beloved wife until my three sons are clear of the above imbarrisements to enjoy it themselves." Lacy was not given property. Instead she was allowed "two thirds part of my personal estate to be husbanded for her interest in the best manner prudence may dictate by my executors." The will further stipulated that the three sons pay their sister $300 at their mother's death.[13]

William died four days later. Although Sidney stayed on the farm for another nine years, until he was twenty-six, he could not quell the restless stirrings to break free of farm life. A neighbor, Isaac King, later affirmed that Rigdon's farming was rewarded with "indifferent success." The general verdict ran that "he was too lazy or too proud to make a good farmer."[14] A more likely possibility—one Sidney suggested—was that God had put his signature on Sidney's brain. In 1868, enraptured in prophetic loquacity, Rigdon intoned: "From his earliest infancy my fear saith the Lord was the ruling principle in his heart. . . . I the Lord called him from his plow as I did Amos from among the herdsmen of Tekoa."[15]

William and Nancy Rigdon had both been born during the apex of the Second Great Awakening, the religious fervor which had spread throughout the colonies by the 1770s. More spectacular perhaps was the religious excitement along the American frontier known as the Great Revival in the West. This new evangelical surge significantly restructured religious bodies and established new sects, culminating in the unprecedented growth of denominations most suited to meet the needs of the ebullient and individualistic frontier society.

Although William's parents, George and Elizabeth Rigdon, were mid-eighteenth century Quakers, that faith became suspect during the Revolution because of its presumed association with Toryism.[16] Baptist congregations, democratically governed to defend religious liberty, were more attuned with the new nation. To people like William Rigdon, fiercely devoted to liberty and highly individualistic, the Baptist church—previously the most despised of all religious sects in colonial America—had strong appeal.[17] At the time of Sidney's birth the Baptists had been transformed from a persecuted and disinherited sect to the largest Protestant denomination in America, although their numbers remained small in Allegheny County.

Baptists had not taken stock of the wilderness west of the Alleghenies until the middle of the eighteenth century, nor was the Ohio watershed territory—the Mississippi and the Great Lakes—known to most evangelical churches, although it had been thoroughly traversed by Jesuits years before. The Baptist church in western Pennsylvania originated from a migration of disaffected and "persecuted members of the church from Virginia" about 1768. These outcasts crossed the Monongahela River into Greene, Gayette, and possibly Washington counties, then likely into Bedford or Cumberland County.[18]

Peters Creek Baptist Church, organized in St. Clair Township, near the Rigdon home, on 10 November 1773, was the first Baptist church established in western Pennsylvania (and still exists today in Library). The Reverend William

H. Whitsitt, a Baptist minister and late-nineteenth-century biographer of Sidney Rigdon, speculated that William Rigdon was a member of the Peters Creek congregation. Circumstantial evidence is persuasive that he was. The minister, Reverend David Philips, witnessed the dictation of William's will, and it is known that William's brothers Thomas and Stephen were Baptists. Furthermore, in an article signed "Titus" in an early *Christian Baptist*, which Whitsitt feels "may be attributed to Sidney," the writer speaks of himself as "the son of a Baptist."[19] Last, and perhaps most convincingly, all Sidney's adult siblings belonged to that denomination.

Although one cannot positively assert that William and Nancy Rigdon were Baptists, it is clear they were God-fearing, Bible-reading Christians. This is the religious tradition that Sidney Rigdon grew up embracing. Late in his life he stated that from his "earliest infancy" the fear of God "was the ruling principle in his heart in consequence of this he was devoted to the study of the bible."[20]

During Sidney's early adolescence revival ferment was still in full swing in western Pennsylvania, and from a young age he likely attended Peters Creek Baptist Church. His own account, given in 1869, simply says, "[I] became acquainted with a Baptist minister . . . [who called my] attention . . . to personal religion."[21] Reverend Philips, a Welsh native, served the Peters Creek congregation from 1780-1824.

Religious experience was important in post-Revolutionary War frontier America. Any unusual agitation of feelings was considered a direct inspiration of the Holy Spirit. Those so inclined had experiences to report and were looked upon as favorites of God. Although Rigdon's mature sense of self was thoroughly and unapologetically religious, he was not baptized until 31 May 1817 at age twenty-four. The delay was due to the fact that he had not yet put forth a conversion experience. Regular or Calvinist Baptists were committed to a membership confined to convinced believers, those who could testify to a personal experience of the miracle of grace.

A true conversion, under Calvinist guidelines, implied

> an exercise of miraculous power on the part of God, which the sinner could neither so control as to bring himself under its influence, nor resist when he was subjected to it. . . . Conversion was as much a mystery to [the preachers] as to their hearers; they might be converted instantaneously or after a long season; the most careless and indifferent might be made to yield when they neither expected nor desired to do so; while others, sincere, earnest, weeping penitents, might seek the same blessing, yet seek in vain.

The experience had to stand the scrutiny of a validation committee and a subsequent confirming vote by the congregation as one of five cardinal prerequisites for full membership in the society.[22]

Preconversion anxiety in young people raised in evangelical circles frequently accompanies their coming-of-age. The symptoms, according to psychologist William James, usually consist of a "sense of incompleteness and imperfection; brooding, depression, morbid introspection, and sense of sin; anxiety about the hereafter; distress over doubts, and the like. . . . Conversion is in its essence a normal adolescent phenomenon, incidental to the passage from the child's small universe to the wider intellectual and spiritual life of maturity."[23] Mormon poet Eliza R. Snow, also raised in the Baptist tradition, recalled that when she asked her minister, "What shall I do to be saved?" he told her she must have a change of heart and "to obtain it, I must feel myself to be the worst of sinners, and acknowledge the justice of God in consigning me to everlasting torment."[24]

Conversions were as varied as individuals. Those with quick sensibilities and lively fancies sometimes surpassed even the most striking cases of a miraculous age, while calm, thoughtful persons were so far from such raptures that they were often reduced to despair. The exact nature of Sidney Rigdon's conversion experience is not known. Years later, as a Mormon, he reportedly said of his Baptist initiation: "When I joined the church I knew I could not be admitted without an experience: so I made up one to suit the purpose, but it was all made up, and was of no use."[25] Peters Creek leaders apparently did have some reservations in 1817 about Sidney's sincerity. The Reverend Samuel Williams, in a derogatory account written after Rigdon became a Mormon, noted that "there was so much miracle about his conversion, and so much parade about his profession, that the pious and discerning Pastor [Philips], entertained serious doubts at the time in regard to the genuineness of the work."[26]

Despite the implied controversy, Rigdon was received by the church, baptized by Father Philips, and later given a favorable letter of recommendation when he separated from the congregation. By this time, and possibly much earlier, Sidney had recognized religion as a way out of the dreary, moribund life of farming. Inculcated with an overwhelming sense of talent and destiny, the ambitious plowman set out to become a Baptist minister.

While Rigdon had a humble, compassionate side, he was also opportunistic and mean-spirited as he single-mindedly sought the esteem he craved. The first evidence of this is in a Baptist minister's retrospective report that Sidney had coveted the aging David Philips's pastorship. The Reverend Samuel Williams, at the time a hostile witness, said that Rigdon "began to put himself forward and seek the preeminence, and was well nigh supplanting the tried and faithful minister who had reared, and nursed, and fed the church, for a long series of years."[27] Rigdon, rare to lift a shade on his personal life, seemed to confirm this assessment when he wrote of himself many years later (speaking in God's voice): "his acquaintence with [the Bible] became so far in advance of all others that they could not contend successfully with him[.] The result of all this was that he was high and lifted up among men but not withstanding this my fear dwelt in his heart."[28]

Philips, who would not retire until 1824, reportedly said of Rigdon at the time that he "was not possessed of the spirit of Christ, notwithstanding his miraculous conversion . . . [and] that as long as he [Rigdon] should live, he would be a curse to the church of Christ."[29] If that sentiment was truly expressed, then Peters Creek Baptist Church could not have accommodated both Rigdon, with his swooping, kinetic ways, and the old-hat style of the Reverend Philips.

Another possibility is that Philips may already have had a ministerial intern and thus could not have accommodated Rigdon. Sidney's three cousins, Charles, Thomas, and John, also became Baptist ministers during this decade. Thomas was known to be in eastern Ohio at this time, but John or Charles may have been serving with Philips. The local pastorship was the only Baptist congregation in the district, and Rigdon had to strike out "boldly from the homestead," as he later put it. Leaving the plantation in his brother Carvel's care, Sidney traveled westward into nearby Beaver County to enter a theological apprenticeship at the home of the Reverend Andrew Clark, minister of the Providence Regular Baptist Church, in North Sewickley, on the Connoquenessing River.[30]

Rigdon did not pursue his "errand into the wilderness" as a journey of solitude. There were no Baptist seminaries in western Pennsylvania, so ministers-in-training developed their styles on the job under the tutelage of established pastors. Prior arrangements for Rigdon's internship were undoubtedly made by his preacher-cousin Thomas Rigdon who had preceded Clark as pastor and who had been living in the area for at least a decade.[31] During 27 February 1819 services at the Providence Church, Clark read to the small congregation Sidney's "letter of Dismission" from the Peters Creek Church specifying his good standing and "received him on the same."[32]

Sidney recalled that at the home of Clark, his "new friend and spiritual counsellor," he discovered what seemed to him "a perfect paradise of books and intellectual companionship." The apprenticeship included an extensive self-improvement course of reading "history, divinity, and general literature" as well as reading and memorizing extensive portions of the Bible.[33] Critics, such as Congregationalist Noah Worcester, argued that Baptists proliferated because, among other things, they had an abundance of unqualified preachers. "Many people are so ignorant as to be charmed with sound [rather] than sense," he argued.

> And to them, the want of knowledge in a teacher . . . may easily be made up, and overbalanced, by great zeal, an affecting tone of voice, and a perpetual motion of the tongue. If a speaker can keep his tongue running, in an unremitting manner . . . and can quote, memoriter, a large number of texts from within the covers of the Bible, it matters not, to many of his hearers, whether he speaks *sense or nonsense*.[34]

The lack of a formal education and training was for rural parishioners an asset. They approved of self-educated men who learned what they knew from listening to other sermons and reading the Bible. Furthermore, despite critics like

Worcester, theatrical, high-camp preachers provided the magic that made religion work. Their rush of words and waterfall of language, punctuated by exaggerated mannerisms, was nineteenth-century performance art, the measure of the minister.

According to his own account, Rigdon was permitted to "exercise his rights" as a preacher in March 1819 when he was awarded a "ministerial license." Two types of Baptist ministers preached on the frontier then: the "licensed" and the "ordained." Licensed preachers, like Rigdon, could sermonize but not administer sacraments or other ordinances. The apprenticeship was always undertaken in a small territory such as the bounds of a single church. If, after a modest period of time, the trainee's "gifts" proved authentic and he seemed qualified for the ministry, he was then permitted to preach within the bounds of the association. "Many a Baptist church on the frontier," according to a prominent history of the movement, "was first gathered and finally organized by these licensed preachers."[35]

Thomas Coke, a Methodist minister contemporary of Rigdon, observed that although Baptist preachers' abilities were often "peculiarly small," their "zeal was much, and God was pleased to own it."[36] Rigdon, whose talents were anything but "small," was definitely life-long material, with room in his mind only for theological ciphers. Piety and drama were for him the very essence of existence. And the various movements with which he affiliated during his long, God-fearing existence amply rewarded his visionary overdrive and flights of fantasy as long as he remained a custodian of their orthodoxy.

Baptist congregations in Rigdon's days were aligned into associations, voluntary unions of churches, for "mutual encouragement, for counsel in church affairs, and for protection against heresy and impostors."[37] Providence Church belonged to the Beaver Baptist Association, an alliance of Calvinist Baptists formed in 1810 from Regular Baptist churches of the border area of Pennsylvania and Ohio. Associations met annually to conduct business, and Rigdon's name first appears in the minutes of the Beaver association when it held its annual meeting in New Lisbon, Columbiana County, Ohio, in 1819. He and another minister cousin, John Rigdon, were invited to seats in the association. Both were also appointed to the committee which later drafted the "Circular Letter" to be sent to all congregations in the association. During this meeting Andrew Clark, Adamson Bentley, and another minister met to consider Sidney's ordination and issued his "Certificate of Ordination" on 1 April 1820.[38]

Sidney's dismissal letter from the Providence Church, ending his apprenticeship with Clark, was dated 4 August 1819.[39] Rigdon then re-trekked the fifty or so miles to St. Clair Township to visit his family and conduct business related to his holdings there. Wickliffe asserts that during this brief hiatus his father preached in the small Pittsburgh Baptist congregation, then under the pastorship of either Obadiah Newcomb or John Davis. This may be wrong, however. Wickliffe's accounts of his father's early history are not always reliable. For example, he refers to David Philips as "a Baptist minister by the name of Peters" and places Andrew Clark in Pittsburgh rather than Beaver County. Furthermore he writes that Rigdon preached his first sermon "at Pittsburgh" when he was twenty-seven (1820). Yet Sidney's own account acknowledges that he was first permitted to "exercise his rights" as a preacher in March 1819 while still under Clark's sponsorship in Beaver County.[40]

Rigdon remained in Peters Creek country for a few months before inner promptings directed his compass towards the new frontier of Ohio's Western Reserve. But he would not grow old in that midland wilderness of blazing stars, Indian pipes, and Buckeye trees. Eighteen years later he would depart on a fast mount during the night's darkest hour, just a step ahead of the constabulary.

Notes

Unless otherwise stated, all primary sources cited are located in the Historical Department of the Church of Jesus Christ of Latter-day Saints, Salt Lake City, Utah.

1. The Rigdon family is of English descent, notably from the Canterbury area in the county of Kent. The name bears an ancient Kentish surname with the various spellings Rigdon, Rigden, Rigdin, and possibly Rigdun. The Rigdon family in Baltimore (now Harford) County can be traced first to George Rigdon, Sidney Rigdon's great-grandfather who was on the Baltimore County tax list from 1699 to 1706. He was a farmer and land owner. In 1704 he married Elizabeth Baker. Their children, as recorded in St. George's Parish records, Harford County, were: Charles (b. 30 June 1705); Elizabeth (b. 7 Feb. 1708; md. Beaven Spain, 6 Jan. 1734); George (b. 5 Apr. 1710; md. Sarah Thompson, 12 Dec. 1734); Thomas Baker (b. 18 Apr. 1713; md. Ann Lacy; d. 9 Aug. 1789); John (b. 17 Apr. 1716; md. Elizabeth Bond); William (b. 17 Jan. 1719); Enoch (b. 4 Jan. 1725/26); Stephen (b. 30 July 1729; never married); and Anne (b. 4 July 1731; d. 31 Dec. 1739).

George Rigdon's will was probated 6 July 1755. Beneficiaries were his wife, Elizabeth, and all his children except son Charles and daughters Elizabeth and Anne, likely deceased, and his estate was worth 137 pounds, 12 shillings, and 8 pence. The will's executors were sons Thomas and William (Ella H. Rowe, *Clark, Rigdon, Wilson and Durham Families of Harford County, Maryland* [Baltimore: Ella H. Rowe, 1987], 17-19).

Sidney Rigdon's grandfather, Thomas Baker Rigdon (b. 18 Apr. 1713; d. 9 Aug. 1789), married Ann Lacy (d. 1 Oct. 1797) who was thought to have come from Ireland to Boston, and later to Maryland. She was the daughter of William and Margaret Lacy.

The children of Thomas Baker and Ann Lacy Rigdon were Alexander (b. 1743; md. Ann Johnson, 11 Dec. 1781; d. 1820); Thomas Baker (d. 1819); William (b. 1748; md. Nancy Gallaher [also spelled Gallagher]—children: Carvel [b. ca. 1790], Sidney [b. 1793], Loammi, also spelled Loamie [b. ca. 1796; d. 1865], Lacy [b. ca. 1799; d. 22 May 1810; St. Clair Township, PA]); Stephen (b. 1749; d. 28 Dec. 1836); Benjamin (b. 1753; md. Elizabeth Forwood [b. 1769; d. 22 Aug. 1857]; d. 20 Dec. 1828); Ann (md. Daniel Preston,

1772); Hannah; Margaret (md. Robert Clark, 4 Dec. 1770); and Elizabeth. Thomas Baker Rigdon's will was probated in 1789 naming his wife and children as beneficiaries (Rowe, 20).

2. Rowe, 20-21.

3. Ibid., 21.

4. Sidney Rigdon, in A. W. Cowles, "The Mormons: Pen and Pencil Sketches, Illustrating Their Early History," *Moore's Rural New Yorker*, 23 Jan. 1869, 61, Special Collections, Harold B. Lee Library, Brigham Young University, Provo, Utah (hereafter Special Collections, BYU).

5. "Records of Early Church Families," *The Utah Genealogical and Historical Magazine* 27 (1936): 156.

6. *History of Allegheny County, Pennsylvania*, 2 vols. (Chicago: A. Warner & Co., 1889), 2:42.

7. Although the records are silent on the matter, it is possible that Stephen was Rigdon's middle name. There are at least three Stephen Rigdons in his ancestry including his father's younger brother (b. 1749, d. 1836), a strict Baptist who never married and drove a stage coach in New Jersey. Sidney also had a particular fondness for his spokesman Stephen Post as well as the New Testament Stephen (Rowe, 22-23).

8. *History of Allegheny County*, 1:366; *History of Pittsburgh and Environs*, 2 vols. (New York/Chicago: American Historical Society, Inc., 1922), 424.

9. Karl Keller, ed., "'I Never Knew a Time When I Did Not Know Joseph Smith': A Son's Record of the Life and Testimony of Sidney Rigdon," *Dialogue: A Journal of Mormon Thought* 1 (Winter 1966): 15-42, cited 20. Although J. W. Rigdon is usually referred to in Mormon accounts as John W. Rigdon, family records usually refer to him as Wickliffe or simply "Wick."

Wickliffe's "Life and Testimony of Sidney Rigdon" was written for a 1906 lecture he delivered at Alfred University and other colleges and communities in the central New York area. Karl Keller, living near Friendship, New York, in 1965, became aware of the existence of the Rigdon lecture (a thirty-one page handwritten manuscript) then owned by Mrs. F. R. Bennett, Wickliffe's granddaughter ("Old Manuscript Tells of Mormon Bank Try," *The Tacoma News Tribune* [Washington], 30 July 1967). The Rigdon lecture notes were first published in an edited form in Arlene Hess, *The History of Friendship* (Friendship, NY: Friendship Sesquicentennial Corporation, 1965). The notes are presently available in the Arlene Hess Papers, Special Collections, BYU. Keller surmised that after Wickliffe joined the LDS church in 1904 he wrote the lecture notes out "in a longer form" (Keller, 16). But this was not so. The notes are a less-controversial abstract of a 200-page manuscript entitled "Life Story of Sidney Rigdon" which Wickliffe wrote as early as 1900, probably earlier.

On 24 September 1900 while visiting friends in Salt Lake City, Wickliffe offered his manuscript to the LDS church First Presidency for $500. It was referred to a committee of readers. On 13 October Rigdon called on President Lorenzo Snow "respecting propositions on manuscript." Snow felt that the "manuscript was of no particular benefit to the church," but because of Rigdon's "very pecuniary circumstances" he felt moved to "offer him $250 or $300 for it," or to "tender him a present of $56 to assist him in case he thought he could do better elsewhere, that is by publishing himself, as he once talked of doing" (Journal History, 24 Sept., 13 Oct. 1900 [a multi-volume daily history of the church compiled by official church historians]). George F. Gibbs, Snow's secretary, discussed the proposal with Rigdon who chose to take the $300. The manuscript, presently retained in the LDS church historical archives, has never been published.

10. Sidney Rigdon, in *Moore's Rural New Yorker* 1869, 61.

11. Keller, 20; J. Wickliffe Rigdon, "Life Story of Rigdon," 4.

12. Keller, 20.

13. Allegheny Co. Wills, Book 1, 300, in Ella Chalfant, *A Goodly Heritage–Earliest Wills on an American Frontier* (Pittsburgh: University of Pittsburgh Press, 1986), 50-51. Witnesses to William's will were Ebenezer Gallaher, Thomas Rigdon, and David Philips. See Helen L. Harriss and Elizabeth J. Wall, *Will Abstracts of Allegheny County Pennsylvania–Will Books I Through V (1789-1844)* (Pittsburgh: n.p., 1986), 22. Nancy Rigdon did not die until 1839.

Loammi graduated from Transylvania Medical College, Lexington, Kentucky, in 1823 and married Rebecca Dunlevy on 9 October 1815. In 1824 he was practicing medicine in Lebanon, Ohio. In March 1826, however, he moved to Hamilton, Ohio, and entered into partnership with Dr. John C. Dunlevy. Early in 1834 Dunlevy removed to Lebanon, and in October of that year Loammi took into partnership, for a term of three years, Dr. Cyrus Falconer. He practiced in Wilmington, Ohio, for eleven years. A respected member of the Baptist church, he died on 10 May 1865 ("History of Butler Co., Ohio," in Hess Papers).

14. In William H. Whitsitt, "Sidney Rigdon, The Real Founder of Mormonism," 1885, 6, Special Collections, Marriott Library, University of Utah, Salt Lake City (hereafter Special Collections, U of U).

15. 1 July 1868 Revelation in Stephen Post Collection, box 1, fd. 16; also listed as Section 37 in Copying Book A in Stephen Post Collection (hereafter cited as Post Collection).

16. Rowe, 19.

17. Excellent works detailing the American Baptist experience include David Benedict, *A General History of the Baptist Denomination In America, and Other Parts of the World*, 2 vols. (Freeport: NY: Books for Libraries Press, 1813); Richard Knight, *History of the General or Six-Principle Baptists in Europe and America* (Providence: Smith and Parmenter, 1827); Isaac Backus, *A History of New England with Particular Reference to the . . . Baptists*, 2 vols. (Newton, MA: Backus Historical Society, 1871); W. T. Thom, *The Struggle for Religious Freedom in Virginia: The Baptists* (Baltimore: Johns Hopkins Press, 1900); Robert G. Torbet, *A History of the Baptists*, 3rd ed. (Valley Forge, PA: Judson Press, 1963); James E. Wood, Jr., *Baptists and the American Experience* (Valley Forge, PA: Judson Press, 1976).

18. Richard C. Wade, *The Urban Frontier: The Rise of Western Cities, 1790-1830* (Cambridge: n.p., 1959), 44, in F. Mark McKiernan, *The Voice of One Crying in the Wilderness: Sidney Rigdon, Religious Reformer–1793-1876* (Lawrence, KS: Coronado Press, 1971), 13. Frank C. Harper, *Pittsburgh of Today*, 2 vols. (New York: American Historical Society, Inc., 1931), 768.

19. Chalfant, 51; Whitsitt, 3, citing *Christian Baptist*, 6:93.

20. 1 July 1868 Revelation, Post Collection, box 1, fd. 16.

21. *Moore's Rural New Yorker* 1869, 61.

22. Mary Agnes Monroe Smith, "A History of the Mahoning Baptist Association," M.A. thesis, West Virginia University, Morgantown, West Virginia, 1943, 8. The five

essential principles are separation of church and state, conversion as a condition of church membership, individual responsibility to God, congregational church government, and immersion as the scriptural form of baptism (cited in Daryl Chase, "Sidney Rigdon—Early Mormon," M.A. diss., University of Chicago, 1931, 12).

23. William James, *The Varieties of Religious Experience–A Study In Human Nature* (New York: Penguin Books, 1985), 199. Starbuck, in his classic 1903 statistical study of conversion, is also insightful on "normal conversion, which he considered to be primarily an adolescent phenomenon. In this type of conversion, the person is motivated by egoistic as well as idealistic considerations. Fear, a sense of sin, and the related phenomenon of depression are the prominent characteristics of the preconversion state" (in Leon Salsman, "The Psychology of Religious and Ideological Conversion," *Psychiatry–Journal for the Study of Interpersonal Processes* 16 [Feb.-Nov. 1953]: 177-87, citing 180).

24. Eliza R. Snow, *Eliza R. Snow–An Immortal* (Salt Lake City: Nicholas G. Morgan, Sr., Foundation, 1957), 5.

25. Harmon Sumner recalled Sidney's statement in J. H. Kennedy, *Early Days of Mormonism* (London: Reeves and Turner, 1888), 64.

26. Williams's reference is in Amos Sutton Hayden, *Early History of the Disciples in the Western Reserve* (Cincinnati: Chase and Hall, 1875), 191-92.

27. Samuel Williams, *Mormonism Exposed* (Pittsburgh: n.p., 1842), 1.

28. 1 July 1868 Revelation in Post Collection, box 1, fd. 16.

29. Williams, 1.

30. Hans Rollmann, "The Early Baptist Career of Sidney Rigdon in Warren, Ohio," *Brigham Young University Studies* 21 (Winter 1981): 37-50, cited, 44).

31. Thomas Rigdon, a licensed minister prior to 1808 when he co-founded the Baptist church in Unity (New Lisbon), Ohio, in what would become the Beaver Baptist Association in 1810, was ordained by Adamson Bentley and David Philips on 27 October 1810 (*Beaver Baptist Association* [1860], 10-11; *Beaver Minutes* [1811], 3, in Rollmann, 44).

Thomas was an influential member of the Beaver Association, serving intermittently as clerk, participating on many committees, drafting circular letters, and preaching sermons during annual meetings. He served as pastor at the following congregations: Unity (1810-13), Providence (1813-14), Anchor (1816-18), Eliza (1818), and Unity (1824). After the division of the Beaver Baptist Association, Thomas and his brothers Charles and John were active in the Mohican Baptist Association. They, along with Sidney, joined Alexander Campbell and Walter Scott in the Reformed Movement later in the decade (Benedict, 547; Hayden, 92; *Beaver Baptist Association* [1860], 7; Rollmann, 44-45).

Thomas Rigdon, father of Thomas, Charles, and John, died on the old St. Clair homestead in the fall of 1819. His will, recorded 25 September 1819, left his farm to his oldest son Stephen, who eventually sold out and moved to Illinois. Additional children in the family were Nancy and Leah Larimer (Harriss and Wall, 44).

32. Providence Church Minutes, MS, 95, in Rollmann, 44.

33. *Moore's Rural New Yorker* 1869, 61.

34. Noah Worcester, *Impartial Inquiries, Respecting the Progress of the Baptist Denomination* (Worcester, MA: 1794), 19-20.

35. *Times and Seasons* 4 (1 May 1843): 177-78; William Warren Sweet, *Religion on the American Frontier: The Baptists 1783-1830* (New York: Henry Holt, 1931), 40.

36. Richard H. Clossman, *A History of the Ohio Baptist Convention* (Granville, OH: Ohio Baptist Convention, 1976), 17.

37. Hayden, 25. Associations were an advisory council only and held no authority over member churches or individual members. To be accepted into an association, a church first sent three representatives with a written creed or articles of faith. If this declaration were considered orthodox a vote would be taken. If accepted, the association's moderator offered the right hand of fellowship to the messengers and invited them to a seat. The messengers were required to be "judicious, well versed in the Scriptures, prudent, men of integrity, and sound in the faith" (Article Three of the Mahoning Baptist Association, cited in Smith, 24).

Baptist Associations were usually named after rivers, but some assumed names with sentimental or historical value such as "Concord" (Warren), "Bethesda" (Nelson), "Mount Hope" (Hubbard), "Zoar" (Youngstown), and a church on the Sandy known as the "Valley of Anchor."

38. *Beaver Minutes* [1819], 4-6 and *Beaver Minutes* [1820], 4, in Rollmann, 45, 47; *Minutes of the Fifty-Eighth Anniversary of the Trumbull Baptist Association* (Niles, OH: News Print, 1897), 22; Hayden, 92.

39. Church Record, Warren Central Christian Church, 69, in Rollmann, 39.

40. Rigdon, 5; Keller, 20; Joel van Meter Stratton, *History of the First Baptist Church of Pittsburgh, Pa.* (Pittsburgh: n.p. 1910), 8.

CHAPTER 2.

The Western Reserve

In northeast Ohio—less than one hundred miles from Sidney Rigdon's Pennsylvania home—the Western Reserve was bestowed on Connecticut colony by King Charles II in 1662. Originally the four million-acre expanse was called New Connecticut or the Connecticut Western Reserve. Bounded on the north by Lake Erie, the east by Pennsylvania, the south by the 41st parallel, and the west by Sandusky and Seneca counties, the district embraced the counties of Ashtabula, Cuyahoga, Erie, Geauga, Huron, Lorain, and the north part of Mahoning, Medina, Portage, Summit, and Trumbull. Initially the King's land grant extended to the Pacific Ocean, but in September 1786 Connecticut ceded to the United States government its claim to all charter lands west of the Reserve. Jurisdictional claims for the remaining parcel were surrendered on 30 May 1801, and nearly the entire real estate package was sold to the Connecticut Land Company, a private entity.

After native American attacks declined with the 1795 Treaty of Greenville, the Connecticut Land Company constructed the Reserve's first toll roads. Settlement was encouraged, and property purchased for as little as 33 cents an acre. The American Dream was as powerful then as any religion of the day. New Englanders, hearing this was a land of perpetual sunshine and easy living, ventured forth in pursuit of prosperity.

Christopher Gore Crary, Jr., an early settler in the Reserve, later described his arrival in Kirtland Township in 1811. "The forest-trees were of endless variety," he wrote, "and of the tallest kinds. A thick growth of underbrush grew beneath, flowers of rare beauty blushed unseen, birds of varied plumage filled the air with their music, the air itself was fragrant and invigorating."[1]

Arriving in the Western Reserve in 1820, Sidney Rigdon found a region of farms and scattered villages. Cleveland, the largest city, had fewer than five thousand settlers. But the land was filling up, and harsh frontier lines began to soften and adjust to civilized New England ways. Roads, like a network of spider webs, soon appeared throughout the wilderness, lumber and grist mills dotted the waterways, and by 1828 crops were shipped to market via the Ohio-Erie Canal.[2] Rigdon's first home was in Warren, where he resided with Adamson Bentley, his future brother-in-law, who had been minister of the local Concord Baptist Church since 1810.[3] Bentley, also from western Pennsylvania, owned a sizeable mercantile and was married to a daughter of Jeremiah Brooks, a prominent local Baptist.

Warren was not only the religious heart of the Western Reserve but also its political center and "seat of justice." Amos S. Hayden, prominent historian of the Campbellite movement, wrote of Bentley and his Warren pastorate:

> For a long time he was popular in that community. The bland dignity of his manners, and his social courtesy, won him many friends. Though his talents as a preacher were above mediocrity, and he was heard with delight and profit by numerous auditors, to his social qualities and moral excellencies, as a man and a citizen, are to be traced the sources of that extensive power which he possessed among the people.[4]

When Rigdon first arrived, the town had no Baptist meetinghouse, and the small congregation met in various homes. His acceptance, noted in the church's minutes, simply states: "Bro. Sidney Rigdon presented his letter of dismission from the Church of Christ called Providence Pa. dated Augt 4th 1819 . . . received into full fellowship."[5] On 1 April 1820 Rigdon preached at the church's "regular monthly meeting." At the same session "Bro Rigdon requested a certificate from the Church stating his standing with us as a Member in fellowship and a li[c]ensed Minister of the Gospel, which was granted."[6] This was also when Rigdon received his "Certificate of Ordination."[7]

Three months after Rigdon's arrival the twenty-seven-year-old bachelor married Phebe (also spelled Phoebe) Brooks on 12 June 1820. The twenty-year-old bride was the daughter of Jeremiah Brooks and Dorcas Smith. Although born in Bridgetown, New Jersey, on 3 May 1800, Phebe and her family had moved to Warren in 1810.[8] Well educated for her day, with a fine mind and exquisite penmanship, Phebe was a remarkable woman. Birthing twelve children, and burying several, she ultimately was ordained a prophetess and served as a ranking leader in her husband's church in the 1860s. Perhaps her crowning achievement, considering the family's chronic poverty, the black bouts of Sidney's mental depression, and the compulsive fanaticism that drove her husband to the edge of religious madness, was the fact that for fifty-six years she never stopped loving him nor believing in his visions and mystical assurances. Unlike virtually everyone else when her "Lord and Master" died, Phebe saw something more than a wasted life in pursuit of a fool's dream of glory.

In 1820, however, the new Mrs. Rigdon quickly learned to adapt, if not embrace, the nomadic ways of her itinerant pastor husband. Although they continued to live in Warren, Rigdon worked as a circuit preacher who semi-regularly traveled to small churches that could not afford a resident minister. Wickliffe Rigdon wrote that while living in Warren his father had no "particular charge," but instead "whenever a vacancy occurred in the country, he always filled it, and in that way acquired a reputation for being a very eloquent preacher."[9]

When a circuit rider like Rigdon went from town to town, he was often thronged, especially after evening meetings when a crowd would sometimes gather at his lodgings seeking further spiritual advice. The Baptist idea of speedy baptism prompted immersions even after dark. During the first six months of his ministry,

Sidney and his brother-in-law, Adamson Bentley, baptized "upward of ninety persons."[10] This dramatic upsurge in membership necessitated the construction of a meetinghouse in Warren during the years 1820-21. The chapel, long a local landmark, was built on the north side of the public square, and Rigdon played a role in its construction and occasionally delivered a sermon from the church's pulpit.[11]

During its 30 August 1820 annual meeting, the Beaver Baptist Association divided into three organizations. The Pennsylvania division, considered the old association, retained the name Beaver. Those churches which had their seats in Ohio—Bazetta, Braceville, Liberty, Mount Hope, Nelson, New Lisbon, Randolph, Salem, Warren, and Youngstown—united to form the Mahoning Association, named after the Mahoning River coursing through the district.[12] Prior to its dissolution the old Beaver Association met a final time from 24 to 26 August 1820, when Rigdon's ordination was announced. He, along with his cousin Charles Rigdon and Adamson Bentley, was requested to draft the "Corresponding Letter" for the year, the means by which various Baptist associations kept in touch. David Benedict, Baptist historian, describes the origin and development of this practice:

> The way in which our people at all distances communicated with each other as to the state of their churches and their general affairs, was by means of corresponding letters for this purpose, from one association to another. In process of time, these letters were printed in the minutes of the associations; but when I first began to attend some of the oldest bodies of this kind [early 1800s], they appointed men on the spot to write to all with which they had agreed to correspond; the letters thus formed were sent to them in manuscript. . . . The next step was to prepare one letter of a general character for all corresponding associations, some of which were in distant States, and to print it in the minutes.[13]

The Mahoning Association was officially organized on 30 August 1820 and was founded on the Philadelphia Confession of Faith of 25 September 1747. This "pattern of faith and of life," originating with the Calvinist or Regular Baptists of seventeenth-century England, was the orthodox creed adhered to by all Baptist churches and associations in America. The Mahoning Association copied, without change, the thirteen articles of faith and practice from the Beaver Association.

Earlier in the same summer of 1820 an incident took place in Mount Pleasant, Ohio, that profoundly altered the course of the Mahoning Association. A June 19-20 theological debate on baptism between classically-trained Alexander Campbell, son of famed religious reformer Thomas Campbell, and the Reverend John Walker, a prominent Seceder Presbyterian minister, resulted in a backlash that eventually inundated Sidney Rigdon and transformed his life as no other single experience had since his birth.

One cannot fully penetrate Rigdon's soul without understanding how the restoration of Christian Primitivism affected his thinking. Known by a variety of names such as the "Back to the Bible Movement," "The Original Gospel," "The Primitive Gospel," "The Pentecostian Gospel," and "The Jerusalem Gospel," the movement in its simplest form sought to restore the "ancient order of things" as pronounced in the New Testament.

Foremost among early American Baptist reformers was the reputed founder, Roger Williams. Early in his ministry Williams became "disturbed as to his right to administer the ordinances of the church, conceiving that a true ministry must derive its authority from apostolic succession and, therefore, he could not assume the office of pastor. . . . He finally came to the conclusion that the church was so corrupt that there could be no recovery out of that apostasy till Christ shall send forth new apostles to plant churches anew."[14]

Shortly afterwards the "Six Point Baptists" arose who held for the "Laying on of Hands." Certain factions in Virginia during this time sought to reproduce apostolic customs of feet-washing, the holy kiss, anointing the sick, love feasts, laying on of hands, and weekly communion. They went so far as to appoint apostles, Samuel Harris being the first chosen. Others were afterwards appointed, but the system was soon abandoned.[15] These reformers plead for the restoration of New Testament Christianity as a basis of unity. In such diverse places as New Hampshire, North Carolina, Kentucky, and Pennsylvania, prophets of the ancient order began seeking the elusive dream of many Christian reformers—the rebirth of the primitive church.

The first voice advocating a return to the "ancient order of things" in western Pennsylvania was Thomas Campbell. A Seceder Presbyterian minister when he left Ireland in 1807, Campbell came under the influence of a radical Scottish reform movement, Independency, which represented a merging of Calvinist and Anabaptist elements. In Scotland, Independency stemmed from the work of John Glas and his son-in-law, Robert Sandeman, who both left the Church of Scotland in 1727 to establish a church that exemplified "the order and discipline of the primitive church." Independent principles were more widely popularized under the prominent evangelistic mission of brothers James and Robert Haldane, who influenced Thomas Campbell.

Teaching that generations of theologians had encrusted Christianity with elaborate creeds, speculation, and unscriptural practices, the Haldanes sought to end the aberrations and called for a return to original, undistorted piety. Thomas Campbell, while living in Rich Hill, Ireland, and ministering to the congregation at Ahorey, often attended nearby Independent church services in Rich Hill where he was exposed to primivitist sermons of John Gibson, Rowland Hill, James Haldane, Alexander Carson, and John Walker.

In 1807, on the advice of a physician, Campbell immigrated to the United States and was assigned to the Presbytery of Chartiers in western Pennsylvania by the North America Synod of the Seceder Presbyterian Church, one of the minority wings of the Scottish church.[16] Campbell's wish for Christian unity led him to admit non-members into communion services, an action that resulted in immediate conflict with superiors. His pronouncement that Jesus Christ died for all humanity, not just the "elect," and that any person could believe on Christ and be saved, was viewed as flagrant heresy. This marked his departure from Presbyterian Calvinism, and he was suspended by the Anti-Burgher Synod in 1808. A year later he and his followers formed "The First Church of the Christian Association of Washington." They desired a more ecumenical church based on the Bible rather than creeds, which they felt were divisive.

The Christian Association initially met at the Cross-roads and Brush Run, Washington County, Pennsylvania. Although loosely organized, the society did not consider itself a church until 4 May 1811. During a sermon at this time, Campbell summarized his religious philosophy in a phrase that ultimately became the rallying cry of the movement: "Where the Scriptures speak, we speak; where the Scriptures are silent, we are silent."

Campbell's philosophy had been well developed in a fifty-six-page essay prepared for the Christian Association. This *Declaration and Address* enumerated the shortcomings of contemporary religion and outlined the steps necessary for the restoration of primitive Christianity. Just as he had finished penning his important work, Campbell was joined by his son, Alexander, who with the remainder of the Campbell family had been summoned to America by his father.

The younger Campbell spent his last months before his departure for America in Scotland at the University of Glasgow where he became acquainted with Greville Ewing, a disciple of Independents Glas, Sandeman, and the Haldanes. Sandemanianism, as Independent thought was known in America, stressed that faith is simple assent to the New Testament testimony of Jesus; the independence of each local congregation; weekly observance of the Lord's Supper on Sunday, "The Lord's Day"; establishment of a lay priesthood; weekly contributions for the poor; mutual exhortation of members; and a claim of the community on private goods.[17]

Campbell was quick to embrace Sandemanian theology, which, unknown to him, was also being taught by his father in America. Alexander was initially concerned that his new-found convictions might be offensive to his father, but when Thomas greeted him and gave him a copy of the *Declaration and Address*, he was overjoyed. He read it by candlelight at a wayside tavern and came to the realization that though he and his father had been separated by time and a great ocean, "they had been lead as if by divine providence to reach the same state in their theological and religious views."[18]

Young Campbell immediately threw his energies and intellectual powers into the Reformed Movement. The first joint crusade of father and son was the repudiation of human creeds as tests of fellowship. They also proposed uniting

Christ's disciples into one church, with the Bible as the single standard of faith and practice. They became convinced that infant membership in the church and baptism by sprinkling were unauthorized of God.

To prevent their new association from becoming another sect opposed to sectarianism, the Campbells sought union with the Presbyterian Synod of Pittsburgh in October 1810. They were refused on grounds that their principles would destroy the local peace. So the thirty-member congregation organized itself in May 1811, erected a simple frame building on Brush Run, and held its first worship services there on 16 June. Thomas Campbell was appointed elder of the Brush Run Church, Alexander was licensed to preach, and four deacons were chosen. On 1 January 1812, Alexander was ordained to the ministry by the laying on of hands. Convinced of the scriptural validity of baptism by immersion, he, his Presbyterian wife, and his father with his family—seven in all—were baptized five months later on 12 June in Buffaloe Creek by a Baptist preacher, Matthius Luce.

In 1814 members of the Brush Run Church decided to move en masse to Zanesville, Ohio, to establish a Christian colony with church, school, and other features. Alexander Campbell, enthusiastic about the project, personally selected the site, but his father-in-law, John Brown, did not want to see his daughter and son-in-law move so far away so he induced the couple to remain in Virginia by deeding them his farm for one dollar. Remaining on the family farm, Alexander added to the original gift until he became the richest, most prosperous farmer in what eventually became West Virginia.

In the fall of 1815 the Brush Run Church applied for membership in the Redstone Baptist Association of Pennsylvania. The Campbells' independence and unwillingness to subscribe to the Philadelphia Confession, and their hostility to the ministers, prompted considerable debate and some protest. Despite the objections, however, the church was received into fellowship.

Friction developed almost immediately. Secluded in the sheltered mountainous areas they occupied, the older churches in the association suffered not only physical isolation but were also insulated against new ideas, smug in the truth they possessed. They considered baptism an outward sign of an inward grace, and that a person's heart must be changed from stone to flesh to be a candidate for baptism. The convert was required formally to renounce the world, the flesh, and the devil before the congregation, having given evidence that he or she was a new creature prepared for baptism.

The Campbells held the doctrine that a person must reform, that repentance was simply a reformation, and that a person was ready for baptism when repentance was resolved. The two parties disagreed on other matters. These included distinctions between laity and clergy, the frequency with which the Lord's Supper should be observed, and the nature of faith itself. The unfriendly element in the Redstone Association regularly brought heresy charges against the Campbells at each annual meeting, but these were voted down.

Thomas Campbell moved to Pittsburgh in 1815 to establish a school in his home. He gathered a group of followers and applied for membership in the Redstone Association, but his affiliation with the stubborn Brush Run Church, now led by his son, caused Campbell's group to be refused admittance. Alexander fumed at his father's rebuff. During the association's annual meeting at Cross Creek in August 1816, he delivered a prepared oration entitled "Sermon on the Law," which spoke of faith and practice based on a new covenant, one "historically connected with the Jewish regime . . . but which is radically different from it." Stressing Jesus' ministry he argued, "There is no need for preaching the law of Moses in order to prepare men to receive the Gospel of Jesus Christ. Christ is the end of the Law for righteousness, and to everyone that believeth."[19] Campbell was criticized for the speech, and many of the orthodox became wary of his teachings. Despite this discomfort, he was still viewed as correct on the proper mode of baptism. Nevertheless, his performance in the 1820 debate with John Walker was closely monitored by fellow ministers in the association.

The precipitating factor in the debate was the baptism of a number of Pedobaptists (believers in infant sprinkling) at Mount Pleasant, Ohio, in 1819 under the direction of John Birch, a Baptist preacher. Walker, the challenger, took the position that the infant children of believers are proper subjects and that sprinkling is the proper mode. His opening statement affirmed that baptism replaced circumcision as "the covenant on which the Christian church is built and to which baptism is the seal." Campbell replied with citations from Greek lexicons and quotations from respected commentators to prove that the root word *baptizein* means "to dip," arguing that the form cannot be modified because the form or act is the very thing commanded.[20]

The general verdict, especially among Regular Baptists, was that Campbell carried the day. But orthodox Baptists were apprehensive about his emphasis on a succession of dispensations. In essence his "antinomianism," declaring the Mosaic law obsolete and freeing Christianity from Judaic precedents, implied throwing away the Old Testament.

Among those to hear of Alexander Campbell's success in the Walker debate were Sidney Rigdon and his brother-in-law, Adamson Bentley. Both read the transcription of the forum when it was published in 1821.[21] Upon learning that the Redstone Association opposed Campbell and wanted to censor him, Bentley said to his friends that in his opinion, "Campbell had done more for the Baptists than any man in the West, and that he intended, on the first opportunity, to go and pay him a visit."[22]

Rigdon probably met Campbell at the annual Redstone Association meeting at Peters Creek in August 1817 and again the following year when Campbell served as association secretary for the meeting in August 1818, more than a year after Rigdon had become a communicant. Bentley had met Campbell when his family was traveling across the mountains of Pennsylvania to their new home.[23] The opportunity to renew acquaintances came when Rigdon and Bentley made a lengthy circuit ride in July 1821, passing south through Ohio and into Kentucky. On their return they stopped at Campbell's residence in Buffaloe Creek, Virginia (now Bethany, West Virginia). Of that visit, Campbell wrote in 1848:

> [W]hile sitting in my portico after dinner, two gentlemen in the costume of clergymen, as then technically called,[24] appeared in my yard, advancing to the house. The elder of them, on approaching me, first introduced himself, saying, "My name, sir, is Adamson Bentley, this is Elder Sidney Rigdon, both of Warren, Ohio."

Bentley told him they wished to "inquire of you particularly on sundry matters of much interest to us set forth in the [Walker] debate." Campbell promised them an audience after the afternoon duties of his seminary were discharged.[25] The three men talked throughout the night. "Beginning with the baptism that John preached," Campbell wrote,

> we went back to Adam and forward to the final judgment. The dispensations—Adamic, Abrahamic, Jewish and Christian—passed and repassed before us. Mount Sinai in Arabia, Mount Zion, Mount Tabor, the Red Sea and the Jordan, the Passovers and the Pentacosts, the law and the Gospel, but especially the ancient order of things and the modern.

Campbell added that "on parting next day, Sidney Rigdon, with all apparent candor, said, if he had within the last year taught and promulgated from the pulpit one error, he had a thousand." But Campbell warned them

> not to pull down anything they had buil[t], until they had reviewed again and again what they had heard; nor even then rashly and without much consideration. Fearing they might undo their influence with the people, I felt constrained to restrain rather than to urge them on in the work of reformation.[26]

Rigdon and Bentley, their senses afire, returned to Warren intending to set the Western Reserve ablaze with their replenished religious conviction. They had assured Campbell "a candid hearing on the part of the uncommitted community, and an immediate access to the ears of the Baptist churches within the sphere of their influence."[27]

Notes

Unless otherwise stated, all primary sources cited are located in the Historical Department of the Church of Jesus Christ of Latter-day Saints, Salt Lake City, Utah.

1. Christopher Gore Crary, Jr., in Williams Brothers, *History of Lake and Geauga Counties, Ohio* (Philadelphia: Press of J. B. Lippencott & Co., 1878), 246.

2. Frederick A. Henry, "History of Centerville Mills and the Old Chillicothe Road"; Amos Sutton Hayden, *Early History of The Disciples in the Western Reserve, Ohio* (Cincinnati: Chase & Hall, 1875), 13-14.

3. Hayden, 93. Rigdon's account (*Times and Seasons* 4 [1 May 1843]:177) that he left Pennsylvania and went to live with Adamson Bentley in July 1819 is wrong as may be seen in the 4 March 1820 Church Record, Warren Central Christian Church, 69, in Hans Rollmann, "The Early Baptist Career of Sidney Rigdon in Warren, Ohio," *Brigham Young University Studies* 21 (Winter 1981): 37-50, cited, 39.

The first sermon preached in Warren was in June 1800 by Henry Speers, a Baptist preacher from Washington County, Pennsylvania, who visited the settlers ("Circular Letter To the Churches of the Trumbull Baptist Association" published in *Minutes of the Fifty-Eighth Anniversary of the Trumbull Baptist Association Held With the Niles Baptist Church* [Niles, OH: News Print, 1897], 21).

4. Hayden, 103-04.

5. Church Record, Warren Central Christian Church, 69, in Rollmann, 39.

6. Church Record, Warren Central Christian Church, 71, in Rollmann, 47.

7. See Arthur B. Deming, *Naked Truths About Mormonism* 1 (Jan. 1888), Oakland, CA: n.p., n.p.; *Trumbull Baptist Association* 1897, 22; William H. Whitsitt, "Sidney Rigdon, The Real Founder of Mormonism," 1885, 18, Special Collections, Marriott Library, University of Utah, Salt Lake City (hereafter Special Collections, U of U).

8. *The Utah Genealogical and Historical Magazine* (Salt Lake City: Deseret News Press, 1936), 27:158.

9. Karl Keller, ed., "'I Never Knew a Time When I Did Not Know Joseph Smith': A Son's Record of the Life and Testimony of Sidney Rigdon," *Dialogue: A Journal of Mormon Thought* 1 (Winter 1966): 15-42, cited, 20.

10. *Beaver Minutes* 1820, 27, in Rollmann, 47.

11. *History of Trumbull and Mahoning Counties with Illustrations and Biographical Sketches*, 2 vols. (Cleveland: H. Z. Williams & Bro., 1882), 1:260.

12. *Minutes of the Mahoning Baptist Association [1820]*, in "Appendix C: Minutes of the Mahoning Baptist Association [1820-1827]," in Mary Agnes Smith, "A History of the Mahoning Baptist Association," M.A. thesis, West Virginia University, Morgantown, 1943, 1-40.

13. David Benedict, *Fifty Years among the Baptists* (New York: Sheldon, 1860), 87.

14. W. W. Sweet, *Religion on the American Frontier* (n.p.: Henry Holt & Co., 1931), 103.

15. P. W. Gates, *The Early Relation and Separation of Baptists and Disciples* (Chicago: n.p., 1904), 124, in Daryl Chase, "Sidney Rigdon—Early Mormon," M.A. diss., University of Chicago, 1931, 34.

16. The Associate, or Seceder, Presbyterians separated from the established branch of the National Presbyterian Church of Scotland in 1733. They promoted each parish's right to select its own minister, a right held by land-owning church patrons. Seceders considered themselves Calvinists. Eventually they became more rigid than the Church of Scotland. The clique later subdivided into "Burghers," who believed that a Holy Oath

could be administered by any magistrate, and "Anti-Burghers," who denied that right (Louis Cochran and Bess White Cochran, *Captives of the Word* [Garden City, NY: Doubleday & Co., 1969], 1).

17. In 1763 Sandeman arrived in America, founded a congregation at Danbury, Connecticut, and remained there the rest of his life. For treatments on Sandeman and Haldane thought, see Lester G. McAllister and William E. Tucker, *Journey in Faith: A History of the Christian Church (Disciples of Christ)* (St. Louis: The Bethany Press, 1975); William H. Whitsitt, *Origin of the Disciples of Christ* (Louisville, KY: Baptist Book Concern, 1891); David Edwin Harrell, Jr., *Quest For A Christian America: The Disciples of Christ and American Society to 1866* (Nashville: The Disciples of Christ Historical Society, 1966); Cochran and Cochran; Dean C. Jessee, ed., *The Papers of Joseph Smith*, 2 vols. (Salt Lake City: Deseret Book Co., 1989), 1:331; Whitsitt, 14-15.

18. Cochran and Cochran, 10.

19. Ibid., 17.

20. *Debate on Christian Baptism Between Mr. John Walker, a Minister of the Secession and Alexander Campbell, held at Mount-Pleasant on the 19th and 20th June, 1820* (Pittsburgh: Eichbaum and Johnston, 1822). See also Winfred Ernest Garrison and Alfred T. DeGroot, *The Disciples of Christ: A History* (St. Louis: Christian Board of Publication, 1948), 168-69.

21. A first edition of 1,000 copies was quickly followed by a second printing of 3,000. Ultimately three versions and five different printings finally appeared, none of them complete or thoroughly accurate (Henry K. Shaw, *Buckeye Disciples: A History of the Disciples of Christ in Ohio* [St. Louis: Christian Board of Publication, 1952], 65).

22. Robert Richardson, *Memoirs of Alexander Campbell*, 2 vols. (Cincinnati: R. W. Carroll & Co., 1872), 2:44.

23. Max Ward Randall, *The Great Awakenings and the Restoration Movement* (Joplin, MO: College Press Publishing Co., 1983), 208.

24. This clothing, according to Senior Pastor Stanley L. Smith, First Baptist Church of Salt Lake City, consisted of a long black frock, a "formal morning coat."

25. Campbell's seminary for boys, conducted in his large home, was discontinued after four years of operation.

26. *The Millennial Harbinger* 5 (1848): 523.

27. Ibid.

CHAPTER 3.

Pittsburgh

Throughout the Great Awakening, Baptists, the most thoroughly American religion of the period, envisioned themselves engaged in a great millenarian work. Members eagerly anticipated the exaltation of righteousness when the lamb and lion would lie down together. Alexander Campbell, a Baptist in name only, recognized this primal religious stirring and skillfully wove theories of Christian primitivism, developed during his Independent training in Scotland, into the fabric of the Mahoning Baptist Association. It was a process in which Sidney Rigdon was a key player. "We want the old gospel back, and sustained by the ancient order of things," Campbell said at the time, "and this alone, by the blessing of the Divine Spirit, is all that we want, or can expect, to reform and save the world."[1]

Many assume that the Campbellites or Disciples of Christ—as the Reformed Baptist Movement of Sidney Rigdon's era is now known—were synonymous with Alexander Campbell.[2] This inaccurate portrayal has often distorted the organization's history. While the Campbells, Adamson Bentley, Walter Scott, and Barton W. Stone are revered today among the Disciples, positive observations about Rigdon, who was once prominent but slammed the door noisily when he left the society in 1830, are more difficult to come by. He is treated with modest respect in only a few Disciple sources, notably Amos S. Hayden's *Early History of The Disciples In The Western Reserve, Ohio*, published in 1875, the year before Rigdon's death in New York. But even that work treats him as an apostate, a visionary too erratic to be trusted.

Rigdon's greatest contribution to the Reformed Baptist Movement was his persuasive rhetoric. Most preachers of the day, unschooled evangelists and itinerant faith healers, held undisciplined, open-air camp meetings, which involved shouting, singing, conversion, and sometimes mass hysteria. But Rigdon was stylish, an eloquent advocate of enlightenment. Alexander Campbell described Sidney as "the great orator of the Mahoning Association." Robert Richardson, Campbell's son-in-law and biographer, added that Rigdon "was a man of more than ordinary ability as a speaker, possessing great fluency and a lively fancy which gave him great popularity as an orator."[3] Hayden's seminal history added that

> Sidney Rigdon was an orator of no inconsiderable abilities. In person, he was full medium height, rotund in form; of countenance, while speaking, open and winning, with a little cast of melancholy. His action was graceful, his language copious, fluent

in utterance, with articulation clear and musical. . . . His personal influence with an audience was very great. . . . He was just the man for an awakening.[4]

And awaken he did, although his crusade was first in Pittsburgh, not in the Western Reserve as generally believed. Even Alexander Campbell, recalling Rigdon's and Bentley's 1821 visit to Buffaloe, incorrectly stated that "in the course of a single year [Rigdon and Bentley] prepared the whole [Mahoning] Association to hear us with earnestness and candor."[5] While both Bentley and Rigdon returned to their Warren, Ohio, home in the Reserve, Rigdon remained there only three months. Wickliffe Rigdon wrote that in November 1821, Sidney, Phebe, and their infant daughter Athalia,[6] born on 11 August, left by horseback to visit Sidney's mother, brother Carvel, and his sister Lacy Boyer, all still living in St. Clair Township, near Pittsburgh.[7]

There was an additional reason Rigdon returned to western Pennsylvania so soon after his visit with Alexander Campbell. Campbell, who visited Pittsburgh occasionally and preached at the small Baptist church there, likely knew the small congregation was in turmoil, having recently lost its minister, John Davis.[8] Rigdon, devoted like Campbell to restoring "the ancient order of things," though retaining the public air of Regular Baptist orthodoxy, was just the disciple to expand Campbell's influence in the smoky city of Pittsburgh where Campbell's father had earlier met rebuff by the Redstone Baptist Association.

Regular Baptist and Disciples of Christ (Campbellite) sources are confident that Rigdon attained his position in Pittsburgh through Alexander Campbell's efforts. Campbell, recalling the period, said

> On my visits to Pittsburg[h] in those days, being a member and minister of the Redstone Baptist Association, I spoke to the Baptist church in that city. The result was, that, with the exception of some twelve persons, the whole church, over a hundred members, were theoretically reformers. In 1822 I induced Sidney Rigdon, then a Baptist minister of Ohio, to accept of a call to the church in Pittsburg[h].[9]

Neither Rigdon's own account nor those of his son Wickliffe mention Campbell's influence, though they do not rule it out either. Rigdon simply said he continued to preach in Trumball County, Ohio, until November, 1821. "At that time," he noted, he was requested by the First Baptist Church of the city of Pittsburgh, to take the "pastorial charge of said Church."[10] Wickliffe, more expansive, writes:

> Soon after his marriage, he and his wife started on their wedding tour to go to Pittsburg[h] to visit his brother, his mother, and his sister, who resided ten miles from Pittsburg[h]. They went on horseback; that is the way they rode in those days. They reached Pittsburg[h] on Saturday night and stayed there overnight. One of the members of the Baptist church who had heard my father preach came to see him and wanted to know if he would not come to the Baptist church and preach to them

Sunday morning. He said that they had one of the largest churches in the city of Pittsburg[h], but the church had become divided and they had no minister and had no preaching in the church, and he would be much pleased if [father] would come and preach to them Sunday morning.

. . . After his discourse was ended and the congregation were dismissed, he told the congregation that he was going out into the country . . . to visit his [family] and should remain out there about four weeks, and if they wished him to come into the city and preach to them every Sunday morning during the time he remained out in the country, he would do so. . . . This offer they gladly accepted and my father preached in the church for four Sundays in succession. When he got ready to go home, he and his wife again came to Pittsburg[h] and stayed overnight, and quite a number of the members of the church called to see them and wanted to know if he would not, when he got back home, come back and take charge of the church and be their pastor. . . . He said to them that he would take the matter under advisement.

When he got home, he told his father-in-law [Jeremiah Brooks] of the offer the church at Pittsburg[h] had made him, and he, being a great Baptist, urged him by all means to accept it, as it was not very often a young minister received such an offer. It might be the making of him and give him a great reputation.[11]

Shortly after the Rigdons' return to Warren, Phebe Rigdon was baptized on 2 December 1821, nearly eighteen months after marriage to Sidney. The church record reads: "Examined Phebe Rigdon in regard to her religious exercise of mind and received her for baptism. Lordsday Dec. 2, Sister Phebe Rigdon was baptised."[12] One month later the Rigdons, during Sunday services, announced their decision to move to Pittsburgh. The 5 January 1822 record notes: "Bro. Bentley being absent Br. Rigdon was appointed moderator and Bro. B. Austin Clerk (pro tem). Br. S. Rigdon and Phebe his wife requested letters of dismission to the Baptist Church at Pittsburgh which was granted."[13]

Rigdon reported on 28 January 1822 as the fourth pastor to the ten-year-old church. He found 113 members who gathered weekly in their own meetinghouse but who were in a state of precarious equilibrium due to the disjointed leadership of the previous minister, John Davis.[14] The details of Rigdon's 1822-23 ministry are provided in his 1838 autobiography. The two accounts of his son, Wickliffe, provide less a story to tell than a case to make. The 1838 autobiography, in particular, is a tidy package of laundered narrative which omits crucial details while presenting Rigdon as the epitome of propriety.

A debate-master and orator, Rigdon was well armed with eloquence and religious savvy. Confident of his abilities, he was well prepared to defend himself during controversy. In his own account, which follows, he seldom uses "I" in connection with anything personal, speaking of himself in the third person:

At the time he commenced his labors in that Church and for some time before, the Church was in a very low state and much confusion existed in consequence of the conduct of their former pastor. However, soon after Elder Rigdon commenced his labors, there was a pleasing change effected, for by his incessant labors and his peculiar style of preaching, the Church was crowded with anxious listeners. The number of members rapidly increased, and it soon became one of the most respectable Churches in that city. He was now a popular minister, and was much respected in that city, and all classes and persuasions sought his society. After he had been in that place some time, his mind was troubled and much perplexed, with the idea that the doctrines maintained by that society were not altogether in accordance with the scriptures. This thing continued to agitate his mind, more and more, and his reflections on these occasions were peculiarly trying; for according to his views of the word of God, no other church that he was acquainted with was right, or with whom he could associate; consequently, if he was to disavow the doctrine of the Church with whom he was then associated, he knew of no other way of obtaining a livelihood except by mental labor, and at that time had a wife and three children to support.

On the one hand was wealth, popularity and honor, on the other, appeared nothing but poverty and hard labor. But, notwithstanding his great ministerial success, and the prospect of ease and affluence, (which frequently swerve the mind, and have an undue influence on too many who wear the sacred garb of religion, who for the sake of popularity and of wealth, can calm and lull to rest their conscientious scruples, and succomb to the popular church,) yet, his mind rose superior to all these considerations. Truth was his pursuit, and for truth he was prepared to make every sacrifice in his power. After mature deliberation, deep reflection, and solemn prayer to his Heavenly Father, the resolve was made, and the important step was taken; and in the month of August, A.D. 1824, after laboring among that people two years and six months, he made known his determination, to withdraw from the church, as he could no longer uphold the doctrines taught and maintained by it. This announcement was like a clap of thunder—amazement seized the congregation . . . which at last gave way in a flood of tears. It would be in vain to attempt to describe the feelings of the church on that occasion, who were zealously attached to their beloved pastor—or the feelings of their minister. On his part it was indeed a struggle of principle over affection and kindness.[15]

The Baptist accounts simply state that Rigdon was excommunicated, not mentioning that the majority of his congregation left with him, nor explaining that he afterwards served as a Baptist minister in several Western Reserve congregations until his conversion to Mormonism in 1830. The official Pittsburgh First Baptist Church account, adapted from the writings of Reverend Samuel Williams, then serving as pastor of that congregation, affirms that within a year after Rigdon's appointment to the pastorship he "began to advance sentiments not in accordance with divine truth. He held to 'baptismal regeneration' [baptism for the remission of sins]." For this, and other errors, he was "condemned by a council of ministers and messengers from neighboring churches, which convened in Pittsburgh on October 11, 1823. By this decision, he was excluded from the Baptist denomination."[16]

The truth of what happened in Pittsburgh seems to fall somewhere between these two positions. That Rigdon was inspired by Alexander Campbell's reformation ideas in 1821 cannot be denied, as both Campbell and Adamson Bentley readily attest. But Rigdon, possibly because of his 1830 rejection and public humiliation by Campbell, never credits in retrospect the "Sage of Bethany" as anything more than an associate. In reality, the Irish divine was his mentor, his theological preceptor, the Master Spirit of the Reformation. Rigdon's role, although significant, particularly as an orator, was subservient. Campbell's periodical, *The Christian Baptist*, first published in 1823, was a clarion call, the fountainhead of much of Rigdon's personal theology for seven years.

In an 1869 interview, Rigdon, true to form, took full credit for his personal reformation in Pittsburgh. Campbell's name never came up. Instead, in Sidney's words, the change came because of "His intense love of investigation and new modes of thought." He added that

> he thoroughly reviewed the Scriptures, and reached down to their profoundest depths. Dissatisfied with all ordinary interpretations, he began a series of new and original explanations of doctrine, of history and of prophecy. These novelties soon appeared in his preaching, and at length he announced to his congregation that he could not preach the doctrines or receive the interpretations of Scripture which the church professed to believe. He resigned his charge: but a large number of the congregation sympathized with him, and wished him to form a new congregation.[17]

Few, if any, of Rigdon's flock were aware at the time that their new pastor intended to introduce the Pittsburgh Regular Baptist congregation to the "ancient order of things," but he had promised Campbell to do exactly that as he departed Buffaloe Creek in the summer of 1821. Their ultimate goal, eventually reached, was to unite the Baptist congregation with the Pittsburgh New Light Presbyterian Society led by Christian reformer Walter Scott.

That Rigdon met with objection from some members should not be surprising. Wickliffe Rigdon sheds light on the matter. "At length an old Scotch divine came to Pittsburg[h]," he wrote, "and wanted to know of my father if he preached and taught the Baptist confession of faith [regarding] infant damnation." The "divine" was likely the Reverend John Winter, newly arrived in Pennsylvania from Great Britain and boarding in the Rigdon home. In their conversation Rigdon replied that infant damnation was not his personal theology, nor did he teach it. Winter argued that he was required to teach it, despite his personal belief, because it was "part of the Baptist confession of faith." Rigdon replied it was "too horrible a doctrine to teach and he would have nothing to do with it."[18] This same position on infant baptism later attracted him to the Book of Mormon.

Wickliffe reported that once this position was known to the congregation, a dispute ensued, but most active members of the group were from Scotland and Ireland and sympathized with Rigdon. According to a Disciple historian, "Debates and dissensions arose frequently between members, while that watchful surveillance, amounting almost to inquisitorial scrutiny, which each thought it his duty to exercise over others occasioned numerous cases of discipline, by which the public religious meetings were disturbed and the cause discredited."[19] While older members advised Rigdon to abide by the Confession Of Faith, younger members thought he acted wisely in refusing to teach the doctrine. Wickliffe concluded his narrative by adding, "my father, seeing there was to be a division in the church, tendered his resignation and the church got another minister."[20]

While this certainly would have been magnanimous on Rigdon's part, it could not have happened quite that way. There could not have been a resignation in 1824 because he had already been released on 11 October 1823. The chain of events that led to his dismissal was initiated by John Winter who formed an opposition coalition of twelve to twenty members. Rigdon's faction of seventy to eighty members and the smaller Winter group each claimed to be the First Baptist Church of Pittsburgh and expelled the other.[21]

The Winter clique struck first on 11 July 1823. Excluding Rigdon and denying him the "liberty of speaking in self defense," as family members later said,[22] these opponents protested his heresy. According to Reverend Williams, who served as minister from 1827-55, Rigdon erred in teaching:

1. [That] Christians are not under obligation to keep the moral law, it having been abolished by the Savior.
2. That the Jewish dispensation was not the best that God might have given to that nation, for it had made them threefold more the children of hell than they were before.
3. That a change of heart consists merely in a change of views and baptism.
4. That there is no such thing as religious experience.
5. That saving faith is a mere crediting of the testimony given by the evangelists such as all persons have in the truth of any other history.
6. That it is wrong to use the Lord's prayer, inasmuch as the reign of Christ has now already commenced.

Williams added that Rigdon also spoke publicly of restoring the "ancient order of things," among which was laying all one's possessions "down at the *Apostles' feet*." At firesides he frequently introduced his "common stock system," as he called it, and "urged with importunity, many of the members to embrace the system." Among other "extravagant expressions" against the regular ministry of the gospel, Rigdon reportedly said that ministers "milched the goats," meaning that because they received money for preaching, theirs were not the sheep of Christ's flock. The greatest of Rigdon's errors, according to Williams, was teaching the doctrine of baptismal regeneration.[23]

Williams's shrill, sectarian accusations were written long after Rigdon had joined the Mormons. Anti-Rigdon fervor was commonfare in Calvinist circles once it was known he had embraced the Reformed Movement, and then the

Mormons. A typical Baptist assessment is I. M. Allen's 1833 sketch of the Pittsburgh First Baptist Church. "Mr. Sidney Rigdon," he began, is "a superficial, flipant man, who for a season promised some usefulness, but, soon embracing the errors of Alexander Campbell, rent the church in pieces, until only fourteen out of ninety-six members remained on the original ground of their constitution. After prosecuting the work of destruction for two years, Mr. Rigdon was excluded from the connection."[24]

Rigdon retaliated by declaring "non-fellowship" with the Winter group.[25] Both factions appeared at the Redstone Association annual meetings, held in Pittsburgh in September 1823, to argue who would be the official Pittsburgh church. This was not the principle item on the agenda, however. The association, angered at Alexander Campbell's liberal *Christian Baptist* periodical and his earlier "Sermon on the Law," had for months sought ways to expel him. Elders Brownfield, Pritchard, and the Stones, members of Redstone affiliates, traveled among the churches urging them to appoint as messengers for the September meeting men who were unfriendly to Campbell and would work to rid the association of him.

Campbell, however, heard of the ploy in August and in a clever stratagem was able to shake off his personal antagonists. He assembled the Brush Run Church and announced that "a crisis of great importance had arrived and great interests which it would be imprudent for me then to disclose, were now pending, and that, without giving any other reason for it, I must request for myself and some twenty other persons, members of that church, letters of dismission, drawn up in Regular Baptist style, for the purpose of establishing a church in Charlestown [now Wellsburg, West Virginia]," a few miles from his residence on Buffaloe Creek.[26]

Quietly, without mentioning his plan to others in the Redstone Association, Campbell persuaded messengers John Brown (his father-in-law) and George Young to apply for membership in the more tolerant Mahoning Association where reforming principles were welcome. Except for this hasty retreat, he would certainly have met Rigdon's fate.

When the Redstone Association convened and announced plans to expel him, Campbell stood up near the rear of the small meetinghouse where he was seated. "Exclude me?" he said in effect. "How can you? I have left you. I have joined a new church in Charleston with thirty-three kindred souls, and we are embraced in the folds of the Mahoning Association."[27] Later recalling his triumph, Campbell wrote: "Never did hunters, on seeing the game unexpectedly escape from their tools at the moment when its capture was sure, glare upon each other a more mortifying disappointment than that indicated by my pursuers at that instant, on hearing that I was out of their bailiwick, and consequently out of their jurisdiction. A solemn stillness ensued, and, for a time, all parties seemed to have nothing to do."[28]

"After dismissing a few minor matters," Campbell later wrote, "they seemed to rally on certain allegations in the letter from a party of dissidents in Pittsburg[h], preferred against the Baptist church in that city for having departed from the Baptist Confession of Faith under the teaching of Sidney Rigdon." Campbell noted that "through the potency of the reasonings and facts alleged by Elder John Rigdon [Sidney's cousin] and the Brush Run delegation, they failed in carrying the point, referring it to a committee to report at their next annual meeting."[29]

The published version of Campbell's previous debate with John Walker included a general challenge for further discussion. "I feel disposed to meet any Pedobaptist minister of any denomination," Campbell crowed, "and I engage to prove in a debate with him, either viva voce, or with the pen, that infant sprinkling is a human tradition and injurious to the well being of society, religious and political."[29] A former attorney, the Reverend W. L. McCalla, a persuasive speaker and Presbyterian minister of Augusta, Kentucky, ventured a response. The debate was scheduled for Washington, Mason County, Kentucky, from 15-21 October. Because the Ohio River was too low for steamboats, Campbell and Rigdon traveled three hundred miles through Ohio and into Kentucky by horseback. During the lengthy ride the men took pleasure in the rich valley of the Scioto and of countryside they had never before visited, though from New Lancaster through the fertile level land to Wilmington the populace was suffering from autumnal fever.[30]

The debate was nevertheless held. Campbell defended not only baptism by immersion but also the meaning of baptism. He argued that it is appropriate only for penitent believers in Christ, not for infants. He argued that the purpose of baptism is not for the forgiveness of original sin but for absolution of personal sin.

After his return from the McCalla debate, Campbell began to assemble from his and Rigdon's notes a version of the proceedings, citing in the preface of the printed debate notes taken by "Bishop Sidney Rigdon of Pittsburgh."[31] Rigdon wrote in the preface, dated 4 May 1824, that his notes were a "fair and full exhibition of both sides of the controversy, of the arguments and topics of illustration, used by the aforesaid gentlemen."[32]

Many Baptist preachers at the debate found Campbell's plea for rejecting creeds and returning to the Bible a heartening tonic. They left more rebellious against the rigid Philadelphia Confession of Faith to which they were obliged to subscribe. But the "ancient order" had, as yet, been introduced only into the churches at Brush Run, Wellsburg, and Pittsburgh.

Rigdon and Campbell were both shocked upon their return from Kentucky to find that instead of waiting a year as the Redstone Association had recommended, dissident members of the Pittsburgh First Baptist Church had turned their wrath on Rigdon on 11 October 1823 while he was absent.[33] Of this action Campbell noted, "[T]hey proceeded to do that which they were not commanded to do, and did, without any authority from the association, call or denominate the excommunicated ones a church."[34] The expulsion of Rigdon's faction reduced the membership to twenty-two who soon lost the meetinghouse "due to non-payment of ground rent."[35]

Undaunted by their loss of official status, Rigdon and followers joined with Walter Scott's small New Light Presbyterian group, which was Campbell's intent all along. The society became known as "Kissing Baptists" for their Separatist Baptist manner of greeting each other with a "Holy Kiss." They had no meetinghouse and met every Sunday in the Allegheny County Court House. Scott, a young single Scot ten years Rigdon's junior, had arrived in Pittsburgh on 7 May 1819 and became affiliated with a small company of Christian Primitivists who had organized under the direction of George Forrester. A former Scotch Baptist, Forrester had prepared for the ministry under the direction of Robert and James Haldane, mentors of Thomas Campbell.

Although Scott was not a Baptist, he, Alexander Campbell, and Rigdon, principle leaders of the Reform, agreed in the "power of the gospel to recover Christendom from its numberless sects and divisions; and to restore the unity of the faith once delivered to the saints." From that day they were engaged in the common cause of "re-proclaiming to the world the gospel as it began in Jerusalem on the first Pentecost after the Lord's ascension."[36]

Rigdon's own account notes that after separating from the Pittsburgh First Baptist Church he, Campbell, and Scott were on "terms of the greatest friendship, and frequently met together to discuss the subject of religion; being yet undetermined respecting the principles of the doctrine of Christ, or what course to pursue."[37]

One thing was certain: Rigdon had lost his job and had no income. Although most of the Pittsburgh First Baptist Church followed him to Scott's Sandemanian Church, the Reformers did not support their ministers financially as had the Baptists. Borrowed directly from the Sandemanians, their creed declared that "the elders of the churches should not look to their brethren for a support, but should obtain it by the sweat of their faces in some kind of manual occupation."[38]

Campbell, speaking of the union between Rigdon and Scott, said, "There is a church in Pittsburgh that would rejoice much more in being a regular church of Christ, than a regular Baptist church; which church has two bishops, who while they watch over and labor among the saints, labor working with their own hands, *according to the apostolic command*; and not only minister to their own wants, but are ensamples to the flock in beneficience and hospitality."[39]

Scott was a school teacher, Rigdon became a tanner. In his third-person narrative, Rigdon discussed his line of work: "Having now retired from the [professional] ministry, and having no way by which to sustain his family, besides his own industry, he was necessitated to find other employment in order to provide for his maintenance, and for this purpose he engaged in the humble capacity of a journeyman tanner."[40] Rigdon apprenticed under his brother-in-law, Richard Brooks. Wickliffe wrote that "My father contributed some money to the business"[41]–likely the proceeds from the sale of Sidney's St. Clair farm. It was purchased by James Means on 28 June 1823.[42]

Status-conscious, Rigdon had a lifelong tendency to put on superior airs, and a tannery bespoke a down-at-heel's life. In addition to being surrounded with vats of lime solution, ammonia, and tanning liquors, tanners scraped the loosened hair and flesh from hides by hand. Rigdon himself called it a "humble occupation," and humiliation seemed to be his primary emotion. He added that when many of his former friends, those "who manifested the greatest love for his society," saw him wearing "the garb suited to the employment of a tanner, there was no longer that freedom, courtesy and friendship manifested."[43]

The indifference of his former associates struck at the core of Rigdon's self-esteem. That it seared his soul is apparent from his recollections fifteen years later. "To a well regulated and enlightened mind," he began, "to one who soars above the arbitrary and vain lines of distinction which pride or envy may draw, such conduct appears ridiculous—while at the same time it cannot but cause feelings of a peculiar nature, in those, who for their honesty and integrity of heart, have brought themselves into situations to be made the subjects of it."[44]

Despite friends' reactions, he did not veer from his purpose. "He had counted the cost before his separation," he explained, "and had made his mind known to his wife, who cheerfully shared his sorrow and humiliation, believing that all things would work together for their good, being conscious that what they had done was for conscience sake, and in the fear of the Lord."[45]

Notes

Unless otherwise stated, all primary sources cited are located in the Historical Department of the Church of Jesus Christ of Latter-day Saints, Salt Lake City, Utah.

1. *Christian Baptist* 1:10.
2. Campbell had no notion of establishing a new sect. It was his followers who brought this about. He wrote: "I have no idea of adding to the catalogue of new sects; this game has been played too long. I labor to see sectarianism abolished and all Christians of every name united upon the one foundation on which the apostolic church was founded" (ibid. 4:217).

He originally thought of his own followers, like himself, as merely nominal Baptists. As the gap widened the terms "Reformers" and "Reformed Baptists" were widely used, but

Campbell rejected them as he did the term "Campbellites." The question of a name did not become a serious issue within the movement until the separation from the Baptists in 1830. He preferred the term Disciples, or Disciples of Christ.

In 1832 Campbell united with the Christian Connection, led prominently by Barton W. Stone. Although their internal organization was not complete until 1849, the Disciples of Christ can be said to have assumed denominational status by the earlier date.

3. Robert Richardson, *Memoirs of Alexander Campbell*, 2 vols. (Philadelphia: J.E. Lippincott and Company 1868, 1872), 2:45, 47.

4. Amos Sutton Hayden, *Early History of the Disciples in the Western Reserve* (Cincinnati: Chase and Hall, 1875), 191-92.

5. *The Millennial Harbinger* 5 (1848): 523.

6. Athalia says she was born in Hartford, Trumbull County. See 10 Oct. 1900 statement of Athalia R. Robinson.

7. J. Wickliffe Rigdon, "Life Story of Sidney Rigdon," 6.

8. Pittsburgh's earliest Baptist church was organized in April 1812 under the direction of Rigdon's former minister, the Reverend David Philips from Peters Creek, and included only twelve members. Edward Jones was the founding minister. At its reception into the Redstone Association in 1816, the membership had dwindled to eight. The society was too poor to build a church and worshiped in private homes and in rented halls (John Newton Boucher, ed., *A Century and a Half of Pittsburgh and Her People* [Pittsburgh: The Lewis Publishing Co., 1908], 243).

9. William H. Whitsitt, "Sidney Rigdon, The Real Founder of Mormonism," 1885, 140-41, Special Collections, Marriott Library, University of Utah (hereafter Special Collections, U of U); Samuel Williams, *Mormonism Exposed* (Pittsburgh: n.p., 1842), 2-3; Richardson, 2:47. Campbell's account is in the *Millennial Harbinger* 5 (Oct. 1848): 553.

10. *Times and Seasons* 4 (4 May 1843): 177.

11. Karl Keller, ed., "'I Never Knew a Time When I Did Not Know Joseph Smith': A Son's Record of the Life and Testimony of Sidney Rigdon," *Dialogue: A Journal of Mormon Thought* 1 (Winter 1966): 15-42, cited, 20-21; Rigdon, "Life Story of Sidney Rigdon," 5-6.

12. Record, Warren Central Christian Church, 79, in Hans Rollmann, "The Early Baptist Career of Sidney Rigdon in Warren, Ohio," *Brigham Young University Studies* 21 (Winter 1981): 37-50, cited, 50.

13. Ibid.

14. Rigdon legally organized the congregation under a charter from the Common-wealth of Pennsylvania which designated his ministry "The First Baptist Church and Congregation of the City of Pittsburgh" (Sarah H. Killikelly, *The History of Pittsburgh: Its Rise and Progress* [Pittsburgh: B. C. & Gordon Montgomery Co., 1906], 377-78; Frank C. Harper, *Pittsburgh of Today*, 2 vols. [New York: The American Historical Society, Inc., 1931], 2:768).

15. This dictated autobiography was published in *Times and Seasons* 4 (1 May 1843): 177-78. The manuscript account is in Manuscript History of the Church, Book A-1, 63-64. Aside from punctuation changes the accounts are virtually identical except for changing the words "manual labor" in the original to "mental labor" in the published version. There is also a partial version of the manuscript account in the Sidney Rigdon Collection.

16. Williams 1842, 2; see also Nancy R. Myler (historian of The First Baptist Church

of Pittsburgh) to Arlene Hess, 17 July 1972, Hess Collection, mss. 1281, fd. 6, item #3, Special Collections, Harold B. Lee Library, Brigham Young University, Provo, Utah (hereafter Special Collections, BYU).

17. A. W. Cowles, "The Mormons: Pen and Pencil Sketches, Illustrating their Early History," *Moore's Rural New Yorker*, 23 Jan. 1869, 61, Special Collections, BYU.

18. Rigdon, 8.

19. Richardson, 2:125.

20. Keller, 22-23.

21. *Christian Baptist* 1:184.

22. Sworn statement by Carvel Rigdon and Peter Boyer, 27 Jan. 1843, in Daryl Chase, "Sidney Rigdon—Early Mormon," M.A. thesis, University of Chicago, 1931, 18.

23. Williams, 2-3.

24. I. H. Allen, *The United States Baptist Annual Register and Almanac* (Philadelphia: T. W. Upstick, 1833), 131.

25. Chase, 18.

26. *Millennial Harbinger* 5 (Oct. 1848): 554.

27. Louis Cochran and Bess White Cochran, *Captives of the Word* (Garden City, NY: Doubleday & Co., 1969), 25.

28. Richardson, 2:70.

29. *Millennial Harbinger* 5 (Oct. 1848): 556.

30. Alexander Campbell, *A Debate on Christian Baptism Between The Rev. W. L. MacCalla, A Presbyterian Teacher, and Alexander Campbell, Held at Washington, KY. Commencing on the 15th and Terminating on the 21st Oct. 1823* (Buffaloe, VA: Campbell & Sala, 1824), 141.

31. Richardson, 2:71.

32. Bishop, in the sense that it is used by the Reformers, implies a leader rather than an office. Alexander Campbell defined a bishop's duties:

> The bishop of a Christian congregation will find much to do that never enters into the mind of a modern preacher or minister. The duties he is to discharge to Christ's flock in the capacity of teacher and president will engross much of his time and attention. Therefore, the idea of remuneration for his services was attached to the office from the first institution. This is indisputably plain, not only from the positive commands delivered to the congregations but from the hints uttered with reference to the office itself. Why should it be so much as hinted that the bishops were not to take the oversight of the flock *"for the sake of sordid gain,"* if no emolument or remuneration was attached to the office? The abuses of the principle have led many to oppose even the principle itself (*Christian Baptist* 3:360).

33. Campbell, ix.

34. Richardson 1872, 2:99.

35. Whitsitt, 145.

36. Nancy R. Myler to Arlene Hess, 17 July 1972, Hess Collection, mss. 1281, fd. 6, item #3, Special Collections, BYU.

37. Hayden, 63.

38. *Times and Seasons* 4 (15 May 1843): 193.

39. Whitsitt, 149.

40. *Christian Baptist* 1:91.

41. *Times and Seasons* 4 (15 May 1843): 193.

42. Keller, 22.

43. Whitsitt, 3.

44. *Times and Seasons* 4 (15 May 1843): 193.

45. Ibid. Although not true, Eber Howe affirmed that "Rigdon resided in Pittsburgh about three years, and during the whole of that time, as he has since frequently asserted, abandoned preaching and all other employment for the purpose of studying the bible" (*Mormonism Unvailed* [Painesville, OH: E. D. Howe, 1834], 289).

CHAPTER 4

Bainbridge

S idney and Phebe Rigdon's family, now including children Athalia (b. 1821), Nancy (b. 1822), Elizabeth or Eliza (b. 1823), and Phebe, Jr. (b. 1824), moved their meager belongings in December 1825 to Bainbridge, Geauga County, Ohio, in the Western Reserve. They settled on a landed estate owned by Phebe's father, Jeremiah Brooks, on the "Chillicothe [Road] just above Taylor Road and a mile north of Centerville."[1]

Unlike the stilted and staid Redstone Association, Baptist organizations in the vigorous Western Reserve not only tolerated new biblical interpretations but welcomed and embraced them. Eastern Ohio settlers had grown weary of hearing they were lost in a world of sin until God at his pleasure rescued them. This theological uneasiness helped free-thinking Baptist ministers like Sidney Rigdon introduce fresh points of view.

The Reformed Baptist Movement did not become a separate denomination, the Disciples of Christ, until 1832—two years after Rigdon had left the movement. Even Campbell did not foresee the founding of a separate sect, initially presuming Christian unity within the liberal arms of the Mahoning Baptist Association. But he was "firmly convinced, fully convinced," as he put it, "that the whole head is sick, and the whole heart faint of modern fashionable Christianity."[2]

Rigdon was in full accord and longed to put a healing hand to the brow of the ailing churches in the Reserve. This desire was satisfied almost immediately upon his arrival. His own account said that it was known "he had been a preacher, and had gained considerable distinction as a public speaker, and the people soliciting him to preach, he complied with their request."[3]

The small Bainbridge congregation embraced a Calvinistic creed, which had become unacceptable to Rigdon, but he was invited to serve without having to endorse their articles of faith. "From this time forward," he noted, he "devoted himself to the work of the ministry, confining himself to no creed, but held up the Bible as the rule of faith, and advocating those doctrines which had been the subject of his, and Mr. Campbell's investigations, viz: Repentence and baptism, for the remission of sins."[4]

He served the area as a circuit preacher, much like his 1820-21 ministry in Warren. "His former success attended his labors," he noted of his six-month sojourn in the area. The largest congregation under his influence was at Mantua Center, Portage County, Ohio, where he preached once a month. The group consisted of disciples from Nelson, Hiram, and Mantua. On 24 August 1824 this congregation passed a resolution "to remove the Philadelphia Confession of Faith and the Church Articles, and to take the Word of God for our Rule of Faith and Practice."[5] This action established the assemblage as "the first Church of Christ of the Restoration Movement in Ohio," according to official Disciple of Christ accounts.[6]

Adamson Bentley and a few other reformers also met with considerable success in the Western Reserve, their work influenced by Campbell's *Christian Baptist*. In 1825 Campbell wrote a series of articles entitled "A Restoration of the Ancient Order of Things" in which he urged abandoning anything not a part of primitive Christianity—creeds and confessions, unscriptural words and phrases, and theological theories. He also urged adopting everything sanctioned by the New Testament such as the weekly breaking of the loaf, Christian fellowship, the simple order of public worship, and the independence of each church under the care of its bishops and deacons.

Rigdon incorporated these innovations in his own preaching. "Large numbers invariably attended his meetings," he related in his autobiography, and

> [t]he doctrines which he advanced being new, public attention was awakened, and great excitement pervaded throughout that whole section of country, and frequently the congregations which he addressed, were so large that it was impossible to make himself audible to all. The subjects he proposed were presented in such an impressive manner to the congregations, that those who were unbiased by bigotry and prejudice, had to exclaim, "we never heard it in this manner before."
> . . . Those by whom he was opposed, well knew that an honorable and public investigation, would inevitably discover the weakness and fatality of their doctrines; consequently they shunned it, and endeavored, by ridiculing the doctrines which he promulgated, to suppress them. But they were unsuccessful, did not turn him from the path which he felt to be his duty. He continued to set forth the doctrines of repentance, and baptism for remission of sins, and the gift of the Holy Ghost, according to the teachings of Peter, on the day of Pentecost, exhorting his hearers in the mean time, to throw away their creeds of faith—to take the Bible as their standard, and search its sacred pages—to learn to live by every word that proceedeth from the mouth of the Lord, and to rise above every sectarian sentiment, and the traditions of the age, and explore the wide and glorious fields of truth which the scriptures holds out to them.[7]

In June 1826, Warner Goodall, venerable Baptist preacher at Mentor, thirty miles from Bainbridge, passed away. Rigdon was invited to deliver Goodall's eulogy. The funeral sermon so impressed the congregation that in the fall they offered Rigdon Goodall's former pastorship. According to Rigdon's autobiography, Mentor had been settled by wealthy and enterprising individuals "who had by their industry and good management made that township one of the most delightful in that country, or probably in the Western Reserve." It was a land of "splendid farms, fertile fields, and stately mansions," and is still one of the most beautiful areas in eastern Ohio.

Although Rigdon and the other reformers had not yet broken openly from the Regular Baptists, their agenda was to continually advocate a restoration of the "ancient order." In Mentor, Rigdon initially encountered the same opposition as in Pittsburgh and Bainbridge. "Many reports were put in circulation," he said, "of a character calculated to lessen him in the estimation of the people, and consequently destroy his influence. Some persons were even wicked enough to retail those slanderous reports which were promulgated, and endeavored to stir up persecution against him; consequently many of the citizens were jealous, and did not extend to him that confidence which he might otherwise have expected."

For the first eight months his Mentor ministry was turbulent, but the "storm subsided" because of his "consistent walk and conversation—his sociability, combined with his overwhelming eloquence." The hearts of his detractors softened, "their evil aprehensions and surmisings were allayed, their prejudices gave way, and the man whom they had looked upon with jealousy was now their theme of praise, and their welcome guest. Those who had been most hostile, now became his warmest admirers, and most constant friends."

Rigdon's teachings were new, he said,

> but at the same time were elucidated with such clearness, and enforced with an eloquence altogether superior to what they had listened to before, that those whose sectarian prejudices were not too deeply rooted, who listened to the deep and searching discourses which he delivered from time to time, could not fail of being greatly affected, and convinced that the principles he advanced were true, and in acordance with the scriptures.

His labors were not confined to Mentor, although he lived there, but over a "vast extent of country." He explained:

> His fame as an orator and deep reasoner in the scriptures continued to spread far and wide, and he soon gained a popularity and an elevation which has fallen to the lot of but few, consequently thousands flocked to hear his eloquent discourses. . . . The churches in the different places, where he preached, were no longer large enough to contain the vast assemblies which congregated from time to time, so that he had to repair to the wide spread canopy of heaven, and in the woods and in the groves, he addressed the multitudes which flocked to hear him.

The popular preacher not only focused on Christ's New Testament teachings but drew attention to "the ancient prophets, particularly those prophesies which had reference to the present and to the future." He proclaimed:

> No longer did he follow the old beaten track, which had been travelled for ages by the religious world, but he dared to enter upon new grounds; called in question the opinions of uninspired men; shewed the foolish ideas of many commentators on the

sacred scriptures—exposed their ignorance and contradictions—threw new light on the sacred volume, particularly those prophesies which so deeply interest this generation, and which had been entirely overlooked, or mystified by the religious world—cleared up scriptures which had heretofore appeared inexplicable, and delighted his astonished audience with things "new and old"—proved to a demonstration the literal fulfilment of prophesy, the gathering of Israel in the last days, to their ancient inheritances, with their ultimate splendor and glory; the situation of the world at the coming of the Son of Man—the judgments which Almighty God would pour out upon the ungodly, prior to that event, and the reign of Christ with his saints on the earth, in the millenium.

These important subjects could not fail to have their weight on the minds of his hearers, who clearly discerned the situation in which they were placed, by the sound and logical arguments which he adduced; and soon, numbers felt the importance of obeying that form of doctrine which had been delivered them; so that they might be accounted worthy to escape those things which were coming on the earth, and many came forward desiring to be baptized for the remission of sins. He accordingly commenced to baptize, and like John of old, there flocked to him people from all the region round about—persons of all ranks and standings in society—the rich, the poor, the noble and the brave, flocked to be baptized of him. Nor was this desire confined to individuals, or families, but whole societies threw away their creeds and articles of faith, and became obedient to the faith he promulgated, and he soon had large and flourishing societies throughout that whole region of country.

He was now a welcome visitor wherever he traveled—his society was courted by the learned, and intelligent, and the highest encomiums were bestowed upon him for his biblical lore, and his eloquence.[8]

During August 1826 the Mahoning Baptist Association annual convocation was held in Canfield, Ohio, in David Hays's barn. Bentley was the moderator, Rigdon a visiting minister. It was customary in the association to have preaching for the public while the messengers were transacting business. Campbell preached the keynote sermon on Saturday. His theme centered on the "Progress of Revealed Thought." This later became known as his "four-ages" sermon based on the conclusion of the prophecies of Malachi. He differentiated between the Starlight, Moonlight, Twilight, and Sunlight ages, and compared them to the Patriarchal and Jewish ages, the times of John the Baptist, and the Modern age.[9]

Rigdon and Scott preached on Sunday morning in the Congregational meeting house, Rigdon using the sixteenth chapter of John as his sermon. One account reported that several people who missed the opening introduction thought they were hearing Alexander Campbell. The eloquence implied by this anecdote is illustrated by James Madison's impression of Campbell's address to the Virginia Constitutional Convention in 1829. The former U.S. president stated that Campbell was "the ablest and most original expounder of the Scriptures" he had ever heard.[10]

Rigdon's vainglorious reports of success, well documented in his own accounts, may not have been far off the mark. Other, less biased sources provide corroborative evidence. The most noted omission in his accounts, however, is the failure to credit others, particularly Campbell and Scott, for their successful ministries. Rigdon went so far on one occasion as to say: "The reason why they were called Campbellites, was, in consequence of Mr. Campbell's publishing the [*Christian Baptist*], and it being the means through which they communicated their sentiments to the world; other than this, Mr. Campbell was no more the originator of that sect than Elder Rigdon."[11]

Rigdon most certainly did triumph, but in terms of overall contributions to the Reformed Movement he must be considered a step behind Walter Scott and Alexander Campbell. Indeed, efforts to unify churches in New Testament Christianity did not firmly take hold until Scott began evangelizing in the Western Reserve in 1828. The groundwork for this was laid during the Mahoning Baptist Association annual meetings held in New Lisbon in 1827. Reports for the year were not encouraging. In the seventeen churches of the association there had only been thirty-four baptisms and thirteen other additions, counteracted by thirteen excommunications.[12]

Campbell became convinced that the association needed an evangelist, a traveling preacher who could ignite the entire Western Reserve with religious fervor. Passing through Steubenville, Ohio, en route to the Mahoning meetings, Campbell called on his old friend Walter Scott, principal of the academy there, and persuaded him to come to New Lisbon. Previous to the meeting, the Braceville church had prepared a petition in consultation with the church at Nelson. The idea, as Campbell had set forth, was to select a suitable person to travel among the churches, preaching the gospel and setting things in order according to the teachings of the primitive church. Rigdon, along with Bentley, Campbell, and others, served on the nomination committee. They recommended that Scott be selected as the organization's evangelist.

One can only speculate why Rigdon was not Campbell's choice. Although his oratorical skills were on a par with Scott's, the latter's education surpassed Rigdon's common school experience, and Scott, like Campbell, was from Great Britain. Or the reason may have been political. Scott had been planning a periodical, the *Millennial Herald*, which would rival Campbell's *Christian Baptist*.[13] When Scott became the evangelist of the Mahoning Association, he was sidetracked—temporarily at least—from pursuing his real goals. This would not be the only time Campbell would effectively block Scott's bid for leadership.[14]

Another possibility, later expressed in Alexander Campbell's memoirs, was that Rigdon was "petulant, unreliable, and ungovernable in his passions, and his wayward temper, his extravagant stories and his habit of self-assertion . . . prevented him from attaining influence as a religious teacher among the disciples."[15] Rigdon is usually viewed through the perspective of his defection, however, and one should note that virtually every unfavorable Baptist, Disciple, and Mormon account of Rigdon was written after he left that particular movement. This "apostasy factor" greatly influenced the way he was analyzed, evaluated, and remembered.

For whatever reason, Scott was appointed and Rigdon was not, and the choice was a wise one. In the words of one historical account, Scott "was not a member of the association, not a Baptist, not a member of any church in the town where he lived, not a resident of the district in which the Mahoning churches were located, not an ordained minister. But it was a good appointment."[16] Scott was in his prime, not yet thirty-one years old. Aside from a classical education, obtained at the University of Edinburgh, he had been a school master for more than a decade. His knowledge of the Bible was extensive, his faith and love genuine. He endeared himself through his fine singing voice, pleasing manner, and storehouse of classical and sacred imagery.

After his appointment Scott left his family in Steubenville, where they had lived since 1826, and began to traverse his territory. Of his position Scott wrote in 1832:

> I never made one objection to the nomination, nor to the appointment but saw in it a providence, I believed no mortal then understood but myself. I immediately cut all other connections, abandoned my projected editorship, dissolved my academy; left my church, left my family, dropped the bitterest tear over my infant household that ever escaped from my eyes, and set out under the simple conduct of Jesus Christ, to make an experiment of what is now styled the Ancient Gospel.[17]

There was no emotional frenzy in Scott's rhetoric as in Rigdon's. Instead he was able to calmly blend rationality and authority, appealing to common sense and to scripture. "The force and freshness of Scott's evangelistic appeal," wrote prominent Disciple historians Winfred E. Garrison and Alfred T. DeGroot, "the exciting sense of discovery, the thought that an ancient treasure of divine truth was just now being brought to light after having been lost for centuries, the sense of witnessing the dawn of a new epoch in the history of Christianity—these things gave to the revival an extraordinary character."[18] A description of Scott's preaching in the winter of 1827-28 said: "He contended ably for the restoration of the true, original apostolic order which would restore to the church the ancient gospel as preached by the apostles. The interest became an excitement; . . . the air was thick with rumors of a 'new religion,' a 'new Bible.'"[19]

Scott's approach, obviously influenced by his background as a master teacher, was unprecedented. When he arrived in a community where he had never preached, he first sought out local children. His after-school conversations and simple gospel games won their confidence. One approach was to gather a group of youngsters together and ask them to raise their left hands. Then he would say, "Now, beginning with your thumbs repeat what I say to you: 'Faith, Repentence, Baptism, Remission of Sins, Gift of the Holy Spirit.' Now again, repeat! Again, faster!" After the children had learned this "five-finger exercise," they were told to inform their parents he would "preach the gospel that night as they had learned it on the fingers of their hands."[20]

Scott's critics accused him of erratic behavior as they had Rigdon, though Scott was certainly more stable. Some people considered him obsessed. A Methodist preacher whose flock Scott invaded claimed several of his former parishioners had been strangled, that a few had drowned during their baptism. Rowdy groups lined the banks of the Mahoning, which became a second Jordan, to greet the newly baptized with derision. Scott's horse was often set loose while he preached, and once when he located the animal he discovered its tail had been cut off.

Campbell, upon hearing unsettling rumors about Scott, persuaded his father Thomas to visit the Evangelist in the Western Reserve. His report praised Scott. "We have long . . . spoken and published many things *correctly concerning* the ancient gospel," he wrote Alexander, "but I must confess that . . . I am at present for the first time upon the ground where the thing has appeared to be *practically* exhibited to the proper purpose."[21]

Scott's success continued. The following year he was re-appointed to the position, but not without considerable discussion. The debate during the Mahoning Association's annual meetings went stale when Rigdon, a messenger from the Grand River Association, said, "You are consuming too much time on this question. One of the old Jerusalem preachers would start out with his hunting shirt and moccasins, and convert half the world while you are discussing and settling plans!" Scott then arose with a smile on his face and said, "Brethren, give me my Bible, my Head, and Bro. William Hayden, and we will go out and convert the world." Rigdon opined, "I move that we give Br. Scott his Bible, his Head, and Bro. William Hayden." Rigdon's resolution was seconded and passed unanimously.[22]

January 1828 saw the "Siege of Warren." This event of major significance in Disciples of Christ history occurred when Adamson Bentley and his entire congregation came into the restoration because of Scott's efforts. Bentley, a reader and agent of the *Christian Baptist*, had "preached well and lived well; but he held not the key to the heart, nor was he skilled to awaken the music of the soul," according to Disciple historian A. S. Hayden.[23] Because of his long-term association with Alexander Campbell, Scott presumed Bentley's flock would immediately come into the fold. But Bentley, although a reformer at heart, was cautious about Scott's approach, particularly when the Evangelist announced, "I have got the saw by the handle, and I expect to saw you all asunder."[24]

Scott requested the use of Bentley's Baptist meetinghouse for preaching, but when Bentley refused Scott addressed a small group at the courthouse instead. The following evening, however, Bentley relented. The Warren church doors were opened and an overflowing crowd gathered to have the "great truths of the gospel [poured] red hot into their ears," as Scott put it.[25] His biographer added that he "presented Christianity in virgin robes of truth and purity, and made it seem like a gospel indeed—glad tidings of great joy to all people."[26] After only eight days the entire Warren congregation, with the exception of six people in two families, embraced the Reformed Movement. Repeat visits brought even more into the gospel net. Within five months 117 new baptisms took place.

Rigdon visited Scott on a trip to Warren in March 1828. Although Rigdon had been with Scott on former occasions and had fully adopted his method of calling awakened and penitent believers to an immediate obedience of their faith for the remission of sins, he held to the Calvinist assertion that baptism, a symbol of acceptance of Christ, did not remit sins: such remission was connected to faith alone. Scott accepted converts on a simple confession of repentance to God and faith in the Lord Jesus after which they were baptized for an immediate acquittal from sins through the blood of Christ and for the Holy Spirit. His baptismal formula was: "For the remission of your sins and the gift of the Holy Spirit, I immerse you in the name of the Father, and of the Son, and of the Holy Spirit!"[27] "The missing link between Christ and convicted sinners seemed now happily supplied," Hayden added. "Rigdon was transported with this discovery."[28]

Rigdon persuaded Bentley to return to Mentor with him where they besieged Rigdon's own congregation. Nearly the entire membership accepted the new doctrines. According to a Disciples historian, they "exchanged their 'articles' for the new covenant as the only divine basis for Christ's church, and abandoned unscriptural titles and church names, choosing to be known simply as disciples of Christ."[29] Rigdon and Bentley received a similar reception in Kirtland, Ohio, where twenty souls entered the waters of baptism, and a separate organization became an immediate necessity. The 2 June 1828 *Christian Baptist* reported that "Bishops Scott, Rigdon, and Bentley, in Ohio, within the last six months have immersed about eight hundred persons."[30] During 1827-29 Rigdon established Reformed congregations at Mantua Center, Perry, Euclid, and Birmingham in Erie County, Waite Hill (the vicinity of Willoughby), and Elyria in Lorain County, and the church at Hamden in Geauga County.[31]

Parley P. Pratt, a Reformed Baptist who would later accompany Rigdon into the Mormon fold, wrote that when he first heard Rigdon preach he was "astonished." He found he "preached faith in Jesus Christ, repentence towards God, and baptism for remission of sins, with the promise of the gift of the Holy Ghost to all who would come forward, with all their hearts, and obey the doctrine!"[32] Not all Baptists accepted Rigdon's teachings. Some former communicants in the Mentor church demeaned him in a piece of homespun doggerel: "A one-story meeting-house without any steeple,/ A roguish priest and foolish people."[33]

Recognizing that Rigdon and most members of his congregation had departed from the Baptist tradition, the Grand River Association, to which Mentor belonged, voted in September 1828 to "withdraw fellowship from the Painesville and Mentor Church." Representatives further resolved that since the "sentiments and practices propagated by the leading men in the Mahoning Association were derogatory to the doctrine of Christ," fellowship with that body was terminated.[34] During the 1829 annual meeting of the Mahoning Association at Warren, Ohio, however, more than one thousand Reformed Baptists, including Sidney Rigdon, assembled in triumph. They were a people possessing one spirit and rejoicing in one hope.

Notes

Unless otherwise stated, all primary sources cited are located in the Historical Department of the Church of Jesus Christ of Latter-day Saints, Salt Lake City, Utah.

1. Frederick A. Henry, "History of Centerville Mills and the Old Chillicothe Road."
2. *The Christian Baptist* 1:33.
3. *Times and Seasons* 4 (15 May 1843): 193.
4. Ibid., 192-93.
5. Amos Sutton Hayden, *Early History of the Disciples in the Western Reserve* (Cincinnati: Chase and Hall, 1875), 22-23.
6. Two years later, in 1826, the Hiram-Nelson-Garrettsville members coalesced into a separate congregation. Alanson Wilcox, *A History of the Disciples of Christ in Ohio* (Cincinnati: The Standard Publishing Co., 1918), 121.
7. *Times and Seasons* 4 (15 May 1843): 194.
8. Ibid. 4 (1 June 1843): 209-10.
9. Henry K. Shaw, *Buckeye Disciples: A History of the Disciples of Christ in Ohio* (St. Louis: Christian Board of Publication, 1952), 41.
10. Winfred Ernest Garrison and Alfred T. DeGroot, *The Disciples of Christ: A History* (St. Louis: Christian Board of Publication, 1948), 28.
11. *Times and Seasons* 4 (15 May 1843): 193.
12. Hayden, 57.
13. Ibid., 37. The preface for the monthly publication was written on 4 July 1823; the first number was issued in August. Edited and printed by Campbell, it was devoted to the "promulgation, exposition and defense of the Christian religion as it is expressly revealed in the New Testament." The seven-volume periodical was issued from Buffaloe Creek (later Bethany), Virginia, from August 1823 to July 1830.

One account refers to *The Christian Baptist* as "the Magna Carta of the new religious movement" (Frederick D. Kershner, *The Restoration Handbook*, Series 1 [San Antonio: Southern Christian Press, 1960], 4). Another cites it as "one of the immortal documents of religious history" (Frederick D. Kershner, *The Christian Union Overture* [St. Louis: The Bethany Press, 1923], 13-14). In January 1830 the publication became *The Millennial*

Harbinger. The first thirty-four volumes, until 1863, were edited by Campbell. The periodical continued another seven volumes, through 1870, with W. K. Pendleton as editor.

14. For other examples, see Henry K. Shaw, *Buckeye Disciples: A History of the Disciples of Christ in Ohio* (St. Louis: Christian Board of Publication, 1952), 44.

15. Robert Richardson, *Memoirs of Alexander Campbell*, 2 vols. (Cincinnati: R. W. Carroll & Co., 1868, 1872), 2:344.

16. Garrison and DeGroot, 187.

17. *The Evangelist*, Apr. 1832, 94.

18. Garrison and DeGroot, 188.

19. William Hayden, in William Alexander Linn, *The Story of the Mormons: From the Date of Their Origin to the Year 1901* (New York: The Macmillan Co., 1923), 65.

20. Shaw, 53-54.

21. Garrison and DeGroot, 198.

22. Hayden, 174.

23. Ibid., 95.

24. Ibid., 96; William Baxter, *Life of Elder Walter Scott* (Cincinnati: Bosworth, Chase & Hall, 1874), 130.

25. Hayden, 96.

26. Baxter, 131.

27. Campbell, in *Millennial Harbinger* 3 (1839): 469.

28. Hayden, 192.

29. Alanson Wilcox, *A History of the Disciples of Christ in Ohio* (Cincinnati: The Standard Publishing Company, 1918), 123-24.

30. Ibid., 263.

31. Evelyn Buzbee and Ruth Whiting, comps., *The Mentor Christian Church Scrapbook* (Mentor, OH: Mentor Christian Church, 1978), 5.

32. Parley P. Pratt, Jr., ed., *The Autobiography of Parley Parker Pratt* (Chicago: Law, King & Law, 1888), 32.

33. Buzbee and Whiting, 16.

34. Grand River Baptist Association Records, 83, 86, 99, in Milton V. Backman, Jr., *The Heavens Resound: A History of the Latter-day Saints in Ohio, 1830-1838* (Salt Lake City: Deseret Book Co., 1983), 14.

CHAPTER 5.

Mentor

And all that believed were together, and had all things common; and sold their possessions and goods, and parted them to all men, as every man had need (Acts 2:44-45).

A merica has been home to repeated religious and social experimentation. Many not wishing to remain in a society where the majority suffer, wanting to reshape civilization, to uplift individuals through alternate models of social harmony, have settled on communitarianism—people together in a self-sufficient group, separate from the surrounding society. Prominent early American religious communal groups include the Labadist Community of Protestant Mystics (established in Maryland in 1680), the Community of the Woman in the Wilderness (Pennsylvania, 1694), the Contented of the God-Loving Soul (1694), Amana Community of Inspirationists (originated in Germany in 1714), United Society of Believers in Christ's Second Appearing (Shakers, who came to America in 1774), the Rappites or Harmonists (who migrated to Pennsylvania in 1804), and the Oneida Perfectionists (1839).

Secular experiments, evolving in the nineteenth century, include Robert Owen's collective in New Harmony, Indiana (1825), George Ripley's transcendental Brook Farm Institute of Agriculture and Education at West Roxbury, Massachusetts (1841), the Fourierists' North American Phalanx in New Jersey (1843), and Bronson Alcott's Fruitlands in Harvard, Massachusetts (1843). Communal ventures were so prolific during his day that Ralph Waldo Emerson wrote to Thomas Carlyle: "We are all a little wild here with numberless projects of social reform. Not a reading man but has a draft of a New Community in his waistcoat pocket."[1]

The communal theories of Robert Owen, a wealthy Scottish reformer and industrialist, profoundly affected Sidney Rigdon. Owen was known throughout Europe and America as a philanthropist and humanitarian, a radical social reformer, and militant atheist. In 1813 he published *A New View of Society* which commanded world attention by his proposals for the cure of poverty. As an experiment to "establish a new Eden in the far west," he bought in 1824 the property of the Rappite colony at New Harmony, Indiana, and was engaged there, along with his father-in-law Robert Dale, in constructing a communist utopia without religion. Other "family commonwealths," based on common ownership and equality of work and profit, were established in Ohio, at Kendal and Yellow Springs.

During April 1829, Alexander Campbell engaged Owen in a famed debate at Cincinnati. The eight-day, sixteen-session forum attracted thousands, including Rigdon, and was held in the largest auditorium in the city, the Methodists' Stone Church on East and Fifth streets. The building's capacity was 1,200, yet people stood in the aisles, sat on the steps of the rostrum, and perched on the window ledges at every session.

Owen's position was that

> all the religions of the world have been founded on the ignorance of mankind; that they have been, and are, the real sources of vice, disunion, and misery of every description; that they are now the only bar to the formation of a society of virtue, of intelligence, of charity in its most extended sense, and of sincerity and kindness among the whole human family; and that they can be no longer maintained except through the ignorance of the mass of the people, and the tyranny of the few over that mass.[2]

Campbell and Owen had immense respect for each other, and despite their differences the debate was genial. Campbell primarily emphasized Owen's skepticism, not his radical social philosophy. Significantly, the New Harmony experiment was not criticized at all, although Campbell had privately complained about it earlier.[3] Morning and evening sessions lasted four hours each, the afternoon session often stretching on until candles were called for. On the last three days Owen surrendered the remainder of time to Campbell, who delivered a remarkable speech of twelve hours, in two-hour periods, from ten to twelve in the mornings and from two to four in the afternoons, for three days.

When Campbell sat down after his final epic speech, the audience rose to its feet in a prolonged tribute to him. Almost overnight he became a national figure. His reputation quickly spread, and before he left Cincinnati he received a letter from a group of admirers in Brooke County, Virginia, urging him to become a delegate to the approaching Virginia State Constitutional Convention.[4]

Rigdon, taken with Owen's system of "family commonwealths," returned to Mentor, convinced that a "common-stock" society, as outlined in Acts 2:44-45, should be implemented among parishioners. The two leaders he convinced in February 1830 to put his communitarian ideas in motion were future Mormons Lyman Wight and Isaac Morley. Morley, who owned a large farm near Kirtland, three miles from Mentor, offered his farm for the collective experiment. Morley and Wight, along with Titus Billings and three other families, covenanted with each other to renounce private property and share all goods. They called their order the "Family" or "Big Family" after Owen's concept of "family common-wealth." By October 1830 the group numbered more than 100 individuals. In addition, Wight had converted five families at Mayfield, about seven miles up river from Kirtland, each of whom also covenanted to abide by the early Christian communal lifestyle.

While both groups took spiritual direction from Rigdon, he did not become a member of either community, although he visited them frequently. His reason for not joining is not known. Perhaps it was to keep harmony among the portion of his congregation that was not committed to the communal goal.

Rigdon's interest in communalism was rivaled only by his belief in millennialism. The habit of looking at the world shaped by biblical prophecy was widespread. From disruptions and bewilderment, many people concluded that the world was on the verge of a great transformation—the second coming of Jesus and the Day of Judgment. Millennialism of various kinds, scholarly and popular, flourished in the decades following the American Revolution and became the means by which many explained and justified the great social changes of the period.

The ardor of religious awakening resulting from the Reformed Baptist Movement led Rigdon and others to hope that the Millennium would soon dawn, that the long-awaited Second Advent, when the Lord would come again in the clouds of heaven, would quickly arrive. They prayed, looked, and sang of the time when the ransomed of the Lord would return to Zion with everlasting joy upon their heads, when sorrow and sighing would be no more.

Walter Scott, according to Disciple historian Amos S. Hayden, was the "origin of millennial views among us." His theology had been shaped by Elias Smith's 1808 *Sermons Containing An Illustration of the Prophecies to Be Accomplished From the Present Time Until the New Heaven and the Earth Are Created*, "the only sensible work on that subject he had seen." Hayden reported that Sidney Rigdon, "who always caught and proclaimed the last word that fell from the lips of Scott or Campbell, seized these views, and with the wildness of his extravagant nature, heralded them every-where."[5]

But even the more stable Campbell, convinced the Millennium was dawning, had during the Cincinnati debate connected Owen's social ideal with his own Christian concept of the Millennium. He suggested that God was using the British philanthropist to hasten that glorious day. In anticipation, in 1830 he changed the name of his periodical from the *Christian Baptist* to the *Millennial Harbinger*. The first issue was headed by a quotation from his own version of Revelation 14:6: "I saw another messenger flying through the midst of heaven, having everlasting good news to proclaim to the inhabitants of the earth."[6]

By 1830—a watershed year in American religious history—the Enlightenment was at a close and evangelical Protestantism prevailed throughout the country. In addition to the inauguration of his *Harbinger*, Campbell was close to establishing his momentous alliance with Barton Stone and founding the Disciples of Christ. Elsewhere, preacher Charles G. Finney traveled to Rochester, New York, then the fastest growing community in the United States, launching a revival that eventually shook the nation. Robert Mätthews (also known as Robert Matthias or Joshua, the Jewish Minister) received the revelation that turned him into a wandering prophet predicting the imminent end of civilization. The Shakers were at the apex of their history. And what would prove to be one of the most significant events in American religious history, Joseph Smith's publication of the Book of Mormon, also occurred in this eventful year.

Despite this firestorm of evangelical enthusiasm, everyday practicalities still had to be attended to. Fields had to be plowed, seeds sowed, meals prepared, and a roof placed over one's head. In early 1830 Sidney Rigdon's reformed congregation in Mentor approached him about a set reimbursement for his services. In his own words:

> the prospect of wealth and affluence was fairly open before him; but he looked upon it with indifference, and made every thing subservient to the promotion of correct principles: and having food and raiment, he learned therewith to be content. As a proof of this, his family were in no better circumstances, and made no greater appearance in the world, than when he labored at the occupation of tanning. His family consisted of his wife and six children, and lived in a very small, unfinished frame house, hardly capable of making a family comfortable; which affords a clear proof that his affections were not set upon things of a worldly nature, or secular aggrandizement.

Although Rigdon, in reality, had no talent for poverty, he told lay leaders "he did not believe in selling his services in that way but would receive what they felt willing to give." They offered him a "suitable habitation in which himself and family could be made comf[o]rtable and one which would accommodate his numerous visitors who were calling upon him." A committee was appointed and a fine farm in the township was purchased. Materials were ordered and work commenced on the house. Years later Wickliffe Rigdon summed up his father's prospects in Mentor. "The honors of the world was within his grasp," the son wrote, "and had he continued on in the way he was going his name would have gone down to posterity as one of the great Baptists of the age in which he lived."[7]

But Rigdon seldom continued on the way he was going. His life-long pattern was to follow his own compass even when it veered towards unknown tangents. Because of this predilection, or perhaps in spite of it, the "fine residence upon a beautiful farm on the Western Reserve" would be a home the Rigdon family would never occupy. Theological dissension between Rigdon and Campbell had been simmering for some time. Their points of disagreement focused on the gifts of the Holy Spirit, authority to perform ordinances, and communitarianism. Campbell held forth that after individuals became children of God through faith and baptism, they would receive the spirit of Christ or Holy Ghost. These converts, he taught, would then be filled with peace and joy and become habitations of God.

He added, however, that those who received the gift of the Holy Ghost would not receive all of the spiritual gifts manifested in the primitive Christian church. The miracles wrought by the Holy Spirit during that early period, such as healing and speaking in tongues, would not reappear in the latter days. Those ancient miracles, he contended, were only to confirm the new religion and prove its divine origin. The manifestations were for a limited time, which had long ago expired.[8]

In contrast, some of Rigdon's followers sought the very gifts and power described in the Holy Scriptures. Edward Partridge, later to become a Mormon bishop, felt it was "absolutely necessary" for God to "again reveal himself to man and confer authority upon some one, or more, before his church could be built up in the last days, or any time after the apostasy." Yet neither Campbell, Rigdon, nor Scott were making claims to a new commission from God.[9]

Parley P. Pratt, also a future Mormon, concluded that "one great link was wanting to complete the chain of the ancient order of things; and that was, the *authority* to minister in holy things—the apostleship, the power which should accompany the form." He noted that Reformers claimed no new commission by revelation or vision from the Lord.[10] Eliza R. Snow, later a plural wife of Joseph Smith and Brigham Young, added, "I heard Alexander Campbell advocate the literal meaning of the Scriptures—listened to him with deep interest—hoped his new life led to a fullness—was baptized, and soon learned that, as well they might, he and his followers disclaimed all authority, and my baptism was of no consequence."[11]

During the 1830 annual meetings of the Mahoning Baptist Association the differences between Rigdon and Campbell boiled over, dousing a considerable amount of Rigdon's fervor. Members of the newly formed Austintown [Ohio] Church hosted the gathering. The village's population of seven hundred was nearly one-fourth Reformed Baptist. With only a single tavern, Austintown saw many visitors sleeping on benches in the new meetinghouse, the first commodious house of worship built by Reformers in the Western Reserve.

The throngs of people in attendance gave a convention-like atmosphere to the three-day conference. Friday was spent singing, fellowshipping, preaching, and giving reports. On Saturday when the Reverend Rigdon had the floor he introduced an argument "to show that our pretensions to follow the apostles in all their New Testament teachings, required a community of goods; that as they established their order in the model church at Jerusalem, we were bound to imitate their example."[12]

Campbell, in attendance, considered any attempt to introduce communal practices highly impractical.[13] Furthermore, he was not a man who could share his "throne" with anyone, and those who challenged his leadership were quickly cut down. Not even best friends were spared if they assumed the prerogatives he felt belonged to him alone.[14]

In a thirty-minute rejoinder Campbell opposed Rigdon, declaring New Testament communitarianism a "special circumstance, that the matter of Ananias and Sapphira put an end to it, and that it was always understood even then to be on a voluntary basis." He quoted passages of later scripture which called for contributions for benevolence, showing that no such communal system prevailed in apostolic times. Rigdon made no rebuttal, and the matter never came up again during the gathering.

That Rigdon would broach the subject of communitarianism at all is surprising, for Campbell's opposition had been made known at least three years before his debate with Owen. Although Campbell technically did not oppose the principle, he believed it could result in confusion and ruin, and that individuals joined such experiments to avoid working for their own living. Perhaps Rigdon felt he could sway the group against Campbell, personally championing a cause he so strongly believed in. Or maybe he remembered Campbell's 1814 interest in removing the Brush Run Church in a body to Zanesville, Ohio, to establish a cooperative Christian colony with church, school, and other features.

Regardless of his reasons, Rigdon was deeply crushed by Campbell's rejection, and he was not the type to feel no rancor. Scorn infuriated him and left him with the urge to retaliate. En route to his home in Mentor, he stopped at a friend's house and commented, "I have done as much in this reformation as Campbell or Scott, and yet they get all the honor."[15]

During the final day of the Austintown assembly, to the shock of many, the Mahoning Association was dissolved. Campbell, through his works and published rhetoric in the *Christian Baptist*, had created a monster which turned on its creator. He had branded denominational ministers as hirelings, as "goat milkers." He had opposed missionary societies, made a caricature of many Christian institutions, and was generally belligerent toward all sects except his own. As the meeting approached its end, John Henry (likely influenced by Walter Scott) introduced a resolution "that the Mahoning Association, as an advisory council, or an ecclesiastical tribunal, should cease to exist." The proposal's supporters thought that nothing in the Baptist association resembled primitive Christianity. Benajah Austin, William Hayden, and Alexander Campbell deplored this action. Campbell arose to oppose the motion but was persuaded not to, and it passed unanimously.[16]

After the motion Campbell got to his feet and asked, "Brethren, what are you going to do? Are you never going to meet again?"[17] Someone suggested that they still meet once a year, but in a meeting with no powers, no evangelistic purpose, no reviewing action—an assembly of brethren for fellowship and mutual encouragement only. In Campbell's own words, "This association came to its end as tranquilly as ever did a good old man whose attenuated thread of life, worn to a hair's breadth, dropped asunder by its own imbecility."[18] He later wrote that the

"Regular Baptist Mahoning Association died of a moral apoplexy, in less than a quarter of an hour."[19]

Most accounts depict Rigdon leaving the Disciple fold after his humiliation in Austintown and retreating into seclusion in Mentor.[20] But this was not the case. Rigdon had not lost his world, he had not suffered an inglorious fall from power, he merely returned home and picked up his ministry where he had left it the week before. The 16 October 1830 *Ashtabula Journal* notes, for example, that "We are requested to state that the Rev. Mr. Rigdon, will preach at the Town House in this Borough on Friday evening next, at early candlelighting. Mr. Rigdon is a Campbellite."

But Rigdon's days as a Campbellite or Reformed Baptist were numbered. A new age of promise had dawned in the East and would soon sweep into his life like an eternal wind. The Book of Mormon, a prophetic voice from the past, was at that moment being carried west in the valise of a fervent young missionary named Oliver Cowdery. The delivery of that sacred opus to Rigdon's Mentor home would prove to be the most consequential moment of his life, an event that would end his long quest for the fullness of the gospel as Jesus had taught it.

Publication of the "Golden Bible," as people were calling it, had been recounted in several Western Reserve and New York newspapers as early as 1827, when Joseph Smith began working on the book. There can be little doubt that Rigdon, an enthusiastic reader of newspapers, was aware of the book before it was placed in his hands. Orson Hyde, a ministerial apprentice who lived for some time in Rigdon's Mentor home and who would later be associated with him in Mormonism, wrote that about 1827 "some vague reports came in the newspapers, that a 'golden bible' had been dug out of a rock in the State of New York. It was treated, however, as a hoax. But on reading the report, I remarked as follows—'who knows but this gold bible may break up all our religion, and change its whole features and bearing?'"[21]

Eliza R. Snow, who like Hyde was a member of one of Rigdon's congregations in Ohio, also noted that prior to 1830 she had "heard of Joseph Smith as a Prophet to whom the Lord was speaking from the heavens; and that a Sacred Record containing a history of the origin of the aborigines of America, was unearthed. . . . I considered it a hoax—too good to be true."[22]

One early account, no doubt referred to by Hyde and Snow, appeared in the nearby *Painesville Telegraph*. Although complete backfiles for that gazette do not exist, the 16 November 1830 issue, in an article entitled "The Golden Bible," noted that "Some two or three years since, an account was given in the papers, of a book purporting to contain new revelations from Heaven, having been dug out of the ground, in Manchester in Ontario Co., N.Y."

Rigdon's brother-in-law and fellow Baptist minister, Adamson Bentley, re-called in a 22 January 1841 letter to Walter Scott: "I know that S[i]dney Rigdon told me there was a book coming out (the manuscript of which had been found engraved on gold plates) as much as two years before the Mormon book made its appearance in this country or had been heard of by me."[23]

Alexander Campbell added in the same account:

> The conversation alluded to in Brother Bentley's letter of 1841, was in my presence as well as his, and my recollection of it led me, some two or three years ago, to interrogate Brother Bentley touching his recollections of it, which accorded with mine in every particular, except the year 1827, and I in the summer of 1826; Rigdon at the same time observing that in the plates dug up in New York there was an account not only of the aborigines of this country, but also stated that the Christian religion had been preached in this country during the first century, just as we were preaching it on the Western Reserve.

William Whitsitt, in his nineteenth-century Rigdon biography, concluded that Rigdon likely mentioned the Book of Mormon to Campbell and Scott in August 1828, during the annual Mahoning convocation at Warren, Trumbell County, Ohio. This agrees with Bentley's statement that Rigdon communicated the information about the Book of Mormon as much as two years before it appeared or had been heard of by him.[24]

Additional evidence is an 26 April 1873 letter to Amos S. Hayden from Darwin Atwater, a Disciples of Christ elder. Atwater recalled that Rigdon, while visiting the Atwater home several years before the Book of Mormon was published, "gave a wonderful description of the mounds and other antiquities found in some parts of America, and said that they must have been made by the aborigines. He said there was a book to be published containing an account of those things. He spoke of these in his eloquent, enthusiastic style, as being a thing most extraordinary."[25]

Stephen S. Harding, a boyhood friend of Joseph Smith and Utah territorial governor during the Civil War, wrote in an 1882 letter to Thomas Gregg:

> When I was a student at Brookville, in the fall of 1827, the Brookville *Enquirer* was laid upon my table, when my eye fell upon a paragraph, credited to some eastern paper, of the finding of a book of metallic plates, called the "Golden Bible." It was found by a young man by the name of Joe Smith, who had spent his time for several years in telling fortunes and digging for hidden treasures, and especially for pots and iron chests of money, supposed to have been buried by Captain Kidd. . . . This boy was about three years older than myself, and it turned out that he was the veritable finder of the "Golden Bible."[26]

Newspapers published at nearby Rochester, New York, on 31 August and 5 September 1829 also mention the Book of Mormon prior to its 1830 release. Both accounts relate the important fact that it was known in Palmyra and vicinity as early as the fall of 1827 that Joseph Smith claimed angelic visitations, had in his possession gold plates, and was working on a book.[27]

This Golden Bible or "ancient record from the dust," according to Smith's earliest public account, "is a record of the forefathers of our western tribes of Indians, having been found through the ministrations of an holy angel, and translated into our own language by the gift and power of God."[28] While Smith remained closed-mouthed regarding his method of "translating" the book, witnesses, including his wife, father-in-law, brother-in-law, and several close friends, provided some details.

According to these accounts, in 1822 at age seventeen Smith found a stone at the bottom of a well he was digging for a neighbor. This chocolate-colored pebble, when placed in the bottom of a hat to exclude light, became a seer stone, providing Smith with clairvoyance—second-sight. For a time young Smith exercised his divination in locating lost animals and misplaced items, fortune telling, and searching for buried Spanish treasure near the Susquehanna River in Pennsylvania. But the seer stone, according to the Book of Mormon, had been prepared for greater use. Alma 37:23 reads: "I will prepare unto my servant Gazelem [Joseph Smith, Jr.] a stone, which shall shine forth in darkness unto light, that I may discover unto my people who serve me, that I may discover unto them the works of their brethren, yea, their secret works, their works of darkness, and their wickedness and abominations."

This stone, still retained by the First Presidency of the LDS church, was the vehicle through which the golden plates were discovered and the medium through which their interpretation came. Smith related in the account later canonized in the LDS Pearl of Great Price that on 23 September 1823, "the vision was opened to my mind that I could see the place where the plates were deposited, and that so clearly and distinctly that I knew the place again when I visited it."[29] Martin Harris, Smith's close friend and financial benefactor, clarified that Smith told him he found the plates' repository "by looking in the stone found in the well of Mason Chase. The [Smith] family told me the same thing."[30]

Henry Harris, another acquaintance, confirmed that "[Smith] said he had a revelation from God that told him they were hid in a certain hill and he looked in his stone and saw them in the place of deposit."[31] Willard Chase, on whose property the stone was discovered, points out that in 1827 Joseph Smith, Sr., explained "that some years ago, a spirit had appeared to Joseph his son, in a vision, and informed him that in a certain place there was a record on plates of gold; and that he was the person that must obtain them. He [Smith] then observed that if it had not been for that stone, he would not have obtained the book."[32] Further corroboration is provided by W. D. Purple, who took notes during an 1826 trial: "Smith, by the aid of his luminous stone, found the Golden Bible, or the book of Mormon."[33]

The Book of Mormon created a new mythology for America. According to the record's narrative, a group of ancient Israelites crossed the seas to the New

World, bringing with them written records and the customs and religious traditions of their ancestors. They continued to keep their own records of events and prophecies, including the visitation of Jesus after his ascension. Ultimately, only a few of these ancient Americans remained true to the faith of their ancestry. The others abandoned God's teachings and became savages of the forests and woods—the ethnic font of the native American Indian. The culture of the faithful came to an end in A.D. 421. The only survivors, Mormon and son Moroni, hid an abridgement of their civilization's records in a hillside vault in what would become New York state, where they were rescued by Joseph Smith. On the basis of this scripture and visions, Smith established a church at Manchester, New York, on 6 April 1830.

During an Erie Canal boat stop en route to Canaan, New York, a Baptist deacon informed Parley Pratt, a member of one of Rigdon's Reformed Baptist congregations in Ohio, that a strange book had recently been published in nearby Palmyra and he had a copy of it at home. Borrowing the deacon's copy of the book, Pratt "opened it with eagerness," he wrote, and read its title page. He then "read the testimony of several witnesses in relation to the manner of its being found and translated. After this I commenced its contents by course. I read all day; eating was a burden, I had no desire for food; sleep was a burden when the night came, for I preferred reading to sleep."

"As I read," he concluded, "the spirit of the Lord was upon me, and I knew and comprehended that the book was true, as plainly and manifestly as a man comprehends and knows that he exists."[34] Overwhelmed, Pratt traveled to Palmyra to meet Joseph Smith, who had since moved to Pennsylvania. After discussing the Book of Mormon with Smith's older brother, Hyrum, Pratt requested baptism into the Church of Christ. Six weeks after his 1 September 1830 baptism, Pratt prepared to leave the Palmyra area as part of a four-man missionary team lead by Joseph Smith's cousin, Oliver Cowdery. Their destination "into the wilderness among the Lamanites [Native Americans]" was some 1,500 miles away in western Missouri.

They did not travel by the most direct route, however. Pratt told the others about his mentor, the Reverend Sidney Rigdon. Hopeful Rigdon would favorably receive their message, the young missionaries journeyed to the Western Reserve. They arrived near Rigdon's Mentor home on Thursday, 28 October. After dividing into pairs, the young elders began to proselyte. Cowdery and Pratt, each carrying a carpetbag full of copies of the Book of Mormon, called on the Rigdon household first. Rigdon at first spurned them and "felt very much prejudiced at their assertions." "He had one Bible," he said, "which he believed was a revelation from God and with which he pretended to have some acquaintance; but with respect to the book they had presented him, he must say that he had considerable doubt."[35]

"You brought truth to me," Pratt responded, "I now ask you as a friend to read this for my sake."[36] Waving aside further argument, Rigdon replied, "No, young gentlemen, you must not argue with me on the subject; but I will read your book, and see what claim it has upon my faith, and will endeavor to ascertain whether it be a revelation from God or not."[37]

His first reaction that night was unfavorable. Matthew Clapp, who replaced Rigdon as minister of the Mentor Disciple congregation, wrote in 1831 that when Rigdon first read the book he "partly condemned it—but, two days afterwards, was heard to confess his conviction of its truth."[38] Rigdon's daughter Nancy, in an 1884 interview, recalled that when Pratt and Cowdery gave her father the book, he "read it and examined it for about an hour and then threw it down, and said he did not believe a word of it."[39] Another account reported that he initially pronounced it a "silly fabrication."[40] But he kept reading, apparently all night.

The next morning the prominent Orris Clapp family was sitting at breakfast. Rigdon stopped to visit and in an excited manner said: "Two men came to my house last night on a c-u-r-i-o-u-s mission," prolonging the word in an histrionic manner. Everyone at the table then looked up while he further explained:

> some men in Palymra, N.Y., had found, by direction of an angel, certain plates inscribed with mysterious characters; that by the same heavenly visitant, a young man, ignorant of letters, had been led into the secret of deciphering the writing on the plates; that it made known the origin of the Indian tribes; with other matters of great interest to the world, and that the discovery would be of such importance as to open the way for the introduction of the Millennium.[41]

Cowdery and Pratt had asked to preach to Rigdon's Mentor congregation. The appointment was accordingly published, and a large congregation assembled. Cowdery and Pratt's message was eloquent in its simplicity. They "professed to be special messengers of the Living God, sent to preach the gospel in its purity, as it was anciently preached by the Apostles."[42] They spoke of a young prophet with divine guidance to correct errors of the Christian churches by calling them to repentance and baptism into the primitive church of Jesus Christ. They propounded the doctrine of divine revelation and asserted that Joseph Smith was a prophet like those of old. They also preached that Christ's advent and the beginning of the millennial reign were imminent.

At the conclusion of his remarks Pratt asked Rigdon if he would like to comment. Sidney arose and stated to the congregation:

> the information they had that evening received, was of an extraordinary character, and certainly demanded their most serious consideration: and as the apostle [Paul] advised his brethren "to prove all things, and hold fast that which is good," so he would exhort his brethren to do likewise, and give the matter a careful investigation; and not turn against it, without being fully convinced of its being an imposition, lest they should, possibly, resist the truth.[43]

After the services ended, Pratt and Cowdery returned home with Rigdon and talked further. Rigdon promised he would finish reading the book, and after completing his investigation would "frankly tell them his mind and feelings on the subject."[44]

Wickliffe Rigdon later remembered that his father "got so engaged in [the book] that it was hard for him to quit long enough to eat his meals. He read it both day and night."[45] When Cowdery and Pratt returned to the Rigdon home after several days of missionary work, Rigdon had read a considerable portion of the book and held a long interview with Cowdery regarding Joseph Smith. Cowdery told him that his cousin was twenty-two years old and had "hardly a common school education," to which Rigdon replied, "if that was all the education he had, he never wrote the book."[46]

Rigdon, in his own account of that conversation, added that he "expressed the utmost amazement that such a man should write a book which seemed to shed a flood of light on all the old scriptures, open all their profoundest mysteries, and give them perfect consistency and complete system. . . . [I]f God ever gave a revelation, surely this must be divine."[47] Earnestly reading, praying for direction, and meditating on the things he heard and read, Rigdon remained ambivalent about the book for some time. Pratt related that Rigdon "had a great struggle of mind before he fully believed and embraced it."[48]

Much of Rigdon's concern lay in his Baptist upbringing that nothing should be accepted on faith alone. While the book affirmed his own beliefs in a literal gathering of Israel and an imminent Millennium, he wanted an omen, a burning bush. Cowdery explained that he, like Rigdon, had also desired a sign and that an angel appeared to him and showed him the gold plates. Rigdon was certainly aware of biblical accounts of angels, and as the Book of Mormon itself affirmed, "neither have angels ceased to minister unto the children of men" (Moroni 7:29). So Rigdon asked for a sign. According to Disciple historian Amos S. Hayden, "the sign appeared, and he was convinced that Mormonism was of God!"[49] Alexander Campbell, always disrespectful to Rigdon after their 1830 affray in Austintown, later wrote that his colleague fasted and prayed for days, until, when "one of his fits of swooning and sighing came upon him, he saw an angel and was converted."[50]

Rigdon left two known accounts of this personal vision. The first, published in 1834, proclaimed:

> to my astonishment I saw the different orders of professing Christians passing before my eyes, with their hearts, exposed to view, and they were as corrupt as corruption itself. That society to which I belonged [the Reformed Baptists] also passed before my eyes, and to my astonishment it was as corrupt as the others. Last of all *that little man who bro't me the Book of Mormon* [Oliver Cowdery], passed before my eyes with his

heart open, and it was as pure as an angel; and this was a testimony from God; that the Book of Mormon, was a Divine Revelation.[51]

The second account of this vision, published in 1843, simply reported that he was "fully convinced of the truth of the work, by a revelation from Jesus Christ, which was made known to him in a remarkable manner, so that he could exclaim 'flesh and blood hath not revealed it unto me, but my father which is in heaven.'"[52]

Much later in his career, long after his presence in the main arena of Mormonism had diminished and religious fanaticism addled his brain, Rigdon, in a 1 July 1868 revelation, assumed God's voice, referred to himself as the "head of the literary world," and pronounced: "There was no man living so well qualified to judge of the divine authenticity of the book of Mormon as he was. His knowledge of the Lord's manner of writing was such as enabled him to detect it when he saw it and thus it was that he received the book of Mormon when I the Lord sent it to him."[53]

Meanwhile Mormon success in the Kirtland area was astounding. News quickly spread throughout the region that an unusual religious message was expounded by prophetic emissaries from New York. On occasion the roads were crowded with people traveling to Kirtland to hear about the restoration. Inquirers exhausted the elders with their constant questions. "The people thronged us night and day," Pratt said, "insomuch that we had not time for rest or retirement." Some came "for curiosity, some to obey the gospel, and some to dispute or resist it. In two or three weeks from our arrival in the neighborhood with the news, we had baptized one hundred and twenty-seven souls."[54]

Although they did not know it at the time, Rigdon and other Reformers had prepared Ohio for the Mormons. Prominent Mormon historian B. H. Roberts considered the Disciples forerunners of the Mormon gospel, regarding Campbell and Scott (like Rigdon) as having been "sent forth to prepare the way before the Lord."[55] Disciple historian Amos S. Hayden explained why the Reformed Baptist Movement was such fertile ground for the Mormon missionaries:

> There were many at the time who believed the millennium was at hand, and in 1830 there were those who were convinced it had dawned. . . . The long-expected day of gospel glory would very soon be ushered in . . . . These glowing expectations formed the staple of many sermons. They were the continued and exhaustless topic of conversation. They animated the hope and inspired the zeal to a high degree of the converts and many of the advocates of the gospel. Millennial hymns were learned and sung with a joyful fervor and hope surpassing the conception of worldly and carnal professors. It was amid a people full of these expectations, and with hearts fired with these things, that Mormonism was brought, and there is small wonder that it found a welcome.[56]

Seventeen members of Isaac Morley's Kirtland communal "Family" were re-immersed in one night into this new dispensation. Lyman Wight wrote that "the whole of the common stock family was baptized."[57] Rigdon was initially displeased, telling the missionaries that what they had done was "without precedent or authority from the Scriptures, as they had baptized for the power of miracles, while the apostles, as he showed, baptized penitential believers for the remission of sins."[58]

When Rigdon ultimately became convinced of the new revelation, restored authority, and the "necessity of obedience thereto," he first informed his wife and asked her, "My dear, you have followed me, once into poverty, are you again willing to do the same?" Recalling their similar experience in Pittsburgh Phebe answered, "I have counted the cost, and I am perfectly satisfied to follow you; it is my desire to do the will of God, come life or come death."[59] Her conviction was based on the fact that her husband "seemed to be altered in demeanor to such an extent that the religion must be of divine origin, else it could not have produced so wonderful an effect."[60]

One day in early to mid-November 1830 (probably the 7th) Rigdon called to assembly a large congregation of his friends and neighbors in the Methodist church at Kirtland. According to Parley Pratt, he

> addressed them very affectionately for near two hours, during most of which time both himself and nearly all the congregation were melted into tears. He asked forgiveness of everybody who might have had occasion to be offended with any part of his former life. He forgave all who had persecuted or injured him in any manner. And the next morning, himself and wife were baptized by Elder O. Cowdery. I was present—it was a solemn scene. Most of the people were greatly affected. They came out of the water overwhelmed in tears.[61]

After Rigdon's baptism, he immediately immersed himself into missionary efforts. John Barr, a one-time sheriff of Cuyahoga County and notable authority on the Western Reserve, later recalled listening to Rigdon's powerful preaching during a Sunday morning service at Mayfield. Taking Varnem J. Card along for company, Barr and his friend sat on a hill overlooking the Chagrin River where they could hear the proceedings. As Rigdon spoke, Barr wrote,

> His voice and manner were . . . imposing. He was regarded as an eloquent man at all times, and now he seemed fully aroused. He said he had not been satisfied in his religious yearnings until now. At night he had often been unable to sleep, walking and praying for more light and comfort in his religion. While in the midst of this agony, he heard of the Book of Mormon. Under this "his soul suddenly found peace. It filled all his aspirations."

At the close of the meeting Rigdon asked if anyone wanted to come forward and be baptized, and one man stepped out of the crowd. While standing in the water of a deep pool "Rigdon gave one of his most powerful exhortations," and, Barr noted, "the assembly became greatly affected. As he proceeded he called for the converts to step forward. They came through the crowd in rapid succession to the number of thirty and were immersed, with no intermission of the discourse on the part of Rigdon." At that point Card took Barr's arm and demanded, "Take me away." Barr turned and saw his friend so pale he thought he might faint. His frame trembled as they walked towards their horses. They rode for a mile towards Willoughby before either uttered a word. Card finally said, "Mr. Barr, if you had not been there I certainly should have gone into the water . . . the impulse was irresistible."[62]

While Rigdon's Kirtland following joined the Mormon fold, his Mentor congregation resisted. They were furious at his defection, saying

> that he might [have] gone down to the grave as one of the great divines of the age, but now he had gone and thrown it all away and was a-going to follow a fool of a boy who claimed an angel had appeared to him. . . . It was nonsense and a man of his knowledge ought to have known better than to have had anything to do with such impostures. He ought not to have let them preach in their church, should not have let them stay overnight in his house, and should have refused to have anything to do with them.

Rigdon replied that they could "talk to him as they pleased," but he was convinced in reading the Book of Mormon that the doctrine preached by the Mormons was true . . . let the consequences be what they may."[63] Rigdon added that at the time he had a "family of small children to provide for but trusted them and himself to the mercy of God. . . . He [also] had . . . the glorious satisfaction of his wife, uniting with him."[64]

As a result of their conversion, the Rigdons lost their small, partially completed house owned by the Mentor congregation. "The church which Sidney Rigdon left at Mentor," remarked Wickliffe Rigdon, "was perfectly horrified and surprised and indignant at his conduct in leaving them in the hasty manner he did but he had gone and the only course for them to pursue was to submit and procure another minister for their church."[65] The new minister was M. S. Clapp, who was married to Alicia Campbell, sister of Alexander Campbell.

The *Painesville Telegraph* during the fall and winter of 1831-32 carried several feature stories about Mormon missionaries, reporting among other things that Cowdery had not only predicted the destruction of the world within a few years but proclaimed that he and his companions were the only ones on earth qualified to administer in the name of Jesus. Furthermore the Saints were going to gather to a certain location, found a city of refuge, and convert the Indians, the lost tribes of Israel.[66]

Before the missionaries left eastern Ohio they ordained Rigdon, Morley, Wight, John Murdock, and others to the ministry and left them to care for the new churches. They also sent a letter to Joseph Smith asking him to send a presiding elder to supervise the group. In the 16 November 1830 edition of the *Painesville Telegraph*, editor Eber D. Howe announced that the Mormon missionary team was "bound for the regions beyond the Mississippi, where [Smith] contemplates founding a 'City of Refuge' for his followers, and converting the Indians under his prophetic authority." On 22 November Cowdery, Pratt, Peter Whitmer, Jr., Ziba Peterson, and Kirtland physician Frederick G. Williams left for Independence, Missouri, the soon-to-be-declared Mormon Zion—the City of New Jerusalem.

Notes

Unless otherwise stated, all primary sources cited are located in the Historical Department of the Church of Jesus Christ of Latter-day Saints, Salt Lake City, Utah.

1. Cited in Richard T. Ely, "Economic Aspects of Mormonism," *Harper's Monthly Magazine* 56 (Apr. 1903): 667-68.

2. Alexander Campbell, *Debate on the Evidences of Christianity . . . Held in the City of Cincinnati, Ohio, From the 13th to the 21st of April, 1829; Between Robert Owen, of New Lanark, Scotland, and Alexander Campbell, of Bethany, Va.*, 2 vols. (Bethany, VA: Alexander Campbell, 1829), cited in Perry E. Gresham, *The Sage of Bethany: A Pioneer in Broadcloth* (St. Louis: The Bethany Press, 1960), 132.

3. David Edwin Harrell, Jr., *Quest for a Christian America: The Disciples of Christ and American Society to 1866* (Nashville: Disciples of Christ Historical Society, 1966), 81.

4. Ibid., 81-83. See also Campbell 1829.

5. Amos Sutton Hayden, *Early History of the Disciples in the Western Reserve* (Cincinnati: Chase and Hall, 1875), 186.

6. Alexander Campbell, *The Sacred Writings of the Apostles and Evangelists of Jesus Christ, Commonly Styled the New Testament. Translated From the Original Greek, by George Campbell, James Macknight, and Philip Doddridge, Doctors of the Church of Scotland. With Prefaces to the Historical and Epistolary Books; and an Appendix, Containing Critical Notes and Various Translations of Difficult Passages* (Buffaloe, VA: Alexander Campbell, 1826).

7. J. Wickliffe Rigdon, "Life Story of Sidney Rigdon," 16-17.

8. *Christian Baptist* 8:89-91, 95.

9. Edward Partridge Papers, 26 May 1839.

10. Parley P. Pratt, Jr., ed., *The Autobiography of Parley Parker Pratt* (Chicago: Law, King & Law, 1888), 32.

11. Eliza R. Snow, *Eliza R. Snow: An Immortal* (Salt Lake City: Nicholas G. Morgan, Sr., Foundation, 1957), 5.

12. Hayden, 298-99.

13. "Extracts from a Variety of Letters," *Christian Baptist* 4:257-60.

14. Henry K. Shaw, *Buckeye Disciples: A History of the Disciples of Christ in Ohio* [St. Louis: Christian Board of Publication, 1952], 58.

15. Hayden, 299.

16. Winfred Ernest Garrison and Alfred T. DeGroot, *The Disciples of Christ: A History* (St. Louis: Christian Board of Publication, 1948), 192.

17. Louis Cochran and Bess White Cochran, *Captives of the Word* (Garden City, NY: Doubleday & Co., 1969), 65.

18. *Millennial Harbinger* 2 (1830):415.

19. Ibid., 1 (1849):272.

20. See summarization in F. Mark McKiernan, *The Voice of One Crying in the Wilderness: Sidney Rigdon, Religious Reformer–1793-1876* (Lawrence, KS: Coronado Press, 1971), 29.

21. *Millennial Star* 26 (19 Nov. 1864): 744.

22. Snow, 6. She added that after she was baptized into Campbell's group, "I was deeply interested in the study of the ancient Prophets, in which I was assisted by the erudite A. Campbell, Walter Scott whose acquaintance I made, but more particularly by Sidney Rigdon who was a frequent visitor at my father's house."

23. Cited in *Millennial Harbinger* 2 (1844): 39.

24. William H. Whitsitt, "Sidney Rigdon, The Real Founder of Mormonism," 1885, 103, Special Collections, Marriott Library, University of Utah (hereafter Special Collections, U of U).

25. William Alexander Linn, *The Story of the Mormons* (London: MacMillan Company, 1923), 65-66.

26. Francis W. Kirkham, *A New Witness For Christ In America–The Book of Mormon*, 2 vols. (Independence, MO: Zion's Printing and Publishing Co., 1942), 1:120-21. In 1857 Harding wrote that "in 1829, I went with Joe Smith, at his special request, to his father's house, in company with Martin Harris and Oliver Cowdery, for the purpose of hearing read his wonderful 'translation' from the sacred plates. This was before these revelations had been given to the world in the printed Book of Mormon" (Pomeroy Tucker, *Origin, Rise, and Progress of Mormonism* [New York: D. Appleton & Co., 1867], 280-84).

27. *Rochester Advertiser and Telegraph*, 31 Aug. 1829, in Kirkham, 151, and the *Gem*, 5 Sept. 1829. Original article is in the *Scrapbook of Early Church History*, by Willard Bean, in Kirkham, 1:152. Another 1829 account in the 22 September *Painesville Telegraph* cited the *Palmyra (N.Y.) Freeman* as saying: "the greatest piece of superstition that has ever come within our knowledge, now occupies the attention of a few individuals of this quarter. It is general[l]y known and spoken of as the 'Golden Bible.'"

28. 1833 letter to N. E. Seaton, in Joseph Smith, *History of the Church of Jesus Christ of Latter-day Saints*, B. H. Roberts, ed., 7 vols. (Salt Lake City: The Church of Jesus Christ of Latter-day Saints, 1902), 1:315; hereafter referred to as *History of the Church.*

29. See Richard S. Van Wagoner and Steven C. Walker, "Joseph Smith: 'The Gift of Seeing,'" *Dialogue: A Journal of Mormon Thought* 15 (Summer 1982): 49-68.

30. *Tiffany's Monthly*, June 1859, 169.

31. Henry Harris Affidavit, in Kirkham, 1:133.

32. Cited in Eber Howe, *Mormonism Unvailed* (Painesville, OH: E. D. Howe, 1834), 246-47.

33. *Chenango Union*, 3 May 1877.

34. Pratt, 37.

35. *Times and Seasons* 4 (15 Aug. 1843): 289; Karl Keller, ed., "'I Never Knew a Time When I Did Not Know Joseph Smith': A Son's Record of the Life and Testimony of Sidney

Rigdon," *Dialogue: A Journal of Mormon Thought* 1 (Winter 1966): 15-42, cited, 23; Rigdon, 20.

36. Anson Call's statement in *Deseret Evening News*, 21 Apr. 1879.

37. *Times and Seasons* 4 (15 Aug. 1843): 289.

38. *Western Reserve Chronicle* (Warren, OH), 3 Mar. 1831, 4, Utah State Historical Society Library.

39. Interview with Wm. H. and E. L. Kelley, 14 May 1884, in *Pittsburgh Leader*, 18 May 1884, in *History of the Reorganized Church of Jesus Christ of Latter Day Saints*, 4 vols. (Independence, MO: Herald House, 1967), 4:452-53.

40. Howe, 102.

41. Hayden, 210-11.

42. John Corrill, *Brief History of the Church of Christ of Latter Day Saints (Commonly Called Mormons) Including an Account of Their Doctrine and Discipline with the Reasons of the Author for Leaving the Church* (n.p.: St. Louis, 1839), 7.

43. *Times and Seasons* 4 (15 Aug. 1843): 289-90.

44. Ibid.

45. Keller, 24.

46. Ibid.

47. Interview with Austin W. Cowles, "The Mormons: Pen and Pencil Sketches, Illustrating their Early History," *Moore's Rural New Yorker*, 23 Jan. 1869, 61, Special Collections, Harold B. Lee Library, Brigham Young University, Provo, Utah (hereafter Special Collections, BYU).

48. Parley P. Pratt, *Mormonism Unveiled* (n.p.: New York, 1838), 41.

49. Hayden, 212.

50. *Millennial Harbinger* 2 (1831): 100.

51. Howe, 217.

52. *Times and Seasons* 4 (15 Aug. 1843): 290.

53. Stephen Post Collection, box 1, fd 16, listed as Section 37 in Copying Book A; hereafter Post Collection.

54. Pratt 1888, 48.

55. Garrison and DeGroot, 300.

56. Hayden, 183.

57. Journal of Lyman Wight, in Joseph Smith III and Heman C. Smith, *The History of the Reorganized Church of Jesus Christ of Latter Day Saints*, 4 vols. (Independence, MO: Herald House, 1967), 1:153.

58. Hayden, 211.

59. Frederick G. Mather, "The Early Days of Mormonism," *Lippincotts Magazine of Popular Literature and Science* 26 (Aug. 1880), 206-207.

60. J. H. Kennedy, *Early Days of Mormonism* (London: Reeves and Turner, 1888), 81.

61. Pratt 1838, 41. Parishioner Matthew S. Clapp later wrote that Rigdon "arose to address the congregation *apparently* much affected and deeply impressed. He seemed exceedingly humble, confessed the sins of his former life, his great pride, ambition, vainglory, etc. etc." While the baptismal date of Sidney, Phebe, and Athalia has been variously given as 14, 15, or 18 November, three references drawn to my attention by H. Michael Marquardt convince me it was actually 8 November. See 15 Feb. 1831 issue of

Painesville Telegraph; Josiah Jones's recollection in *Brigham Young Studies* 12 (Spring 1972): 309; and Oliver Cowdery to "Our beloved brethren," 12 Nov. 1830, in Newel Knight Journal, copy of letter in my possession. See discussion of the Rigdon baptism date in Richard L. Anderson, "The Impact of the First Preaching in Ohio," *Brigham Young University Studies* 11 (Summer 1971): 486-87.

62. Mather, "The Early Days of Mormonism."

63. Keller, 24.

64. 1 July 1868 Revelation, Post Collection, box 1, fd 16, listed as Section 37 in Copying Book A.

65. Rigdon, 6.

66. See particularly the *Painesville Telegraph*, 16 Nov. 1830 and 15 Feb. 1831.

Section 2.

Ohio

CHAPTER 6.

Prelude to Kirtland

After Sidney Rigdon's baptism into Mormonism and expulsion from his Mentor pastorship, he preached for a time without a parish, the head of a large household without a home. Soon, however, he obtained quarters in an old log cabin on John Johnson's property in Hiram, Ohio, thirty-five miles southeast of Mentor. Here, with some twenty other converts, Rigdon formed a congregation.[1] Wickliffe Rigdon later wrote that his father "had now [e]mbraced a new religion[,] one on which he had always looked and hoped for and one which satisfied his mind and belief."[2] Although he had found in Mormonism a religion to match his manner, Sidney had not yet met the Mormon prophet. Possibly to satisfy some remaining doubts, particularly those of his wife, who "wished him to go to Palmyra to see Joseph Smith,"[3] he went to Manchester, New York, along with Edward Partridge, a Painesville hatter and one of Rigdon's Reformed Baptist followers.

When Rigdon and Partridge arrived at the Smith home in mid-December, the prophet was not there but was visiting his parents, who had moved a few miles to the small community of Kingdon, near Waterloo. So the two Ohio travelers walked around the Smith farm and became convinced of the "good order and industry" of the family. They also made inquiries in the neighborhood to gain "further information respecting the doctrine which [Smith] preached." Neighbors reportedly testified to the Smiths' integrity on all matters except religion, wherein young Joseph was said to have deceived his family about the Book of Mormon. Both Rigdon and Partridge waved the criticisms aside as prejudice.[4]

When they arrived at Kingdon that evening, the prophet was conducting a religious service. Partridge, after listening to him, requested immediate baptism. Joseph Smith recommended the immersion be delayed until the fatigued Partridge had rested, and the next day, 11 December, Smith baptized him in nearby Seneca Lake. The prophet welcomed Rigdon and Partridge into the young Church of Christ, particularly pleased that a religious bellwether of Rigdon's stature, seemingly motivated by pure faith, would be heaven sent to further the work. As God's spokesman, Smith had a message from the Lord for the former Baptist minister:

> Behold, verily, verily I say unto my servant Sidney, I have looked upon thee and thy works. I have heard thy prayers, and prepared thee for a great work. Thou art blessed, for thou shalt do great things. Behold thou wast sent forth, even as John [the Baptist]—to prepare the way before me, and before Elijah, which should come, and thou knew it not. . . .

[T]he time of my coming . . . is nigh at hand . . . and I have sent forth the fulness of my gospel by the hand of my servant Joseph: and in weakness have I blessed him. . . . Wherefore watch over him, that his faith fail not . . . and a commandment I give unto thee, that thou shalt write for him: and the scriptures shall be given, even as they are in mine own bosom, to the salvation of mine own elect. . . .

Tarry with him, and he shall journey with you—forsake him not, and surely these things shall be fulfilled. And inasmuch as ye do not write, behold it shall be given unto him to prophesy: and thou shalt preach my gospel, and call upon the holy prophets to prove his words, as they shall be given him. . . . Fear not, little flock—the kingdom is yours, until I come. —Behold I come quickly.[5]

Rigdon was deeply impressed by this prophetic augury. His destiny seemed assured by cosmic powers, and it was as though he had returned from Mount Sinai with his purpose fixed in stone. All zest and fire, he was anxious to federate with Smith and save the elect in a glorious crusade. The two elders were quick to accomplish a merger of their talents.

The first project they focused their joint energies on was a revision of the Bible on which Smith had been working intermittently since finishing the Book of Mormon. John Whitmer, historian of the new church, wrote that once the celestial edict was given to Rigdon "he went to writing the things which the Lord showed unto his servant the Seer."[6] Although Mormon usage designates this Bible revision as the Joseph Smith Translation (JST), ancient manuscripts were not used, nor were Smith or Rigdon familiar with foreign languages. From Smith's description of the process the procedure was an "inspired revision," not a translation.

Between 1777 and 1833 more than 500 separate editions of the Bible or New Testament were published in the United States. Many of these were revisions of the King James Version (1611), containing modernizations of language, paraphrases, and alternate readings based on comparisons with Greek and Hebrew. Even Rigdon's classically-trained mentor, Alexander Campbell, had issued his own New Testament translation in 1826. Although Rigdon was not involved with the project, he was familiar with it.

Alexander Campbell had heartfelt reverence for the Bible but no special respect for the King James Version, being too well-grounded in first-century Greek to accept 1611 English as inviolable. As a basis for his personal interpretation of sacred writings, Campbell used renderings of the four gospels published by George Campbell in Edinburgh in 1778, James MacKnight's translation of the Epistles, published first in London in 1795, and the translation of Acts and Revelation by Phillip Doddridge, first published in London in 1776. These works were issued together in a London publication in 1818. Campbell made various emendations, added a preface, and included 100 pages of critical notes and appendices. As a wealthy gentleman farmer, he was able to publish his new edition from his own printing office in Buffaloe, Virginia.[7]

Mirroring Campbell's perspective on biblical translation, Joseph Smith believed in the Bible as it "came from the pen of the original writers," but that "ignorant translators, careless transcribers, or designing and corrupt priests have committed many errors."[8] He added that "many important points touching the salvation of men, had been taken from the Bible, or lost before it was compiled." Thus Smith's version is viewed by Mormon faithful as "a restoration of lost material—material once known to the ancient prophets but then lost, material now made known again in these last days through the Prophet Joseph Smith."[9]

Smith began his biblical innovations six months before he met Rigdon. But the former minister, often called a "walking Bible" by his peers in the Reformed Baptist Movement, made an immediate impact on the work. The material of the early manuscripts, which extended at least through the first seven chapters of Genesis in the handwriting of Oliver Cowdery and John Whitmer, was further revised and rewritten by Rigdon.[10] Mormons believed that Rigdon had been sent to Smith for such projects. David Whitmer, a close friend of Smith and one of the Three Witnesses to the Book of Mormon, wrote:

> Rigdon was a thorough Bible scholar, a man of fine education, and a powerful orator. He soon worked himself deep into Brother Joseph's affections, and had more influence over him than any other man living. He was Brother Joseph's private counsellor, and his most intimate friend and brother for some time after they met. Brother Joseph rejoiced[,] believing that the Lord had sent to him this great and mighty man S[i]dney Rigdon, to help him in the work.[11]

That Rigdon could have been merely "Sidney the Scribe," a penman whose sole function was to take down dictation, is implausible. A biblical scholar with a reputation for erudition, he was more learned, better read, and more steeped in biblical interpretation than any other early Mormon, despite his common school education. Any number of Smith's followers could have served as clerk, but only Rigdon could have functioned as a scribe in the historical Jewish sense of the word: "a man of learning; one who read and explained the law to the people."[12]

Smith's own description of Rigdon's fortuitous arrival in New York states for December 1830:

> It may be well to observe here, that the Lord greatly encouraged and strengthened the faith of His little flock, which had embraced the fulness of the everlasting Gospel, as revealed to them in the Book of Mormon, by giving some more extended information upon the Scriptures, a translation of which had already commenced. . . . To the joy of the little flock . . . did the Lord reveal the following doings of olden times, from the Prophecy of Enoch.[13]

The Prophecy of Enoch refers to a lost book, the history of Enoch, the "Seventh from Adam," who, according to the Bible, was "translated" up to heaven without first dying. Smith's elaboration of this passage was one of the longest and most remarkable revelations of his career. Enoch, he said, founded Zion, the fabled

City of Holiness, where the inhabitants were "of one heart and of one mind, and dwelt in righteousnes[s]; and there were no poor among them" (JST Gen. 7:23; Moses 7:18). Subsequently, this city was translated, taken from the earth, but would literally be brought back to earth in the last days and joined with a new Zion, the New Jerusalem, which the people of God would build (JST Gen. 7:70-72; Moses 7:62-64).[14]

Once the Enoch prophesy was received, Rigdon could not rest until Smith agreed to move church headquarters to the Western Reserve. He argued that while the foundling church in New York was harassed and persecuted, the Mormon congregations in Ohio enjoyed considerable peace, missionary efforts were amazingly fruitful, and Ohio was much closer to native American nations on the frontier, making missionary efforts there more feasible. Finally, engaging his full powers of persuasion, Rigdon appealed to Smith's sense of futurity. Just as the young nation was manifestly destined ever westward, the newly-formed Church of Christ was similarly compelled. After all, the Book of Mormon prophesied America as the promised land, the nation to usher in the Millennium.

The most important factor in the eventual migration west, however, may have been the fact that most Rigdon followers in the Kirtland area believed in communalism. Smith and Rigdon, both indigent visionaries with no visible sources of income, generally sought their bread from the sweat of their followers' brows. Amos S. Hayden, wielding a vengeful knife, points this out as he flayed them in his history of the Disciples in the Western Reserve. Calling the area the Mormon "promised land," he observed that "in it their long cherished hopes and anticipations of living without work were to be realized. Thus, from almost a state of beggary . . . they were immediately well furnished with the 'fat of the land' by their fanatical followers, many of whom were wealthy."[15]

Smith throughout his life saw God's guiding hand in his every action and was quick to assume God's voice to amplify his own verities. Beginning with the organization of the Church of Christ on 6 April 1830 he began calling himself "the prophet" and used the term "having a revelation" when referring to the statements he issued in response to specific questions or crises. Rigdon was privy to the same epiphanies, and several early revelations were given to both men simultaneously. When the two enquired about moving to the Western Reserve, for example, word came back:

> Behold, I say unto you that it is not expedient in me that ye should translate any more until ye shall go to the Ohio, and this because of the enemy and for your sakes. And again, I say unto you that ye shall not go until ye have preached my gospel in those parts, and have strengthened up the church whithersoever it is found, and more especially in Colesville ("A Revelation to Joseph and Sidney, given in Canandaigua, New-York, December, 1830" [BC 39; also see D&C 37:1]).

John Corrill documented Smith's and Rigdon's travels throughout upstate

New York preaching and prophesying "great judgments that should come in the last days, and destruction upon the wicked."[16] Apocalyptic rhetoric and doomsday hysteria abounded in early Mormon preaching. A century and a half of Mormon history has seen it fall to the wayside. But to Rigdon and Smith, the dark pronouncements were necessary. The existing system of social, economic, and political interfaces had to be recast in the image and likeness of a vision compelling enough to draw adherents away from their daily routines to a life that assumed heroic quality. They would become a peculiar people seeking to achieve the Millennium.

Many of the seventy or so members of the Church of Christ in New York were relatively prosperous farmers. Short of being convinced the sky was falling, these land owners would likely not have been willing to relocate. But Smith told them that "God is about to destroy this generation, and Christ will descend from Heaven in power and great glory, with all the holy angels with him, to take vengeance upon the wicked, and they that know not God."[17]

Rigdon proved the prophet's words with biblical references and added fatalistic predictions of his own. One surviving newspaper account has him levying malevolent prophecies on the town of Waterloo and further warning all New Yorkers to rise up and "flee the wrath to come."[18] Together the two men were so powerful, church historian John Whitmer wrote, "that the people who heard them speak were amazed, and trembled, and knew not whereunto this thing would grow."[19]

After Smith and Rigdon returned to Fayette, New York, a general conference was held at the Whitmer farm on 2 January 1831. While conducting rudimentary business, Smith was requested by the audience to tell them more about the Ohio venture. He "enquired of the Lord in the presence of the whole congregation," wrote Whitmer. The seer then sat at a table dictating the Lord's words while Rigdon wrote them. In part the message said:

> But behold, verily, verily, verily I say unto you, that mine eyes are upon you; I am in your midst, and ye cannot see me, but the day soon cometh that ye shall see me and know that I am; for the vail of darkness shall soon be rent, and he that is not purified shall not abide the day; Wherefore gird up your loins and be prepared. Behold the kingdom is yours and the enemy shall not overcome. . . . And now I show unto you a mystery, a thing which is had in secret chambers. . . . And I hold forth and deign to give unto you greater riches, even a land of promise; a land flowing with milk and honey, upon which there shall be no curse when the Lord cometh, and I will give it unto you for the land of your inheritance, if you seek it with all your hearts: And this shall be my covenant with you, ye shall have it for the land of your inheritance, and for the inheritance of your children forever, while the earth shall stand, and ye shall possess it again in eternity, no more to pass away: But verily I say unto you, that in time ye shall have no king nor ruler, for I will be your King and watch over you. Wherefore, hear my voice and follow me, and you shall be a free people, and ye shall

have no laws but my laws, when I come, for I am your Lawgiver, and what can stay my hand. . . .

And again I say unto you, that the enemy in the secret chambers, seeketh your lives: Ye hear of wars in far countries, and you say in your hearts there will soon be great wars in far countries, but ye know not the hearts of them in your own land: And that ye might escape the power of the enemy, and be gathered unto me a righteous people, without spot and blameless: Wherefore, for this cause I gave unto you the commandment, that ye should go to the Ohio: and there I will give unto you my law, and there you shall be endowed with power from on high. And if ye seek the riches which it is the will of the Father to give unto you, ye shall be the richest of all people, for ye shall have the riches of eternity: And it must needs be that the riches of the earth is mine to give.[20]

Whitmer wrote that when the revelation was first read, "the solemnities of eternity rested on the congregation." But shortly, he added, some fought it, believing "that Joseph had invented it himself to deceive the people that in the end he might get gain."[21] For several weeks Smith argued with his small group of followers, using Rigdon as his ally. They spoke longingly of "the promised land . . . the land of your inheritance . . . a land flowing with milk and honey, upon which there shall be no curse when the Lord cometh." Ultimately their powers of persuasion, bolstered by the fear they had instilled in the Saints, prevailed.

Whitmer was dispatched to Ohio to carry the commandments and revelations with him to "comfort and strengthen my brethren in that land."[22] Rigdon sent a letter of introduction with Whitmer advising the Western Reserve Saints to "receive him, for he is a brother greatly beloved, and an Apostle of this church." He also wrote:

With him we send all the revelations we have received; for the Lord has declared unto us that you pray unto Him that Joseph Smith and myself go speedily unto you. . . . The Lord has made known unto us some of his great things which he has laid up for them that love Him, among which the fact that you are living on the land of promise and that there at Kirtland is the place of gathering, and from that place to the Pacific Ocean, God has dedicated to himself, not only in time, but through eternity, and he has given it to us and our children, not only while time lasts, but we shall have it again in eternity, as you will see by one of the commandments, received day before yesterday.[23]

Rigdon followed Whitmer to the Western Reserve within a matter of weeks. The 26 January 1831 *Palmyra Reflector* printed his adieu from New York state:

Elder S. Rigdon left this village on Monday morning last in the stage, for the "Holy Land" where all the "Gold Bible" converts, have recently received a *written* command from God, through J. Smith, junior, to repair with all convenient speed after selling off the property.— This command was at first resisted by such as had property, (the brethren from all the neighboring counties being all assembled by special summons,) but after a night of fasting, prayer and trial, they all consented to obey the holy messenger. Rigdon has for some time past been arranging matters with Smith for the final departure of the *faithful* for the "far west." This man of many CREEDS [Rigdon] appears to possess colloquial powers to a considerable degree, and before leaving this vicinity left us his *blessing*. He delivered a discourse at the Court House immediately preceding his departure; wherein he depicted in strong language, the want of "charity and brotherly love" among the prevailing sects and denominations of professing christians. . . . After denouncing dreadful vengeance on the whole State of New York, and this village in particular, and recommending to all such as wish to flee from "the wrath to come," to follow him beyond the "western waters," he took his leave. The *Prophet, Spouse*, and whole "holy family" as they style themselves, will follow Rigdon as soon as their . . . followers shall be able to dispose of what little real property they possess.

Notes

Unless otherwise stated, all primary sources cited are located in the Historical Department of the Church of Jesus Christ of Latter-day Saints, Salt Lake City, Utah.

1. John and Elsa Johnson, along with their four children, had moved from the cabin into their new large New England colonial-style house in 1826 (see Linda King Newell and Valeen Tippetts Avery, *Mormon Enigma: Emma Hale Smith* [Garden City, NY: Doubleday & Co., 1984], 41).

2. J. Wickliffe Rigdon, "Life Story of Sidney Rigdon," 26.

3. Karl Keller, ed., "'I Never Knew a Time When I Did Not Know Joseph Smith': A Son's Record of the Life and Testimony of Sidney Rigdon," *Dialogue: A Journal of Mormon Thought* 1 (Winter 1966): 15-42, cited, 25.

4. Preston Nibley, ed., *History of Joseph Smith by His Mother Lucy Mack Smith* (Salt Lake City: Bookcraft, 1958), 192.

5. *Times and Seasons* 4 (15 Sept. 1843): 320-21. See also Book of Commandments, chap. 37 (hereafter BC), and Doctrine and Covenants 35 (hereafter D&C).

6. F. Mark McKiernan and Roger D. Launius, eds., *An Early Latter Day Saint History: The Book of John Whitmer–Kept By Commandment* (Independence, MO.: Herald Publishing House, 1980), 31. On 8 March 1831 John Whitmer was commanded to "write and keep a regular history, and assist my servant Joseph, in transcribing all things which shall be given you" (D&C 47:1). He wrote his twenty-two-chapter history over a period of several years. He retained the manuscript until his death, after which the Reorganized Church of Jesus Christ of Latter Day Saints purchased it in 1903.

7. S. Morris Eames, *The Philosophy of Alexander Campbell* (Bethany, WV: Bethany College, n.d.), 100. During the Virginia Constitutional Convention of 1829, in the middle of a heated argument over the issue of free public schools and libraries, Randolph pointed his finger at Campbell and declared, "That man is never satisfied. God Almighty could not satisfy him with the Bible which He gave and Mr. Campbell went and wrote a Bible of his own" (Henry K. Shaw, *Buckeye Disciples: A History of the Disciples of Christ in Ohio* [St. Louis: Christian Board of Publication, 1952], 68).

8. Joseph Fielding Smith, ed., *Teachings of the Prophet Joseph Smith* (Salt Lake City: Deseret Book Co., 1938), 327.

9. Ibid., 10.

10. Robert J. Matthews, "The 'New Translation' of the Bible, 1830-33: Doctrinal Development During the Kirtland Era," *Brigham Young University Studies* (Summer 1971): 401-22, cited 406.

11. David Whitmer, *An Address to All Believers in Christ* (Richmond, MO: David Whitmer, 1887), 35.

12. *Webster's New Twentieth Century Dictionary of the English Language* (New York City: Prentice Hall Press, 1979), 1,630.

13. Joseph Smith, *History of the Church of Jesus Christ of Latter-day Saints*, B. H. Roberts, ed., 7 vols. (Salt Lake City: The Church of Jesus Christ of Latter-day Saints, 1902), 1:131-33; hereafter referred to as *History of the Church.*

14. The "Prophecy of Enoch," the Mormon apocalyptic blueprint of the nineteenth-century, is now part of the book of Genesis 7:1-78 in the JST. The 1835 D&C did not include this prophecy, but it became part of a later publication called the Pearl of Great Price as the Book of Moses 7:1-69. For a detailed discussion of the JST, see Robert J. Matthews, *A Plainer Translation: Joseph Smith's Translation of the Bible, A History and Commentary* (Provo, UT: Brigham Young University Press, 1975). Also see Richard P. Howard, *Restoration Scriptures: A Study of Their Textual Development* (Independence, MO: Herald Publishing House, 1969), 70-193.

15. Amos Sutton Hayden, *Early History of the Disciples in the Western Reserve* (Cincinnati: Chase and Hall, 1875), 214.

16. John Corrill, *A Brief History of the Church of Christ of Latter Day Saints, (Commonly Called Mormons); Including an Account of their Doctrines and Discipline* (St. Louis: by the author, 1839), 8.

17. McKiernan and Launius, 31-32.

18. *Palmyra Reflector*, 1 Feb. 1831.

19. McKiernan and Launius, 32-33.

20. This is section 12 in the 1835 D&C—section 38 in modern LDS editions—and is entitled: "A Revelation to the churches in New-York, commanding them to remove to Ohio" (BC 10).

21. McKiernan and Launius, 32-35.

22. Ibid., 36.

23. Eber Howe, *Mormonism Unvailed* (Painesville, OH: E. D. Howe, 1834), 111; J. H. Kennedy, *Early Days of Mormonism* (London: Reeves and Turner, 1888), 84. The *Painsville Telegraph*, 18 Jan. 1831, in commenting on Whitmer's arrival, stated that the more important part of Whitmer's mission was "to inform the brethren that the boundaries of the promised land, or the New Jerusalem, . . . the township of Kirtland, a few miles west of this, is the eastern line and the Pacific Ocean the western line."

CHAPTER 7.

The Law of the Lord

The prophet's syncretic ability to blend others' ideas with his own intuition was a conspicuous feature of his career. It was not surprising that Joseph Smith's communal vision began evolving within days of meeting Rigdon, who discussed with Smith the range of his own religious experience, including communitarianism. Smith's first of a host of revelations on financial matters, the "law of the Lord," as it was subsequently called, was withheld from public view from 2 January 1831 until both Rigdon and Smith were in the Western Reserve.

Rigdon, who traveled by stage, arrived back in Ohio a week or so before Smith. On his first day in Hiram two former parishioners from Mentor visited and requested a "reason for his present hope, and for his belief in the Book of Mormon." Rigdon complained he was weary, exhausted from having lost so much sleep on the journey, but the men persisted, one avowing "he thought there was no more evidence to confirm the Book of Mormon, than the Koran of Mohamet." Rankled, Rigdon replied, "Sir, you have insulted me in my own house—I command silence—if people come to see us and cannot treat us with civility, they may walk out of the door as soon as they please." Mumbling a reluctant apology, the men left.

Two days later the more respectful of the two men returned with several other Mentor acquaintances and pleaded with Rigdon to "give some reason for his present faith." Their former pastor then commenced a lengthy history of his investigations into Joseph Smith's background. "Even his enemies had nothing to say against his character," he reported. For evidence he showed them a transcript from the dockets of two New York magistrates, where Smith had been tried earlier that year for "being a disorderly person and setting the country in an uproar by preaching the Book of Mormon." Both documents testified that the young prophet had been acquitted.[1]

Rigdon further spoke of the "supernatural gifts with which he said Smith was endowed; he said [Smith] could translate the scriptures from any language in which they were now extant, and could lay his finger upon every interpolation in the sacred writings, adding that he had proven him in all these things." When Rigdon was asked by his friends why they should receive the new scripture he replied, "The Book of Mormon, is to form and govern the Millennial Church; the old revelation was never calculated for that, nor would it accomplish that object; and without receiving the Book of Mormon there is no salvation for any one into whose hands it shall come." He avowed that faith in the book could only be obtained by asking for divine confirmation. When scriptural objections to sign seeking were made, Rigdon replied, "If we have not familiarity enough with our Creator to ask of him a sign, we were no Christians; and that, if God would not condescend to his creatures, in this way, *he was no better than Juggernaut!!!*"[2]

Rigdon's belief in the Book of Mormon as the real millennial harbinger is evidenced in a 15 January 1831 letter from New York newspaper man W. W. Phelps to *Painesville Telegraph* editor Eber D. Howe: "I had ten hours discourse [on Mormonism] with a man from your State named Sidney Rigdon, a convert to its doctrines and he declared it was true, and he knew it by the power of the Holy Ghost, which was again given to men in preparation for the Millennium; he appeared to be a man of talents and sincere in his profession."[3]

Rigdon preached at Kirtland on Sunday, 30 January, and told his audience that Joseph Smith, their latter-day oracle, was en route to their little community. During his sermon he fulminated a challenge to the world to "refute the divine pretensions of the *Book of Mormon*." This caught the attention of his old associate, Alexander Campbell's father Thomas, who wrote him from nearby Mentor where he was visiting at the home of his daughter Alicia and her new husband, Reverend Matthew Clapp:

> DEAR SIR:—It may seem strange, that instead of a confidential and friendly visit, after so long an absence, I should thus address, by letter, one whom for many years I have considered not only as a courteous and benevolent friend, but as a beloved brother and fellow-laborer in the gospel; but, alas! how changed, how fallen! Nevertheless, I should now have visited you, as formerly, could I conceive that my so doing would answer the important purpose, both to ourselves and to the public, to which we both stand pledged, from the conspicuous and important stations we occupy—you as the professed disciple and public teacher of the infernal book of Mormon, and I as a professed disciple and public teacher of the supernal book of the Old and New Testaments of our Lord and Saviour Jesus Christ, which you now say is superceded by the book of Mormon. . . . To the disproof of this assertion, I understand you to defy the world. . . . This, I understand from your declaration on last Lord's day, you are abundantly prepared and ready to do. I, therefore, as in duty bound, accept the challenge, and shall hold myself in readiness, if the Lord permit, to meet you publicly, in any place, either in Mentor or Kirtland, or in any of the adjoining towns that may appear most eligible for the accommodation of the public. The sooner the investigation takes place the better for all concerned.

Campbell forewarned that he intended to expose the claims of Mormonism "by examining the character of its author and his accomplices . . . expose their pretensions to miraculous gifts, and the gift of tongues; and . . . test them in three or four foreign languages." He planned to expose their assertion

> that the authority for administering baptism was lost for fourteen hundred years till restored by the new prophet, by showing it to be a contradiction to Matt. xvi:18 . . .

that the pretended duty of "common property" is anti-scriptural, and a fraud upon society, that re-baptizing believers is making void the law of Christ; and the pretension of imparting the Holy Spirit by imposition of hands, is an unscriptural intrusion on the exclusive prerogative of the primary apostles . . . that its pretentious visions, humility and spiritual perfection, are nowise superior to those of the first Shakers, Jememia Wilkson, the French prophets, etc.

Campbell concluded by declaring that "in the last place we shall examine the internal evidence of the book of Mormon itself, pointing out its evident contradictions, foolish absurdities, shameless pretensions to antiquity, restore it to its rightful claimant as a production beneath contempt, and utterly unworthy the reception of a school-boy." The letter ends with Campbell declaring himself the champion "of all who do not wilfully and blindly submit to become the dupes of a shameless combination of unprincipled religious swindlers—whose unhallowed design is to rob the simple both of their salvation and their property."[4]

Kirtland Reformers Nathan P. Goodall and Isaac Moore delivered Campbell's letter to Rigdon. Their testimony in the 15 February 1831 *Painesville Telegraph* reported that "when [Rigdon] had read about half a dozen lines he came to the epithet 'infernal,' which he found applied to his beloved book, he committed it to the flames." Rigdon, perhaps out of fear, possibly out of disdain, never met the Reverend Campbell in open debate.

Rigdon's one-time spiritual mentor and erstwhile nemesis, Alexander Campbell, followed his father's stinging criticism of Rigdon with his own rebuke in the *Millennial Harbinger*. "It was with mingled emotions of regret and surprise," he began, "that we have learned that Sidney Rigdon has renounced the ancient gospel, and declared that he was not sincere in his profession of it; and that he has fallen into the snare of the Devil in joining the Mormonites. He has led away a number of disciples with him." Campbell then disparaged his former lieutenant by referring to his eccentricity—the first public assessment of Rigdon's possible manic-depressive illness. "His instability," the Reverend Campbell wrote,

I was induced to ascribe to a peculiar mental and corporeal malady, to which he has been subject for some years. Fits of melancholy succeeded by fits of enthusiasm accompanied by some kind of nervous spasms and swoonings which he has, since his defection, interpreted into the agency of the Holy Spirit, or the recovery of spiritual gifts, produced a versatility in his genius and deportment which has been increasing for some time. I was willing to have ascribed his apostasy to this cause, and to a conceit which he cherished that within a few years, by some marvellous interposition, the long lost tribes of Israel were to be collected, had he not declared that he was hypocritical in his profession of the faith which he has for some time proclaimed.[5]

Campbell's insult was not soon forgotten by Rigdon. Prone to hold long-time grudges, Rigdon would later in the pages of Kirtland's Mormon newspapers attack Campbell and his followers on several occasions.

Despite Rigdon's public reservations regarding his once-professed Reformed Baptist beliefs, there is no convincing evidence that he ever harbored similar doubts about the Book of Mormon. Although he later lost faith in Smith, Rigdon was a steadfast believer in Mormonism's holy book. Five years before his death, in a letter to an associate, he declared his commitment to Mormon scripture and warned that "rejecting it or . . . corrupting it after pretending to receive it is as heaven-daring and soul-dam[n]ing as any other thing can be, yea, more than it is possible for anything else to be."[6]

Rigdon welcomed the prophet and his wife to his Kirtland stronghold on 1 February 1831, where the Smiths established temporary residency with the family of local merchant Newel K. Whitney. The town then was a small farming community of 1,000 people. It boasted a few stores and shops, a grist mill, a post office, one hotel, and several other buildings and homes. Three days after his arrival in Kirtland Smith pronounced God's word that "it is meet that my servant Joseph Smith, Jun., should have a house built, in which to live and translate." The divine disclosure revealed financial benefits for Rigdon as well: "And again, it is meet that my servant Sidney Rigdon should live as seemeth him good, inasmuch as he keepeth my commandments" (D&C 41:7-8 [4 Feb. 1831]).

Cyrus Smalling, a Mormon living in the community at the time, believed that church officials "imagined that God was about to make them rich . . . and then they would make the *whole Church rich*."[7] But despite financial dreams the two engineered during their union, Rigdon and Smith were often impoverished. As early as 13 January 1831, even before Rigdon had returned from New York, Jotham Maynard and Asa Ayres, Jr., overseers of the poor in Kirtland, signed a writ authorizing the constable to require, among others, Rigdon and his destitute family to "Depart out of this Township."[8] Before the year's end Smith, two of his brothers, and a host of other Mormons were also warned out of town. George A. Smith, a cousin of Joseph Smith, later said that this was done to prevent the Saints from becoming a town charge. "The law of Ohio," he explained, "being that if a person, who had been warned out of town, applied for assistance, he was to be carried to the next town and so on till he was taken out of the state or to the town from which he formerly came."[9]

In addition to financial plans, Smith and Rigdon began to subdue the radical religious excesses in which newly baptized Mormons in Kirtland had become entangled. The restoration of ancient Christianity, including spiritual gifts as taught by the missionaries who had converted Rigdon, had invited misunderstanding and bizarre conduct in the neophyte society. In his official account, Smith noted that the nearly 100 church members "were striving to do the will of God, so far as they knew it, though some strange notions and false spirits had crept in among them. With a little caution and some wisdom, I soon assisted the brethren and sisters to overcome them."[10]

These "strange notions and false spirits" were explained in more detail elsewhere. The 15 February 1831 *Painesville Telegraph* reported that the Saints

> would fall, as without strength, roll upon the floor, and, so mad were they that even the females were seen on a cold winter day, lying under the bare canopy of heaven, with no couch or pillow but the fleecy snow. At other times they exhibited all the apish actions imaginable, making grimaces both horrid and ridiculous, creeping upon their hands and feet, etc. Sometimes, in these exercises the young men would rise and play before the people, going through all the Indian maneuvers of knocking down, scalping, ripping open, and taking out the bowels. At other times, they are taken with a fit of jabbering after which they call speaking foreign languages by divine inspiration. At other times, they would start and run several furlongs, then get upon stumps and preach to imagined congregations, baptize ghosts, etc.

Such stories cannot all be dismissed as mere barbs by anti-Mormon editors. Parley Pratt, a fervent Mormon, wrote that as he visited the different branches of the church in the Kirtland area

> some very strange spiritual operations were manifested, which were disgusting, rather than edifying. Some persons would seem to swoon away, and make unseemly gestures, and be drawn or disfigured in their countenances. Others would fall into ecstasies, and be drawn into contortions, which were not edifying, and which were not congenial to the doctrine and spirit of the gospel. In short, a false and lying spirit seemed to be creeping into the Church.[11]

Extreme behavior was also documented by John Whitmer, who wrote that

> some had visions and could not tell what they saw. Some would fancy to themselves that they had the sword of Laban, and would wield it as expert as a light dragoon, some would act like an Indian in the act of scalping, some would slide or scoot on the floor, with the rapidity of a serpent, which [they] termed sailing in the boat to the Lamanites, preaching the gospel. And many other vain and foolish mane[u]vers, that are un[seem]ing, and unprofitable to mention. Thus the devil blinded the eyes of some good and honest disciples.[12]

Joseph Smith's cousin, George A. Smith, added detail not found elsewhere. According to him, "Black Pete," a former slave and self-proclaimed revelator, lived in "the family" on the Morley farm. The diviner one evening thought he caught sight of a black angel passing through the heavens. In his dash after the seraph he fell off a steep cliff and landed in a tree on the banks of the Chagrin River below. "He came out with a few scratches," Smith recalled, "and his ardor somewhat cooled." He added that "many strange visions were seen, and wild enthusiastic notions were entertained; men ran out of doors under the influence of this spirit, and some of them got upon the stumps of trees and shouted, and all kinds of extravagances were entered into by them."[13]

The prophet eventually assembled the Saints

in order to show them the difference between the Spirit of God, and the spirit of the devil. He said, if a man arose in meeting to speak, and was seized with a kind of paroxysm that drew his face and limbs in a violent and unnatural manner, which made him appear to be in pain; and if he gave utterence to strange sounds, which were incomprehensible to his audience, they might rely upon it, that he had the spirit of the devil.[14]

In addition to devilish manifestations, the Kirtland "family commonwealth" was disintegrating. John Whitmer wrote: "The disciples had all things common and were going to destruction very fast as to temporal things, for they considered from reading the scripture that what belonged to one brother, belonged to any of the brethren, therefore they would take each other's clothes and other property and use it without leave, which brought on confusion and disappointments."[15] Another contemporary account in the 1 February 1831 *Geauga Gazette* noted that "as to matters [of] apparel, and indeed other things, where any one wants what he has not [they take it] where [they] can find it unoccupied."

And even when it was occupied some felt free to pirate. Levi Hancock, visiting Kirtland in February 1831, observed:

> While I was in the room at "Father Morleys" as we all called him, . . . Herman Bassett came to me and took my watch out of my pocket and walked off as though it was his. I thought he would bring it back soon but was disappointed as he sold it. I asked him what he meant by selling my watch. "O," said he, "I thought it was all in the family." I told him I did not like such family doings and I would not bear it.[16]

Such radical behavior did little to dignify the young church's public image. Prominent voices in the area, particularly the press, stepped up their ridicule. The *Chardon Spectator* reported, "The idle, foolish whim whams of this sect excite, and very properly, we suppose, the ridicule of the people generally."[17] Criticism of fanatical Mormon doings continued after the Kirtland era. Many verbal fusillades targeted various church financial experiments instigated through Smith's and Rigdon's joint revelations.

Rigdon was, on many occasions, the catalyst for these pronouncements. David Whitmer, "a man of the highest integrity, and of undoubted truth and veracity," according to citizens of his hometown,[18] witnessed Rigdon's influence on Smith on several occasions. "Rigdon would expound the Old Testament scriptures of the Bible and Book of Mormon (in his way)," Whitmer affirmed, and whatever his interests, he would have "Brother Joseph inquire of the Lord about it, and they received an answer according to their erring desires."[19]

A few days after Smith's and Rigdon's New York meeting, revelations regarding economic matters surfaced. Their first pronouncement advised: "And again I say unto you, let every man esteem his brother as himself: For what man among you, having twelve sons, and is no respecter to them, and they serve him obediently, and he saith unto the one, be thou clothed in robes and sit thou here;

and to the other, be thou clothed in rags and sit thou there, and looketh upon his sons and saith I am just[?]" The scripture stipulated that "certain men among you" should be appointed to "look to the poor and the needy, and administer to their relief, that they shall not suffer." These select men, who included Rigdon and Smith, were to "govern the affairs of the property of this church" (Book of Commandments 40, pp. 82-83; cf. D&C 38:26-27).

Scores of subsequent revelations—many unpublished, uncanonized, and unknown to modern Mormons—were uttered during this period. Substantial textual changes later made by Smith, Rigdon, and others resulted in a convoluted narrative of nineteenth-century church financial policy. Complicating the account, neither Smith nor Rigdon were competent financial leaders, yet they considered their judgment superior to worldly wisdom. Their naivete brought the church to the brink of financial ruin more than once.

Perhaps the greatest miscalculation, both in Kirtland and later, was the false assumption that an influx of immigrants would bring prosperity. The exact opposite proved to be the case. Most Mormon converts were of the lower economic classes, and like Smith and Rigdon had few worldly tangible resources to add to the community's financial base. Paupers were eager to "share all things in common," anticipating that some wealth would trickle down. John Whitmer noted "some of the disciples who were flattered into this church . . . thought that all things were to be common, therefore they thought to glut themselves upon the labors of others."[20]

Because it was not right "that one man should possess that which is above another," spoke the young prophet, "Wo unto the rich men, that will not give your substance to the poor, for your riches will canker your souls!" (Book of Commandments LII:19, p. 118; cf. D&C 49:20; Book of Commandments LVIII:19, p. 132; cf. D&C 56:16). Furthermore, the "riches of those who embrace my gospel among the Gentiles" would be given "unto the poor of my people" (1835 D&C 13:11, p. 122; cf. D&C 42:39).

Communitarianism, Smith's utopian dream, arose out of the conversion of Rigdon and his Kirtland congregation. Smith later said, "[T]he plan of 'common stock,' which had existed in what was called 'the family' . . . was readily abandoned for the more perfect law of the Lord."[21] This economic blueprint was put to writing on 9 February 1831 during a gathering of twelve elders who met together in "mighty prayer." The principles of consecration differed little from those of other communitarian schemes of the day. For the most part they all required that one's possessions go to a common fund for the explicit purpose of eliminating poverty and for payment of common debts through personal sacrifice.

The implementation of the 1831 Mormon system, however, differed considerably from other idealistic communities of the nineteenth century. Smith's vision combined elements of both individualism and collectivism. All things belonged to God, but church members were stewards of God's property rather than owners or profiteers. Through cooperation the Saints would acquire land in and around Kirtland, then build an egalitarian Kingdom of God. Stewards were assigned real estate for which they alone were responsible. Control over receiving and allocating stewardships was assigned to a bishop, a management-level supervisor. In case of differences of opinion, he had the authority to make all final decisions regarding a steward's inheritance. To discourage theft that plagued Rigdon's "family commonwealth," Mormons were counseled not to "take thy brother's garment [but] pay for that which thou shalt receive of thy brother" (D&C 42:54).[22] Community dwellings were also unacceptable for "every family shall have a place, that they may live by themselves" (Book of Commandments 44:57, pp. 95-96).

While Smith counseled against a community of goods, property was to be donated for the benefit of the poor, which included himself and Rigdon, and for general church expenditures: "If thou loveth me, thou shalt serve me and keep all my commandments; and behold, thou shalt consecrate *all* thy properties, that which thou hast unto me, with a covenant and a deed which cannot be broken" (Book of Commandments 44:26, p. 92). This was later amended to read: "If thou lovest me thou shalt serve me and keep all my commandments. And behold, thou wilt remember the poor, and consecrate of thy properties for their support that which thou hast to impart unto them, with a covenant and a deed which cannot be broken" (D&C 42:29-30).[23]

Members possessing capital would invest it. Those owning no real estate, like Rigdon and Smith, would contribute labor or serve as managers. Ultimately, the possessions of all within the community would be united because all would have contributed equally, whether in money or labor, to the common stock. As a reward, if the steward remained faithful to his trust, he would, in the next life, receive an eternal "inheritance and be made equal with [the Lord]" (D&C 88:107).

Private accumulation of wealth was impossible under this system because faithful stewards consecrated surplus profits or production to the common storehouse. This redistribution of each year's excess was intended to discourage luxurious living and preclude competitive expansion. The Saints were to strive for equality, to "be alike," and to "receive alike."[24]

To prevent debt, members were advised to be self-sufficient and independent. "How far is it the will of the Lord that we should have dealings with the world," Smith prayed, and how should we "conduct our dealings with them?" The answer: "Thou shalt contract no debts with them."[25] As the church slipped into severe financial distress a few years later and had to borrow immense sums to stay afloat, this clause was deleted and is not included in modern editions of the Doctrine and Covenants.[26]

By spring 1831 the church in Kirtland and vicinity had increased to more than 1,000 members. The Arcadian community was a mixture of new and landless converts, old settlers reluctant to deed their lands to the church, and a penniless hierarchy that had no regular income. Despite Mormon efforts to pool their resources in Ohio, Missouri, and later in Utah, success never came. John Whitmer, after the Kirtland failure, rationalized: "The time has not yet come that the law [of Consecration and Stewardship] can be fully established, for the disciples live scattered abroad and are not organized; our [numbers] are small, and the disciples untaught, consequently they understand not the things of the kingdom."[27]

The reasons for failure may have been more sinister than Whitmer's simplification. But social historian Klaus J. Hansen agrees with Whitmer that

> Joseph Smith, the originator of these [communitarian] ideas, soon discovered, like Marx after him, that it was as easy to commit them to paper as it was difficult for fallible humans to follow them. Early attempts to put these economic principles into operation quickly faltered, as much because of the imperfections of the practitioners as because of flaws in the principles themselves.[28]

Notes

Unless otherwise stated, all primary sources cited are located in the Historical Department of the Church of Jesus Christ of Latter-day Saints, Salt Lake City, Utah.

1. Although the South Bainbridge and Colesville judicial systems were unable to convict Smith, he received rough treatment before being released (see Wesley P. Walters, *Joseph Smith's Bainbridge, N.Y. Court Trials* [Salt Lake City: Modern Microfilm Company, 1974]), and H. Michael Marquardt and Wesley P. Walters, *Inventing Mormonism: Tradition and the Historical Record* (San Francisco: Smith Research Associates, 1994), 63-87.

2. Eber Howe, *Mormonism Unvailed* (Painesville, OH: E. D. Howe, 1834), 112-14.

3. Cited in Journal History (15 Jan. 1831), a multi-volume daily history of the church compiled by official church historians, hereafter Journal History.

4. *Painesville Telegraph*, 15 Feb. 1831.

5. *Millennial Harbinger*, 1 (1831): 100-101.

6. Sidney Rigdon to Stephen Post, 24 Jan. 1871, Stephen Post Collection, box 2, fd. 3; hereafter Post Collection.

7. Cyrus Smalling letter, 10 Mar. 1841, in E. G. Lee, *The Mormons, or Knavery Exposed* (Philadelphia: n.p., 1841), 12-15.

8. "Kirtland Township Record," 1:76, cited in Anne B. Prusha, *A History of Kirtland, Ohio* (n.p.: Lakeland Community College, n.d.) 42.

9. Ibid. Smith's first statement is in his journal, cited in Max H. Parkin, *A Study of the Nature and Causes of External and Internal Conflict of the Mormons in Ohio Between 1830 and 1838* (Salt Lake City: Department of Seminaries and Institutes of Religion, 1967), 163.

The second statement is in *Journal of Discourses*, 26 vols. (London: Latter-day Saints' Book Depot), 1854-86), cited 13 (8/9 Oct. 1868): 106; hereafter as *Journal of Discourses*.

10. Joseph Smith, *History of the Church of Jesus Christ of Latter-day Saints*, B. H. Roberts, ed., 7 vols. (Salt Lake City: The Church of Jesus Christ of Latter-day Saints, 1902), 1:146-47; hereafter as *History of the Church*.

11. Parley P. Pratt, Jr., ed., *The Autobiography of Parley Parker Pratt* (Chicago: Law, King & Law, 1888), 61.

12. F. Mark McKiernan and Roger D. Launius, eds., *An Early Latter Day Saint History: The Book of John Whitmer–Kept by Commandment* (Independence, MO: Herald House, 1980), 62.

13. *Times and Seasons* 3 (1 Apr. 1842): 747. See also G. A. Smith's address in *Journal of Discourses* 11 (15 Nov. 1864):1-12.

14. Journal History, Feb. 1831, 2.

15. McKiernan and Launius, 37.

16. Levi Hancock Journal, 45, Special Collections, Harold B. Lee Library, Brigham Young University, Provo, Utah; hereafter Special Collections, BYU.

17. *Chardon Spectator and Geuga Gazette*, 10 Aug. 1833.

18. Statement of Alexander W. Doniphan et al., 19 Mar. 1881 in David Whitmer, *An Address to All Believers in Christ* (Richmond, MO: David Whitmer, 1887), 9-10.

19. Ibid., 35.

20. McKiernan and Launius, 42. The most sophisticated treatment of early Mormon economic experiments is Lyndon W. Cook, *Joseph Smith and the Law of Consecration* (Orem, UT: Keepsake Paperbacks, 1991).

21. *History of the Church*, 1:146-47.

22. Initially no provisions were made for the financial support of the bishop and his counselors. Because he was to devote his whole time to the temporal matters of the church, a verse was later inserted in section 42 of the 1835 D&C which explained that the bishop "shall receive his support, or a just remuneration for all his services," and his counselors were to "have their families supported out of the property which is consecrated to the bishop."

23. Donating one's property to the group by giving up the deed was a Shaker concept. When Kentucky Reformer Barton Stone began his crusade against the Shakers, he attacked their economic radicalism, claiming they were "world-minded, cunning deceivers." "The *Shakers* are come to take people's land—Everyone that joins them must immediately give up his deed to the elders!" (Richard M'Nemar, *The Kentucky Revival* [Albany: E. and E. Hosford, 1808], 95-101).

24. Uncanonized revelation received by Joseph Smith in March 1832, Newel K. Whitney Papers, Special Collections, BYU. D&C 70:3-18 (Nov. 1831) provides the theological justification for church leaders receiving special consideration within the Mormon framework of equality.

25. Manuscript copy of D&C 42.

26. Also see Zebedee Coltrin diaries (1832-34). "The Articles Covenants & Law of the Church of Christ Independence, Jackson County Missouri January 12th 1832 Copied by P. Whitmer for Zebedie Coltrin Harvy Whitlock Elders of the Church of Christ" is

essentially the same version as in the Book of Commandments and is called "The Church Law."

27. McKiernan and Launius, 42.

28. Klaus J. Hansen, *Mormonism and the American Experience* (Chicago: University of Chicago Press, 1981), 127.

CHAPTER 8.

The New Jerusalem

We believe in the literal gathering of Israel and in the restoration of the Ten Tribes; that Zion (the New Jerusalem) will be built upon the American continent; that Christ will reign personally upon the earth; and that the earth will be renewed and receive its paradisiacal glory.

—Joseph Smith, Article of Faith, No. 10 (1841)

Every age has its delusions. For early Mormons these included eventually discarded communitarian plans as well as hope in the imminent second coming of Jesus Christ. That return, promised by the apocalyptic voice of the young prophet, stranded the Saints in an advent season—the eleventh hour—which has endured for more than a century and a half. These prophetic failures were at the very root of Sidney Rigdon's eventual loss of faith in Joseph Smith.

Rigdon was obsessed with prophecies of Armageddon and was convinced his generation was doomed long before he met the Mormon prophet. Alexander Campbell referred to Rigdon as a "flaming literalist of the school of *Elias* [Smith], a Millennarian of the first water."[1] The fact that the Book of Mormon, according to Rigdon, was to "form and govern the Millennial Church," was precisely the reason it appealed to him so profoundly.[2]

When it came off the press in late March 1830, the Book of Mormon not only described the destruction of vast ancient American civilizations but contained ominous and foreboding predictions about Rigdon's Jacksonian America. No millenarians ever identified the New Jerusalem so particularly and so concretely with America as did Mormons. Their Holy City of Zion was to arise literally within the borders of the United States. The Book of Mormon warned early readers to flee to that land of refuge or be destroyed (see 3 Ne. 20:22, 21:21-29; Ether 13:1-11).

That apocalyptic admonition overshadowed nineteenth-century Mormonism. It dominated daily life, the hopes and fears of the people, their view of the world. Rigdon summed it up precisely when he said: "The Scriptures informed us of perilous and distressing times, great judgments that should come in the last days, and destructions upon the wicked: and now God had sent along his servants to inform us of the time."[3] Smith's revelations made it clear the time was now. "I come quickly" was his frequent prediction in the name of the Lord.

The vision was not unique to Book of Mormon people, however. Establishing the Kingdom of Christ dominated all American evangelicalism contemporary to the Mormon restoration. Believers were filled with spiritual fervor, religious unrest, and were easily swayed by fanaticism as revelations, dreams, prophecies, and anticipation of the Millennium were astir. In Mormonism these hopes gave rise to the concept of Zion, a just and stable society, where all would be of one heart, one mind, and dwell in righteousness. From its apex Zion would emanate outward like a wave rippling across the country. The New Jerusalem would be the wonder of its time. Its streets would be paved with gold and all who fled there to escape the great destruction about to befall the world would find "a land of peace, a city of refuge, a place of safety for the saints of the most high God," as a 7 March 1831 revelation declared (D&C 45:66).

The anticipation became increasingly dramatic. The lost ten tribes of Israel were to migrate south from the North Pole, where they had for ages been secluded by immense barriers of ice. When the ice melted, those tribes, with John the Beloved and the Three Nephites—scriptural figures who never tasted of death—would arrive in the New Jerusalem, loaded with immense quantities of gold and silver. The gathered elect would greet Jesus as he descended in glory to direct the ideal society in its ideal state. That vivid image eventually impaled the church in an unwinnable situation in Missouri.

Smith had Missouri in mind as the land of Zion before he met Rigdon. The foundation of his utopianism was in place prior to an 1830 missionary foray to western Missouri led by Oliver Cowdery. In the 1820s the federal government, for the first time in U.S. history, began to move native Americans, indigenous to the Atlantic states, west across the Mississippi to the "permanent Indian frontier." Large numbers were relegated to the western borders of Missouri, important to the Church of Christ because newly converted "Lamanite" (native American) members of the church were to play a significant role in building Zion.

Before the Lamanite missionaries left New York, Smith directed a revelation to Cowdery, who, as Second Elder, stood next to the prophet in church government:

> [B]ehold I say unto you, that you shall go unto the Lamanites and preach my gospel unto them, and cause my church to be established among them. . . . And now behold I say unto you, that it is not revealed, and no man knoweth where the city [Zion] shall be built, but it shall be given hereafter. Behold, I say unto you, that it shall be on the borders by the Lamanites (BC 30).[4]

On 2 January 1831 the Lord revealed he had prepared a "land of promise, a land flowing with milk and honey" (D&C 38:18-20). Subsequent revelations provided glimpses of the futuristic heavenly abode and specified Kirtland as a jumping-off place "until the time shall come when it shall be revealed unto you from on high, when the city of the New Jerusalem shall be prepared, that ye may be gathered in one, that ye may be my people, and I will be your God" (D&C 42:9). Cowdery spoke vaguely of the planned Mormon utopia when he first passed through Ohio's Western Reserve at the time of Sidney Rigdon's conversion. The *Painesville Telegraph*'s earliest mention of Mormons stated, "We understand that [Cowdery] is bound for the regions beyond the Mississippi, where he contemplates founding a 'City of refuge' for his followers."[5]

M. S. Clapp, after listening to the message of the Cowdery-Pratt-Whitmer-Peterson missionary team, provided an additional account linking Zion with the Lamanites. He reported the emissaries as saying the Book of Mormon "chiefly concerned the western Indians, as being an account of their origin, and a prophecy of their final conversion to christianity, and make them a *white* and delightsome people, and be reinstated in the possession of their lands of which they have been despoiled by the whites."[6]

The missionaries were convinced that American Indians, allegedly descendants of ancient Israelites—in fact, called "Jews" by Joseph Smith—would play an important role in establishing Zion. Believing their darker brothers and sisters would accept their destiny as outlined in the Book of Mormon, the proselytizers hurried to an appointment in Missouri they viewed as divinely determined.

While awaiting good word from the "western countries" in the spring of 1831, Rigdon and Smith also returned to revising the Bible in the newly completed Smith cabin on Father Morley's property. From early February through 7 March they worked on Genesis 6-19. The original handwritten document shows that they turned their attention to the New Testament on 8 March 1831. The title of that page of the manuscript is "A Translation of the New Testament by the power of God." From 8 March until 3 April they devoted their energies to Matthew 1-9. The following day they returned to Genesis 19:30 and brought their work up to chapter 24:41. From 7 April until early June they focused on Matthew 9:2 and 26:71. Work then halted until the fall.

Their labors on the Bible were not continuous. Many interruptions arose, several related to Smith's and Rigdon's indigence. Contemporary and reminiscent accounts agree that the Mormons as a group were in an impoverished situation in Kirtland from 1831 to 1835. The plan for getting out of these straits, formed in the earliest days of the church, was to seek new converts, preferably wealthy and willing to share their surplus with the "the house of Israel," the revelation delicately phrased it (D&D 42:39).

The first Gentiles to test the revelation were a group of Shaking Quakers living communally in North Union, a few miles southwest of Kirtland. This society seemed to epitomize the "ancient order of things." In addition to sharing property, the Believers claimed visions, faith healings, revelations, and the ability to speak in tongues. Like the Disciples of the Western Reserve, who joined the Church of Christ by the hundreds, the Shakers seemed prepared by the hand of the Lord for the higher message.

In early March 1831 the prophet directed a revelation to Rigdon and Parley P. Pratt, his two most dynamic spokesmen, along with a recently converted Shaker from the North Union commune, Leman Copley. The men were commanded to warn the Shakers that the Second Coming was nigh at hand and refuge could be found only in Mormondom. "Behold I will go before you," the trio was promised, "and be your reward; and I will be in your midst, and you shall not be confounded. Behold I am Jesus Christ, and I come quickly" (D&C 49:27-28).

Despite assurances that the missionaries need only "knock and it shall be opened," the door slammed abruptly in their faces. John Whitmer's history noted that "the above-named brethren went and proclaimed according to the revelation given them, but the Shakers hearkened not to their words and received not the Gospel [at] that time, for they are bound in tradition and priestcraft, and thus they are led away with foolish and vain imaginations."[7] Pratt himself wrote, "this strange people . . . utterly refused to hear or obey the gospel."[8]

The Shakers saw it differently. Ashbel Kitchel, leader of that community, recorded in his journal the interaction between his group and the Mormons:

> We continued on friendly terms in the way of trade and other acts of good neighborship untill the spring of 1831 when we were visited on Saturday evening by Sidney Rigdon and Leman Copley, the latter of whom had been among us; but not likeing the cross [celibacy] any to[o] well, had taken up with Mormonism as the easier plan and had been appointed by them as one of the missionaries to convert us.
>
> They tarried all night, and in the course of the evening, the doctrines of the cross and the Mormon faith were both investigated; and we found that the life of . . . self denial corresponded better with the life of Christ, than Mormonism. . . . Thus the matter stood and we retired to rest, not knowing that they had then in possession what they called a revelation or message from Jesus Christ to us, which they intended to deliver to day (sabbath) and which they supposed would bring us to terms.
>
> Sabbath morning, matters moved on pleasantly in sociable chat with the Brethren, untill I felt to give them all some council, which was for neither to force their doctrine on the other at this time; but let the time be spent in feeling of the spirit, as it was Rigdon's first visit, for it might be possible that he would yet see that the foundation he was now on, was sandy. . . .
>
> A little before meeting, another one came from the Mormon camp as an assistant, by the name of Parley Pratt. He called them out, and enquired how they had got along? and was informed by Rigdon and Leman, that I had bound them to silence, and nothing could be done. Parley told them to pay no attention to me, for they had come with the authority of the Lord Jesus Christ, and the people must hear it, &c.
>
> They came into meeting and sat quietly untill the meeting was through, and the people dismissed; when Sidney Rigdon arose and stated that he had a message from the Lord Jesus Christ to this people; could he have the privilege of delivering it? He

was answered, he could. He then said it was in writing; could he read it? He was told he might. He then read the following Message. [The text of D&C 49—with a few wording changes from the way it appears in Book of Commandments LII.]

At the close of the reading, he asked if they could be permitted to go forth in the exercise of their gift and office.—I told him that the piece he had read, bore on its face, the image of its author; that the Christ that dictated that, I was well acquainted with, and had been, from a boy; that I had been much troubled to get rid of his influence, and I wished to have nothing more to do with him; and as for any gift he had authorized them to exercise among us, I would release them & their Christ from any further burden about us, and take all the responsibility on myself.

Sidney made answer—This you . . . cannot do; I wish to hear the people speak. I told him if he desired it, they could speak for themselves, and step[p]ed back and told them to let the man know how they felt; which they did in something like these words; that they were fully satisfied with what they had, and wished to have nothing to do with either them or their Christ. On hearing this Rigdon professed to be satisfied, and put his paper by; but Parley Pratt arose and commenced shakeing his coattail; he said he shook the dust from his garments as a testimony against us, that we had rejected the word of the Lord Jesus.

Before the words were out of his mouth, I was to him, and said;—You filthy Beast, dare you presume to come in here, and try to imitate a man of God by shaking your filthy tail; confess your sins and purge your soul from your lusts, and your other abominations before you ever presume to do the like again, &c. While I was ministering this reproof, he settled trembling into his seat, and covered his face; and I then turned to Leman who had been crying while the message was reading, and said to him, you hypocrite, you knew better;—you knew where the living work of God was.[9]

After the promises of the mission were not fulfilled, Copley lost faith in Mormonism, returned to the Shakers, and begged for reunion. His request was granted.

As time drew near for the emigrating New York Saints to arrive in Kirtland, Smith had yet to hear from cousin Cowdery in Missouri, a fact which postponed the announcement of the precise location of the city of refuge. "The place is not yet to be revealed," spoke God's advocate, "but after your brethren come from the east, there are to be certain men appointed and to them it shall be given to know the place . . . and they shall be appointed to purchase the lands and to make a commencement to lay the foundations of the City."[10]

Meanwhile, church leaders finally heard from Cowdery. In an 8 April 1831 report from Independence, Missouri, he enthusiastically, albeit prematurely, wrote of the mission's success. The "God of hosts has not forsaken the earth," he began,

> but is in very word about to redeem his ancient covenant people & lead them with the fulness of the Gentiles to springs yea fountains of living waters to his holy hill of zion . . . the principl[e] chief says he believes every word of the Book [of Mormon] & there are many now in the Nation who believes & we trust that when the Lord Shall open our way we shall have glorious time for truly my brethren my heart sorrows for

them for they are cast out & dispersed and know not the God in whom they should trust.[11]

Cowdery's optimism turned out to be ill-founded. The missionaries did not have proper credentials or authorization to preach on Indian land and their teachings were viewed as incendiary by federal agents. The Elders had disclosed to the recently relocated Delaware tribe that the "great Spirit" designed

> in this generation, to restore them to the possession of their lands, now occupied by the whites; and the Indians shall go forth among the white people, as a lion among the beasts of the forests, and as a young lion among the flocks of sheep, who, if he goeth through, both treadeth down and teareth to pieces, and no man can deliver. Thy hand shall be lifted up against thy adversaries, (the whites) and all their enemies (the whites) shall be cut off.[12]

Once federal agents heard these impolitic teachings, they threatened the missionaries with prison if they did not withdraw. Although they appealed to General Clark, superintendent of Indian Affairs west of the Mississippi, their objections were in vain. The Lamanite mission failed to bring a single Native American to the Mormon fold. The missionaries settled for proselyting activities in nearby Independence, Missouri, where they established a small branch of women.[13]

Pratt returned from Missouri in May, enthusiastic about the prospects of the Saints settling in Jackson County. The need to declare the chosen land was pressing on Smith, but he wanted to reconnoiter the area personally. Meanwhile the New York Saints arrived in Kirtland. Eber Howe, editor of the nearby *Painesville Telegraph*, wrote on 17 May 1831 that "About two hundred men, women, and children, of the deluded followers of Jo Smith's Bible speculation, have arrived on our coast during the last week, from the state of New York, & are about seating themselves down upon the 'promised land' in the county." Mormon historian John Whitmer recorded that "there was no preparation made for [them]."[14] They were destitute, having followed the prophet's commandment to sell their property—at a loss if necessary—or abandon it.

Lemon Copley, the disillusioned Shaker missionary, owned a considerable tract of land at Thompson, sixteen miles northeast of Kirtland, and agreed to share his land with the new arrivals for half value. Despite the revealed word not to engage in debt, Bishop Edward Partridge was commanded to secure a contract with Copley for 1,000 acres. Partridge hesitated. He was again directed to secure the land to relieve the hardship of the New York Saints and consented. Following the Law of Consecration, Partridge designated family properties according to need. Cabins were built, and the new arrivals prepared to plant crops. Still uncertain of the prospects in Missouri, Smith announced in a May 1831 revelation that the Copley property was to be consecrated "for a little season, until I, the Lord, shall provide for them otherwise. . . . Let them act upon this land as for years, and this shall turn unto them for their good" (D&C 51:17-18).

Copley, the immigrants' benefactor, after abandoning the faith decided to renege on his contract and ordered the Saints to vacate his farm. He also demanded sixty dollars from each family, claiming they had made alterations to his houses and planted crops. So the Colesville emigrants had nowhere to go. Frantic, Smith found himself with no alternative but to send them to Missouri, hoping it was indeed "a land flowing with milk and honey" as they were promised.[15]

While plans were underway for a Missouri expedition, Rigdon spent much time in missionary work. After failing to convert the Shakers, he proselyted in more receptive areas. Traveling with Luke Johnson in mid-May, Rigdon first went to New Portage, Ohio, and baptized "about fifty or sixty." The two then continued to Rigdon's old homestead near Pittsburgh, where they converted Sidney's mother, Nancy G., and his older brother Carvel, along with several others in the area.[16]

In late May or early June, Rigdon arrived back in Kirtland and there encountered his former friend, Alexander Campbell, then conducting a tour of the Western Reserve to assess Mormonism's damage to his movement. Preaching throughout Ohio, the sage consistently referred to Mormonism as "delusions and religious imposition." In a confrontation with "the far-famed Alexander Campbell," Rigdon's summary contended that Campbell's "wonted shrewdness and presence of mind forsook him" so that he was "quite confused and silly." Rigdon claimed he told his former mentor, "You have lied, Alexander . . . you are a child of the Devil, you are an enemy to all righteousness, and the spirit of the Devil is in you . . . and if you do not receive the Book of Mormon, you will be damned."[17] Campbell's summary had Rigdon put it differently: "Were Joseph to be proved a liar, or say himself that he never found the Book of Mormon as he had reported, still he would believe it, and believe that all who do not believe it shall be damned."[18]

After Campbell departed for his home in Virginia, Joseph Smith's Church of Christ held its fourth general conference, the first in Ohio. During the three-day gathering (3-6 June 1831) a profound change was inaugurated in the church's organization. Prior to 1831 the only major division of authority was between elders and all others (see D&C 20:1-12, 38-45; 21:1-12); members did not recognize two priesthoods within the church.

On Friday, 3 June 1831, the first day of the convocation, while Joseph Smith was prophesying to the congregation, "The Lord made manifest to Joseph that it was necessary that such of the elders as were considered worthy, should be ordained to the high priesthood."[19] He then laid his hands on Lyman Wight and ordained him to the "High Priesthood after the Holy Order of God." Wight then arose and according to one account "presented a pale countenance, a fierce look, with his arms extended, and his hands cramped back, the whole system agitated, and a very unpleasant object to look upon."[20] He called upon those around him, "if you want to see a sign, look at me," and then climbed up on a bench and pronounced in a loud voice that he saw the Savior. Waxing prophetic, he pronounced "there were some in the congregation that should live until the Savior should descend from heaven, with a Shout, with all the holy angels with him."[21]

Wight, still enraptured in vision, then ordained Rigdon, John Whitmer, and Joseph Smith to the High Priesthood even though Smith had previously ordained him.[22] The official history compiled under Smith's direction until his 1844 death records that on this date "the authority of the Melchisedek Priesthood was manifested and conferred for the first time" on twenty-three elders.[23] Traditional Mormon history holds that Smith and Cowdery had been ordained to the Higher Priesthood in May 1829 under the direction of ancient apostles Peter, James, and John, though like other supernal events this detail was added later. It was first mentioned years later in a 7 September 1834 letter from Cowdery to William W. Phelps.[24]

Mormon historian and theologian B. H. Roberts later tried to clarify confusion on the matter in his edition of the official *History of the Church*. "A misapprehension has arisen in the minds of some," he wrote,

> respecting the statement—"The authority of the Melchisedek Priesthood was manifested and conferred for the first time upon several of the Elders." It has been supposed that this passage meant that the higher or Melchisedek Priesthood was now for the first time conferred upon men in this dispensation. This of course is an error. . . . The Prophet [meant] . . . that the special office of High Priest was for the first time conferred upon men in this dispensation.[25]

But Roberts, despite his usually exact approach to Mormon history, put words in Smith's mouth, and he was incorrect. An array of Smith's close associates testified that the Higher or Melchizedek Priesthood was not conferred until 3 June 1831. These include brothers Parley P. and Orson Pratt, Book of Mormon witnesses David and John Whitmer, plus Lyman Wight, William E. McLellin, John Corrill, J. C. Brewster, and William Smith, the prophet's younger brother.[26]

Lyman Wight, later to become a member of the Quorum of Twelve Apostles, recorded in his personal diary of this June conference: "here for the *first time* I saw the Melchizedek priesthood introduced into the Church of Jesus Christ, as anciently, whereunto I was ordained under the hands of Joseph Smith, and they ordained sixteen others, such as he chose, unto the same priesthood."[27]

Parley Pratt's account is equally precise. He wrote that during the meeting,

> Several were then selected by revelation, through President Smith, and ordained to the High Priesthood after the order of the Son of God; which is after the order of Melchizedek. This is the first occasion in which this priesthood had been revealed and conferred upon the Elders in this dispensation, although the office of an Elder is the same in a certain degree, but not in the fulness.[28]

In September 1832, Smith received a revelation (D&C 84) which added significant detail to the understanding of priesthood authority. The high priesthood introduced in June 1831 had been associated with Melchizedek. In the new revelation, the office of elder was linked for the first time with the high priesthood. A "lesser priesthood," resembling that "confirmed" on Aaron, was mentioned (vv. 6-18). That the office of elder was not originally included in the Melchizedek Priesthood was pointed out by church president Brigham Young shortly before his death in 1877. In discussing the ordination of the original 1835 Quorum of Twelve Apostles he said that he and Heber C. Kimball "*were elders. The fact that we were not high priests and had never been ordained to the high priesthood* was taken to Brother Joseph. . . . [who said that] the apostleship holds all the keys of the priesthood upon the face of the earth."[29] Earlier Orson Pratt on 27 December 1847 had clarified that "there was a time when this Church was governed by the Lesser Priesthood."[30]

To his death David Whitmer insisted the idea of a higher priesthood was an afterthought, an error introduced "at the instigation of S[i]dney [Rigdon]."[31] "Authority is the word we used for the first two years in the church," he added, "until S[i]dney Rigdon's days in Ohio. This matter of the two orders of priesthood in the Church of Christ, and lineal priesthood of the old law being in the church, all originated in the mind of S[i]dney Rigdon. He explained these things to Brother Joseph in his way, out of the old Scriptures, and got Brother Joseph to inquire, etc."[32]

On Sunday, 6 June, the final day of the conference, twenty-eight elders were appointed to travel through the west in pairs, preaching the gospel along the way. They were to meet in conference in western Missouri, "upon the land," said the revelation, "which I will consecrate unto my people, which are a remnant of Jacob [Native Americans], and those who are heirs according to the covenant [non-Indian Mormons]." Smith and Rigdon were among those called to "take their journey as soon as preparations can be made to leave their homes." The two were told that if they remained faithful "ye shall assemble yourselves together to rejoice upon the land of Missouri, which is the land of your inheritance, which is now the land of your enemies" (D&C 53:2).

According to one scholar's account, Joseph Smith made fourteen excursions outside Ohio from 1831 to 1838. Rigdon, his most frequent companion, was with him on half of these trips.[33] On 19 June 1831 Rigdon, Smith, Martin Harris, Edward Partridge, William W. Phelps, Joseph Coe, Ezra Booth, and A. Sidney Gilbert and his wife left Kirtland for the promised land. They traveled by wagon, canal boat and stagecoach to Cincinnati, where they met Rigdon's former friend and fellow reformer, Walter Scott. The official Mormon account of the visit noted that Scott, unlike many Disciples, was not interested in their message. The narrative added that he showed a bitter spirit "against the doctrine of the New

Testament (that 'these signs shall follow them that believe,' as recorded in Mark the 16th chapter.)"[34]

After leaving Cincinnati the travelers landed at Louisville, Kentucky, where they waited three days for a steamer to convey them upriver to St. Louis. Weary of waiting at that historic city, Smith, Harris, Phelps, Partridge, and Coe went on foot to Independence, where they arrived about mid-July. The rest of the company, including Rigdon, came by water a few days later.

Church leaders were disappointed in western Missouri, particularly by the uncultured residents of Independence, the county seat of Jackson County, where they had anticipated success as promised in the revelations. A rough frontier settlement and a point of departure for western explorers, traders, and trappers, the fledgling village had a new brick courthouse, two or three stores, and fifteen to twenty dwelling houses, mostly cabins of logs hewed on both sides. It was a far cry from the "highly cultivated state of society" in Kirtland, as Smith later declared, and "how natural it was," he added, "to observe the degradation, leanness of intellect, ferocity, and jealousy of a people that were nearly a century behind the times . . . without the benefit of civilization, refinement, or religion."[35] This may be why neither Rigdon nor Smith ever made his residence in Jackson County, the divinely proclaimed "land of their inheritance."

Further chagrin—particularly in the case of Rigdon, Partridge, and Ezra Booth—was caused by an errant prophecy of Smith. In vision he had seen a "large church" in Independence built up by Cowdery. Yet when the Kirtland travelers arrived the envisioned congregation consisted of a mere "three or four females." Booth noted that Rigdon was so disappointed he commented that "Joseph's vision was a bad thing." Booth added that Partridge complained that the land that Smith and Cowdery had selected in the area "was inferior in point of quality to other lands adjoining." When the prophet became irate, Partridge argued, "I wish you not to tell us any more, that you know these by the spirit when you do not; you told us, that Oliver had raised up a large church here, and there is no such thing." Undaunted, the prophet replied, "I see it, and it will be so."[36] Partridge withdrew but later locked horns with Rigdon on the still unresolved issue.

Despite his outward optimism, Smith also harbored concerns about the Promised Land. After contemplating the degraded state of the Lamanites and the lack of civilization in general, the prophet asked in prayer, "When will the wilderness blossom as the rose? When will Zion be built up in her glory, and where will Thy temple stand, unto which all nations shall come in the last days?" In answer, God proclaimed that Missouri was "the land which I have appointed and consecrated for the gathering of the Saints. Wherefore, this is the land of promise, and the place for the city of Zion. . . . Behold, the place which is now called Independence is the center place; and the spot for the temple is lying westward, upon a lot which is not far from the court-house" (D&C 52:1-3). This temple site was a sixty-four-acre tract one-half mile west of the Jackson County courthouse, located in the center of the village.

On 1 August 1831 Smith made known a revelation which stated in part: "And I give unto my servant Sidney a commandment, that he shall write a description of the land of Zion, and a statement of the will of God, as it shall be made known by the Spirit, unto him: and an epistle and subscription, to be presented unto all the churches, to obtain moneys, to be put into the hands of the bishop, to purchase lands for an inheritance for the children of God" (Book of Commandments LIX:63). Rigdon was further designated to "concecrate and dedicate this land, and the spot of the temple, unto the Lord."

The next day, while Smith was helping the Colesville Saints lay the first log for a house of worship in Kaw Township, twelve miles west of Independence, Rigdon fulfilled his obligation to dedicate the glorious city of New Jerusalem. Ezra Booth, in attendance that day, later wrote that the event was "attended with considerable parade and an ostentatious display of talents, both by Rigdon and Cowdery."[37]

Historian John Whitmer, recounting Cowdery's description of the consecration ceremony, wrote that Rigdon addressed the dozen or so assembled Saints:

> Do you receive this land for the land of your inheritance with thankful hearts from the Lord? answer from all we do, Do you pledge yourselves to keep the laws of God on this land which you have never kept in your own lands? We do. Do you pledge yourselves to see that others of your brethren who shall come hither do keep the laws of God? We do. After prayer he arose and said, I now pronounce this land consecrated and dedicated for the Lord for a possession and inheritance for the Saints, (in the name of Jesus Christ, having authority from him.) And for all the faithful servants of the Lord to the remotest ages of time. Amen.[38]

Next a specially prepared oak log, ten inches in diameter, was carried to the spot by twelve men using handspikes. Cowdery then selected a small rough stone, the best he could find, and carried it in one hand to the spot. He removed the surface of the earth, prepared a spot for the symbolic rock, and delivered an address suited to the occasion. The stone in place, one end of the oak log was laid on it, and thus was installed a symbolic claim on the splendid city of Zion. Joseph Smith's account of the event recorded: "Through prayer, the land of Zion was consecrated and dedicated for the gathering of the Saints by Elder Rigdon; and it was a season of joy to those present, and afforded a glimpse of the future, which time will yet unfold to the satisfaction of the faithful."[39]

The next day, 3 August, seven elders, including Smith, Cowdery, Peter Whitmer, Jr., Frederick G. Williams, William W. Phelps, Martin Harris, and Joseph Coe, assembled on the ten-acre temple site for Smith's dedication and reading of the 87th Psalm. The prophet laid a figurative cornerstone near a sapling distinguished from others by removal of the bark on the north and east sides. On the south side of the treelet was engraved the letter "T" for temple and on the east side "ZOM" for Zomas, which Smith said was the original word for Zion.[40]

Their principal work accomplished, the Kirtland elders desired to "return speedily to the land from whence they came" (Book of Commandments LXI:1). Ezra Booth, who became disaffected during the trip, later wrote that

> none appeared more anxious to return home than Rigdon and Smith, whose plans for future subsistence were considerably frustrated. They expected to find a country abounding with the necessaries and comforts of life. But the prospect appeared somewhat gloomy, and will probably remain so for some years to come. . . . Before they went to Missouri, their language was, "we shall winter in Ohio but one winter more;" and when in Missouri, "it will be many years before we come here, for the Lord has a great work for us to do in Ohio."[41]

The 8 August instructions on how to return to Ohio are recorded in the Book of Commandments, chapter LXI. The men were told to obtain a boat and "journey speedily for the place which is called St. Louis." From there Smith, Rigdon, and Cowdery were to continue to Cincinnati by water while the others were to hike the remaining distance, preaching by the wayside.

Trouble erupted on 10 August, the day after the brethren left Independence in several canoes. According to Ezra Booth's account, Cowdery and several others argued. "As the Lord God liveth, if you do not behave better, some accident will befall you," Cowdery promised. The mishap happened two days later near McIlwaine's Bend. Irritated with the prophet's rowing instructions, several men in his canoe, apparently Phelps and Sidney Gilbert, refused to power the craft and the boat ran into a fallen tree and nearly swamped. In an attempt to reconcile the contending parties, the group stopped for the night on the riverbank, where the conflict continued. Booth, although a hostile witness, left the only contemporary account of the affair:

> Oliver's denunciation was brought into view; his conduct and equipage, were compared to "a fop of a sportsman;" he and Joseph were represented, as highly imperious and quite dictatorial; and Joseph and Sidney were reprimanded for their excessive cowardice. Joseph seemed inclined to arm himself, according to his usual custom, in case of opposition, with the judgment of God, for the purpose of pouring them, like a thunder bolt upon the rebellious Elders; but one or two retorted, "none of your threats" which completely disarmed him, and he reserved his judgment for a more suitable occasion.[42]

By early morning an accommodation had been reached. But the prophet had lost interest in traveling on the "rough and angry current of the Missouri," as Booth put it. A way out was provided when Phelps "in open vision by daylight saw the destroyer in his most horrible power, ride upon the face of the waters."[43] Smith then pronounced the Missouri the "river of Destruction" and added, "[I]t is not needful for this whole company of mine Elders to be moving swiftly upon the waters, whilst the inhabitants on either side are perishing in unbelief." And now, "concerning my servants Sidney, and Joseph, and Oliver," the disclosure continued, "let them come not again upon the waters, save it be upon the canal, while journeying unto their homes. . . . And again, verily I say unto you, my servants Sidney, and Joseph, and Oliver, shall not open their mouths in the congregations of the wicked, until they arrive in Cincinnati" (D&C 61).

Smith and his two scribes booked passage by stagecoach. It was expensive, and they had not received enough money from Bishop Partridge in Independence. "The Lord don't care how much *money* it takes to get us home," Rigdon reportedly said as they gathered up sufficient cash from the others, telling them "you can beg your passage on foot, but as we are to travel in the stage, we must have money." Even then the men did not have enough and had to pawn their trunk in Cincinnati to continue the journey.[44]

Rigdon, Smith, and Cowdery arrived in Ohio on 27 August. Rigdon quickly followed Smith's directive and by 31 August had a lengthy "description of the land of Zion" as it was "made known by the Spirit unto him":

I, Sidney, a servant of Jesus Christ by the will of God the Father and through the faith of our Lord Jesus Christ unto the Saints which are scattered abroad in these last days, may grace, mercy and peace, rest upon you from God the father and from our Lord Jesus Christ, who is greatly to be feared, among his saints and to be had in reverence of all them who obey him.

Beloved Brethren,—

It has pleased God even the Father to make known unto us in these last days the good pleasure of his will concerning his Saints; and to make known unto us, the things which he has decreed upon the nations even wasting and destruction until they are utterly destroyed, . . . so in these last days, he has commenced to gather together, into a place provided before of God and had in reserve in days of old being kept by the power and providence of God, . . . this land ["provided" by "our heavenly Father"] himself because it was the one which was best adapted for his children, where Jew and Gentile might dwell together . . .

This land being situated in the center of the continent on which we dwell with an exceeding fertile soil and cleared ready for the hand of the cultivator bespeaks the goodness of our God, in providing so goodly a heritage, and its climate suited to persons from every quarter of this continent, either East West North and South yea I think I may say, for all constitutions from any portion of the world, and its productions nearly all varieties of both grain and veg[e]tables which are common in this country, together with all means, clothing: in addition to this it abounds with fountains of pure water the soil climate and surface all adapted, to health indeed I may say that the whole properties of the country [i]nvite the Saints to come, and partake of their blessings but what more need I say about a country, which our Heavenly Father holds in his own hands, for if it were unhealthy he could make it healthy and if barren he could make if fruitful. Such is the land which the Lord God has provided for us, in the last days for an inheritance, and truly it is a goodly land, and none other as well suited for all the saints as this and all those who have faith and confidence in God who has ever seen this land will bear the same testimony. In order that you may understand the will of God respecting this land and the way and means of possessing it, I can only refer you to commandments which the Lord had delivered by the mouth of his prophets which will be read, to you, by our brethren Oliver Cowdery and Newel K. Whitney whom the Lord has appointed, to visit the churches and obtain means for purchasing this land of our inheritance that we may escape in the day of tribulation which is coming on the earth. I conclude by exhorting you to hear the voice of the Lord your God, who is speaking to you in much mercy and who is sending forth his word and his revelation in these last days in order that we may escape impending vengeance; and the judgments which await this generation, and which will speedily overtake the—Brethren pray for me, that I may be counted worthy to obtain an inheritance in the land of Zion and to overcome, the World through faith, and dwell with the sanctified forever, and ever Amen.[45]

Rigdon's predilection for tortuous prose and interminably long sentences was evident, and Smith did not like his colleague's stem-winding epistle. His dislike was further triggered by the fact that Rigdon had been commanded merely to provide a description of Jackson County, not an apocalyptical essay calling sinners to repentance. A divine reprimand was quickly issued. "I, the Lord, am not pleased with my servant Sidney Rigdon," came the word. "He exalted himself in his heart, and received not counsel, but grieved the Spirit; Wherefore his writing is not acceptable unto the Lord, and he shall make another; and if the Lord receive it not, behold he standeth no longer in the office to which I have appointed him" (D&C 63:55-57).

The express purpose of Rigdon's description was "to obtain moneys . . to purchase lands for an inheritance" (D&C 58:51), to anchor the advertising campaign like a modern real estate brochure. Abiding counsel, Rigdon wrote another tract. This time he left out the doomsday rhetoric and focused on the task at hand—convincing eastern Saints to emigrate to the newly designated Promised Land:

> Unlike the timbered States in the East, except upon the rivers and water courses, which were verdantly dotted with trees from one to three miles wide, as far as the eye can glance, the beautiful rolling prairies lay spread around like a sea of meadows. The timber is a mixture of oak, hickory, black walnut, elm, cherry, honey locust, mulberry, coffee bean, hackberry, box elder, and basswood, together with the addition of cottonwood, buttonwood, pecan, soft and hard maple, upon the bottoms. The shrubbery was beautiful, and consisted in part of plums, grapes, crab apples, and persimmons. The prairies were decorated with a growth of flowers that seemed as gorgeous and grand as the brilliancy of stars in the heavens, and exceed description. The soil is rich and fertile, from three to ten feet deep, and generally composed of rich black mold, intermingled with clay and sand. It produces in abundance, wheat, corn, and many other commodities, together with sweet potatoes and cotton. Horses,

cattle, and hogs, though of an inferior breed, are tolerably plenty, and seem nearly to raise themselves by grazing in the vast prairie range in summer, and feeding upon the bottoms in winter. The wild game is less plenty where man has commenced the cultivation of the soil than it is a little distance farther in the wild prairies. Buffalo, elk, deer, bear, wolves, beaver, and many lesser animals roam at pleasure. Turkeys, geese, swans, ducks, yea, a variety of the feathered race are among the rich abundance that graces the delightful regions of this goodly land of the heritage of the children of God. Nothing is more fruitful, or a richer stockholder in the blooming prairies, than the honey bee; honey is but about twenty-five cents per gallon.

The season is mild and delightful nearly three quarters of the year, and as the land of Zion, situated at about equal distances from the Atlantic and Pacific oceans, as well as from the Allegheny and Rocky Mountains, in the thirty-ninth degree of north latitude, and between the tenth and seventeenth degrees of west longitude. It bids fair to become one of the most blessed places on the globe, when the curse is taken from the land, if not before. The winters are milder than in the Atlantic States, of the same parallel of latitude; and the weather is more agreeable, so that were the virtues of the inhabitants only equal to the blessings of the Lord, which he permits to crown the industry and efforts of those inhabitants, there would be a measure of the good things of life, for the benefit of the saints, full, pressed down and running over, even an hundredfold. The disadvantages here, like all new countries, are self-evident, lack of mills and schools, together with the natural privations and inconveniences, which the hand of industry and the refinement of society with the polish of science overcome. But all these impediments vanish when it is recollected that the prophets have said concerning Zion in the last days how the glory of Lebanon is to come upon her; the fir tree, the pine tree, and the box together, to beautify the place of his sanctuary, that he may make the place of his feet glorious; where for brass he will bring gold, and for iron he will bring silver, and for wood brass, and for stones iron; and where the feast of fat things will be given to the just; yea, when the splendor of the Lord is brought to one consideration, for the good of his people; the calculations of men and the vain glory of the world vanishes; and we exclaim: God will shine—the perfection of beauty out of Zion.[46]

In 1844, when Brigham Young and other members of the Quorum of the Twelve spearheaded an organized effort to undercut Rigdon's claims to church leadership, one of the items they charged him with was that in 1831, "Having a fruitful imagination [Rigdon] became very extravagant in his description of the upper country. He expatiated on the beauties of Jackson county in such a profuse manner, that fears were entertained by the brethren that it would cause the saints from the east to apostatize, as soon as they should arrive, not finding things as set forth by Elder R[igdon]."[47] This charge, leveled by Jedediah Grant, is particularly interesting in view of the fact that Rigdon's second draft is the more exaggerated version. Ezra Booth, in an 1831 letter to Bishop Partridge, commented on this same point when he wrote that Rigdon's description of Zion

differs essentially from that which you wrote; so much so, that either yours or his must be false. Knowing him to be constitutionally inclined to exaggerate, and suspecting that this habit would be as likely to preponderate, in his written as in his oral communications, you cautioned him against it. "What I write will be written by the most infallible inspiration of the holy spirit," said he with an air of contempt.[48]

The second version was accepted as the "will of the Lord" and printed. Immediately afterwards Oliver Cowdery and Newel K. Whitney went from place to place, preaching and soliciting money to buy land for the Saints. They carried with them copies of Rigdon's "description of Zion" and Smith's revelations concerning the gathering. According to John Whitmer's account, "the Saints . . . truly opened their hearts, and thus there has been lands purchased, for the inheritance of the Saints."[49]

Rigdon and Smith still preferred their inheritance in the more cultivated Kirtland.[50] The essence of that was etched in stone on 11 September 1831, when Smith, shortly after arriving at his Ohio homestead, announced that Kirtland was to be retained as a "stronghold . . . for the space of five years" (D&C 64:21). With this pronouncement the call to gather to the New Jerusalem lost some of its urgency. Although the Saints of that generation did not know it, their "shining city on a hill," where the downtrodden would find refuge and bring about the Advent, was a mirage, an air castle that would ultimately become part of the lost world of utopian dreams.

Notes

Unless otherwise stated, all primary sources cited are located in the Historical Department of the Church of Jesus Christ of Latter-day Saints, Salt Lake City, Utah.

1. *Millennial Harbinger* 1 (Dec. 1837): 578.

2. Eber Howe, *Mormonism Unvailed* (Painesville, OH: E. D. Howe, 1834), 112-14. For a thorough study of Mormon millenarian views, see Grant Underwood, *The Millenarian World of Early Mormonism* (Urbana: University of Illinois Press, 1993).

3. Marvin S. Hill, *Quest for Refuge: The Mormon Flight from American Pluralism* (Salt Lake City: Signature Books, 1989), 33.

4. Several important changes were made in this revelation when it was published in the 1835 D&C. For comparison, see D&C 28:8-9.

5. *Painesville Telegraph*, 16 Nov. 1830.

6. *Western Reserve Chronicle* (Warren, OH), 3 Mar. 1831, 4, Utah State Historical Society (hereafter cited as USHS).

7. F. Mark McKiernan and Roger D. Launius, eds., *An Early Latter Day Saint History: The Book of John Whitmer-Kept by Commandment* (Independence, MO: Herald House, 1980), 61.

8. Parley P. Pratt, Jr., ed., *The Autobiography of Parley Parker Pratt* (Chicago: Law, King & Law, 1888), 65.

9. Ashbel Kitchel Diary, Special Collections, Harold B. Lee Library, Brigham Young

University, Provo, Utah. Copley was restored to Mormon fellowship by October 1832. During a 27-29 December 1833 trial at Kirtland, and again at Chardon on 2-3 April 1832, Copley testified against Joseph Smith in his dispute with Philastus Hurlbut. Copley was again disfellowshipped for his testimony against the prophet (Lyndon W. Cook, *The Revelations of the Prophet Joseph Smith* [Provo, UT: Seventy's Mission Bookstore, 1981], 66-67).

10. McKiernan and Launius, 54.

11. Oliver Cowdery to Joseph Smith, Jr., 1 Apr. 1831, Joseph Smith Letterbooks.

12. Ezra Booth, cited in Howe, 197.

13. David Whitmer later said, "How many Indians did Brother Joseph convince? He never preached a sermon to them in his life to my knowledge" (David Whitmer, *An Address to All Believers in Christ* [Richmond, MO: David Whitmer, 1887], 27).

14. McKiernan and Launius, 54.

15. Although the group resettled together in Missouri under Newel Knight's leadership, they were ultimately driven from their homes in 1833. See Newel K. Knight, *Scraps of Biography: The Tenth Book of the Faith-Promoting Series* (Salt Lake City: Juvenile Instructor Office, 1883), chap. 6.

16. *Millennial Star* 26:835.

17. Ezra Booth's written account of Rigdon's memory of the event is in Howe, 209-10.

18. *Millennial Harbinger*, 2 (1831): 332.

19. McKiernan and Launius, 66.

20. Booth in Howe, 188.

21. McKiernan and Launius, 66.

22. "Minutes of a general Conference held in Geauga County Ohio June 3, 1831," in Donald Q. Cannon and Lyndon W. Cook, eds., *The Far West Record* (Salt Lake City: Deseret Book Co., 1983), 6-7.

23. Joseph Smith, *History of the Church of Jesus Christ of Latter-day Saints*, B. H. Roberts, ed., 7 vols. (Salt Lake City: The Church of Jesus Christ of Latter-day Saints, 1902), 1:176; hereafter referred to as *History of the Church*.

24. Published in *Latter Day Saints' Messenger and Advocate*, Oct. 1834.

25. *History of the Church*, 1:176.

26. See R. Kent Fielding, "The Growth of the Mormon Church in Kirtland, Ohio," Ph.D. diss., University of Indiana, 1957, 111-13; Hill, 25.

27. Diary quoted in Joseph Smith III and Heman C. Smith, *The History of the Reorganized Church of Jesus Christ of Latter Day Saints*, 4 vols. (Independence, MO: Herald Publishing House, 1967 reprint), 1:193; emphasis in original.

28. Pratt, 72.

29. *Deseret News*, 6 June 1877 (sermon delivered on 21 May 1877, emphasis added).

30. Cited in Juanita Brooks, ed., *On the Mormon Frontier: The Diary of Hosea Stout*, 2 vols. (Salt Lake City: University of Utah Press, 1964), 1:292.

31. Whitmer, 35.

32. Ibid., 64. Whitmer added in an interview printed in the 17 October 1886 *The Omaha Herald* that Smith manifested an "alarming disposition to get revelations to cover every exigency that would arise, and in this he was eagerly urged on by some of his associates

who would frequently come to him with the request that he 'ask the Lord' about this thing or the other."

33. Milton V. Backman, Jr., *The Heavens Resound: A History of the Latter-day Saints in Ohio, 1830-1838* (Salt Lake City: Deseret Book Co., 1883), 115.

34. *History of the Church*, 1:188.

35. Ibid., 1:189.

36. Howe, 176-77, 202.

37. Ibid., 198.

38. McKiernan and Launius, 79.

39. Dean C. Jessee, ed., *The Papers of Joseph Smith*, 2 vols. (Salt Lake City: Deseret Book Co., 1989), 1:358.

40. Howe, 199.

41. Ibid., 198-99.

42. Ibid., 204-05.

43. *History of the Church*, 1:202-203.

44. Howe, 206.

45. McKiernan and Launius, 81-83.

46. Smith and Smith, 1:205-209.

47. Jedediah M. Grant, *Collection of Facts, Relative to the Course Taken By Elder Sidney Rigdon, in the States of Ohio, Missouri, Illinois, and Pennsylvania* (Philadelphia: Brown, Bicking & Guilbert, 1844), 7.

48. Howe, 208.

49. McKiernan and Launius, 84.

50. *History of the Church*, 1:189.

CHAPTER 9.

Tarred and Feathered

A religious life, exclusively pursued, does tend to make the person exceptional and eccentric. . . . Religious geniuses have often shown symptoms of nervous instability. . . . Often they have led a discordant inner life, and had melancholy during a part of their career. They have known no measure, been liable to obsessions and fixed ideas; and frequently they have fallen into trances, heard voices, seen visions, and presented all sorts of peculiarities which are ordinarily classed as pathological. Often, moreover, these pathological features in their career have helped to give them their religious authority and influence.

—William James[1]

Nancy Towle, a free-lance evangelist, visited Kirtland, Ohio, in September 1831, shortly after Sidney Rigdon and Joseph Smith rejoined their families. Her published account provides a window on the tentative foothold Mormons had established in the Western Reserve:

[The Mormons] believe, according to the Book [of Mormon], that a day of great wrath, is bursting upon all the kindreds of the earth; and that, in Mount Zion, *and in Jerusalem*, alone, *shall be deliverance in that day*; (even in the land, which the Lord Jesus had given to them, for a dwelling-place *and an everlasting possession.*) The place where they then had their stay [Kirtland], was not the "Land of Promise;" but *that*, lay, on the western boundary of the State of Missouri. In which place, they were then assembling; and where they believed that in process of time, they should have a temple; and a city, of great magnificence, and wealth; and that shortly, they should increase, and tread down all their enemies, and bruise them beneath their feet. After which period, Christ Jesus should descend, and reign with them, personally, 1000 years upon the earth. And then their enemies should be loosed for a season, for, as one said to me, for the space of three months, when should take place, the General Judgment; and the final consummation of all created things.[2]

The seer and the scribe, as the Mormon torch bearers Smith and Rigdon were then called, remained in Kirtland only briefly that fall of 1831. Anxious to return to their Bible revision, they relocated to nearby Hiram, Ohio, in mid-September. Their board and room, while they engaged in their literary calling, was partly subsidized by new convert John Johnson, whom Rigdon had known for several years during his Baptist ministry in the Hiram area. But Johnson's contribution was insufficient to support the families. During an 11 October 1831 conference at Hiram, Oliver Cowdery made "known the [unfavorable financial] situation of brs Joseph Smith Jr and Sidney Rigdon." David Whitmer, Reynolds Cahoon, Simeon Carter, Orson Hyde, Hyrum Smith, and Emer Harris were appointed to look after their needs so they could continue translating the Bible.[3]

The Rigdon family, now consisting of at least six and possibly seven children (a son George was born and died sometime in 1831), settled into the Johnson family's old log cabin where Sidney and Phebe had lived a year earlier. The Smith family—Joseph, Emma, and their newly adopted twins—moved into a spare room in the nearby Johnson farmhouse.

The village of Hiram had been a stronghold of the Reformed Baptist movement, and the Reverend Rigdon had achieved considerable success in the area during the late 1820s. The Mantua congregation, to which Hiram initially belonged, was organized on 27 January 1827. In the Disciples of Christ creed it is revered as the "first Church of Christ of the Restoration movement in Ohio."[4] During the winter of 1831 Rigdon and Smith held a meeting in the south school house in Hiram. A chronicler of the period wrote that "Such was the apparent piety, sincerity and humility of the speakers, that many of the hearers were greatly affected."[5]

Ezra Booth, a Methodist minister in nearby Mantua, converted to Mormonism in 1831 and went to Hiram on a brief missionary tour. There he encountered Symonds Ryder, a Reformed Baptist minister. Booth requested the opportunity to speak after a Ryder sermon, and Ryder consented. Deeply affected by the Christian simplicity of Booth's sermon, Ryder visited Kirtland but was unfavorably impressed when he happened to hear a young Mormon girl predict the destruction of Peking, China. A month later, however, after reading of the destruction of that city, Ryder joined the Mormon church and was ordained an elder in June 1831.

On 7 June 1831 Booth was commissioned by Joseph Smith to participate in the first missionary tour to Missouri. When his commission arrived late with his name misspelled, Ryder—skeptical of revelation deficient in orthography—began to doubt Smith was called of God and eventually refused to carry out his preaching orders. When his friend Booth returned from Missouri in September they compared notes and came to a similar conclusion. In fairness to Booth, he met with Rigdon, Smith, and Cowdery on several occasions to discuss his concerns. "The various shifts and turns, to which they resorted in order to obviate objections and difficulties," he later wrote, "produced in my mind additional evidence, that there was nothing else than a deeply laid plan of craft and deception."[6]

Although Booth was "silenced from preaching as an Elder in this Church" on 6 September 1831, five days after returning from Missouri, he would not be muzzled.[7] Booth's former colleague, the Reverend Ira Eddy of Nelson, Portage County, asked Booth to publicly voice his criticisms of the church. Booth complied in a series of nine letters to Reverend Eddy which appeared in the *Ohio Star* (Ravenna) from 13 October to 8 December 1831.

The ex-Mormon began his narrative by relating that his thousand-mile journey to "the promised land" in Missouri

> taught me quite beyond my knowledge, the *imbecility* of human nature. . . . It has unfolded in its proper character, a *delusion* to which I had fallen a victim, and taught me the *humiliating,* truth, that I was exerting the powers of both my mind and body, and sacrificing my time and property, to build up a system of delusion, almost unparalleled in the annals of the world.
>
> When I embraced Mormonism, I conscientiously believed it to be of God. The impressions of my mind were deep and powerful, and my feelings were excited to a degree to which I had been a stranger. Like a ghost, it haunted me by night and by day, until I was mysteriously hurried, as it were, by a kind of necessity, into the vortex of delusion.[8]

The extensive circulation of these letters had dramatic impact on the public mind for several months. Booth's opposition was based on several factors, including the inconsistencies and failures of Smith's revelations, and what he saw as the despotic personalities and personal weaknesses of Smith, Rigdon, and others.

Many expected Booth's letters to have a ruinous effect on the church. Ambrose Palmer, who was converted by Booth earlier in the year, felt the letters gave Mormonism "such a coloring, or appearance of falsehood, that the public feeling was, that 'Mormonism' was overthrown."[9] To counteract Booth's letters a 1 December 1831 revelation told Smith and Rigdon to stop translating "for the space of a season" and preach roundabout. "Verily thus saith the Lord," came the word, "there is no weapon that is formed against you that shall prosper; and if any man lift his voice against you, he shall be confounded in mine own due time" (1835 D&C 91:1 [now D&C sec. 71]).

For the next six weeks the irrepressible duo preached in Shalersville, Ravenna, Kirtland, and elsewhere. The official church history recounts that they spent their time

> setting forth the truth, vindicating the cause of our Redeemer; showing that the day of vengeance was coming upon this generation like a thief in the night; that prejudice, blindness and darkness filled the minds of many, and caused them to persecute the true Church, and reject the true light; by which means we did much towards allaying the excited feelings which were growing out of the scandalous letters then being published in the *Ohio Star,* at Ravenna, by the before-mentioned apostate, Ezra Booth.[10]

Rigdon was Booth's principal opponent. Although the prophet's "tongue was loosed to speak," as David Whitmer pointed out,[11] Rigdon was superior in eloquence and more audacious in debate. Even Jedediah Grant, a caustic Rigdon critic in later years, admitted that he "was truly a man of talents, possessing a gift for speaking seldom surpassed by men of this age."[12] In this war of words with Booth, Rigdon was the designated Goliath.

On 15 December 1831 Rigdon addressed a "To The Public" letter to the *Ohio Star* announcing that he intended to deliver a "Lecture on the Christian Religion" on Christmas Day. He specifically requested that Ezra Booth be present as "I shall review the letters written by him and published in the Ohio Star." Rigdon said the letters "are unfair and false representation of the subject on which they treat," and also issued a special challenge to Simonds Ryder to debate him in the township of Hiram "that if I am deluded in receiving this book as a revelation from God, I may be corrected, and the public relieved from anxiety."[13]

Booth did not attend the 25 December lecture, and Rigdon, in a bad-tempered rhetorical assault, skewered his antagonist's character. He maintained that Booth's letters contained a "bundle of falsehoods" and asserted that the former Mormon "dare not appear in their defense because he knew his letters were false, and would not bear the test of investigation."[14] Booth was not a total milksop; he merely preferred the safer medium of the newspaper. But editor Lewis L. Rice, upon receiving Booth's next letter, announced his intention of discontinuing, although most certainly not diffusing, the controversy.

Symonds Ryder, described in one account as someone who "did not drift on the current, but rather one who sets currents in motion,"[15] also avoided Rigdon in public. He wrote in the 29 December *Ohio Star*: "To undertake to correct [Rigdon] of his errors before the public, would be a most arduous task for me. His irascible temper, loquacious extravagance, impaired state of mind, and want of due respect to his superiors, I fear would render him in such a place, unmanageable, and I therefore fear of accomplishing the desired object."

Ryder further noted that since the elders had returned from Missouri most Mormons in Hiram had left the faith and the debate would only serve "to save, if possible, a sinking cause." Although Ryder and Rigdon, like Booth and Rigdon, never met face to face, they continued to spar in the *Ohio Star*. Rigdon wrote a letter, published 12 January 1832, misspelling Ryder's name "Simons Rider," and taunting him to debate. "He presented himself before the public as an accuser," Rigdon wrote. "[H]e had been called upon before the same public, to support his accusations; and does he come forward and do it? nay, but seeks to hide himself behind a battery of reproach, and abuse, and low insinuations."

Meanwhile, by 10 January 1832 an overly-confident Rigdon and Smith thought they had won the day against their adversaries. A revelation of that date told them "it is expedient to translate again" (D&C 73:3), and they returned vigorously to their work in Hiram. In mid-January they momentarily halted their labors and traveled to Amherst, Lorain County, Ohio, to conduct a small conference of elders. During this 25 January convocation the prophet was acknowledged president of the High Priesthood, in effect president of the church, and, according to Orson Pratt's journal, "hands were laid on him by Elder Sidney Rigdon, who sealed upon his head the blessings which he had formerly received."[16]

Back in Hiram on 16 February, while engaged in "translating St. John's Gospel," Rigdon and Smith, enraptured in heavenly ecstasy, jointly experienced "in spirit" an apparition they called "The Vision," or "vision of the Three Degrees of Glory," now published as Doctrine and Covenants 76. In 1892 Philo Dibble, an eye-witness to this important episode, wrote a description:

> The vision which is recorded in the Book of Doctrine and Covenants was given at the house of "Father Johnson," in Hyrum, Ohio, and during the time that Joseph and Sidney were in the spirit and saw the heavens open, there were other men in the room, perhaps twelve, among whom I was one[.] [D]uring a part of the time—probably two-thirds of the time—I saw the glory and felt the power, but did not see the vision.
>
> The events and conversation, while they were seeing what is written (and many things were seen and related that are not written,) I will relate as minutely as is necessary.
>
> Joseph would, at intervals, say: "What do I see?" as one might say while looking out the window and beholding what all in the room could not see. Then he would relate what he had seen or what he was looking at. Then Sidney replied, "I see the same." Presently Sidney would say "what do I see?" and would repeat what he had seen or was seeing, and Joseph would reply, "I see the same."
>
> This manner of conversation was repeated at short intervals to the end of the vision, and during the whole time not a word was spoken by an other person. Not a sound nor motion made by anyone but Joseph and Sidney, and it seemed to me that they never moved a joint or limb during the time I was there, which I think was over an hour, and to the end of the vision.
>
> Joseph sat firmly and calmly all the time in the midst of a magnificent glory, but Sidney sat limp and pale, apparently as limber as a rag, observing which, Joseph remarked, smilingly, "Sidney is not used to it as I am."[17]

In addition to seeing the Father and the Son and the creation of other worlds whose inhabitants are "begotten sons and daughters unto God," Rigdon and Smith scanned the past and gazed into the future. They beheld the rebellion of Lucifer, his expulsion from heaven, and everlasting contention against the children of God. Then they witnessed an afterlife that shattered usual Christian beliefs. The published text of "The Vision" declared that God saves all men and women "except those sons of perdition who deny the Son after the Father has revealed him" (D&C 76:43-44) and described those who are saved as "they whose bodies are celestial, whose glory is that of the sun" (v. 70), as "the terrestrial, whose glory differs . . . even as that of the moon differs from the son" (v. 71), or as "the glory of the telestial, which glory is that of the lesser, even as the glory of the stars" (v. 81).[18] While still enraptured in spirit, the two diviners wrote a description of their vision. Afterwards they sent the recorded revelation to Independence, Missouri, for publication, and in July 1832 the vision of the degrees of glory was printed in *The Evening and the Morning Star.*

The three-tiered gradation of glory could only have been viewed by Rigdon's and Smith's contemporaries in 1832 as three heavens. For conventional Christians heaven was a single place, despite Paul's reference to "the third heaven" (2 Cor. 12:2). To traditionalists, any concept of universal salvation implied Universalism, a "dangerous heresy," a threat to the fabric of moral conduct in society. Consequently, many converts steeped in denominational Protestantism faced a crisis when they learned of this vision. Brigham Young's brother Joseph, a former Methodist minister, recalled: "[W]hen I came to read the vision of the different glories of the eternal world, and of the sufferings of the wicked, I could not believe it at first. Why, the Lord was going to save every body!"[19] Brigham Young himself remembered:

> When God revealed to Joseph Smith and Sidney Rigdon that there was a place prepared for all, according to the light they had received and their rejection of evil and practice of good, it was a great trial to many, and some apostatized because God was not going to send to everlasting punishment heathens and infants, but had a place of salvation, in due time, for all, and would bless the honest and virtuous and truthful, whether they ever belonged to any church or not. It was a new doctrine to this generation and many stumbled at it.[20]

The *History of the Church* makes no mention of the concerns of rank and file over the new doctrine. "Nothing could be more pleasing to the Saint," began the formal treatment,

> than the light which burst upon the world, through the foregoing vision. Every law, every commandment, every promise, every truth, and every point, touching the destiny of man, from Genesis to Revelation, where the purity of the scriptures remains unsullied by the folly of men, go to show the perfection of the theory and witnesses the fact that the document is a transcript from the records of the eternal world. The sublimity of the ideas; the purity of the language; the scope for action; the continued duration for completion, in order that the heirs of salvation may confess the Lord and bow the knee; the rewards for faithfulness, and the punishments for sins, are so much beyond the narrow-mindedness of men, that every honest man is constrained to exclaim: "*It came from God.*"[21]

Three weeks after "The Vision," in an unpublished revelation, found in the Kirtland Revelation Book, Smith learned that the office of president of the High Priesthood is vested with authority to preside, assisted by counselors, over all the concerns of the church.[22] On 8 March the prophet "ordained brother Jesse Gause and Brother Sidney to be my councellors of the ministry of the presidency of the high Priesthood."[23] Gause, virtually unknown to modern Mormons, had only been a member of the church a few weeks. He had three years' of leadership experience with Shaker communes in Massachusetts and Ohio, and for twenty-three years previously had been a Quaker. To Smith and Rigdon, Gause must have seemed a godsend to assist them in keeping afloat the floundering economic system.

There has been some question as to which man was senior advisor to Smith. Gause was a decade older than Rigdon in an era when church seniority was determined on the basis of age, and his name was listed first in the revelation. More importantly, Rigdon, mentioned more frequently in the Doctrine and Covenants than any other man except Smith and Cowdery, was recipient of at least eight revelations dictated by Smith between 1830 and 1832. Gause, on the other hand, was recipient of only one revelation, dated 15 March 1832.[24] By the time the divine enunciation was ready for printing, Gause, who was excommunicated 3 December 1832, had been replaced by Frederick G. Williams. The introductory words "my servant Jesse" were altered without explanation to read "my servant Frederick G. Williams" (see D&C 81). All published copies of the revelation have failed to note this revision.[25]

The John Johnson property in Hiram, where "The Vision" and at least fourteen other revelations were received, is today a revered site in Mormon history. Rigdon later said of the few months he and Smith spent there: "these were the beginning of good days; shut up in a room, eating nothing but dry johnny cake and buttermilk. . . . I had little to eat, little to wear, and yet it was the beginning of good days."[26] The agreeable farmstead was also site of his and Smith's personal humiliation, the location of a threatening assault by vigilantes who issued their own prediction of the future.

The miscreants in the Hiram area were primarily local Reformed Baptists (Campbellites), many of whom viewed Rigdon, their former pastor, as a schemer, out "to get their property into a common fund, and allow certain persons to live without work."[27] Brothers Olmstead and John Johnson, Jr., viewed Rigdon and Smith as grafters intent on defrauding them of their future inheritance. Samuel F. Whitney, brother of prominent Mormon Newel K. Whitney, reported that the Johnson boys were angry because Joseph and Sidney continually urged their father to "let them have his property."[28] Evidence supporting a property dispute was provided by Mormon apostle Orson Hyde, who married a Johnson sister, Nancy Marinda. In 1844 Hyde accused Rigdon of holding an old grudge against the Johnson family because "Father [John] Johnson, after giving him and his family a living for a long time, building a stone house for them to live in, etc., would not give him his farm and all his property; for he once demanded of Father Johnson a deed of all his property with offering one dollar as an equivalent."[29]

Symonds Ryder, probable ringleader of Campbellite mischief,[30] clarified that

Rigdon and Smith were not assaulted because of their beliefs. "The people of Hiram were liberal about religion and had not been averse to Mormon teaching," he said afterwards. What infuriated the evildoers were some official documents they found, possibly a copy of the revelation outlining the "Law of Consecration and Stewardship," which instructed new converts about "the horrid fact that a plot was laid to take their property from them and place it under the control of Smith."[31]

Intimidation of the Rigdon and Smith families lasted several weeks. One contemporary account reported that in response to threats, Smith and Rigdon proclaimed that no harm could befall them, "that it could not be done—that God would not suffer it; that those who should attempt it, would be miraculously smitten on the spot."[32] Then the threats escalated into violence. The 15 February 1860 *Portage County Democrat* (Ravenna, Ohio) reported that "someone bored an auger hole into a log of the house in which Rigdon lived, and filling it with powder, tried to blow it up."[33]

Rigdon, later remembering the siege during general conference on 6 April 1844, recounted that he and Smith "had been locked up for weeks and had no time only to eat." But

> bandittis came to the place—some 20 or 30 men came rushing to the place cursing & blaspheming. This was the reason why we were shut up. They never cease[d] their warfare. . . . A gentleman from Mexico having heard rumors of the Mormons came to see us[.] One night he went out of my house and found in the fence one after another a dozen men—he returned into the house in fury and got his pistols and said he would kill them but they r[a]n away.[34]

During the darkest hour of Saturday, 24 March, infuriated Campbellites—some accounts say fortified by a keg of whiskey—stepped up their intimidation. A company from Shalersville, Garrettsville, and Hiram assembled outside Rigdon's cabin. One account reported that when the door was forced, Rigdon, to no avail, tried to reason with the intruders, presuming "they were gentlemen."[35] But Rigdon recalled that "they broke into my house[,] drag[ged] me out of my bed—out of the door my head beating on the floor. [T]hey drag[ge]d me over the wood pile[,] and on they went my head thumping on the frozen ground, after which they threw tar and feathers on me—and endeavored to throw aqua fortes [nitric acid] in my face but I turned my face and it missed me."[36]

Wickliffe Rigdon's account noted that by the time his 225-pound father was dragged by his heels to the place where he was tarred and feathered "he was insensible," yet his assailants "pounded him till they thought he was dead and then went to get Joseph Smith."[37] Smith, then only twenty-seven, was more inclined to fight than Rigdon. But he was quickly overpowered and carried to the spot where Rigdon lay unconscious, stretched out naked on the ground. "I supposed he was dead," Smith later wrote, and "I began to plead with them, saying,

'You will have mercy and spare my life, I hope.'"[38] They did, but not before stripping him, threatening castration, and smearing him with tar and feathers.

Smith was not permanently injured. He was bruised around the head and suffered a chipped tooth but was able to carry out his normal Sunday duties the following day. Rigdon, on the other hand, was badly hurt and lay on the ground for some time before he regained consciousness. "At last he got up in a dazed condition," Wickliffe wrote, "and did not know where he was nor where to go[.] . . . [H]e went reeling along the road not knowing where he was; he would have passed his house but my mother was out the door watching for him and went out as he came along and got him in the house. She got the tar and feathers off from him as best she could and got him to bed."[39]

Mormon accounts imply that the Hiram mob intended to kill Rigdon and Smith. Had this been their intent they would have brought weapons and succeeded. But the fact that they came prepared with a bucket of hot tar (they got feathers from Rigdon's pillow) suggests they were proffering a warning. Symonds Ryder wrote, "This had the desired effect, which was to get rid of them. They soon left for Kirtland."[40] No one was ever brought to trial. Such action, particularly against curious religious beliefs, was tolerated in America during Rigdon's lifetime.[41] For example, despite the fact that a 17 April 1832 letter to the editor in the *Geauga Gazette* (Painesville) called the events of 24 March "a base transaction, an unlawful act, a work of darkness, a diabolical trick," one writer noted that vigilantism proved "one important truth which every wise man knew before, that is, that Satan hath more power than the pretended prophets of Mormon."

Rigdon was slow to recover. Smith recalled that when he visited his injured friend on Monday morning he

> found him crazy, and his head highly inflamed, for they had dragged him by his heels, and those, too, so high from the ground that he could not raise his head from the rough, frozen surface, which lacerated it exceedingly; and when he saw me he called to his wife to bring him his razor. She asked him what he wanted of it; and he replied, to kill me. Sister Rigdon left the room, and he asked me to bring his razor; I asked him what he wanted of it, and he replied he wanted to kill his wife; and he continued delirious some days.[42]

This was the second known head trauma suffered by Rigdon. His brother Loammi, a physician, reported that when Sidney was seven years old he had been thrown from a horse. His foot got caught in a stirrup and he was dragged some distance before being rescued. "In this accident," reported Dr. Rigdon,

> he received such a contusion of the brain as ever afterward seriously affected his character, and in some respects his conduct. His mental powers did not seem to be impaired, but the equilibrium of his intellectual exertions seems thereby to have been

sadly affected. He still manifested great mental activity and power, but was to an equal degree inclined to run into wild and visionary views on almost every question.[43]

Ample evidence from Rigdon's contemporaries supports this medical opinion. Alexander Campbell was the first to make public mention of Rigdon's "peculiar mental and corporeal malady," as he called it.[44] Another contemporary account noted that Rigdon "spoke very rapidly, and used to get tremendously excited, so that he foamed at the mouth" when preaching.[45] Newel K. Whitney, an early Mormon bishop, said of Rigdon in 1844: "I was well acquainted with Elder Rigdon a number of years before he came into this church. . . . He was always either in the bottom of the cellar or up in the garret window."[46] Jedediah Grant confirmed in 1844 Rigdon's mood swings: "Elder R. would not only soar as it were to the highest Heaven in raptures of delight, but when dark clouds overspread his horizon he would also sink into the lowest state of despondency."[47]

These retrospective accounts attempted to disparage Rigdon. A narrative by his son, Wickliffe, provides clearer insight into his father's eccentric nature. "Being of a bilious temperament," said Wickliffe of his father, he was sick most of the time in Nauvoo, Illinois: "for weeks at a time he would not be able to leave his bed."[48] While addressing the Saints on 6 April 1844, Sidney verified his son's observation when he reported that "Want of health and other circumstances have kept me in silence for nearly the last five years."[49]

Years after the Kirtland era, Rigdon, like most of Nauvoo's lowland settlers, would suffer from malaria, the "ague" as it was called. But the mosquito-borne disease rarely incapacitates for lengthy periods. Rigdon's biographer F. Mark McKiernan wrote that "During the five years he lived at Nauvoo Rigdon suffered the poorest health of his life. He contracted an unspecified disease (not malaria) which disabled him for months at a time."[50]

Using modern clinical criteria to diagnose the illness of a historical figure is risky, but "bilious temperament" was a specific disease. In nineteenth-century America the malady was best known as melancholia, a syndrome encompassing dramatic mood changes and madness. While the ailment today is usually designated "manic-depression illness," it has also been called "mood disorder," "affective disorder," "chronic bipolar disorder," and "bipolar affective disorder."[51]

In the modern medical world Rigdon would had been aided pharmaceutically and perhaps stabilized. But in his day there was no effective treatment available. Thus when a major bout of depression hit, as it evidently did in Nauvoo, Rigdon was unable to work, preach, interact, or get out of bed for weeks at a time. Even today in 20-35 percent of all cases like Rigdon's, social impairment persists and depression never completely lifts.[52]

An inventory of symptoms taken from the *Diagnostic and Statistical Manual of Mental Disorders* (DSM-III-R) provides a clinical overview of Rigdon's presumed debility. The depressive phase includes: "Dysphoric mood or loss of interest or pleasure in all or almost all usual activities and pastimes. The dysphoric mood is characterized by symptoms such as the following: depressed, sad, blue, hopeless, low, down in the dumps, irritable. The mood disturbance must be prominent and relatively persistent."

The manic phase of the illness includes a wide range of symptoms, such as:

[I]nflated self-esteem or grandiosity (which may be delusional), decreased need for sleep, pressure of speech, flight of ideas, distractibility, [and] increased involvement in goal-directed activity. . . . The elevated may be described as euphoric, unusually good, cheerful, or high, often having an infectious quality for the uninvolved observer, but recognized as excessive by those who know the person well. . . . [T]he predominant mood disturbance may be irritability, which may be most apparent when the person is thwarted. . . . Grandiose delusions involving a special relationship to God. . . . If the person's mood is more irritable than expansive, his or her speech may be marked by complaints, hostile comments, and angry tirades. . . .

When delusions or hallucinations are present, their content is usually clearly consistent with the predominant mood (mood-congruent). God's voice may be heard explaining that the person has a special mission. Persecutory delusions may be based on the idea that the person is being persecuted because of some special relationship of attribute.[53]

Despite the severity of the 24 March 1832 injury, Rigdon recovered well enough to move to Kirtland the following Wednesday, 28 March, with his family. All his children had the measles and were transported the thirty miles in an open wagon. On 1 April, again accosted by a mob, he left his family with friends and escaped to Chardon. The following day he arrived at Warren where he, Smith, Whitney, and Gause fled to the relative safety of Zion, the land of their promised inheritance. They arrived in Independence, Missouri, on 24 April.[54]

Notes

Unless otherwise stated, all primary sources cited are located in the Historical Department of the Church of Jesus Christ of Latter-day Saints, Salt Lake City, Utah.

1. William James, *The Varieties of Religious Experience–A Study in Human Nature* (1902) (New York: Penguin Books, 1985), 6-7.

2. Nancy Towle, *Vicissitudes Illustrated* (Charleston: James L. Burgess, 1832), 137-47; emphasis in original.

3. Donald Q. Cannon and Lyndon W. Cook, eds., *Far West Record–Minutes of The Church of Jesus Christ of Latter-day Saints, 1830-1844* (Salt Lake City: Deseret Book Co., 1983), 17.

4. Alanson Wilcox, *A History of the Disciples of Christ in Ohio* (Cincinnati: Standard Publishing Company, 1918), 121.

5. Symonds Ryder, "Letter to A. S. Hayden," 1 Feb. 1868, in Amos Sutton Hayden,

Early History of the Disciples in the Western Reserve (Cincinnati: Chase and Hall, 1875), 220-21.

6. Eber Howe, *Mormonism Unvailed* (Painesville, OH: E. D. Howe, 1834), 177.

7. Cannon and Cook, 11-12.

8. Howe, 176; emphasis in original.

9. Journal History (31 Dec. 1831)—a multi-volume daily history of the church compiled by official church historians; hereafter Journal History.

10. Joseph Smith, *History of the Church of Jesus Christ of Latter-day Saints*, B. H. Roberts, ed., 7 vols. (Salt Lake City: The Church of Jesus Christ of Latter-day Saints, 1902), 1:241; hereafter referred to as *History of the Church*.

11. David Whitmer, *An Address to All Believers in Christ* (Richmond, MO: David Whitmer, 1887), 70.

12. Jedediah M. Grant, *Collection of Facts Relative to the Course Taken by Elder Sidney Rigdon in the States of Ohio, Missouri, Illinois, and Pennsylvania* (Philadelphia: Brown, Bicking & Guilbert, 1844), 6.

13. This newspaper clipping is in the Mormon Retrieval Project, box 3, fd. 3, Special Collections, Harold B. Lee Library, Brigham Young University, Provo, UT; hereafter Special Collections, BYU.

14. *Messenger and Advocate* 2 (Jan. 1836): 242.

15. B. A. Hindsdale, "Life and Character of Symonds Ryder," in Hayden, 257.

16. Elden J. Watson, *The Orson Pratt Journals* (Salt Lake City: Elden J. Watson, 1975), 11.

17. *The Juvenile Instructor*, 15 May 1882, 303-304. Dibble's account should be viewed with some caution, however. Dibble was an early showman and story teller who traveled about the Great Basin displaying artifacts. If his earlier 1882 recounting is accurate, he was not present during the reception of "The Vision." He wrote: "I arived at Father Johnson's just as Joseph and Sidney were coming out of the vision alluded to in the Book of Doctrine and Covenants, in which mention is made of the three glories" (Philo Dibble, "Early Scenes in Church History," *Faith Promoting Series* No. 8 [Salt Lake City: Juvenile Instructor Office, 1882], 81).

18. More than a decade later Smith would also reveal that "In the celestial glory there are [also] three heavens or degrees" (D&C 131:1).

19. *Deseret News*, 18 Mar. 1857.

20. *Journal of Discourses*, 26 vols. (London: Latter-day Saints' Book Depot, 1854-86), 16 (18 May 1873): 42; hereafter as *Journal of Discourses*.

21. *History of the Church*, 1:252-53.

22. "Duty of Bishops, March 1832," Newel K. Whitney Collection, Special Collections, BYU.

23. "Kirtland Revelation Book," 10-11. The term First Presidency was first used in 1835 to identify the presidency over the entire church and not just the priesthood.

24. "Kirtland Revelation Book," 17-18.

25. See D. Michael Quinn, "Organizational Development and Social Origins of the Mormon Hierarchy, 1832-1932: A Prosopographical Study," M.A. thesis, University of Utah, 1973, 13; D. Michael Quinn, "Jesse Gause: Joseph Smith's Little-Known Counselor," *Brigham Young University Studies* 4 (Fall 1983): 487-93.

26. Journal History, 6 Apr. 1844, 1.

27. Alanson Wilcox, A History of the Disciples of Christ in Ohio (Cincinnati: Standard Publishing Co., 1918), 126.

28. Naked Truths About Mormonism 1 (Jan. 1888): 1, in Donna Hill, Joseph Smith: The First Mormon (Garden City, NY: Doubleday & Co., 1977), 466. One account related that the mobbing occurred because "Eli Johnson" "suspected Joseph of being intimate with his sister, Nancy Marinda Johnson" (Fawn Brodie, No Man Knows My History: The Life of Joseph Smith, the Mormon Prophet, 2d ed. [New York: Alfred A. Knopf, 1975], 119). This anecdote is likely apocryphal for John Johnson's only sons were John Jr., Luke, Olmstead, and Lyman (Linda King Newell and Valeen Tippetts Avery, Mormon Enigma: Emma Hale Smith [Garden City, NY: Doubleday & Co., 1984], 41).

29. Speech of Elder Orson Hyde, Delivered Before the High Priest's Quorum in Nauvoo, April 27th, 1845 (City of Joseph, IL: John Taylor, 1845), 54.

30. Ryder's son Hartwell, defending his father's innocence, later wrote, "I can well remember that my father was sick in bed until late the next morning" ("Short History of the Foundation of the Mormon church based on personal memories and facts collected by Hartwell Ryder, Hiram, Ohio, at the Age of 80 years," copied by Minnie M. Ryder in 1903-1904, from the manuscript written by her uncle, Hartwell Ryder. Library of Hiram College [Hiram, Ohio]; cited in Stanley B. Kimball, "Sources on the History of the Mormons in Ohio: 1830-38," Brigham Young University Studies 11 [Summer 1971]: 528).

Contrary to young Ryder's memory, Joseph Smith said Simonds Ryder was present during the Sunday morning sermon delivered by the battered prophet (History of the Church, 1:264).

31. Symonds Ryder, "Letter to A. S. Hayden," 1 Feb. 1868, in Hayden, 220-21.

32. Geauga Gazette (Painesville), 17 Apr. 1832.

33. Ms 19, Mormon Manuscript Retrieval Project, box 3, fd 3, Special Collections, BYU.

34. Manuscript minutes of 6 Apr. 1844, General Minutes Collection.

35. Hill, 145.

36. Manuscript minutes of 6 Apr. 1844, General Minutes Collection.

37. Karl Keller, ed., "I Never Knew a Time When I Did Not Know Joseph Smith," Dialogue: A Journal of Mormon Thought 1 (Winter 1966): 25-26.

38. History of the Church, 1:162.

39. Keller, 26.

40. Symonds Ryder, "Letter to A. S. Hayden," 1 Feb. 1868, in Hayden, 220-21.

41. Even god-fearing women were not exempt from testosterone-fueled attacks on their piety. Mother Ann Lee, an immigrant from England who claimed visions which resulted in the formation of her Church of Christ's Second Appearance (Shaking Quakers), was so treated. While on a mission to New Lebanon in New England in 1783 she stopped to rest among her disciples. These followers, who believed that the Christ Spirit was making his second appearance in her, persuaded her to demonstrate some of her religious zeal in dance and spiritual operations. Following this she went to the home of an adherent, where a mob gathered. Her followers were attacked, dragged from the house by their hair, beaten, and hurled into the mud. Mother Ann had been hiding in a sealed closet from which she was ejected and dragged by her heels to her carriage. Beaten and whipped, she and her

group were harassed by the mob all the way to the ferry opposite Albany (Theodore E. Johnson, *Hands to Work and Hearts to God* [Brunswick, ME: Bowdoin Museum of Art, 1969], chap. 4).

42. *History of the Church*, 1:265.

43. *Baptist Witness*, 1 Mar. 1875, in J. H. Kennedy, *Early Days of Mormonism* (London: Reeves and Turner, 1888), 62.

44. *Millennial Harbinger* 1 (1831): 100-101.

45. W. Wyl, *Mormon Portraits or the Truth About the Mormon Leaders from 1830 to 1886* (Salt Lake City: Tribune Printing and Publishing Co., 1886), 122.

46. *Times and Seasons* 5 (15 Sept. 1844): 686.

47. Grant, 7.

48. J. Wickliffe Rigdon, "Life Story of Sidney Rigdon," 161.

49. *History of the Church*, 6:288.

50. F. Mark McKiernan, *The Voice of One Crying in the Wilderness: Sidney Rigdon, Religious Reformer–1793-1876* (Lawrence, KS: Coronado Press, 1971), 108.

51. Diane and Lisa Berger, *We Heard the Angels of Madness* (New York: William Morrow and Co., 1991), 43. Hippocrates, a fifth-century B.C. physician, first identified this indisposition as "an aversion to food, despondency, sleeplessness, irritability, and restlessness." He believed that human health was determined by the relative levels of the four humors: blood, yellow bile, black bile, and phlegm. To these ancient scientists, specific diseases stemmed from imbalances in these humors. Melancholia indicated trouble with black bile—hence came "bilious temperament." (See Dianne Hales, *Depression* [New York and Philadelphia: Chelsea House Publishers, 1989], 24.)

The Greek physician Galen (C.E. 129-ca. 199) thought the spleen cleared black bile out of the body. If there was an excess of this humor, it congealed in the stomach and caused melancholia. He broke with tradition by proposing for the first time that melancholia and mania, a condition characterized by intense euphoria and delusions of grandeur, might be related symptoms of a single disorder (ibid., 26).

In the late seventeenth century, the humoral gave way to more scientific explanations. One reason was that melancholia had become a fashionable ailment, a mark of distinction and intelligence. The illness seems to strike the exceptionally creative more than other classes. Poets and writers such as Goethe, Coleridge, Wordsworth, and Blake declared it was a necessary foundation for much of their work (Berger and Berger, 235). The German scientist Wilhelm Griesinger (1817-68) maintained that melancholia was caused by psychic, mixed, and physical causes including grief, loss of fortune, injury, illness, or even a spoiled love affair, nervous disorders, and head injuries (Hales, 26).

By the late twentieth century Sidney Rigdon would have been recognized as suffering from an illness with a biochemical cause, often triggered by stress, which leads to cycles of mood swings. Experts believe that true manic depression does not appear at least until age thirteen, although it has been detected in children as young as six years of age. Recent reports estimate that 10-30 percent of adult manic-depressives are detectable by age eighteen (Berger and Berger, 239; see also "The 'Atypical' Clinical Picture of Adolescent Mania," *American Journal of Psychiatry* 139 [1982]: 602-605). Physicians have recently found links between head trauma and manic-depression (Sashi Shukla, M.D., "Failure to Detect Organic Factors in Mania," *Journal of Affective Disorders* 15 [1988]: 17-20).

52. Hales, 38-39.

53. *Diagnostic and Statistical Manual of Mental Disorders*, 3d ed. rev. (Washington, D.C.: American Psychiatric Association, 1987), 214-17.

54. Sidney Rigdon, "Statement of Journey to Missouri, 1832," ms d 713, fd 2, Sidney Rigdon Collection.

CHAPTER 10.

The Literary and United Firms

The Missouri trip not only removed Rigdon and Smith from further peril in Ohio, it allowed them to inspect affairs and attend to business in Zion. On 26 April 1832, soon after their arrival in Independence, the faithful Saints convened. Between morning and afternoon sessions a protracted affray involving Rigdon and Edward Partridge, the bishop in Zion, was diffused. Problems between the erstwhile friends first arose when Rigdon and Smith were in Jackson County the summer of 1831. Partridge had criticized the prophet for his allegedly failed prophecy regarding the church in Zion and had then withheld money from Rigdon and Smith for their passage back to Ohio. The official pronouncement simply reported Partridge's errors as "unbelief and blindness of heart."[1]

To chastise the bishop, Rigdon had sent Missouri church leaders John Corrill and Isaac Morley a letter on 14 November 1831. Chief among Rigdon's charges against Partridge was "His having insulted the Lord's prophet in particular & assumed authority over him in open violation of the Laws of God."[2]

Partridge's backers, led by stalwarts John Whitmer and Oliver Cowdery, disliked Rigdon's critical tone. In a 10 March 1832 rejoinder, penned by Cowdery, they urged him to assume a more Christian posture. "[W]hereas the duty of a disciple of Christ is to promote union harmony & brotherly love," the churchmen stated, "[we] earnestly entreat our br. Sidney for the good of the cause in which we labor & for which we suffer persecutions, to candidly reflect upon the subject of the aforementioned letter and ask himself whether he was not actuated by his own hasty feelings rather than the Spirit of Christ when indicting the same."

Partridge was "willing to make every confession which br. Sidney as a disciple of Christ could require & forever bury the matter," wrote Cowdery, advising that "such may be the resolution" whereby "the wound in the Church [may] be healed" and the two gospel brothers could "walk together . . . filling the important stations in the Kingdom of God in honor to themselves & the advancement of our Redeemer's Cause."[3]

Meanwhile, as Saints reassembled after lunch, Smith alluded to the Rigdon/Partridge reconciliation in the voice of revelation: "[I]nasmuch as you have forgiven one another your trespasses, even so I, the Lord, forgive you" (D&C 82:21). After a few laudatory accolades intermixed with chastisement, the edict focused on business matters, specifically the organization of Zion's Literary and United firms which had been divinely mandated in Ohio on 1 March 1832. The revelation announced: "[F]or verily I say unto you the time has come, and is now at hand, and behold and lo it must needs be that there be an organization of the literary and mercantile establishments of my church both in [Ohio] and in the land of Zion for a permanent and everlasting establishment and firm unto my Church to advance the cause which ye have espoused."[4]

The original source manuscript for this revelation (D&C 78) was substantially altered, the verse explicitly referring to these business concerns deleted, prior to publication to offset subsequent developments.[5] David Whitmer, an original witness to the Book of Mormon, later wrote to Joseph Smith's son that "Oliver Cowdery told me that Rigdon was the cause of those changes being made [in the revelations]: by smooth talk he convinced Joseph, Oliver, and F. G. Williams that it was all right."[6] While others, including Whitmer's brother John, his brother-in-law Oliver Cowdery, and church printer W. W. Phelps, also are known to have influenced retroactive changes in various revelations,[7] Rigdon was most likely responsible for modifying edicts governing the Literary and United firms, since he had most often written official church circulars on these matters.[8]

The changes obfuscated the original purpose and function of these organizations. Mormon scholar Lyndon W. Cook notes that because Brigham Young and most of his contemporaries were not fully aware of the early history of the mercantile firm they confused the terminology regarding the "Law of Consecration" and the "United Firm." Published Doctrine and Covenants references to "United Firm" were changed to read "United Order." Thus "it was easy to assume," writes Cook, "though erroneously, that 'United Order' in the Doctrine and Covenants referred to a religio-socio-economic law instead of a business partnership."[9]

To understand Rigdon's function, an overview may be helpful. In July 1830, while Rigdon was still a Reformed Baptist minister in Ohio, Joseph Smith and John Whitmer began to "arrange and copy" for publication the prophet's revelations. In September 1831 W. W. Phelps was directed to purchase a printing press in Cincinnati for use in Missouri. During the October-November 1831 conference at Hiram, Ohio, church members, after a request from the prophet, decreed that he, Rigdon, Martin Harris, Oliver Cowdery, John Whitmer, and W. W. Phelps "have claim on the Church for recompense" for their work in preparing the revelations for publication.[10]

The Literary Firm, established by revelation, employed these churchmen to manage the "literary concerns of my church [and] have claim for assistance upon the bishop or bishops in all things" (D&C 72:20).[11] This specific stewardship included printing Smith's revelations, the yet-to-be-completed revision of the Bible, the church hymnal, children's literature, church newspapers (*The Evening and the Morning Star, Latter-day Saints' Messenger and Advocate, The Northern Times*), and a church almanac.

On 1 March 1832 the United Firm, a mercantile partnership, was organized through revelation (D&C 78) as a private business alliance to create additional personal income for the temporal "salvation" of church leaders, including Rigdon. A second purpose, which never reached fruition, was generating surplus wealth to support the economic needs of the entire church. In addition, firm members were to oversee the "affairs of the poor" in both Kirtland and Missouri. Rigdon also made it clear in a 25 June 1833 letter from the First Presidency that the Literary Firm, considered of greater importance, would be supported by the United Firm if necessary.[12]

The United Firm was established with just three members: Smith, Rigdon, and Newel Whitney. When they arrived in Independence on 24 April, a Missouri branch of the firm was organized, with partners in Zion: Edward Partridge, Oliver Cowdery, W. W. Phelps, Sidney Gilbert, John Whitmer, and Jesse Gause. During a 27 April meeting of the firm, the sharers, bonded by mutual covenant, resolved to do business under the names "Gilbert, Whitney & Company" (Missouri) and "Newel K. Whitney & Company" (Ohio). W. W. Phelps and A. Sidney Gilbert were assigned to draft the bond for the business. During a joint meeting of the two branches in Independence on 30 April, the group gave Gilbert and Whitney power of attorney to "act in the name of this firm," and decided the Kirtland branch of the firm should negotiate a loan for $15,000. With this, business in Zion was completed.

Before returning to Ohio Rigdon preached, according to the prophet's account, "two . . . powerful discourses, which, so far as outward appearance is concerned, gave great satisfaction to the people."[13] Benton Pixley, a non-Mormon living in Independence, was in Rigdon's audience for at least one of the sermons. Pixley's account, a contemporary synopsis of Mormon teachings, said that

> Rigdon tells us that we are to look for and expect about these day[s] a new revelation—that the precepts inculcated and given by the Apostles to other people and in other ages are by no means to be applied to us. Those promises are not to be received by us as a matter of comfort nor those threatenings as a matter of alarm—for neither one nor the other belong to us—Promises given to a people very different from us and under very different circumstances eighteen hundred years ago away off on the Cont[i]nent of Asia can with no consistency be applied to the people of these United States. We are without a rev[e]lation and must wait upon God and pray for one suited to our times and circumstances.[14]

On 6 May 1832, Rigdon, Smith, and Whitney left Independence by stage for Kirtland. En route a runaway occurred and the agile prophet jumped from the coach. Whitney tried to follow suit but became entangled in a wheel, seriously mangling his leg and foot. Rigdon, who remained inside the conveyance, was unharmed. Smith and Whitney spent four weeks in a public house in Greenville, Indiana, while Rigdon proceeded home to Kirtland where his nine-year-old daughter, Nancy, was seriously ill.[15]

During his absence, Rigdon's large family had been shuffled from home to home, relying on the generosity of neighbors, and were boarding at Reynolds Cahoon's place when Sidney arrived.[16] These quarters were apparently unsatisfactory. Cahoon noted in his 26 May 1832 diary, "Br. Sidney arrived hear with much intiligence from Zion. Thursday Br. Sidney moved to the flats."

Apparent worry over his daughter's illness and despair over living quarters precipitated another virulent mood swing in Rigdon. Joseph Smith's mother, writing of the 5 July incident years later, said that a group had gathered in Joseph Smith Sr.'s barn for a Thursday evening prayer meeting, anticipating a sermon from Rigdon. "We waited a long time before he made his appearance," Lucy wrote, then

> at last he came in, seemingly much agitated. He did not go to the stand, but began to pace back and forth through the house. My husband said, "Brother Sidney, we would like to hear a discourse from you today." Brother Rigdon replied, in a tone of excitement, "The keys of the kingdom are rent from the Church, and there shall not be a prayer put up in this house this day." "Oh! no," said Mr. Smith, "I hope not." "I tell you they are," rejoined Elder Rigdon, "and no man or woman shall put up a prayer in this place today."
>
> This greatly disturbed the minds of many sisters, and some brethren. The brethren stared and turned pale, and the sisters cried. Sister Howe, in particular, was very much terrified: "Oh dear me!" she said, "what shall we do? what shall we do? The keys of the kingdom are taken from us, and what shall we do?" "I tell you again," said Sidney, with much feeling, "the keys of the kingdom are taken from you, and you never will have them again until you build me a new house."[17]

Joseph Smith's older brother Hyrum, also present on the occasion, said he did not believe Rigdon's assertion and borrowed a horse to ride to the town of Hiram, where the prophet was again living at John Johnson's, possibly in the Rigdon family's former quarters. On Saturday evening the brothers rode back into Kirtland. Charles C. Rich wrote that on Sunday morning, "everybody turned out to meeting." Joseph preached, "denouncing the doctrine of Rigdon as being false." Rich wrote that Smith "took [Rigdon's] licence from him and said, 'The Devil would handle him as one man handles another—the less authority he had the better.'"[18]

Lucy Smith's account, which like Rich's was retrospective, added that "Joseph went upon the stand, and informed the brethren that they were under a great mistake, that the Church had not transgressed; and, as for the keys of the kingdom," he said, "I, myself, hold the keys of this Last Dispensation, and will for ever hold them, both in time and eternity; so set your hearts at rest upon that point, all is right." She added that after her son preached a comforting discourse, he appointed a council to try Sidney for "having lied in the name of the Lord":

> In this council Joseph told him, he must suffer for what he had done, that he should

be delivered over to the buffetings of Satan, who would handle him as one man handleth another, that the less Priesthood he had, the better it would be for him and that it would be well for him to give up his license.

This counsel Sidney complied with, yet he had to suffer for his folly. After he had sufficiently humbled himself, he received another license; but the old one was retained, and is now in the hands of Bishop Whitney.[19]

Lucy's account is supported by Charles Rich's recollection which stated, "Before I left Kirtland[,] at the house of Father Smith, Joseph and Hyrum reordained [Sidney] to the Priesthood."[20] One non-Mormon account reported that Rigdon "contrived to be out of his mind, in order to mislead the saints into the belief that the goods of the kingdom had been taken from the church and must not be restored, as he said, until they had built him a new house."[21]

Considering similar manic or depressive periods throughout Rigdon's life, it is unlikely he contrived this drama. The derangement, as documented by several witnesses, lasted much longer than after the mobbing in Hiram. While viewing his psychopathology from a religious rather than a medical perspective, and thus considering the episode a "buffeting of Satan," bystanders were convinced of his sentence. Rich reported that "the devil did handle him by pulling him out of bed and other rough methods."[22] Philo Dibble writing in 1882 noted that towards the end of July,

> Sidney was lying on his bed alone. An unseen power lifted him from his bed, threw him across the room, and tossed him from one side of the room to the other. The noise being heard in the adjoining room, his family went in to see what was the matter, and found him going from one side of the room to the other, from the effects of which Sidney was laid up for five or six weeks.[23]

Oliver Huntington recorded in a similar account in an 1883 journal entry that "the folks heard a noise . . . in Sidneys room, went in and found him thrown down and about the room from one place to another as a strong man could throw a very weak one; and no visible hand by which he was thrown. He was handled by the devil as one man handles another and was as sore and bruised as if it had been by the hand of man."[24]

Rigdon's disfavor lasted less than three weeks. In a relatively unknown contemporary account of Rigdon's breakdown, Joseph Smith is more sympathetic. Writing to W. W. Phelps in a 31 July 1832 letter, the prophet said that

> when Bro Sidney learned the feelings of the Brethren in whom he had placed so much confidence for whom he had endured so much fateague & suffering & whom he loved with so much love his heart was grieved his spirits failed & for a moment he became frantick & the advisary taking the advantage, he spake unadvisedly with his lips[.] after receiving a severe chastisement [he] resigned his commision and became a private member in the church, but has since repented like Peter of old and after a

little suffering by the buffiting of Satan has been restored to his high standing in the church of God.[25]

The Rigdon family did receive a church-provided home after this incident, and, despite the transitory loss of his senses, Sidney's stock rose again. On 8 March 1833, Smith pronounced in revelation: "I say unto thy brethren Sidney Rigdon, and Frederick G. Williams, their sins are forgiven them also, and they are accounted as equal with thee in holding the keys of this last kingdom. . . . And this shall be your business and mission in all your lives to preside in counsel and set in order all the affairs of this church and kingdom" (D&C 90:6, 16).

Ten days later, during a gathering of the High Priesthood, Rigdon requested that he and Williams be ordained to the office "to which they had been called . . . those of Presidents of the High Priesthood, and to be equal in holding the keys of the kingdom with Brother Joseph Smith, Jun., according to the revelation given on the 8th of March, 1833."[26]

Seven months later, after Rigdon's request was fulfilled, he and the prophet, while at Perrysburg, New York, shared a 12 October epiphany wherein Rigdon was told:

> And it is expedient in me that you, my servant Sidney, should be a spokesman unto this people; yea, verily I will ordain you unto this calling, even to be a spokesman unto my servant Joseph. And I will give unto him power to be mighty in testimony. And I will give unto thee power to be mighty in expounding all scriptures, that thou mayest be a spokesman unto him, and he shall be a revelator unto thee, that thou mayest know the certainty of all things pertaining to the things of my kingdom on the earth (D&C 100:9-12).

Despite his eccentricity, Rigdon was more polished, logical, and verbally gifted than Smith. For years he had been Mormonism's unofficial pitch man, and his designation as "spokesman unto my servant Joseph" satisfied Book of Mormon prophecy (see 2 Ne. 7, 15, 17). This became Rigdon's crowning touchstone. Despite a ministry overshadowed by mental illness, unsuccessful efforts to effect the Second Advent, and failed attempts to build the New City of Jerusalem, Rigdon felt that God had anciently foretold his role as spokesman. That belief caused him to rise, phoenix-like, again and again.

Notes

Unless otherwise stated, all primary sources cited are located in the Historical Department of the Church of Jesus Christ of Latter-day Saints, Salt Lake City, Utah.

1. See Ezra Booth's 20 Sept. 1831 letter to Partridge in Eber Howe, *Mormonism Unvailed* (Painesville, OH: E. D. Howe, 1834), 201-202. The official pronouncement is D&C 58:14-16.

2. Donald Q. Cannon and Lyndon W. Cook, eds., *Far West Record–Minutes of The Church of Jesus Christ of Latter-day Saints, 1830-1844* (Salt Lake City: Deseret Book Co., 1983), 41.

3. Ibid., 42. Partridge still harbored concerns over Smith's behavior, as well, as evidenced by a 14 January 1833 letter from Orson Hyde and Hyrum Smith, chastising Partridge:

> At the time Joseph, Sidney, and Newel left Zion, all matters of hardness and misunderstanding were settled and buried (as they supposed), and you gave them the hand of fellowship but, afterwards you brought up all these things again, in a cens[u]rious spirit, accusing Brother Joseph in rather an indirect way of seeking after monarchial power and authority. This came to us in Brother Corrill's letter of June 2nd. We are sensible that this is not the thing Brother Joseph is seeking after, but to magnify the high office and calling whereunto he has been called and appointed by the command of God (Joseph Smith, *History of the Church of Jesus Christ of Latter-day Saints*, B. H. Roberts, ed., 7 vols. [Salt Lake City: The Church of Jesus Christ of Latter-day Saints, 1902], 1:317-19; hereafter referred to as *History of the Church*).

4. "Kirtland Revelation Book," 16.

5. Ibid. Upgrading revelations and retrospectively editing the past are hallmarks of early Mormonism. Thousands of substantive alterations were made between the time many revelations were received, their first publication in various sources, and later propogations in the Book of Commandments (1833) and various editions of the Doctrine and Covenants since 1835.

6. David Whitmer to Joseph Smith, III, 9 Dec. 1886 (in *Saints Herald*, 5 Feb. 1887). For discussions of altered Mormon revelation, see Melvin J. Peterson, "A Study of the Nature and Significance of the Changes in the Revelations as Found in a Comparison of the Book of Commandments and Subsequent Editions of the Doctrine and Covenants," M.A. thesis, Brigham Young University, 1955; Richard P. Howard, *Restoration Scriptures: A Study of Their Textual Development* (Independence, MO: Department of Religious Education, Reorganized Church of Jesus Christ of Latter Day Saints, 1969), 196-263; and Karl F. Best, "Changes in the Revelations, 1833 to 1835," *Dialogue: A Journal of Mormon Thought* 25 (Spring 1992): 87-112.

7. At a 30 April 1832 meeting in Missouri, the Literary Firm designated Phelps, Cowdery, and John Whitmer to review and select revelations "as dictated by the Spirit" to be included in the Book of Commandments and "make all necessary verbal corrections" (Cannon and Cook, 46). While authority for making changes was given to Phelps, Cowdery, and Whitmer, the prophet did warn Phelps in a letter to "be careful not to alter the sense of any" of the revelations (Dean C. Jessee, *The Personal Writings of Joseph Smith* [Salt Lake City: Deseret Book Co., 1984], 247).

8. See his 25 June 1833 letter to W. W. Phelps (*History of the Church*, 1:362-64); also his 25 June 1833 letter to Edward Partridge (ibid., 364-65); and his 2 July 1833 letter "To the Brethren in Zion" (ibid., 368-70).

9. Lyndon W. Cook, *Joseph Smith and the Law of Consecration* (Orem, UT: Keepsake Paperbacks, 1991), 65-67.

10. Cannon and Cook, 32.

11. Shortly after the organization of the Literary Firm, Jesse Gause was added. In 1833 Frederick G. Williams, who had replaced Gause in the presidency of the High Priesthood, also became a member.

12. *History of the Church*, 1:365-66.

13. Ibid., 270-71.

14. Benton Pixley to A. Peters, 1 June 1832 (Ms 4802). On 12 October 1832, Pixley wrote another letter from Independence (published in the 30 Nov. 1832 *The Standard* [Cincinnati]) which provides a further look at Mormon activity in Jackson County:

> Dwelling as I do among a people called Mormonites, and on the very land which they sometimes call Mount Zion, at other times the New Jerusalem; and where, at no distant period, they expect the re-appearing of the Lord Jesus to live and reign with them on earth a thousand years. . . . One woman, I am told, declared in her sickness, with much confidence, that she should not die, but here live and reign with Christ a thousand years; but unfortunately she died, like other people, three days after. They tell indeed of working miracles, healing the sick, &c.&c. These things, however, are not seen to be done, but only said to be done. People therefore who set their faces for the Mount Zion of the West, (which by the by is on a site of ground not much elevated,) must calculate on being disappointed, if they believe all that is said of the place, or expect much above what is common in any new country of the West.
>
> . . . Their first, best, great, and celebrated preacher, Elder Rigdon, tells us the Epistles are not and were not given for our instruction, but for the instruction of a people of another age and country, far removed from ours, of different habits and manners; and needing different teaching: and that it is altogether inconsistent for us to take the Epistles written for that people at that age of the world, as containing suitable instruction for this people at this age of the world. The Gospels, too, we are given by them to understand, are so mutilated and altered, as to convey little of the instruction which they should convey. Hence we are told a new revelation is to be sought, it to be expected, indeed is coming forthwith. Our present Bible is to be altered and restored to its primitive purity, by Smith, the present prophet of the Lord, and some books to be added of great importance, which have been lost (Mormon Manuscript Retrieval Project, ms 19, box 3, fd 3, Special Collections, Harold B. Lee Library, Brigham Young University, Provo, Utah; hereafter Special Collectios, BYU).

15. Nancy Rigdon's illness is mentioned in Smith's 31 July 1832 letter to Phelps, in Jessee, 249.

17. See Cahoon's 18 May 1832 diary (ms d 1115).

16. Leonard J. Arrington, *Charles C. Rich: Mormon General and Western Frontiersman* (Provo, UT: Brigham Young University Press, 1974), 332, noted that Lucy Smith mistakenly placed this incident before Smith's second trip to Missouri, "about three months earlier than it occurs as [Charles C.] Rich told it." Reynolds Cahoon's diary entry for Thursday, 5 July 1832, precisely dates the event: "at the meeting Br. Sidney remarked that he had a revelation from the Lord & said that the kingdom was taken from the Church and left with him[.] [F]ryday Br. Hiram went after Joseph when he came he affirmed that the kingdom was ours & never should be taking from the faithful."

17. Preston Nibley, ed., *History of Joseph Smith by His Mother Lucy Mack Smith* (Salt Lake City: Bookcraft, 1958), 221-23.

18. Arrington, 21.

19. Nibley, 222-23. Philo Dibble, writing in 1882, said that "Joseph arose in our midst and spoke in mighty power, saying: 'I can contend with wicked men and devils—yes with angels. No power can pluck those keys from me, except the power that gave them to me; that was Peter, James, and John. *But for what Sidney has done, the devil shall handle him as one man handles another.*'" Rigdon was not present at the time, Dibble added, but was informed of Joseph's prophecy immediately after the meeting by the wife of Thomas B. Marsh. His reply: "Is it possible that I have been so deceived? But if Joseph says so, it was so" (Philo Dibble, "Early Scenes in Church History," *Faith Promoting Series* No. 8 [Salt Lake City: Juvenile Instructor Office, 1882], 80).

20. Arrington, 332.

21. J. H. Kennedy, *Early Days of Mormonism* (London: Reeves and Turner, 1888), 107-108.

22. Arrington, 21.

23. Dibble, 80.

24. Oliver B. Huntington diary, 202, Special Collections, BYU.

25. Jessee, 246-47.

26. *History of the Church*, 1:334.

CHAPTER 11.

Book of Mormon Authorship

It is the conviction of nearly all of the opponents of Mormonism, who have paid particular attention to the history of its origin, that the Church of Jesus Christ of Latter-day Saints was not an emanation from the mind of Joseph Smith, but that it was first conceived of by Sidney Rigdon, and that Smith was merely his tool in giving the movement publicity while he played his part behind the scenes until his pretended conversion in the year 1830.

—Charles Shook (1914)[1]

Antagonists have expended considerable energy attempting to discredit the Book of Mormon, which gave Joseph Smith's prophesying a concrete legitimacy that the visions and predictions of other seers of the day could not match. The Book of Mormon had a particular appeal for people emerging from a twilight of visionary dreams and folk magic, men and women looking to demonstrate their literacy and enlightenment. It fit the popular belief that what was written was a greater truism and more authentic than the spoken word.

Throughout his life Joseph Smith gave one explanation for the origin of the Book of Mormon. He summed it up best in a 4 January 1833 letter to N. E. Seaton, a Rochester, New York, newspaper editor: "The Book of Mormon is a record of the forefathers of our western tribes of Indians, having been found through the ministrations of an holy angel, and translated into our language by the gift and power of God, after having been hid up in the earth for the last 1,400 years."[2]

Mormonism's success in Ohio, particularly among Sidney Rigdon's Reformed Baptists, spelled conspiracy in some people's eyes. While eleven of Smith's friends and relatives signed affidavits that they had examined the gold plates and seen the angel who delivered them to the prophet, many did not accept this supernatural explanation. To cynics it seemed improbable that a semi-literate farm boy could author a literary work so intricate in plot and steeped in biblical lore as the Book of Mormon.

The logical explanation for the holy book was that Smith must have collaborated behind the scenes with someone better educated and more sophisticated. A former school teacher, Oliver Cowdery, Smith's major copyist during the project, was considerably better schooled than his prophet-cousin. Cowdery was touted in the press as co-author of the Book of Mormon in the 25 November 1830 *Cleveland Herald*. But as soon as Sidney Rigdon made his late 1830 trip to New York to meet Smith, rumors surfaced that he, not Cowdery, was the mastermind behind the new scripture.[3]

The earliest New York publication linking Rigdon with Book of Mormon authorship was the 1 September 1831 issue of the *New York Courier and Enquirer*, reprinted in the 29 October 1831 *Hillsborough Gazette* (Ohio). The article describes Smith as "the son of a speculative Yankee peddler, and was brought up to live by his wits." Rigdon is characterized as

> perfectly *aufait* with every species of prejudice, folly of fanaticism, which governs the mass of enthusiasts. In the course of his experience, he had attended all sorts of camp-meetings, prayer meetings, anxious meetings, and revival meetings. He knew every turn of the human mind in relation to these matters. He had a superior knowledge of human nature, considerable talent, great plausibility, and knew how to work the passions as exactly as a Cape Cod sailor knows how to work a whale ship. . . . There is no doubt but the ex-parson from Ohio is the author of the book which was recently printed and published in Palmyra, and passes for the new Bible.[4]

During the spring of 1833 or 1834, while visiting the home of Samuel Baker near New Portage, Ohio, Rigdon stated in the presence of a large gathering that he was aware some in the neighborhood had accused him of being the instigator of the Book of Mormon. Standing in the doorway to address the audience in the yard, he held up a Book of Mormon and said:

> I testify in the presence of this congregation, and before God and all the Holy Angels up yonder, (pointing towards heaven), before whom I expect to give account at the judgment day, that I never saw a sentence of the Book of Mormon, I never penned a sentence of the Book of Mormon, I never knew that there was such a book in existence as the Book of Mormon, until it was presented to me by Parley P. Pratt, in the form that it now is.[5]

Such was Rigdon's stance even on his deathbed. He confirmed that position repeatedly, as did his wife and at least three of his children, two of whom were non-believers in Mormonism. His oldest child, Athalia R. Robinson, in a notarized statement of 10 October 1900, said that the missionaries presented the book to her father in the presence of "My mother and myself. . . . This was the first time father ever saw the book of Mormon."[6] His son Wickliffe added in a 1905 interview that during a visit with his father,

> then in his last years . . . I found him as firm as ever in declaring that he himself had nothing whatever to do in writing the book, and that Joseph Smith received it from an angel. On his dying bed he made the same declaration to a Methodist minister.

. . . My mother has also told me that Father had nothing whatever to do with the writing of the book, and that she positively knew that he had never seen it until Parley P. Pratt came to our home with it.[7]

Nancy R. Ellis, Rigdon's most anti-Mormon offspring, recalled in an 1884 interview the arrival of the missionaries in her Mentor, Ohio, home when she was eight years old: "I saw them hand him the book, and I am as positive as can be that he never saw it before. . . . She further stated that her father in the last years of his life called his family together and told them, as sure as there was a God in heaven, he never had anything to do in getting up the Book of Mormon, and never saw any such thing as a manuscript written by Solomon Spaulding."[8]

This Spalding (also Spaulding) manuscript, as far as most nineteenth-century—and some contemporary—Book of Mormon antagonists were concerned, was the true source of the sacred Mormon book. Born in Connecticut in 1761, graduated from Dartmouth College (New Hampshire) in 1785, Spalding for a time was a Congregational minister in New York before becoming a Presbyterian. After moving to Ohio in 1809 he wrote a historical novel about aboriginal America, narrated by a shipwrecked Roman named Fabius. The work was never published and Spalding died in 1816.

On 13 March 1833 a Methodist minister from Jamestown, New York, with the given name of Doctor Philastus Hurlbut (also Hurlburt or Hurlbert), visited Joseph Smith in Kirtland and embraced his message. He qualified his conversion, however, by warning the prophet that if he ever "became convinced that the Book of Mormon was false, he would be the cause of [Smith's] destruction."[9] Church leaders did not seem concerned. Rigdon ordained Hurlbut an elder on 18 March and sent him on a mission to Pennsylvania. He was soon recalled and excommunicated on 3 June 1833 for making an obscene comment to a young woman.[10]

Angry over what he viewed as mistreatment, Hurlbut sought revenge. He returned to Pennsylvania and spent several months lecturing against Mormonism. There he became acquainted with a family named Jackson who told Hurlbut that years before, when Solomon Spalding had lived near them in Amity, Washington County, Pennsylvania, he admitted authoring a romantic, historical fiction that like the Book of Mormon contained an account of an early immigration to America. Hurlbut returned to Kirtland and announced a lecture on what he called "Anti-Mormonism." To this group he recounted his travels in Pennsylvania where "he had learned that one Mr. Spaulding had written a romance, and the probability was, that it had, by some means, fallen into the hands of Sidney Rigdon, and that he had converted it into the Book of Mormon."[11]

Several of Rigdon's old Campbellite nemeses—Judge Orris Clapp, and both sons, Thomas J. and Matthew S. Clapp, and Adamson Bentley—advanced Hurlbut a large sum to begin searching for the Spalding manuscript.[12] He traveled first to New Salem (formerly Conneaut), Ohio, where Spalding was living when he wrote the manuscript and where several family members still resided. He called a meeting and announced to those gathered his theory of the origin of the Book of Mormon. "This idea was new to them," explained one account, "however, they were pleased with it, and Mr. H[urlbut]'s project seemed to them a good one."[13]

While in New Salem Hurlbut obtained a collection of affidavits from the deceased writer's brother John Spalding, John's wife Martha, and several other former friends and neighbors. The consensus of the witnesses supported Hurlbut's theory that Solomon Spalding had written a historical novel. According to their collective recall the work of fiction detailed the settlement of America, "endeavoring to show that the American Indians are the descendants of the Jews, or the lost tribes."[14]

Hurlbut learned from John Spalding that his brother's widow lived in Monson, Massachusetts. The sleuth set out to find her and en route stopped at Palmyra, New York, for two months where he collected derogatory depositions from more than a hundred of Joseph Smith's acquaintances. Hurlbut's activities in upstate New York were well-known that season. On 20 December, the local newspaper, the *Wayne Sentinel*, published the first announcement of his theory of Book of Mormon origins:

> The original manuscript of the Book was written some thirty years since, by a respectable clergyman, now deceased, whose name we are not permitted to give. It was designed to be published as a romance, but the work has been superadded by some modern hand—believed to be the notorious Rigdon. These particulars have been derived by Dr. Hurlbert from the widow of the author of the original manuscript.[15]

When Hurlbut finally met Spalding's widow, Matilda Davison, and explained his hypothesis, she told him the manuscript he wanted was likely stored in a trunk of papers left with relatives in Harwick, New York. Securing her permission to retain the manuscript if he found it, Hurlbut traveled to Harwick where he indeed discovered the novel and took it back to Ohio for closer examination.

On his return to the Western Reserve, the successful investigator joined forces with a committee of non-Mormon Kirtland citizens who were concerned that Smith was "collecting about him an impoverished population, alienated in feeling from other portions of the community, thereby threatening us with an insupportable weight of pauperism."[16]

The plan formulated by the civic leaders, according to their own account, was to employ "D. P. Hurlbut to ascertain the real origin of the Book of Mormon, and to examine the validity of Joseph Smith's claims to the character of Prophet."[17] To stir up additional support Hurlbut exhibited his numerous affidavits in Kirtland, Mentor, and surrounding communities, lecturing wherever he could assemble an audience. His activities caused sufficient furor for the Mormon First Presidency to write to Missouri Saints warning them of Hurlbut's speculations which had "fired the minds of the people with much indignation against Joseph and the Church."[18]

Smith and Rigdon were quick to defend the Mormon cause. And at some point in the passion of a heated exchange, Hurlbut publicly threatened that he would "wash his hands" in the prophet's blood.[19] In January 1834, Smith filed a legal complaint bringing Hurlbut to trial on 1 April. The court found him guilty, fined him $200, and ordered him to keep the peace for six months.

The notoriety surrounding Hurlbut, compounded by an embarrassing incident when his wife was discovered in bed with Judge Orris Clapp, tarnished his image. He sold his research to Eber D. Howe, editor of the *Painesville Telegraph*, who held a long-term grudge against Mormonism for converting his wife and daughter.[20] The Kirtland committee that commissioned Hurlbut's research announced in the 31 January 1834 *Painesville Telegraph* that it was

> now making arrangements for the *Publication* and extensive *circulation* of a work which will prove the "Book of Mormon" to be a work of *fiction* and *imagination*, and written more than twenty years ago, in Salem, Ashtabula County, Ohio, by Solomon Spalding, Esq. and completely divest Joseph Smith of all claims to the character of an honest man, and place him at an immeasurable distance from the high station which he pretends to occupy.

Mormonism Unvailed, published by Howe, was first advertised in the *Telegraph* on 28 November 1834. The volume contained a lengthy critique of the Book of Mormon, a reprint of Ezra Booth's nine letters, disparaging affidavits provided by Joseph Smith's old New York neighbors, and an introduction to the Spalding theory of the origin of the Book of Mormon. While Howe admitted he had Spalding's manuscript,[21] it was obvious that the former minister's work, a secular text, was not the source for the Book of Mormon, a lofty religious tome, although the introduction, ethnological assumptions, and mystical lore were undeniably similar.[22] To explain the enigmatic gaps in genre and plot, Howe wrote that his witnesses claimed Spalding had "altered his first plan of writing, by going farther back with dates, and writing in the old scripture style, in order that it might appear more ancient."

Howe further purported that through some unspecified means, Rigdon must have secured this hypothetical second, revised manuscript while he was living in Pittsburgh. He concluded: "We, therefore, must hold out Sidney Rigdon to the world as being the original 'author and proprietor' of the whole Mormon conspiracy, until further light is elicited upon the lost writings of Solomon Spaulding."[23]

Rigdon's numerous and consistent denials to the contrary, speculation regarding his acquisition of a second Spalding manuscript dominated secular investigation into the twentieth century. It became especially useful following the 1884 rediscovery of the original manuscript Hurlbut had obtained from Matilda

Spalding Davison. The document was inadvertently located in Hawaii among papers of Eber D. Howe's *Painesville Telegraph* successor, Lewis L. Rice. It was eventually donated to Oberlin College (Ohio), where it remains today.[24]

The weight of scholarly studies since Fawn Brodie's seminal 1945 *No Man Knows My History* biography of Joseph Smith has all but eliminated the Spalding theory and Rigdon's complicity.[25] Other options have been suggested over the years. The earliest Book of Mormon critic, Rigdon's former mentor Alexander Campbell,[26] opined in 1831 that Joseph Smith, profoundly affected by the salvationist Christianity of nineteenth-century Protestant America, was, in fact, the author of the work. "This prophet Smith," speculated Campbell,

> through his stone spectacles, wrote on the plates of Nephi, in his book of Mormon, every error and almost every truth discussed in New York for the last ten years. He decides all the great controversies—infant baptism, ordination, the trinity, regeneration, repentance, justification, the fall of man, the atonement, transubstantiation, fasting, pennance, church government, religious experience, the call to the ministry, the general resurrection, eternal punishment, who may baptize, and even the question of free masonry,[27] republican government, and the rights of man.[28]

For those skeptical of the supernatural, answers must be sought elsewhere (see Appendix 5 for further discussion). As William McLellin, an early Mormon leader and later apostate, affirmed years after he had left Mormonism:

> You seem to think S. Rigdon the bottom of all M[ormon]ism. Many people know better. He never heard of the work of Smith & Cowdery, until C[owdery] and P[arley] P. Pratt brought the book to him in Mentor, O[hio]. True enough, I have but little confidence in S. Rigdon, but I know he was more the tool of J. Smith than his teacher and director. He was docile in J. S. hands to my knowledge.[29]

If any one single item defined Rigdon it was his untiring belief in the authenticity of that "ancient voice from the dust." It provided him the shelf on which he rested his soul. And in the end, when he was disillusioned and bereft of faith in Joseph Smith, he still avowed that the Book of Mormon was precisely what it claimed to be—the word of God.

Notes

Unless otherwise stated, all primary sources cited are located in the Historical Department of the Church of Jesus Christ of Latter-day Saints, Salt Lake City, Utah.

1. Charles A. Shook, *The True Origin of The Book of Mormon* (Cincinnati: The Standard Publishing Co., 1914), 126.

2. Joseph Smith, *History of the Church of Jesus Christ of Latter-day Saints*, B. H. Roberts, ed., 7 vols. (Salt Lake City: The Church of Jesus Christ of Latter-day Saints, 1902), 1:315; hereafter referred to as *History of the Church*.

A sampling of recent scholarship dealing with possible origins of the Book of Mormon (not included elsewhere in this chapter) include: Edward H. Ashment, "The Book of Mormon–A Literal Translation?" *Sunstone* 5 (Mar.-Apr. 1980): 10-14; Richard S. Van Wagoner and Steven C. Walker, "Joseph Smith: 'The Gift of Seeing,'" *Dialogue: A Journal of Mormon Thought* 15 (Summer 1982): 49-68; Blake T. Ostler, "The Book of Mormon as a Modern Expansion of an Ancient Source," *Dialogue: A Journal of Mormon Thought* 20 (Spring 1987): 66-124; D. Michael Quinn, *Early Mormonism and the Magic World View* (Salt Lake City: Signature Books, 1987); John W. Welch, *The Collected Works of Hugh Nibley: Volume 7, the Book of Mormon* (Salt Lake City: Deseret Book Co. and F.A.R.M.S., 1988); Dan Vogel, ed., *The Word of God: Essays on Mormon Scripture* (Salt Lake City: Signature Books, 1990); Robert N. Hullinger, *Joseph Smith's Response to Skepticism* (Salt Lake City: Signature Books, 1992); Brent Lee Metcalfe, ed., *New Approaches to the Book of Mormon: Explorations in Critical Methodology* (Salt Lake City: Signature Books, 1993); Daniel C. Peterson, ed., *Review of Books on the Book of Mormon* [F.A.R.M.S.] 6 (1994).

3. See Parley P. Pratt, *Mormonism Unveiled*, 2d ed. (New York: O. Pratt and E. Fordham, 1838), 2; *Cleveland Herald*, 15 Sept. 1831.

4. The newspaper article is available at LDS church archives and is cited in Leonard J. Arrington, "James Gordon Bennett's 1831 Report on 'The Mormonites,'" *Brigham Young University Studies* 10 (Spring 1970): 353-64.

5. Signed 14 Mar. 1872 affidavit of Phineas Bronson, Hiel Bronson, Mary D. Bronson, in R. Etzenhouser, *From Palmyra, New York, 1830 to Independence, Missouri, 1894* (Independence, MO: Ensign Publishing House, 1894), 387-88.

6. 10 Oct. 1900 notarized statement.

7. In *Elders' Journal* (Chattanooga, TN) 2 (1905): 267-68.

8. Interview with Wm. H. and E. L Kelley, 14 May 1884, in *Pittsburgh Leader*, 18 May 1884, cited in Joseph Smith III and Heman C. Smith, *The History of the Reorganized Church of Jesus Christ of Latter Day Saints*, 4 vols. (Independence, MO: Herald House, 1967 reprint), 4:453. Rigdon's minister cousin, John Rigdon, also left testimony denying his cousin's involvement in producing the Book of Mormon, as recorded by Sidney Knowlton for John Page:

> I hereby certify that I heard Rev. John Rigdon, a member of the Church of Disciples, known by the name of Campbellites, sometime in March, 1840, at his own residence in Fulton Co., Illinois, say in answer to a question propounded to him by Elder John E. Page, as follows, to wit: Question by Mr. Page–"Sir, what are your views in relation to Sidney Rigdon having any connection with the origin of the Book of Mormon, as it is reported, that he, Rigdon had access to the Spaulding manuscript, from which he transcribed or originated the Book of Mormon?" Answer by Rigdon–"I do not believe from my acquaintance with him, (S. Rigdon) having known him from his infancy till after the publication of said Book of Mormon, as well as one can know another, being on the greatest terms of intimacy at the time said book was printed, and from all the circumstances connected with his life, character and conduct, that Sidney Rigdon had any thing whatever to do with it" (statement of Sidney A. Knowlton in John E. Page, *The Spaulding Story, Concerning the Origin of the Book of Mormon,*

Duly Examined, and Exposed to the Righteous Contempt of a Candid Public [Pittsburgh: n.p., 1843], 8).

9. While this reference was noted in Joseph Smith's diary under this date (Scott H. Faulring, ed., *An American Prophet's Record: The Diaries and Journals of Joseph Smith* [Salt Lake City: Signature Books in association with Smith Research Associates, 1989], 20), it is not mentioned in the published *History of the Church*.

10. *History of the Church*, 1:352.

11. Benjamin Winchester, *Plain Facts, Shewing the Origin of the Spaulding Story, Concerning The Manuscript Found, and its Being Transformed into the Book of Mormon with A Short History of Dr. P. Hurlbert, the Author of the Said Story* (Bedford, MA: C. B. Merry, 1841), 9.

12. Ibid., 9, 21.

13. Ibid., 10. Orson Hyde made his own study of the matter. He concluded that during the time he lived in the Rigdon home, when Sidney was his pastor and mentor, there was not a single hint that Rigdon was working on a manuscript. Furthermore, he explained: "Forgery, deception, and romance formed no part of the principles which Mr. Rigdon taught me during the time that I was under his tuition, and I must say, that I should not have been more surprised if they had accused the Lord Bishop of London of the same things which they charge against Mr. Rigdon." Hyde also recalled that when he had visited New Salem in the spring of 1832 and organized a branch of the church there, he had met no one who claimed to have found similarities between the Book of Mormon and the Spalding work (Orson Hyde to George J. Adams, 7 June 1841, in Winchester, 25-27).

14. Eber Howe, *Mormonism Unvailed* (Painesville, OH: E. D. Howe, 1834), 279.

15. This article was reprinted in the *Chardon* (Ohio) *Spectator*, 18 Jan. 1834.

16. See 31 Jan. 1834 letter "To the Public" in the *Painesville Telegraph*. The group was comprised of O. A. Crary, Amos Daniels, John F. Morse, Samuel Wilson, Josiah Jones, Warren Corning, Jr., James H. Paine, Jos. H. Wakefield, Sylvester Cornwall, and Timothy D. Martindale.

17. Ibid. The editor of the Apr. 1834 *Latter Day Saints' Messenger and Advocate* wrote of the "celebrated committee, residing in our country . . . who have employed this Hurlbut to expose, the 'origin of the book of mormon'."

18. *History of the Church* 1:475.

19. George A. Smith's testimony in *Journal of Discourses*, 26 vols. (London: Latter-day Saints' Book Depot, 1854-86), 11 (15 Nov. 1864):8; hereafter *Journal of Discourses*.

20. Lewis L. Rice letter to James H. Fairchild, 30 Jan. 1885, noted that Howe's wife was a Mormon, "but he was deadly opposed to it and got up and published a book purporting to show that Spalding was the orginator of the Mormon Bible" (in Dale Broadhurst Collection, Special Collections, Marriott Library, University of Utah). See also Robert C. Webb, *The Real Mormonism: A Candid Analysis of an Interesting but Much Misunderstood Subject in History Life and Thought* (New York: Sturgis & Walton Co., 1916), 406.

21. The title "Manuscript Found," often given to this manuscript, is not based on wording found in the original. A faint notation, "Manuscript Story-Conneaut Creek," was penciled on the document's paper wrapper sometime before it came into the possession

of Lewis L. Rice, according to his statement to James H. Fairchild, 12 June 1885 (Broadhurst Collection).

22. Spaulding's fictitious narrative described a shipload of Romans in the days of Constantine who were blown off course during a voyage to the British Isles. They safely reached the east coast of North America, after which one of them, Fabius, began writing a history of their activities.

Spalding's introduction is nearly identical to the Joseph Smith story. While out for a mid-day stroll, wrote Spalding, he "hap[pen]ed to tread on a flat Stone" with a badly worn inscription. "With the assistance of a leaver I raised the Stone . . . [and found] that it was designed as a cover to an artificial cave." Descending to the bottom, he discovered "a big flat Stone fixed in the form of a do[o]r." Moving the obstacle he saw an earthen box within which were "eight *sheets* of parchment." Written on the pages "in an eligant hand with Roman Letters & in the Latin Language" was "a history of the author[']s life & that part of America which extends along the great Lakes & the waters of the Mississippy."

If Spalding's and Smith's recountings have a common antecedent, it seems to be the Masonic "Legend of Enoch." In this saga, Enoch, the seventh patriarch, the son of Jared, and the great-grandfather of Noah, according to Masonic tradition, became disgusted with wickedness surrounding him. Fleeing to the "solitude and secrecy of Mount Moriah" he became engaged in prayer and contemplation. Here the Shekinah (sacred presence) appeared to him with instructions to preserve the wisdom of the antediluvians to their posterity. He then made a gold plate and engraved in characters the true, ineffable name of Deity. The plate was then placed in a specially prepared subterranean vault, along with other treasure, and covered with a stone door. Enoch was then only allowed to visit the site once a year. After his death all knowledge of this sacred treasure was lost.

Years later when King Solomon and his masons were excavating in Jerusalem to build the great temple they discovered the treasure trove. Hiram Abif (also Abiff), a widow's son, was killed defending the spot. Solomon's temple received these treasures, including the gold plate and the Urim and Thummin. See Albert G. Mackey, *An Encyclopaedia of Freemasonry and Its Kindred Sciences: Comprising the Whole Range of Arts, Sciences and Literature as Connected With the Institution* (Philadelphia: L. H. Everts & Co., 1887), 255-56; Mervin B. Hogan, ed., *An Underground Presidential Address [of Reed C. Durham, Jr.]* (Salt Lake City: Research Lodge of Utah, F. & A. M., 16 Sept. 1974), privately circulated; Don McDermott, "Joseph Smith and the Treasure of Hiram Abiff," *The Cryptic Scholar* (Winter/Spring 1991); Jack Adamson, "The Treasurer of the Widow's Son," ca. 1970, privately circulated.

23. Howe, 290. Rigdon's most poignant denial of involvement with the Book of Mormon is found in his 27 May 1839 letter to the *Boston Journal* reprinted in Winchester, 25-27.

24. The Spalding manuscript was first published by the Reorganized Church of Jesus Christ of Latter Day Saints in 1885 under the title, *The "Manuscript Found," or "Manuscript Story"* (Lamoni, IA: Herald Publishing House, 1885).

25. The best analysis of this topic is Lester E. Bush, Jr., "The Spalding Theory Then and Now," *Dialogue: A Journal of Mormon Thought* 10 (Autumn 1977): 40-69. Other well-known treatments include: Benjamin Winchester, *Plain Facts, Shewing the Origin of the Spaulding Story, Concerning The Manuscript Found, and its Being Transformed into the*

Book of Mormon with A Short History of Dr. P. Hurlbert, the Author of the Said Story (Bedford, MA: C. B. Merry, 1841); John E. Page, *The Spaulding Story Concerning the Origin of the Book of Mormon* (Pittsburg, 1843); "Reply to Chicago Inter-Ocean on The Spaulding Story, in *The Saints' Herald*" 24 (15 Feb. 1877): 49-52); J. E. Mahaffey, *Found at Last! "Positive Proof" That Mormonism is a Fraud and the Book of Mormon a Fable. Including a Careful Comparison of the Book of Mormon with the original Spalding MS, which shows Twenty-Two Points of Identity!* (Augusta, GA: Chronicle Job Office, 1902); John Henry Evans, *One Hundred Years of Mormonism* (Salt Lake City: Deseret Sunday School Union, 1909), 89-103; Charles A. Shook, *The True Origin of the Book of Mormon* (Cincinnati: Standard Publishing Co., 1914); Robert C. Webb, *The Real Mormonism* (New York: Sturgis & Walton Co., 1916), 400-26; Francis W. Kirkham, *A New Witness for Christ in America: The Book of Mormon* (Independence, MO, 1942), esp. vols. 1 and 2; Leonard Arrington and James Allen, "Mormon Origins in New York: An Introductory Analysis," *Brigham Young University Studies* 9: 241-74; Marvin S. Hill, "The Role of Christian Primitivism in the Origin and Development of the Mormon Kingdom, 1830-1844," Ph.D. diss., University of Chicago, 1968, 80-97; Richard P. Howard, "Beating Solomon Spaulding's Poor, Dead Horse One More Time," *Saints' Herald*, Sept. 1977, 37; and the unpublished work of Dale R. Broadhurst, especially his 1982 "The Secular and the Sacred: An Examination of Selected Parallels in the Writings of Solomon Spalding and The Book of Mormon" and "A New Basis for the Spalding Theory" (Broadhurst Collection).

26. The similarity between early Mormonism and some of Alexander Campbell's teachings has led some to suggest that Smith purloined his primitive gospel from the Disciples through Rigdon. But long before he met Rigdon, Smith was exposed to the Primitivism and Seekerism of his parents and other family members. See Dan Vogel, *Religious Seekers and the Advent of Mormonism* (Salt Lake City: Signature Books, 1988), and Marvin S. Hill, *Quest for Refuge: The Mormon Flight from American Pluralism* (Salt Lake City: Signature Books, 1989).

27. When Martin Harris, who had served on Palmyra's anti-Masonic vigilance committee, first arrived in Ohio he announced that the Book of Mormon is "the Anti-masonick Bible" (*Geauga Gazette*, 15 Mar. 1831). "The Mormon Bible is anti-masonic," added the editor of the *Ohio Star* the following week, "and it is a singular truth that every one of its followers, so far as we are able to ascertain, are anti-masons" (*Ohio Star*, 24 Mar. 1831).

Joseph Smith's anti-Masonic stance at the time the Book of Mormon was dictated can be explained by the fact that his father, a member of Ontario Masonic Lodge No. 23 (Canandaigua, NY) since 1817, left the craft in the aftermath of the notorious 1826 abduction of anti-Masonic crusader William Morgan and was considered a seceder Mason. See Mervin B. Hogan, "The Two Joseph Smiths' Masonic Experiences," 1987, privately circulated, and Stanley Upton Mock, *The Morgan Episode in American Free Masonry* (East Aurora, NY: Roycrofters, 1930).

28. *Millennial Harbinger* 1 (10 Feb. 1831): 93.

29. Cited in LDS *Church News*, 8 Dec. 1985, 10.

CHAPTER 12.

Loss of Zion

Verily this is the word of the Lord, that the city of New Jerusalem shall be built
by the gathering of the saints, beginning at this place [Independence, Missouri], even
the place of the temple, which temple shall be reared in this generation. For verily this
generation shall not all pass away until an house shall be built unto the Lord (D&C
84:4-5).

Mormonism in its purest distillation is the fused product of Joseph Smith's
and Sidney Rigdon's revolutionary thinking condensed into the prophet's
revelations. Their joint vision recast existing American social, economic, and
political systems into an apocalyptic model they called Zion. Faced with the
uncertainty, if not the menace of the future, their followers were drawn from daily
routines into a larger-than-life existence in which the group's endeavors took on
an epic quality.

The original Smith/Rigdon vision of Zion, their shared plan of an insular
and self-reliant community, was nothing new to nineteenth-century America,
permeated as it was with secular and religious communitarian societies. What was
more or less unique about the Mormon religious commonwealth was the
application of biblical prophecies and events to the American scene. Jackson
County, Missouri, at the heart of the continent, was the site of the fabled city of
New Jerusalem. And that sacred ground, declared the prophet—not Mesopotamia
or the Great Rift Valley of Africa—had been old Eden, the cradle of humanity.[1]

America, according to Mormon teachings, had been held in special trust since
the dawn of time. This majestic land was again ready to fulfill its role as a sanctuary,
a place of refuge and inheritance. What for other millenarian faiths was the
imminent end, for the Mormons was a new beginning. "Fired by a Biblical
imagination which fused history and myth, Old Testament and New, into one
consuming vision," wrote one later observer, Mormonism reflected high-wrought
millenarian excitement:

> The Prophet would re-enact an old drama, rehearsed in every gospel dispensation
> when the righteous sought to separate themselves from the wicked in special
> gatherings: Enoch's holy city, Noah's seaworthy ark, Abraham's intrepid family, the

142

great migration of the tribes under Moses, the flights of *Book of Mormon* peoples under Lehi, Mulek, and the brother of Jared, the establishment of the Primitive Church—momentous gatherings followed all too often by heartbreaking captivities and dispersions or dissolutions. But now, in the fulness of times, after the long night of Christian apostasy, Israel by blood and by adoption was being called home. Rachel would weep no more for her children, Ezekiel's dry bones were being quickened, the clay of Jeremiah's potter reworked, Isaiah's remnant ransomed. It was Daniel's stone ready to roll forth, and St. John's heavenly city about to come to earth.[2]

Sidney Rigdon, on behalf of the First Presidency, sent an elaborate draft of plans for Zion, this idealized city of New Jerusalem, to church leaders in Jackson County, Missouri, on 25 June 1833. He included extensive architectural details "of the house to be built immediately . . . for the [First] Presidency."[3] The heart of the city of New Jerusalem, as specified in Rigdon's packet of information, would be three large blocks set apart for a twelve-building temple complex. Most studies incorrectly presume that Rigdon's disenchantment with Joseph Smith began later in Nauvoo when the prophet sought Rigdon's daughter as a plural wife. To the contrary, his loss of faith was gradual, a discontent that initially erupted when the prophet's vision of the New Jerusalem and subsequent promises of Mormon redress proved failures of epic proportion. While Copernicus reversed the early Christian belief that the earth was the center of the universe, Missouri mobs annulled desultory Mormon plans to build utopia in Jackson County and evoke the second advent of Jesus Christ.

From their earliest years, Mormons in both Ohio and Missouri began to isolate themselves. To validate their uniqueness they minimized socialization with outsiders and emphasized their differences. Being eccentric made them feel special, and they did not understand that what seemed to be solidarity to them appeared to be insularity to outsiders, an exclusivity that would provoke tragic misunderstandings, persecution, and bloodshed.

Beliefs radically different from those of orthodox denominations have escaped armed opposition in America even when they have outraged generally accepted social norms. Harmonists in Pennsylvania and Indiana as well as Shaker congregations in several areas advocated a community of goods and proclaimed the imminent coming of Christ. They did so without exciting neighbors or arousing the enmity of outsiders. The Wallingford Community in Connecticut and the Oneida Community in New York State practiced free love without persecution. The deciding distinction between such groups and Mormons was that the former neither sought political power nor pressed their opinions on outsiders through newspapers or proselyting.

The political aims of Mormons and Missourians were on a collision course, a clash of disparate cultures, from the beginning. What separated them until it fused them in violence was a profound disagreement, a glitch in the moral

geography that permits parallel lives to meet and explode. "Missourians," according to one study of the culture of this period, "were . . . emotional, quick-tempered,
quarrelsome, and ruthless. . . . Rugged individualism and ill-temper were problems
whenever the men met together at muster for the militia, for work on the public
roads, at political gatherings, and on other occasions."[4] Missouri Mormons,
cocooned in a superiority complex, were arrogant and self-righteous. Their zeal
was viewed as presumptuous and contemptuous by local non-Mormons.[5]

According to early LDS historian John Whitmer, problems in Jackson County
started as early as March 1832 when "the enemies held a counsel . . . how they
might destroy the saints."[6] Another account noted that when the meeting came
to a close the leaders of the group determined to rid the country of "this tribe of
locusts that . . . threaten to scorch and wither the herbage of a fair and good portion
of Missouri."[7]

The contemporary opinion on the Mormon mass migration into Jackson
County was expressed clearly in a 31 August 1833 *Cleveland Herald* article (citing
the *St. Louis Republican*) entitled "The Mormonites—Persecution":

> [T]he citizens have been daily told that they are to be cut off and their lands
> appropriated to the Mormons for inheritances; but they are not fully agreed among
> themselves as to the manner in which this shall be accomplished, whether by the
> destroying angel, the judgment of God, or the arm of power. The committee express
> their fears that, should this population continue to increase, they will soon have all
> the offices of the country in their hands; and that the lives and property of other
> citizens would be insecure, under the administration of men who are so ignorant and
> superstitious as to believe that they have been subjects of miraculous and supernatural
> cures; hold converse with God and his angels and possess and exercise the gift of
> divination, and of unknown tongues; and are, withal, so poor as to be unable to
> procure bread and meat. The committee says, that "one of the means resorted to by
> them, in order to drive us to emigrate, is an indirect invitation to the free brethren of
> color in Illinois, to come like the rest to the land of Zion."[8]

Within days of the citizens' committee gathering, vigilantes, "in the deadly
hours of the night, commenced stoning or brick-batting some of the [Saints']
houses."[9] Covert harassment continued until 15 July 1833 when the vigilance
committee of Jackson County residents openly advocated driving the Saints from
the county. In a lengthy epistle they charged Mormons with a multitude of offenses,
including religious fanaticism, introducing to Missouri the "dregs of that society
from which they came lazy, [i]dle and vicious," tampering with slaves, and "enviting
free negroes and mulatoes from other States to become Mormons, and remove
and settle among us."[9]

They were further accused of blaspheming "the *most* high God, and cast
contempt on his holy religion, by pretending to receive revelations direct from
heaven by pretending to speak in unknown tongues, by direct inspiration, and by

divine pretentions derogatory of God and religion, and to utter subversion of human reason." They also cited the Saints as openly declaring that "God has given them this country of land and that sooner or later they must and will have the possession of our lands, for an inheritance."[10]

The issue of slavery has been overplayed in the Jackson County expulsion. The primary dispute centered on blood-and-soil nationalism, a discord similar in intensity and perspective to the modern Moslem world's anger over Israel. Mormons, without the prior-rights claims of twentieth-century Jews, simply viewed the Promised Land as their God-given entitlement. They proclaimed that high-minded belief to native Missourians, who naturally took umbrage.

Alexander Majors, who spent his youth in Jackson County, later wrote: "The cause of all this trouble was solely from the claim that they had a new revelation direct from the Almighty, making them the chosen instruments to go forward, let it please or displease whoever it might, to build the New Jerusalem on the spot above referred to, Temple Lot."[11] Colonel Pitcher, one of the principles in the Missouri difficulties, gave a newspaper writer an interview in 1881 on the troubles in Jackson County, where he had resided since 1826. He stated that Mormons and old settlers got along well until W. W. Phelps began to publish "the so called revelations of Joseph Smith" in The Morning and Evening Star. "The Mormons, as a rule," he wrote,

> were an ignorant and a fanatical people, though there were some very intelligent men among them. The troubles of 1833, which led to their expulsion from the county, were originated by these fanatics making boasts that they intended to possess the entire county, saying that God had promised it to them and they were going to have it. This of course caused ill feeling toward them, which continued to grow more and more bitter, until the final uprising.[12]

When specifically asked whether slavery was a factor he answered, "No, I don't think that matter had anything to do with it. The Mormons, it is true, were northern and eastern people, and 'free soilers,' but they did not interfere with the negroes and we did not care whether they owned slaves or not."[13]

Once the Jackson County vigilance committee framed its written opposition to the Mormon presence, the group placed a copy of its proceedings at the post office and sent copies to principal newspapers in the eastern and middle states so "the Mormon brethren may know at a distance that the gates of Zion are closed against them—that their interests will be best promoted by remaining among those who know and appreciate their merits."[14]

Five days later the committee called on Mormon leaders in Independence and asked them to leave the county, allowing them fifteen minutes to formulate a reply. Meanwhile a crowd gathered at Independence Square and demanded the discontinuance of the church printing establishment, the church storehouse, and the "cessation of all mechanical labors." When church members refused to comply, the group destroyed the printing office and tarred and feathered Bishop Edward Partridge and Charles Allen.[15]

Under threat of destruction, Sidney Gilbert closed the doors of the storehouse to business. Three days later, church leaders were forced to sign a written agreement to leave the county by 1 January 1834. Despite firm assurances that God would protect the Mormon people, the Missourians had beaten their hand, so to speak, and won the pot.

Oliver Cowdery went to Kirtland to inform Smith and Rigdon of the turn of events in Missouri. Shortly after Cowdery's arrival, Smith issued a revelation. In omniscient-sounding language the revelation (now D&C 101) explained why the promised Mormon plans of a just and stable society in the New Jerusalem ended so disastrously. Even though Missouri Saints had given up prior lives, profitable ventures, families, and friends, the revelation proclaimed their sacrifices inadequate, their efforts to seek a renewed sense of community and spiritual nourishment not enough. The manifestation criticized the Saints for their "jarrings, and contentions, and envyings, and strifes, and lustful and covetous desires." They had been "slow to hearken unto the voice of the Lord," and in their sins had "polluted their inheritances."

Nevertheless, the beleaguered adherents were promised relief through redress. "Let them importune at the feet of the judge," the revelation continued. "And if he heed them not, let them importune at the feet of the governor; and if the governor heed them not, let them importune at the feet of the president; and if the president heed them not, then will the Lord arise and come forth out of his hiding place, and in his fury vex the nation" (D&C 101:86-89).

In response to this admonition, several petitions were sent to John F. Ryland, judge of the Fifth Circuit Court, Missouri governor Daniel Dunklin, and U.S. president Andrew Jackson. One petition to Dunklin, bearing 114 signatures, related the burning of Mormon homes, the destruction of their lands and labor, "savage barbarities" with clubs, sticks, firearms and knives, of hunger, and of "mangled bodies."[16]

Dunklin responded instructing the Saints to organize themselves and apply for public arms "unless exempted by religious scruples." He addressed their civil injuries thus:

> I must refer you to the courts; such questions rest with them exclusively. The laws are sufficient to afford a remedy for every injury of this kind, and whenever you make out a case entitling you to damage, there can be no doubt entertained of their ample reward. Justice is somewhat slow in its progress, but it is not less sure on that account.[17]

Under the governor's protective guard, Mormons were escorted into Independence to bring criminal charges against the committee, which provoked a violent response on the outskirts of town. On 31 October 1833, rabble-rousers demolished houses and whipped several Mormons. Intimidated judges refused to issue warrants and the violence continued. On 4 November a skirmish on the Big Blue River resulted in the deaths of one Mormon and two Missourians. The Missouri attorney general, realizing the potent force of the mobocrats, advised Mormons to "relinquish all hope of criminal prosecution to effect anything against the band of outlaws." The Mormons returned under guard dejected and fearful of ever obtaining their rights and possessions. Compelled to leave their "Promised Land," they fled across the Missouri River into LaFayette and Clay counties. Parley Pratt wrote that the waterway shore

> began to be lined on both sides of the ferry with men, women, and children; goods, wagons, boxes, provisions, etc., while the ferry was constantly employed; and when night again closed upon us the cottonwood bottom had much the appearance of a camp meeting. Hundreds of people were seen in every direction, some in tents and some in the open air around the fires, while the rain descended in torrents. Husbands were inquiring for their wives, wives for their husbands; parents for their children, and children for parents. Some had the good fortune to escape with their families, household goods, and some provisional goods. The scene was indescribable, and, I am sure, would have melted the hearts of any people on the earth, except our blind oppressors, and a blind and ignorant community.[18]

As soon as the prophet received word of the plight he issued a revelation on 16 December 1833 which thundered in God's voice: "I have sworn, and the decree hath gone forth by a former commandment which I have given unto you, that I would let fall the sword of mine indignation in the behalf of my people; and even as I have said, it shall come to pass." Through a parable the revelation explained church leaders were to gather

> all the strength of mine house, which are my warriors, my young men, and they that are of middle age . . . and go ye straightway unto the land of my vineyard, and redeem my vineyard; for it is mine; I have bought it with money. Therefore . . . break down the walls of mine enemies . . . and scatter their watchmen. And inasmuch as they gather together against you, avenge me of mine enemies, that by and by I may come with the residue of mine house and possess the land (D&C 101:55-58).

An additional edict, issued 24 February 1834, explained why the Jackson County mobs had driven out the Mormons:

> I will pour out my wrath without measure in mine own time. For I have suffered [the Missourians] thus far, that they might fill up the measure of their iniquities, that their cup might be full[.] . . . [T]hey are as salt that has lost its savor, and is thenceforth good for nothing but to be cast out and trodden under foot of men. But verily I say unto you, I have decreed that your brethren which have been scattered shall return to the lands of their inheritances, and shall build up the waste places of Zion.
> For after much tribulation, as I have said unto you in a former commandment, cometh the blessing. Behold, this is the blessing which I have promised after your tribulations, and the tribulations of your brethren—your redemption, and the redemp-

tion of your brethren, even their restoration to the land of Zion, to be established, no more to be thrown down. . . . Behold, I say unto you, the redemption of Zion must needs come by power (D&C 103:2-15).

The "big stick" by which church leaders intended to gain the "victory and glory" promised to them in the revelation was a quasi-military campaign subsequently known as Zion's Camp, a portent of Mormon militaristic aggression to come. Missouri church leaders Sidney Gilbert, W. W. Phelps, Edward Partridge, John Corrill, and John Whitmer wrote to Governor Dunklin in April to advise him that "a number of our brethren, perhaps two or three hundred, would remove to Jackson [C]ounty in the course of the coming summer." They wrote that the camp's objective was "purely to defend ourselves and possessions . . . inasmuch as the executive of this state cannot keep up a military force 'to protect our people in that county, without transcending his power.'"[19]

Smith's role in redeeming Zion was drawn from biblical mythology and announced in the 24 February 1834 revelation: "I will raise up unto my people a man, who shall lead them like as Moses led the children of Israel. For ye are the children of Israel, and of the seed of Abraham; and ye must needs be led out of bondage by power, and with a stretched out arm. . . . Mine angels shall go up before you, and also my presence, and in time ye shall possess the goodly land" (D&C 103:15-20). Rigdon's role was also specified: "It is my will that my servant Sidney Rigdon shall lift up his voice in the congregations in the eastern countries, in preparing the churches to keep the commandments which I have given unto them concerning the restoration and redemption of Zion" (v. 29).

Rigdon and Lyman Wight, along with three other sets of missionaries designated as recruiters for Zion's Camp, left Kirtland on 26 February 1834 for upstate New York. At conference after conference they asked young men to assist in the campaign. They also sought to gather funding to purchase more land in Zion and to "obtain money for the relief of the brethren in Kirtland, say two thousand dollars, which sum would deliver the Church in Kirtland from debt."[20] Instead of collecting $2,000 during their three-week excursion, donations amounted to just $189. Their recruiting efforts fell short also. Commanded to raise a 500-man army of liberation, church leaders were barely able to raise 100 volunteers and the necessary provisions to equip them.

Smith's disappointment was reflected in a 1 April 1834 letter to Orson Hyde who was still in New York. The prophet lamented that if the Saints would not help their brethren "when they can not do it without sacrifice, with those blessings which God had bestowed upon them, I prophesy, I speak the truth, I lie not, God shall take away their talent, and shall prevent them from ever obtaining a place of refuge, or an inheritance upon the land of Zion." He closed his letter by writing: "I therefore adjure you to beseech them in the name of the Lord, by the Son of God, to lend us a helping hand; and if all this will not soften their hearts to administer to our necessity for Zion's sake, turn your back on them, and return speedily to Kirtland; and the blood of Zion be upon their heads, even as upon the heads of their enemies."[21]

The quest for donations and recruits continued throughout the spring of 1834. On Friday, 19 April, Smith and Rigdon left for a campaign in Medina County, Ohio. During a conference at Norton two days later Smith prophesied that "the time is near when desolation is to cover the earth." Without the redemption of Zion "we must fall." He predicted that "the time is near when the sun will be darkened, and the moon turn to blood, and the stars fall from heaven, and the earth reel to and fro." He added that "if we are not sanctified and gathered to the places God has appointed . . . we must fall." Rigdon took the stand and continued in the same apocalyptic line of thought in discussing the gathering, deliverance of Zion, and the Second Advent "now just before us."[22]

On 1 May, Zion's Camp began to assemble at Kirtland. Recruiters sought money, horses, wagons, guns, clothing, bedding, other supplies, and able-bodied men. Three days later Smith and Rigdon held Sunday services under the shade of the new school house. Joseph spoke briefly, followed by Sidney, who, in militant rhetoric, urged the men to deeds of valor and promised them the glory of Christian martyrs and the victories of the ancient Hebrew legions. He then announced that the prophet and high council had agreed to his suggestion to change the name of the church from "The Church of Christ" to "The Church of the Latter-day Saints," emphasizing the proximity of the Millennium.

The following day the main body of 100 members of Zion's Camp left Kirtland. Ultimately the group swelled to 205 men led by Smith. Prior to the exodus, Smith and others placed their hands on Rigdon and "confirmed upon him the blessings of wisdom and knowledge to preside over the Church" in the prophet's absence. He was promised the "blessing of old age and peace, till Zion is built up and Kirtland established, till all his enemies are under his feet, and of a crown of eternal life in the Kingdom of God with us."[23]

Rigdon's first official communication as acting president was a 10 May circular letter co-authored by his assistant Oliver Cowdery. The document requested more volunteers to join Zion's Camp and explained the rationale for not turning a Christian cheek to Jackson County:

> Should we quietly submit to this abuse, none embracing this gospel would be safe in any part of our country; for the adversary of righteousness would influence this wicked generation to slay us where ever we could be found, and we should be left without a place to lay our heads in safety. We have the right of citizenship and of the protection of the laws while we conduct ourselves circumspectly, and God has never required that we should submit to these abuses without exerting ourselves against them. If we were to remain quiet, when our property and homes were taken from us by wicked

men, where would our women, and our helpless infants look for support, and whither would they flee for protection?

The letter further explained that the governor of Missouri, who was aware of their march, would feel duty bound to call out the militia to aid and protect them:

> The privilege of being among those who redeem and prepare the land, upon which unborn generations are to rejoice in the salvation of God ought to inspire every heart, and stimulate every saint in action in the great work. Our brethren should remember, that it is not the work of a few days, but that they are laying the foundation of an order of things which is to remain while time endures. And what can be more pleasing, than the reflection, that by our diligence we prepare a habitation and a place of security where our children can be preserved among the shock which is to dissolve the nations?[24]

The camp's thousand-mile trek across Ohio, Indiana, Illinois, and Missouri was made in forty-six days. Missouri governor Dunklin had promised to reinstate the Saints upon the "lands of their inheritance" provided they could defend themselves afterwards. But when Mormon emissaries Orson Hyde and Parley Pratt visited the governor and informed him that the Saints were on their way, he announced that he had changed his mind. He could see that a prolonged armed conflict would ensue if Mormons were returned to their homes.[25]

Even before Dunklin's decision took the wind out of their sails, Smith and others came to realize that the camp could not succeed. In a 4 June 1834 letter to his wife he wrote:

> Our numbers and means are altogether too small for the accomplishment of such a great enterprise, . . . our holy hope is that whilst we deter the enemy, and terrify them for a little season (for we learn by means of some spies we send out for that purpose that they are greatly terrified) notwithstanding they are endeavoring to make a formidable stand.[26]

After a siege of cholera brought on by contaminated water, intimidation from a larger force of Missourians, and a terrible storm, the prophet was ready to return his disheartened force to Ohio. Newspaper accounts incorrectly reported that during a battle with Jackson County citizens Smith had been wounded in the leg, the shattered limb amputated, and that he had died three days later.[27] To the contrary, neither Smith nor any of his liberation force set foot in Jackson County.[28]

Before departing for home, the prophet issued an elaborate rationalization for the unsuccessful effort to redeem Zion. Their failures were attributed to "the transgressions of my people. . . . [T]hey have not learned to be obedient to the things which I required at their hands, but are full of all manner of evil, and do not impart of their substance, as becometh saints, to the poor and afflicted among them."[29]

For many, the bugle call to redeem Zion was a hurried march to disillusionment. From the beginning men presumed they were "going to fight the battle of the Lord and redeem Zion."[30] Nathan Tanner wrote that "sum of the camp became angry & said they had rather die than return without a fite."[31] To assuage the discontent, the prophet in his revelation on the subject admonished the men to "wait for a little season . . . to let my army become very great . . . and that her banners may be terrible unto all nations" (D&C 105:31). He promised the failed liberators that "within three years they should march to Jackson County and there should not be a dog to open his mouth against them."[32]

On 1 August Smith and other Zion's Camp members finally arrived back in Kirtland. The *Painesville Telegraph* wrote the week of 8 August:

> Gen. Joe Smith, with his army of fanatics returned to his old head quarters in this country on Saturday last, after an absence of three months, during the most of which time they have been on the march to and from Missouri. This expedition may be considered as one of the veriest "wild goose chases" to be found upon record. . . . [S]everal hundred armed men have been dragged nearly 800 miles, in the heat of the Summer, for the express purpose of "taking Zion."

Gentiles were not the only ones to take a dim view. Sylvester Smith, a disgruntled camp member, accused Joseph Smith of "prophesying lies in the name of the Lord."[33] After a lengthy examination the high council exonerated the prophet on 11 August. But Sylvester Smith continued his complaints. Rigdon came to the prophet's aid by preferring charges against Sylvester on 23 August 1834. The Kirtland High Council met five days later and again vindicated Joseph.

In an effort to settle problems arising from the abortive march, Smith called a special gathering of all camp members on 14 February 1835. After explaining that God had commanded him to arrange the meeting, he said, "God had not designed all this for nothing, but He had it in remembrance yet; and it was the will of God that those who went to Zion, with a determination to lay down their lives, if necessary, should be ordained to the ministry, and go forth to prune the vineyard for the last time, or the coming of the Lord, which was nigh—even fifty-six years should wind up the scene."[34]

Most nineteenth-century Mormons seemed not to notice when ill-fated predictions about the end of the world or the redemption of Zion misfired. Prophetic failures ripple into the future like echoes in time. In 1890, for example, it was widely believed among Utah Mormons that Joseph Smith's 1835 end-of-the-world prediction would find immediate fulfillment. Oliver Huntington, writing in his 1875 diary, recalled the prophet saying that "God had revealed to him that the coming of Christ would be within 56 years, which being added to 1835 shows that before 1891 and the 14th of Feb. the Savior of the world would make his appearance again upon the earth and the winding up scene take place."[35] Apostle Moses Thatcher believed the same,[36] as did B. H. Roberts, who noted in general conference on 27 October 1890 that "Before another General Conference shall be reached we shall have entered upon the year 1891. He then read from D&C 130 and also commented on the prophet's statements of 14 February 1835 where he said 'even 56 years should wind up the scene.'"[37] But as 1891 passed, enthusiasm for the prophet's prophecy diminished. In 1903, Patriarch Benjamin F. Johnson, a close friend of Joseph Smith, could not conceal his disappointment when he remarked "we were over seventy years ago taught by our leaders to believe that the coming of Christ and the millennial reign was much nearer than we believe it to be now."[38]

An important part of that failed dream was the expectation, fostered now for over 160 years, that the expulsion from Jackson County, Missouri, was only temporary. John Whitmer, early Mormon historian, noted the tradition among early Saints that "those who obeyed the covenant in the last days, would never die: but by experience, they have learned to the contrary."[39] Mormons today face the reality that the generation of Saints alive in 1832 did not live to see the redemption of Zion, the establishment of the holy city of New Jerusalem, or the second coming of Christ, all of which were promised in revelations, patriarchal blessings, and numerous pronouncements by church leaders.

On 6 April 1845, for example, Brigham Young, who never set foot in Independence, Missouri, stated: "As the Lord lives we will build up Jackson County in this generation."[40] Folklore has it that in the big barn on his estate behind the Eagle Gate in downtown Salt Lake City, Young kept a carriage in readiness for the return which, for unknown reasons, he thought would take place around 1869.[41] Wilford Woodruff recorded in his 23 August 1862 diary that while standing on the Salt Lake temple block President Young said:

> If we do not Hurry with this I am afraid we shall not get it up untill we have to go back to Jackson County which I Expe[c]t will be in 7 years. I do not want to quite finish this Temple for there will not be any Temple finished untill the One is finished in Jackson County Missouri pointed out by Joseph Smith. *Keep this a secret to yourselves* lest some may be discouraged. Some things we should keep to ourselves.[42]

Speaking to the survivors of Zion's Camp on 10 October 1864 Young further expounded on the imminence of the return, promising that "if that Company behaved v[e]ry well they should be the first Company Chosen to go back to Jackson County."[43]

Orson Pratt, a member of Zion's Camp, was another prominent leader who continually reminded congregations that the revelations promised a return in his generation. On 20 May 1855 he said:

> When the Saints were driven out from Jackson County, almost all in the Church expected that they would speedily be restored; and a person was considered almost an apostate that would say, they would not come back in five years, or ten at the furthest; but the prevailing opinion seemed to be that it would take place immediately. . . .

Now . . . twenty-two years have passed since that time, and we look around now. . . . The people think of almost everything else but the redemption of Zion . . . so far as the revelations go, in speaking of this subject, I think that this event is nearer than this people are aware of.

Again, take the subject of the coming of Christ, and as far back as 1831 . . . I found many Saints thinking that Christ would come immediately. . . . No doubt they felt exceedingly anxious to have him come, as we all do, and this anxiety overcame them, and hence they were mistaken. I have no doubt that there are others in the Church that think it is a far off event, an event that will probably take place in the days of their youngest children; but from what is written, I look upon it as an event that is much nearer than is generally supposed. . . . Christ seems to be near at hand, yet Zion must be redeemed before that day; the temple must be built upon the consecrated spot, the cloud and glory of the Lord rest upon it, and the Lamanites, many of them, brought in, and they must build up the NEW JERUSALEM![44]

Elder George Q. Cannon, a powerful member of the LDS First Presidency during the administrations of John Taylor and Wilford Woodruff, said in 1864 general conference: "The day is near when a Temple shall be reared in the Center Stake of Zion, and the Lord has said his glory shall rest on that House in this generation, that is the generation in which the revelation was given, which is upwards of thirty years ago."[45]

Wilford Woodruff, future church president, prophesied during a two-day meeting in Logan, Utah, that "thirty years hence in *1898*" all would have been fulfilled.[46] So confident was Woodruff that the church would return to Jackson County in his lifetime that he approved a $20,000 loan to the Hedrickites, Jackson County owners of the temple lot, to build a meeting house on the block with the temple block as security, hoping the group would default and Mormons would become the rightful owner.[47]

Lorenzo Snow, commenting on the return in an 1870 address, said "when we returned from Provo [during the move] I believed we were on our return to Jackson Co & I shall still believe it untill I learn to the Contrary."[48] Later, Snow said in general conference:

The time is speedily coming—we do not want to talk very much though about going to Jackson County, Missouri. . . . We are not going tomorrow, nor next day, this week or next week; but we are going, and there are many hundreds and hundreds within the sound of my voice that will live to go back to Jackson County and build a holy temple to the Lord our God.[49]

While president of the church in 1900, Snow again affirmed during a special priesthood meeting in the Salt Lake temple that "there are many here now under the sound of my voice, probably a majority, who will live to go back to Jackson County and assist in building that temple."[50]

In patriarchal blessings and other prophetic pronouncements Latter-day

Saints have been similarly promised they would witness the Second Coming in the flesh. When Brigham Young's brother Phineas was so ill doctors told him he would die, "Brother Joseph Smith came to see me, and blessed me, and told me that I should live to see the redemption of Zion."[51] Lydia Knight was also promised in 1830 by Joseph Smith, Sr., "You shall be preserved in life . . . thou shalt stand to see Israel gather from their dispersion, the ten tribes come from the land of the north country; the heavens rend, and the Son of Man come in all the glory of His Father. And thou shalt rise to meet Him and reign with Him a thousand years."[52]

In 1837 Wilford Woodruff was promised that he would "stand in the flesh & witness the winding up scene of this generation," that he would "remain on the earth to behold thy Savior Come in the Clouds of heaven."[53] And James M. Workes's patriarchal blessing assures: "Thou shalt come to thy inheritance in the land of Zion before you die, or are translated which shall be according to thy faith."[54] Other examples include blessings for William Goates, Sr.,[55] Amman Rowan,[56] Lyman Johnson,[57] Heber C. Kimball,[58] William Smith,[59] and Orson Hyde whose promise that "he *shall* stand on the earth and bring souls till Christ comes"[60] was changed in the *History of the Church* to read "he *may* stand on the earth and bring souls till Christ comes."[61]

Countless end-of-the-world scares, starting as far back as A.D. 534 and continuing to the present, have resulted from precise interpretations of ambiguous scriptural texts and mystical readings of changes in nature or numerology. At the turn of the last millennium, in 999, people were convinced that the Day of Judgment, prophesied in the book of Revelation was at hand. It was widely preached and believed that Christ would make his promised reappearance in Jerusalem, so vast numbers of people began streaming toward the Holy Land after selling their possessions to finance their pilgrimage:

> Buildings of every sort were suffered to fall into ruins. It was thought useless to repair them, when the end of the world was so near. Many noble edifices were deliberately pulled down. Even churches, so well maintained, shared the general neglect. Knights, citizens and serfs, travelled eastward in company, taking with them their wives and children, singing psalms as they went, and looking with fearful eyes upon the sky, which they expected each minute to open, to let the Son of God descend in his glory.[62]

Even though the faith of these legions ended in disillusionment and poverty, the same mistakes on smaller scales were repeated again in 1100, 1200, and 1245.

A millennial enthusiast known to both Rigdon and Smith was William Miller (1782-1849), also dubbed "Crazy Miller, the end-o-the-worldman," "that fanatic," or "Miller the Prophet." In 1818, following two years of intensive study of the scriptures, he reached the conclusion that the time of Christ's second advent would be in 1843. When 1843 passed without incident, Miller explained that he had erred in following the Hebrew rather than the Roman chronology. Instead of 1843, he predicted, the date of the Second Advent was 22 October 1844. As the date drew near a quickened tempo and greater urgency possessed believers. Some Millerites, dressed in white robes, left their shops, homes and farms to await the coming of Christ on rooftops and hills. But as one account put it, "Their Lord came not, and the day of sweet expectation had become the day of bitter disappointment."[63]

Psychologists have long recognized that when prophecies fail, followers often bounce back with greater faith than before.[64] When Mormon prophecies fail, members resort to self-blame. The loss of Zion, the city of New Jerusalem, was a consequence of their misdeeds.

In 1838-39 both Rigdon and Smith would come to realize that the city of New Jerusalem was a glittering improbability and that Zion would likely not be redeemed in the near future. Alanson Ripley reported that "Joseph Smith, Jr., counseled to sell all the land in Jackson, and all other land in the state."[65] This countered the earlier position that the lands could not be sold because "to sell our land would amount to a denial of our faith as that land is the place where the Zion of God shall stand, according to our faith and belief in the revelations of god and upon which Israel will be gathered according to the prophets."[66] Eventually Zion was metaphorically enlarged to include the entire American continent, despite a previous 10 October 1833 declaration: "At this time the evil and designing circulated a report that *Zion* was to be *extended* as far east as Ohio, which in some degree tended to distract the minds of the saints, and produced a momentary indecision about removing thither, according to the commandments; but the report was soon corrected."[67] While a modern Zion in Missouri represented the longings of Joseph Smith, Jr., and Sidney Rigdon, other concerns gnawed at the membership. When the dream of a temple and Christ's second coming suffered an irreversible setback, attention shifted back to Kirtland where Smith and Rigdon planned and executed a "sort of sacred space in exile."[68]

Notes

Unless otherwise stated, all primary sources cited are located in the Historical Department of the Church of Jesus Christ of Latter-day Saints, Salt Lake City, Utah.

1. Wilford Woodruff recorded in his diary on 30 March 1873 that President Brigham Young said:

Joseph the Prophet told me that the garden of Eden was in Jackson Co Missouri, & when Adam was driven out of the garden of Eden He went about 40 miles to the Place which we Named Adam Ondi Ahman, & there built an Altar of Stone & offered Sacrifice. That Altar remains to this day. I saw it as Adam left it as did many others & through all the revolutions of the world that Altar had not been disturbed. Joseph also said that when the City of Enoch fled & was translated it was whare the gulf of

Mexico now is. It left that gulf a body of water (Scott G. Kenney, ed., *Wilford Woodruff's Journal–Typescript*, 9 vols. [Midvale, UT: Signature Books, 1983], 7:129).

2. William Mulder, "Mormonism's 'Gathering': An American Doctrine With A Difference," *Church History* 23 (Sept. 1954): 8.

3. Joseph Smith, *History of the Church of Jesus Christ of Latter-day Saints*, B. H. Roberts, ed., 7 vols. (Salt Lake City: The Church of Jesus Christ of Latter-day Saints, 1902), 1:363; hereafter referred to as *History of the Church*.

4. Max H. Parkin, *A Study of the Nature and Causes of External and Internal Conflict of the Mormons in Ohio Between 1830 and 1838* (Salt Lake City: Department of Seminaries and Institutions of Religion, 1967), 76.

5. For excellent discussions of the causes underlying the conflict in Jackson County, see Warren A. Jennings, "The City in the Garden: Social Conflict in Jackson County, Missouri," in F. Mark McKiernan, Alma R. Blair, and Paul M. Edwards, eds., *The Restoration Movement: Essays in Mormon History* (Lawrence, KS: Coronado Press, 1973), 99-119; and Warren A. Jennings, "Zion is Fled: The Expulsion of the Mormons from Jackson County, Missouri," Ph.D. diss., University of Florida, 1962.

6. F. Mark McKiernan and Roger D. Launius, eds., *An Early Latter Day Saint History: The Book of John Whitmer: Kept By Commandment* (Independence, MO: Herald Publishing House, 1980), 86.

7. Alphonso Wetmore, *Gazetter of the State of Missouri* (St. Louis: C. Keemle, 1837), 94.

8. Mormon Manuscript Retrieval Project, box 3, fd 3, Special Collections, Harold B. Lee Library, Brigham Young University, Provo, Utah; hereafter Special Collections, BYU.

9. *Evening and Morning Star* (Kirtland, OH), Dec. 1833.

10. McKiernan and Launius, 88-90.

11. Alexander Majors, *Seventy Years on the Frontier, Being Memoirs of a Lifetime on the Border* (Chicago, N.P., 1893), 53.

12. R. Etzenhouser, *From Palmyra, New York, 1830 to Independence, Missouri, 1894* (Independence, MO: Ensign Publishing House, 1894), 323.

13. Ibid., 324.

14. Ibid., 332-33.

15. *History of the Church*, 1:390.

16. McKiernan and Launius, 99.

17. Ibid., 101-102.

18. Parley P. Pratt, Jr., ed., *Autobiography of Parley Parker Pratt* (Salt Lake City: Deseret Book Co., 1976), 101. About 1,000 Mormons (including unbaptized children) fled Jackson County in the fall of 1833 (Max H. Parkin, "A History of the Latter-Day Saints In Clay County, Missouri, From 1833 to 1837," Ph.D diss., Brigham Young University, 1976, 33).

19. McKiernan and Launius, 104. For a detailed treatment of Zion's Camp, see Peter Crawley, "The Political and Social Realities of Zion's Camp," M.A. thesis, Brigham Young University, 1973; and Roger D. Launius, "Zion's Camp and the Redemption of Jackson County, Missouri," M.A. thesis, Louisiana State University, 1978.

20. *History of the Church*, 2:44.

21. Roger D. Launius, *Zion's Camp: Expedition to Missouri, 1834* (Independence, MO: Herald Publishing House, 1986), 47.

22. Journal History, 21 Apr. 1834, 1-2—a multi-volume daily history of the church compiled by official church historians.

23. Scott H. Faulring, ed., *An American Prophet's Record: The Diaries and Journals of Joseph Smith* (Salt Lake City: Signature Books in association with Smith Research Associates, 1989), 27.

24. Sidney Rigdon and Oliver Cowdery to "Dear Brethren," 10 May 1834, Sidney Rigdon Collection.

25. Peter Crawley and Richard L. Anderson, "The Political and Social Realities of Zion's Camp," *Brigham Young University Studies* 14 (Summer 1974): 413-14.

26. Dean C. Jessee, *The Personal Writings of Joseph Smith* (Salt Lake City: Deseret Book Co., 1984), 323.

27. See 17 July 1833 article entitled "The Mormons" in *Ohio Atlas and Elyria Advertiser.*

28. Brothers Luke and Lyman Johnson actually did step on Jackson County soil, albeit briefly. Luke's retrospective account noted that the brothers "procured a boat, and rowed over the Missouri River and landed in Jackson Co., where they discharged three rounds of their small arms, and immediately got into the boat, and with all our energies rowed back. Meanwhile the mob . . . lined the shores, and commenced firing upon us, their balls skimming the waters near us. After landing I returned fire and shot across the Missouri River" (*Latter-day Saints' Millennial Star* 26 [Nov. 1864]).

29. This revelation (D&C 105:2-3) was not included in the 1835 edition of the Doctrine and Covenants, and to guard against the possibility of retaliation against anyone mentioned in the revelation and affiliated with the expedition, code names were used in referring to participants. Joseph Smith, for instance, is called Baurak Ale. Sidney Rigdon's code name is Pelagoram.

Brigham Young also blamed the Saints for failing to redeem Zion. On 30 August 1846 he said: "If we had done right & known how to have Magnifyed the Priesthood we should not have been driven from Jackson County" (Kenney, 3:73). On 10 February 1867 he added:

[W]e are not yet prepared to go and establish the Centre Stake of Zion. The Lord tried this in the first place. He called the people together to the place where the New Jerusalem and the great temple will be built, and where He will prepare for the City of Enoch. And He gave revelation after revelation; but the people could not abide them, and the Church was scattered and peeled, and the people hunted from place to place till, finally they were driven into the mountains, and here we are (*Journal of Discourses*, 26 vols. [London: Latter-day Saints' Book Depot, 1854-86], 11 [10 Feb. 1867]: 324; hereafter *Journal of Discourses*).

30. Launius, 51.

31. "Nathan Tanner Biographical History," 13, Special Collections, BYU.

32. Reed Peck, "Mormons So Called" (Quincy, IL: 1839), 3.

33. *History of the Church*, 2:142.

34. Ibid., 182. Futile efforts to raise an army of redemption continued through 1836;

attempts at redress lasted far beyond that. On 24 September 1835, for example, Joseph Smith noted in his diary: "This day the High Council met at my house to take into consid[e]ration the redeem[p]tion of Zion. It was the voice of the spirit of the Lord that we petition to the Governer [of Missouri]. That is those who have been driven out should do so to be set back on their Lands next spring. We [should] go next season to live or dy in Jackson County." That day Smith and Rigdon drew up an Article of Enrollment "for the redem[p]tion of Zion that we may obtain volunteers to go next spring to M[iss]o[uri]. I ask God in the name of Jesus that we may obtain Eight hundred men or one thousand well armed and that they may ac[c]omplish this great work" (Faulring, 34-35).

35. Huntington added that

> in connection with this event, was related by my brother Dimick Huntington, the fact that when Joseph and Hyrum Smith submitted in their feelings to consent to give themselves up to the state mob at Nauvoo Illinois, after they had passed the Mississippi River. Joseph said "if they shed my blood it shall shorten this work 10 years." That taken from 1891 would reduce the time to 1881 which if the true time within which the Saviour should come must be crowded into 6 years (Oliver Huntington diary, 129, Special Collections, BYU).

36. Abraham H. Cannon diary, under date, Utah State Historical Society.

37. *Latter-day Saints' Millennial Star* 43 (27 Oct. 1890): 675.

38. Benjamin F. Johnson to George S. Gibbs, Apr.-Oct., 1903, 18, Special Collections, BYU.

39. McKiernan and Launius, 45.

40. *Times and Seasons* 6 (1 July 1845):956.

41. Mulder, 17.

42. Kenney, 6:71; emphasis in original.

43. Ibid., 192-93.

44. *Journal of Discourses* 3 (20 May 1855): 17.

45. Ibid., 10 (23 Oct. 1864): 344.

46. Kenney, 6:422-23. At Tooele Stake conference on 29 July 1889 Woodruff said: "Many of these young men and maidens that are here to-day will, in my opinion, if they are faithful, stand in the flesh when Christ comes in the clouds of heaven. These young people from the Sabbath Schools and from the Mutual Improvement Associations, will stand in the flesh while the judgments of the Almighty sweep the nations of the earth . . . in fulfilment of the revelations of God" (*Latter-day Saints' Millennial Star* 51 [23 Sept. 1889]: 595).

47. Diary entry for 14 Aug. 1890, in Kenney, 8:118.

48. Wilford Woodruff diary, 23 June 1870, in ibid., 6:559.

49. *Latter-day Saints' Millennial Star* 40 (10 Apr. 1878):64.

50. Cited in Klaus J. Hansen, "The Metamorphosis of the Kingdom of God: Toward a Reinterpretation of Mormon History," *Dialogue: A Journal of Mormon Thought* 1 (Autumn 1966):74.

51. Elden Jay Watson, comp., *Manuscript History of Brigham Young* (Salt Lake City: Elden Jay Watson, 1968), xxvii.

52. "Homespun," *Lydia Knight's History* (Salt Lake City: Juvenile Instructor Office, 1883), 36-37.

53. Kenney, 1:143.

54. Copy in my possession.

55. Kenneth Joseph Goates, *William Goates, Sr. and His Family* (Salt Lake City: Goates Family, 1990), 34.

56. Copy in my possession.

57. *History of the Church*, 2:188.

58. Ibid., 188.

59. Ibid., 191.

60. *Latter-day Saints' Millennial Star* 15 (26 Mar. 1853):206.

61. *History of the Church*, 2:189, emphasis added.

62. Omar V. Garrison, *The Encyclopedia of Prophecy* (Secaucus, NJ: Citadel Press, 1979), 6.

63. Ibid., 170.

64. Leon Festinger, Henry W. Riechen, and Stanley Schachter, *When Prophecy Fails* (Minneapolis: University of Minnesota Press, 1956).

65. *Latter-day Saints' Millennial Star* 16 (16 Dec. 1854): 788.

66. McKiernan and Launius, 121.

67. *Times and Seasons* 5 (15 Apr. 1845): 865.

68. Roger D. Launius, *The Kirtland Temple: A Historical Narrative* (Independence, MO: Herald Publishing House, 1986), 23.

CHAPTER 13.

The Kirtland Temple

And again, verily I say unto you, my friends, a commandment I give unto you,
that ye shall commence a work of laying out and preparing a beginning and foundation
of the city of the stake of Zion, here in the land of Kirtland (D&C 94:1).

Kirtland—provisional Zion—was the apex of Sidney Rigdon's religious triumphs. During his later life, especially when seized in melancholia's black talons, Rigdon often floated back nostalgically to the rich loam and tall trees of Ohio's fabled lands. In Kirtland Sidney found his place in the sun, a pinnacle from which he viewed the world for nearly a decade.

The window of opportunity, during which Rigdon achieved co-equal billing with Joseph Smith, lasted from 1831-39. During this era he and the prophet, both gifted visionaries, jointly developed the church's infrastructure and its governing agenda. Retrospectively the duo seem mismatched. Rigdon was highly educated and well read while Smith possessed only a rudimentary education. Rigdon was pessimistic while Smith demonstrated a *joie de vivre*. Smith was remarkable for his charisma, Rigdon for his eloquence. But despite occasional friction, they were virtually inseparable. Their burdens, in fact, were their bonds.

Both the impassioned prophet and his spokesman longed deeply for public recognition. Except for Zion's Camp march to Missouri when he remained behind to supervise activities in Ohio, Rigdon was extensively involved in virtually every enterprise in Kirtland. His keen intellect and superior training oriented him toward enhancing the general educational level of the populace. He was equally zealous to improve the church's awareness of revelations fresh from its prophet's lips.

The first step, beginning just weeks after Sidney first met Joseph, had been to publish Smith's revelations in book form. Both Rigdon and Smith felt printing the scriptures would help centralize authority, thus stabilizing the young church. According to David Whitmer, however, he and several others raised strong objections against publication. "Brothers Joseph and S[i]dney would not listen to us," Whitmer later wrote, "and said they were going to send [the writings] to Independence to be published."[1]

The reluctant objected principally because the revelations depicted Jackson County residents as "intruders upon the land of Zion . . . enemies to the church

. . . [who] should be cut off . . . [from] the land of Zion and sent away." Whitmer prophesied that Missourians would "come upon [the Mormon settlers] and tear down the printing press, and the church would be driven out of Jackson County."[2]

On 20 November 1831, John Whitmer and Oliver Cowdery were dispatched from Ohio with the manuscript revelations, arriving in Independence on 5 January 1832. The printing of the Book of Commandments had progressed to chapter 65 when, on 20 July 1833, a mob demolished the printing office just as David Whitmer had predicted.[3] A few hundred copies of the unfinished book, in makeshift bindings, were used by the Saints until 1835 when it was replaced by the Doctrine and Covenants.

In addition to influencing publication of early Mormon scriptures, Rigdon, drawing on a lifetime of Baptist experience, advocated an educated lay ministry. Many if not most of those attracted to Mormonism early on, including Joseph Smith and Brigham Young, had limited education. So, following instructions in Doctrine and Covenants 88 (given 27 December 1832), an institution sub-sequently known as the School of the Elders or School of the Prophets was established with Rigdon as principal instructor. The school's mission was to teach the ministry—not only fundamental subjects such as reading and writing but also advanced studies in theology, ancient languages, and Christian history.

Students were expected to acquire knowledge through serious study and also through revelation. Zebedee Coltrin, a student in the school, stated: "The School of the Prophets began in Kirtland, January 24, 1833, much instruction received by the gift of tongues and the interpretation thereof." He added, "[T]he science we engaged in for the winter was English grammar, of which we obtained a general knowledge."[4]

The concept of the school ultimately expanded into a broader educational effort, the "Kirtland School," established in December 1834 to foster spiritual and secular knowledge among all Saints, including children. Trustees of the organiza-tion, which sponsored a number of programs over several years, were Joseph Smith, Jr., Frederick G. Williams, Sidney Rigdon, and Oliver Cowdery. Subjects emphasized in the Kirtland School, mostly by Rigdon and his associate William McLellin, included grammar, reading and writing, geography and history, politics and philosophy, and foreign languages.[5] The main emphasis, however, particu-larly for adult male priesthood holders, was religious studies. Perhaps the most significant aspect of this instruction was Rigdon's preparation and delivery of a seven-part series of theological lectures to a group of prospective missionaries, "the first laborers of the Kingdom," during the 1834-35 winter term of the School of Elders.[6]

The purpose of the lectures, as noted in the first lesson, was "to unfold to the understanding the doctrine of Jesus Christ." These discourses, systematically arranged with accompanying script designed for missionaries to memorize and teach, developed fully the Mormon position on faith, miracles, sacrifice, the gift of the Holy Spirit, as well as the character and attributes of the Godhead. Relatively unknown to modern Mormons, Rigdon's theological discourses, later called the Lectures on Faith, were removed from the Doctrine and Covenants in 1921 by LDS church leaders despite the fact that the 1835 First Presidency had designated the lectures "the Doctrine of the Church of the Latter Day Saints." The second part of the book, the portion that comprises current editions, was labeled "PART SECOND Covenants and Commandments."[7]

Publication of the Doctrine and Covenants was initiated on 24 September 1834 when the Kirtland High Council nominated a committee composed of Joseph Smith, Sidney Rigdon, Oliver Cowdery, and Frederick G. Williams, principles in the Literary Firm, to "arrange the items of doctrine" for publication. Although this new scripture had not yet been returned from the bindery on 17 August 1835, a general church assembly was convened to introduce the publishing committee's labors. After a hymn, Cowdery arose and introduced the "Book of doctrine and covenants of the church of the Latter Day Saints" on behalf of the committee. Rigdon then spoke briefly, after which Elder John Smith, leader of the Kirtland high council, "bore record that the revelations in said book were true, and that the lectures [on faith] were judiciously arranged and compiled, and were profitable for doctrine." The entire work was then canonized by common consent.[8]

The trusting church membership, which had not yet examined the completed work, was unaware of a number of textual changes between the publication of the Book of Commandments and the new book of scripture (fifteen times the number of all changes that would subsequently be made in all Doctrine and Covenants editions from 1835 to 1921).[9] Lyman Wight, an early Mormon apostle, was so affected by the alterations that he said: "The Book of Doctrine and Covenants was a telestial law; and the Book of Commandments . . . was a celestial law."[10]

David Whitmer, at that time a close associate of Rigdon and Smith in the Literary Firm, expressed his view of why so many changes were made. "Some of the revelations in the Book of Commandments had *to be changed*," he explained, "because the heads of the church had gone too far, and had done things in which they had already gone ahead of some of the former revelations."[11] According to Whitmer, the revelations were changed to match later actions. Rigdon and Cowdery attributed the necessity of changing God's printed word to such minor factors as transcription errors, poor copy, or sloppy printers. But the omissions, additions, and corrections were far too extensive to be attributed wholly to these causes, a fact not lost on Whitmer. The Book of Mormon witness wrote:

> Some of the revelations as they are now in the Book of Doctrine and Covenants have been changed and added to. Some of the changes being of the greatest importance as the meaning is entirely changed on some very important matters; as if the Lord had changed his mind a few years after he gave the revelations.

. . . These changes were made by the leaders of the church, who had drifted into error and spiritual blindness. Through the influence of S[i]dney Rigdon, Brother Joseph was led on and on into receiving revelations every year, to establish offices and doctrines which are not even mentioned in the teachings of Christ in the written word. In a few years they had gone away ahead of the written word, so that they had to change these revelations.[12]

Whitmer had already had his differences with Rigdon, as evident in his explanation of who was behind these significant changes. "Many of the brethren objected seriously to it," he wrote, "but they did not want to say much for the sake of peace, as it was *Brother Joseph and the leaders* who did it. . . . I was told that Sidney Rigdon convinced Brother Joseph and that committee that it was all right."[13]

While prophet and spokesman did not consider their revelations flawless, thus making them eligible for amendment, they were consistent in their view of the Bible, which they also believed could be improved. Wanting to understand the Old Testament by reading it in the original, a Hebrew class was organized on 4 January 1836, and two days later Elder William McLellin, a teacher in the Kirtland School, returned from an excursion to nearby Hudson Seminary and reported that he had hired Jewish scholar, Joshua Seixas, to teach them Hebrew for a term of seven weeks for the sum of $320. By 15 February sixty to seventy fledgling scholars were ready to begin translating the Hebrew language. Four days later Seixas divided the class to allow the gifted students to work at a faster pace. The advanced group of Sidney Rigdon, Joseph Smith, Jr., Oliver Cowdery, W. W. Phelps, Edward Partridge, William McLellin, Orson Hyde, Orson Pratt, Sylvester Smith, and Warren Parrish continued to study under Seixas until 29 March 1836.

In addition to Rigdon's profound influence on educational programs, he was still the church's principal advocate with the masses. He authored most of the consequential essays published in the *Messenger and Advocate*, the Mormon newspaper at Kirtland; preached at religious services, funerals, weddings, and other public functions; and bestowed personal blessings on grateful Saints. On 13 January 1835, for example, all newly-elected members of the Kirtland High Council were ordained by Rigdon, Joseph Smith, and Hyrum Smith. Joseph Smith's personal diary records that "Many great and glorious blessings were pronounced upon the heads of these councilors by President S[idney] Rigdon who was spokesman of the occasion."[14]

But Rigdon, who had difficulty containing his fervency, could also easily become belligerent, particularly when challenged. Joseph Smith, who did not immediately gain the upper hand, recognized early on that his prickly and arrogant spokesman could quickly erupt. The prophet's 19 November 1833 diary entry, written in his own hand, depicts his thoughts on Rigdon's disposition after the two returned from a lengthy mission to New York and Canada:

> Brother Sidney is a man whom I love but [he] is not capa[b]le of that pure and ste[a]dfast love for those who are his benefactors as should posess the breast of a man a President of the Church of Christ. This with some other little things such as a selfish and ind[e]pendance of mind which [are] to[o] often manifest[,] d[e]stroys the confidence of those who would lay down their lives for him. But notwithstanding these things he is a very great and good man. A man of great power of words and [he] can gain the friendship of his hearers very quick[ly]. He is a man whom God will uphold if he will continue faithful to his calling. O God grant that he may for the Lord's sake.

Continuing in Oliver Cowdery's handwriting, the journal entry reads:

> . . . And again, blessed be Brother Sidney, also notwithstanding he shall be high and lifted up, yet he shall bow down under the yoke like unto an ass that coucheth beneath his burthen [burden], that learneth his master's will by the stroke of the rod, Thus saith the Lord. Yet the Lord will have mercy on him and he shall bring forth much fruit. . . . Blessed are his generations. Nevertheless, one shall hunt after them as a man hunteth after an ass that hath strayed in the wilderness, and straitway findeth him and bringeth him into the fold. Thus shall the Lord watch over his generation that they may be saved.[15]

His contrariness aside, Rigdon's harangues, delivered both from the pulpit and in writing, were perhaps the most potent early weapon against forces intent on destroying Mormonism and the credibility of Joseph Smith, Jr. Campbellites, former associates in the Disciple of Christ movement, were a favored target of this deft vivisectionist. He particularly loathed his wife's brother-in-law, Adamson Bentley, a prominent Disciple minister who had convinced his wealthy father-in-law, Jeremiah Brooks, to disinherit Phebe Rigdon because of her conversion to Mormonism. Responding publicly to this action Rigdon wrote:

> I have an old uncle in the state of Maryland, that was never married, and he possesses a large property. I would say to . . . Adamson Bentley (for he is an animal of his own kidney) . . . go there; he is now about eighty years of age, & of course it is will-making time, and about the right age for Bentley to prevail on him to make a will that will disinherit a monstrous heretic. I think it is probable there will be no difficulty . . . seeing he has been so successful in his former attempt with old Mr. Brooks, my wife's father, and got his own wife so well fattened on other people's property. Be sure my uncle is not a Cambellite in religion, but a regular Baptist.[16]

In another virulent attack, Rigdon called the Campbellites behind the anti-Mormon book *Mormonism Unvailed* "the smaller animals of this species" and attacked their character:

> The scheme of Messrs. Campbell and Scott is the most barefaced and impudent imposition ever attempted to be pawned on any generation, and those who are stupid

enough to continue to follow them, will cast a shade upon the character of this generation as long as the name of it is known among the living. . . .

If it were to be asked why did not the Lord choose Messrs. Campbell and Scott, to lay the foundation of his work in the last days the answer would be, that God who knows the hearts of all living, knew that they were corrupt to the very core, and destitute of that nobleness of soul which would entitle them to this honor.[17]

Rigdon's gruff, arrogant style can be seen in his written exchange with Oliver Barr, several letters of which were published in the *Messenger and Advocate*. The non-Mormon, in a 24 May 1836 letter printed in the newspaper, had responded to Rigdon's essay on revelation and apostasy. Barr's temperate epistle reasoned that "[T]he whole gospel has been revealed, and is now recorded in the New Testament; hence not lost, but in our possession." Rigdon had asked in his letter, "if the world has departed from the gospel, how is it to be restored but by revelation?" Barr responded: "I answer, the gospel does not need to be restored to the world. Let the world return back to the gospel, and its order, and all will be well."[18]

Rigdon's response was to label Barr's letter a "plow and drag story, [which] savors of anything but christian propriety and decorum." After strenuously debating Barr's position, and warning him to repent and be baptized, Rigdon ended with an invective scolding:

> Before you ever present yourself again as a braggadocio challenging with a high hand, people to investigate with you the subject of religion, I would seriously recommend to you to get some Yankee school master to give you some lessons on english grammar, that you may know that them apostles is not quite according to the rules of grammar, and also get some country girl to give you a few lessons on logic, so that you may be enabled to tell the difference, between a man's first ideas and his knowledge.
>
> By way of conclusion I say sir that I feel myself insulted by being brought into contact with such a man and the correspondence between you and I closes. Farewell.[19]

In later life, when Rigdon seemed a cast-off has-been living in the reflected glow of the past, he became strangely impotent in fending off attacks on his own character and ability. The fading Rigdon is far more familiar to modern Mormons than the early power-behind-the-throne. Interestingly, for more than a century and a half, while Rigdon has been consigned to the historical Mormon closet, LDS myth-makers have built up Joseph Smith's mystique, revising it, often radically, for each generation. Like other charismatic luminaries who die young, devotees tailor them to their own needs, molding them to fit their own hopes and disappointments like second skins. Accordingly, the Quorum of the Twelve Apostles, promoting its own agenda after Joseph Smith's 1844 death, rewrote Mormon history so radically that Rigdon never again mattered.

An intriguing example of this retroactive revisionism was the aggrandisement of the Quorum of Twelve Apostles, which has resulted in a twentieth-century misunderstanding of the original intent and authority of this quorum. During a 16 January 1836 discussion, Joseph Smith said "the 12 are not subject to any other than the First Presidency, viz, myself, S Rigdon, and F G. Williams."[20] The reason for this was that members of the Twelve, also known as the traveling high council, were the church's evangelists. Their authority was in the missions rather than in the organized stakes. In the latter they had not authority; in the former, where there was no standing high council, they functioned in lieu of a stake organization. When Joseph Smith's statement was published later in the *History of the Church*, a significant wording change enhanced the Twelve's claim to supremacy. The entry now reads: "The Twelve are not subject to any other than the first Presidency, viz. myself . . . Sidney Rigdon, and Frederick G. Williams, who are now my Counselors; and where I am not, there is no First Presidency over the Twelve."[21]

The record respecting Rigdon's successful efforts to bring the Kirtland temple project to completion has not been altered. A Mormon house of God was alluded to during Rigdon's first meeting with Joseph Smith. The prophet's revelation pronounced: "I am Jesus Christ, the Son of God; wherefore, gird up your loins and I will suddenly come to my temple" (D&C 36:8). Further specifics were announced 2 January 1831 wherein the revelation promised that in Ohio "you shall be endowed with power from on high" (D&C 38:32).

In June 1833, six months after the Saints were commanded to build a temple, they had purchased the land but not yet begun construction. On 1 June they were chastised in a revelation for delaying the project. "Ye have sinned against me a very grievous sin," the disclosure began, "in that ye have not considered the great commandment in all things, that I have given unto you concerning the building of mine house." Church members were admonished to keep the commandments, whereby they would find the means necessary to build the temple. "Let the house be built," the revelation continued, "not after the manner of the world," but "after the manner which I shall show unto three of you [Smith, Rigdon, Williams], whom ye shall appoint and ordain unto this power." The revelation then gave a general description of the edifice (D&C 95:3, 11-17).

Church leaders exhorted the Saints that Zion could not be redeemed until the temple in the stake of Zion was completed. A letter from Oliver Cowdery, read into the 4 August 1835 "Minutes of the High Council at Kirtland," explained "the Lord has commanded us to build a house, in which to receive an endowment, previous to the redemption of Zion; and that Zion could not be redeemed until this takes place."[22] When construction began, detailed architectural plans had not yet been completed. On 3 June, a conference of high priests called on the First Presidency to discuss the situation. Smith asked the men their views. Some favored a frame building, others a log house. Lucy Smith, the prophet's mother, wrote that he reminded them they were not building an abode for themselves but for God.

"Shall we brethren build a house for our God, of logs?" he asked. "No," he replied, "I have a better plan than that. I have a plan of the house of the Lord, given by himself; and you will soon see by this, the difference between our calculations and his idea."[23]

Truman O. Angell, later to become official church architect in Salt Lake City, confirmed Mother Smith's account:

> I did not go to Kirtland until the fall of 1835. At this time I went to work upon the Kirtland Temple. . . . F. G. Williams came into the Temple about the time the main hall first floor was ready for dedication. He was asked, how does the house look to you. He answered that it looked to him like the model he had seen.
>
> He said President Joseph, Sidney Rigdon, and himself were called to come before the Lord and the model was shown to them. He said the vision of the Temple was thus shown them and he could not see the difference between it and the House as built.[24]

Orson Pratt added this important confirmation:

> When the Lord commanded this people to build a house in the land of Kirtland . . . he gave them the pattern by vision from heaven, and commanded them to build that house according to that pattern and order; to have the architecture, not in accordance with architecture devised by men, but to have everything constructed in that house according to the heavenly pattern that he by his voice had inspired to his servants.[25]

Despite church leaders' claims that Smith's, Rigdon's, and Williams's collective vision depicted the design of the temple, the elements of the still-extant sacred structure are traceable to standard, early nineteenth-century buildings. The exterior was a basic adaptation and modification of earlier plans completed for the never-built temple in the City of New Jerusalem.[26] Alterations in the plans succeeded in blending Greek Revival, Federal, Gothic, and Georgian motifs into an architectural style similar in form to structures throughout Connecticut, western Massachusetts, and New York. Since most of Kirtland's settlers and artisans came from those areas, such borrowings were not unexpected, especially by an architecturally inexperienced group.

Historian Laural B. Andrew has written that "clearly the Mormons did not start out with an *a priori* concept of 'style'" when they initiated the Kirtland temple. They merely adopted features of several styles, the combination of which created a beautiful building, "following the usual pattern of the migrant, who tends to construct in his new environment the architectural forms with which he is familiar and that remind him of home."[27]

Several well-known architects had published complete building guides by 1830. Certainly the Kirtland temple building committee relied on the "how-to-do-it" architectural books of Asher Benjamin, a renowned Greek Revival architect during the first part of the nineteenth century. Kirtland craftsmen had access to some of his five architectural books and used them with apparent relish, particularly on the ornamental woodworking, window casings, and stress supports. The decorative patterns used throughout the interior, for instance, were described and pictured in considerable detail in Benjamin's pattern books. His publications also purposed identical engineering schemes for the support beams of the vaulted ceilings used in the temple. He described an identical design for the double-hung windows, the distinctive wall-supported, wrap-around staircases, and other internal features incorporated into the building.[28] Features adapted from additional sources include the steeple and belfry, a variant of a popular New England style developed by Charles Bulfinch in a Congregational church at Pittsfield, Massachusetts, during the 1790s, and the large Venetian window located in the center of the temple, derived from other Bulfinch-designed churches.[29]

Joseph Smith displayed an early interest in architecture and may have gathered design ideas for the Kirtland temple during an October 1832 business trip to New York City. On the lower east side of Manhattan, New York, there were at least five Georgian Gothic churches similar to the temple. It is likely that Smith saw at least one of these structures during that trip. A letter to his wife describes his interest in New York City architecture:

> This day I have been walking through the most splendid part of the city of New York. The buildings are truly great and wonderful to the astonishing of every beholder. . . . Can the great God of all the earth maker of all things magnificent and splendid be displeased with man for all these great inventions sought out by them. My answer is no it can not be, seeing these great works are calculated to make man wise and happy, therefore not for these works can the Lord be displeased . . .[30]

Among the New York City structures Smith may have seen are the Northeast Reform Dutch, or Market Street Church (now the Sea and Land Church), built by Henry Rutgers between 1814 and 1817, and the All Saints Free Church, built during 1827-29. Both are similar in appearance to the Kirtland temple.

Like other religious groups, the Mormons built their temple on a hilltop, a high plateau overlooking the East Chagrin Valley where the terrain to the summit served as a continual reminder of how difficult the path is to heaven. Construction did not get underway until the summer of 1833. Thereafter, nearly every able-bodied man and woman in Kirtland contributed to the massive public works project. During the Zion's Camp march, when most men were absent from town between 5 May and mid-August 1834, work continued under the supervision of Rigdon and Joseph Smith, Sr., but little was accomplished until the labor force returned. Rigdon's role in exhorting the Saints to complete the edifice was pivotal. Mormon apostle Heber C. Kimball, speaking of Rigdon's involvement with the temple project, later said that "he frequently used to go upon the walls of the building both by night and day frequently wetting the walls with his tears, crying aloud to the Almighty to send means whereby we might accomplish the building."[31]

The completed structure was impressive; from basement to tower its height is approximately 110 feet. The heavy stucco exterior over the mortared rubble stone was a variation of the time-honored building finish called "rough cast." Another feature of the stucco was the use of crushed china and glassware which caused the bluish-tinted walls to glisten in sunlight.[32]

Even before completion, the Kirtland temple hosted educational classes, priesthood meetings, and church councils, as well as other activities. The rather traditional appearance of the structure is an accurate reflection of the relatively uncomplicated Mormon behavioral and theological tenets of the 1830s. For all practical purposes the temple functioned as a meetinghouse. The prophet in his diary often called it a chapel. Very little uniquely Mormon ritual existed when the building was begun, despite frequent hints from the prophet about a "glorious endowment that God has in store for the faithful."[33] Smith promised followers bountiful blessings upon completion as a palliative to those who objected to committing meager resources to such a vast enterprise. But the eventual conferring of specific endowments in Illinois in a prescribed ritual and the development of the sealing ceremony were not yet contemplated and did not impact the planning of the temple.

In preparation for the more general endowment of the Holy Spirit, Smith and Rigdon presided over a series of ceremonies involving washings and anointings designed to purify priesthood holders. The first ordinance conducted in the partially completed temple was a foot-washing ceremony. Mentioned in the New Testament, the feat is also a remnant of Sandemanian theology from Rigdon's late 1820s ministry with Walter Scott in Pittsburgh. Joseph Smith first mentioned this early Christian practice during a 5 October 1835 meeting of the First Presidency and Quorum of the Twelve. He was more specific on 12 November. Discussing the future washings and anointings, he remarked:

> [T]here is on[e] great deficiency or obstruction in the way that deprives us of the greater blessings. And in order to make the foundation of this Church complete and permanent, we must remove this obstruction which is to attend to certain duties that we have not as yet attended to. . . . The item to which I wish the more particularly to call your attention to-night is the ordinance of washing of feet. This we have not done as yet, but it is necessary now as much as it was in the days of the Saviour. We must have a place prepared that we may attend to this ordinance aside from the world.
>
> . . . We must have all things prepared and call our Solem[n] Assembly as the Lord has commanded us that we may be able to accomplish his great work. . . . All who are prepared and are sufficiently pure to abide the presence of the Saviour will see him in the Solem[n] Assembly.[34]

The first ordinance administered in the temple was on 21 January 1836. "At about three o'clock P.M.," Oliver Cowdery wrote, we "assembled in our office garret [in the temple], having all things prepared for the occasion, with presidents Joseph Smith, [J]r.[,] F. G. Williams, Sidney Rigdon, Hyrum Smith, David Whitmer, John Whitmer, and [E]lder John Corrill, and washed our bodies with pure water before the Lord, preparatory to the anointing with the holy oil." He added that "after we were washed, our bodies were perfumed with a sweet smelling oderous wash [whiskey, perfumed with cinnamon]."[35] At early candlelight Rigdon and the other members of the First Presidency met in the temple's west room to "attend to the ordinance of anointing our heads with holy oil." The Kirtland and Zion high councils met in two adjoining rooms in prayer while the ordinance was performed.

Joseph Smith's diary records that visions were opened, allowing some to see "the face of the Saviour" while others were "ministered unto by holy angels." In a rare first-hand account of his own ability as a seer, the prophet described the glories of the Celestial Kingdom of God, where he saw, in addition to his deceased brother Alvin, all children who died before arriving at the age of accountability, as well as Sidney Rigdon and Frederick G. Williams, despite the fact that both would later be expelled from the faith. The vision of heaven also included members of the 1835 Quorum of the Twelve, most of whom would ultimately leave Mormonism. Intriguingly, the prophet also envisioned "the armies of heaven protecting the Saints in their return to Zion" to reclaim the promised land and the ultimate "Redemption of Zion."[36]

On the following day, after the remarkable visions and manifestations had waned, the participants regrouped and spent their entire study hour "rehearsing to each other the glorious scenes that occurred on the preceding evening, while attending to the ordinance of holy anointing." Later that evening, the same blessing and anointing was administered for the Quorum of the Twelve and the presidency of the Seventy. Rigdon then concluded the services by "invoking the benediction of heaven upon the Lord's anointed which he did in an eloquent manner." Afterwards the congregation shouted a loud hosannah and "[t]he gift of [tongues] fell upon us in mighty pow[e]r, angels mingled their voices with ours, while their presence was in our midst and un[c]easing pra[i]ses swelled our bosoms for the space of half an hour."[37]

Such spiritual manifestations attended most meetings conducted during this period. It was a time of rejoicing, long to be remembered by those in attendance. The pentecostal manifestations enjoyed during these temple services would shortly thereafter be imparted to the general Saints during the building's dedicatory services. On 27 March 1836, Rigdon, who had prayed so fervently for the Lord to send means for the temple's completion, co-presided with Joseph Smith during the dedicatory exercises and appears to have been in charge of the proceedings. The newspaper account published in the *Messenger and Advocate* noted that the congregation began to assemble before 8:00 a.m. The first floor sanctuary filled within minutes of the doors opening. The vestibule then filled, after which more of the faithful gathered around open windows. The rest were urged to hold services of their own in a schoolhouse west of the temple. So many were unable to attend the first service that church leaders promised to repeat the agenda the following Sunday.

"One thousand persons were now silently and solemnly waiting to hear the word of the Lord from the mouth of his servants in the sacred desk," the newspaper noted.[38] Rigdon began by reading the 96th and 24th Psalms. The choir then rendered "Ere Long The Vail," after which Rigdon, "in an able, devout and appropriate manner, addressed the throne of Grace." After the prayer the choir sang "O Happy Souls." Rigdon, ever a cornucopia of biblical interpretation, then took the stand and delivered a two-and-one-half-hour dedicatory sermon, his text Matthew 8:18-20:

> Now when Jesus saw great multitudes about him, he gave commandment to depart unto the other side. And a certain scribe came, and said unto him, Master, I will follow thee whithersoever thou goest. And Jesus saith unto him, The foxes have holes, and the birds of the air have nests; but the Son of man hath not where to lay his head.

Later in his career, after fanaticism burned holes in his soul, Rigdon would bury listeners under avalanches of verbiage. At the Kirtland temple dedication, however, he was in top form. Edmund Flagg described Rigdon during this period, writing that he had "a face full of fire, a fine tenour [sic] voice, and a mild and persuasive eloquence of speech."[39] A. S. Hayden, in another account, described the Mormon spokesman as "full medium height, rotund of form . . . with a little cast of melancholy . . . his language [was] copious, fluent in utterance, with articulation clear and musical."[40]

During his dedicatory sermon, a newspaper reporter noted, Rigdon "drew tears from many eyes" by rehearsing the toils, privations, and anxieties of those who had labored on the building. Waxing poetic he recalled the travail of "those who had wet [the walls] with their tears, in the silent shades of night, while they were praying to the God of Heaven, to protect them, and stay the unhallowed hands of ruthless spoilers, who had uttered a prophecy when the foundation was laid, that the walls would never be reared."[41] When Rigdon referred to the Savior's lament that he "hath nowhere to lay his head," the reporter noted, "his whole soul appeared to be fired with his subject." By the time he reached his conclusion, "we can truly say," added the reporter,

> no one unacquainted with the manner of delivery and style of our speaker can, from reading f[or]m any adequate idea of the powerful effect he is capable of producing in the minds of his hearers: And to say on this occasion he showed himself master of his subject and did well, would be doing him injustice; to say he acquitted himself

with honor or did very well, would be detracting from his real merit; and to say that he did *exceeding* well; would be only halting praise.[42]

After bringing the audience to this pinnacle, Rigdon introduced Joseph Smith, Jr., and presented him to the church as a prophet and seer. After the various quorums voted to sustain Smith, the congregation sang "Hosanna—Now Let Us Rejoice." Following a twenty-minute intermission the service reconvened and the prophet read the dedicatory prayer. He thanked God for the means to complete the temple, for the Saints' dedication, and for the gospel of Jesus. He prayed for the welfare of the church, for the members of the presiding bodies, for the leaders of nations, for the children of Israel, and for all humankind.

Following his prayer, the choir sang W. W. Phelps's "The Spirit of God Like a Fire Is Burning," after which the Saints partook of the sacrament of the Lord's Supper. The hymn and sacred ritual thrilled the congregation. At this point in the services, many later attested, an extraordinary outpouring of spiritual power was bestowed on the faithful. Eliza R. Snow wrote, "The ceremonies of that dedication may be rehearsed, but no mortal language can describe the heavenly manifestations on that memorable day. Angels appeared to some, while a sense of divine presence was realized by all present, and each heart was filled with 'joy inexpressible and full of glory.'"[43]

Others testified to divine manifestations during various portions of the dedicatory program. During Rigdon's first prayer President Frederick G. Williams saw an angel enter a window, take a seat beside Joseph Smith, Sr., and remain throughout most of the service. Heber C. Kimball described the individual: "He was tall, had black eyes and white hair, and stooped shoulders, and his garment was whole, extending to near his ankles on his feet he had sandals. He was sent to accept of the dedication."[44] Lydia Knight remembered that Smith arose during the service and told the congregation "the personage was Jesus, as the dress described was that of our Savior, it being in some respects different to the clothing of the angels."[45]

David Whitmer reported seeing three angels pass through the south aisle and seat themselves in the congregation. George A. Smith summarized the experience: "There came a shock on the house like the sound of a mightily rushing wind, and almost every man in the house arose, and hundreds of them were speaking in tongues, prophesying or declaring visions, almost with one voice."[46] The service was brought to a close about 4:00 p.m. Hyrum Smith and Sidney Rigdon made a few closing remarks prior to Rigdon's short benediction. The congregation then ended the meeting with a shout, "Hosanna! Hosanna! Hosanna to God and the Lamb." They repeated this exclamation three times, sealing each series with three amens.

Two days after the dedication, 29 March 1836, the foot washing ceremony, the only ordinance performed in the solemn assembly after the dedication of the temple, was performed. Rigdon, Williams, Cowdery, and Hyrum Smith "met in the most holy place in the Lord's House, and sought for a revelation from Him concerning the authorities of the Church going to Zion." The men felt inspired to call other leaders to join them in fasting through the day and the night to seek further communications. The prophet insisted that "those who had entered the holy place, must not leave the house until morning." They were further instructed during their stay to "cleanse our feet and partake of the Sacrament that we might be made holy before Him, and thereby be qualified to officiate in our calling, upon the morrow, in washing the feet of the elders."[47]

Accordingly each man first cleansed his face and feet. Then Rigdon, who had years before officiated in a similar ordinance as a Reformed Baptist minister, first washed the prophet's feet. Smith then reciprocated after which the ordinance was performed for the rest of the group by Smith and Rigdon. Smith's diary entry for the following day, 30 March, records:

> I then observed to the quorums that I had now completed the organization of the Church and we had passed through all the necessary ceremonies, that I had given them all the instruction they needed and that they now were at liberty after obtaining their [evangelical] licenses to go forth and build up the Kingdom of God.[48]

One week after the dedication, on 3 April 1836, the prophet and Oliver Cowdery, his principle assistant in transcribing the Book of Mormon, went to a pulpit in the west end of the Kirtland temple. Lowering curtains that hung from the ceiling, they knelt and began to pray. As they meditated, Smith later recorded, the Savior appeared before them, standing on the breastwork of their pulpit, and formally restored to them the fullest authority to conduct his work. Following this vision, the prophet attested to seeing Moses, Elias, and Elijah, each entrusting to them the power of the holy priesthood.

Elijah said that "the keys of this dispensation are committed into your hands, and by this ye may know that the great and dreadful day of the Lord is near, even at the doors" (D&C 110). The pronouncement, claimed to fulfill the final prophecy of the Old Testament found in Malachi 4:5-6, implied that a significant restoration had occurred. A holy temple existed where Christ could dwell and manifest himself on the earth at will. The last days were officially inaugurated, and God's authority was fully restored to the first authentic prophet since Biblical times.

The temple seemed to possess its own spirit, an intrinsic sacredness. Orson Pratt later wrote:

> God was there, his angels were there, the Holy Ghost was in the midst of the people, the visions of the Almighty were opened to the minds of the servants of the living God; the veil was taken from the minds of many; they saw the heavens opened; they beheld the angels of God; they heard the voice of the Lord; and they were filled from the crown of their heads to the soles of their feet with the power and inspiration of the Holy Ghost. . . . In that Temple, set apart by the servants of God, and dedicated

by a prayer that was written by inspiration, the people were blessed as they never had been blessed for generations and generations.[49]

Nevertheless this edifice, the spiritual touchstone of the period, was savored only briefly. Just six months after the dedication, discontent within the fold became evident. By late 1837 internal unrest turned into open dissension, culminating in the abandonment of Kirtland and the temple the Saints had struggled so ardently to build.[50]

Notes

Unless otherwise stated, all primary sources cited are located in the Historical Department of the Church of Jesus Christ of Latter-day Saints, Salt Lake City, Utah.

1. David Whitmer, *An Address to All Believers in Christ* (Richmond, MO: David Whitmer, 1887), 54-55.

2. Ibid.

3. Whitmer added that after this event Smith had confidence in his [Whitmer's] ability as a prophet and in July 1834, while on Fishing River, Missouri, during the Zion's Camp march, "ordained me his successor as 'Prophet Seer and Revelator' to the Church" (Whitmer, 55).

4. Journal History, 24 Jan. 1833—a multi-volume daily history of the church compiled by official church historians; hereafter Journal History.

5. William McLellin's description of the school is found in *Latter Day Saints Messenger and Advocate* 1 (Apr. 1835): 80.

6. The authorship of the lectures has long been debated. Recent studies ascribe the wording primarily to Rigdon with some contributions made by Smith (see J. Bonner Ritchie, "Lectures on Faith," in Daniel H. Ludlow, ed., *Encyclopedia of Mormonism*, 4 vols. [New York: Macmillan Publishing Co., 1992], 4:819; Wayne A. Larsen, Alvin C. Rencher, and Tim Layton, "Who Wrote the Book of Mormon? An Analysis of Wordprints," *Brigham Young University Studies* 20 [Spring 1980]: 225-51; Alan J. Phipps, "The Lectures on Faith: An Authorship Study," M.A. thesis, Brigham Young University, 1972).

The authorship question is ultimately academic. Whatever Smith's original position, he was involved in preparing the lectures for publication: "During the month of January [1835]," the *History of the Church* reads, "I was engaged in the School of the Elders, and in preparing the lectures on theology for publication in the book of Doctrine and Covenants" (Joseph Smith, *History of the Church of Jesus Christ of Latter-day Saints*, B. H. Roberts, ed., 7 vols. [Salt Lake City: The Church of Jesus Christ of Latter-day Saints, 1902], 2:180; hereafter *History of the Church*). He underscored his personal support of the lectures by noting in the introduction to the 1835 edition that he accepted responsibility for "every principle advanced." Furthermore, the First Presidency's introduction makes no distinction between the inspirational quality of the lectures, which significantly occupy the first part of the book, and the second part which contains the covenants and commandments.

7. For treatments of this matter, see Richard S. Van Wagoner, Steven C. Walker, and Allen D. Roberts, "The 'Lectures on Faith': A Case Study in Decanonization," *Dialogue:*

A *Journal of Mormon Thought* 20 (Fall 1987): 71-77; Robert J. Woodford, "The Historical Development of the Doctrine and Covenants," 3 vols., Ph.D. diss., Brigham Young University, 1974; John William Fitzgerald, "A Study of the Doctrine and Covenants," M.A. thesis, Brigham Young University, 1940.

8. *History of the Church*, 2:243-51.

9. Melvin J. Petersen "A Study of the Nature of and the Significance of the Changes in the Revelations as Found in a Comparison of the Book of Commandments and Subsequent Editions of the Doctrine and Covenants," M.A. thesis, Brigham Young University, 1955.

10. *History of the Church*, 2:481.

11. Whitmer, 56 (emphasis in original).

12. Ibid., 56, 59.

13. Ibid., 61 (emphasis in original).

14. Scott H. Faulring, ed., *An American Prophet's Record: The Diaries and Journals of Joseph Smith* (Salt Lake City: Signature Books in association with Smith Research Associates, 1989), 100-101.

15. Ibid., 15-16.

16. Sidney Rigdon to Oliver Cowdery, in *Latter Day Saints' Messenger and Advocate* 2 (June 1836): 334-35.

17. Ibid., 297-99.

18. Ibid., 325.

19. Ibid., 326-29.

20. Faulring, 110.

21. *History of the Church*, 2:374.

22. Ibid., 239.

23. Preston Nibley, ed., *History of Joseph Smith by His Mother Lucy Mack Smith* (Salt Lake City: Bookcraft, 1958), 30.

24. Truman O. Angell to John Taylor and Counsel, 11 Mar. 1885, in Laurel B. Andrew, *The Early Temples of the Mormons: The Architecture of the Millennial Kingdom in the American West* (Albany, NY: State University of New York Press, 1978), 36.

25. *Journal of Discourses*, 26 vols. (London: Latter-day Saints' Book Depot, 1854-86, 14 (9 Apr. 1871): 273; hereafter *Journal of Discourses*.

26. The original plans of the Jackson County temple, principally rendered by Frederick G. Williams, are retained in LDS archives.

27. Andrew, 41. See also Frank Ross, "Ohio: Architectural Cross-Road," *Journal of the Society of Architectural Historians* 12 (Spring 1953): 3.

28. See Asher Benjamin, *The Country Builder's Assistant* (Greenfield, 1797), plates 6, 13; Asher Benjamin, *The American Builder's Companion* (Boston, 1806), plates 19, 35; Asher Benjamin, *The Rudiments of Architecture* (Boston, 1814), plates, 30, 31; Asher Benjamin, *The Practical House Carpenter* (Boston, 1830), plates 27, 28, 32, 48, 52, 62. Cited in Roger D. Launius, *The Kirtland Temple: A Historical Narrative* (Independence, MO: Herald Publishing House, 1986), 150.

29. Andrew, 41.

30. Ibid., 44.

31. *Times and Seasons* 6 (15 Apr. 1845): 867.

32. While a wondrous element of Mormon folklore, such a practice was not uncommon. For instance, in novelist Nathaniel Hawthorne's *The Scarlet Letter*, Governor Bellingham's mansion was finished in like manner: "It had, indeed, a very cheery aspect; the walls being overspread with a kind of stucco, in which fragments of broken glass were plentifully intermixed; so that, when the sunshine fell aslantwise over the front of the edifice, it glittered and sparkled as if diamonds had been flung against it by the double handful" (Nathaniel Hawthorne, *The Scarlet Letter* [Boston and New York: Houghton Mifflin Co., 1850], 128-29.

33. Smith's diary entry for 3 Nov. 1835, in Faulring, 47.

34. Ibid., 57-58.

35. Leonard J. Arrington, ed., "Oliver Cowdery's Kirtland, Ohio, 'Sketch Book,'" *Brigham Young University Studies* 12 (Summer 1972): 416-18.

36. Faulring, 120.

37. Ibid., 121.

38. The full contemporary account of the temple dedication is in *Latter Day Saints' Messenger and Advocate* 2 (Mar. 1836): 274-78.

39. Edmund Flagg, *The Far West* (New York: Harper and Brothers, 1838), 113.

40. Amos S. Hayden, *Early History of the Disciples in the Western Reserve, Ohio* (Cincinnati: Chase & Hall, 1875), 191-92.

41. *Latter Day Saints' Messenger and Advocate* 2 (Mar. 1836): 275.

42. Ibid., 276.

43. Eliza R. Snow, in Edward W. Tullidge, *The Women of Mormondom* (New York: Tullidge and Crandall, 1877), 99.

44. Heber C. Kimball, "Autobiography," 66.

45. *Lydia Knight's History, The First Book of the Noble Women's Lives Series* (Salt Lake City: Deseret News, 1883), 33.

46. *Journal of Discourses* 11 (15 Nov. 1864): 10.

47. *History of the Church*, 2:430.

48. Faulring, 155.

49. *Journal of Discourses* 18 (9 Oct. 1875): 132.

50. The temple was subsequently used as a stable and then as a public school for four decades. The building, long ago restored by the Reorganized Church of Jesus Christ of Latter Day Saints, was awarded to them by legal decision in 1880 by Judge L. S. Sherman, who decreed that "The Reorganized Church of Jesus Christ of Latter Day Saints, is the True and Lawful successor of, and successor to the said original Church of Jesus Christ of Latter Day Saints, organized in 1830, and is entitled in law to all its rights and property." See the full history of the Kirtland temple, including legal and real estate transactions, in Launius, 100-35.

CHAPTER 14.

Financial Disaster

While reflecting upon the goodness and mercy of the Lord, this evening, a prophecy
was put into our hearts, that in a short time the Lord would arrange his providences
in a merciful manner and send us assistance to deliver us from debt and bondage.
                                                           —Joseph Smith, Jr., 30 November 1834[1]

Efforts to establish a self-contained community in Kirtland, Ohio, during the
1830s failed as dramatically as attempts to institute Zion in Jackson County,
Missouri. But Kirtland Saints were not driven from the land by malevolent
vigilantes. They voluntarily sought sanctuary in Missouri to dwell with their
expatriate prophet and his spokesman, who had fled Kirtland in early 1838 to
elude creditors and probable imprisonment.

Neither Joseph Smith nor Sidney Rigdon demonstrated at any time during
their careers the financial acumen that became the hallmark of millionaire Brigham
Young's thirty-year administration in the Rocky Mountain Basin.[2] Joseph's and
Sidney's fiscal ventures—first in Kirtland and later in Nauvoo, where both
ultimately filed for bankruptcy—proved disastrous forays into high finance and real
estate management, areas in which they had little knowledge and less expertise.
Rigdon's and Smith's implications that God devised their financial plans left no
room for mistakes in the minds of followers who became disillusioned and
antagonistic.

The church in Kirtland was poor from the beginning. In the spring of 1833,
for example, only ten Mormons in the entire town owned enough assets to be
levied either personal property or real estate taxes. These assessments represented
less than one percent of all taxable assets held by individuals in Kirtland Township.
Furthermore, except for prosperous merchant Newel K. Whitney, no Mormon
was assessed taxes for both land and personal property.[3]

Rigdon's and Smith's personal incomes accrued from the Literary Firm and
the United Firm, two private business concerns underwritten by general church
revenues. The Literary Firm had published the Doctrine and Covenants, Book of
Mormon, and several newspapers, and planned to publish Smith's and Rigdon's
completed revision of the Bible. But heavy operating expenses, scant returns from
sales, and destruction of its Missouri office caused the company to fail before it

could undertake the mammoth project. In early 1834 Smith wrote Literary Firm members that "we have run into debt for the press" and "have received but a very few dollars for the [Evening and Morning] Star and printing."[4] The prophet's younger brother, Samuel H. Smith, and David Whitmer were appointed agents to sell newspaper subscriptions and collect money. Their efforts saved the enterprise until the partners terminated their stewardships in 1836 and the Literary Firm dissolved.

Publication projects continued under the name "Oliver Cowdery & Co.," however, until February 1837. During this period the second edition of the Book of Mormon was printed. Upon completion of the printing, Cowdery sold his interest to Rigdon and Smith. Warren A. Cowdery, acting as their agent in the printing office and bookbindery, also served as editor of the periodical *Messenger and Advocate*. Unable to keep the enterprise afloat, Rigdon and Smith were forced to sell the office, bookbindery, and contents three months later.

The United Firm, another multi-faceted church enterprise, floundered for several reasons—overextension in mercantile goods, entering real estate transactions, constructing the Kirtland temple, and assisting Mormon poor. United Firm debts were substantial, with estimates ranging from a high of $150,000[5] to a more probable $102,300.[6] Newel Whitney, the firm's chief agent, worked feverishly to maintain credit arrangements and procure large quantities of store goods from the east for resale to Kirtland Saints. Large sums were borrowed, mostly from New York creditors, to acquire real estate, operate and maintain a brickyard, a tannery, and an ashery in Kirtland, as well as to disperse extra funds to the Literary Firm. John Corrill wrote:

> Notwithstanding they were deeply in debt they had so managed as to keep up their credit, so they concluded to try mercantile business. Accordingly, they ran in debt in New York, and elsewhere, some thirty thousand dollars, for goods, and shortly after, some fifty or sixty thousand more, as I was informed; but they did not fully understand the mercantile business, and, withal, they suffered pride to arise in their hearts, and became desirous of fine houses, and fine clothes, and indulged too much in these things, supposing for a few months that they were very rich.[7]

The combined proceeds from the United Firm's enterprises were insufficient to offset its overall operating costs, further precipitated by over-extending credit purchases. Rigdon met with other members of the faltering Ohio business on 11 January 1834. Uniting in prayer, they petitioned the Lord to assist "the Bishop of this Church with means sufficient to discharge every debt that the [United] Firm owes, in due season. That the Church may not be br[o]ught into disrepute, and the Saints be afflicted by the hands of their enemies."[8] Despite these fervent entreaties, Mormon poverty worsened, a concern to the non-Mormon populace.[9] The Mormon newspaper concluded: "The Saints have neglected the necessary preparation beforehand; they have not sent up their wise men with money to purchase land, but the rich have generally sta[ye]d back and withheld their money, while the poor have gone first and without money. Under these circumstances what could be expected but the appalling scene that now presents itself?"[10]

On 3 April 1834 Rigdon gathered with Smith, Frederick Williams, Newel Whitney, John Johnson, and Oliver Cowdery and "united in asking the Lord to give Elder Zebedee Coltrin influence over Brother Jacob Myers, to obtain the money which he has gone to borrow for us, or cause him to come to this place and bring it himself."[11] Orson Hyde, who had previously clerked in Gilbert & Whitney Mercantile, volunteered to help, feeling he could raise the money quickly in the eastern branches of the church. When his efforts failed, he wrote Rigdon and Smith on 31 March 1834 to inform them he was "not likely to succeed according to [your] expectations."[12] The First Presidency responded, "We adjure you to beseech [the Saints in that region], in the name of the Lord, by the Son of God, to lend us a helping hand." They warned that should the Saints "not help us, when they can do it without sacrifice . . . God shall take away" their wealth.[13]

Lean donations reflected hard times rather than a lack of faith. On 10 April 1834, still unable to secure needed funds, members of the United Firm gathered and agreed to dissolve their association. Partners were indebted for more than $3,000. Rigdon's share of the debt was $777.98, a huge sum in 1834 and equal to two years's average pay at one dollar a day.[14] Smith requested that the partners simply "give up all notes & demands that they had against each other and all be equal."[15] On 23 April the firm's properties were divided among the partners. Rigdon received the home in which he was living (the home still stands directly across the street east from the temple). He also received a tannery on lot 17, from which he was to draw his future financial support.[16]

Despite continued efforts to meet obligations, by 1835 a portion of the United Firm's notes remained unpaid. When the second edition of the Doctrine and Covenants was prepared with five previously unpublished revelations pertaining to the United Firm (secs. 78, 82, 92, 96, 104), the firm and partner names were replaced with codes because of potential lawsuits. The defunct business itself became both *United Order* and/or *Order of Enoch* to disguise its nature as a private business.[17]

Debts continued to mount and church leaders' worries escalated. On 23 October 1835 Rigdon met with the prophet, Oliver Cowdery, Frederick Williams, David Whitmer, Hyrum Smith, John Whitmer, Samuel Smith, and W. W. Phelps. They again pleaded with the Lord to

> give us means sufficient to deliver us from all our afflictions and difficulties, wherein we are placed by means of our debts; that He will open the way & deliver Zion in the appointed time and that without the shedding of blood . . . that he will give us the blessings of the earth sufficient to carry us to Zion and that we may purchase

inheritances in that land, even enough to carry on and accomplish the work unto which he has appointed us.[18]

As church finances worsened, leaders began expelling from the society those they viewed as covetous and lacking in benevolence. In June 1836 Preserved Harris was charged with "want of benevolence to the poor and charity to the church." Considered to be rich like his brother Martin in New York, Harris was charged with not being "liberal" in his offerings. He was found guilty and disfellowshipped.

During Harris's trial Frederick G. Williams acknowledged the church's poverty and that its debts were an embarrassment to church leaders. Additional contributions, he said, were needed to alleviate this distress. Rigdon emphatically declared the "law of God" regarding property: "it is the duty of the saints to offer their all to the will of God for the building up of the Kingdom & for the sustenance of the poor." A true believer, he asserted, consecrates his "property, life & all he possesses." Christ suffered the "loss of all things, that he might save all," he reasoned. "We must follow him and be made perfect through sufferings also, or lose all."[19]

By the summer of 1836 the Saints' financial plight appeared so hopeless that Smith and Rigdon embarked on an unusual quest. They left Kirtland, along with Hyrum Smith and Oliver Cowdery, on 25 July 1836, and boarded the steamer *Charles Townsend* at nearby Fairport. Their junket was by boat and rail through Buffalo, Utica, Schenectady, Albany, New York City, and Boston. While business matters were investigated en route, their ultimate destination was Salem, Massachusetts, where they arrived the afternoon of 5 August. The following day Smith proclaimed a cryptic revelation. "I, the Lord your God, am not displeased with your coming [on] this journey, notwithstanding your follies," the pronouncement began. Promising that Salem's "gold and silver shall be yours," the revelation then alluded to a clandestine residence: "And the place where it is my will that you should tarry, for the main, shall be signalized unto you by the peace and power of my Spirit, that shall flow unto you. This place you may obtain by hire" (D&C 111).

The official account in the *History of the Church* describes the venture as a missionary and sight-seeing excursion:

> [W]e hired a house, and occupied the same during the month, teaching the people from house to house, and preaching publicly, as opportunity presented; visiting occasionally, sections of the surrounding country, which are rich in the history of the Pilgrim Fathers of New England, in Indian warfare, religious superstition, bigotry, persecution, and learned ignorance.[20]

Contemporary records do not support this sketch. Although they did sight-see,[21] apparently only one public address was given by anyone in the group. Four local newspapers, the *Register*, *Observer*, *Gazette* and *Commercial Advertiser*, mentioned Rigdon's 20 August lecture at the lyceum. The *Register* of 22 August described Rigdon as "a man of very respectable appearance, apparently about 40 years of age and very fluent in his language." His stated topic was not Mormonism but "Christianity." And he introduced that topic by proclaiming he had not come "to engage in the religious disputes of the day" nor to "discuss the authenticity of the scriptures." Although Smith was present at the lecture, he remained silent. The 27 August *Observer* merely noted that Rigdon was accompanied by "three or four of his disciples." And when the group left town the 25 August *Register* noted that "Mr. Rigdon, the Mormon preacher, who introduced himself at our Lyceum last week, has since left the city, with three or four of his associates."[22]

Ebenezer Robinson, a prominent Nauvoo newspaper editor, citing the prophet's younger brother, Don Carlos, later wrote of the reason these leaders converged on Salem when circumstances in Kirtland were so critical. "We speak of these things with regret," Robinson began:

> A brother in the church, by the name of Burgess,[23] had come to Kirtland and stated that a large amount of money had been secreted in the cellar of a certain house in Salem, Massachusetts, which had belonged to a widow, and he thought he was the only person now living, who had knowledge of it, or to the location of the house.
> . . . We were informed that Brother Burgess met them in Salem, evidently according to appointment, but time had wrought such a change that he could not, for a certainty point out the house, and soon left.[24]

A 19 August 1836 letter Smith wrote to his wife Emma confirms the basic elements of Robinson's account:

> With regard to the great object of our mission, you will be anxious to know. We have found the house since Bro. Burgess left us, very luckily and providentially, as we had [during] one spell been most discouraged. The house is occupied, and it will require much care and patience to rent or buy it. We think we shall be able to effect it; if not now[,] within the course of a few months.[25]

According to Robinson, the men ultimately "found a house which they felt was the right one, and hired it. Needless to say, they failed to find either that treasure, or the gold and silver spoken of in the revelation."[26] Disheartened, the small company returned empty-handed to Kirtland in mid-September, having spent precious church assets in their futile search for the treasure.

On 22 December 1836 Rigdon met with other church leaders to resolve one of the sources of their collective poverty: the persistent practice of eastern churches sending their poor to Kirtland. After "deliberate discussion upon the subject," the leaders labeled the practice "unchristianlike" and resolved that it was the duty of all churches abroad not to send their poor to Kirtland, "to burden the church in this place, unless they come and prepare a place for them and means for their support . . . as our houses are full, and our lands mostly occupied."[27] But the poor continued to come. One observer noted:

> One almost wondered if the whole world were centering at Kirtland. They came, men, women, and oxen, [in] vehicles rough and rude, while others had walked all or part of the distance. The future "City of the Saints" appeared like one beseiged. Every available house, shop, hut, or barn was filled to its utmost capacity. Even boxes were roughly extemporized and used for shelter until something permanent could be secured.[28]

Meanwhile Rigdon and Smith pushed ahead with another financial scheme. Given the accepted barter system of the day, when the basic unit of exchange was often a bushel of wheat, neither of the former farm hands had probably handled currency, stock certificates, or bonds. Yet they formulated a bold plan for financial salvation based on the belief that God would back them fiscally and bring success to their economic plans. According to Wickliffe Rigdon, his father initially opposed the idea of the Kirtland Safety Society Bank, arguing "it would not be legal as they had no charter."[29] Others opposed the bank as well. William McLellin, at the time a member of the Quorum of the Twelve, noted that Smith, Rigdon, and other church leaders did not wait for a charter. They forged ahead thinking that "everything must bow at their nod—thus violating the laws of the land."[30] McLellin, who left the church shortly after, said that the three witnesses to the Book of Mormon warned Smith against "this evil course" but managed only to rouse his anger.[31]

The first recorded activity of the proposed Kirtland Safety Society Bank occurred early in August 1836 when Smith, Cowdery, and Rigdon visited a New York City firm to discuss acquisition of bank plates.[32] Rigdon, whose name is listed first in the Safety Society stock ledger, purchased 2,000 shares of stock for $12 on 18 October 1836. The following month he added another 1,000 shares. Rigdon, Smith, and two others subsequently held 3,000 shares each, making them the largest stockholders.[33] The constitution for the depository was drawn up on 2 November 1836. Rigdon was elected president and Smith cashier. Cashiers at that time were commonly the chief operating officers, responsible for daily operations including transactions, bookkeeping, accounts, records, and personnel, answering to the president.

Despite their official designations, Rigdon and Smith were co-equals in the Kirtland Safety Society. Their signatures were affixed to nearly every bank note issued by the firm. After Smith's 1844 murder, church leaders under Brigham Young's direction closed ranks and retrospectively attributed full blame for the society's demise to Rigdon. Jedediah M. Grant, Young's close associate, wrote later that during the summer and fall of 1835 Rigdon

> commenced lecturing the saints on the subject of getting rich. His flights [of fancy]

were so rapid that Elder Smith was unable to keep him within the bounds of reason, many others, also, protested against his course, Elder R[igdon] in order to convince the multitude that he was right, expatiated in the most extravagant manner on the . . . Scripture[s], applying them to the saints.

Rigdon's lectures, Grant insisted, were "directed to the passions of the people," and "caused many in indigent circumstances to imagine themselves rich." Furthermore, Grant continued, Rigdon's

analogies, resemblances, illustrations, paintings, and figures, were superlatively brilliant, and captivating in the extreme, but alas! when a few months had passed away, they found that their riches were like Jonah's gourd, they had sprung up in a night, and perished in a day. . . . Elder Rigdon's imaginary schemes of wealth and grandeur having all vanished into insignificance, he was under the necessity of leaving Ohio, in search of another place of abode. He finally located himself among the Saints in Caldwell County, Missouri.[34]

Grant's inaccurate assessment of Rigdon is but one example of misrepresentation characteristic of the Illinois period of Mormon history. Under the guise of denying polygamy, protecting "the Lord's anointed," or advancing the Quorum of the Twelve to the pinnacle of ecclesiastical power, the character of many good men and women was assailed by forces of fanatical religious allegiance.

But in October 1836, when Oliver Cowdery and Orson Hyde were dispatched on missions for the Kirtland Safety Society, Joseph Smith and Sidney Rigdon together inaugurated the chain reaction that ensued. Cowdery traveled to Philadelphia to obtain bank note plates from the firm of Underwood, Bald, Spencer, and Huffy. Hyde, a member of the pro-banking Whig party, traveled to Columbus to petition the Ohio thirty-fifth General Assembly for a bank charter. Cowdery's task was relatively easy: to make payment and bring back the plates. Hyde's chore, however, was impossible. Despite Hyde's political connections, the Kirtland community for the most part favored the Democrat party. All three legislators representing the Kirtland area were Whigs, politicians too savvy to support a Mormon bank in a Democrat stronghold. Furthermore, these three Geauga legislators were closely linked to Grandison Newell, a rabid anti-Mormon who in 1837 practically singlehandedly drove Rigdon and Smith from Ohio under a barrage of legal encumbrances.

Ohio passed a law on 27 January 1816 prohibiting the issue and circulation of unauthorized money.[35] Although the prudent state legislature denied the petition to charter a bank, the press of short-term loans and other financial stresses caused Rigdon and Smith to abandon prudence and establish their financial institution under the guise of a "mutual stock association." On 2 January 1837 officers of the Kirtland Safety Society met in their new building just south of the temple. Assuming they could assign banking functions to a private corporation as had been done in other areas, they executed a revised "Articles of Agreement."

Rigdon was called as chair and Warren Parrish secretary. "After much discussion and investigation," the group reorganized. Its amended mission statement read:

> We, the undersigned subscribers [Rigdon's name was first], for the promotion of our temporal interests, and for the better management of our different occupations, which consist in agriculture, mechanical arts, and merchandising; do hereby form ourselves into a firm or company for the before mentioned objects, by the name of the "Kirtland Safety Society Anti-Banking Company."[36]

The list of subscribers was impressive: everyone from Elijah Abel to Lucy Smith to Brigham Young was listed. To emphasize Joseph Smith's endorsement of the new bank, the local newspaper contained his personal admonishment that "It is wisdom and according to the mind of the Holy Spirit, that you should call at Kirtland. . . . [W]e invite the brethren from abroad, to call on us, and take stock in our Safety Society."[37]

On the morning of 6 January the firm first issued "stock certificates" in varying denominations from $1 to $100. By month's end, $15,000 in bank notes were circulating throughout the community as paper currency. As one study of the Safety Society noted, "The founders of the bank did not realize that because Oliver Cowdery arrived with pieces of paper with dollar signs and numbers on them which summed to $150,000 this did not add one penny to Kirtland's wealth."[38] Mormons accepted Safety Society notes as legal tender because they believed the bank was created by God, that it had a sacred mission, and thus was invincible. Both Rigdon and Smith contributed liberally to the creation of this impression. Wilford Woodruff, present at the grand opening of the bank, wrote in his diary,

> I . . . he[a]rd President Joseph Smith, Jr., declare in the presence of F. Williams, D. Whitmer, S. Smith, W. Parrish, and others in the Deposit office that he had received that morning the word of the Lord upon the subject of the Kirtland Safety Society. He was alone in a room by himself and he had not only [heard] the voice of the Spirit upon the Subject but even an audible voice. He did not tell us at that time what the LORD said upon the subject but remarked that if we would give heed to the Commandments the Lord had given this morning all would be well.[39]

Warren Parrish, Smith's personal secretary as well as an officer in the Safety Society, later wrote that the prophet said "that the audible voice of God instructed him to establish a Banking-Anti-Banking Institution, which, like Aaron's rod, should swallow up all other Banks . . . and grow and flourish and spread from the rivers to the ends of the earth, and survive when all others should be laid in ruins."[40]

Within a matter of weeks the desperately-conceived nineteenth-century savings and loan institution began to flounder. The 12 January 1837 *Cleveland Daily Gazette* announced:

> During the past two days an emission of bills from the society of Mormons, has been

showered upon us. As far as we can learn there is no property bound for their redemption, no coin on hand to redeem them with, and no responsible individuals whose honor or whose honesty is pledged for their payment. They seem to rest upon a spiritual basis. —Aside from the violation of the statute rendering them void, and of course the notes given for them, we look upon the whole as a more reprehensible fraud on the public, and cannot conceal our surprise that they should circulate at all. We do not object to private or company banking, as a system, provided it is done *upon a system and made safe*, but we consider this whole affair a deception.[41]

Less than a week later, in a stronger denunciation, the 18 January 1837 *Cleveland Weekly Gazette* called the Kirtland Safety Society Anti-Banking Company a "stupendous fraud in the community" and editorialized further: "We know that Rigdon, a notorious hypocrite and knave, is at the head of the concern, for ourselves, we are anxious to see some guaranty that there is good faith and property in this banking matter—something to protect the community against a revelation that Joe Smith should take up what little money they have, and depart hence."

A consortium of Pittsburgh bankers was perhaps the first to test the soundness of the Kirtland bank. Loading a hand-satchel with Safety Society notes, a representative of the Pittsburgh group arrived in Kirtland and called on Rigdon. Producing the bundle of bills, he asked for their immediate redemption in coin. Rigdon declined to exchange, however, stating that the paper had been put forth as a "circulating medium for the accommodation of the people," and that it would be "thwarting that purpose to call any of it in."[42]

The stock ledger of the Safety Society reveals that 200 persons subscribed to 79,420 shares of stock at a face value of approximately $3,854,000. Yet the paid-up cash reserve totalled a meager $20,725.[43] Lacking sufficient cash reserves to back its currency, bank officials offered inflated real estate instead of coin for scrip exchanges when put to the test. On 27 January the *Painesville Telegraph* notified readers of Rigdon's announcement that no specie would be given for Kirtland bank notes thereafter.[44] To improve cash flow, Smith as bank cashier publicly appealed to church members to acquire stock by payment of specie. He promised that "if the elders will remember the Kirtland Safety Society and do as they should Kirtland will become a great city."[45] But people sensed they might be on a sinking ship and began trading off currency. By 1 February the $70,000 worth of notes were being discounted at 12.5 cents on the dollar.

On 9 April 1837, during Sunday services in the Kirtland temple, Rigdon sermonized that "the Presidency had used every means for the deliverance of the Church but as many of the Church had refused Kirtland Currency[,] which was their temporal salvation[,] . . . they [had] put strength in the hands of their enemies . . . and must suffer by it." Smith then "arose like the lion of the tribe of JUDAH," Wilford Woodruff recorded, and promised that those "who had turned traitors,

[and] opposed the currency and consequently the prosperity of Kirtland," would be severely dealt with by the Lord.[46]

Nonetheless, Smith and Rigdon soon found themselves entrapped in a hopeless vortex of legal entanglements. The 1 February 1837 *Cleveland Weekly Gazette* first raised serious questions about the Kirtland Safety Society bank which, despite several attempts, was never legally chartered.[47] Recognizing this, Samuel D. Rounds, a front man for a prosperous Kirtland farmer and businessman, Grandison Newell, swore out a writ against Rigdon and Smith shortly after the bank's opening.[48] The writ accused the two of illegal banking in defiance of the 1816 Ohio statutes. A hearing on 24 March 1837 postponed the trial until the fall session of the court. At the jury trial in October 1837 Rigdon and Smith were both found guilty and fined $1,000 each plus court charges. Although they appealed, both fled the state before their court date.[49]

Rounds's writ was only one of a deluge filed against Rigdon, Smith, and other church leaders in 1837. E. D. Howe, editor of the nearby *Painesville Telegraph*, later explained the reasoning behind the legal harassment:

> All [the Mormons'] vain babblings and pretensions were pretty strongly set forth and noticed in the columns of the TELEGRAPH. In view of all their gaseous pretensions the surrounding country was becoming somewhat sensitive, and many of our citizens thought it advisable to take all the legal means within their reach to counteract the progress of so dangerous an enemy in their midst, and many law suits ensued.[50]

Despite the flurry of law suits, charges, countercharges, arrests, and personal threats submerging the bank, the institution continued operation with adjustments in its official staff until it closed its doors in November 1837. Joseph Smith was still signing bills as late as June 1837; Frederick Williams was then listed as secretary and Smith as treasurer.[51] In March 1838 the Kirtland Safety Society Bank was numbered in newspaper accounts among seventeen "Broken Banks and Fraudulent Institutions."[52] The bank's failure reverberated throughout the Mormon economy. Land speculators were unable to pay creditors, merchants who purchased goods on credit from Buffalo and New York became insolvent, consumers were unable to pay bills or make purchases, and the job market dried up because employers would not hire Latter-day Saints. The entire economy quickly folded.[53]

Neither Rigdon nor Smith foresaw the disaster, nor did they predict the even greater disintegration of the American economy generally which came to be known as the "Panic of '37." As late as the spring of 1837 Smith was still expounding grand visions of Kirtland, such as one recorded by Wilford Woodruff:

> Joseph presented us in some degree the plot of the city of Kirtland . . . as it was given him by vision. It was great[,] marvelous & glorious. The city extended to the east, west, North, and South. Steam boats will come puffing into the city. Our goods will be conveyed upon railroads from Kirtland to many places & probably to Zion. Houses

of worship would be reared unto the most high. Beautiful streets [were] to be made for the Saints to walk in. Kings of the earth would come to behold the glory thereof & and many glorious things not now to be named would be bestowed upon the saints.[54]

May 1837 nevertheless brought disaster to the entire country. Within a single month 800 banks with $120,000,000 in deposits suspended operations. Historian Samuel E. Morrison wrote:

[Martin] Van Buren was no sooner seated in the White House than American mercantile houses and banks began to fail, and there were riots in New York over the high cost of flour. In May [1837], after almost every bank in the country had suspended specie payments, and the government had lost $9 million through the collapse of pet banks, the President summoned Congress for a special session. In the meantime, there was widespread suffering.[55]

Even with a legitimate bank charter, the Kirtland Bank would likely have failed during the economic turmoil of 1837-42. But compliance with a charter could have prevented the rash of lawsuits lodged against Rigdon and Smith and may have diminished the mass apostasy in the wake of the failure as many Saints held the leaders personally responsible for the economic mayhem. Financial reverses sustained by church members were not the only cause for the anger and victimization many felt. The prophet and his spokesman had said that the bank, established by divine mandate, could not fail. Where now was the guarantee? Between November 1837 and June 1838 approximately 300 Kirtland members, representing perhaps 15 percent of all Mormons, withdrew or were excommunicated from the church. Included were nearly one-third of the church's leading officers, the three witnesses to the Book of Mormon, four members of the Quorum of the Twelve, three original presidents and three current presidents of Seventy, as well as Frederick G. Williams, a member of the First Presidency.[56]

Notes

Unless otherwise stated, all primary sources cited are located in the Historical Department of the Church of Jesus Christ of Latter-day Saints, Salt Lake City, Utah.

1. Scott H. Faulring, ed., *An American Prophet's Record: The Diaries and Journals of Joseph Smith* (Salt Lake City: Signature Books in association with Smith Research Associates, 1989), 30-31.

2. Brigham Young's 1859 personal property assessments of $100,000 were only slightly less than the church's entire assessment in Salt Lake County. By his death, Young estimated his personal wealth at approximately $1,000,000. See D. Michael Quinn, "The Mormon Hierarchy, 1832-1932: An American Elite," Ph.D. diss., Yale University, 1976, 105-106; also George Q. Cannon's 1872 statement that Young had deposited "a hundred thousand dollars tithing—the tithing of his own personal means" in Zion's Cooperative

Mercantile Institution (*Journal of Discourses*, 26 vols. [London: Latter-day Saints' Book Depot, 1854-86] 15 [8 Oct. 1872]: 106; hereafter *Journal of Discourses*).

3. Roger D. Launius, *The Kirtland Temple: A Historical Narrative* (Independence, MO: Herald Publishing House, 1986), 36.

4. Joseph Smith, Jr., to "Edward [Partridge], William [Phelps] and others of the firm," 30 Mar. 1834, Joseph Smith Collection.

5. Fawn M. Brodie, *No Man Knows My History*, 2d ed. rev. (New York: Alfred Knopf, 1971), 202.

6. Marvin S. Hill, C. Keith Rooker, and Larry T. Wimmer, "The Kirtland Economy Revisited: A Market Critique of Sectarian Economics," *Brigham Young University Studies* 17 (Summer 1977): 416.

7. John Corrill, *Brief History of the Church of Christ of Latter Day Saints* (St. Louis: n.p., 1839), 26, 27. The 19 January 1837 edition of *The Aurora* (Lisbon, OH) contained an article, "Mormonism in Ohio" (dated 14 Nov. 1836), in which an observer wrote:

> Last week I passed through Kirtland, and I was astonished to see that a city had sprung up since I was there last March. I should think there were between 100 and 200 houses (perhaps more) new buildings, most of them are small and plain, but some of them are elegant. . . . Most of the farms between the centre of Kirtland and the centre of Chester, they own; they also own a large store in Chester, and do business under the firm of Rigdon, Smith, & Co., they trade on a large scale, and made market for every thing that can be raised about here. . . . They have procured plates from New York, for issuing Bank notes payable in 30 days after demanded (Mormon Manu-scripts Retrieval Project, Special Collections, Harold B. Lee Library, Brigham Young University, Provo, Utah; hereafter Special Collections, BYU).

8. Faulring, 19-20.

9. *Painesville Telegraph*, 31 Jan. 1834.

10. *Latter Day Saints Messenger and Advocate*, Sept. 1836, 379.

11. Joseph Smith, *History of the Church of Jesus Christ of Latter-day Saints*, B. H. Roberts, ed. 7 vols. (Salt Lake City: The Church of Jesus Christ of Latter-day Saints, 1902), 2:54; hereafter *History of the Church*.

12. Ibid., 48.

13. Ibid.

14. Dale W. Adams, "Chartering the Kirtland Bank," *Brigham Young University Studies* 4 (Fall 1983): 468.

15. Undated Frederick G. Williams statement, Williams Collection.

16. Geauga Deed Records, Book 18, 487-88, in Milton V. Backman, Jr., *The Heavens Resound: A History of the Latter-day Saints in Ohio, 1830-1838* (Salt Lake City: Deseret Book Co., 1983), 73; D&C 104:20.

17. As Mormon historian Lyndon W. Cook has noted, few Mormons were aware of the United Firm in the 1830s. Even prominent leaders like Brigham Young, who was not a firm member, later confused terms regarding "law of consecration" and "United Firm." Consequently in the 1870s "United Order" and "Order of Enoch" were used by Saints to refer to churchwide communitarian programs instituted by Young. The stated agendas of these plans sought to elevate the poor, achieve a self-sufficient economy, and establish

spiritual unity. Twentieth-century usage of "Law of Consecration," "Law of Consecration and Stewardship," "United Order," and "Order of Enoch" have become synonymous to Mormons. "It is often assumed, erroneously," Cook asserts, "that these terms refer to a single economic program revealed to Joseph Smith in the 1830s, and that this same program will be practiced by the Saints in the future" (Lyndon W. Cook, *Joseph Smith and the Law of Consecration* [Orem, UT: Keepsake Paperbacks, 1991], 65-67).

18. Dean C. Jessee, ed., *The Papers of Joseph Smith, Volume 1, Autobiographical and Historical Writings* (Salt Lake City: Deseret Book Co., 1989), 147-48.

19. "Kirtland Council Minute Book," 212-14.

20. *History of the Church*, 2:464.

21. Rigdon and Cowdery toured the East India Marine Society museum on 6 August; the Smiths did likewise three days later. See "Album for the Use of Visitors, Salem East India Marine Society, October 7, 1834 to August 26, 1837," Peabody Museum of Salem, in David R. Proper, "Joseph Smith and Salem," *Essex Institute Historical Collections* 100 (Apr. 1964): 94.

22. Ibid., 93-94.

23. This is likely a reference to Jonathan Burgess. Box 5, fd 6, of "Promissory notes by Joseph Smith" contains a $100 note signed by Cowdery and Rigdon promising to pay Jonathan Burgess "one year from date with use." The item was signed in Salem, Massachusetts, on 17 August 1836.

24. Ebenezer Robinson, "Items of Personal History of the Editor," *The Return* (Davis City, IA), July 1889, 105-106. See also James Colin Brewster, *Very Important to the Mormon Money Diggers* (Springfield, IL: 20 Mar. 1843).

25. Dean C. Jessee, *The Personal Writings of Joseph Smith* (Salt Lake City: Deseret Book Co., 1984), 350.

26. *The Return*, 105-106.

27. *History of the Church*, 2:468-69.

28. A. G. Riddle, cited in Williams Brothers, *History of Lake and Geauga Counties, Ohio* (Philadelphia: J. B. Lippencott & Co., 1878), 248.

29. Karl Keller, ed., "I Never Knew a Time When I Did Not Know Joseph Smith," *Dialogue: A Journal of Mormon Thought* 1 (Winter 1966): 27-28.

30. Donna Hill, *Joseph Smith: The First Mormon* (New York: Doubleday, 1977), 206.

31. Ibid.

32. *Latter Day Saints Messenger and Advocate* 2 (Sept. 1836): 375.

33. Stanley B. Kimball, "Sources on the History of the Mormons in Ohio: 1830-38," *Brigham Young University Studies* 11 (Summer 1971): 531-32.

34. Jedediah M. Grant, *A Collection of Facts Relative to the Course Taken by Elder Sidney Rigdon, in the States of Ohio, Missouri, Illinois and Pennsylvania* (Philadelphia: Brown, Bicking & Guilbert, 1844), 10.

35. Charles Clifford Huntington, *A History of Banking and Currency in Ohio before the Civil War* (Columbus, OH: Ohio Archaeological and Historical Publications, 1915).

36. *Latter Day Saints Messenger and Advocate* 3:475.

37. Ibid., 443.

38. Adams, 476.

39. Scott G. Kenney, ed., *Wilford Woodruff's Journal–Typescript*, 9 vols. (Midvale, UT: Signature Books, 1983), 1:120.

40. 5 Feb. 1838 letter from Warren Parrish to the editor of *The Painesville Republican*, re-printed in the 22 Mar. 1838 *The Ohio Repository*.

41. Article is found in Mormon Manuscripts Retrieval Project, Special Collections, BYU.

42. J. H. Kennedy, *Early Days of Mormonism* (London: Reeves and Turner, 1888), 163.

43. Kimball, "Mormons in Ohio," 531-32. Brigham Young purchased 2,000 shares on 9 December 1836 for a deposit of $7.00 and was shocked to later receive one of his endorsed notes as part of a financial transaction, thinking they would have been stored like stock certificates. Because his notes were circulating, he concluded that something was amiss (Andrew Jenson, *Historical Record* [9 vols.] [Salt Lake City: Published by author, 1888], 5:433-40).

44. See also the *Cleveland Herald and Gazette*, 25 Jan. 1837, and the *Western Reserve Chronicle* (Warren, OH), 7 Feb. 1837.

45. *Latter Day Saints' Messenger and Advocate* 3 (Jan. 1837): 443.

46. Kenney, 1:142.

47. Rigdon and Smith must have been encouraged by trusted associates outside the Mormon community, perhaps local Democratic party leaders, to expect they would be granted a charter. After the first attempt failed, Orson Hyde again applied on 10 February 1837. The eleven Mormon names attached to this application included Rigdon, Smith, Whitney, Warren Cowdery, Hyrum Smith, and Oliver Cowdery. Non-Mormon signatures included Benjamin Adams (Painesville postmaster and local Democrat leader), Nehemiah Allen (prominent citizen of nearby Willoughby), Benjamin Bissell (Rigdon's and Smith's personal lawyer, also a prominent Democrat), Horace Kingsbury (prominent Painesville citizen and Democrat), and H. A. Sharp (prominent Willoughby citizen). Despite this list of supporters, the charter bid again failed.

Church leaders did obtain a charter for the Monroe Bank in Michigan territory at this time, which added to their circulation of currency. According to Wilford Woodruff, during a meeting in the Kirtland temple on 31 January 1837, Smith announced that the First Presidency had "bought the Monroe charter & we all lent a hand in establishing it, that it might be ben[e]ficial to us in forwarding the building of the temporal Kingdom" (Kenney, 1:124).

48. Newell, who claimed to have spent $1,000 in court actions against Mormons during 1837, gave Rounds $100 for his trouble (see unpublished manuscript by Mrs. Mary Newell, "Thomas Newell and His Descendants," 1878, on file in the Lake County Historical Library, Mentor, Ohio).

49. See Common Pleas, *Record Book U*, Geauga County, Ohio, 353f.

50. E. D. Howe, *Autobiography and Recollections of a Pioneer Printer* (Painesville, OH: Telegraph Steam Printing House, 1878), 45.

51. See a sample bill in Joseph Smith III and Heman C. Smith, *The History of the Reorganized Church of Jesus Christ of Latter Day Saints*, 4 vols. (Independence, MO: Herald House, 1967 reprint), 2:n.p.

52. *The Republican* (Willoughby, OH), 15 Mar. 1838.

53. For other references on the Kirtland economy, see Brodie; Robert K. Fielding, "The Growth of the Mormon Church in Kirtland, Ohio," Ph.D. diss., Indiana University, 1957; Max H. Parkin, "The Nature and Causes of External and Internal Conflict of the Mormons in Ohio between 1830 and 1838," M.A. thesis, University of Utah, 1966; Elizabeth G. Hitchcock, "Grandison Newell, A Born Trader," *Historical Society Quarterly* (Lake County, OH) 10 (May 1968); Paul Sampson and Larry D. Wimmer, "The Kirtland Safety Society: The Stock Ledger Book and the Bank Failure," *Brigham Young University Studies* 12 (Summer 1972): 427-36; Anne B. Prusha, "A History of Kirtland, Ohio," M.A. thesis, Kent State University, 1971; Scott H. Partridge, "The Failure of the Kirtland Safety Society Anti-Banking Company," *Journal of Economic History* 30 (Dec. 1971): 848-53; and Hill, Wimmer, and Rooker.

54. Kenney, 1:134.

55. Samuel E. Morrison, *The Oxford History of the American People* (New York: Oxford University Press, 1965), 455.

56. Launius, 84.

CHAPTER 15.

Exiled to the Land of Milk and Honey

*Beware of such as attack you as soon as you enter [Kirtland], and begin to
interrogate you about the amount of money you have, and to importune you for it, with
assurances that you shall have it refunded with interest, and that the Lord shall bless
you abundantly; yea, and multiply blessings upon you. Of such we say beware. They
take advantage of your honest simplicity, obtain your available means, and then desert
you.*

—Warren Cowdery, *Latter Day Saints' Messenger and Advocate*, May 1837[1]

Possessing entirely different personalities in most respects, Sidney Rigdon and
Joseph Smith were surprisingly alike in other ways. One of their most
intriguing similarities was a powerful belief in their own correctness. Neither
readily conceded personal error or misconduct. Plans that went awry were
attributed to someone else. The collapse of the Kirtland Safety Society Anti-Banking Company illustrates this as well as any example. Although Rigdon and Smith
were principal officers and stockholders in the failed bank, neither accepted
culpability. Strategies for shifting blame involved a convoluted reconfiguring of
events whereby Warren Parrish, the prophet's personal secretary, and Frederick
G. Williams, a member of the First Presidency, were made villains.

Legal difficulties aside, problems within the Mormon flock erupted as early
as 19 February 1837 when some church members, murmuring that they had been
fleeced, divested themselves of Kirtland bank notes at a substantial discount.
Wilford Woodruff noted in his journal that Smith, just back from a business trip,
spoke to a congregation in the temple for several hours to suppress the rising storm
of concern among adherents. "Although he had not been away half as long as
Moses was on the Mount," said Woodruff, "yet many were stirred up in their
hearts and some were against him."[2]

During a 6 April 1837 Kirtland conference, church leaders concentrated
considerable energy on the church's perilous financial position. The prophet
began by explaining:

> There are many causes of embarrassment, of a pecuniary nature now pressing
> upon the heads of the Church. They began poor; were needy, destitute, and were truly

afflicted by their enemies; yet the Lord commanded them to go forth and preach the gospel, to sacrifice their time, their talents, their good name, and jeopardize their lives; and in addition to this, they were to build a house for the Lord, and prepare for the gathering of the Saints. . . . Large contracts have been entered into for lands on all sides, where our enemies have signed away their rights. We are indebted to them, but our brethren from abroad have only to come with their money, take these contracts, relieve their brethren from the pecuniary embarrassments under which they now labor, and procure for themselves a peaceable place of rest among us. This place must and will be built up, and every brother that will take hold and help secure and discharge those contracts that have been made, shall be rich.

Hyrum Smith and Oliver Cowdery then spoke briefly, after which Rigdon took the stand, focusing on the unliquidated debt of the church. He defined that obligation as $6,000 from the Jackson County calamity, a $13,000 deficit on the Kirtland temple, and an unspecified debit, probably the largest single item, for real estate purchases. The justification was "that there might be a place of rest, a place of safety, a place that the Saints might lawfully call their own."[3]

Fearing arrest and harassment from impatient creditors, Rigdon and Smith were forced into hiding frequently during the remaining months of 1837. Lorenzo Brown, writing of this period, said his family was "visited by Presidents Joseph Smith and Sidney Rigdon, who on account of persecution heaped upon them often stayed three days and nights in the woods concealed."[4] On 13 April both missed the wedding of Wilford Woodruff and Phebe Carter and the nuptials of George W. Robinson and Athalia Rigdon, Sidney's oldest daughter, because, as Woodruff recorded, their lives were "sought for by wicked and ungodly men."[5]

One of the malevolent men Woodruff alluded to was evidently Grandison Newell, the wealthy industrialist who lived in nearby Mentor. For unknown reasons, Newell made the oppression of Mormonism his personal vendetta and wanted Rigdon in his camp. "Your bosom associate," began his 1837 letter to Rigdon, "is the imposture[r] Smith, the impious fabricator of gold bibles—the blasphemous forger of revelations, with which he swindles ignorant people out of their hard-earned property." Newell's diatribe claimed that two well-armed men "under the express direction of their prophet" had waited outside the Newell home, and "in a moment when I was defenseless and suspecting no danger" planned to assassinate him. The two alleged gunmen, Solomon H. Denton and a Mr. Davis, lost their nerve and, according to Newell, left the scene.[6]

Newell brought charges against Smith before Judge Flint of Painesville. A group of Newell's friends rode to Kirtland to apprehend the prophet, but he eluded the vigilantes. The 3 June trial, *The State of Ohio, vs. Joseph Smith, Jr., alias The Prophet*, was held in Painesville's Methodist church before a large crowd of spectators anxious to witness a disclosure of the "murderous projects of the modern prophet," reported the 5 July 1837 *Ohio Statesman*. Rigdon testified that "information came to him from some quarter" that Davis and Denton "entertained designs against" Newell's life. He told Smith, he said, and afterwards the prophet informed him that "through his influence Davis and Denton had laid aside their purpose."[7] Despite the lack of incriminating evidence, Justice Flint ordered Smith bound over to the Court of Common Pleas.

The second trial was held at Chardon on 9 June, presided over by Judge Humphrey. After hearing the evidence, the judge acquitted the defendant on grounds that Newell's hatred for Smith induced his action against the defendant rather than fear of assassination.[8] Newell, dissatisfied with the decision, wrote a plea to the citizenry which was published in the 30 June 1837 *Painesville Telegraph*. Public opinion rested unexpectedly in Smith's favor, and the matter was quietly dropped.[9]

While Rigdon's and Smith's attentions were focused on the prophet's trials, defections within Mormonism's highest circles were brewing. Later compilers of the *History of the Church*, using Smith's narrative voice, provided the historical backdrop for this period:

> At this time the spirit of speculation in lands and property of all kinds, which was so prevalent throughout the whole nation, was taking deep root in the Church. As the fruits of this spirit, evil surmisings, fault-finding, disunion, dissension, and apostasy followed in quick succession, and it seemed as though all the powers of earth and hell were combining their influence in an especial manner to overthrow the Church at once, and make a final end. Other banking institutions refused the "Kirtland Safety Society's" notes. The enemy abroad, and apostates in our midst, united in their schemes, flour and provisions were turned towards other markets, and many became disaffected toward me as though I were the sole cause of those very evils.[10]

The most formidable Kirtland dissenter was Warren Parrish, pronounced the "Lord's Scribe" in an unpublished 14 November 1835 revelation.[11] Teller of the Kirtland bank, Parrish quickly became disenchanted with Smith's and Rigdon's management and "prophetic pretensions." Subsequently explaining his reasons for dissent, he confessed:

> I have listened to [the prophet] with feelings of no ordinary kind when he declared that the audible voice of God instructed him to establish a Banking-Anti-Banking Institution, which, like Aaron's rod, should swallow up all other Banks . . . and grow and flourish and spread from the rivers to the ends of the earth, and survive when all others should be laid in ruins. I have been astonished to hear him declare that we had $30,000 in our vaults, and $600,000 at our command, when we had not to exceed $6,000, and could not command any more: also, that we had but about $10,000 of our bills in curculation, when he, as Cashier of the institution, knew that there was at least $150,000. . . . [His and Rigdon's] management in this place has reduced [the] society to a complete wreck.[12]

According to Wickliffe Rigdon, another underlying cause of difficulty was

Rigdon's and Smith's inability to pay Parrish back the "hard money" he had loaned to them to "start the bank with." Presumably basing his account on what his father told him, Wickliffe said that on their default Parrish threatened he would "get judgment against [them], and if judgment was not paid, he would put them in jail where they would stay until judgment was paid."[13] Perhaps seeking money to appease Parrish, Smith put pressure on Apostle Parley P. Pratt by calling due a debit. Pratt exploded in anger. In a furious 23 May 1837 letter to the prophet, Pratt criticized his and Rigdon's leadership in the bank:

> Having long pondered the path in which we as a people, have been led in regard to our temporal management, I have at length become fully convinced that the whole scheme of speculation in which we have been engaged, is of the devil. I allude to the covetous, extortionary speculating spirit which has reigned in this place for the last season; which has given rise to lying, deceiving and taking advantage of one's neighbor, and in short every evil work.
>
> And being as fully convinced that you, and president Rigdon, both by precept and example, have been the principal means in leading this people astray, in these particulars, and having myself been led astray and caught in the same snare by your example, and by false prophesying and preaching, from your own mouths, yea, having done many things wrong and plunged myself and family, and others, well nigh into destruction, I have awoke to an awful sense of my situation, and now resolve to retrace my steps and get out of the snare, and make restitution as far as I can.
>
> And now dear brother, if you are still determined to pursue this wicked cause, until yourself and the church shall sink down to hell, I beseech you at least, to have mercy on me and my family, and others who are bound with me for those three lots which you sold to me at the extortionary price of 2000 dollars, which never cost you 100 dollars. For if it stands against me it will ruin me and my helpless family, as well as those bound with me: for yesterday president Rigdon came to me and informed me, that you had drawn the money from the bank, on the obligations which you held against me, and that you had left it to the mercy of the bank, and could not help whatever course they might take to collect it; not withstanding the most SACRED PROMISE on your part, that I should not be injured by those writings. I offered the three lots for the writings; but he wanted my house and home also.
>
> Now, dear brother, will you take those lots and give me up the writings, and pay me the 75 dollars, which I paid you on the same? Or will you take the advantage of the neighbor because he is in your power? If you will receive this admonition of one who loves your soul, and repent of your extortion and covetousness in this thing, and make restitution, you have my fellowship and esteem, as far as it respects our dealings between ourselves.
>
> But if not, I shall be under the painful necessity of preferring charges against you for extortion, covetousness, and taking advantage of your brother by an undue religious influence. For it is this kind of influence which led us to make this kind of trades in this society. Such as saying it was the will of God that lands should bear with such a price; and many other prophesyings, preachings and statements of a like nature.[14]

Opposition to Smith and Rigdon threatened the foundation of the church. Wilford Woodruff, writing of "murm[u]ring, complaining, & of mutiny" in his 28 May 1837 diary, spoke of efforts "to overthrow [the prophet's] influence & cast him down untill Joseph was grieved in spirit to stand in such perils among fals brethren."[15] Despite this "thick cloud of darkness standing over Kirtland," Smith faced his followers and detractors in the temple and "spake to the people in the name of the Lord in his own defence."[16] Rigdon followed with an eloquent plea, and others also spoke in the prophet's favor. "But, Alas," wrote Woodruff, Warren Parrish "arose, once a friend, (not now) in the blackness of his face & corruption of his heart stretched out his puny arm and proclaimed against Joseph."[17]

Not only were Parrish and Pratt contesting the prophet's leadership, but on 29 May apostles Orson Pratt and Lyman Johnson brought charges against him before a bishop's court condemning him for "lying and misrepresentation—also for extortion—and for speaking disrespectfully against his brethren behind their backs."[18] The same day Parrish brought charges against Rigdon before the bishop and high council: "[F]or expressing an unbelief in the revelations of God, both old and new. Also an unbelief in the agency of man and his accountability to God, or that there is such a principle existing as sin—and also for lying & declaring that God required it at his hands."[19]

To counter the charges against Rigdon and Smith, the Kirtland High Council that evening summoned Isaac Rogers, Artemas Millet, Abel Lamb, and Harlow Redfield to testify against dissidents Frederick G. Williams, David Whitmer, Parley P. Pratt, Lyman Johnson, and Warren Parrish. The prophet, in his own words, was so afflicted "I was unable to raise my head from my pillow" and was absent.[20] Rigdon, the presiding officer at the hearing, read the charges:

> We, the undersigned, feeling ourselves aggrieved with the conduct of [the above named men] believing that their course for some time past has been injurious to the Church of God, in which they are high officers, we therefore desire that the High Council should be assembled, and we should have an investigation of their behavior, believing it to be unworthy of their high calling.[21]

After considerable discussion of proper church procedure, the council determined "they could not conscientiously proceed to try Presidents Williams and Whitmer, and they were accordingly discharged." After an adjournment the group reassembled and engaged in an intense discussion. The clerk noted that "the Council and assembly then dispersed in confusion."[22]

The matter did not end there. Mary Fielding, in a 15 June 1837 letter to her sister, stated that the two previous Sundays were "consumed by internal dissension."[23] Oliver Huntington added that the Parrish faction created a disturbance at the temple "every day of the week, Sunday not excepted."[24] Eliza R. Snow later recalled a remarkable fray on one of those days, possibly 4 June:

[Warren Parrish] with several of his party, came into the Temple armed with pistols and bowie-knives, and seated themselves together in the Aaronic pulpits, on the east of the Temple, while Father [Joseph] Smith [Sr.] and others, as usual, occupied those of the Melchizedek Priesthood on the west. Soon after the usual opening services, one of the brethren on the west stand arose, and just after he commenced to speak, one of the east interrupted him. Father Smith, presiding, called to order—he told the apostate brother that he should have all the time he wanted, but he must wait his turn—as the brother on the west took the floor and commenced to speak, he must not be interrupted. A fearful scene ensued—the apostate speaker became so clamorous, that Father Smith called for the police to take that man out of the house, when Parrish, John Boynton, and others, drew their pistols and bowie-knives, and rushed down from the stand into the congregation; J. Boynton saying he would blow out the brains of the first man who dared to lay hands on him. Many in the congregation, especially women and children, were terribly frightened—some tried to escape from the confusion by jumping out of the windows. Amid screams and shrieks, the policemen, in ejecting the belligerents, knocked down a stovepipe, which fell helter-skelter among the people; but although bowie-knives and pistols were wrested from their owners, and thrown hither and thither to prevent disastrous results, no one was hurt, and after a short, but terrible scene to be enacted in a Temple of God, order was restored, and the services of the day proceeded as usual.[25]

Lucy Mack Smith, apparently describing this same scene, varies in a few details. She recalled that the chaos began when Joseph Smith, Sr., speaking of "the bank affair . . . reflected somewhat sharply upon Warren Parrish." Parrish rushed to the stand, grabbed the elderly Smith, and began to drag him from the stand. Smith's appeals to Oliver Cowdery did no good. William Smith jumped up to assist his father, but Apostle John F. Boynton drew a sword and held it against his chest threatening, "if you advance one step further, I will run you through." At this point Mother Smith noted she, along with many others, fled the temple in fear.[26]

The following Sunday Parley P. Pratt, not yet reconciled with Smith, continued his public attack on the First Presidency. He charged that the entire church had departed from God's ways and that the prophet had committed "great sins."[27] Benjamin Winchester stood and challenged the assumption that Smith "was authorized by God almighty to establish his kingdom—that he was God's prophet and God's agent and that he could do whatever he should choose to do, therefore the Church had NO RIGHT TO CALL INTO QUESTION anything he did, or to censure him for the reason that he was responsible to God Almighty only."[28] At this point Rigdon arose and announced he shared the reproach being heaped on the prophet. He said if the fault-finding continued he would leave. When the criticism persisted, he and several others filed out of the building.

The verbal attacks on Smith were so devastating he became incapacitated for many days—brought "to the borders of the grave"—as he put it.[29] Upon recovering, one of the first steps he and Rigdon took was to distance themselves from the Safety Society. Despite the fact that an estimated 82 percent of bank notes were issued during their tenure,[30] they resigned their offices on 8 June, sold their interests, and walked away from the institution.[31]

Their positions were then assumed by Frederick G. Williams, the other member of the First Presidency, and Warren Parrish. In an attempt to salvage what remained of the ravaged institution, the new officers dispensed another $15,000 of notes to supplement the $70,000 Rigdon and Smith had issued. This action merely depreciated the value of the bills further. The 15 July 1837 *Cleveland Gazette* warned: "LOOK OUT. We learn by the *Painesville Telegraph* of yesterday, that the 'Mormon Banking Company' is about making a new emission of their worthless trash, using *old paper* and signed by Williams and one Par[r]ish, by the redemption of a few dollars of which they expect to get the *old emission* as well as the new, again into circulation."

To escape lawsuits, dissent, and financial distress, Rigdon and Smith traveled to Canada on a five-week fund-raising excursion.[32] En route to Fairport, a nearby harbor on Lake Erie, Smith was served writs. He, Rigdon, and Thomas B. Marsh, president of the Quorum of the Twelve, were forced to return to Painesville, four miles away. Anson Call, passing through on his way to Kirtland, saw a gathering of fellow Mormons at the office of Smith's attorney, Benjamin Bissell. He stopped and was told that the sheriff had "refused to take any person living in Kirtland for [Joseph's] bondsman." Call, a personal friend of sheriff Abel Kimball, told him he would stand for the bond. But Kimball feared Smith and Rigdon were permanently fleeing the country. Call told him he was "willing to run all risks and according to his oath he was under obligation to take me."[33] The bonds were signed and Rigdon and Smith returned to Fairport.

Sheriff Kimball arrived almost immediately and served another writ on the prophet, forcing the travelers back to Painesville where Smith stood trial and was acquitted at 10:00 p.m. Too tired to continue their journey, the company returned to Kirtland. They made a second start the next evening in S. B. Stoddard's wagon and arrived at Ashtabula after daybreak. They stayed till afternoon, relaxing on the beach and swimming in the lake. At 4:00 p.m. they took deck passage on board a steamer for Buffalo. After arriving the next morning they started for Toronto and spent more than a month in Canada visiting various branches of the church in an effort to raise money.

In late August as they returned home through Painesville, writs were again served on both Rigdon and Smith. Bissell took the two aside in the tavern where they were held and warned them "they had better make their escape for there was a mob gathering and it was out of his power to protect." After exiting the kitchen door the men sprinted for safety. As Mary Fielding wrote to her sister:

> The first step they took was to find the Woods as quick as possible where they thought

they should be safe. But in order [to reach] thereto they had to lay down . . . by an old log just w[h]ere they happened to be[,] so determinately were they pursued by their mad enemy in every direction. . . . Br[other] J[oseph] was obliged to entreat Bro Rigdon, after his exertion in running . . . to breath[e] more softly if he meant to escape.

Under cover of darkness they began their trek back to Kirtland, first taking each other by the hand and covenanting to "live and die together." Their pursuers searched for them with the aid of lighted torches. Ultimately the two men were driven into an area locally known as the Manti Swamps. Rigdon became exhausted and wanted to be left behind. The younger and more athletic Smith carried him piggyback for several miles until they encountered a safe road to Kirtland where they arrived at daybreak.[34]

During the leaders' absence from Kirtland, Warren Cowdery, editor of the *Latter Day Saints' Messenger and Advocate*, critiqued the Kirtland economy with sophisticated aplomb in a surprisingly candid essay in the July 1837 issue. After a lengthy discussion of the contributing factors he diagnosed what he and many others felt was the major reason for the failure of the Safety Society: "We believe that banking or financiering is as much a regular science, trade or business, as those of law, physic or divinity, and that a man may be . . . a celebrated divine . . . and be as liable to fail in the management of a bank as he would in constructing a balloon or the mechanism of a watch if he had never seen either." He further editorialized his views of the hazards of autocratic leadership, and the potential dangers it posed to American freedoms:

> If we give all our privileges to one man, we virtually give him our money and our liberties, and make him a monarch, absolute and despotic, and ourselves abject slaves or fawning sycophants. . . . Whenever a people have unlimited confidence in a civil or ecclesiastical ruler or rulers, who are but men like themselves, and begin to think they can do no wrong, they increase their tyranny and oppression and establish a principle that [that] man, poor frail lump of mortality like themselves, is infallible. Who does not see a principle of popery and religious tyranny involved in such an order of things? Who is worthy the name of a freeman, who thus tamely surrenders the rights, the privileges, and immunities of an independent citizen?[35]

Responding to Cowdery's editorial, Rigdon announced in the August issue that the *Messenger and Advocate* would be terminated with the September edition and replaced by a new periodical, *The Elder's Journal*, to be edited by Joseph Smith, Jr. The August newspaper contained a letter from Smith denouncing the Safety Society and its new officials. The dispatch, addressed "To the brethren and friends of the Church of the Latter-day Saints," proclaimed:

> I am disposed to say a word relative to the bills of the Kirtland Safety Society Bank. I hereby warn them to beware of speculators, renegades, and gamblers, who are duping the unsuspecting and unwary and by palming upon them, those bills, which are of no worth here. I discountenance and dissaprove of any and all such practices. I know

them to be detrimental to the best interests of society, as well as to the principles of religion.[36]

This was the first of a series of events that would ultimately place blame for the bank failure on Frederick Williams and Warren Parrish.[37] George A. Smith, Joseph's cousin and later church historian, expressed what by 1864 had become the official position on the causes behind the bankruptcy:

> Warren Parrish was the teller of the bank, and a number of other men who apostatized were officers. They took out of its vault, unknown to the President or Cashier, a hundred thousand dollars, and sent their agents around among the brethren to purchase their farms, wagons, cattle, horses, and everything they could get hold of. The brethren would gather up this money put it into the bank, and those traitors would steal it and send it out to buy again, and they continued to do so until the plot was discovered and the payment stopped. It was the cursed apostates—their stealing and robberies, and their infernal villainies [sic] that prevented that bank being conducted as the Prophet designed. If they had followed the counsel of Joseph, there is not a doubt but that it would have been the leading bank in Ohio, probably of the nation.[38]

This account conflicts with the contemporary stories Joseph Smith told. Although neither Rigdon nor Smith ever pressed charges against Parrish, in an 8 August 1838 editorial in the *Elder's Journal* the prophet accused his former scribe of stealing from the Safety Society. According to Joseph Smith's mother, the prophet asked Frederick Williams, his counselor and a justice of the peace, for a warrant to search Parrish's trunk. Williams refused. "I insist upon a warrant," Smith threatened, "for if you will give me one, I can get the money, and if you do not, I will break you of your office [in the First Presidency]." "Well, break it is, then," replied his counselor, "and we will strike hands upon it." "Very well," answered Joseph, "from henceforth I drop you from my quorum, in the name of the Lord." The two men struck hands on the bargain and Williams was dropped from the First Presidency.[39]

Ezra Granger Williams, Frederick's son, and an eyewitness to the above incident, related the matter differently. He admitted that the prophet approached Williams but not for a search warrant. Evidently Smith unsuccessfully attempted to convince Williams, the Safety Society's treasurer, to let him withdraw additional funds from the bank for "speculative purposes." Williams refused and suggested that he knew more about the rules of banking. An ugly quarrel erupted. "I did not think that the Prophet had any faults," young Williams later wrote, "but heard him as he greatly condemned my father." According to Williams, shortly thereafter the contrite prophet

> returned and on bended knees, crying like a child, humbly asked my father's forgiveness, admitting that he was wrong and that my father was right. He pleaded with him to still be friends and to continue by his side as usual [in the First Presidency].

My father gladly forgave him, but answered, "No, as the people would never have the confidence in him again that they had had before."[40]

Smith's other published account of the matter merely implied Parrish's theft. The prophet's "caution to the public" was published on 6 June 1844, just a few weeks before his murder:

> Having once notified the public against receiving a certain currency called "Kirtland Safety Society;" I again caution all persons against receiving or trading in said paper money, as all that was issued as genuine was redeemed. After the first officers who signed said bills retired, a new set of officers were appointed, and the vault of the instutition was broken open and robbed of several hundred thousand dollars, the signatures forged upon the said stolen bills, and those bills are being slyly bartered or had in trade, for the purpose of wilful and malicious prosecution and collection.
>
> In the first place the bills are not collectable by law in an unchartered institution. In the second place, they are spurious, the signature being a forgery, and every person passing or trading a bill is guilty of passing counterfeit money, because the bare-faced act of swindling. And lastly, he that uses said bills in any way, as a medium of trade is guilty of fraud, and shows a wicked and corrupt determination to wilfully, maliciously and feloniously rob the Latter-day Saints.[41]

Conflict over the Kirtland Safety Society Anti-Banking Company resulted in a leadership crisis by the time Rigdon and Smith returned from their Canadian trip. On 3 September a conference was scheduled to resolve the predicament. Brigham Young and others were fearful that Smith and Rigdon would not be sustained in their First Presidency callings, so faithful members were personally encouraged to attend the meeting. When a vote of support was taken, Smith and Rigdon were accepted. But counselor Frederick Williams and apostles Luke S. Johnson, Lyman E. Johnson, and John F. Boynton were objected to. Boynton then made a confession, "justifying himself in his former conduct by reason of the failure of the [Kirtland] bank."

Rigdon arose and attributed the men's difficulties to their "leaving their calling to attend to other occupations." But Boynton, shaking his head to the contrary, complained that "he understood the Bank was instituted by the will of God and he had been told that it should never fail let men do what they would." The prophet stood and stated that "if this had been declared no one had authority from him for So doing. For he had allways Said that unl[e]ss the instutition was conducted on ri[g]h[t]eous principals it would not Stand."[42]

One week later the Johnson brothers and Boynton asked for forgiveness and were received into fellowship and allowed to retain their apostleships. Thomas Marsh, visiting Kirtland at this time, reported that even Warren Parrish appeared "satisfied with Brother Joseph and the Church."[43] These impressions of harmony proved to be only a lull between storms. Nevertheless, Rigdon and Smith believed their problems with dissenters had been resolved and felt sufficiently secure in their positions to leave Kirtland on 27 September. Their travels were "to fulfill the mission appointed us on the 18th of September by a conference of Elders, in establishing places of gathering for the Saints."[44]

While stopped at Terre Haute, Indiana, the half-way point on their trip, Rigdon wrote a 13 October letter to the *Elder's Journal.* Basically a travelogue, the letter comments on the Millennium, a favorite topic throughout Rigdon's life:

> A person who is acquainted with the purposes and work of God in the last days, by traveling only increases his desire, that the great work of God may be spe[e]dily accomplished; for the amelioration of the world depends [e]ntirely on the accomplishment of the purposes of God. For this cause, the intel[l]igent saint earnestly desires the gathering of the elect; to be completed; that the scene of wretchedness may ce[a]se in the world, and the remainder of man may have rest.[45]

The wayfarers arrived at Far West, Missouri, about forty miles northeast of Independence, in late October or early November. During a 7 November general assembly of the Saints there, Rigdon explained "the object of the meeting, giving a relation of the recent reorganization of the Church in Kirtland." Smith and Rigdon were then nominated and "unanimously chosen" though Williams was replaced by Hyrum Smith.[46] While addressing the throng, Rigdon also preached on the temperance sweeping the nation, a proposition he highly favored. A year earlier his preaching to a Kirtland gathering had prompted a vote to discontinue the use entirely "of all liquors from the Church in Sickness & in health except wine at the Sacraments & for external Washing."[47] After a few similar remarks from Rigdon, the Far West audience "unanimously voted not to support Stores and Shops selling spirituous liquors, Tea, Coffee or Tobacco."[48] The congregation seemed enthusiastically united with Rigdon. In his closing prayer he asked the Lord to "dedicate this land for the gathering of the Saints, and their inheritances."[49]

When Rigdon and Smith arrived back in Kirtland about 10 December they found that all was not well. The former dissenters had again renounced Smith and Rigdon as heretics and announced the establishment of a new organization, the Church of Christ. Claiming to be the "old standard," they announced plans to install David Whitmer as president. The group had achieved considerable stature in the community by obtaining physical control of the Kirtland temple. Claiming that the building's significance had been trivialized, they asserted that the prophet often made light of worship experiences. They cited Smith's introduction of Rigdon on one occasion: "The truth is good enough without dressing up, but Brother Rigdon will now proceed to dress it up."[50] Another avowed charge was that Smith had "privately trained a pet dove to fly through an open window, light upon his shoulder, and pick grains of wheat" from his ear while he stood at the pulpit. Thus he supposedly could procure a visit from the dove at his pleasure.

"When the dove appeared," the account continued, "he would very gravely and solemnly announce to his credulous audience that it was the dove of the 'Holy Spirit' sent from heaven to communicate to his ear a divine message."[51]

To wrest control from the dissidents, Smith and Rigdon called for a public meeting in the temple. Dissenters arrived in force. The prophet demanded the excommunication of several who were in rebellion, but it was apparent the votes would not be forthcoming. Smith stood his ground. L. E. Miller, who was present, related afterward that Joseph convened the gathering "with a resolution and courage that the situation seemed to demand, and carried himself as one who felt that his soul and being had found themselves set firmly on the rock, while all else was but the shifting of sand or the swaying of reeds in the summer wind."[52]

Rigdon, weakened from a bout with an undisclosed illness, approached the stand and gripped the sides of the pulpit for support. As the prophet's right-hand man for seven years, deriving much support from his fellow Baptist and Campbellite converts, whose leaders scorned him, he felt the glories of the restored gospel were as much his personal triumph as Smith's. Completely misunderstanding his role in the economic forces that had contributed to Kirtland's financial chaos, Rigdon resorted to witchhunting. In his wrath he accused dissenters of a long inventory of crimes including lying, stealing, adultery, counterfeiting, and swindling. His ruthless verbal assault rose in a crescendo of violent epithets. Finally, when his might was spent, Rigdon was assisted down the long aisle to the eastern vestibule. The congregation sat in silence while he was escorted away and the temple doors closed behind him. During the rancorous fight that ensued after his departure, an exhausting cacophony of charges and counter-charges were hurled back and forth. The meeting eventually adjourned and the disheartened prophet left the temple sensible to the fact that the unity he and Rigdon had built together since the church's 1830 organization was now lost.

In early January 1838, Grandison Newell, who would later relate with gusto how he "run the Mormons out of the country," started the rumor that he intended to file charges against Smith and Rigdon again.[53] On 12 January, Kirtland constable Luke Johnson heard a report that Sheriff Kimball was about to arrest Smith. Johnson "went to the French farm, where he then resided, and arrested him on an execution for his person, in the absence of property[,] to pay a judgment of $50, which I had in my possession at the time, which prevented Kimball from arresting him."[54]

Although the prophet settled the execution and thanked Johnson for intervening, previous experience suggested that he and Rigdon must soon disappear. Plans were made to leave that night, and a revelation was received in the presence of Rigdon, Vinson Knight, and George W. Robinson, pronouncing:

Thus saith the Lord, let the Presidency of my church, take their families as soon as it is practicable, and a door is open for them, and move to the west, as fast as the way is made plain before their faces, and let their hearts be comforted for I will be with them, verrily [sic] I say unto you, the time has come, that your labors are finished, in this place for a season. Therefore arise and get yourselves into a land which I shall show unto you, even a land flowing with milk & honey, you are clean from the blood of this people, and wo, unto those who have become your en[e]mies, who have professed my name saith the Lord, for their judgement lingereth not, and their damnation slumbereth not. Let all your faithfull friends arise with their families also, and get out of this place and gather themselves together unto Zion and be at peace among yourselves, O ye inhabitants of Zion, or there shall be no safety for you even so amen.[55]

Wickliffe Rigdon later recalled his family's last day in Kirtland. On returning home from school that fateful 12 January 1838, he saw "considerable commotion about my father's house." He asked his mother the reason and Phebe replied "nothing that concerned me." Later that evening young Rigdon saw several men come into the house, whisper to his father, and then leave. "I wanted to know of Mother what was the trouble, but [still] could get no reply. . . . And I and my brother Sidney went to bed." The boys were later awakened by a man who put their shoes on them and explained they were going to "a land flowing with milk and honey."[56] They started in an open lumber wagon at midnight unaware that two hours earlier Rigdon and Smith had left Kirtland on the fastest horses obtainable. The official pronouncement, written as though uttered by Smith, noted:

A new year dawned upon the Church in Kirtland in all the bitterness of the spirit of apostate mobocracy; which continued to rage and grow hotter and hotter, until Elder Rigdon and myself were obliged to flee from its deadly influence, as did the Apostles and Prophets of old, and as Jesus said, "when they persecute you in one city, flee to another." On the evening of the 12th of January, about ten o'clock, we left Kirtland, on horseback, to escape mob violence, which was about to burst upon us under the color of legal process to cover the hellish designs of our enemies, and to save themselves from the just judgment of the law.[57]

Notes

Unless otherwise stated, all primary sources cited are located in the Historical Department of the Church of Jesus Christ of Latter-day Saints, Salt Lake City, Utah.

1. *Latter Day Saints' Messenger and Advocate* 8 (May 1837): 506.
2. Scott Kenney, ed., *Wilford Woodruff's Journal–Typescript*, 9 vols. (Midvale, UT: Signature Books, 1983), 1:125.
3. Joseph Smith, *History of the Church of Jesus Christ of Latter-day Saints*, B. H. Roberts,

ed., 7 vols. (Salt Lake City: The Church of Jesus Christ of Latter-day Saints, 1902), 2:478-80; hereafter *History of the Church.*

4. Lorenzo Brown Journal, 3, Special Collections, Harold B. Lee Library, Brigham Young University, Provo, Utah; hereafter Special Collections, BYU.

5. Kenney, 1:140. The Woodruff marriage was to have been pronounced by Smith. Rigdon was to have performed the nuptials for the Robinsons. Instead, both couples were wed by Frederick G. Williams, local justice of the peace. Because the Church of the Latter Day Saints was not a recognized legal entity in Ohio, Rigdon had been indicted in 1835 for performing the 4 September 1834 marriage of Orson Hyde and Marinda N. Johnson (see "Criminal Records, Common Pleas," Book T, 3, Geauga County Courthouse, Chardon, OH). The 30 Oct. 1835 *Chardon Spectator and Geauga Gazette* announced that during the trial, however,

> Rigdon produced a license of the Court, which had been granted to him several years ago, as a minister of the gospel of that sect usually called Campbellites. . . . It appeared that the society of disciples kept written minutes of their proceedings, and no church record of his dismissal being offered, the Court rejected the testimony, and a *nolle prosequi* was entered.

6. Newell to Rigdon, published in the 26 May 1837 *Painesville Telegraph.*

7. *Painesville Telegraph*, 30 June 1837.

8. Ibid., 16 June 1837.

9. For a full treatment of this incident, see Max H. Parkin, *Conflict at Kirtland: A Study of the Nature and Causes of External and Internal Conflict of the Mormons in Ohio Between 1830 and 1838* (Salt Lake City: Department of Seminaries and Institutes of Religion, 1967), 213-19.

10. *History of the Church*, 2:487-88.

11. Scott H. Faulring, ed., *An American Prophet's Record: The Diaries and Journals of Joseph Smith* (Salt Lake City: Signature Books in association with Smith Research Associates, 1989), 59.

12. Letter published in the 15 Feb. 1838 *Painesville Republican*, re-printed in *The Ohio Repository*, 22 Mar. 1838.

13. Karl Keller, ed. "I Never Knew a Time When I Did Not Know Joseph Smith," *Dialogue: A Journal of Mormon Thought* 1 (Winter 1966): 28.

14. Parley P. Pratt to Joseph Smith, 23 May 1837, in Richard Livesey, *An Exposure of Mormons, Being a Statement of Facts Relative to the Self Styled LDS and the Origin of the Book of Mormon* (Preston, Eng.: J. Livesey, 1838), 9; emphasis in original.

After his defection, Warren Parrish sent a copy of Pratt's letter to the editor of *Zion's Watchman*, a non-Mormon publication, which printed it on 6 March 1838. By then Pratt had amended his differences with Smith, felt that a clarification was necessary to exonerate himself, and apologized for his rash words. According to Pratt's account, the printed letter was "not a true copy" of his, but was "altered, so as to convey a different idea from the original." Although he did not say precisely what was altered and in what manner, he did admit to writing the letter in "great severity and harshness, censuring them both." He further acknowledged that his letter "was not calculated to admonish them in the spirit of meekness, to do them good, but rather to injure them and wound their feelings." Yet he insisted that

> I did not however believe at the time and never have believed at any time before, or since, that these men were dishonest or had wrong motives or intentions, in any of their undertakings, either temporal or spiritual; I have ever esteemed them from my first acquaintance, as men of God. . . . But I considered them like other men, and as the prophets and apostles of old liable to errors, and mistakes, in things which were not inspired from heaven; but managed by their own judgment.

He added, "I censure myself for rashness, excitement, imprudence, and many faults which I would to God, that I had avoided" (*Elders' Journal* 4 [Aug. 1838]: 50).

The matter did not end there, however. Richard Livesey, a Methodist Episcopal minister in Massachusetts, had the letter reprinted in his anti-Mormon pamphlet. When the letter was brought to Pratt's attention in 1840 while serving a mission in England he wrote, "Messrs. Smith and Rigdon . . . are servants of the Most High God, for whom I would lay down my life if necessary. These letters from apostates and dissenters are wicked lies and misrepresentations" (Parley P. Pratt, *A Reply to Mr. Thomas Taylor's "Complete Failure" &C and Mr. Richard Livesey's "Mormonism Exposed"* [Manchester, Eng.: N.p., 1840], n.p.).

15. Kenney, 1:147.

16. Ibid.

17. Ibid., 1:148.

18. Orson Pratt and Lyman Johnson, "Charges Against Joseph Smith, Jr., n.d.," Newel K. Whitney Collection, Special Collections, BYU.

19. Vault–Ms 76, box 2, fd 2, Special Collections, BYU.

20. *History of the Church*, 2:492.

21. Ibid., 484-85.

22. Ibid., 486.

23. This letter, in possession of Stephen Pratt, is cited in Marvin S. Hill, *Quest for Refuge: The Mormon Flight from American Pluralism* (Salt Lake City: Signature Books, 1989), 59.

24. Oliver Huntington Journal, 28, Special Collections, BYU.

25. Eliza R. Snow, comp., *Biography and Family History of Lorenzo Snow* (Salt Lake City: George Q. Cannon & Sons, 1884), 20-21.

26. Preston Nibley, ed., *History of Joseph Smith by His Mother, Lucy Mack Smith* (Salt Lake City: Bookcraft, 1958), 241.

27. Hill, 59.

28. Charles L. Woodword, "The First Half Century of Mormonism," 195, New York Public Library; emphasis in original.

29. *History of the Church*, 2:493. Mary Fielding, in an 8 July 1837 letter to her sister Mercy Thompson, wrote of Smith's illness: "[O]ur beloved Brother Joseph Smith appeared to be so far gone that [we doubted he would] live till next morn" (Thompson Collection).

30. See Marvin S. Hill, C. Keith Rooker, Larry T. Wimmer, *The Kirtland Economy Revisited: A Market Critique of Sectarian Economics* (Provo, UT: Brigham Young University Press, 1977), 58.

31. *Latter Day Saints' Messenger and Advocate* 3 (July 1837): 537.

32. See Daniel Allen, "Minutes of School of the Prophets, Parowan, Utah," 10 Aug. 1872, 168, Special Collections, BYU.

33. Anson Call Diary, 27 July 1837.

34. My narrative here is a composite of two accounts: Anson Call's diary of the period and Mary Fielding's letter cited in Karl Ricks Anderson, *Joseph Smith's Kirtland: Eyewitness Accounts* (Salt Lake City: Deseret Book Co., 1987), 218-19.

35. *Latter Day Saint's Messenger and Advocate* 3 (July 1837): 536-41.

36. Ibid. (Aug. 1837): 560. The official Mormon account, which editors stylistically wrote as if in Joseph Smith's words, notes:

> Some time previous to this [7 July] I resigned my office in the "Kirtland Safety Society," disposed of my interest therein, and withdrew from the instutition; being fully aware, after so long an experiment, that no institution of the kind, established upon just and righteous principles for a blessing not only to the Church but the whole nation, would be suffered to continue its operations in such an age of darkness, speculation, and wickedness (*History of the Church*, 2:497).

37. Ex-Mormon Cyrus Smalling wrote an extensive letter concerning some of the problems of the Kirtland Bank which included the allegation that Smith had

> one or two hundred boxes made, and gathered all the lead and shot that the village had or that part of it that he controlled, and filled the boxes with lead, shot, &c, and marked them, one thousand dollars each. Then, when they went to examine the vault, he had one box on a table partly filled for them to see, and when they proceeded to the vault, Smith told them that the church had two hundred thousand dollars in specie, and he opened one box and they saw that it was silver, and they hefted a number and Smith told them that they contained specie ("Letter to Mr. Lee," 10 Mar. 1841, in John A. Clark, *Gleanings By the Way* [Philadelphia: W. I. and I. K. Simon, 1842], 334).

Warren Parrish, however, did not mention this deception in his extensive letter of criticism against Smith and the bank in the 15 February 1838 *Painesville Republican*.

38. *Journal of Discourses*, 26 vols. (London: Latter-day Saints' Book Depot, 1854-86) 11 (15 Nov. 1864): 11; hereafter *Journal of Discourses*.

39. Nibley, 240-41.

40. Nancy Clement Williams, *After 100 Years* (Independence, MO: Zion's Printing and Publishing Co., 1951), 44.

41. *Nauvoo Neighbor*, 19 June 1844.

42. "The Scriptory Book of Joseph Smith," 4 Sept. 1837 entry, in Faulring, 164. Ira Ames's first journal entry for 1837 noted that in the bank failure, John Boynton and Lyman E. Johnson lost everything they owned.

43. *Elders' Journal* 3 (July 1838): 38.

44. *History of the Church*, 2:518. Church historian John Whitmer reported that because Rigdon and Smith knew their days in Kirtland were numbered, their trip to Missouri was merely "to prepare a place for themselves and families" (F. Mark McKiernan

and Roger D. Launius, *An Early Latter Day Saint History: The Book of John Whitmer, Kept by Commandment* [Independence, MO: Herald House, 1980], 159).

45. *Elders' Journal* (1837-38): 7-8.

46. Donald Q. Cannon and Lyndon W. Cook, eds., *Far West Record: Minutes of The Church of Jesus Christ of Latter-day Saints, 1830-1844* (Salt Lake City: Deseret Book Co., 1983), 122.

47. Kenney, 1 (4 Dec. 1836): 110-11.

48. Cannon and Cook, 124.

49. Ibid., 124.

50. *New York Times*, 25 Dec. 1887.

51. Harvey Rice, *Pioneers of the Western Reserve* (Boston: n.p., 1883), 303.

52. James H. Kennedy, *Early Days of Mormonism* (London: Reeves and Turner, 1888), 166-67.

53. Ibid., 168. Others did file suit, however. The Halsted, Haines Company brought suit against Smith, Rigdon, Hyrum Smith, Oliver Cowdery, Brigham Young, and others for "redress in connection with questionable business practices." The defendants failed to appear when summoned and the plaintiffs were awarded $2337.35, plus expenses, which they never collected (Geauga County Court of Common Pleas [1839], Special Collections, BYU).

54. Luke Johnson Papers, under date.

55. "The Scriptory Book of Joseph Smith," 51-52, in Faulring, 192-93.

56. Keller, 29.

57. *History of the Church*, 3:1.

Section 3.

Missouri

CHAPTER 16.

Victims No More

Although trials, persecutions, privations and sorrows await the Saints, yet God will not forsake them; yea, in the hour of their greatest need, he will stand by them to deliver. . . . Bro Joseph is truly a wonderful man he is all we could wish a prophet to be–and Bro. Sidney what Eloquence is his, and think how he has sacrificed for the Truth.

—William Law (1837)[1]

The day after their flight from Kirtland, Sidney Rigdon and Joseph Smith arrived on 13 January 1838 at Norton Township, Medina County, Ohio– sixty miles away. There they waited thirty-six hours for their families, and on the 16th the small wagon train began its slow westward trek towards Missouri. Neither Rigdon nor Smith felt safe; both concealed themselves under blankets during most of the trip. The *History of the Church*, written in Smith's voice, reported that men pursued them more than two hundred miles from Kirtland "seeking our lives":

> They frequently crossed our track, twice they were in the houses where we stopped, once we tarried all night in the same house with them, with only a partition between us and them; and heard their oaths and imprecations, and threats concerning us, if they could catch us; and late in the evening they came into our room and examined us, but decided we were not the men. At other times we passed them in the streets, and gazed upon them, and they on us, but they knew us not.[2]

Only when the company reached Dublin, Indiana, a stop on the National Road, did the two men dare to walk about freely. After resting and replenishing supplies, the Smith party drove on, agreeing to wait for the Rigdons at Terre Haute. Rigdon waited in Dublin another week for his son-in-law George W. Robinson and other family members, including his seventy-nine-year-old mother. When Robinson arrived he brought two span of horses, a carriage, and another wagon.

As the small train rolled across Indiana, bad roads and frequent storms slowed them down. Progress was excruciatingly tedious. Phebe Rigdon, pregnant with her eleventh child, was often ill, as was Sidney's elderly mother, and the Rigdon children also suffered from the bitter weather. On the east banks of the Wabash at Terre Haute they rejoined the Smiths, ferried across the river, and commenced their westward journey.

Arriving at Paris, Illinois, Rigdon and Smith applied for lodging at several taverns. At each hostel they were turned away because they "were Mormons and could not be received." One innkeeper boasted he would not board them "for love or money," and neither would any other innkeeper, for they had all pledged to refuse them. The cold was so extreme, however, that Sidney and Joseph were afraid their families would suffer. They concluded that "we might as well die fighting as freeze to death" and returned to the tavern. We "must and [will] stay," they announced. "[We] have men enough to take the town, and if we must freeze, we will freeze by the burning of these houses." Intimidated, the tavern owners accommodated the travelers. Smith's account noted that "[we] received many apologies in the morning from the inhabitants for their abusive treatment."[3]

Fearing the same treatment elsewhere, Rigdon and Smith decided to divide the company again, each group taking a different route. A day out of Paris, on the vast Illinois prairie, the Rigdon party encountered a fierce blizzard which obliterated the roadway. Local residents had warned them against crossing the area in such a fierce storm, but the group, short on provisions, was anxious to move ahead quickly. George W. Robinson took the lead, driving a covered carriage. Riding with him was his pregnant wife Athalia, Rigdon's mother Nancy, and pregnant Phebe Rigdon. Following Robinson were four open wagons, including the one driven by Sidney who was forced to return to Paris for repairs when a wheel came off his wagon. The others pressed on into the storm. Wickliffe Rigdon many years later remembered that by the time his father reached town again, the children were "so cold we had to be carried into the house."[4]

Sidney so feared his family's fate in the blizzard that night, Wickliffe wrote, that he did not sleep. Instead he prayed continually and "walked the house till morning." When the storm abated, he began crossing the snow-covered prairie at daybreak, despite the cold. After three hours he came to a house, the owner of which told him that a covered carriage and an open wagon had stopped there and "their women had come into his house to get warm as they were nearly frozen to death." The group was staying two miles farther down the road. This information was joyously received, wrote Wickliffe, as "the agony was over and the lost ones were alive."[5]

The grateful group continued on. After several days' travel they were again forced to stop some thirty miles west of Paris because of Athalia Robinson's and Mother Rigdon's poor health. They found comfortable lodging at a farm house where a large stock of winter corn lured prairie chickens by the hundreds. Wickliffe later described this bountiful resting spot as "the happiest three weeks I ever spent."[6]

Arriving at the Mississippi opposite Louisiana, Missouri, the Rigdon party had to wait ten days for the ice to clear before the ferry could operate. Finally, after a trip of nearly three months, the Rigdons arrived at Far West, Missouri, on 4 April and joined the several hundred Jackson County Mormons who had settled in the area. The prophet, who had arrived there on 13 March, accompanied by well-wishers, met the travelers at the edge of town. Wickliffe later remembered that Smith shook "hands with my father and my mother with tears in his eyes and thanked God that we had got to the journey's end."[7]

A conference honoring the eighth anniversary of the church had been scheduled for that weekend at the large schoolhouse outside the village. On 7 April Rigdon gave the keynote address. Wickliffe remembered that the school house was filled to capacity and windows were opened to allow the speakers to be heard on the grounds. During Rigdon's ninety-minute sermon he proclaimed "he had found a home at last[,] he should never move again[,] here was his resting place where he hoped he should be permitted to worship God according to the dictates of his conscience."[8]

That new-found home was a large two-story log structure near the town's center. Despite Rigdon's hope for blissful refuge, however, within a matter of months his family, along with virtually every other Mormon family in the state, including hundreds who relocated from Ohio, was again homeless, driven into the wilderness by rancorous Missourians. Psychologist William James retrospectively attributed the persistent abhorrence of Mormons to "aboriginal human neophobia . . . that inborn hatred of the alien and of eccentric and non-conforming men."[9] But the more immediate historical catalyst of the 1838-39 crisis in Missouri was unresolved internal dissent that spilled over from Ohio, dissent which had its roots in the failure to redeem Jackson County.

Even before Rigdon and Smith reached Far West in the spring of 1838, newspapers were trumpeting the fugitives' failed commercial activities in Ohio. "We learn from a source to be relied on," wrote the 30 January 1838 *Western Reserve Chronicle* (Warren, Ohio), "that the Mormon Society at Kirtland is breaking up. Smith and Rigdon, after prophecying the destruction of the town, left with their families in the night, and others of the faithful are following. . . . An exposure of the proceedings of the Society is in course of preparation by one Par[r]ish, the former confidential secretary of the prophet Smith."[10]

Warren Parrish's expose, published the following month, was a devastating disclosure of the failed financial workings of the church. Of Rigdon and Smith he concluded: "I believe them to be confirmed infidels who have not the fear of God before their eyes. . . . They lie by revelation, swindle by revelation, cheat and defraud by revelation, run away by revelation, and if they do not mend their ways, I fear they will at last be damned by revelation."[11]

Realizing their reputations had been sullied by the Kirtland cataclysm, Smith and Rigdon sought to refurbish their images through public relations and more

elaborate biographies. A principal obstacle to their revisionist perspective was the
record of official church historian John Whitmer, who had been excommunicated
on 10 March. The two leaders sent a letter to their former friend and co-worker
requesting the history he had been keeping. The tone of the letter, probably written
by Rigdon, was condescending:

> We were desirous of honoring you by giving publicity to your notes on the history of
> the Church of Latter-day Saints, after making such corrections as we thought would
> be necessary, knowing your incompetency as a historian, and that writings coming
> from your pen, could not be put to press without our correcting them, or else the
> Church must suffer reproach. . . . We are still willing to honor you, if you . . . give
> up your notes . . . but if not, we have all the materials for another, which we shall
> commence this week to write.[12]

Whitmer refused.[13] Smith's diary indicates he and Rigdon began their own
history on 27 April: "This day was chiefly spent writing a history of this Church
from the earliest period of its existance up to this date, by Presidents Joseph Smith,
Jr., Sidney Rigdon [and] myself [George W. Robinson] also engaged in keeping
this record."[14] The opening paragraphs of both Rigdon's and Smith's biographies
were written in a defensive tone. Smith's account begins:

> Owing to the many reports which had been put in circulation by evil-disposed and
> designing persons, in relation to the rise and progress of the Church of Jesus Christ
> of Latter-day Saints, all of which have been designed by the authors thereof to militate
> against its character as a Church and its progress in the world—I have been induced
> to write this history, to disabuse the public mind, and put all inquirers after truth into
> possession of the facts, as they have transpired, in relation both to myself and the
> Church, so far as I have such facts in my possession.[15]

Rigdon's statement also attempted to calm troubled waters: "As there has been
a great rumor, and many false statements have been given to the world respecting
Elder Rigdon's connection with the Church of Jesus Christ, it is necessary that a
correct account of the same be given, so that the public mind may be disabused
on the subject."[16]

In 1838 Far West, however, both Rigdon and Smith were struggling to
maintain their threatened positions of power in the hierarchy. Several LDS
luminaries living in Far West, including W. W. Phelps, Lyman Johnson, Frederick
G. Williams, John Whitmer, David Whitmer, and Oliver Cowdery, presented a
united front that seriously challenged Rigdon's and Smith's doings. During a 30
January 1838 protest meeting at Cowdery's home, they planned their opposition
to Joseph's and Sidney's fund raising, warning members against being forced into
using "their earthly substance contrary to their own interest and privilege" under
the "pretense of incurring the displeasure of God."[17]

Realizing that Zion would not be established in Jackson County, several of these men had sold all or portions of their property there. This looked to Smith and Rigdon like a denial of the faith. Cowdery and the others, however, viewed the right to control personal property as a cherished American freedom. Cowdery made that position clear in a 4 February 1838 letter to his brothers Warren and Lyman:

> The radical principles taught by Messrs. Smith and Rigdon here [are] subversion of the liberties of the whole church. . . . I told them if I had property, while I live and was sane, I would not be dictated, influenced, or controlled by any man or set of men, by no tribunal of ecclesiastical pretenses whatsoever. . . . My soul is sick of such scrambling for power and self-aggrandisement. . . . I came to this country to enjoy peace. If I cannot I shall go where I can.[18]

During Mormonism's early years, when Cowdery was Second Elder, the church had been characterized by democratic vigor. In the turmoil of 1838, whatever egalitarian style existed was supplanted by a command-and-compliance culture. On 10 March, four days before Smith reached Far West, W. W. Phelps was excommunicated along with John Whitmer. A month later Cowdery and David Whitmer met the same fate.[19] Phelps and Cowdery initially retained control over the press, however, and in May began assembling it, intending to publish an opposition newspaper.

Rigdon's and Smith's actions over the next six months constitute one of the darker chapters in Mormon history. Declaring "they were fed up with dissenter criticism, and with being harassed to death,"[20] the duo initiated a concerted effort to undermine their antagonists through character assassination. The prophet alleged that the dissidents were guilty of "Lying, Cheating, Defrauding, and Swindeling," seeking "the lives of the First Presidency and to overthrow the Kingdom of God."[21] Rigdon claimed that after David Whitmer and Oliver Cowdery came to Far West they "set up a nasty, dirty, pettifoggers office, pretending to be judges [attorneys] of the law." Addressing the ex-Mormons directly, he ranted:

> You began to interfere with all the business of the place, trying to destroy the character of our merchants, and bringing their creditors upon them, and break them up. In addition to this, you stirred up men of weak minds to prosecute one another, for the vile purpose of getting a fee for pettifogging for one of them. You have also been threatening continually to enter into a general system of prosecution determined, as you said, to pick a flaw in the titles of those who have bought city lots and built upon them.[22]

Still reeling from Grandison Newell's legal harassment in Ohio, Smith and Rigdon were not about to let the same thing happen in Mormon-controlled Caldwell County, Missouri. Viewing themselves immune, they refused legal writs, and in April, according to John Whitmer, Smith publicly asserted that "he did not intend in [the] future to have any process served on him, and the officer who attempted it should die."^{23} Rigdon, similarly disposed, told the Saints that "he would suffer no process of law to be served on him hereafter."^{24}

The prophet and his spokesman ventured beyond mere boastful rhetoric. John Whitmer's account of the period notes that the First Presidency called together a council of church leaders to discuss how to deal with dissidents. Smith stated "that any person who said a word against the heads of the church should be driven over these prairies as a chased deer by a pack of hounds."^{25} Putting teeth into the rhetoric, a clandestine Army of Israel was formed from organizational remnants of Zion's Camp. Bound together by Machiavellian artifice into a brotherly union, members swore fraternal oaths to "always uphold the [First] Presidency, right or wrong," and to assist in the "utter destruction of apostates."^{26}

According to later court testimony and other first-hand corroborative accounts, this secret brotherhood was initially known by various titles as: "The Daughter of Zion" (from Micah 4:13), "Brother of Gideon" (a veiled reference to Jared Carter's brother), and "The Big Fan" or "The Thresher" (to separate the wheat from the chaff).^{27} Eventually, they settled on "The Sons of Dan" or Danites. "Dan shall judge his people," read Genesis 49:16-17, as "a serpent by the way, an adder in the path, that biteth the horse heels, so that his rider shall fall backwards." Later in Deuteronomy 33:22 "Dan is a lion's whelp." At first the group acted as secret "thought police," charged to ferret out any who were critical of the hierarchy, then force them out of the community through intimidation. Their thinking was, reported John Corrill, that the sect "would never become pure unless these dissenters were routed from among them. Moreover, if they were suffered to remain, they would destroy the Church."^{28}

Sampson Avard, Major General of the Danites, later testified during a court hearing that the intent of the band "was to drive from the county of Caldwell all that dissented from the Mormon Church."^{29} This assessment was confirmed by George W. Robinson, Joseph Smith's scribe, who (presumably under the prophet's direction) wrote in "The Scriptory Book of Joseph Smith, Jr.": "[W]e have a company of Danites in these times [27 July 1838], to put right physically that which is not right, and to cleanse the Church of verry great evils which hath hitherto existed among us inasmuch as they cannot be put to right by teachings & persuas[ions]."^{30} Corrill's sworn court testimony provided further insight:

> I think the original object of the Danite band was to operate against the dissenters; but afterwards it grew into a system to carry out the designs of the Presidency; and, if necessary to use physical force to build up the Kingdom of God, it was to be done by them. This is my opinion as to their object; and I learned it from various sources connected with the band.^{31}

Once Mormon dissidents were driven from Far West, the Danites became a home guard militia of nearly 300 men. They then evolved into a punitive force that raided and plundered native Missourians. The group also acquired the popular name of the "Destroying Angels." This society's constitution, prescribed in a "Bill of Rights and Articles of Organization," was allegedly authored by Sidney Rigdon. Initiates promised to be "governed by such laws as shall perpetuate these high privileges of which we know ourselves to be the rightful possessors" and pledged to resist all tyranny "whether it would be in kings or in the people." The order's executive power was vested in "the President of the whole church and his counsellors." The legislative branch included "the President and his counsellors, together with the Generals and Colonels of the society."[32]

In forcefully separating chaff from wheat, the Danites applied to their own brethren the same tactics used against them previously. Reed Peck, in a candid account of Danite activities, wrote that they were organized during a clandestine 10 June meeting when Jared Carter, George W. Robinson, and Sampson Avard, "under the instruction of the [First] [P]residency, formed a secret military society, called the 'daughter of Zion.'"[33] Avard was the group's spokesman. He addressed newly inducted members in unmistakable Masonic overtones:

> As the Lord had raised up a prophet in these last days like unto Moses it shall be the duty of this band to obey him in all things, and whatever he requires you shall perform being ready to give up life and property for the advancement of the cause[.] When any thing is to be performed no member shall have the privilege of judging whether it would be right or wrong but shall engage in its accomplishment and trust God for the result[.][34]

Yet when a proposition was made and "supported by some as being the best policy to kill [the dissenters] that they would not be capable of injuring the church,"[35] this was strenuously opposed by John Corrill and Thomas B. Marsh, president of the Quorum of the Twelve. A modified plan of intimidation and minor violence was instead adopted. Violent opposition to dissent was officially pronounced during a Sunday sermon on 17 June by Sidney Rigdon, whose hatred of dissenters amounted to an obsession.

Later accounts have implied that Rigdon spoke on his own behalf that day in the town square at Far West. But evidence suggests that he was, in fact, serving as official spokesman for the First Presidency. From Smith came the concept, from Rigdon the words, and from the people the power. Designated "spokesman unto the Lord . . . all the days of his life," in a 13 December 1833 blessing pronounced by the prophet,[36] Rigdon was acting in that capacity on 17 June 1838 when he made public "The Political Motto of the Church of Latter-day Saints," formulated by Smith and others on 14 March 1838:

> The Constitution of our country [was] formed by the Fathers of liberty [to promote] peace and good order in society[,] love to God, and good will to man. All good and wholesome laws, virtue and truth above all things, and aristarchy, live for ever! But woe to tyrants, mobs, aristocracy, anarchy, and toryism, and all those who invent or seek out unrighteous and vexatious law suits, under the pretext and color of law, or

office, either religious or political. Exalt the standard of Democracy! Down with that of priestcraft, and let all the people say Amen! that the blood of our fathers may not cry from the ground against us. Sacred is the memory of that blood which bought for us our liberty.[37]

Although a complete text of Rigdon's speech is not extant, several listeners recorded portions of this pivotal call to arms at the time it was given. Reed Peck recalled Rigdon in his introduction declaring that "some certain characters" in Far West had been crying "you have broken the law you have acted contrary to the principles of republicanism." Resorting to his trademark exclusivist ideology, Rigdon reasoned that "when a county, or body of people have individuals among them with whom they do not wish to associate and a public expression is taken against their remaining among them and such individuals do not remove, it is the principle of republicanism itself that gives that community a right to expel them forcibly and no law will prevent it."[38]

Rigdon focused his intense hatred for dissenters by adapting Matthew 5:13 (D&C 101:39-40; 103:10) in defense of his political purposes: "Ye are the salt of the earth. If the salt has lost its savor, it is thenceforth good for nothing, but to be cast out and trodden under the feet of men." Observers noted that the eloquent preacher then whipped the crowd to a frenzy by proclaiming that it was "the duty of this people to trample [dissenters] into the earth and if the county cannot be freed from them any other way I will assist to trample them down, or to erect a gallows on the square of Far West and hang them up as they did the gamblers at Vicksburg and it would be an act at which the angels would smile with approbation."[39]

The prophet delivered a short speech sanctioning Rigdon's address. "Though," said he, "I don't want the brethren to act unlawfully; but I will tell them one thing, Judas was a traitor, and instead of hanging himself was hung by Peter." With this hint the subject was dropped for the day having created a "great excitement, and prepared the people to execute anything that should be proposed."[40]

Immediately following the "Salt Sermon," as it was subsequently known, John Corrill sought out Mormon dissenter John Whitmer and advised him that in the wake of Rigdon's address Whitmer's safety might be in question. Whitmer did not believe that the Saints as a body would turn on him, but he went to the prophet for advice. He was told that he and W. W. Phelps would have to surrender their property in Far West, real estate they were accused of purchasing with church funds. He advised Whitmer to "place the property in the hands of the bishop and high council to be disposed of according to the laws of the church, and things will quiet down."[41]

Whitmer refused. In consequence he, Oliver Cowdery, David Whitmer, W. W. Phelps, and Lyman E. Johnson received a lengthy ultimatum drafted by

Rigdon[42] demanding that they leave Far West in three days. Eighty-four of Far West's most influential Mormons, including Hyrum Smith of the First Presidency, signed the document which reads in part:

> [O]ut of the county you shall go, and no power shall save you. And you shall have three days after you receive this communication to you, including twenty-four hours in each day, for you to depart with your families peaceably; which you may do undisturbed by any person; but in that time, if you do not depart, we will use the means in our power to cause you to depart; for go you shall. . . .
>
> We have solemnly warned you, and that in the most determined manner, that if you did not cease that course of wanton abuse of the citizens of this county, that vengeance would overtake you sooner or later, and that when it did come it would be as furious as the mountain torrent, and as terrible as the beating tempest; but you have affected to despise our warnings, and pass them off with a sneer, or a grin, or a threat and pursued your former course; and vengeance sleepeth not, neither does it slumber; and unless you heed us this time, and attend to our request, it will overtake you at an hour when you do not expect it, and at a day when you do not look for it; and for you there shall be no escape; for there is but one decree for you, which is depart, depart, or a more fatal calamity shall befall you.[43]

On Tuesday, when dissidents were informed that preparations were being made to "hang the[m] up" that night, they fled town with only the clothes on their backs. George W. Robinson wrote that the men were "soon seen bounding over the prairie like the scape goat to carry of[f] their own sins we have not seen them since, their influence is gone, and they are in a miserable condition, so also it [is] with all who turn from the truth to lying[,] cheating[,] defrauding & Swindeling."[44] One account attempted to justify "The wrath of the presidency": "threats of han[g]ing &.c. were undoubtedly a farce acted to frighten these men from the county that they could not be spies upon [the First Presidency's] conduct or that they might deprive them of their property." But even before they left, George Robinson swore out writs of attachment against the men and took possession of "all their personal property, clothing & furniture," leaving their families homeless.[45]

In years to come, after Rigdon dissented from Brigham Young's brand of Mormonism, blame for these civil rights violations was heaped squarely on his shoulders. Jedediah M. Grant, for example, wrote in 1844 that Rigdon began to "pour his wrath in torrents upon the heads" of the dissenters who had "made shipwreck concerning the faith."[46] But John Whitmer focused the situation more accurately when he wrote regarding the persecution of apostates, "J. Smith S. Rigdon & Hiram Smith were the instigators & G. W. Robinson was the prosecutor."[47] Book of Mormon witness David Whitmer confirmed this perspective in an 1881 interview: "Smith and Rigdon . . . issued a decree organizing what was termed the 'Danites, or Destroying Angels,' who were bound by the most fearful oaths to obey the commandments of the leaders of the church. The Danites consisted only of those selected by Smith and Rigdon."[48]

While Rigdon later testified that neither he nor Smith was a Danite,[49] insider Reed Peck substantiated David Whitmer's view by writing that the secret society was "under the instruction of the presidency."[50] While the First Presidency did not regularly attend Danite meetings, John Corrill admitted under oath that they participated in at least one conclave. He related that the First Presidency was introduced to officers and pronounced blessings on them.[51] "The time has come," the prophet said to his Danite charges,

> when the Lord has willed for us to take up arms in our own defense. We wish to do nothing unlawful. If the people of the world will but let us alone, we will preach the gospel and live in peace. All we ask is that you place your trust in the presidency—in Brother Sidney, Brother Hyrum and myself—and I will give you a pledge that if we lead you into any difficulty I will give you my head for a foot-ball to be kicked about in Missouri dust.[52]

On 4 July 1838 Rigdon delivered the most consequential speech of his lengthy public career, a proclamation of Mormon independence from mob rule and legal process. While Rigdon could, and often did, deliver memorable extemporaneous political-religious oratory, this pivotal speech was carefully prepared, written before delivery, and pre-approved by presiding elders of the church.[53] After a Danite-led parade[54] and the laying of cornerstones at the Far West temple site,[55] Rigdon rose and, sprinkling his rhetoric with patriotic eulogy, delivered a provocative notice to enemies of the church:

> We take God and all the holy angels to witness this day, that we warn all men in the name of Jesus Christ, to come on us no more forever, for from this hour, we will bear it no more, our rights shall no more be trampled on with impunity. The man or the set of men, who attempts it, does it at the expense of their lives. And that mob that comes on us to disturb us; it shall be between us and them a war of extermination, for we will follow them, till the last drop of their blood is spilled or else they will have to exterminate us; for we will carry the seat of war to their own houses, and their own families, and one party or the other shall be utterly destroyed—remember it then all Men.
>
> We will never be the aggressors, we will infringe on the rights of no people; but shall stand for our own until death. We claim our own rights, and are willing that all others shall enjoy theirs.
>
> No man shall be at liberty to come into our streets, to threaten us with mobs, for if he does, he shall atone for it before he leaves the place, neither shall he be at liberty, to vilify and slander any of us, for suffer it we will not in this place.
>
> We therefore, take all men to record this day, that we proclaim our liberty on this day, as did our fathers. And we pledge this day to one another, our fortunes, our lives, and our sacred honors, to be delivered from the persecutions which we have had to endure, for the last nine years, or nearly that. Neither will we indulge any man,

or set of men, in instituting vexatious law suits against us, to cheat us out of our just rights, if they attempt it we say wo be unto them.

We this day then proclaim ourselves free, with a purpose and a determination, that never can be broken, no never! no never! NO NEVER!!![56]

At the conclusion of Rigdon's oration, hundreds of Saints, led by their prophet, waved their hats high above their heads and delivered the Hosanna Shout: "Hosanna! Hosanna! Hosanna to God and the Lamb!"[57]

Rigdon and Smith were elated at the response. The speech was immediately printed in *The Far West*, a weekly non-Mormon newspaper published at Liberty, and issued in pamphlet form by Ebenezer Robinson. The prophet recommended in the August *Elder's Journal* that all church members purchase copies for their families to read. He reaffirmed his approval of the central point of the declaration, that the Saints were determined to retaliate against further persecution: "We are absolutely determined no longer to bear [mobbing] come life or come death for to be mob[b]ed any more without taking vengeance, we will not."[58]

Publication of Rigdon's 4th of July sermon eroded Mormon relations with neighbors. Many who read Rigdon's rhetoric were especially agitated by the final paragraph, which was labeled both impolitic and treasonous.[59] A citizen of nearby Liberty commented in the *Western Star*:

> Until July 4th, we heard no threats being made against [the Mormons] in any quarters. The people had all become reconciled to let them remain where they are. . . . But one Sidney Rigdon, in order to show himself a great man, collected them all together in the town of Far West, on the 4th of July, and there delivered a speech containing the essence of, if not treason itself.[60]

The discourse stirred up so much excitement in the surrounding territory that, Emily Austin recalled, "Rigdon's life could not have been insured for five coppers [pennies]."[61] As *the* symbol of Mormon militancy in Missouri, Rigdon became after Smith's death a scapegoat within the church for all the misfortune that befell the movement during this period, despite the prophet's explicit approval of both his 17 June and 4 July addresses.

Church leaders Brigham Young, Wilford Woodruff, Orson Hyde, and Jedediah Grant, with the benefit of hindsight, condemned Rigdon's speech as overly aggressive and violent. In making his own case for church leadership Young specifically asserted that "Elder Rigdon was the prime cause of our troubles in Missouri, by his fourth of July oration."[62] Grant, citing a portion of the sermon, was equally critical:

> The foregoing extract from his oration, as anticipated by the judicious, was the main auxiliary that fanned into a flame the burning wrath of the mobocratic portion of the Missourians. They now had an excuse, their former threats were renewed, and soon

executed, we were then . . . all made accountable for the acts of one man; death and carnage, marched through the land in their most terrific forms.[63]

In fairness to Rigdon, however foolish and impolitic the 4th of July declaration of independence, the responsibility rests not alone with him but equally on the shoulders of those who approved and accepted it. Whoever was responsible for the Missouri wrath, it was quick in coming: a few days after the oration, "the thunder rolled in awful majesty over the city of Far West, the arrows of lightning fell from the clouds and slivered the liberty pole from top to bottom; thus manifesting to many that there was an end to liberty and law in that state."[64] Ebenezer Robinson wrote that the lightning's destruction of the liberty pole which had been erected in the town square for the celebration "struck dismay into the hearts of some, but," he continued, "we were told at the time, that Joseph Smith, Jr., walked over the splinters and prophesied that as he walked over these splinters, so we will trample our enemies under our feet."[65]

Notes

Unless otherwise stated, all primary sources cited are located in the Historical Department of the Church of Jesus Christ of Latter-day Saints, Salt Lake City, Utah.

1. William Law to Isaac Russell, 10 Nov. 1837, William Law Collection.
2. Joseph Smith, History of the Church of Jesus Christ of Latter-day Saints, B. H. Roberts, ed., 7 vols. (Salt Lake City: The Church of Jesus Christ of Latter-day Saints, 1902), 3:3; hereafter referred to as History of the Church.
3. Journal History, 29 Dec. 1842—a multi-volume daily history of the church compiled by official church historians; hereafter Journal History.
4. John W. Rigdon, "Life Story of Sidney Rigdon," 62-65; Karl Keller, ed., "I Never Knew a Time When I Did Not Know Joseph Smith," Dialogue: A Journal of Mormon Thought 1 (Winter 1966): 29.
5. Rigdon, 66.
6. Keller, 30.
7. Ibid.
8. Rigdon, 68.
9. William James, The Varieties of Religious Experience: A Study in Human Nature (New York: Longmans, Green, and Co., 1902), 338.
10. Hepzibah Richards, in an 18 January 1838 letter to her brother Willard, on a mission to the British Isles, described the Kirtland turmoil:

You had an opportunity to learn something of the spirit which was beginning to prevail here last spring, that spirit has continued to increase. . . . If at any time it has appeared to be quelled, it now appears that it was only preparing to operate with greater virulence, until it is generally believed that this place will soon be trodden down by the enemies of the Gospel which you preach. For some days past the spirit of things has been rapidly changing, and to the view of all appears to be gathering blackness. A large number have dissented from the body of the Church and are very violent in their opposition to the President and all who uphold him. They have organized a Church and appointed a meeting in the house [the temple] next Sabbath; they say they will have it, if it is by the shedding of blood. They have the keys of the House already (cited in "History of the Great Lakes Mission, Ohio," 18 Jan. 1838).

11. *Painesville Telegraph*, 22 Feb. 1838.

12. *History of the Church*, 3:15-16.

13. Following John Whitmer's 1878 death, his twenty-two-chapter history was given to his brother David. Prior to his death in 1888 he willed the manuscript to his son, David J. In 1893 LDS church historian Andrew Jenson visited young Whitmer and copied the manuscript (Andrew Jenson, "Memoranda, attached to copy of manuscript, October 1893").

14. Scott H. Faulring, ed., *An American Prophet's Record: The Diaries and Journals of Joseph Smith* (Salt Lake City: Signature Books in association with Smith Research Associates, 1989), 176-77. During the 6 April 1838 general conference, Rigdon's son-in-law George W. Robinson was appointed "general Church Clerk & Recorder." His specific assignment was to "keep a record of the whole Church also as scribe for the first Presidency" (Faulring, 172). The original Smith and Rigdon biographies, in the handwriting of Robinson, are recorded in Book A of the "Manuscript History of the Church."

15. *History of the Church*, 1:1. This account also contains the official version of Joseph Smith's controversial "First Vision." Interestingly, Rigdon never referred to this incident in the many letters and speeches that survive. In a little known account he did, however, relate an unusual version of Smith's discovery of the gold plates (see Appendix 2).

16. *Times and Seasons* 4 (24 Apr. 1843): 172. Neither Smith's nor Rigdon's history was published until later in Nauvoo. The prophet's account in 1902 became the foundation of the official *History of the Church of Jesus Christ of Latter-day Saints*, edited by prominent Mormon historian B. H. Roberts and copyrighted by church president Joseph F. Smith. Rigdon's lengthy personal account was condensed into a mere footnote, a reflection of his diminished importance in the eyes of twentieth-century church leaders.

17. "Oliver Cowdery Letterbook," 30 Jan. 1838, Huntington Library, San Marino, California.

18. Ibid.

19. Williams was not excommunicated until 17 March 1839 for "leaving the saints in time of peril, persecution and dangers, and acting against the interests of the Church" (*History of the Church*, 3:284).

Burr Riggs, Williams's son-in-law, testified that Rigdon suspected Frederick of disloyalty: "About the latter part of July, I heard Sidney Rigdon say, [that] Wm. W. Phelps and Dr. Williams, and he strongly suspected John Corrill, were using their influence against the presidency of the church . . . and [that] their influence must be put down" (Senate Document 189, p. 28, in Frederick G. Williams, "Frederick Granger Williams of the First Presidency of the Church," *Brigham Young University Studies* 12 [Spring 1972]: 258).

20. John Corrill, *Brief History of the Church of Christ of Latter Day Saints* (St. Louis: n.p., 1839), 59.

21. Faulring, 187.

22. *Document Containing the Correspondence, Orders &c., in Relation to the Disturbances with the Mormons and the Evidence Given Before the Hon. Austin A. King, Judge of the Fifth Judicial Circuit of the State of Missouri, at the Court-House in Richmond, in a Criminal Court of Inquiry, Begun November 12, 1838, on the Trial of Joseph Smith Jr., and Others for High Treason and Other Crimes Against the State* (Fayette, MO: Published by order of the General Assembly at the office of *Boon's Lick Democrat* 1841), 103-106; hereafter *Correspondence and Orders*.

While some have been inclined to dismiss the testimony of witnesses against church leaders in this court of inquiry, a leading scholar on this period has written:

> The evidence that is available . . . substantiates most of the testimony by the prosecution's witnesses regarding key issues and events, such as the Salt Sermon and expulsion of dissenters from Far West, the teachings and activities of the Danite band, the burning and plundering committed by Mormon soldiers in Daviess County, and Joseph Smith's leading role in the Mormon military organizations (Stephen C. LeSueur, "High Treason and Murder: The Examination of Mormon Prisoners at Richmond, Missouri, in November 1838," *Brigham Young University Studies* 26 [Spring 1986]: 17-18).

23. *Correspondence and Orders*, 138-39.

24. Ibid. Hearing John Whitmer protest after Rigdon's 4th of July declaration that state laws must be obeyed, Alanson Ripley replied that "as to the technical niceties of the law of the land, he did not intend to regard them; that the kingdom spoken of by the prophet Daniel had been set up, and that it was necessary every kingdom should be governed by its own laws." George W. Robinson added that "when God spoke he must be obeyed, whether his word came in contact with the laws of the land or not; and that, as the kingdom spoken of by Daniel has been set up, its laws must be obeyed" (ibid.).

While still in the First Presidency later in Nauvoo, Illinois, Rigdon acknowledged that a principal reason for harassment in Missouri was because the Saints would not have anything to do with the laws—"we did not break them we were above them" (Scott G. Kenney, ed., *Wilford Woodruff's Journal—Typescript* [9 vols] [Midvale, UT: Signature Books, 1983-85], 2:378).

25. F. Mark McKiernan and Roger D. Launius, eds., *An Early Latter Day Saint History: The Book of John Whitmer—Kept by Commandment* (Independence, MO: Herald House, 1980), 162.

26. *Correspondence and Orders*, 101-102. The full oath, according to one published account, was:

> In the name of Jesus Christ, the Son of God, I now promise and swear, truly, faithfully, and without reserve, that I will serve the Lord with a perfect heart and a willing mind, dedicating myself, wholly, and unreservedly, in my person and effects, to the upbuilding of His kingdom on earth, according to His revealed will. I furthermore promise and swear that I will regard the First President of the Church of Jesus Christ of Latter Day Saints, as the supreme head of the Church on earth, and obey him the same as the Supreme God, in all written revelations given under the solemnities of a "Thus saith the Lord," and that I will always uphold the Presidency, right or wrong.

I furthermore promise and swear that I will never touch a daughter of Adam, unless she is given me of the Lord. I furthermore promise and swear that no Gentile shall ever be admitted to the secrets of this holy institution or participate in its blessings. I furthermore promise and swear that I will assist the Daughters of Zion in the utter destruction of apostates, and that I will assist in setting up the kingdom of Daniel in these last days, by the power of the Highest and the sword of His might. I furthermore promise and swear that I will never communicate the secrets of this degree to any person in the known world, except it be to a true and lawful brother, binding myself under no less a penalty than that of having my blood shed. So help me God and keep me faithful (Achilles, *The Destroying Angels of Mormondom, or a Sketch of the Life of Orrin Porter Rockwell, the Late Danite Chief* [San Francisco: n.p., 1878], 8-9).

27. For Mormon references to Danite activities from participants themselves, see Allen Joseph Stout, "Journal," 8-9; Dimick B. Huntington, "Journal from 1808 to Salt Lake City," n.p.; Anson Call, "Statement December 30, 1885," 2; Moses Clawson, "Reminiscences," 9, all in Special Collections, Harold B. Lee Library, Brigham Young University, Provo, Utah; hereafter Special Collections, BYU; and Luman A. Shurtliff, "History of Luman Andros Shurtliff," 120-25.

28. Corrill, 31.

29. *Document Showing the Testimony Given Before the Judge of the Fifth Judicial District of the State of Missouri, on the Trial of Joseph Smith, Jr., and others, for High Treason and Other Crimes Against that State* (Washington, D.C.: U.S. Government Printing Office, 1841), 12; hereafter *Document.*

30. Faulring, 198.

31. *Document,* 1.

32. When William E. McLellin, a former apostle, led an October 1838 search of Smith's Far West home to confiscate books and papers that might prove damaging to the Mormons, the Danite constitution was reportedly found in a trunk filled with the prophet's personal papers (see *Missouri Republican,* 20 Nov. 1838). The complete "Bill of Rights of the Daughters of Zion, and Articles of Organization" was published by Ebenezer Robinson in his "Items of Personal History of the Editor," *The Return* (Davis City, IA), 1 (Oct. 1889): 145.

33. Reed Peck, "Mormons So Called" (Quincy, IL: 1839), 10.

34. Ibid., 9-10. In Freemasonry the government of Grand Lodges includes the same emphasis on loyalty: "The first duty [of a Freemason] . . . is to obey the edicts of his Grand Lodge. Right or wrong, his very existence as a Mason hangs upon obedience to the powers immediately set above him. . . . The one unpardonable crime in a Mason is contumacy, or disobedience" (M. N. Butler, comp., *The Government of Freemasonry, and Its Relation to Both Church and State* [Albany, MO: Freeman Printing Office, 1881], 4).

35. Peck, 22-23.

36. Patriarchal Blessing Book 1, 12, in Richard L. Anderson, "The Mature Joseph Smith and Treasure Searching," *Brigham Young University Studies* 24 (Fall 1984): 529.

37. *History of the Church,* 3:9.

38. Peck, 8.

39. Ibid., 6-7.

40. Ibid., 7. Joseph Smith had earlier used the same "Salt Sermon" imagery in a 24 February 1834 revelation now D&C 103:2-15.

41. *Correspondence and Orders*, 138-39.

42. Sampson Avard testified during an 1838 court hearing that Rigdon was the author of the paper (Journal History, 13 Nov. 1838). Whereas Avard's signature is the first on the document, and Rigdon's does not appear, Avard had been in Far West for less than a month and the document begins, "Whereas the citizens of Caldwell county have born [sic] with the abuse received from you at different times and on different occasions, until it is no longer to be endured."

43. *Correspondence and Orders*, 138-39.

44. Faulring, 187.

45. John Whitmer wrote that

when we were on our way home from Liberty, Clay County [where they had gone to secure legal aid], we met the families of Oliver Cowdery and L. E. Johnson, whom they had driven from their homes. . . . While we were gone Jo. and Rigdon and their band of Gadiantons had kept up a guard, and watched our houses and abused our families, and threatened them, if they were not gone by morning, they would be drove out and threatened our lives if they ever saw us in Far West (in McKiernan and Launius, 165).

46. Jedediah M. Grant, *Collection of Facts, Relative to the Course Taken By Elder Sidney Rigdon, in the States of Ohio, Missouri, Illinois, and Pennsylvania* (Philadelphia: Brown, Bicking & Guilbert, 1844), 10.

47. McKiernan and Launius, 163-64.

48. *Kansas City Daily Journal*, 5 June 1881. Whitmer added elsewhere the statement:

If you believe my testimony to the book of Mormon; if you believe that God spake to us three witnesses by his own voice, then I tell you that in June, 1838, God spake to me again by his own voice from the heavens, and told me to "separate myself from among the Latter Day Saints, for as they sought to do unto me, so should it be done unto them" . . . . In June, 1838, at Far West, Mo., a secret organization was formed, Doctor Avard being put in as the leader of the band; a certain oath was to be administered to all the brethren to bind them to support the heads of the church in *everything they should teach*. All who refused to take this oath were considered dissenters from the church, and certain things were to be done concerning these dissenters, by Dr. Avard's secret band (David Whitmer, *An Address to All Believers in Christ* [Richmond, MO: David Whitmer, 1887], 27; emphasis in original).

Interestingly, Rigdon's grandson, Sidney Ellis, a prominent Pittsburgh and New York actor, founded the "Danites Dramatic Company," a traveling troupe (see 9 June 1880, *Friendship [New York] Register*).

49. *Times and Seasons* 4 (15 July 1843): 271.

50. Peck, 9-10.

51. *Correspondence and Orders*, 111.

52. Corrill's testimony was substantiated by Reed Peck and John Cleminson in *Correspondence and Orders*, 114-20. In addition, Joseph Smith, speaking later on 3 January

1844, said, "The Danite system . . . was a term made use of by some of the brethren in Far West, and grew out of an expression I made use of when the brethren were preparing to defend themselves from the Missouri mob, in reference to the stealing of Macaiah's images (Judges, Chapter 18)—If the enemy comes, the Danites will be after them, meaning the brethren in self-defense" (*History of the Church*, 6:165). Rigdon, in later years, also acknowledged the existence of the society but maintained that neither he nor Joseph was actually a member of the brotherhood. His explanation was that the group was organized merely for self-defense (*History of the Church*, 3:453-54).

53. W. W. Phelps said that a few days before the holiday he heard David Patten say that Rigdon was writing a declaration to proclaim the church independent (*Correspondence and Orders*, 122; Ebenezer Robinson, *The Return* 1 [Nov. 1889]: 170).

54. That the parade was a Danite display of horsemanship can be seen by examining the *Elders' Journal* 1 (Aug. 1838): 60. It describes the protocol for the 4th of July parade staged two weeks after the brotherhood was formed:

> [T]hat Reynolds Cahoon, be marshal of the day, and Col. George M. Hinkle and Major Jefferson Hunt, be assistant marshals. . . . that George W. Robinson act as Colonel for the day; Philo Dibble, as Lieut. Colonel; Seymour Brunson as Major, and Reed Peck as Adjutant. . . . that Jared Carter, Sampson Avard, and Cornelius P. Lott, act as Generals before whom the military band shall pass in review.

55. A 26 April 1838 revelation given to Smith, Rigdon, and Hyrum Smith not only changed the church's name to "The Church of Jesus Christ of Latter-day Saints" but also commanded them to build a temple at Far West so that the gathering "may be for a defense, and for a refuge from the storm, and from wrath when it shall be poured out without mixture upon the whole earth" (D&C:115:3, 6).

56. Peter Crawley, "Two Rare Missouri Documents," *Brigham Young University Studies* 14 (Summer 1974): 527.

57. Robinson, "Items of Personal History," 149; Parley P. Pratt, Jr., ed., *Autobiography of Parley P. Pratt* (Salt Lake City: Deseret Book Co., 1976 [1874], 173; *Times and Seasons* 1 (Apr. 1840): 81; Faulring, 186-87.

58. *Elders' Journal* 1 (Aug. 1838): 54.

59. *Niles' National Register* (Washington D.C.) 55 (6 Oct. 1838): 83.

60. *Missouri Argus*, 27 Sept. 1838.

61. Emily Austin, *Mormonism: or, Life Among the Mormons* (Madison, WI: M. J. Cantwell, Book and Job Printer, 1882), 88.

62. "Elder Rigdon's Trial," *Times and Seasons* 5 (1 Oct. 1844): 667.

63. Grant, 11-12; see also *Times and Seasons* 5 (15 Sept. 1844): 651, and 5 (1 Nov. 1844): 698; John Jacques, "The Life and Labors of Sidney Rigdon," *Improvement Era* 3 (June 1900): 583.

64. *Times and Seasons* 1 (Apr. 1840): 81.

65. Ebenezer Robinson, *The Return* 1 (Oct. 1889): 145-51. During April conference 1876 Dimick Huntington related that "after the celebration of the independence of our nation was over, one hour; a small cloud came from the west and passed over the town, and from it was discharged [a] thunderbolt which struck the liberty pole that had been set up on the public square for that occasion, and shivered it into atoms." Dimick said that

"Joseph looked at the scene and his face shone white as snow as he said, 'thus saith the Lord as this pole has been shivered to atoms, so shall this Nation be shivered, and as I walk over these slivers (suiting the movement to the words) so will I walk over the ashes of my enemies" (Oliver Huntington Diary, 1875, 129, Special Collections, BYU).

CHAPTER 17.

Zion

The emigration to this land is very extensive and numerous[.] . . . [T]he First
Presidency are chiefly engaged in counciling and settling the emigrants to this land.
The [prophecies] are fulfilling very fast upon our heads and in our day and generation.
They are gathering from the North, and from the South, from the East, and from [the]
West unto Zion for safety against the day of wrath which is to be poured out without
mixture upon this generation according to the prophets.

—Joseph Smith (1838)[1]

The Missouri era (1831 to 1839) casts a deep shadow over the history of Mormonism.[2] Joseph Smith taught that the area was the land of antediluvian Old Testament narration, that Jackson County was old Eden. Adam-ondi-Ahman, in nearby Daviess County, was the place where Adam and Eve fled when driven from the idyllic garden, and Far West, in Caldwell County, was the "spot where Cain Killed Abel."[3] Mormons hoped initially and perhaps naively that Jackson County, the fabled "land of their inheritance," would be rescued from non-believing hordes. Joseph Smith advised Lyman Wight and others of the Missouri High Council on 16 August 1834 "to be in readiness to move into Jackson County in two years from the 11th of September next, which is the appointed time for the redemption of Zion."[4]

With the passing of time it became clear that Zion would not be redeemed nor would the Saints be redressed for their Jackson County losses. The Missouri legislature moved in 1836 to organize Caldwell County for Mormon settlement; thus most Saints left Clay and Ray counties and established new lives in Caldwell. John Whitmer and W. W. Phelps chose the county's center for a new city of refuge which they named Far West. Developed on large tracts of wild prairie lands, the village eventually became home to 2,500 people, the largest Mormon population in the state. Between December 1837 and mid-July 1838 more than 1,600 Kirtland Saints migrated to Far West, abandoning homes and flocking to this new colonizing adventure in the wilderness of western America. Land was cheap. In Caldwell County the Saints purchased nearly 250,000 acres of federal lands for $1.25 an acre; nearly thirty townsites were eventually settled.

Far West at its apex consisted of hundreds of log cabins, four dry goods stores, nine groceries, six blacksmith shops, and two hotels. The schoolhouse, where Sidney Rigdon preached shortly after settling in the area, was moved to the center of the town square for use as a combination church, town hall, and courthouse.[5] The Rigdon dwelling, a two-story log cabin directly across the street from the town square, was the village's largest home. Upon leaving Kirtland, Rigdon lost virtually everything he owned, including twelve acres of property valued at $4,211.[6] He rebounded financially in Missouri, however, quickly finding sustenance from church coffers.

Mormonism's theological preoccupation with economics has been evident since the earliest days of the movement. The Book of Mormon implied that the rewards for righteous living included material wealth (Alma 1:29, 31). While the Mormon work ethic, as pointed out by historian D. Michael Quinn, was "communitarian rather than individualistic, and socialistic rather than entrepreneurial or capitalistic," church leaders such as Rigdon, Smith, and later Brigham Young, seldom went without.[7] Rigdon and Smith, upon arriving in Caldwell County, presented their financial plight to the Far West High Council on 12 May 1838. Both leaders indicated that during the previous eight years they had spent their "time[,] tallents[,] & property, in the service of the Church, and are now reduced as it were to absolute beggery, and still were detained in service of the Church." They had now reached the point, they expressed, where either something "should be done for their support . . . by the Church" or they "must do it themselves."

After a lengthy discussion, during which George M. Hinkle forcefully opposed "a salaried ministry," the high council voted eleven to one to give the two men eighty acres of land each and to contract with them for their services, "not for preaching or for receiving the word of god by revelation, neither for instructing the Saints in righteousness," but for work rendered in the "[p]rinting establishment, in translating the ancient records &c, &c." After negotiations, they ultimately agreed to offer Rigdon and Smith an annual contract of $1,100 apiece, more than three times what the average worker of the day could earn.[8] Ebenezer Robinson, the high council's clerk, later wrote that "when it was noised abroad that the Council had taken such a step, the members of the church, almost to a man, lifted their voices against it. The expression of disapprobation was so strong and emphatic that at the next meeting of the High Council the resolution voting them a salary, was rescinded."[9]

Angered by this refusal, Rigdon and Smith sought additional sources of church revenues. A revelation given to them in Kirtland on 12 January 1838, but not yet public, was dusted off and presented to the membership. In response to the question: "O Lord, show unto thy servants how much thou requirest of the properties of thy people for a tithing," the Saints were told: "I require all their surplus property to be put into the hands of the Bishop of my Church of Zion, for the building of mine house and for the laying the foundation of Zion, and for the priesthood and for the debts of the presidency of my church."[10]

Ten days later another revelation explained that surplus tithing was to be "disposed of by a Council composed of the First Presidency . . . and of the Bishop and his Council; and by my High Council" (D&C 120). On 26 July still further instruction declared that the "first presidency [should] keep all their properties, that they can dispose of to their advantage and Support and the remainder be put into the hands of the Bishop or Bishops agreeably to the commandments, and revelations."[11] For those unwilling to be so "tithed," the 8 July revelation threatened: "If my people observe not this law, to keep it holy, and by this law sanctify the land of Zion . . . behold verily I say unto you, it shall not be a land of Zion unto you."[12]

Rigdon expanded on the revelation's warning, adding that noncompliers would be "delivered over to the brother of Gideon and be sent bounding over the Prairies as the dissenters were a few days ago."[13] But fate failed to discriminate between non-tithers and tithe payers. Within four months the entire body of Mormons was driven from their promised land by looting, pillage, and gratuitous violence. Trouble began on 6 August 1838 at Gallatin, the county seat of Daviess County. During the third week of July, Judge Josiah Morin, a Democratic candidate for state senator, informed John D. Lee and Levi Stewart of a Whig plot to prevent Mormons—who voted Democrat en masse—from casting ballots in Daviess County on election day.

Shortly after polls opened on 6 August, William Peniston, a Whig candidate for the state legislature, mounted a barrel and began castigating Mormons. Calling church leaders "horse thieves, liars, counterfeiters," the agitator asserted that "he did not consider [that] Mormons had any more right to vote than the niggers." Goaded into action by Peniston's rhetoric, several Missourians attempted to bully the eight or ten Mormons waiting to vote. A brawl quickly erupted. John L. Butler noted that when he saw what was happening he "hollowed out to the top of my voice . . . O yes, you Danites, here is a job for us." He picked up a large oak bludgeon, and "When I got in reach of them, I commenced to call out loud for peace and at the same time making my stick to move to my own utter astonishment, tapping them as I thought light, but they fell as dead men."[14]

In the brief skirmish the heavily outnumbered Mormons prevailed. Nearly thirty Missourians were wounded by Butler and others. Fearing vengeance by the regrouped ruffians, Mormons retreated to their cabins, gathered up their families, and hid as a group in a hazel thicket until morning. Word of the fray soon reached Far West. Judge Morin, passing through town, informed Smith and Rigdon that he had heard that "two or three of our brethren were killed by the Missourians, and left upon the ground, and not suffered to be interred . . . and [that] a majority of the inhabitants of Daviess county were determined to drive the Saints from that county."[15]

The signal drum sounded and a Danite company, including the First Presidency, assembled in the town square. One observer said that Rigdon addressed the troops with sword in hand. "Now we as the people of God do declare and decree," he shouted, brandishing the cutlass, "by the Great Jehovah, the eternal and omnipotent God, that sits upon his vast and everlasting throne, beyond that ethereal blue, we will bath our swords in the vital blood of the Missourians or die in the attempt!"[16] Under the command of Danite regimental Colonel George W. Robinson, the well-armed company, which had grown to nearly one hundred men, reached Lyman Wight's home at Diahman by nightfall. There the men listened to a more accurate report of the election day fight. Instead of returning home the next morning, however, they decided to visit prominent Daviess County men to assess their view of the incident at Gallatin.

Three Danite leaders, Lyman Wight, Sampson Avard, and Cornelius P. Lott, called on Judge Adam Black, a local justice of the peace whom George W. Robinson, the prophet's scribe, attested was "[manifestly] an en[e]my of ours."[17] The group demanded the judge sign a prepared statement renouncing his affiliation with vigilantes and pledging not to molest Mormons in the future. He refused. In thirty minutes Danite emissaries, including Rigdon and Smith, surrounded the house. "We have come to be plain with you," threatened Avard, the group's spokesman: "the only alternative is for you to sign this obligation." Fearing the large company of armed men, Black signed a statement of his own which satisfied the Danites.[18] Other principal men in the area were visited and enjoined to discuss peace. Robinson added that the company arrived home about midnight and "found all well in Far West."[19]

But all was not well outside the Mormon stronghold, particularly in Daviess County. Squire Black, incensed at his treatment by the militia, immediately filed a complaint stating that Mormons had demanded his signature or suffer "instant death."[20] The next day William Peniston also swore before Judge Austin A. King that Mormons not only threatened Black's life but intended to "drive from the county all the old citizens, and possess themselves of their lands, or to force such as do not leave, to come into their measures and submit to their dictation."[21]

The situation quickly exploded. One observer wrote that the standoff could "not be settled without a fight, and the quicker they have it the better for the peace and quiet of the county."[22] While neither Smith nor Rigdon at this point sought confrontation, they were likewise resolved not to back away from one. The 1 September 1838 entry in the "Scriptory Book of Joseph Smith" reaffirms their stance, earlier elucidated in Rigdon's 4th of July oration: "[I]n the name of Jesus Christ the Son of the Living God we will endure [persecution] no longer. . . . Our rights and our liberties shall not be taken from us, and we peacably submit to it as we have done heretofore, but we will avenge ourselves of our enemies, inasmuch as they will not let us alone."[23]

Rigdon wrote lengthy requests for assistance to the governor and to Judge Austin A. King, imploring them to "protect the citizens of Davies[s] against the threatened violence of the mob." The letters were accompanied by affidavits, Rigdon later testified, which "could leave no doubt on the mind of the governor or judge, that the citizens before mentioned were in eminent danger."[24] Rigdon's efforts were partially successful. Major General Atchison and Brigadier Generals Doniphan and Parks marched troops into Daviess County and momentarily defused the situation. Once they left, however, the harassment resumed. Missouri miscreants scoured the countryside for Mormons, forcing them from their homes. "They calculated to drive the people into Far West," Hyrum Smith later stated, "and then drive them to hell."[25] Mormon messengers sought assistance from the governor but were reportedly told "the quarrel was between the Mormons and the mob," and that they "might fight it out."[26]

Rather than fight, the besieged citizens of DeWitt in Daviess County loaded their wagons and abandoned the town on 11 October. Their arrival in Far West infuriated local church leaders, who urged retaliation. On 15 October, while advising several companies of Mormon fighting men en route to Diahman, an irate Joseph Smith asserted:

> The law we have tried long enough! Who is so big a fool as to cry, the law! the law! when it is always administered against us and never in our favor. I do not intend to regard the law hereafter. . . . We will take our affairs into our own hands and manage for ourselves. We have applied to the Governor and he will do nothing for us; the militia of the county we have tried and they will do nothing. All are mob. . . . I am determined that we will not give another foot . . . God will send us angels to our deliverance and we can conquer 10,000 as easily as ten!

Rigdon joined Smith, chastising the "oh, don't men" who refused to fight "while others are out on expeditions to other counties doing all they can to support the cause." In the heat of the moment he proposed that "blood should first run in the streets of Far West," that "traitors among [us] who had always opposed [our] doings should be slain." He subsequently mellowed and insisted instead that pacifists simply be forced to march with troops the next day. If they refused, he exclaimed, "they should be pitched on their horses with bayonets and placed in front of the battle." A hearty "amen" from the congregation sealed his senti-ments.[27] Reed Peck noted that he, John Corrill, W. W. Phelps, John Cleminson, and several other "anti Danites had the honor of being enrolled in one of these companies and under the *bayonet resolutions* marched to Daviess County."[28]

Smith and Rigdon instructed the "Army of Israel," lacking sufficient proven-der and supplies, to live off the land while they battled. Prior to their departure, Major General Sampson Avard informed his captains that it soon will be your privilege to take your respective companies and go out on a scout on the borders of the settlements, and take to yourselves spoils of the goods of the ungodly Gentiles[.] . . . [I]t is written, the riches of the Gentiles shall be consecrated to my people, the house of Israel; and thus you will waste away the Gentiles by robbing and plundering them of their property; and in this way we will build up the kingdom of God.[29]

When some of the inductees opposed these aggressive plans, Avard asserted "there were no laws that were executed in justice . . . this being a different dispensation" wherein the Lord would personally reign, "and His laws alone were the laws that would exist." Further protests were silenced when Avard announced that he had received his authority on the matter from President Rigdon the previous evening.[30]

The company marched to Daviess County resolved to drive their enemies out a final time. This strategy was delayed by a massive snowstorm. *The Far West*, a non-Mormon newspaper in nearby Liberty, felt "the snow and cold weather will be the best mediator of peace between the parties."[31] On 18 October, however, Mormon raiders were able to ride out. Apostle David W. Patten, known by his Danite title "Captain Fearnought," descended on Gallatin with a large contingent of men and, after plundering the small village, burned most of it to the ground. Then the marauders pillaged the Daviess County countryside, depositing their spoils, which they termed "consecrated property," in the bishop's storehouse at Diahman. "It should not be supposed," wrote Oliver B. Huntington, "that we were common robbers because we took by reprisal that with which to keep from starvation our women and children."[32]

During the evening of 23 October, 130 Mormon cavalry returned to Far West. According to Albert P. Rockwood, Rigdon gave these "horsemen of Isreall" a "short address suited to the occasion when all the people said Amen."[33] A courier had also conveyed a letter to Rigdon from the prophet which caused him to celebrate, Mormon James C. Owens noted. The letter stated: "[T]he enemy was delivered into [our] hands, and that they need not fear; that this had been given to him by the spirit of prophecy, in the name of Jesus Christ."[34]

For a time Daviess County was in the hands of Mormon raiders. "The citizens," wrote Reed Peck,

men, women and children, fled through the snow in wagons, on horseback and on foot after the plundering and burning commenced, as precipitately as though they had been invaded by a hostile band of Indians: but with this flood of testimony their calamitous report was not generally credited until men expecially appointed for the purpose had visited Daviess Co. and returned with a confirmation of their story.[35]

Danite atrocities would be confirmed by such prominent Mormons as Thomas B. Marsh, Orson Hyde, Reed Peck, William Swartzell, John Cleminson, W. W. Phelps, and John Corrill. Swartzell, a recent convert living at Diahman, chose to leave the church: "I concluded that I had been fed on such stuff long enough," he wrote in his diary, "the idea of such a band attacking a State which could call to its aid twenty-five other free and independent sovereignties, more densely populated than itself, was preposterous. God (thought I) can have no dealings with this people, who have been led away by imposters; and I, for one, will leave them to their fate."[36]

The most prominent Mormon defectors of this period were Quorum of the Twelve President Thomas B. Marsh and outspoken Apostle Orson Hyde. After witnessing the burning and plundering in Daviess County, Marsh and Hyde traveled to Richmond, in Ray County, where on 24 October Marsh, in a lengthy affidavit, confirmed that a company of Mormons under Apostle David Patten had burned Gallatin. "They have among them," Marsh continued, "a company consisting of all that are considered true Mormons, called the Danites, who have taken an oath to support the heads of the church in all things that they say or do, whether right or wrong." After exposing future Danite plans for scourging the countryside, Marsh added:

> The plan of said Smith, the prophet, is to take this State, and he professes to his people to intend taking the United States, and ultimately the whole world. . . . I have heard the prophet say that he should yet tread down his enemies, and walk over their dead bodies; that if he was not let alone he would be a second Mahomet to this generation, and that he would make it one gore of blood from the Rocky Mountains to the Atlantic Ocean; that like Mohomet, whose motto, in treating for peace, was "the Alcoran, or the Sword," so should it be eventually with us, "Joseph Smith or the Sword."[37]

Hyde, in a second affidavit, attested that "most of the statements in the foregoing disclosure of Thomas B. Marsh, I know to be true, the remainder I believe to be true."[38]

These affidavits, in addition to Danite activities in the surrounding countryside, caused considerable hysteria in Richmond where citizens expected an imminent Danite attack. Richmond Judge E. M. Ryland in an 25 October express to Governor Lilburn Boggs stated: "the city is expected to be sacked and burned by the Mormon banditti tonight."[39] Judge Austin A. King confirmed Ryland's position by letter to the governor, adding: "Until lately, I thought the Mormons were disposed to act only on the defensive; but their recent conduct shows that they are the aggressors, that they intend to take the law into their own hands."[40] Sashiel Woods and Joseph Dickson reported to Boggs that Mormons had massacred a fifty-man Missouri militia company. Richmond, they said, was to be attacked at any moment. "We know not the hour and minute we will be laid in ashes—our country ruined—for God's sake give us assistance as quick as possible."[41]

The previous evening a militia company, led by a Methodist minister, Captain Samuel Bogart, had been patrolling the borders of Caldwell County when it encountered a small group of Mormons. They were disarmed, three taken hostage, and the rest allowed to return to Far West where they spread the horrific news that the captives would be shot at sunrise. The prophet, now commander-in-chief of all Mormon military units, dispatched a company of men under Apostle David Patten to "Go and kill every devil of them" and rescue the trio.[42] The cavalry unit discovered the Missourians bivouacked on Crooked River, twelve miles south of Far West. Patten's men dismounted a mile from the militia, left their horses with a small guard, and approached the camp silently on foot. At dawn they rushed upon their enemies, echoing their war cry, "God and Liberty!" The militia fled, leaving one of their number dead. The gunfight also resulted in the deaths of Mormons Gideon Carter, David W. Patten, and eighteen-year-old Patrick O'Banion.

The command post for the operation was Rigdon's home, although, according to his account, he "was not connected with the militia, being over age."[43] He later recalled that early the next morning the county sheriff reported several Mormons dead in the battle. Rigdon and an unnamed horseman (possibly Joseph Smith) rode out onto the prairie to meet the returning company. Young O'Banion was taken to Sidney's house where, according to Wickliffe Rigdon, he "lingered in great agony for two days and then died."[44]

Although Governor Boggs had done virtually nothing to protect Mormons from predatory Missourians, the Danite assault on the militia at Crooked River put the politician into action. On 27 October 1838 Boggs issued a directive to Major-General John B. Clark, which read in part:

> Since the order of this morning to you . . . I have received, by Amos Rees, Esq., of Ray county and Wiley C. Williams, Esq., one of my aid[e]s, information of the most appalling character, which changes entirely the face of things, and places the Mormons in the attitude of an open and avowed defiance of the laws, and of having made war upon the people of this State. Your orders are therefore, to hasten your operations and endeavor to reach Richmond in Ray County, with all possible speed. The Mormons must be treated as enemies, and must be exterminated, or driven from the State, if necessary for the public peace.[45]

The governor's "extermination order," as it subsequently became known, was supported by the unwritten—though frequently avowed—right of American citizens to expel unwanted groups or individuals from their midst. Rigdon himself had used this reasoning to justify forcing Mormon dissidents from Far West.[46] Boggs later said his principal desire was to quell Mormon insurrection without bloodshed. The muster of such a massive military force from his perspective was merely to "awe [the Saints] into submission."[47] Initially Mormons, unaware of the size of the military contingent, were not awed. Responding to a rumor that the governor had called out the militia, Smith scoffed:

> I care not a fig for the coming of the troops. We've tried long enough to please the Gentiles. If we live together they don't like it; if we scatter they massacre us for it. The

only law they know here is that might makes right. They are a damned set, and God will blast them into hell!

If they try to attack us we will play hell with their applecarts. Before now, men, you've fought like devils. But now I want you to fight like angels, for angels can whip devils. And for every one we lack in number to match the mob, the Lord will send an angel to fight alongside.[48]

Albert Rockwood, impressed with Smith's bravado, recorded in his diary that "the Prophet goes out to the battle as in days of old. He has the sword that Nephi took from Laban. . . . The Prophet has unsheathed his sword and in the name of Jesus declares that it shall not be sheathed again untill he can go into any County or state in safety and in peace."[49]

Far West was elevated sufficiently for a commanding view of the terrain. On 30 October, an hour before sunset, Missouri militia leader General Samuel Lucas and his army, a cortege more than a mile long, was spotted approaching Far West from the south. After crossing Goose Creek the military formed a line of battle as if to attack the city. Wickliffe Rigdon, later recalling the reaction of Far West residents, wrote that "the women were greatly excited and the men showed great fear as to what might happen." Young Rigdon saw Joseph Smith in front of the Rigdon home loading a weapon. He was soon surrounded by a panicked throng of forty or fifty men seeking instructions. The prophet told them to get their weapons and come with him. Eight-year-old Wickliffe and his ten-year-old brother Sid tagged along with the men as they established a skirmish line to oppose what they wrongly thought was an undisciplined mob of Missourian rabble.

Within moments Sidney Rigdon arrived on the scene and asked his boys what they were doing. Wickliffe told his father they were there "to see what was going to be done." "You and your brother go home. You may get killed here," he ordered. When young Wickliffe argued they were in no more danger of getting killed than he was, Sidney exploded "in anger for us to go home at once and we started."[50] Rigdon, attempting to survey the army through his telescope, was so unnerved, Lorenzo D. Young later reported, that he "could not hold the glass still enough to see anything."[51] Meanwhile, seeing that the Mormons intended to fight, the militia withdrew into nearby woods until morning to await approaching reinforcements and general orders.

Some Mormons, misinterpreting the army's actions, thought the battalion had been intimidated into retreat. One account alleged the withdrawal occurred because hundreds of angels, bearing the appearance of "legions of armed men," stood beside the Mormons, visible only to the Missourians.[52] Oliver Huntington claimed the troops "all turned and ran pell mell back to their camp, in great fright, declaring they saw too many thousands of soldiers to think of attacking the city," speculating that they had seen the "Three Nephites, armed for battle, leading the hosts of heaven."[53]

Despite rumors of miraculous relief, Mormon leaders were frightened. John Corrill and Reed Peck were secretly sent to scour the area in search of General Doniphan, Smith's and Rigdon's friend and personal lawyer, to "beg like a dog for peace."[54] But the couriers did not locate the general until his command was encamped outside Far West. Peck was assured the army would hold off an attack until militia leaders had met with Mormon emissaries the following day.

Few Far West residents slept that night. "If we must fight," Rigdon was heard to lament, "[we must] sell our lives as dear as we could."[55] Accordingly all hands went to work. Rails, logs, and wagons were formed into a protective breastwork. Women and children, after concealing valuables, lay awake in fear. The vacant second story of Rigdon's home was "packed as full of women and children as could get into it," Wickliffe Rigdon later wrote. "[W]e all sat on the floor as close as we could get and there we sat all night."[56] When morning came the Mormon mediators—George M. Hinkle, Arthur Morrison, Reed Peck, John Corrill, W. W. Phelps, and John Cleminson—were briefed by the First Presidency. Peck noted the prophet said "a compromise must be made on some terms honorable or dishonorable."[57] Hinkle added they were told to obtain a treaty "on any terms short of a battle."[58] Corrill said the prophet stated he would "go to prison for twenty years or even die rather than allow his people to be exterminated."[59]

The interview between Mormon negotiators and General Lucas and his staff—generals Wilson, Doniphan, and Graham—did not take place until 2:00 p.m. outside the city. After a brief parley wherein Hinkle, the Mormon's chief negotiator, sued for peace, General Lucas read Governor Boggs's "extermination order" to the astonished men. "I expected we should be exterminated without fail," John Corrill recalled of this moment: "There lay three thousand men, highly excited and full of vengeance, and it was as much as the officers could do to keep them off from us any how; and they now had authority from the executive to exterminate."[60]

Lucas assured the negotiators that blood would not be shed if Mormons agreed to his demands. The general insisted that they give up their leaders to be tried and punished, appropriate their property to pay for the costs of the expedition and assessed damages in upper Missouri, leave the state en masse, and give up their arms.[61] Hinkle argued strenuously against the harsh terms, requesting they be given until morning to decide. Lucas agreed but demanded that Joseph Smith, Sidney Rigdon, Lyman Wight, Parley P. Pratt, and George W. Robinson be surrendered as hostages to insure faithful compliance. Failure to deliver them within thirty minutes, he threatened, would result in the destruction of the city. Far West would be "consumed by fire and . . . its contents would soon be in ashes."[62]

Returning to Far West, the representatives explained the militia's terms to Rigdon and the four others. "There is no time for controversy," Hinkle argued when the men hesitated to give themselves up. "If you go not into the camp immediately, they are determined to come upon Far West before the setting of the sun."[63] A runner then interrupted the huddle and reported that the Missourians, in full battle array, were advancing towards the town. Parley P. Pratt later recalled the urgency of the situation: "There was no alternative but to put ourselves into the hands of such monsters, or to have the city attacked, and men, women and children massacred. We, therefore, commended ourselves to the Lord, and voluntarily surrendered as sheep into the hands of wolves."[64]

Colonel Hinkle, escorting the hostages to General Lucas, met him within six hundred yards of the city. Hinkle said: "Here, general, are the prisoners I agreed to deliver to you."[65] Smith and Wight asked for a postponement until morning, but Lucas refused. "You are my prisoners," he declared, "and there is no time for talking at the present."[66] As the Missourians surrounded the knotted group of men, several militiamen threatened them, forcing Lucas to place a protective guard of thirty soldiers in a double ring around the men. When the hostages entered the encampment, they were met by unnerving clamor from the assembled militia, many of whom were dressed like Native Americans. "The loud cries and yells of more than one thousand voices," Smith later wrote, "and the horrid and blasphemous threats and curses which were poured upon us in torrents, were enough to appall the stoutest heart."[67]

Back in Far West Hyrum Smith and Brigham Young advised all the "Crooked River boys" to flee northward out of the state "for, if found, they will be shot down like dogs."[68] Nearly seventy left. All Mormon plunder, Oliver Huntington later wrote, was "gathered together in one house, lest every man who was found with a saddle or a blanket not his own be hanged for stealing."[69]

When night fell Rigdon and the other captives were forced to sleep on the ground in the open air with no bedrolls in a strong rain. Pratt wrote that during the night the guards kept up a constant tirade of mockery, demanding miracles and signs. "Come, Mr. Smith, show us an angel," one jested. "Give us one of your revelations," sneered another. "Or, if you are Apostles or men of God, deliver yourselves, and then we will be Mormons."[70]

The next morning Hyrum Smith and Amasa Lyman also joined the weary hostages. When General Lucas finally got around to meeting the men, he astounded them by refusing to discuss surrender terms. Their options were Lucas's terms or a battle. Joseph Thorp, a member of Doniphan's brigade, wrote that Lyman Wight was the only Mormon who wanted to return to town and fight. "They were about as badly scared set as I ever saw," Thorp said of the hostages, "except old [Wight] who stood like a lion and said fight, without a sign of fear about him."[71]

At 8:00 a.m., Smith sent a message to Far West instructing the Saints to surrender. Although Rigdon and the other hostages felt they had been betrayed by their own negotiators, what they failed to understand was that the surrender agenda had been dictated with no room for negotiation; the terms were unconditional.[72]

Initially the men feared they would be executed. Lucas held a secret court martial on the eve of 1 November. Mormon T. B. Foote recalled that prior to the hearing he saw the prisoners seated in a wagon, "from all of whom I received a bow of recognition except from S[idney] Rigdon, who sat with his head down and his face buried in his hands." The dramatic despondency foreshadowed the delirium and anxiety attacks that would soon engulf Rigdon.[73]

General Doniphan, General Parks, Colonel Hinkle, and a number of other officers during the tribunal argued strenuously for the prisoners, but about two-thirds of the officers voted for conviction. At midnight, Lucas directed the following order to Doniphan: "Sir: You will take Joseph Smith and the other prisoners into the public square of Far West, and shoot them at 9 o'clock tomorrow morning."[74] But Doniphan, later a Mexican War hero, refused the order in a note to Lucas: "It is cold-blooded murder. I will not obey your order. My brigade shall march for Liberty to-morrow morning, at 8 o'clock; and if you execute those men, I will hold you responsible before an earthly tribunal, so help me God!"[75] Hyrum Smith later related that about sunrise the next morning Doniphan ordered his brigade to take up the line of march and leave the camp. As he passed by the Mormon prisoners he said, "By God you have been sentenced by the court martial to be shot this morning; but I will be damned if I will have any of the honor of it, or any of the disgrace of it; therefore I have ordered my brigade to take up the line of march and to leave the camp, for I consider it to be cold blooded murder, and I bid you farewell."[76]

Doniphan's courageous response, supported by his brigade, prevented the execution.[77] Neither Lucas nor any of his officers pursued the matter further. Instead of proceeding with their military tribunal of the civilians, Lucas and his force of 2,500 men marched for Far West at 9:30 a.m. to receive the prisoners and their arms. The Mormon detachment of 600 men marched out of the town into a hollow square formed by the militia, then grounded their arms. Colonel Hinkle rode forward and delivered his sword and pistols to Lucas. The general, in order to gratify the army and let the Mormons see his troops, paraded around the town through the main streets and then marched back to headquarters.

Rigdon and the other prisoners were allowed to see their families, who feared they had been killed. They were given two minutes to get a change of clothing. Wickliffe Rigdon later wrote that when Sidney and George W. Robinson came to bid their families goodbye "the house was so crowded with Missourians that it was nearly impossible to get in or out of the house." "We also suppose[d]," he added, "it was the last time we should ever see them."[78]

The Rigdon family was destitute. Sidney later recalled that when he was allowed to go into his house he found his family

> so completely plundered of all kinds of food that they had nothing to eat but parched corn which they ground with a hand mill, and thus were they sustaining life. I soon pacified my family and allayed their feelings by assuring them that the ruffians dared not kill me. I gave them strong assurances that they dared not do it, and that I would return to them again.[79]

The prisoners were led to two large wagons in the town square. Pratt later recalled watching Rigdon take leave of his wife and daughters "who stood at a little distance, in tears of anguish indescribable."[80] As the men prepared to enter the wagons, hundreds of Mormons crowded around them, anxious to take a parting look or offer a farewell handshake. In the midst of these dismal scenes the orders were given, and the procession, under the command of General Wilson, moved slowly away towards Independence, the erstwhile Mormon City of Refuge.

Notes

Unless otherwise stated, all primary sources cited are located in the Historical Department of the Church of Jesus Christ of Latter-day Saints, Salt Lake City, Utah.

1. Scott H. Faulring, ed., *An American Prophet's Record: The Diaries and Journals of Joseph Smith* (Salt Lake City: Signature Books in association with Smith Research Associates, 1989), 193.

2. The Mormon population in the state during this period reached nearly 15,000. The best demographic study estimates the following peak percentages of Latter-day Saints by county: Jackson (57 percent), Clay (15 percent), Carroll (30 percent), Daviess (70 percent), and Caldwell (virtually 100 percent). See Wayne J. Lewis, "Mormon Land Ownership as a Factor in Evaluating the Extent of Mormon Settlements and Influence in Missouri, 1831-1841," M.A. thesis, Brigham Young University, 1981, 72-74.

3. Reed Peck, "Mormons So Called" (Quincy, IL: 1839), 5.

4. Joseph Smith, *History of the Church of Jesus Christ of Latter-day Saints*, B. H. Roberts, ed., 7 vols. (Salt Lake City: The Church of Jesus Christ of Latter-day Saints, 1902), 2:145; hereafter *History of the Church*.

5. *History of Caldwell and Livingston Counties, Missouri* (St. Louis: n.p., 1886), 120-22; hereafter *History of Caldwell and Livingston Counties*.

6. "Kirtland Saints Land and Tax Records," in Milton V. Backman, Jr., *A Profile of Latter-day Saints of Kirtland, Ohio and Members of Zion's Camp–1830-1839* (Provo, UT: Brigham Young University, 1982), 157.

7. D. Michael Quinn, "The Mormon Hierarchy, 1832-1932: An American Elite," Ph.D. diss., Yale University, 1976, 81-82.

8. Ebenezer Robinson, "Items of Personal History of the Editor," *The Return* (Davis City, IA), 1 (Oct. 1889): 145-51; Faulring, 182-83; *History of the Church*, 3:32.

9. Robinson, 145-51.

10. The revelation was given at the "French Farm" in Kirtland in the presence of Smith, Rigdon, Vinson Knight, and George W. Robinson (Faulring, 191, 194-95).

11. Ibid., 197.

12. Ibid., 195.

13. Peck, 8-9.

14. Journal History, 6 Aug. 1838—a multi-volume daily history of the church compiled by official church historians; hereafter Journal History. Other accounts of the Gallatin affair are Reed C. Durham, Jr., "The Election Day Battle at Gallatin," *Brigham Young University Studies* 13 (Autumn 1972): 36-61; Stephen C. LeSueur, *The 1838 Mormon War in Missouri* (Columbia, MO: University of Missouri Press, 1987), 58-64; John D. Lee, *Mormonism Unveiled; or The Life and Confessions of the Late Mormon Bishop, John D. Lee* (St Louis: Bryan, Brand, & Co., 1877), 56-60; and Sidney Rigdon, *An Appeal to the American People: Being an Account of the Persecutions of the Church of Jesus Christ of Latter Day Saints; and of the Barbarities Inflicted on Them by the Inhabitants of the State of Missouri* (Cincinnati: Printed By Shepard & Sterns, 1840), 15-18.

15. Journal History, 7 Aug. 1838.

16. William Swartzell, *Mormonism Exposed; Being A Journal of a Residence in Missouri from the 28th of May to the 20th of August, 1838* (Pekin, OH: William Swartzell, 1840), 29.

17. Faulring, 202.

18. *Document Showing the Testimony Given Before the Judge of the Fifth Judicial District of the State of Missouri, on the Trial of Joseph Smith, Jr., and others, for High Treason and Other Crimes Against that State* (Washington, D.C.: U.S. Government Printing Office, 1841), 161; hereafter *Document.*

19. Faulring, 202.

20. Missouri State Dept., Commission Dept., Mormon War, 1838-41, in Marvin S. Hill, *Quest for Refuge: The Mormon Flight from American Pluralism* (Salt Lake City: Signature Books, 1989), 85.

21. *History of the Church,* 3:61.

22. *Missouri Republican,* 11 Oct. 1838.

23. Faulring, 210-11.

24. *Times and Seasons* 4 (15 July 1843): 271.

25. Hyrum Smith statement, *Times and Seasons* 4 (15 July 1843): 247.

26. *History of the Church,* 3:157.

27. Peck, 19.

28. Ibid., 20.

29. *History of the Church,* 3:180-81. John Whitmer explained that the Danites "commenced a difficulty in Davies[s] Co. . . . in which they began to rob and burn houses &c. &c. took honey which they (the Mormons) called Sweet oil & hogs which they called bear, and Cattle which they called Buffalo. Thus they would Justify themselves by saying we are the people of God, and all things are god[']s, therefore they are ours" (F. Mark McKiernan and Roger D. Launius, eds., *An Early Latter Day Saint History: The Book of John Whitmer—Kept by Commandment* [Independence, MO: Herald House, 1980], 165).

30. The official position was that "When a knowledge of Avard's rascality came to the Presidency of the Church, he was cut off . . . and every means proper used to destroy his

influence, at which he was highly incensed, and went about whispering his evil insinuations, but finding every effort unavailing, he again turned conspirator, and sought to make friends with the mob" (*History of the Church*, 3:181). This stance is not accurate. Avard was not excommunicated until 17 March 1839 for testifying in court about Danite activities rather than for the activities themselves.

31. As reported in the *Missouri Argus*, 1 Nov. 1838.

32. Oliver B. Huntington Journal, 33 (Special Collections, Harold B. Lee Library, Brigham Young University, Provo, Utah; hereafter Special Collections, BYU).

33. Dean C. Jessee and David J. Whittaker, "The Last Months of Mormonism in Missouri: The Albert Perry Rockwood Journal," *Brigham Young University Studies* 28 (Winter 1988): 23.

34. James H. Hunt, *Mormonism, Embracing the Origin, Rise and Progress of the Sect, With an Examination of the Book of Mormon; Also Their Troubles in Missouri, and Final Expulsion From The State* (St. Louis: Ustick & Davies, 1844), 226.

35. Peck, 21-22.

36. Swartzell, 33.

37. *Correspondence and Orders*, 57-59.

38. Ibid. The following day, in a letter to "Bro & Sister Abbott," Marsh explained that "I have left the Mormons & Joseph Smith jr. for conscience sake and that alone." He then added that "the disposition in J. Smith and S. Rigdon to pillage, rob, plunder, assassinate and murder, was never equalled, in my estimation, unless by some desperado Bandit. O my what principles to be called the religion of Jesus Christ." Hyde concurred, "I can say with him that I have left the church . . . for conscience sake, fully believing that God is not with them" (copy in the Kirtland Letter Book, cited in Hill, 96). Although both Marsh and Hyde later rejoined the church, neither ever denied the truthfulness of the statements made in their affidavits or the 25 October 1838 letter.

39. *Correspondence and Orders*, 57.

40. Cited in *Missouri Argus* (St. Louis), 8 Nov. 1838.

41. *Correspondence and Orders*, 60.

42. Ebenezer Robinson, *The Return* 2 (Feb. 1890): 216.

43. *Times and Seasons* 4 (15 July 1843): 274.

44. Karl Keller, ed., "I Never Knew a Time When I Did Not Know Joseph Smith," *Dialogue: A Journal of Mormon Thought* 1 (Winter 1966): 32.

45. *Document*, 61.

46. Peck, 8.

47. Governor Boggs to the Missouri General Assembly, 5 Dec. 1838, in *Document*, 14.

48. *Correspondence and Orders*, 117.

49. Jessee and Whittaker, 25.

50. Keller, 34.

51. Journal History, 16 Aug. 1857.

52. "Elder John Brush, By Two Friends," *Autumn Leaves* 4 (Apr. 1891): 173.

53. Oliver B. Huntington Journal, 162, Special Collections, BYU.

54. Peck, 24-25; Corrill, 41.

55. *Times and Seasons* 4 (15 July 1843): 275.

56. Keller, 35.

57. Peck, 25.

58. Hinkle to W. W. Phelps, 14 Aug. 1844, *Messenger and Advocate* (Pittsburgh), 1 Aug. 1845.

59. Corrill, 41.

60. Ibid.

61. General Lucas to Governor Boggs, 2 Nov. 1838, in *Document*, 73.

62. 9 Jan. 1840 Arthur Morrison affidavit, in LeSueur, 170.

63. *History of the Church*, 3:445.

64. Parley P. Pratt, Jr., ed., *The Autobiography of Parley Parker Pratt, one of the Twelve Apostles of the Church of Jesus Christ of Latter-Day Saints* (Chicago: Law, King & Law, 1888), 203.

65. *History of the Church*, 3:445.

66. Ibid.

67. Journal History, 31 Oct. 1838.

68. Ibid., 1 Nov. 1838.

69. Oliver B. Huntington Journal, 34, Special Collections, BYU.

70. Journal History, 31 Oct. 1838.

71. Joseph Thorp, *Early Days in the West: Along the Missouri One Hundred Years Ago* (Liberty, MO: Liberty Tribune, 1924), 89.

72. Five days after the surrender at Far West, Smith wrote to his wife: "Colonel Hinkle, proved to be a tra[i]tor to the Church, he is worse than a [H]ull who betra[yed] the army at [D]etroit, he decoyed us unawares[,] God reward him" (Joseph Smith, Jr., to Emma Smith, 4 Nov. 1838, archives, The Auditorium, Reorganized Church of Jesus Christ of Latter Day Saints, Independence, Missouri).

Reed Peck eloquently related his perspective of the Hinkle team:

> The very men who risked their lives at [Smith's] request to open a communication with the army are now branded as traitors[.] When no others would venture we stepped forward and were instrumental in saving the lives of hundreds . . . by bringing about a treaty[.] Propositions were made to us and we faithfully reported the same to the presidency and they understood the whole matter, still Joseph pretends to the church that he was betrayed by us as Christ was by Judas (Peck, 32).

Peck elaborated that Hinkle and the other members of his committee were held up as scapegoats because Smith and Rigdon had delivered so many brave speeches yet were taken without a fight. The prophet's most noted embarrassment, Peck pointed out, was the failed 14 October 1838 boast that "I am determined that we will not give another foot and I care not how many come against us, 10 or 10000[.] God will send his Angels to our deliverance and we can conquer 10000 as easily as 10" (Peck, 32, 19).

In his own defense Hinkle wrote to W. W. Phelps on 14 August 1844 that the negotiators were appointed by Smith to

> go and confer with the commanding officers of the Missouri Militia, and effect a treaty if possible, on any terms short of a battle. . . . Our object was (at least I felt so) to prevent the effusion of blood, which we all saw must inevitably take place, unless

something could be immediately done. . . . When the facts were laid before Joseph, did he not say, "I will go" and did not the others go with him, and that too voluntarily, so far as you and I were concerned, my understanding was, that those men were to be taken and kept till next morning as hostages. —And if they did not, upon reflection and consultation with the officers in the camp of the enemy, during the night, conclude to accept of the terms proposed to us, but chose to fight, then they were to be kept safely, and returned to us in the city next morning, unharmed; and time given us to prepare for an attack by the Militia. During this whole interview and transaction, were not thousands of troops drawn up near the city, ready to fall upon us, provided those demanded as hostages refused to go! . . . Were we not advised next day, by word sent expressly from Joseph Smith to us, to surrender! When that intelligence was received, did I not draw up the forces under my command, and explain to them the nature of the whole affair, and then request all who were in favor of surendering, to make it known by marching three paces forward! They made a very slow start, but finally all came forward. We then marched out with slow and solemn step, into a partial hollow square of the enemy, faced inward, grounded arms, and marched away and left them. The town was laid under martial law and guarded. Then the authorities commenced taking others as prisoners, and kept them under guard to be tried, as they said, by civil law.

. . . I have been informed that one of your number is now in an adjourning neighborhood to this, asserting that I sold the heads of the church, in Missouri, for $700.00. Now Sir, as you are the man who was engaged in the whole affair with me, I request that you write a letter for publication . . . and in it exempt me from those charges, and correct the minds of that people and the public on this subject (Hinkle to W. W. Phelps, 14 Aug. 1844, *Messenger and Advocate* [Pittsburgh], 1 Aug. 1845).

73. Journal History, 28 May 1868.

74. *History of Caldwell and Livingston Counties*, 137.

75. Ibid. Wickliffe Rigdon's account, possibly based on information from his father, wrote that Doniphan said to Lucas: "You have got those men into your possession by promising them protection and fair treatment and now you are going to shoot them in the presence of their families[?]" Looking Lucas "square in the eyes," he said, "you hurt one of these men if you dare and I will hold you personally responsible for it, and at some other time you and I will meet again when in mortal combat and we will see who is the better man." Lucas reportedly replied, "If that is the way you feel about it, they shall not be shot" (Keller, 36).

76. *Times and Seasons* 4 (15 July 1843): 251.

77. Peter H. Burnett, *Recollections and Opinions of an Old Pioneer* (New York: D. Appleton and Co., 1880), 63.

78. Keller, 36.

79. *Times and Seasons* 4 (15 July 1843): 275.

80. Pratt, 208.

CHAPTER 18.

Jail

Thus, within the short space of four months from the time the church made that threatening boast that if a mob should come upon us again, "we would carry the war to their own houses, and either one party or the other should be utterly destroyed," we found ourselves prisoners of war, our property confiscated, our leaders in close confinement, and the entire church required to leave the state or be exterminated.

—Ebenezer Robinson[1]

Charismatic movements, such as Mormonism, maximize events by coloring them with an indelible strain of folklore. Myth is frequently more powerful than the historical reality that engenders it. Thus Sidney Rigdon's and the other Mormon prisoners' mundane two-day wagon trip to Independence became a morality play peopled by the irredeemably evil and the entirely righteous. Prisoner Hyrum Smith, playing upon the passions of the public during sworn court testimony, alleged that the conditions of travel during the forced excursion were inhumane. "We traveled about twelve miles that evening, and encamped for the night [at Crooked River]," he began his deposition. The weather was inclement, snow had fallen, and the prisoners were forced to "sleep on the ground . . . and for want of covering and clothing, we suffered extremely with the cold."[2]

Others viewed the trip more positively. Fellow prisoner Parley P. Pratt wrote his wife that on the march to Jackson County the prisoners were "treated with every kindness and respect which we could desire."[3] Whereas Hyrum complained "our provision was fresh beef roasted in the fire on a stick,"[4] Pratt noted that they fared better than the troops: "[O]ur meals were served to us in the best manner with plenty of coffee and sugar. We had the privilege of sleeping in a tent with the officers, while many of the troops slept in the open air."[5]

General Wilson, according to Pratt's account, viewed his charges as "wonderful . . . royal prisoners," and en route he often "halted the whole brigade to introduce us to the populace, pointing out each of us by name."[6] Rigdon's more peevish account likened it to a sideshow where "we served the same purpose that a caravan of wild animals would."[7] Probably the wayside spectators were merely curious. Pratt added that Wilson allowed no person to "insult us, or treat us with disrespect in the least."[8] When they arrived in Independence, Rigdon and the others were initially quartered in a vacant house prepared for them. Although under guard, they were well-treated. "Were it not for the absence of our families," Pratt wrote, "we should almost forget that we are prisoners." With an almost audible sigh of relief he added: "we believe that this journey saved our lives from the hands of furious men."[9]

The prisoners were free to walk the streets of Independence without guard, visiting former haunts at will. The most sacred site in the vicinity was the place they had dedicated seven years earlier for a temple in Zion, their City of New Jerusalem. What had been a beautiful rise of ground, heavily timbered in 1831, now lay desolate, a melancholy reminder of their shattered dreams.

Meanwhile, back in Far West on Tuesday, 6 November, General Clark assembled the citizenry at the town square to deliver a stern speech:

> The orders of the governor to me were, that you should be exterminated, and not allowed to remain in the state, and had your leaders not been given up, and the terms of the treaty complied with, before this, you and your families would have been destroyed and your houses in ashes.
>
> There is a discretionary power vested in my hands which I shall exercise in your favor for a season; for *this* lenity you are indebted to *my* clemency. I do not say that you shall go now, but you must not think of staying here another season, or of putting in crops, for the moment you do this the citizens will be upon you. . . . As for your leaders, do not once think—do not imagine for a moment—do not let it enter your mind that they will be delivered, or that you will see their faces again, for their *fate is fixed—their die is cast their doom is sealed.*[10]

Although Mormons and non-Mormons alike were guilty of deplorable crimes during the fall of 1838, the older settlers and Missouri officials were inclined to blame all the disturbances on the newcomers. Had the Saints turned their cheek to gentile atrocities perhaps they would eventually have been left alone. But Rigdon's and Smith's combustible rhetoric, the clandestine Danite band's illicit operations, and the candid anti-Mormon testimony by prominent dissidents—all of which clearly contributed to the conflict—stood as evidence that the Saints posed a bona fide threat to the peace and well-being of society.

Crimes against the Mormons, for which no one was ever charged, were regarded as an unfortunate by-product of the passion of a Mormon-instigated conflict. This one-sided view led Missouri officials to focus exclusively on the malfeasance of Mormon elders, as though they alone were responsible for the uproar. For example, when General Wilson arrived in Daviess County after the surrender of Diahman he reacted only to Mormon depredations:

> It is perfectly impossible for me to convey to you any thing like the awful state of things which exist here—language is inadequate to the task. The citizens of a whole county, first plundered, and then their houses and other buildings burnt to ashes, without

houses, beds, furniture or even clothing in many instances, to meet the inclemency of the weather. I confess that my feelings have been shocked with the gross brutality of these Mormons, who have acted more like demons from the infernal regions than human beings.[11]

Two weeks after the surrender at Far West, Rigdon and the other Mormon prisoners at Independence were told they were being transferred to Richmond, Ray County. Generals Lucas and Wilson tried for days to arrange a military escort for the group. Finally a small entourage was assembled and the men left, some riding in carriages, others on horseback. Their first night was spent in a "very hostile neighborhood," Pratt wrote. When their guards retired for the night they armed the prisoners to defend themselves in case of attack.[12]

Continuing their journey the following morning, 9 November, the party was met by a large troop of soldiers under the command of Colonel Sterling Price, later to serve as Missouri's governor and as a prominent Confederate general during the Civil War. The prisoners were taken to an old log house on the north side of the square, which had served as the Ray County jail. Shortly after their arrival, Colonel Price and guard entered the house with blacksmith John Fulkerson, who fettered the seven men together with a trace chain that extended from one man's ankle to another's, fastened with a padlock. Heavily guarded at night, the men slept on the floor stretched in a row. Sleep, difficult to manage in such a rigid position, was even less likely because of the noise of the guards.

On Saturday, 10 November, General Clark paid the captives a visit. When asked why they were jailed, Clark told them he would let them know in a few days. Rigdon's retrospective account portrays the general as a bumbling buffoon. "The awkward manner in which he entered and his apparent embarrassment was such as to force a smile from me," Sidney wrote. When he asked a guard "what was the matter with General Clark, that made him appear so ridiculous?" he was told that the man was very near-sighted. Rigdon's retort did nothing to endear him to his keeper: "I replied that I was mistaken if he were not as near witted, as he was near sighted."[13] But General Clark proved to be a man suited to the task. After studying the military Code of Laws which he obtained from Fort Leavenworth's commanding officer, Richard P. Mason, Clark asked Governor Boggs to forward to him the Missouri attorney general's opinion on proper jurisdiction. Within the week Boggs's orders arrived: "You will not attempt to try them by court-martial, the civil law must govern."[14]

Sometime during the weekend prior to his arraignment Rigdon overheard his guards scheming to travel to Far West, thirty miles away, and "commit violence on the persons of [Emma Smith] and my wife [Phebe] and daughters."[15] As the father of four teenage girls (Athalia, seventeen; Nancy, fifteen; Sarah, fourteen; Eliza, twelve), he was terrorized. Fortunately he was able to convey a message to Far West urging Phebe and Emma to secure a guard. Unaware of whether his notice was received in time, Rigdon, in his own words, "waited with painful anxiety for [the soldiers'] return." He then "listened to all they said, to find out, if possible, what they had done." To his immense relief he heard the men report to others that "they had passed and repassed both houses, and saw the females, but there were so many men about the town, that they dare not venture for fear of being detected, and their numbers were not sufficient to accomplish anything if they had made the attempt, and they came off without trying."[16] Rigdon was so over-whelmed by the news that he "finally lost his reason," wrote Pratt.[17] Lyman Wight described how "Rigdon, who was of a delicate constitution, received a slight shock of apoplectic fits, which excited great laughter and much ridicule in the guard and mob-militia."[18]

This stress-induced loss of equilibrium, like earlier deliriums, affected Rigdon for as long as two weeks. Phebe, at home in Far West caring for eight children, including newborn Hortense Antoinette, was unable to go to her husband. But their seventeen-year-old daughter Athalia, herself nursing an infant,[19] volunteered to go to the jail to care for her ailing father and her husband George W. Robinson. Pratt wrote that when Athalia first entered the room,

> amid the clank of chains and the rattle of weapons, and cast her eyes on her sick and dejected parent and sorrow worn husband, she was speechless, and only gave vent to her feelings in a flood of tears. This faithful lady, with her little infant, continued by the side of her father till he recovered from his sickness, and till his fevered and disordered mind resumed its wonted powers.[20]

Rigdon's own account of the period states: "Being taken sick at the early stage of the trial, I had not the opportunity of hearing but a small part of the testimony when it was delivered before the court."[21] Strictly speaking the hearing was not a trial but a preliminary court of inquiry before Missouri Fifth Judicial Circuit Court Judge Austin A. King. King, already well-known to Mormons, had earlier denounced Danite destruction and condemned Mormon aggression in both the 3 November *Jeffersonian Republican* and again in the 8 November *Missouri Argus*.

The prosecution during a court of inquiry need only demonstrate that a crime was committed and that sufficient evidence exists to bind over the defendants for trial. Mormon assessment of this hearing has been harsh. Parley P. Pratt called it a "mock Court of Inquiry,"[22] and Rigdon referred to it as "a new kind of Court: it was not an inquisition, nor yet a criminal court, but a compound between."[23] Although the hearing was in accordance with legal procedures of the day, and probable cause was proven, justice was not fully served. Culpability for the disturbances in the state fell solely on the Mormons, while the actions of non-Mormons were ignored by law enforcement officials. "This outcome," according to Stephen C. LeSueur, foremost scholar on this period, "illustrates how the dominant community can use the law to enforce local customs and values—and to preserve the power of the existing elite—against groups of people perceived as threatening to that community."[24]

In addition to Rigdon and other Mormon leaders, fifty-three other defendants, identified during a two-day investigation at Far West, were brought to Richmond. Eleven others were added during the hearing. The prisoners' request to be tried individually was denied. Satisfied that they were all "poor persons, unable to employ counsel to assist them in their defense," the court appointed Amos Rees, Alexander W. Doniphan, and John R. Williams to defend them.[25] The seventeen-day Richmond hearing began on 12 November. The charges, according to Rigdon's account, were "treason, murder, burglary, arson, larceny, theft and stealing."[26] But state prosecutor Thomas C. Burch focused mainly on "overt acts of treason" such as the Mormon assault on Missouri state militia units.

During the hearing the defendants stood behind a long pole that separated them from Judge King. Although a cordon of guards surrounded the prisoners, defendant Morris Phelps reported that many spectators were allowed to gather menacingly around them. One onlooker, no doubt referring to Rigdon, said this "one is a great preacher and leader amongst them, he ought to be hung, or sent to the penitentiary." Phelps noted that the gawkers "would examine and view us as critical as if we were ravenous wolves, and they were about to purchase us for our fur."[27]

The prosecution provided testimony about Mormon raiding expeditions into Daviess County, the 25 October bloodshed at Crooked River, and the establishment of a "theocratic kingdom" considered above Missouri law. When the hearing began, many in attendance were surprised when the state called Sampson Avard as its first witness. Most expected that the Danite Major-General, who had been captured on 2 November a few miles from Far West, would be a suspect rather than a key witness. But Avard had become disillusioned when the prophet's promised victory over the Missourians failed to materialize. Prosecutor Wood claimed the moment Avard heard Smith had surrendered Far West he proclaimed: "I at once lost all faith and am no longer a Mormon."[28]

Avard's deposition was of paramount importance to the state. General John B. Clark, reporting Avard's capture to Governor Boggs, wrote: "I will here remark that but for the capture of Sampson Avard, a leading Mormon, I do not believe I could have obtained any useful facts. No one disclosed any useful matter until he was brought in."[29] Avard's recital, embodying 20 percent of the court record, lasted two days. Peter Burnett, a newspaper editor and lawyer present at the hearing, reported:

> [Avard] was a very eccentric genius, fluent, imaginative, sarcastic, and very quick in replying to questions put by the prisoners' counsel. His testimony was very important, if true; and, as he had lately been himself a Mormon, and was regarded by them as

a traitor from selfish motives, his testimony labored under some apparent suspicion. For these reasons he was cross-examined very rigidly.[30]

Particularly damaging was Avard's assertion that "about four months ago, a band called the Daughters of Zion, since called the Danite Band, was formed of the members of the Mormon Church, the original object of which was, to drive from the county of Caldwell, all those who dissented from the Mormon Church, in which they succeeded admirably." Avard explicitly accused the prophet: "I consider Joseph [Smith], jun. as the prime mover and organizer of this Danite Band." Imposing in his recall of detail, Avard maintained that each Danite considered himself duty-bound to obey the First Presidency "as to obey the Supreme God." He also added the damaging particular that the prophet, in blessing Danite officers, prophesied "they should be the means, in the hands of God, of bringing forth the millenial kingdom,"[31] at which point Judge King turned to the court clerk and said: "Write that down; it is a strong point for treason."[32]

Although compelling evidence linked Rigdon and Smith directly to Danitism, the Mormon position, delineated in numerous accounts since 1838, holds that Avard alone was responsible for the organization and activities of the clandestine brotherhood. According to Rigdon, Avard was so anxious to save himself that he advised a potential Mormon witness to "swear hard" against the heads of the church, since they were the ones the court wanted. "I intend to do it," he said, "in order to escape, for if I do not they will take my life."[33]

But Avard's testimony did not stand alone. During the remainder of the tribunal, the prosecution called forty-one witnesses, twenty Missourians and twenty-one Mormons, several of whom supported the Danite chief's statement. To downplay the significance of the corroborative Mormon testimony, Parley P. Pratt, reflecting the position undoubtedly held by most Mormons, condemned the witnesses as "dissenters and apostates who wished to save their own lives and secure their property at the expense of others."[34] This assessment was neither fair nor accurate. John Corrill, Reed Peck, John Cleminson, W. W. Phelps, and George Hinkle, all of whom were subsequently excommunicated, were not mean-spirited scoundrels intent on destroying Mormonism. Their dissent stemmed from a sincere opposition to what they perceived as criminal acts. The dissidents' warnings of calamitous consequences, though they would all too soon prove true, had brought only threats and condemnation from their leaders.

Surprisingly, the Mormons' distinguished defense team advised their clients not to respond in their own behalf to the witness of Avard and others. "It would avail us nothing," Rigdon said of Doniphan's counsel, "for the judge would put us into prison, if a cohort of angels were to come and swear that we were innocent."[35] Rigdon later observed that "if we were to give to the court the names of our witnesses, there was a band there ready to go, and they would go and drive them out of the country, or arrest them and have them cast into prison, to prevent them from swearing, or else kill them."[36]

But seven witnesses—Malinda Porter, Delia F. Pine, Jonathan W. Barlow, Thoret Parsons, Ezra Chipman, Arza Judd, Jr., and Rigdon's feisty mother, Nancy G. Rigdon—testified for the defense. Unintimidated by the court and the some- times rowdy gallery, the seventy-nine-year-old widow stood by her son, avowing that Sidney was not involved in the Crooked River battle, that George W. Robinson did not have the clock he allegedly stole in Daviess County, and that Sampson Avard "would swear to a lie to accomplish an object; that he had told many a lie, and would do so again."[37]

At the conclusion of Judge King's court of inquiry on 29 November, twenty-nine defendants were released for lack of evidence. Twenty-four others were held over to stand trial on suspicion of arson, burglary, robbery, and larceny. Their bail bonds were forfeited when, with all other Mormons, the men were forced to leave the state. Morris Phelps, Lyman Gibbs, Darwin Chase, Norman Shearer, and Parley P. Pratt were committed to the Richmond jail on charges of murder for their alleged participation in the Crooked River fray. Sidney Rigdon, Joseph Smith, Hyrum Smith, Lyman Wight, Caleb Baldwin, and Alexander McRae were imprisoned in the Clay County jail, without bail, on charge of treason, "until they be delivered therefrom by due course of law."[38] A grand jury trial for the detained men was scheduled for March 1839.

On 30 November Rigdon and others were conveyed to their new quarters in the Clay County jail at Liberty, Missouri. Lyman O. Littlefield, who at the time worked in the office of the *Missouri Enquirer*, wrote that the bulky wagon conveying the prisoners entered the town from the east, passed through the center of the village, and halted close to the platform in front of the jail. A large gathering of citizens had assembled hoping to catch a glimpse of the notorious prisoners. They were not disappointed. The men, under the direction of Sheriff Samuel Hadley and his deputy Samuel Tillery, exited the wagon one by one and ducked into the low door of the jail. The prophet, the last to enter, turned briefly, surveyed the multitude of spectators, doffed his hat, and in a distinct voice said: "Good afternoon, gentlemen." The heavy iron door then closed.[39]

Liberty Jail was built in 1833 at a cost of $600. The formidable twenty-two-foot square limestone structure had four-foot-thick walls. Inside the outer wall was a second wall of hewn oak logs separated from the limestone by a twelve-inch space filled with loose rock to prevent tunneling under. The prison was divided into an upper room and a lower earthen-floored dungeon, lighted by two small windows grated with heavy iron bars.[40]

The confined men were permitted to write letters and receive correspondence and visitors. Immediately after receiving a 30 November letter from her husband, Emma Smith took her young son Joseph and Phebe and Wickliffe Rigdon to

Liberty, where they spent a night in the jail. Up to this point the men had been generally sequestered in the lower dungeon, where the temperature was as cold as outside. Although a small fire could be maintained, there was no chimney and choking smoke caused serious eye irritation. But Wickliffe wrote that "the jailer seemed to feel sorry for them and brought them up stairs and this is where we found them. . . . We remained with them two days."[41]

The chief highlight for the incarcerated men was visitors. Many brought delicacies. Most came with the intent of cheering up the downcast group. Joseph Smith III, recalling a night spent in the gloomy place, remembers Erastus Snow visiting and entertaining with the songs "The Massacre at the River Raisin" and a parody called "Mobbers of Missouri," sung to the tune of "Hunters of Kentucky."[42] Although no Liberty Jail letters from Rigdon to his family are extant, Joseph Smith's 4 April 1839 note to Emma provides a window into the ordeal. Describing the jail and inmates as "grates . . . and screaking iron doors," "weary joints and bones," "dirty straw couches," a "nauseous smell," "this hell surrounded with demons," the prophet concluded that "pen, or tongue, or angels could never describe what took place here."[43]

As in most penal institutions of the day, the food was revolting. Alexander McRae remembered the victuals as "very coarse, and so filthy that we could not eat it until we were driven to it by hunger."[44] Lyman Wight recalled that the "mercies of the jailor were intolerable, feeding us with a scanty allowance, on the dregs of coffee and tea, from his own table, and fetching the provisions in a basket, on which the chickens had roosted the night before, without being cleaned."[45] Hyrum Smith testified that the food was "anything but good and decent." He felt that on several occasions attempts were made to poison the prisoners. "The effect it had upon our system was, that it vomited us almost to death, and then we would lay some two or three days in a torpid, stupid state, not even caring or wishing for life."[46] McRae suspected the poison was administered in either tea or coffee since he did not use either and did not become ill. Those that drank the beverages, however, "were sorely afflicted, some being blind two or three days, and it was by much faith and prayer that the effect was overcome."[47] Both Hyrum Smith and Lyman Wight suspected that on one occasion they were given human flesh to eat. Except for Wight, who was suffering from "extreme hunger," none of the others ate the mysterious fare.[48]

Hyrum Smith reported in his diary that curiosity seekers often crowded about the barred door to catch a glimpse of the caged prisoners: "We are often inspected by fools who act as though we were elephants or dromedarys or sea hogs or some monstrous whale or sea serpents. We have never had our teeth examined like an old horse, but expect [to] every day when . . . a new swarm come[s] that have never seen us." He added that the prisoners were frequently taunted by street urchins who banged on the door, yelling such jeers as "come out here damn ye, I'll kill you," or "prophesy you damd rascals."[49]

Imprisonment was emotionally as well as physically trying. Joseph Smith lamented "our souls have been bowed down and we have suffered much distress . . . and truly we have had to wade through an ocean of trouble."[50] Hyrum Smith later complained that because of "my close and long confinement, as well as from the sufferings of my mind, I feel my body greatly broke[n] down and debilitated, my frame has received a shock from which it will take a long time to recover."[51] Forty-five-year-old Rigdon, a fretful hand-wringer under stressful circumstances, was not a good companion. While the others bore the taunts, bad food, unsanitary and crowded quarters, and the fear of lynching, Rigdon's frequent bouts of mania, followed by melancholic periods of whining, wore heavily on the others' nerves. "The sufferings of Jesus Christ," he was heard to mutter, "were a fool to [mine]."[52]

In 25 January 1839, after petitioning to have their case heard on a plea of habeas corpus, the prisoners were brought before Judge Joel Turnham, a Clay County judge. The Smith brothers, along with McRae, Wight, and Baldwin, were represented by their previous counsel, Alexander Doniphan.[53] Rigdon, who considered himself a capable barrister, chose to present his own plea. His unique rhetorical skills served him well. When summoned to address the court, the still-infirm spokesman spoke from a cot on which he reclined. After pleading innocent to the charges of high treason and murder, Rigdon began to relate the hardships and degradations he had suffered trying to serve God. He spoke of tar and feathers, homeless children, mobbings, hunger, cold, and of destitution. Doniphan, who was unsuccessful in obtaining release for his clients,[54] later said of Rigdon's petition: "Such a burst of eloquence it was never my fortune to listen to, at its close there was not a dry eye in the room, all were moved to tears."[55]

Judge Turnham, affected by the persuasive narrative, admitted Sidney to bail and immediate release. As soon as the magistrate had imposed his decision, a gentleman in the crowd stood and called out: "We came here to do injury to this man. He is innocent of this crime, as has been made to appear. And now, gentlemen, out with your money and help the man return to his destitute family."[56] The spectators, most of them hardened Mormon haters, contributed $100 to the primary instigator of Mormon militancy many of them had previously wanted to lynch. Despite the goodwill of the courtroom spectators, Rigdon was afraid to leave the security of Liberty Jail. Wickliffe Rigdon wrote that his father heard from friends that some Missourians were saying that even though he had been legally discharged he would never get away, for "they had him and they were going to kill him."[57]

Returning to confinement with the rest of his brethren, Rigdon waited ten days, until 5 February, for a favorable opportunity to put into effect the escape plan he had masterminded with the assistance of Sheriff Samuel Hadley and jailor Samuel Tillery. A carriage, probably driven by his son-in-law George W. Robinson, was ready to "take me in and carry me off with all speed," wrote Rigdon. Arrangements had also been made for a guide "who was well acquainted with the country—to pilot me through the country so that I might not go on any of the public roads."[58] Phebe had come to the jail earlier in the day to accompany her husband out of the state to safety in Illinois.

When darkness fell, the sheriff and jailer brought supper to their charges. After Sidney and Phebe had eaten, Rigdon whispered to the jailor to blow out all the candles but one, and step away from the door with that one. The sheriff then took him by the arm, and a pre-arranged scuffle ensued. During the mock shoving match the sheriff pushed Rigdon out the door onto the street, then shook his hand and bade him farewell, advising him to make his escape with all possible speed. After sprinting a short distance Rigdon heard someone running behind him. Thinking his escape had been discovered he drew his pistol, cocked it, and assumed a defensive posture, determined not to be taken alive. But as his pursuer drew near and spoke, Rigdon recognized it was George W. Robinson. A few moments later another ally, the guide, arrived with horses.

In the rush of adrenalin and confusion of the moment, Rigdon had forgotten his wife in the jail. Robinson returned to get her while Rigdon and his squire left town as fast as their horses could manage. Three miles outside town Robinson and Phebe, riding in an open carriage, caught up with the horsemen. Phebe and her son-in-law then drove to Far West to gather their families while Rigdon and his guide spared no horseflesh racing eastward across Missouri to an anticipated safe haven.

At daybreak Rigdon and his escort arrived at the house of an acquaintance. They slept throughout the day, then rode again under cover of darkness until they reached Tenny's Grove. To their surprise the Rigdon and Robinson families awaited them, having traveled faster, more public byways. A hiding place was secured in the rear of the wagon where Rigdon hid during daylight hours as the conveyance rolled easterly. When the travelers reached the western banks of the Mississippi after dark, Rigdon was so apprehensive about remaining in Missouri overnight that he paid two canoeists to transport him across the mighty river, where, wrote his son Wickliffe, he "was free from his persecutors . . . and could rest in peace."[59]

Notes

Unless otherwise stated, all primary sources cited are located in the Historical Department of the Church of Jesus Christ of Latter-day Saints, Salt Lake City, Utah.

1. Ebenezer Robinson, "Items of Personal History of the Editor," from *The Return* (Davis City, IA), 2 (Feb. 1890): 66.
2. *Times and Seasons* 4 (15 July 1843): 251.

3. Journal History, 4 Nov. 1838—a multi-volume daily history of the church compiled by official church historians; hereafter Journal History.

4. *Times and Seasons* 4 (15 July 1843): 251.

5. Journal History, 4 Nov. 1838.

6. Parley P. Pratt, Jr., ed., *The Autobiography of Parley Parker Pratt, one of the Twelve Apostles of the Church of Jesus Christ of Latter-Day Saints* (Chicago: Law, King & Law, 1888), 210-11.

7. Sidney Rigdon, *An Appeal to the American People: Being an Account of the Persecutions of the Church of Jesus Christ of Latter Day Saints; and of the Barbarities Inflicted on Them by the Inhabitants of the State of Missouri* (Cincinnati: Printed By Shepard & Sterns, 1840), 63.

8. Journal History, 4 Nov. 1838.

9. Ibid.

10. Joseph Smith, *History of the Church of Jesus Christ of Latter-day Saints*, B. H. Roberts, ed., 7 vols. (Salt Lake City: The Church of Jesus Christ of Latter-day Saints, 1902), 3:202; emphasis in original; hereafter *History of the Church*.

11. General Wilson to General Clark, 12 Nov. 1838, in *Document Showing the Testimony Given Before the Judge of the Fifth Judicial District of the State of Missouri, on the Trial of Joseph Smith, Jr., and others, for High Treason and Other Crimes Against that State* (Washington, D.C.: U.S. Government Printing Office, 1841), 78; hereafter *Document*.

12. Pratt, 216.

13. *Times and Seasons* 4 (15 July 1843): 276.

14. Governor Boggs to General Clark, 19 Nov. 1838, in *Document*, 81.

15. *Times and Seasons* 4 (15 July 1843): 276. It was perhaps on this occasion that the prophet, edgy because of a toothache, vented his growing frustration on the crowing guards by bellowing his command to be silent, which they then were (Pratt, 229).

16. *Times and Seasons* 4 (15 July 1843): 277.

17. Pratt, 228.

18. John Jaques, "The Life and Labors of Sidney Rigdon," *Improvement Era* 3 (Feb. 1900): 265-66.

19. This baby was evidently Sidney R. Robinson, who died in infancy (see Lyman De Platt, "Nauvoo—Early Mormon Records Series" 1 [1842 Census of Nauvoo]: 21-22, LDS Family History Library, Salt Lake City).

20. Pratt, 228.

21. *Times and Seasons* 4 (15 July 1843): 277. Smith made no mention of Rigdon's condition in a 12 November 1838 letter to his wife: "Brother Robinson is chained next to me he has a true heart and a firm mind, Brother Wight, is next, Br. Rigdon, next Hyram, next, Parley, next Amasa, next, and thus we are bound together in chains as well as the cords of everlasting love, we are in good spirits and rejoice that we are counted worthy to be per-secuted for [C]hrist['] sake" (Dean C. Jessee, *The Personal Writings of Joseph Smith* [Salt Lake City: Deseret Book Co., 1984], 368).

22. Pratt, 230.

23. J. Wickliffe Rigdon, "Life Story of Sidney Rigdon," 66.

24. Stephen C. LeSueur, *The 1838 Mormon War in Missouri* (Columbia, MO: University of Missouri Press, 1987), 217. Also see Stephen C. LeSueur, "'High Treason

and Murder:' The Examination of Mormon Prisoners at Richmond, Missouri, in November 1838," *Brigham Young University Studies* 26 (Spring 1986): 3-30.

25. Journal History, 12 Nov. 1838.

26. *Times and Seasons* 4 (15 July 1843): 277.

27. Morris Phelps, "Reminiscences," 17.

28. "Mormon Memoirs," *Liberty* (Missouri) *Tribune*, 9 Apr. 1886.

29. *Correspondence and Orders, etc., in Relation to the Recent Disturbances with the Mormons* (Jefferson City, MO: Office of the Jeffersonian, 1840), 90.

30. Peter Burnett, *Recollections and Opinions of an Old Pioneer* (New York: D. Appleton and Co., 1880), 63-64.

31. *Document*, 97-98.

32. Pratt, 230. This refers to Daniel 2:44; 7:27. The official LDS account of this phase of the hearing, written by member of the First Presidency, Willard Richards, in the 1850s, reads: "Our Church organization was converted, by the testimony of the apostates, into a temporal kingdom, which was to fill the whole earth, and subdue all other kingdoms" (*History of the Church*, 3:211). Richards's position was misleading. Since 1844 he had been a member of the secret Council of Fifty whose members were dedicated to establishing "a government within a government" (see D. Michael Quinn, "The Council of Fifty and Its Members, 1844-1945," *Brigham Young University Studies* 20 [Spring 1980]: 163-97).

33. Rigdon, 47-48.

34. Pratt, 230.

35. *Times and Seasons* 4 (15 July 1843): 277.

36. Ibid.

37. *Document*, 147.

38. Judge King's 29 Nov. 1838 mittimus in *History of the Church*, 3:214-15.

39. Lyman Littlefield, "Reminiscences," 79-80.

40. For an extensive description of the jail, see Leonard J. Arrington, "Church Leaders in Liberty Jail," *Brigham Young University Studies* 13 (Autumn 1972): 20-26.

41. Rigdon, 151.

42. Mary Audentia Smith Anderson, "The Memoirs of President Joseph Smith III (1832-1914)," in *Saints' Herald*, 6 Nov. 1934, 1414.

43. Joseph Smith, Jr., to Emma Smith, 4 Apr. 1839, in Arrington, 22.

44. Alexander McRae, "Incidents," *Deseret News*, 2 Nov. 1854.

45. *Times and Seasons* 4 (15 July 1843): 269.

46. Ibid., 254.

47. McRae, "Incidents."

48. *Times and Seasons* 4 (15 July 1843): 269.

49. Hyrum Smith Diary, 18 Mar. 1839.

50. "The Prophet's Letter to the Church," 16 Dec. 1838, in *History of the Church*, 3:226-33.

51. *Times and Seasons* 1 (Dec. 1839): 22-23.

52. Journal History, 25 Feb. 1839.

53. Doniphan eventually rose to prominence as western Missouri's foremost defense lawyer.

54. Smith and the others later regretted not having Rigdon plead their cases as well.

The prophet wrote in a 25 March letter from Liberty Jail: "we should have been liberated at the time Elder Rigdon was, on the writ of habeas corpus, had not our own lawyers interpreted the law, contrary to what it reads, against us; which prevented us from introducing our evidence before the mock court" (Journal History, 25 Mar. 1839).

55. *Saints' Herald*, 2 Aug. 1884.

56. Ibid.

57. Karl Keller, ed., "'I Never Knew a Time When I Did Not Know Joseph Smith': A Son's Record of the Life and Testimony of Sidney Rigdon," *Dialogue: A Journal of Mormon Thought* 1 (Winter 1966): 15-42, cited 38.

58. *Times and Seasons* 4 (15 July 1843): 278.

59. Rigdon, 158.

Illustrations

Earliest known image of Sidney Rigdon (no date), photograph by J. Gurney & Son, 707 Broadway, New York City (courtesy Utah State Historical Society).

Sidney Rigdon's boyhood home in St. Clair Township, Pennsylvania (courtesy Vaughn Chapman).

Pittsburgh at the time Sidney Rigdon lived there (Mrs. James Gibson sketch, in History of Allegheny County Pennsylvania, *2 vols. [Chicago: A. Warner & Co., 1889], 1:frontispiece).*

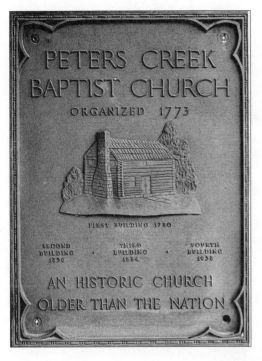

Historic plaque marking site of Peters Creek Baptist Church which the young Sidney Rigdon attended (1991 photograph by Richard S. Van Wagoner).

The Kirtland Temple (from a Frank Taylor Sketch, in 7 April 1883 Harper's Weekly, 212).

Sidney Rigdon house in Kirtland, Ohio (date unknown) (courtesy Special Collections, University of Utah Library).

Site of Sidney Rigdon's tannery in Kirtland, Ohio (1991 photography by Richard S. Van Wagoner).

The Rigdon family's first Nauvoo, Illinois, house, built by James White in 1825 (courtesy Archives, Church of Jesus Christ of Latter-day Saints).

Sidney Rigdon's still-extant house and Nauvoo Post Office next door to Joseph Smith's Mansion House (1991 photograph by Richard S. Van Wagoner).

SUPER HANC PETRAM ÆDIFICABO.

FOR PRESIDENT,
GEN. JOSEPH SMITH,
OF NAUVOO, ILLINOIS.
FOR VICE PRESIDENT,
SIDNEY RIGDON,
OF PENNSYLVANIA.

1844 flyer for Joseph Smith's and Sidney Rigdon's political campaign (courtesy Utah State Historical Society).

The Conococheague Creek Bridge, in Antrim Township, Pennsylvania, from which Sidney Rigdon and William McLellin first viewed "Adventure Farm" (courtesy Archives, Church of Jesus Christ of Latter-day Saints).

Adventure Farm barn used by Rigdonites as an auditorium in Antrim Township, Pennsylvania (photograph by George L. Zundel, in Improvement Era 47 [Apr. 1944]: 247).

George W. Robinson built this house in Friendship, New York. It was the Rigdon family's first home in that community (1991 photograph by Richard S. Van Wagoner).

Friendship Academy in Friendship, New York, where Sidney Rigdon delivered a series of lectures on geology (courtesy Friendship Public Library).

To whom this may concern...
This may certify that the bearer Jane Post has been received into the Church of Jesus Christ of the Children of Zion; and has been ordained an elder and set apart to preside over the office of an elder in the female priesthood among the children of Zion and also appointed to preside as an elder in the branch of Zion in Attica and to attend to all duties pertaining to her calling in the gospel of our Lord Jesus Christ. And it being her desire to work righteousness, and follow after truth: We give this our sister this certificate and letter of commendation, praying for her prosperity in Our Redeemer's cause. March 1869

Sarah Newton
Joseph H. Newton   *Presiding officers of the Operative priesthood in Zion*
Stephen Post

Jane Post's ordination certificate as an elder in the Church of Jesus Christ of the Children of Zion (courtesy Archives, Church of Jesus Christ of Latter-day Saints).

PREACHER'S LICENSE.

TO WHOM THIS MAY CONCERN:

This is to Certify, That the bearer *Stephen Post* has been received into the church of Jesus Christ of the children of Zion, and has been ordained and set apart as a member of the quorum *of the Presidency* in the evangelical ministry, to preach the everlasting gospel of our Lord Jesus Christ in the new covenant. And it being his desire to work righteousness, and to teach his fellow men truth, we give this our brother this certificate and letter of commendation to all to whom he may come, praying for his success in our Redeemer's cause.

Given under our hands, at *Attica Iowa* the *22nd* day of *Feb.* 1870.

Sidney Rigdon
PRESIDENT.

Stephen Post
Jane Post
Assistant Presidents

Isaac Huffaker

Stephen Post's "Preacher's License," signed by Sidney Rigdon and other members of the First Presidency of the Church of Jesus Christ of the Children of Zion (courtesy Archives, Church of Jesus Christ of Latter-day Saints).

Sidney Rigdon's gravesite in Maple Grove Cemetery, Friendship, New York (1991 photograph by Richard S. Van Wagoner).

Section 4.

Illinois

CHAPTER 19.

Appeals for Redress

[T]he saints of the last days have been made to know, in all places where they have made their appearance . . . that there is not a State in this UNION, where a man is at liberty to worship God according to the dictates of his conscience; neither is there a society in this nation, that will suffer the saints of God to enjoy their rights undisturbed. . . . Governors and rulers will refuse to discharge the duties of their offices, notwithstanding they are bound by the solemnities of an oath to do so; but oaths nor any thing else can bind men to do their duty, when the rights of the saints are concerned.

—Sidney Rigdon, November 1836[1]

Sidney Rigdon's life was a catalogue of failed dreams and religious angst, fueled by naive faith in the imminent second coming of Jesus Christ. Rigdon viewed the loss of Zion, coupled with the indignity of incarceration in Richmond and Liberty jails, as God's failed promise to bless and nurture his children. Rigdon reportedly lamented the entire Missouri experience: "If God did not care anything more about us than He seemed to do, [allowing] us to be hauled around as we had been, [I] did not care about serving such a God."[2]

Once safe and situated with his family in the Quincy, Illinois, home of the benevolent Judge John Cleveland and his wife Sarah,[3] Rigdon's faith and reason returned and his animosity toward God mellowed. Citizens of Quincy opened their hearts and homes to the Missouri expatriates, who soon began swarming into the area by the hundreds. On 23 February 1839, during a meeting of the Quincy Democratic Association, a committee was appointed to seek relief for the refugees. Four days later a large gathering of Quincy citizens and Mormons, including Rigdon, met in the court house to further discuss the Saints' plight. Several resolutions were adopted, one of which declared in part: "That the strangers recently arrived here from the State of Missouri, known by the name of the 'Latter Day Saints,' are entitled to our sympathy and kindest regard, and that we recommend to the citizens of Quincy to extend all the kindness in their power to bestow, as persons who are in affliction."[4]

After church historian Elias Higbee presented a document which outlined the needs of his people, Rigdon arose and faced the group. The *Quincy Whig* reported that he read "the memorial which his people had presented to the Legislature of Missouri,"[5] then

> in a very eloquent and impressive manner related the trials, sufferings and persecutions which his people have met with at the hands of the people of Missouri. We saw the tears standing in the eyes of many of his people while he was recounting their history of woe and sorrow, and, in fact, the gentleman himself was so agitated at different periods of his address that his feelings would hardly allow him to proceed.[6]

Rigdon's efforts to aid the regrouping Saints and seek redress for Mormon losses were substantial. The official LDS record does not adequately acknowledge this. Brigham Young, John Taylor, Orson Hyde, Willard Richards, and George A. Smith, in a power play to secure the Quorum of the Twelve's leadership after Joseph Smith's death, devalued Rigdon's contributions while enhancing their own. Taylor, for example, in an 11 December 1864 address to the Saints in Salt Lake City, accused Rigdon of "not liv[ing] his religion" and of advising the Missouri exiles following arrival in Illinois: "Brethren, every one of you take your own way, for the work seems as though it had come to an end."[7] Young similarly said that Rigdon "exhorted the Saints to scatter and every man do the best he could for himself . . . this work of the gathering . . . we shall not accomplish, these Saints will never be gathered again."[8]

In reality, such statements against gathering reflect Joseph Smith's early 1839 sentiments. If Rigdon did indeed make such claims, and there is no certainty he did, he would have been reflecting what the prophet was saying. While Rigdon was examining possible settlement sites in Iowa and Illinois, the still-imprisoned Smith reversed his previous position on Missouri real estate sales. Authorization was given by the prophet to sell all consecrated properties in Jackson County, Far West, and vicinity. He counseled in a 25 March 1839 circular letter that the scattered Saints should settle "in the most safe and quiet places they can find" between Kirtland and Far West. Additionally, there must be "no organization of large bodies upon common stock principals."[9]

Future church leader Albert Rockwood in two 1839 letters to his father provided evidence that the prophet's early position was dispersion not gathering. "It is thought by some we shall not gather again in large bodies at present," Rockwood initially wrote, "still we do not know[.] [O]ur leader is gone, we have none to tell us what to do by direct Revelation."[10] In a second letter Rockwood explicitly stated that "last night we heard that the Prophet[']s advise for the Brethren [is] to scatter, hold no meetings in [Quincy] & be wise servants that the wrath of the enemy be not kindled against us."[11] Throughout this Sidney Rigdon was still pursuing a safe haven for his fellow outcasts.

The most promising regrouping site was Commerce, Illinois, and a nearby expanse on the Iowa side of the Mississippi called the "Half-Breed Tract," approximately 119,000 acres given to mixed-bloods of Fox and Sauk tribes as part of an 1824 land-cession treaty. These sparsely settled lands were being promoted by Isaac Galland, former Indian agent and frontier opportunist associated with the New York Half-Breed Land Company. Galland, who conveniently joined the Mormon church and became its chief real estate agent, first became aware of Mormons in late 1838 when Israel Barlow, a destitute Missouri exile, made his acquaintance in Iowa. The land promoter expressed sympathy and interest in the plight of the expatriates, a concern conveyed to Rigdon in mid-February when Barlow arrived in Quincy.

Rigdon, Edward Partridge, Elias Higbee, and Barlow immediately left for Commerce to discuss real estate prospects with Galland, but he was not at home. In a 26 February letter to Mormon Daniel W. Rogers, Galland advised that about fifty families could be accommodated in the area but that a shortage of cultivated land existed due to the newness of the tract. He wrote that he would be available in mid-March and wished Rigdon or other "leading members of your Church to spend some time with me in traveling through the tract, and in hearing and learning the state of the public mind, and feelings of the community, in relation to the location of the Church."[12]

Although Galland seemed genuine, offering "assurance of my sincere sympathy in your sufferings and wrongs, and deep solicitude for your immediate relief from present distress,"[13] his ensuing actions proved him to be more of a scoundrel. Rigdon and Smith, on behalf of the church, purchased $18,000 worth of land in and about Commerce, trading Mormon-owned Missouri property in payment. They also exchanged additional Missouri real estate for $80,000 worth of the Half-Breed Tract in Iowa. Although Galland's title to the Nauvoo properties was bona fide, his deeds to the Iowa territory were not. The extent of Galland's double dealings were unknown until 1841 when the tangled Half-Breed Tract litigation was finally settled and his deeds court-certified as worthless.

Initially "of the opinion that it is not wisdom to effect a trade with [Galland] at present,"[14], Rigdon opted, along with son-in-law George W. Robinson and Elias Higbee, to rent a farm forty miles northeast of Quincy. This area was commonly called "Big Neck Prairie" or "The Great Bend Country" because of the configuration of the Mississippi River. Rigdon's cousin and boyhood chum, Stephen Rigdon, had lived in the vicinity at Harris Township in Fulton County since at least 1817 and was likely one reason Sidney chose to relocate there.[15]

Sidney's plans changed within the month, however, after the prophet advised him and others "that the Church would do well to secure to themselves the contract of the land which is proposed to them by Mr. Isaac Galland . . . inasmuch as he shall prove himself to be a man of honor and a friend to humanity."[16] During a 9 March meeting of the Democratic Association of Quincy, Rigdon was appointed to lead a delegation to meet with Galland and inspect his proffered real estate.

Wickliffe Rigdon recalled that "Galland was willing to give immediate possession" of his own house, the most imposing residence in Commerce. Sidney on either 11 or 12 March apparently agreed in principle to buy the property on behalf of the church[17] and wrote to George W. Robinson, telling him of his change in plans. His son-in-law leased the Big Neck Prairie farm to a Mormon named Herrick and joined the Rigdons in Commerce early in May.

The splendid two-story stone house of Isaac Galland, built by James White in 1827 on an old Spanish land claim, was situated near an abundant spring. The village where the house was located was first called Quashquema, then Venus in 1823, and finally Commerce in 1837.[18] Wickliffe Rigdon described his family's new home as a "beautiful place on the banks of the river . . . nicely shaded with locust trees and considerable land lying back [behind] it on the flats."[19] Joseph Smith III later remembered the house as being "in excellent condition."[20]

Rigdon's position as the only First Presidency member not in jail, his literacy and eloquence, and his fortitude in pursuing Mormon interests gained him considerable stature among leading area citizens, including Illinois governor Thomas Carlin and Iowa governor Robert Lucas. Encouraged by Galland, Rigdon conceived and set in motion an aggressive plan to seek Mormon redress for property losses in Missouri as well as to impeach that state and expel it from the Union.

Meanwhile Joseph Smith, still languishing in Liberty Jail, had received no communications from his counselor since his escape. "We feel to inquire after Elder Rigdon," the prophet's 25 March 1839 epistle to the Saints noted, "if he has not forgotten us, it has not been signified to us by his writing. . . . A word of consolation and a blessing would not come amiss from anybody."[21] Prompted by Smith's admonition, Rigdon responded with a warm 10 April letter to his former cellmates using the plural voice that was a trademark of his writing style. "We wish you to know that our friendship is unabating," he began, "and our exertions for your delivery, and that of the Church unceasing." Getting to business, he explained his strategy for impeaching the state of Missouri:

> Our plan of operation is to get all the governors, in their next messages, to have the subject brought before the legislatures; and we will have a man at the capital of each state to furnish them with the testimony on the subject; and we design to be at Washington to wait upon Congress, and have the action of that body on it also; all this going on at the same time, and have the action of the whole during one session.[22]

Rigdon's exertions were substantial. Alanson Ripley, writing to the Liberty Jail prisoners on 10 April, expressed the sentiment of most Mormons in Quincy when he wrote: "President Rigdon is wielding a mighty shaft against the whole host of foul calumniators and mobocrats of Missouri."[23] Most likely the prisoners had escaped before they received either Rigdon's or Ripley's letters. Disheartened when Rigdon was freed and they were still detained, the incarcerated men attempted two abortive jail breaks, one on 6 February and another on 4 March.

Accompanied by a fifteen-man guard, the Mormon captives were moved to Daviess County on 8 April, where a grand jury indicted them for all crimes previously charged against them. After securing a change of venue, the group, escorted by Sheriff William Morgan and four deputies, left for Boone County on 15 April. That night the prisoners escaped from custody by bribing some guards with a promise of $800. Taking back roads where they would not be seen, the men arrived in Quincy on 22 April.[24]

Once the prophet returned to his flock, he assumed the dominant position that had been temporarily conceded to Rigdon. On 30 April the two men and others met at Commerce where they confirmed their intent to purchase the 123.4-acre Hugh White farm and the 47.17-acre Galland property. The consensus was to deed both properties to Alanson Ripley to protect church interests. But Rigdon, who along with the Smith brothers had signed promissory notes for $23,000, bristled at that suggestion and asserted that "no committee should control any property which he had anything to do with." To appease Rigdon the Galland purchase was accordingly deeded to George W. Robinson with the "express understanding that he should deed it to the Church, when the Church had paid for it according to their obligation in the contract."[25]

On 4-6 May a general conference of the church was held at the Presbyterian campground near Quincy. On the first day Rigdon spoke briefly, explaining the recent land purchase from Galland. Among other matters discussed, the conference sanctioned a mission to Europe for members of the Quorum of the Twelve and resolved to send President Rigdon to Washington, D.C., to present the church's petition for redress to federal officials. Iowa governor Robert Lucas, a former resident of Ohio, had previously given Rigdon two letters of recommendation to assist him in breaching the Capitol's circles of political power. One was addressed to Ohio governor Wilson Shannon, the other to U.S. president Martin Van Buren. "I have the honor to introduce to your acquaintance," began Lucas's endorsement to "His Excellency":

> the bearer, Doctor Sidney Rigdon, who was for many years a citizen of the State of Ohio, and a firm supporter of the administration of the General Government.
>
> Doctor Rigdon visits Washington (as I am informed) as the representative of a community of people called Mormons, to solicit from the Government of the United States, an investigation into the cause that led to their expulsion from the State of Missouri: together with the various circumstances connected with that extraordinary affair.
>
> I think it due to that people to state, that they had for a number of years a community established in Ohio, and that while in that state they were (as far as I ever heard) believed to be an industrious, inoffensive people; and I have no recollection

of ever having heard of any of them being charged in that state as violators of the laws.[26]

Other letters of support were provided by a prominent group of Quincy citizens, including U.S. senator Richard M. Young and Governor Thomas Carlin.

Rigdon postponed his trip east for six months. His poor health interfered, and his aged mother died in Commerce on 6 October. The greatest reason for the delay, however, was probably the difficulty of scheduling an appointment with President Van Buren, then in the midst of planning the 1840 campaign with a political machine badly crippled by defections and factional strife. Meanwhile Rigdon immersed himself in providing for his family and establishing the church in Commerce and Montrose, Iowa. The Rigdon "family school in Commerce" was taught by Eliza R. Snow, a well-educated young sophisticate who had been a member of Rigdon's Reformed Baptist congregation in Ohio.[27]

As the work of building a new community progressed, Orson Hyde emerged from an unhappy exile to request reinstatement in the church and Quorum of the Twelve. Wilford Woodruff wrote: "[A] more humble & penitant man I never saw, & well he might be for in the time of the persecution in Zion or [F]ar [W]est, he deserted the Cause, denied the faith & betrayed his brethren."[28] Despite Hyde's contrition, Rigdon managed to make a life-long enemy of his former apprentice when he "vary plain & forcably" opposed forgiveness, saying "he feared that if Br[.] H[y]de returned to his quorum that when the next trial came he would desert the Church as he had done before but . . . if it was the will of God he was willing that Br[.] H[y]de should return to his quorum."[29] The following day Hyde was restored to the church and Twelve by a full vote of the council, "after making an humble Confession & acknowledgement of his sins."[30]

Rigdon, during the summer of 1839, worked arduously on a lengthy entreaty to the public: *An Appeal To The American People: Being An Account Of The Persecutions Of The Church Of Latter Day Saints; And Of The Barbarities Inflicted On Them By The Inhabitants Of The State of Missouri*. The small, elegantly bound book, published by the church in early 1840, sold for "25 cents per copy, or 10 copies for two dollars."[31] Rigdon meanwhile retained his position as Mormondom's most popular preacher. At an open-air meeting in Commerce on Sunday, 7 July 1839 hundreds of Saints gathered to hear the farewell addresses of the Quorum of the Twelve who were preparing to leave for missions to Europe. After Page, Taylor, Woodruff, Hyde, and Young spoke, Rigdon addressed the meeting. Woodruff recorded that "his address was of such a nature in appealing to our affections, in parting with our wives, and Children, & the peculiarity of our mission, the perils that we might meet with, & the blessings that we should receive . . . that tears was brought from many eyes."[32]

Before the missionary cadre left Commerce, illness struck them, as well as hundreds of others, including Rigdon. Conventional wisdom held that the ague-like symptoms resulted from the effects of fetid air ascending from the humid, marshy regions along the Mississippi. What was not known until British army physician Ronald Ross discovered it in 1897 was that the *mal aria* ("bad air" in Italian) was caused by the bite of the *Anopheles* mosquito, rather than swamp vapors. Malaria's assault begins shortly after the insect deposits a parasite into its victim's bloodstream. The parasite travels to the liver and re-emerges, in vastly increased numbers, as a ring-shaped particle. It then burrows into red blood cells, feeding on hemoglobin and continuing to reproduce. At regular intervals, the infected red cells explode, unleashing a new generation of parasites into the bloodstream. At this point the infected person suffers aches and fever, often accompanied by vomiting. Drenching sweats and shaking chills ensue, followed by months or even years of anemia and periodic fevers.

On 22 July, having suffered for several days himself, Joseph Smith determined to surmount the malady and instill an element of hope in his followers. He arose from his bed and began administering to the sick in his own home and door yard. Walking towards Rigdon's house a quarter-mile northward, he blessed and comforted scores of sick lining the river's banks. While some Saints experienced temporary relief, a healing they viewed as miraculous, Rigdon and many others suffered episodic bouts of the illness until the formation of natural immunities gave them a measure of lasting alleviation.

The morbidity rate on the upper Mississippi was so high that year that Rigdon would later preach a general funeral sermon for all who had succumbed. Wickliffe Rigdon wrote of the period: "We found Commerce very sickly. We all got well except Father's mother, who was 81."[33] Nancy G. Rigdon's funeral was on 6 October 1839, the first day of the first general conference held at Commerce. Although Sidney did not attend the convocation, Elias Higbee, then serving as church historian, was appointed at the conference to accompany Rigdon as church envoy to Washington, D.C. Two weeks later, during a 20 October meeting of the Nauvoo High Council, Joseph Smith, Jr., was also appointed an emissary to accompany Rigdon and Higbee. On 28 October documents drawn up by Henry G. Sherwood "recommending, constituting, and appointing" Rigdon, Higbee, and Smith "delegates for the Church, to importune the President and Congress of the United States for redress of grievances" were signed by the Nauvoo High Council.[34]

The three political neophytes had high hopes for their sacred mission to the seat of American democracy. Trusting that fellow Democrat Martin Van Buren would sympathize with their predicament, the delegates also believed that their articulate spokesman Rigdon could persuade the president, as steward of public welfare, to tap his reservoir of implied powers and punish Missouri for its treatment of Mormons. Leaving Commerce on 29 October in a two-horse carriage driven by Orrin P. Rockwell, the men would return several months later disillusioned, their hopes for redress dashed on the shoals of what they viewed as religious bigotry.

Spending the first night of their excursion at Higbee's home in Carthage, the travelers stayed at Quincy until 31 October to "complete the necessary papers for their mission."[35] Although weakened by malarial chills, Rigdon pushed on with the others. The following day they stopped in Kingston at the tavern of Mormon Benjamin S. Wilber. Dr. Robert Foster, who had a medical practice in the area, was retained as Rigdon's personal physician and agreed to accompany the group to Springfield, a three-day journey east. On 4 November the group arrived there, boarding with Mormon John Snyder for several days while Foster treated his ailing patient. While waiting for a remission of Rigdon's malaria, the Mormon leaders met with James Adams, Sangamon County Probate Justice of the Peace. The official Mormon account, in the voice of Joseph Smith, states that "James Adams, judge of probate, heard of me, sought me out, and took me home with him, and treated me like a father."[36] This visit, which had likely been arranged the previous month by Apostle Heber C. Kimball, a fellow freemason, was a portentous one for the fledgling church in Illinois.

American Masonry, rejuvenated after its pummeling in the late 1820s over the alleged murder of William Morgan by Masonic conspiracy, again surged with power in 1839. After the Mormons' bruising in Missouri, Smith and Rigdon had concluded that protection for the Saints could occur under an umbrella of political influence, a power that would command deference. Masonry, the self-proclaimed universal fraternity of men of goodwill, embodied that potency. Judge James Adams, a lawyer, insurance agent, land speculator, and official in the Grand Masonic Lodge of Missouri, had been installed as Worshipful Master of the Springfield Masonic Lodge one week prior to meeting the Mormon committee. On 9 November, after his visit with church leaders, Adams wrote them a letter of recommendation to carry eastward.[37]

After resting five days in Springfield under Foster's care, Rigdon was still ailing. Smith wrote to his wife, Emma, on 9 November:

> [P]erhaps you may think strange That we are not fu[r]ther on our Jou[r]ny at this date. . . . I will say that we have done all that we could for the saf[e]ty of Elder Rigdon on account of his we[a]k state of hea[l]th. . . . [T]his morning we are under the ne[c]es[s]ity of leaveing him at Brother Snyders and p[ur]suing our Journ[e]y without him[.] [W]e think he will soon recover his health as he is not dangerously sick we regret that he cannot go on with us . . . but cannot help ourselves [we] must comm-it him into the hands of God and go on.[38]

All letters of recommendation, except Judge Adams's, introduced Sidney Rigdon, since he was the designated leader of the delegation. No mention was made of either Smith or Higbee. To rectify this deficiency, Rigdon arose from his sick bed on 9 November and wrote a letter introducing Smith and Higbee:

I have the honor of introducing to you Messr. Joseph Smith Jun. and Elias Higbee who have gone to Washington for the purpose of obtaining redress for the abuses received by the Church of Latter-day Saints in Missouri. They are also the bearers of a package of letters of recommendation given to myself[.] [T]he object of those letters were not for any individual advantage but for the benefit of the whole Church of Latter day Saints[.] [M]yself being sick and unable to travel[,] I have placed them in their hands for the same purpose for which they were put into mine. As they have been deputed to take my place in consequence of sickness I wish you to consider those letters as much theirs as mine and to place all confidence in them as gentlemen who have the confidence of those sending them and that your confidence in them may be as strong as the confidence that one man can place in another. I can assure you gentlemen that they are men of integrity and piety in whom the greatest confidence can be placed.[39]

After this letter was written, plans evidently changed. According to a 14 February 1874 letter from Foster to Joseph Smith III, the prophet approached Foster, declaring that if the doctor "was willing to obey the will of God, and be obedient to his commandments, I must quit my practice and start the next day with them to the city of Washington."[40] Foster complied, and with the physician on hand to attend to Rigdon, the five men were able to pursue their journey through Indiana to Columbus, Ohio. En route Smith and Rigdon traveled incognito. "If their real names had been made public," wrote Foster, "we should have been very much annoyed by the inquisitive."[41] On 18 November they arrived in the Ohio capital. Fearing they would miss their scheduled appointment with Van Buren, Smith and Higbee boarded a stagecoach on the most expeditious route to Washington, leaving Rigdon, Foster, and Rockwell to "come on at their leisure in the carriage."[42]

Smith and Higbee arrived in Washington on 28 November and rented a room at the Gadsby Hotel on the corner of Missouri and Third streets. The following day, according to Smith's account, they proceeded to the White House, knocked on the front door, announced themselves, and "requested to see the President." Ushered into his presence in an upper apartment, they presented him with their letters of introduction. "As soon as he had read one of them," Smith wrote, "he looked upon us with a kind of half frown and said, What can I do? I can do nothing for you! If I do anything, I shall come in contact with the whole State of Missouri."[43] Smith and Higbee refused to be intimidated. According to the prophet, they "demanded a hearing, and [our] constitutional rights." The president reportedly then "promised to reconsider what he had said, and observed that he felt to sympathize with us on account of our sufferings."[44] But Van Buren, known by such sobriquets as "the Little Magician" and "the Red Fox of Kinderhook," had a reputation for "non-commitalism," evasion, and double-talk.[45]

Despite Van Buren's professed empathy, the Mormon emissaries were not impressed with the Jacksonian Democrat. In comments omitted from the published version of the prophet's 5 December 1839 letter to his brother, Joseph belittled the plump and dapper president, who had a reputation for elegance. Calling Van Buren "His Majesty," Smith scoffed:

> On the whole we think he is without body or parts, as no one part seems to be proportioned to another. . . to come directly to the point, he is so much a fop or a fool (for he judged our cause before he knew it) we could find no place to put truth into him.
>
> We do not say the Saints shall not vote for him, but we do say boldly . . . that we do not intend he shall have our votes.[46]

Smith also commented that he had received a letter on 20 November from Rigdon, Foster, and Rockwell, who were then resting near Rigdon's boyhood home in Washington County, Pennsylvania, at his brother Carvel's house. "He has occasionally a chill yet," commented Joseph on the status of his friend's health, "but is not dangerous. We expect him here soon."[47]

Meanwhile Smith and Higbee began lobbying for the Mormon cause. "We believe our case will be brought before the House," Smith wrote his brother Hyrum, "we will leave the event with God; he is our Judge, and the Avenger of our wrongs."[48] Instead of a hearing in the House of Representatives, the Mormon petition was referred to the Senate Judiciary Committee, then approaching its year-end adjournment. During the hiatus between sessions, Smith traveled by rail to Philadelphia on church business, arriving on 21 December. Rockwell and Higbee, traveling by carriage, reached the city two days later. Rigdon and Foster remained in Washington at the Gadsby Hotel until late December while Rigdon continued convalescing. His health allowed travel to Philadelphia to participate in a 13 January 1840 church conference. Parley P. Pratt brought up the question of printing the Book of Mormon in New York, to which Rigdon preferred having the work done "in the west among the brethren and thereby keep the pro[f]its in the Society." Rigdon then discussed the "pecuniary embarassments" under which the Illinois committee was laboring, and a collection was taken for their cause.[49]

On 27 January, Smith, Rockwell, Higbee, and Foster left Philadelphia for Washington by rail, having sold their carriage for expenses. Rigdon, too sick to travel, remained in Philadelphia for an additional six weeks.[50] Back in the capitol, the Mormon delegation again implored Van Buren to intercede on their behalf. "It was with great reluctance [Van Buren] listened to our message," Smith later wrote. After hearing their plea he allegedly replied, "Gentlemen, your cause is just, but I can do nothing for you." Mindful of the upcoming elections he added, "If I take up for you I shall lose the vote of Missouri."[51]

After this interview with Van Buren and a similarly discouraging one with presidential candidate John C. Calhoun, Smith left Washington, along with Foster and Rockwell, and began the arduous trip back to Illinois. En route the prophet frequently vented his anger against Van Buren, holding him responsible for the church's failed mission.[52] Shortly after arriving in Commerce Smith granted a newspaper interview to the *Quincy Whig* contending that the president "was not as fit as my dog, for the chair of state; for my dog will make an effort to protect his abused and insulted master, while the present chief magistrate will not so much as lift his finger to relieve an oppressed and persecuted community of freemen."[53]

In fairness to Van Buren, who sympathized somewhat with the Saints, the question of redress was a legal issue, hence the referral to the Senate Judiciary Committee. Furthermore, neither Van Buren, who would lose the 1840 election, nor any other prominent politician was in a position to assist the Saints in restoring them to their property when Native American genocide and the horrors of slavery failed to excite widespread public outrage.[54] And the most important and largely overlooked factor in any examination of the issue is the conclusion drawn during the investigative hearings of the Senate Judiciary Committee. The Mormons' own vengeful and unlawful activities in Missouri, well-documented in Judge King's 1838 court of inquiry, served as damning evidence against their petition for recompense. Elias Higbee, the only Mormon representative still in Washington, forwarded regular updates to Rigdon, recovering in Philadelphia, and to Smith.[55] Missouri's congressional delegation, alarmed by Mormon demands for more than a million dollars in damages,[56] aggressively presented their state's position. Governor Boggs forwarded to Washington a transcript of the testimony given by Sampson Avard and others at the Richmond court. Evidence of militancy and lawlessness on the part of Mormons was the foundation for Missouri's successful defense.

Higbee was informed on 26 February by General Wall, who chaired the Senate Judiciary Committee, that the panel had ruled to proceed no further with the Mormon petition. The official 4 March 1840 recount to the U.S. Senate, after providing a brief background narrative of the situation in Missouri, reported that the case was "not such a one as will justify or authorize any interposition by this government." None of the wrongs attested to in the Mormons' petition were "alleged to be committed by any of the officers of the United States, or under the authority of its government in any manner whatever." Therefore the committee, under the circumstances, did not consider it justified to inquire further "into the truth or falsehood of the facts charged in the petition." Respecting the accusations against Missouri, the decision advised:

> If they are true, the petitioners must seek relief in the courts of judicature of the state of Missouri, or of the United States, which has the appropriate jurisdiction to administer full and adequate redress for the wrongs complained of, and doubtless will do so fairly and impartially or the petitioners may, if they see proper, apply to the justice and magnanimity of the state of Missouri—an appeal which the committee feel justified in believing will never be made in vain by the injured or oppressed.[57]

Higbee conveyed the disheartening news in letters to Rigdon and Smith. "I feel now that we have made our last appeal to all earthly tribunals," he wrote, "that we should now put our whole trust in the God of Abraham, Isaac, and Jacob. We have a right now which we could not heretofore so fully claim—that is, of asking God for redress and redemption, as they have been refused us by man."[58]

On 5 March Rigdon left Philadelphia for New Jersey, where many relatives resided. A letter from Higbee, informing Rigdon of the decision in Washington, reached him there on 2 April. Writing to Smith the following day, Rigdon informed him that the Senate

> has decided that they have no constitutional right to interfere in the case between us and the people of Missouri; and refer us to the courts for redress; either those of Missouri or the United States. Now I am confident, that there is but one person in Missouri that we can sue with safety, and that is Boggs, and he is known to be a bankrupt, and unable to pay his debts; that if we should sue him, we will have the cost to pay, as he has nothing to pay it with. We are therefore left to bear the loss without redress, at present.

Sidney added that Higbee, having borrowed money from Illinois senator Richard Young, was on his way home. "I am up to this time without means to get home," Rigdon added of his own financial dilemma, but "I shall doubtless get means as soon as my health will admit of my going. My health is slowly improving, and I think if I have no relapse, I will be able to leave for home some time in the month of May."[59]

Notes

Unless otherwise stated, all primary sources cited are located in the Historical Department of the Church of Jesus Christ of Latter-day Saints, Salt Lake City, Utah.

1. "Persecution," in *Latter Day Saints' Messenger and Advocate* 3 (Nov. 1836): 436.

2. John Taylor's account in *Journal of Discourses*, 26 vols. (Liverpool, Eng.: Latter-day Saints' Book Depot, 1855-86), 23 (5 Feb. 1882): 12. Orson Hyde, who felt personal animosity towards Rigdon, reported that after Missouri Sidney claimed "he would never follow any revelation again that did not tend to his comfort and interest, let it come from Joseph Smith, God Almighty, or any body else" (*Speech of Elder Orson Hyde, Delivered Before the High Priest's Quorum in Nauvoo, April 27th, 1845* [City of Joseph, IL: John Taylor, 1845], 7).

3. See Joseph Smith III's account in *Saints' Herald*, 6 Nov. 1934, 1416.

4. *Quincy Argus*, 16 Mar. 1839, in John P. Green, *Expulsion of the Mormons—Facts Relative to the Expulsion of the Mormons or Latter Day Saints From the State of Missouri, Under the "Exterminating Order"* (Cincinnati: R. P. Brooks, 1839), 11.

5. This lengthy "Memorial of a Committee to the State Legislature of Missouri in Behalf of the Citizens of Caldwell County" was drafted on 10 December 1838 while Rigdon and Smith were in jail. The nine-man committee included Edward Partridge, Heber C.

Kimball, John Taylor, Theodore Turley, Brigham Young, Isaac Morley, George W. Harris, John Murdock, and John M. Burk (Joseph Smith, *History of the Church of Jesus Christ of Latter-day Saints*, B. H. Roberts, ed., 7 vols. [Salt Lake City: The Church of Jesus Christ of Latter-day Saints, 1902], 3:217-24; hereafter referred to as *History of the Church*).

6. Account of 27 Feb. 1839 "Meeting of the Democratic Association of Quincy," in Journal History, 9 Jan. 1839–a multi-volume daily history of the church compiled by official church historians; hereafter Journal History.

7. John Taylor, in *Journal of Discourses* 11 (1867): 25.

8. Ibid., 11:17.

9. Joseph Smith to "The Church at Quincy Illinois," 20 Mar. 1839, *History of the Church*, 3:301. No further common stock programs were established during Joseph Smith's life. The prophet shaded the truth during his 1839-40 trip to Washington, D.C., when he stated that Mormons would not share property in common. "'It has been reported by some vicious or de[s]igning characters,' he said, 'that the church of Latter Day Saints believe in having their pro[p]erty in common and also the leaders of sa[id] church controlls said propperty. . . . This is a base fabrication,' he insisted, 'on the contrary no person's feelings can be more repugnant to such a principle than mine[,] every person in this Church has a right to controll his own proppe[r]ty'" (Joseph Smith to Mr. Editor [of the *Chester County Register and Examiner*], 22 Jan. 1840, in Dean Jessee, *The Personal Writings of Joseph Smith* [Salt Lake City: Deseret Book Co., 1984], 457-58).

10. Albert P. Rockwood 30 Jan. 1839 letter to his father, in Dean C. Jessee and David J. Whittaker, "The Last Months of Mormonism in Missouri: The Albert Perry Rockwood Journal," *Brigham Young University Studies* 28 (Winter 1988): 34.

11. Mid-February 1839 Rockwood letter to "Dear Beloved Father," in Jessee and Whittaker, 34.

12. *History of the Church*, 3:265-67.

13. Ibid.

14. 5 Mar. 1839 Edward Partridge letter to Joseph Smith, Jr., in *History of the Church*, 3:272.

15. See "Historical Notes—An Ancient Burial Ground," *Journal of the Illinois State Historical Society* 26 (Oct. 1933): 310-11.

16. "The Prophet's Epistle to the Church, Written in Liberty Prison, 25 Mar. 1839," *History of the Church*, 3:298.

17. Karl Keller, ed., "I Never Knew a Time When I Did Not Know Joseph Smith," *Dialogue: A Journal of Mormon Thought* 1 (Winter 1966): 38.

18. See Constantine Kreymeyer article (originally written in 1874) in *Nauvoo Independent*, 14 Nov. 1923.

19. J. Wickliffe Rigdon, "Life Story of Sidney Rigdon," 159.

20. Joseph Smith, III, "Memoirs," *Latter Day Saints' Herald*, 13 Nov. 1934, 1454. After the Rigdons moved from the home in 1841, the place became known as the Nauvoo Ferry Hotel, managed by Charles Ivins and Samuel Bennett. The lot was subsequently engulfed by the Mississippi after the Keokuk Dam was built in 1913 (see *Times and Seasons*, 2 Aug. 1841, and Richard N. Holzapfel and T. Jeffery Cottle, *Old Mormon Nauvoo–1839-1846* [Provo, UT: Grandin Book Company, 1990], 134-35).

21. *History of the Church*, 3:298.

22. Ibid., 310-11. Rigdon's strategy can be seen as early as 23 February 1839 when he wrote to Felix Grundy, U.S. Attorney General, who had gained a large following by favoring laws for relief of the poor: "My object in writing to you is to as[c]ertain if recourse can be had to the federal [government] and whether or no[t] we can enter suit in the court not only against individual inhabitants of Missouri but against the state also for the unconstitutional acts of the executive of said state" (in Clark V. Johnson, ed., *Mormon Redress Petitions: Documents of the 1833-1838 Missouri Conflict* [Provo, UT.: Brigham Young University Religious Studies Center, 1992], 737-38).

23. *History of the Church*, 3:312.

24. See Joseph Smith III, "Memoirs," 1454; Ebenezer Robinson, "Items of Personal History," *The Return* (Davis City, IA) 2 (Apr. 1890): 243; and Joseph H. McGee, "The Mormons in Missouri," an 1898 newspaper clipping in the Library of the State Historical Society of Missouri (Columbia, Missouri), in Stephen C. LeSueur, *The 1838 Mormon War in Missouri* (Columbia, MO: University of Missouri Press, 1987), 243.

In response to charges of bribery, Sheriff Morgan signed an affidavit asserting that the Mormons "made the escape without the connivance consent or negligence of myself or said guard," but disbelieving Daviess citizens assaulted him so severely that he died (William Morgan statement, 6 July 1839, and Joseph McGee, "Some of the Waste Places of Zion," in *Deseret News*, 10 Sept. 1904, 23, in LeSueur, 244).

25. *History of the Church*, 3:341-42. Robinson's privilege on the property also included ferry rights and an option on additional parcels of land. The deed is recorded in Hancock County Deed Book G, 247. On 23 March 1840 Ripley deeded the White farm to Joseph Smith and his heirs. On 5 October 1841 the property was deeded to Joseph Smith as trustee-in-trust for the church. George W. Robinson turned the Galland property over to Smith as trustee-in-trust on 5 October 1841 (Hancock County Records, "Mortgage I," 95).

26. *History of the Church*, 3:333.

27. *Eliza R. Snow: An Immortal* (Salt Lake City: Nicholas G. Morgan, Sr., Foundation, 1957), 12. Snow mentions that she was with Rigdon's mother (who lived with Sidney) at her death, and attended her funeral on 6 October.

28. Scott Kenney, ed., *Wilford Woodruff's Journal*, 9 vols. (Midvale, UT: Signature Books, 1983), 1:340.

29. Ibid.

30. Ibid., 341.

31. The completed manuscript was first read to the assembled Saints in Quincy on 1 November 1839. Robinson was appointed special agent to see the book published. Hyde, en route to his European mission in mid-November, teamed with Robinson at Springfield to unite their exertions in publishing Rigdon's appeal. Eventually printed by the Cincinnati firm of Shepard & Stearns, the books were available for distribution in Nauvoo in mid-January 1840.

32. Kenney, 1:345.

33. Keller, 38.

34. *History of the Church*, 4:18.

35. Ibid., 19.

36. Ibid., 20.

37. This letter, along with other letters of introduction, is in the Martin Van Buren

Collection, Library of Congress, Washington, D.C. A copy is found in the Mormon Manuscript Retrieval Project, Special Collections, Harold B. Lee Library, Brigham Young University; hereafter Special Collections, BYU.

38. Jessee, 1984, 448.

39. Original in Martin Van Buren Collection, copy in Manuscript Retrieval Project.

40. R. Etzenhouser, *From Palmyra, New York, 1830 to Independence, Missouri, 1894* (Independence, MO: Ensign Publishing House, 1894), 308-309.

41. Ibid., 309.

42. *History of the Church*, 4:21.

43. Joseph Smith, Jr., and Elias Higbee to Hyrum Smith and the Nauvoo High Council, 5 Dec. 1839, in *History of the Church*, 4:39. The credential Van Buren first read was likely an introduction signed by Rigdon, Smith, and Higbee. The document attests to the "Cruel Outrages and injustice inflicted upon the said Church by the Citizens of the State of Missouri and also their Suffering Condition in Consequence" (undated letter in Joseph Smith Collection).

44. Ibid.

45. For general treatments of President Van Buren, see James C. Curtis, *The Fox at Bay: Martin Van Buren and the Presidency, 1837-1841* (Lexington, KY: University Press of Kentucky, 1970); John Niven, *Martin Van Buren: The Romantic Age of American Politics* (London: Oxford University Press, 1983); John Fitzpatrick, ed., *The Autobiography of Martin Van Buren* (1920; reprint, New York: DaCapo, 1973).

46. Journal History, 5 Dec. 1839.

47. Joseph Smith, Jr., to Hyrum Smith and High Council, Journal History, 5 Dec. 1839.

48. Ibid.

49. "Minutes of a Conference Held at Philadelphia January 13th 1840" in "Record Book of Philadelphia Branch, Eastern States Mission."

50. *History of the Church*, 4:77.

51. Ibid., 80.

52. Elias Higbee's 24 Mar. 1840 letter to Smith noted that some Washington, D.C., newspapers were reporting that the prophet had "come out for [William Henry] Harrison," who won the 1840 election (ibid., 98).

53. *Quincy Whig*, 17 Oct. 1840.

54. Although the issue of "states rights" was not definitely decided until the Civil War, the office of president did have sufficient power to quell disturbances in the states. Early in American history Congress had deemed it necessary to endow the president with such powers. On 2 May 1792, the office of chief executive was empowered to call up state militia to suppress insurrections "Whenever the laws of the United States shall be opposed or the execution thereof obstructed, in any state, by combinations too powerful to be suppressed by the ordinary course of judicial proceedings or by the power vested in the marshals" (Edward S. Corwin, *The President, Office and Powers, 1787-1957*, 4th ed. rev. [New York: New York University Press, 1957], 131).

The president was first required to be notified of the difficulties by an associate justice or district judge of the United States, something that was not done in Missouri. A proclamation was then required to be issued to the "insurgents" to "disperse and retire peaceably." If this step failed then troops could be dispatched, as in 1794 when President George Washington crushed the famous Whiskey Rebellion in Pittsburgh. Presidents Jefferson and Jackson also made use of these and ensuing powers during their administrations.

55. Higbee's 20, 21, 22, 26 Feb., and 9, 24 Mar. 1840 letters to Joseph Smith are found in *History of the Church*, 4:81-98.

56. The claims of 451 individuals totaled $1,381,044 (ibid., 74). The best single source for background on the Mormon redress issue is Johnson, *Mormon Redress Petitions*.

57. *History of the Church*, 4:91-92.

58. Higbee to Smith, 26 Feb. 1840, ibid., 88.

59. Rigdon to Smith, 3 Apr. 1840, ibid., 102.

CHAPTER 20.

From Swamp to City

[Commerce in 1839] was literally a wilderness. The land was mostly covered with trees and bushes, and much of it was so wet that it was with the utmost difficulty that a footman could get through, and totally impossible for teams. Commerce was unhealthy, very few could live there; but believing that it might become a healthy place by the blessing of heaven to the saints, and no more eligible place presenting itself, I considered it wisdom to make an attempt to build up a city.

—Joseph Smith, Jr.[1]

On 21 April 1840, one month before Sidney Rigdon returned to Illinois from the East, the U.S. Post Office Department designation for Commerce was changed to Nauvoo, "a Hebrew term signifying a beautiful place," wrote Wickliffe Rigdon.[2] Although credit for the inventive name is usually given to Joseph Smith, Wickliffe attributed it to George W. Robinson, his brother-in-law. The versatile Robinson, appointed Nauvoo's first postmaster, had studied under Kirtland's Jewish tutor and was "quite a Hebrew scholar," according to Wickliffe.[3] While still in the East, Sidney had used his influence with U.S. senator Richard M. Young to secure Robinson's governmental appointment. Having served briefly as postmaster in Far West, Missouri, Rigdon understood the financial benefits of the position in a boom town where the postmaster received a fee for each mail item handled.

Eventually a wealthy and powerful banker in Friendship, New York, Robinson was a sagacious businessman. Much of his income in early Nauvoo came from lucrative ferry rights between Commerce and Mormon settlements across the Mississippi in Iowa. During a 15 March 1840 Nauvoo High Council meeting, convened within days after Joseph Smith's return from Washington, the ferry's operation was removed from Robinson's control and placed under Smith's. Rigdon, possibly made aware of the prophet's impending seizure while the two were in Washington, took immediate action to secure another source of income for his son-in-law. Senator Young wrote Elias Higbee on 9 April that he had "received from Mr. Rigdon the Petition and papers in relation to a change of postmaster at Commerce, with an affidavit from Doctor Galland [the former postmaster].[4] Two weeks later Robert Johnstone, Second Assistant Postmaster General, informed Senator Young that Robinson had been appointed.[5] He served in this position until 24 February 1841, when Rigdon himself was appointed to the post, an action that would cause considerable friction between him and Smith.

Although Nauvoo's population increased dramatically in the early 1840s, much of its short-lived prosperity was based on the same perilous real estate speculation that brought down Kirtland's economy. Rigdon and the Smiths once again pinned their financial aspirations on hopes that new converts, aware of the prophet's dark visions of America's future, would flee their homelands, gather to Nauvoo—proclaimed city of refuge—and purchase property from the real estate arm of the church. But of the more than 3,000 British converts who arrived in Nauvoo before 1846, most were poverty-stricken refugees from the English working class.[6] Sobering to the First Presidency was that real estate sales fell far below their expectation, forcing the brethren to default on the promissory notes they had co-signed. Because the church was not yet a legal entity in 1839, Rigdon, the Smith brothers, and their wives were personally liable for the organization's nearly $150,000 debt.[7]

The earliest hint of impending financial crisis was Smith's 27 May 1839 letter to Hancock County businessman Mark Bigler, from whom the prophet hoped to borrow money. Although the price for an average lot in Nauvoo was set at $500, the prophet worried that "money seems to come in too slowly."[8] In an attempt to impede fiscal calamity, the First Presidency appointed the church's foremost financial talent to serve as their agents. On 13 May 1839 they reaffirmed administrative proxy Oliver Granger's earlier charge "to contend earnestly for the redemption of the First Presidency of my Church." Church members were admonished to "entrust him with moneys, lands, chattels, and goods . . . saith the Lord."[9] Later that month Stephen Markham was appointed to "go forth among the faithful, as our agent to gather up and receive such means in money and otherwise, as shall enable us to meet our engagements which are now about to devolve upon us in consequence of our purchases here for the Church."[10] And during the October 1839 general conference Elder Lyman Wight preached on the importance of raising funds and paying for the lands "which had been contracted for as a settlement for the Church."[11]

To pay for the vast acreage, Mormon property owners in the East were advised to sign their real estate over to the church, through agents Isaac Galland and William Smith, in exchange for an equivalent value of land in Nauvoo. The eastern property was to be sold outright or transferred to the Commerce City Company, also known as the Hotchkiss, Gillett, & Tuttle Syndicate, for payment against the church's indebtedness with that coalition. Despite entreaties of the First Presidency and efforts of their agents, the paltry revenues were insufficient even to make interest payments on the promissory notes. Overwhelmed by their obligations,

Rigdon and the Smith brothers sought a way out of their financial problems: bankruptcy. In April 1842 they engaged the services of Calvin A. Warren, a Quincy lawyer, to pursue their individual petitions. The prophet, in a 13 May letter to Horace R. Hotchkiss on behalf of himself, his brother, and Rigdon, informed the Connecticut promoter that "money is out of sight . . . it cannot be had." And although all creditors would "have to fare alike," Smith added, "I have no doubt you will yet, and in a short time, be enabled to have your pay in full."[12]

Shocked at the church leaders' tactic, Hotchkiss wrote at once to Smith demanding "immediately upon receipt of this letter, your precise meaning in saying that 'all your creditors would fare alike' . . . I wish to know exactly how [my] bond stands in your inventory."[13] The prophet responded a month later: "Your papers are inventoried along with all other property."[14] When Hotchkiss objected in an 8 November letter to Rigdon,[15] Smith, now trustee-in-trust for the church, wrote: "I knew not but what the law required of me to include you amongst the list of my creditors. . . . I have since learned, from a decision of the judge of the supreme court . . . that the [bankruptcy] law had no jurisdiction over such a contract. . . . I shall yet endeavor to make up the payments as fast as possible, and consider the contract as still good between us."[16] Hotchkiss ultimately arrived at the conclusion that under the prevailing conditions in Nauvoo he could not hope for a completely satisfactory settlement. On 7 April 1843 he wrote Smith, then serving as Nauvoo city recorder, that "I wish it understood distinctly by them who have built upon [my property] that I shall not attempt to take their buildings from them, but shall be ready at any time to give them a lease of their lots for a very long period, at a reasonable rent."[17]

Illness prevented Sidney Rigdon from playing a major role in this and most other Nauvoo activities from 1840-44. Ague again brought him low during the season of 1840. His old adversary malaria, coupled with other stress-related factors, triggered the longest depression Rigdon would suffer in his anxiety-ridden life. Overwhelmed with financial worries and dazed by his dashed hopes of federal redress and return to Missouri, Rigdon imploded under the weight of despair. His son Wickliffe characterized the sad state of Sidney's health: "Sidney Rigdon being of a bilious temperament was sick most of the time while he remained at Nauvoo . . . for weeks at a time he would not be able to leave his bed. . . . [S]ome times he would be able to be around and at such times he would on Sundays preach to the people."[18]

Rigdon was able to take care of a few business matters, although forced to rely extensively on family members, particularly George W. Robinson, to do so. In July 1840 he declined a challenge to debate his Campbellite minister cousin John Rigdon in nearby Adams County because, as he put it:

My health continues very bad, and it is only at intervals that I am able to write . . . it is known through the country, generally, that I am unable to get five miles from my house, let alone discuss a subject of importance with any person. And it is also a fact that my attendent Physician, has forbid my using any exertions, either mental or physical, except very moderate exercise, as it will endanger my life.[19]

In addition, Rigdon had cause to worry that the long arm of Missouri's legal system would force his extradition. The prophet had earlier advised Mormons bent on revenge to wait until the "proper time came to take back their rights." When the time was right, he promised, we will "take the whole State of Missouri like men."[20] But some Mormons, burning with hatred towards their arch enemies, began organizing punitive raiding parties into Missouri. Devout churchman Joel H. Johnson told of a "secret combination" consisting of a bishop, a councilor, four high councilmen, and ten or twelve elders who advocated "that it was no harm to steal from Missourians."[21] In early July 1840 a Missouri posse seized four suspected Mormon raiders on the Illinois side of the Mississippi, took them to Tully, Missouri, beat them, and temporarily jailed the men without due process. Mormon leaders appealed to Illinois governor Carlin to take steps to correct this injustice.

In retaliation, Missouri governor Thomas Reynolds, encouraged by ex-governor Boggs, requested Governor Carlin to extradite Smith, Rigdon, Lyman Wight, Parley P. Pratt, Caleb Baldwin, and Alanson Brown "as fugitives from justice."[22] The *Quincy Whig* responded in a scathing denunciation of the extradition request:

Fudge! We repeat; Smith and Rigdon should not be given up. The law requiring the Governor of our State [Carlin] to deliver up fugitives from justice, is a salutary and wise one, and should not in ordinary circumstances be disregarded, but as there are occasions that authorize the citizens of a State to resent a tyranical and oppressive government, so there are occasions when it is not only the privilege, but the duty of the Governor of the State to refuse to surrender the citizens of his State upon the requisition of the Executive of another,—and this we consider as the case of Smith and Rigdon.[23]

Carlin, despite the protests, complied with Reynolds's request. But when a sheriff rode into Nauvoo on 15 September to serve the warrant, Rigdon, despite his illness, along with all the others, was "gone from home."[24] In a caustic editorial of its own, the church's *Times and Seasons* argued that "[Reynolds] has no business with them; they have not escaped from justice, but from the hands of a cursed, infuriated, inhuman set, or race of beings who are enemies to their country, to their God, to themselves, and to every principle of righteousness and humanity."[25] Fear of extradition or abduction by Missouri officers was a constant concern for both Rigdon and Smith. The prophet's resulting emotional distress became so acute in 1843 that he began to suspect Rigdon, his bosom friend, and wrongfully accused him of collusion with Missouri authorities—this despite the fact that his counselor was a fugitive from justice as well.

The principal wellspring of Smith's paranoia was Dr. John C. Bennett, a former Campbellite and acquaintance of Rigdon in Willoughby (Chagrin), Ohio, three miles from Kirtland. On 25 July 1840 Bennett wrote to Rigdon and Smith: "Some months ago I resigned my office [Brigadier-General of the Invincible Illinois Dragoons], with an intention of removing to your town, and joining your people; but hitherto I have been prevented. I hope, however, to remove to Commerce, and unite with your Church next spring. I believe I should be much happier with you."[26] Two days later he again wrote the two Mormons of his wish to relocate his medical practice to Nauvoo. The physician offered the Saints "all the benefit of my speaking powers, and my untiring energies." Then he gushed, "I hope that time will soon come when your people will become my people, and your God my God."[27] Three days later the doctor advised Rigdon and Smith: "My anxiety to be with you is daily increasing, and I shall wind up my professional business immediately, and proceed to your blissful abode, if you think it best."[28]

Although Smith and Bennett had never met, the prophet was impressed by the "frank and noble mindedness breathed in your letter," and added, "I am brought to the conclusion that you are a friend to suffering humanity and truth." Smith then concluded, "Elder Rigdon is very sick, and has been for nearly twelve months with the fever and ague, which disease is very prevalent here at this time. At present he is not able to leave his room."[29]

One week later Bennett, who had not yet received the prophet's letter, again wrote:

> I have come to the conclusion to join your people immediately, and take up my abode with you. Let us adopt as our motto—*Licut patribus sit Deus nobius*—(as God was with our fathers, so may He be with us). . . . I shall be with you in about two weeks, and shall devote my time and energies to the advancement of the cause of truth and virtue, and the advocacy of the holy religion which you have so nobly defended, and so honorably sustained.[30]

Bennett's rise to the pinnacles of Mormon prominence was comparable to Rigdon's earlier ascent. But Bennett's contributions were political. A month after arriving in Nauvoo, Bennett addressed a general conference, urging continued appeals for Missouri redress. At that same convocation he was appointed to draft a bill for the incorporation of Nauvoo[31] and was chosen as delegate to facilitate the passage of that bill through the Illinois legislature. A 15 January 1841 circular from the First Presidency avowed that Bennett, "one of the instruments . . . in procuring the city charter[,] . . . is calculated to be a great blessing to our community."[32] Four days later a gullible Smith, unaware of Bennett's sordid past, evoked a blessing upon the rake: "And for his love he shall be great," pronounced the prophet in the Lord's voice, "I have seen the work which he hath done, which I accept if he continue, and will crown him with blessings and great glory" (D&C 124:17).

That revelation of 19 January 1841 also contained an intriguing reference to

Rigdon's incapacity. Rigdon, enveloped in the dark folds of despair, was talking about relocating to the healthier environs of his boyhood Pittsburgh. Earlier in Kirtland Smith had pronounced a revelation that promised "my servant Sydney must go sooner or later to Pittsburg."[33] Rigdon now wished to take up that pledge. But the prophet wanted his old friend by his side, and in a dramatic display of divine assurance guaranteed him a restoration of his health if he refrained from moving to Pennsylvania:

> If my servant Sidney will serve me, and be counselor unto my servant Joseph, let him arise and come up, and stand in the office of his calling, and humble himself before me.
>
> And if he will offer unto me an acceptable offering, and acknowledgements, and remain with my people, behold, I, the Lord your God, will heal him . . . and he shall lift up his voice again on the mountains, and be a spokesman before my face (D&C 124:103-104).

The Rigdons still lived in the lower stone house, the former Galland residence on Block 132,[34] but Smith wanted the family closer. "Let [Sidney] come and locate his family in the neighborhood in which my servant Joseph resides," the revelation continued; "let him not remove his family unto the eastern lands . . . it is not my will that he shall seek to find safety and refuge out of Nauvoo" (D&C 124:105-109). Heeding "the Lord's word," Rigdon vacated the lower stone house by July 1841, when it became the "Nauvoo Ferry Hotel," managed by Charles Ivins and Samuel Bennett.[35] The February 1842 Nauvoo census lists the Rigdon family living in the Nauvoo First Municipal Ward, well north of the lower stone house and Joseph Smith's neighborhood.[36] But the Rigdons, along with the Robinsons, were likely living temporarily at the Hiram Kimball residence while their new home was being built on Main Street, immediately north of Joseph Smith's nearly completed "Mansion House."[37]

Rigdon's contemporaries, many of them unaware of his depression, often criticized his deportment in Nauvoo. Apostle Orson Hyde, for example, frequently complained of Rigdon's "peculiar ebbings and flowings." On one occasion, Hyde unknowingly provided a classical description of Rigdon's bipolar illness. "Sometimes," Hyde began, "in a gust of passion or a flight of fancy . . . [Elder Rigdon] takes the comet's track and flies almost 'beyond the bounds of time and space' [but] at other times, he is completely in the jaws of despair."[38] Amasa Lyman, later of the First Presidency, said disapprovingly that when Rigdon was not sick, he was merely content "to sleep and smoke his pipe, and take his drink all the while."[39] Manic depression does ebb and flow, and one would expect Rigdon's activities to have been erratic. Still, his voice was not muted; neither did he become a recluse. The public record shows him to be engaged in numerous activities, although certainly not with the same fervor he displayed in Kirtland and Far West.

By the time the Rigdons moved from the lower stone house, Nauvoo had developed into a remarkable oasis. The community had two sawmills, a steam flour mill, a foundry, a tool factory, schools, bridges, paved streets, a host of shops, a planned hotel, dozens of cultivated fields, gardens, and orchards, and a cooperative farm on the outskirts of the town. In February 1841 Rigdon was elected a city councilman. He also became a regent of the "University of the City of Nauvoo," where he was appointed professor of "Rhetoric and Belles Letters and Church History."[40] In addition to teaching and serving as chaplain of the Nauvoo Legion (the city's military appendage), and postmaster as of 24 February, he was a founding member of the Board of Directors of the Nauvoo Agricultural and Manufacturing Association. Chartered by Governor Carlin, the association promoted "agriculture and husbandry in all its branches, and for the manufacture of flour, lumber, and such other useful articles as are necessary for the ordinary purposes of life."[41]

On the eleventh anniversary of the church, 6 April 1841, the cornerstones of the Nauvoo temple were laid. Rigdon, whose normal body weight of 212 pounds had been reduced to 165 pounds,[42] delivered the keynote discourse to the large throng of Saints. He began by pointing out that the occasion was the third time he had addressed the Saints at a cornerstone dedication. The Saints had gathered in Nauvoo, he continued, "not to violate law and trample upon equity and good social order; not to devastate and destroy; but to lift up the standard of liberty and law, to stand in defence of civil and religious rights, to protect the innocent, to save mankind, and to obey the will and mandate of the Lord of Glory." He then testified that "the glorified Savior . . . is again revealed, [that] he speaks from the heavens, that he reigns . . . that is the reason why we are here, and why we are thus . . . that the Saints have sacrificed all things for the testimony of Jesus Christ."[43]

Robert B. Thompson chronicled Rigdon's discourse in the 15 April 1841 *Times and Seasons.* "From the long affliction and weakness of body," began the reporter,

> we hardly expected the speaker to have made himself heard by the congregation, but he succeeded beyond our most sanguine expectations, and being impressed with the greatness and solemnities of the occasion, he rose superior to his afflictions and weakness, and for more than an hour occupied the attention of the assembly.
>
> It was an address worthy a man of God, and a messenger of salvation. . . . [N]ever did we hear him pour out such pious effusions; in short it was full to overflowing, of christian feeling and high-toned piety.
>
> He called to review the scenes of tribulation and anguish through which the saints had passed, the barbarous cruelties inflicted upon them for their faith and attachment to the cause of their God, and for the testimony of Jesus, which, they endured with patience, knowing that they had in heaven a more enduring substance, a crown of eternal glory.[44]

After architects lowered the southeast cornerstone into position, the prophet pronounced a brief blessing. Rigdon added: "May the persons employed in the erection of this house be preserved from all harm while engaged in its construction, till the whole is completed; in the name of the Father, and of the Son, and of the Holy Ghost; even so, *Amen.*"[45]

The day's activities exhausted Rigdon. The following day, as meetings continued, he arose and stated that "in consequence of weakness from his labors of yesterday, he would call upon General John C. Bennett to officiate in his place." On 8 April, the conference's final day, Bennett was presented "with the First Presidency, as Assistant President until President Rigdon's health should be restored."[46] Rigdon was present during the 8 April meeting, offering the benediction. After a two-hour adjournment he addressed the afternoon session on "Baptism for the Dead," the first known public sermon on the topic although it had been mentioned in Smith's 19 January 1841 revelation (D&C 124:29-36). The newspaper account of Rigdon's treatise states that the subject "was set forth in a manner new and interesting, and with an eloquence peculiar to the speaker, which was listened to with intense interest by the assembly."[47] During services the following Sunday, 11 April, Rigdon again "made some observations on baptism for the remission of sins."[48] William Huntington's diary notes that "Joseph and Sidney baptised each other for the remission of their Sins as this order was then Instituted in the church."[49] Other members were then baptized in turn.

Rigdon was evidently feeling well enough to begin writing an extensive theological essay for the *Times and Seasons.* On 15 April the periodical stated that he had promised them "a lengthy communication, for our next number," which would be devoted to "an expose of the false systems of the day, an exhibition of the true Priesthood, [and] a vindication of the claims of the Saints, drawing the contrast between true and false prophets."[50] But the 1 May issue of the paper related that in consequence of "the sickness of Pres[ident] Rigdon," the article "could not be got ready for the present number, but as soon as his health will admit, we shall take pleasure in giving it publicity."[51]

Rigdon's relapse into depression worried church leaders. According to Jedediah Grant, they "would visit him and pray for his recovery, and comfort him all they could, knowing he had suffered many afflictions."[52] Hyrum Smith felt that a contributing factor to Rigdon's despondency was the feeling that he had been slighted by Smith. Although Rigdon had been guaranteed along with the prophet in an 8 March 1833 revelation that it would be "your business and mission . . . all your lives, to preside in council, and set in order all the affairs of this church and kingdom" (D&C 90:16), one holy promise had not yet been bestowed upon him. Hyrum approached his brother, saying: "Br. Joseph, you have ordained me and Br. Don Carlos [Smith] and others, to be Prophets, Seers, and Revelators, but you have not ordained Br. Sidney, and I have thought that he feels that you have slighted him, I want you to go . . . and ordain him to the same office."[53] Shortly afterwards the prophet and Nauvoo Stake president William Marks performed the ordinance. In its next issue the local newspaper contained the brief mention: "We have to announce that Sidney Rigdon has been ordained a Prophet, Seer and Revelator."[54]

Notes

Unless otherwise stated, all primary sources cited are located in the Historical Department of the Church of Jesus Christ of Latter-day Saints, Salt Lake City, Utah.

1. In B. H. Roberts, *A Comprehensive History of the Church of Jesus Christ of Latter-day Saints*, 6 vols. (Salt Lake City: Deseret News Press, 1930), 2:9.

2. J. Wickliffe Rigdon, "Life Story of Sidney Rigdon," 160.

3. Karl Keller, ed., "I Never Knew a Time When I Did Not Know Joseph Smith: A Son's Record of the Life and Testimony of Sidney Rigdon," *Dialogue: A Journal of Mormon Thought* 1 (Winter 1966): 15-42, cited 39.

4. Joseph Smith, *History of the Church of Jesus Christ of Latter-day Saints*, B. H. Roberts, ed., 7 vols. (Salt Lake City: The Church of Jesus Christ of Latter-day Saints, 1902), 4:111-12; hereafter *History of the Church*.

5. Johnstone to Young, 21 Apr. 1840, ibid., 121.

6. The prophet, convinced of imminent disaster in 1841, ordered his missionary cadre in Great Britain home. Apostle Heber C. Kimball received a letter from his wife dated 30 December 1840. She informed him that "Joseph had written for the Twelve to come immediately home for our personal Safety, as great Judgments are nigh in this land even at the Door" (Scott Kenney, ed., *Wilford Woodruff's Journal*, 9 vols. [Midvale, UT: Signature Books, 1983], 2:47).

Wilford Woodruff's diary brims with lament over the cataclysm that never happened. On 15 February 1841 he wrote: "Their is no doubt but what troubles will soon arise between England & America but may the Lord prepare his Saints for the worst" (ibid.). The next day he anguished: "*War War* is [at] the door between England & America. O Lord Deliver us" (ibid., 48). On 15 March he again commiserated that the English Saints "universally feel that the Judgments of God are near in this land & are anxious to gather with the Saints in Nauvoo as soon as possible" (ibid., 62-63). By 22 August, after returning to Nauvoo, Woodruff, in an apocalyptic frenzy, wrote: "an awful storm is gathering over the heads of a guilty generation which is spe[e]dily to burst upon the nations by the power & wrath of God which will engul[f] millions of the human family in ruin & destruction" (ibid., 118-19).

Smith did not seem worried about the failure of his prophecy. Pleased with the conversion rate in Great Britain, the prophet, in a heady burst of enthusiasm, told apostles in 1843 that he planned to go with them to England and from there throughout the world conducting a great revival: "I will yet take these brethren through the United States and through the world, and will make just as big a wake as God Almighty will let me; we must send kings and governors to Nauvoo, and we will do it" (*Deseret News*, 9 Apr. 1856).

7. See David E. Miller and Della S. Miller, *Nauvoo: The City of Joseph* (Santa Barbara/Salt Lake City: Peregrine Smith, 1974), 27-33.

8. Smith and Vinson Knight to Bigler, 27 May 1839, in *History of the Church*, 3:366.

9. Joseph Smith, Sidney Rigdon, and Hyrum Smith, "Letter of Recommendation to Oliver Granger," in *History of the Church*, 3:350.

Smith, in a 15 August 1841 letter to Horace R. Hotchkiss, complained:

> I presume you are no stranger to the part of the city plat we bought of you being a deathly sickly hole, and that we have not been able in consequence to realize any valuable consideration from it, although we have been keeping up appearances, and holding out inducements to encourage immigration, that we scarcely think justifiable in consequence of the mortality that almost invariably awaits those who come from far distant parts (*History of the Church*, 4:407).

Despite his acknowledgement that the mosquito-infested Mississippi bottom lands were a "deathly sickly hole," the prophet was so financially desperate he continued to promote real estate sales in the unhealthy tract. As late as 13 April 1843, while addressing a company of newly-arrived English Saints, he knew better than to announce: "Some persons may perhaps inquire which is the most healthful location. I will tell you. The lower part of the town is most healthful. In the upper part of the town are the merchants, who will say that I am partial . . . but the lower part of the town is much the most healthful; and I tell it [to] you in the name of the Lord" (*History of the Church*, 5:357).

10. Ibid., 3:367.

11. Ibid., 4:13.

12. Smith to Hotchkiss, 13 May 1842, ibid., 5:7.

13. Hotchkiss to Smith, 27 May 1842, ibid., 51.

14. Smith to Hotchkiss, 30 June 1842, ibid., 52.

15. Hotchkiss to Rigdon, 8 Nov. 1842, ibid., 195.

16. Smith to Hotchkiss, 26 Nov. 1842, ibid., 195. On 30 January 1841 Smith was elected sole trustee of the church "to hold my office during life (my successors to be the First Presidency of said church), and vested with plenary powers . . . to receive acquire, manage, or convey property, real, personal, or mixed, for the sole use and benefit of said church" (Hancock County Records, Book No. 1 of Bonds and Mortgages, p. 95, No. 87, in ibid., 4:287).

17. Hotchkiss to Smith, 7 Apr. 1843, ibid., 5:382-83.

18. Keller, 161.

19. *Times and Seasons* 1 (July 1840): 134-36.

20. John D. Lee, *Mormonism Unveiled; or the Life and Confessions of the late Mormon Bishop* (St. Louis: Bryan, Brand & Co., 1877), 173.

21. "Diary of Joel Hills Johnson," 1:24-25. See also *Times and Seasons* 1 (15 Nov. 1840): 221; *The Wasp*, 29 Mar. 1843, 1, 3; and *History of the Church* , 4:219-20, 461, 469.

22. *History of the Church*, 4:198.

23. Cited in *Times and Seasons* 1 (Sept. 1840): 188-89.

24. *History of the Church*, 4:198.

25. Ibid., 199.

26. Ibid., 172.

27. Bennett to the "Reverends Sidney Rigdon and Joseph Smith, Jun.," ibid., 170.

28. Bennett to Rigdon and Smith, 30 July 1840, ibid., 172.

29. Smith to Bennett, 8 Aug. 1841, ibid., 177.

30. Bennett to "Reverends Joseph Smith, Jun., and Sidney Rigdon," 15 Aug. 1840, ibid., 179.

31. The Nauvoo City Charter bears Bennett's unmistakable stamp, but the official history of Mormonism, written in Joseph Smith's voice, maintains: "The City Charter of Nauvoo is of my own plan and device. I concocted it for the salvation of the Church, and on principles so broad, that every honest man might dwell secure under its protective influence without distinction of sect or party" (ibid., 249).

32. Ibid., 270.

33. David Whitmer, in a 9 December 1886 letter to Joseph Smith III, wrote: "I will tell you of a revelation received through Joseph at Kirtland, which was the cause of me leaving Kirtland to come to Missouri. It was received in the presence of Hyrum Smith, Sydney Rigdon, Frederick G. Williams, and others. It was not printed, as many others were never printed; so I give you part of it from memory." The essence of that prophecy, as recalled by Whitmer, was: "That my servant Sydney must go sooner or later to Pittsburg; that I, Joseph, must remain here in Kirtland, for this is my appointed place; and the brethren must not keep my servant David here any longer, for he is needed in Missouri, for that is his appointed place" (in *Saints' Herald*, 5 Feb. 1887).

34. This property was located at the west end of present Parley Street.

35. *Times and Seasons*, 2 Aug. 1841. The "lower stone house" was engulfed by the Mississippi after the Keokuk Dam was built in 1913 (see Richard N. Holzapfel and T. Jeffery Cottle, *Old Mormon Nauvoo–1839-1846* [Provo, UT: Grandin Book Co., 1990], 134-35).

36. The census lists Sidney and Phebe and eight children: Nancy, Sarah, Eliza, Algernon Sidney, John Wickliffe, Lacy Ann, Phebe D., and Hortense Antoinette. Phebe was then pregnant with her twelfth child who would be named Ephraim Robinson Marks Rigdon. Also listed in the first ward are George W. and Athalia Robinson and their children Sidney R., Ephraim G., and Sophia (Lyman De Platt, *Nauvoo–Early Mormon Records*, 1:21-22, LDS Family History Library, Salt Lake City).

37. James Kimball, to whom I am indebted for my understanding of Rigdon's Nauvoo residences, speculated that the Rigdons and Robinsons vacated the lower stone house in May or June 1841. Hiram Kimball was a partner with George W. Robinson in the Nauvoo Foundry (see *Wasp*, 13 Aug. 1842).

The extant Rigdon home in Nauvoo, on the east side of Main between Water and Sidney streets (south half of lot 2, block 147), was purchased from Joseph and Emma Smith by George W. Robinson on 5 August 1841 (recorded 30 Oct. 1841, Hancock County Records, Deed Book I, 514). The Rigdons likely moved here in November 1842 when Willard Richards moved into their former quarters in the Hiram Kimball house.

The 1842 tax tabulations (made about November) show a $300 real property listing for the south half of lot 2 of block 147, indicating a house was there. Other items on Rigdon's 1842 tax inventory include $7 for cattle and $52 for other personal property.

38. *Speech of Elder Orson Hyde, Delivered Before the High Priest's Quorum in Nauvoo, April 27th, 1845* (City of Joseph, IL: John Taylor, 1845), 6-7.

39. *Times and Seasons* 5 (15 Sept. 1844): 654.

40. The editor of the *Times and Seasons* wrote of him: "Professor Rigdon is too well known to require any commendatory article to introduce him to public consideration, and popular favor. He has long been regarded, by both enemies and friends, as an accomplished Belles Letters scholar, and eloquent orator,—deeply learned in that department of collegiate education which has been assigned to him in the university" (*Times and Seasons* 2 [15 Dec. 1841]: 631).

41. The "Act to Incorporate the Nauvoo Agricultural and Manufacturing Association in the County of Hancock," signed by Governor Thomas Carlin on 27 February 1841, is cited in *History of the Church*, 4:303-305.

In a 20 June 1843 *Nauvoo Neighbor* letter Rigdon discussed the affairs of the association: The first great object of the company was to establish a pottery for the manufacturing of the various kinds of crockery in common use in the country. After clay and other resources were located, land was purchased and a stone building was put under construction. The building was nearly up one story when work stopped because of electioneering intrigue that "if certain persons were elected, all the charters granted by a previous Legislature to the citizens of Nauvoo would be repealed." Proven to be the case, this clique paralized the exertions of the company; many who were about to contribute to the funds of the society paused, not knowing what was best; and in consequence the work stopped (*History of the Church*, 5:436-38).

42. Veritas to James G. Bennett in 19 Feb. 1842, *New York Herald*, described Rigdon as

five feet, nine and a half inches high, weighing one hundred and sixty-five pounds—his former weight, until reduced by sickness, produced by the Missouri persecution, was two hundred and twelve pounds. He is a mighty man in Israel of varied learning, and extensive and laborious research. There is no divine in the west more deeply learned in biblical literature, and the history of the world, than he; an eloquent orator, chaste in his language, and conclusive in his reasoning; any city would be proud of such a man. By his proclamation, thousands on thousands have heard the glad tidings and obeyed the word of God; but he is now in the "sear and yellow leaf," and his silvery locks fast pining for the grave (*Latter-day Saints' Millennial Star* 3 [May 1842]: 8-9).

43. *History of the Church*, 4:327-29.

44. *Times and Seasons* 2 (15 Apr. 1841): 381-82.

45. *History of the Church*, 4:329.

46. Ibid., 341.

47. *Times and Seasons* 2 (15 Apr. 1841): 387.

48. Journal History, 11 Apr. 1841—a multi-volume daily history of the church compiled by official church historians.

49. Journal of William Huntington, 12, Special Collections, Harold B. Lee Library, Brigham Young University, Provo, Utah. I am indebted to H. Michael Marquardt for drawing this reference to my attention.

50. *Times and Seasons* 2 (15 Apr. 1841): 383.

51. Ibid., 2 (1 May 1841): 404.

52. Jedediah M. Grant, *A Collection of Facts Relative to the Course Taken by Elder Sidney*

Rigdon, in the States of Ohio, Missouri, Illinois and Pennsylvania (Philadelphia: Brown, Bicking & Guilbert, 1844), 14.

53. Ibid., 15.

54. *Times and Seasons* 2 (1 June 1841): 431.

CHAPTER 21.

Between Family and Friends

The sound has gone, her to oppress;
Yes, Miss Rigdon now has to bear the slang,
Because she did not conform
To Joseph Smith's word of God;
But barely a youth, she for herself spoke,
And showed that she was not to be duped.
                                        —Oliver Olney[1]

F ew years in the life of Sidney Rigdon's family were more momentous than 1842. Apostasy and bankruptcy impacted the clan as did the healthy squall of newborn Ephraim Robinson Marks Rigdon, the last of Sidney's and Phebe's twelve children. Moreover, teenager Eliza, clenched in the jaws of death, miraculously revived with haunting messages from beyond the grave. None of these could compare, however, to the sensation precipitated by Joseph Smith's proposal of plural marriage to nineteen-year-old daughter Nancy.

Perhaps the greatest ambiguity in Smith's thorny persona was his proclivity to test conventions, to live on the edge of his impulses. In an 1834 letter to Oliver Cowdery the prophet wrote, "I do not, nor never have, pretended to be any other than a man 'subject to passion,' and liable, without the assisting grace of the Savior, to deviate from that perfect path in which all men are commanded to walk!"[2]

Smith's boundless appetite for life dogged him from his earliest years. He knew he was not what people expected of a prophet. His language was course, full of epithets, taunts, and braggadocio. His backwoods savoir-faire sometimes impressed visitors whom he lavished with food, wine, and tall tales, but his frequent misuse of Latin, Hebrew, and German were plainly pedantic. His relish for competition in sports, matched by his ambition in commerce and politics, was not what people expected from a divine. Nor could Smith resist the flourishes of military dress and parade, or dramatic staging of ritual and ceremony of all kinds. Embracing friends and lashing out verbally and physically at enemies, he was no Buddah. But perhaps the most scandalous manifestation of Smith's lust for manly achievement was his inclination toward extra-marital romantic liaisons, which he believed were licensed by the Old Testament and countenanced by God's modern revelation.

For example, his abrupt 1830 departure from Harmony, Pennsylvania, was attributed in part to accusations that he had dallied with a local girl. Nearly fifty years later Emma Smith's cousin Hiel Lewis still repeated stories that Joseph attempted to "seduce E[liza] W[inters]."[3] Benjamin F. Winchester, a close friend of the prophet, later recalled the charges of "licentious conduct" hurled against Smith in Kirtland, "especially among the women." He added that Smith's name was "connected with scandalous relations with two or three families."[4] Stalwart Benjamin F. Johnson noted that the uproar was "one of the Causes of Apostacy & disruption at Kirtland altho[ugh] at the time there was little Said publickly upon the subject."[5]

The name most frequently linked with Smith's in Kirtland was Fanny Ward Alger. Miss Alger, "a varry nice & Comly young woman," according to Benjamin Johnson,[6] was nineteen years old when she became the Smiths' maid in 1835. Martin Harris, one of the Three Witnesses to the Book of Mormon, recalled that the prophet's "servant girl" claimed he had made "improper proposals to her, which created quite a talk amongst the people."[7] Mormon Fanny Brewer similarly reported "much excitement against the Prophet . . . [involving] an unlawful intercourse between himself and a young orphan girl residing in his family and under his protection."[8]

Former Mormon apostle William McLellin later wrote that Emma Smith substantiated the Smith-Alger affair. According to McLellin, Emma was searching for her husband and Alger one evening when through a crack in the barn door she saw "him and Fanny in the barn together alone" on the hay mow.[9] McLellin, in a letter to one of Smith's sons, added that the ensuing confrontation between Emma and her husband grew so heated that Rigdon, Frederick G. Williams, and Oliver Cowdery had to mediate the situation. After Emma related what she had witnessed, Smith, according to McLellin, "confessed humbly, and begged forgiveness. Emma and all forgave him."[10] While Cowdery may have forgiven his cousin, he did not forget the incident. Three years later, when provoked by the prophet, Cowdery countered by calling the episode "a dirty, nasty, filthy affair."[11]

Gossip in Ohio's Western Reserve linked Smith to Athalia and Nancy Rigdon, Sidney's sixteen- and fifteen-year-old daughters. Clark Braden, prominent RLDS Mormon, later testified in court that a "bitter quarrel between Rigdon and Smith shortly before they left Kirtland was because Smith wanted to have Nancy Rigdon a girl of 16 sealed to him."[12] William C. Smith (not Joseph's brother) added that "I went to school with Athalia Rigdon, and there was talk among the boys about sealing. I think there was difficulty between Joseph Smith and Rigdon with reference to having Rigdon's daughter sealed to Smith."[13]

The Mormon newspaper of the period published a letter from editor Warren

Cowdery to quell the gossip that had traveled to Milton and Palmyra in nearby Portage County:

> Having learned from a respectable source that rumors were afloat and had gained some credence in your towns, that were derogatory to the characters of Joseph Smith Jr. and the family of Sidney Rigdon[,] we therefore deemed it our duty to say in defence of injured innocence, that we have the best of reasons for saying that the reports to which we have alluded, are without any foundation in truth. Since our acquaintance with J. Smith Jr. there has been the strongest ties of friendship existing between himself and S. Rigdon. And we hazard nothing in saying, were those reports true that must have originated in our vicinity, the bonds of friendship would have been severed forever between them. We . . . pronounce the whole a sheer fabrication.
>
> Relative to the family of Sidney Rigdon, we have to say, that it is large, consisting mostly of females, young, innocent, unsuspecting, without reproach and for ought we know, above suspicion.[14]

Smith's career, in many respects, was the equivalent of a held breath. A sense of urgency attended every aspect of his life. Early accounts of his moral ambivalence—reflections of his youthful passions or romantic liaisons—were self-interpreted as divine promptings towards enlightenment. The orthodox Mormon interpretation of early references to Smith's sexual activities is that such incidents are proof of his involvement in the heaven-sanctioned Old Testament model of polygamy. The official stance, however, is muddied by the fact that Smith never claimed to have received the sealing power of plural marriage until 3 April 1836.[15] Furthermore, the divinely mandated laws of the church, spelled out in both the Book of Mormon and Doctrine and Covenants, labeled polygamy a sin. The prophet's public denunciations of plural marriage were specific and unmistakable. During a 30 March 1842 meeting of the Female Relief Society of Nauvoo, President Emma Smith read a personal letter to the group from Joseph. The prophet warned against "iniquitous characters . . . [who] say they have authority from Joseph or the First Presidency" and advising them not to "believe any thing as coming from us, contrary to the old established morals & virtues & scriptural laws, regulating the habits, customs & conduct of society." The sisters were urged to denounce any man who made polygamous proposals and to "shun them as the flying fiery serpent, whether they are prophets, Seers, or revelators: Patriarchs, Twelve Apostles, Elders, Priests, Majors, Generals, City Councillors, Aldermen, Marshals, Police, Lord Mayors or the Devil, [they] are alike culpable & shall be damned for such evil practices."[16]

The prophet's most pointed denial of plural marriage occurred on 5 October 1843 in instructions pronounced publicly in the streets of Nauvoo. Willard Richards wrote in Smith's diary that Joseph "gave instructions to try those who were preaching, teaching, or practicing the doctrine of plurality of wives. . . . Joseph forbids it and the practice thereof. No man shall have but one wife."[17] Four months later, Joseph and brother Hyrum co-authored a letter for the 1 February 1844 *Times and Seasons* which "cut off from the Church for his iniquity" Hyrum Brown, a Mormon in Michigan, who was "preaching polygamy and other false and corrupt doctrines."

Despite the prophet's barbed attack on spiritual wifery, plural marriage, polygamy, "the blessings of Abraham, Isaac, and Jacob," the practice was the central focus of his private life. William Clayton, Smith's scribe, made that point clear when he wrote:

> During the last year of his life we were scarcely ever together, alone, but he was talking on the subject, and explaining that doctrine and principles connected with it. . . . From him I learned that the doctrine of plural and celestial marriage is the most holy and important doctrine ever revealed to man on the earth, and that without obedience to that principle no man can ever attain to the fulness of exaltation in celestial glory.[18]

A multitude of Mormon records provides irrefutable evidence for Smith's prerogative with an array of women, many of them just a few years older than his own children.[19] And while the prophet now stands astride the Mormon world like a colossus, in Nauvoo he maneuvered within the charisma of his own mystique to defy both church,[20] Nauvoo City,[21] and Illinois[22] marriage laws, as well as to conceal his behavior from his wife Emma. This equivocal deportment, secreted by a deferential and circumspect group of men and women,[23] created two cultures in Nauvoo—one where monogamy and fidelity prevailed—the other where eros and duplicity seemed to subvert the highest moral values, and where exonerating the "Lord's Anointed" became more important than telling the truth.[24]

This dichotomy left Joseph's and Emma's marriage hanging by a thread. Emma spent the last three years of her husband's life jealously battling his errant yearnings, more than once threatening to return to her family in New York.[25] On one occasion, according to Smith's private secretary, she threatened that if he continued to "indulge himself she would too."[26] Although Emma apparently countenanced two of her husband's 1843 sealings—to Emily and Eliza Partridge— she recanted within a day and demanded that Joseph give them up or "blood should flow."[27] Her change of heart came after she found Joseph and Eliza Partridge secluded in an upstairs bedroom at the Smith home. The realization that the sealing represented more than a "spiritual marriage"[28] or "adoptive ordinance"[29] devastated her.[30]

Smith used this ruse that same month, May 1843, to convince another young woman, Helen Mar Kimball, that her sealing to him would be of a "spiritual order and not a temporal one." Helen, fifteen-year-old daughter of Apostle Heber C. Kimball, reported that the prophet admonished her: "If you will take this step, it will insure your eternal salvation & exaltation and that of your father's household & all of your kindred." "This promise was so great," Helen later remembered, "that I willingly gave myself to purchase so glorious a reward."[31] Lamenting her decision, Helen confided to a close Nauvoo friend: "I would never have been sealed to Joseph had I known it was anything more than ceremony. I was young, and they deceived me, by saying the salvation of our whole family depended on it."[32]

Sidney Rigdon's family was likewise drawn into the labyrinth of spiritual wifery on 9 April 1842. At the funeral of young Ephraim R. Marks, Nancy Hyde, wife of Apostle Orson Hyde, gave nineteen-year-old Nancy Rigdon a message that Joseph wanted to talk with her at the Hyde residence. Nancy Marinda Johnson Hyde, a trusted friend of the Rigdons, was a clandestine facilitator for spiritual wifery, a role she espoused apparently to amend for her husband's 1838 apostasy. The conditions imposed on Orson Hyde to obtain his former standing, according to one account, were to relinquish his money and his wife to Joseph Smith "as a ransom for his transgression."[33]

On 2 December 1841, while Orson Hyde was absorbed in his historic mission to the Holy Land, Smith revealed a divine directive ordering church printer Ebenezer Robinson to take Nancy Hyde and her children into his home, the first floor suite of the *Times and Seasons* office on the corner of Bain and Water streets. The revelation concluded: "[L]et my handmaid Nancy Marinda Hyde hearken to the counsel of my servant Joseph in all things whatsoever he shall teach unto her, and it shall be a blessing upon her and upon her children after her, unto her justification, saith the Lord."[34] An entry four months later in the prophet's personal diary notes that Nancy was sealed to him in April 1842, one of several relationships contracted with married women during his lifetime.[35]

Evidently Hyde, although sealed to the prophet, was shared with Smith's scribe, Apostle Willard Richards, whose wife was in Massachusetts. Ebenezer Robinson wrote that in late January 1842, after his family was forced to vacate the printing office, "Willard Richards nailed down the windows, and fired off his revolver in the street after dark, and commenced living with Mrs. Nancy Marinda Hyde."[36] John C. Bennett, former member of the First Presidency, wrote of Richards "Hyde-ing" and "Mrs. Hyde and Dr. Richards" residing at the printing office "on special business."[37]

Sidney Rigdon, later commenting on Hyde's and Richard's illicit relationship, exclaimed in an 1845 letter:

> If R[ichards] should take a notion to H[yde]'s wife in his absence, all that is necessary to be done is to be sealed. No harm done, no adultery committed; only taking a little advantage of rights of priesthood. And after R[ichards] has gone the round of dissipation with H[yde]'s wife, she is afterwards turned over to S[mith] and thus the poor silly woman becomes the actual dupe to two designing men, under the sanctimonious garb of rights of the royal priesthood.[38]

In April 1842, however, the Rigdon family knew nothing of Apostle Richards's and Nancy Hyde's relationship. Thus Nancy Rigdon had no qualms about meeting Joseph Smith at the Hyde residence with Sister Hyde as chaperon. On arriving at the printing office, Willard Richards informed her that Joseph was detained elsewhere and wished her to return the following Thursday. In the meantime she discussed the situation with Francis M. Higbee, twenty-three-year-old son of Elias Higbee, who was courting her. Higbee, forewarned by John C. Bennett that Smith had confided to him a romantic interest in Nancy, cautioned her "not to place too much reliance on revelation,"[39] but did not counsel her against going.

The various accounts of Nancy's second visit to the printing office are convoluted. The general consensus, however, is that upon her arrival Smith greeted her, ushered her into a private room, then locked the door. After swearing her to secrecy, wrote George W. Robinson, Smith announced his "affection for her for several years, and wished that she should be his . . . the Lord was well pleased with this matter . . . there was no sin in it whatever . . . but, if she had any scruples of conscience about the matter, he would marry her privately."[40]

But Nancy, a "buxom and winsome" girl according to one account,[41] was not cooperative. Despite her tender age, she did not hesitate to express herself. The prophet's seductive behavior shocked her; she rebuffed him in a flurry of anger.[42] Wickliffe Rigdon wrote that Smith, flustered, beckoned Mrs. Hyde into the room to help win Nancy over. Hyde volunteered that she too was surprised upon first hearing of the tenet, but was convinced it was true, and that "great exaltation would come to those who received and embraced it."[43] Incredulous, the feisty Nancy countered that "if she ever got married she would marry a single man or none at all."[44] Grabbing her bonnet, she ordered the door opened or she would "raise the neighbors." She then stormed out of the Hyde-Richards residence.

Within a day or two Willard Richards delivered a private letter to Nancy. The prophet, as was his custom, had dictated the personal communication through his scribe. The essence of that message made an intriguing appendage to Sidney Rigdon's 9 April Ephraim Marks funeral sermon. According to observer Wilford Woodruff, President Rigdon took as his text: "When we see a principle that makes us the most Happy if we will Cultivate that principle & practice it ourselves it will render others Happy."[45] The prophet, who habitually used language as much to conceal as he did to express, began his letter to Nancy with the cheerful assertion: "Happiness is the object and design of our existence." After a brief discussion on keeping the commandments, the message cut to the chase:

> That which is wrong under one circumstance, may be, and often is, right under another. . . . Everything that God gives us is lawful and right; and it is proper that we should enjoy His gifts and blessings. . . . Blessings offered, but rejected, are no longer blessings. . . . Our Heavenly Father is more liberal in his views, and boundless in his mercies and blessings, than we are ready to believe or receive.

Citing God, Smith further declared "no good thing will I withold from them who . . . will listen to my voice and to the voice of My Servant whom I have sent; for I delight in those who seek diligently to know my precepts, and abide by the laws of my kingdom; for all things shall be made known unto them in mine own due time, and in the end they shall have joy."[46]

Although the timetable hereafter is sketchy, Nancy apparently first told her boyfriend Francis Higbee about the prophet's behavior. Higbee, who ultimately obtained the letter, spread the word through his circle of friends, including John C. Bennett, his superior officer in the Nauvoo Legion. Wickliffe Rigdon later wrote that "the story got out and it became the talk of the town that Joseph had made a proposition to Nancy to become his wife, and that she refused him."[47] The prophet himself later admitted to Samuel James, Rigdon's cousin, that "he had approached Nancy Rigdon and asked her to become his spiritual wife and she had to go and blab it[.]"[48]

Sidney and Phebe, who had given birth to Ephraim Robinson Marks Rigdon on 9 April, were incensed at the prophet's insolence. Convention dictated that women be addressed only through their fathers. Rigdon perceived he had been hoodwinked by friend Smith. J. Gibson Divine, a close associate of Rigdon in 1845, asked in a newspaper letter: "[I]s it not a system of oppression to lead a man, standing at the head of a family of interesting children, into a covenant to obey every revelation or every order coming from a certain source, asking no questions, and in a few days after one of his daughters to be demanded as a wife for a married man, and not a question to be asked by the father[?]"[49] George W. Robinson wrote that when Sidney confronted Smith at the Rigdon home, the enraged father demanded an explanation of the prophet's behavior. Smith "attempted to deny it at first," Robinson said, "and face [Nancy] down with the lie; but she told the facts with so much earnestness, and the fact of a letter being present, which he had caused to be written to her, on the same subject, the day after the attempt made on her virtue," that ultimately "he could not withstand the testimony; he then and there acknowledged that every word of Miss Rigdon's testimony was true."[50]

Wickliffe Rigdon, twelve years old at the time, later remembered additional details. He recalled that "Smith came to Rigdon[']s house and mentioned the subject and attempted to deny it[.]" Nancy was one of those "excitable women," he added, and when she heard the prophet's denials from an adjacent room, she stormed into the parlor and said, "Joseph Smith you are telling that which is not true[.] you did make such a proposition to me and you know it." Another unnamed person said, "Nancy are you not afraid to call the Lord[']s anointed a cursed liar[?]" "No," the strong-willed girl replied, "I am not for he does lie and he knows it."[51]

Robinson wrote that Smith, after acknowledging his proposition, sought a way out of the crisis by claiming he had approached Nancy "to ascertain whether she was virtuous or not, and took that course to learn the facts!"[52] But Sidney found that rationalization feeble. Convinced of Smith's involvement in the "spiritual wife business," as Sidney later termed it,[53] Rigdon concluded that Smith had "contracted a whoring spirit."[54] This is why, according to Wickliffe, Rigdon told family members immediately after the prophet left their home that Smith "could never be sealed to one of his daughters with his consent as he did not believe in the doctrine."[55]

Still unwell in the spring of 1842, Sidney was caught in a double bind over the situation.[56] On the one hand he was obligated to defend his daughter's honor, on the other he wished to avoid trouble. Wickliffe wrote that after the private confrontation with the Rigdon family, a "bad feeling exist[ed] between Joseph Smith and Sidney Rigdon they did not often meet although they lived within a few rods of each other they did not seem to be on Verry friendly terms."[57]

By late April gossip about the prophet and Nancy, and perhaps others, began causing problems in the Smith household. Smith's account of 29 April notes "a conspiracy against the peace of my household was made manifest, and it gave me some trouble to counteract the design of certain base individuals, and restore peace."[58] Two weeks later Joseph dictated a letter to Sidney "concerning certain difficulties, or surmises which existed."[59] The following day his neighbor responded by letter. Although the contents of those letters are not known,[60] that evening the prophet and Willard Richards walked next door to the Rigdon home and, according to Smith's account, "had a private interview with Prest[.] Rigdon with much apparent satisfaction to all parties[,] concerning certain evil reports put in circulation by F[rancis] M. [Higbee] about Prest[.] Rigdon[']s family & others."[61]

Meanwhile Rigdon focused his energies on an unsuccessful bid for the Illinois state senate, a race he lost to Jacob C. Davis. The 14 June 1842 *Wasp* contains a letter to the Hancock County citizenry announcing Rigdon's candidacy. "Fellow-citizens," began the formal declaration,

> should you honor me with your suffrage, at the election in August next, and I should be the object of your choice, in the Senate chamber, I will be yourselves as nearly as I can. Your interest shall be my interest, and your will the rule of my action. As far as my abilities will admit, I will look closely to the interest of every part of the county, without partiality, or sectional feelings, in the smallest degree. These are the pledges, and the only ones, which I make, or am willing to make.

Ten days later, during the "Celebration of St. John's," a ritual of the Nauvoo Masonic Lodge into which Rigdon had recently been initiated,[62] he was the featured speaker before an estimated crowd of 6,000 and apparently delivered a political oration.

To all appearances, the imbroglio involving Rigdon and Smith seemed settled for awhile. But on 28 June, Smith again visited the Rigdon home. The official Mormon account of the incident, written by Willard Richards, states that although "much unpleasant feeling was manifested by Elder Rigdon's family . . . [they] were confounded and put to silence by the truth."[63] Three days later Rigdon wrote to Smith, suggesting a private meeting. "I write this in the greatest confidence to yourself and for your own eye and no other," wrote Sidney. "I am your friend and not your enemy as I am afraid you suppose. I want you to take your horse and carriage on tomorrow and take a ride with me out to the Prairie." Stressing secrecy, Rigdon added: "Say not a word to any person living but to Hiram only. [A]nd no man shall know it from me."[64]

Apparently, during their rendezvous Rigdon asked the prophet to stop slandering his family. According to Robinson, Smith agreed to "take back what was said."[65] But during his 3 July Sunday sermon Smith instead denounced both Rigdon and Robinson by name, saying that "any man that would suffer [John C.] Bennett to come into their houses, was just as bad as he."[66] Robinson, fearing for his safety, moved to La Harpe in the adjoining county of McDonough. Rigdon apparently intended to denounce Joseph in writing as soon as his health allowed. As time passed, however, Rigdon's course remained conservative. When inquiries came, he attempted to allay the prevalent excitement, evading direct answers insofar as possible.

Despite Rigdon's reluctance to expose Smith's involvement in spiritual wifery, John C. Bennett kicked open the prophet's bedroom door, exposing his foibles publicly. In orthodox Mormon circles, Bennett was a scabby opportunist who tried to camouflage his own sexual adventures. Yet much of what Bennett wrote about Mormonism's inner circles was factual. As a member of the First Presidency, he was clearly in a privileged position to witness much of Joseph's personal behavior. Bennett, like Willard Richards, Brigham Young, Heber C. Kimball, and others early in 1842, may have been taking spiritual wives with the prophet's permission as well.[67] William Law, also a member of the First Presidency (1841-44), wrote in 1871, though unaware in 1842 of Smith's involvement in spiritual wifery, "I believe now that John C. Bennett did know it, for he at the time was more in the secret confidence of Joseph than perhaps any other man in the city."[68] And Oliver Olney, prominent observer of the Nauvoo scene, confirmed in his 16 June 1842 diary entry that Smith and Bennett had "moved together in all their windings. If Bennett had not moved ahead so fast all would have been well now."

From May through August 1842, the Nauvoo High Council—the governing ecclesiastical body over local church matters—tried to ascertain the truth of the spiritual wifery controversy. Mormon Catherine Fuller Warren, responding to charges of "unchaste and unvirtuous conduct with John C. Bennett," admitted the actions during her 20 May testimony. She also confessed to intercourse with others, including Joseph Smith's younger brother, Apostle William Smith, rationalizing that the men had "taught the doctrine that it was right to have free intercourse with women and that the heads of the church also taught and practised it which things caused her to be led away thinking it to be right."[69]

William Smith's atonement for spiritual wifery was to serve a mission to Pennsylvania. John Bennett became the designated scapegoat for sexual misadventures, according to George W. Robinson, because of "the affair with Miss Rigdon." Smith had "suspicions that Bennett had cautioned her on the matter and he was further afraid that [he] would make disclosures of other matters."[70] As part of the campaign to smear Bennett, who was then mayor of Nauvoo, the prophet and others named both Sarah Pratt (wife of apostle Orson Pratt)[71] and Nancy Rigdon as Bennett's lovers.

A Mormon newspaper, *The Wasp*, printed on 20 July a petition signed by prominent Nauvoo citizens affirming Joseph Smith's "high moral character." Orson Pratt, Sidney Rigdon, and George W. Robinson refused to sign it, infuriating Smith. Addressing the Saints on 25 August, he admonished them to "support the character of the Prophet, the Lord's anointed." Lashing out at Pratt, Rigdon, and Robinson, he boasted, "I can kick them off my heels, as many as you can name."[72]

The bedeviling paradox for many regarding the Nancy Rigdon incident is that while Smith's fame as a prophet of God makes the charges against him hard to believe, her steadfast reputation makes them difficult to dismiss.[73] Corroborative evidence exists in the accounts of at least three other Nauvoo women who similarly rejected the prophet's advances that spring of 1842. Sarah M. Kimball, wife of a prominent non-Mormon, told Smith merely to "teach it to someone else" when he approached her with his new ideas.[74] Sarah Pratt and Martha Brotherton, however, were not intimidated by prophetic aura and went public with their tales of attempted exploitation. Their grievances were not taken seriously within the male-dominated Mormon society. Smith, Brigham Young, and others were deeply esteemed by the community and had at their disposal a number of adherents who would corroborate in their defense as proof of religious faith.

Inevitably, Nancy Rigdon, Sarah Pratt, and Martha Brotherton saw their reputations impugned by an avalanche of slander.[75] The prophet labeled Sarah Pratt a "[whore] from her mother's breast."[76] Martha Brotherton was branded a "mean harlot,"[77] while Nancy was tagged a "poor miserable girl out of the very slough of prostitution."[78] Despite the drama of these events, neither Rigdon, Pratt, nor Brotherton stood to gain from exposing the prophet's prurience; none had obvious political motives to hurt him. Furthermore, documentation from orthodox Mormon sources provides evidence of the prophet's passion for women. In 1843, for example, he was sealed to at least nine Nauvoo women.[79] The frenzied tempo of his life in 1843 may have merely reflected his need for new passion and challenges. In a 14 May 1843 sermon he declared, "Excitement has almost become the essence of my life. When that dies away, I feel almost lost."[80]

Another possibility is that Smith privately feared the predictions of a contemporary adventist prophet, William Miller, who predicted that the "apocalyptic moment," the end of the world, was to come in his own age, "about the year 1843."[81] It may be significant that Smith took no more plural wives after November 1843 after seeing that Miller's predictions had failed.

In the midst of that tumultuous summer of 1842 a stressed and emaciated Sidney Rigdon, during Sunday services on 21 August, addressed those gathered in the grove near the temple. He was "not upon the stand to renounce his faith in Mormonism," he began, but "to bear his testimony of its truth, and add another to the many miraculous evidences of the power of God." He then unfolded "a scene of deep interest which had occurred in his own family." Although he had witnessed many instances of the power of God in his life, "never before had he seen the dead raised." His sixteen-year-old daughter Eliza, critically ill with typhoid pneumonia, after being declared dead by the attending physician, "rose up in the bed and spoke in a very powerful tone." Rigdon related that she told of a message from the Lord, after which she would return to his presence. She summoned the family around her and bade them farewell, with "a composure and calmness that defies all description."

At the time of her death she had expressed a "great unwillingness to die," but after her return "she expressed equally as strong a desire to go back." Addressing her older sister Nancy she said, "[I]t is in your heart to deny this work, and if you do, the Lord says it will be the damnation of your soul." After delivering other messages for each of her sisters, "she swooned, but recovered again." Sidney explained that during this episode "she was as cold as when laid in the grave, and all the appearance of life was the power of speech." She remained this way for thirty-six hours then called her father to her bedside. Whispering in Rigdon's ear she said that the Lord had revealed that because he had "dedicated her to God, and prayed to him for her, that he would give her back again." She then admonished him to "dry up his tears," go to bed and rest, "for in the morning she should be getting better, and should get well," a promise that proved true.

Rigdon then commented on the "many idle tales and reports abroad concerning him," saying that, rumors to the contrary, he had not denied the faith. Neither had he labeled Joseph Smith "a fallen prophet." He closed his testimony by declaring that "he had no controversy with the world, having an incontrovertible evidence, that through the obedience to the ordinances of the religion he now believes, the Lord had actually given back his daughter from the dead."[82]

Hyrum Smith, the peacemaker in Joseph's family, was elated at Rigdon's dedication. In his address Hyrum "cited Elder Rigdon's mind back to the revelation concerning him, that if he would move into the midst of the city and defend the truth, he should be healed . . . and showed that what Elder Rigdon felt in regard to the improvement in his health was a fulfilment of the revelation." He further told Rigdon that "inasmuch as he had seen the mercy of the Lord, exerted in his behalf, it was his duty to arise and stand in defence of the truth and innocence."[83] Six days later, the 27 August *Wasp* contained an engaging letter to the editor from Rigdon. "I am fully authorized by my daughter, Nancy," began the communication,

> to say to the public through the medium of your paper, that the letter which has appeared in the Sangamo Journal, making part of General Bennett's letters to said paper, purporting to have been written by Mr. Joseph Smith to her, was unauthorized by her, and that she never said to Gen. Bennett or any other person that said letter was written by said Mr. Smith, nor in his hand writing, but by another person, and in another person's handwriting.

Failing to mention that the "other person" was the prophet's scribe Willard Richards, Rigdon also stated that Nancy had not given Bennett permission to "use her name in the public papers," classifying that as "a flagrant violation of the rules of gallantry." In a postscript Rigdon further added that "Mr. Smith denied to me the authorship of that letter."[84] The newspaper's editor, commenting that Rigdon's explanation was unsatisfactory, wrote that the *Sangamo Journal* had not concluded that Smith wrote the letter. "Nevertheless," the editor added, "it was written to accomplish his purposes."

Despite Rigdon's efforts to calm troubled waters, Nancy continued to suffer abuse from those around her. Stephen Markham, for example, a close friend of Smith, certified in the 31 August 1842 *Wasp* that he had witnessed Nancy early on in a compromising situation with John Bennett. Markham claimed "many vulgar, unbecoming and indecent sayings and motions" passed between them and testified that he was convinced they were "guilty of unlawful and illicit intercourse with each other." George W. Robinson, on Nancy's behalf, issued a sworn statement on 3 September 1842 that Markham had lied. Explaining that he was present on the occasion Markham referred to, he pointed out that Nancy was sick and that "Dr. John C. Bennett was the attending physician." Sidney Rigdon also swore out a refutation of Markham's story and employed an attorney to sue him.

Other Rigdon family friends rushed to defend Nancy's reputation. Oliver Olney testified in an 18 September 1842 letter to the *Sangamo Journal* (published 7 October) that "every person knows . . . that Stephen Markham's affidavit was for the express purpose and design of helping the elders . . . to refute the statements of Bennett." In Nancy's defense he added: "I have been personally acquainted with Miss Nancy Rigdon from her infancy to the present time, and a more virtuous lady I believe never lived. I do not believe that any act in her life could give the least suspicion to the most designing, and eager of mischief makers."[85] Olney's brother John, in a 14 September 1842 letter to the *Sangamo Journal*, announced his withdrawal from the church because "polygamy, lasciviousness, and adultery, are practised by some of its leaders." He added, "I have heard the circumstances of Smith's attack upon Miss Rigdon, from the family as well as herself; and knowing her to be a young lady who sustains a good moral character, and also of undoubted veracity, I must place implicit confidence in her statement."

Joseph H. Jackson added that: "When, as happens in the cases of Miss Martha Brotherton and Miss Nancy Rigdon, [the prophet's] overtures were rejected[,] with disdain and exposure [he] threatened he would set a hundred hell hounds on them, to destroy their reputations."[86] Significantly in the 3 September *Wasp* a small notation read: "We are authorized to say, by Gen. Joseph Smith, that the affidavit of Stephen Markham, relative to Miss Nancy Rigdon, as published in the handbill of affidavits, was unauthorized by him: the certificate of Elder Rigdon relative to the letter being satisfactory."

To the church's advantage, Bennett dramatically overstated his case in white-washing his own behavior, making it possible to discredit him in the eyes of the Saints and effectively equating his name with licentiousness and betrayal. A *Wasp* extra published on 27 July 1842 declared him "a spoiler of character and virtue, and a living pestilence, wailing in darkness to fester in his own infamy." A special pamphlet, *Affidavits and Certificates Disproving the Statements and Affidavits Contained in John C. Bennett's Letters*, denounced him for seduction, pandering, buggery, and abortion. But Bennett, like George W. Robinson, was sorely underestimated. Both men became formidable opponents and would play principal, although relatively unknown, roles in events culminating in Joseph Smith's 1844 imprisonment and subsequent murder.

Notes

Unless otherwise stated, all primary sources cited are located in the Historical Department of the Church of Jesus Christ of Latter-day Saints, Salt Lake City, Utah.

1. Oliver H. Olney, *The Absurdities of Mormonism Portrayed* (Hancock County, IL: by the author, 1843), 16.

2. *Latter Day Saints' Messenger and Advocate* (Kirtland, OH) 1 (Nov. 1834): 40.

3. Linda King Newell and Valeen Tippetts Avery, *Mormon Enigma: Emma Hale Smith* (Garden City, NY: Doubleday & Co., 1984), 64.

4. Benjamin F. Winchester, "Primitive Mormonism—Personal Narrative of It," *Salt Lake Tribune*, 22 Sept. 1889.

5. Dean R. Zimmerman, *I Knew the Prophets: An Analysis of the Letter of Benjamin F. Johnson to George F. Gibbs, Reporting Doctrinal Views of Joseph Smith and Brigham Young* (Bountiful, UT: Horizon, 1976), 39.

6. Ibid., 38.

7. A. Metcalf, *Ten Years Before the Mast* (N.p.: n.p., n.d.), 72.

8. Max H. Parkin, "The Nature and Causes of Internal and External Conflict of the Mormons in Ohio Between 1830 and 1838," M.A. thesis, Brigham Young University, 1966, 174.

9. McLellin to Joseph Smith III, 8 July-Sept. 1872, archives, Reorganized Church of Jesus Christ of Latter Day Saints, Independence, Missouri (hereafter RLDS archives). Also see McLellin's account of this liaison in the 6 Oct. 1875 *Salt Lake Tribune.*

10. McLellin to Joseph Smith III, 8 July-Sept. 1872.

11. Oliver Cowdery to Warren Cowdery, 21 Jan. 1838, original in Huntington Library, San Marino, California; copy in Oliver Cowdery Collection.

12. *The Braden and Kelley Debate* (Saint Louis, MO: Christian Publishing, ca. 1884), 202. In 1884 Nancy Rigdon was asked in an interview by RLDS Elder E. L. Kelley to respond to the rumor that she was sealed to Joseph Smith in Kirtland. "It is absolutely false," she responded. "I never heard of such a thing while in Kirtland as sealing" (14 May 1884 interview with Elders William H. and E. L. Kelley, cited in Joseph Smith III and Heman C. Smith, *The History of the Reorganized Church of Jesus Christ of Latter Day Saints,* 4 vols. [Independence, MO: Herald House, 1967 reprint], 4:452-53).

13. *The Braden and Kelley Debate,* 391.

14. *Latter Day Saints' Messenger and Advocate* (Kirtland, OH) 3 (Sept. 1837): 566.

15. The first polygamous marriage in Mormonism solemnized by a third party was not performed until Joseph Smith was "sealed" to plural wife Louisa Beaman by Joseph Bates Noble on 6 April 1841. Apostle Erastus Snow spoke in 1883 of "his first wife's sister: Louisa Beeman [sic], being the first Morm[o]n that entered Plural Marr[ia]ge in this last dispensation, Br[other] Nobles officiating in a grove Near Main Street in the City of Nauvoo. The Prophet Joseph dictating the ceremony and Br[other] Nobles repeating it after him" (Andrew Karl Larson and Katharine Miles Larson, eds., *Diary of Charles Lowell Walker,* 2 vols. [Logan, UT: Utah State University Press, 1980], 2:610).

Erastus's wife, Artimesia Beaman Snow, added elsewhere: "My sister, Louisa Beman, next older than myself, was the first woman given in plural marriage" (Andrew Karl Larson, *Erastus Snow: The Life of a Missionary and Pioneer for the Early Mormon Church* [Salt Lake City: University of Utah Press, 1971], 747).

For extensive treatments of Mormon plural marriage, see Daniel W. Bachman, "A Study of the Mormon Practice of Plural Marriage Before the Death of Joseph," M.A. thesis, Purdue University, 1975; Lawrence Foster, *Religion and Sexuality: Three American Communal Experiments of the Nineteenth Century* (New York: Oxford University Press, 1981); Richard S. Van Wagoner, *Mormon Polygamy: A History* (Salt Lake City: Signature Books, 1986); and B. Carmon Hardy, *Solemn Covenant: The Mormon Polygamous Passage* (Urbana: University of Illinois Press, 1993).

16. "A Record of the Organization and Proceedings of the Female Relief Society of Nauvoo," Joseph Smith Collection.

17. Scott H. Faulring, ed., *An American Prophet's Record: The Diaries and Journals of Joseph Smith* (Salt Lake City: Signature Books in association with Smith Research Associates, 1989), 417. When incorporating Smith's journal into the *History of the Church,* church leaders, under Brigham Young's direction, deleted ten key words from this significant passage and added forty-nine others so that it now reads:

Gave instructions to try those persons who were preaching, teaching, or practicing the doctrine of plurality of wives; for, according to the law, I hold the keys of this power in the last days; for there is never but one on earth at a time on whom the keys are conferred; and I have constantly said no man shall have but one wife at a time, unless the Lord directs otherwise (Joseph Smith, *History of the Church of Jesus Christ of Latter-day Saints*, B. H. Roberts, ed., 7 vols. [Salt Lake City: The Church of Jesus Christ of Latter-day Saints, 1902], 6:46; hereafter *History of the Church*).

18. Andrew Jenson, *Historical Record* 6 (July 1887): 226.

19. For a lengthy treatment of this, see Van Wagoner, 4-14.

20. Monogamy was the divinely declared law of the church throughout Joseph Smith's lifetime. This was clearly outlined to him by revelation on 9 February 1831: "Thou shalt love thy wife with all thy heart, and shall cleave unto her and none else" (D&C 42:22). A month later, another heavenly mandate declared: "[i]t is lawful that [a man] should have one wife, and they twain shall be one flesh."

A "Chapter of Rules for Marriage among the Saints," canonized by the church on 17 August 1835, read: "we believe, that one man should have one wife; and one woman, but one husband, except in the case of death, when either is at liberty to marry again." Furthermore, although a reading of the Old Testament provides ample evidence that polygamy was an acceptable lifestyle in ancient Israel, the practice is strongly denounced in several Book of Mormon passages (Jacob 1:15; 2:23-27; 3:5; Mosiah 11:2-4, 14; Ether 10:5).

21. The Nauvoo City Council, of which Smith was a member, on 17 February 1842 passed "An Ordinance Concerning Marriages" which required persons solemnizing marriages to return a record of them to the city recorder within thirty days or face a twenty-dollar fine ("Nauvoo City Council Minutes").

22. *Revised Laws of Illinois* (Vandalia: Greiner & Sherman, 1833), 198-99.

23. This secret organization was called the "Endowment Council," the "Endowment Quorum," the "Holy Order," the "Quorum of the Anointed," "Joseph Smith's Prayer Circle," or simply the "Quorum." Its primary function was to introduce a select group of men and women to instructions the prophet said would help them obtain full salvation with God. A secondary function was to "test" initiates' ability to keep a secret prior to their introduction to plural marriage. The introduction of Masonry to Mormonism in 1842 provided another vehicle for swearing adherents to secrecy. See D. Michael Quinn, "Latter-day Prayer Circles," *Brigham Young University Studies* 19 (Fall 1978): 79-105.

24. Parley P. Pratt, in speaking of the means by which church leaders should sustain Joseph Smith, advised that "we must lie to support brother Joseph, it is our duty to do so" (Sidney Rigdon in *Latter Day Saints' Messenger and Advocate* [Pittsburgh], 18 June 1845).

25. For a treatment of the personal difficulties between Joseph and Emma, see Van Wagoner, 47-59.

26. William Clayton Diary, 23 June 1843, cited in George D. Smith, ed., *An Intimate Chronicle: The Journals of William Clayton* (Salt Lake City: Signature Books in association with Smith Research Associates, 1991), 108. Emma's threat to "be revenged and indulge herself" may have been merely a warning to the prophet to give up his spiritual wives. But Joseph H. Jackson, a non-Mormon opportunist who gained the confidence of the prophet in Nauvoo, recorded in an 1844 expose of Mormonism: "Emma wanted [William] Law for a spiritual husband," and because Joseph "had so many spiritual wives, she thought it but fair that she would at least have one man spiritually sealed up to her and that she wanted

Law, because he was such a 'sweet little man'" (Joseph H. Jackson, *A Narrative of the Adventures and Experiences of Joseph H. Jackson in Nauvoo: Disclosing the Depths of Mormon Villiany Practiced in Nauvoo* [Warsaw, IL: n.p., 1844], 20).

Although there is nothing to suggest that Law and Emma were more to each other than friends, Law later confirmed that Joseph "offered to furnish his wife Emma with a substitute for him, by way of compensation for his neglect of her, on condition that she would forever stop her opposition to polygamy and permit him to enjoy his young wives in peace and keep some of them in his house and to be well treated etc." ("The Mormons in Nauvoo—Three Letters from William Law on Mormonism," *Salt Lake Tribune*, 3 July 1887).

27. E[mily]. D. P. Young, "Incidents in the Life of a Mormon Girl." In a ploy to appease his wife's fury, William Clayton wrote, the prophet told Emma "he would relinquish all [others] for her sake." He nevertheless told Clayton privately, who recorded it immediately in his diary, that "he should not relinquish anything" (Clayton diary, 16 Aug. 1843, cited in Smith, 117).

28. Spiritual wifery was a Swedenborgian concept whereby people who could not be lawfully united in this world might be enjoined in the afterlife. It was not expected that the union in question would be anything more than a spiritual connection; the notion that it should be consummated was especially disclaimed by Swedenborgians. Although "spiritual wifery" in Mormon usage much later came to be equated with promiscuous intercourse or "free love," this was not the contemporary Nauvoo meaning. "Polygamy," "spiritual wifery," "spiritual marriage," and "plural marriage" were all apparently interchangeable terms in Mormon and non-Mormon contexts during the early 1840s. Emily Dow Partridge, a plural wife to both Smith and later to Brigham Young, uses "spiritual wife" as a reference to herself and others: "Spiritual wives, as we were then termed, were not very numerous in those days and a spiritual baby was a rarity indeed" (Emily D. P. Young, "Autobiographical Sketch," 72).

Helen Mar Kimball Whitney, another of Smith's plural wives, added that in Nauvoo "spiritual wife was the title by which every woman who entered into this order [plural marriage] was called" (Whitney, 15). Heber C. Kimball, of the First Presidency in 1855, utilized that term in chiding the Saints for opposing the "spiritual wife doctrine the Patriarchal Order, which is of God" (*Journal of Discourses*, 26 vols. [London: Latter-day Saints' Book Depot, 1854-86], 3 [6 Oct. 1855]: 125; hereafter as *Journal of Discourses*).

Joseph H. Jackson, for a brief period a close friend and confidante of Joseph Smith, added that "a spiritual wife is a woman, who by revelation is bound up to a man, in body, parts and passions, both for this life and for all eternity, whereas the union of a carnal wife and her husband ceases at death" (Jackson, 12-13).

29. The "Law of Adoption," a Mormon adaptation of "Adoptive Freemasonry," allowed Mormon men, women, or entire families to be adopted into the eternal family of a prominent church leader. For a treatment of "Adoptive Masonry," see Albert G. Mackey, *An Encyclopaedia of Freemasonry and its Kindred Sciences: Comprising the Whole Range of Arts, Sciences and Literature as Connected with the Institution* (Philadelphia: L. H. Everts & Co., 1887), 27-28. For a treatment of the Mormon "Law of Adoption," see Marvin S. Hill, *Quest for Refuge: The Mormon Flight from American Pluralism* (Salt Lake City: Signature Books, 1989), 113-14.

30. This 22 May 1843 encounter is described in William Clayton's journal entry for 23 May (see Smith, 105-106). In addition, Emma also learned that the Partridge sisters had actually been sealed to the prophet two months earlier. The second ceremony, according to Emily, was merely effected "to save family trouble" (Young, "Incidents in the Life of a Mormon Girl," 185). In 1846, two years after Joseph's death, Emma Smith, in a conversation with Joseph W. Coolidge, family friend and administrator of the prophet's estate, remarked that "Joseph had abandoned plurality of wives before his death." Coolidge indicated that from personal experience he knew otherwise. After a heated exchange Emma retorted with exasperation, "Then he was worthy of the death he died" (Joseph F. Smith diary, 28 Aug. 1870).

31. Helen Mar Kimball, "Helen Mar Kimball's Retrospection About Her Introduction to the Doctrine and Practices of Plural Marriage in Nauvoo at Age 15" (a sealed letter to be opened after her death).

32. Catherine Lewis, *Narrative of Some of the Proceedings of the Mormons* (Lynn, MA: n.p., 1848), 19.

33. William Hall, *The Abominations of Mormonism Exposed, containing many facts and doctrines concerning that singular people, during seven years membership with them; from 1840 to 1847* (Cincinnati: I. Hart, 1852), 22.

34. *History of the Church*, 4:467.

35. Faulring, 396.

36. Ebenezer Robinson, *The Return* (Davis City, IA) 2 (Oct. 1890): 347.

37. John C. Bennett, *The History of the Saints: Or an Expose of Joe Smith and Mormonism* (Boston: Leland and Whiting, 1842), 241.

38. Cited in Rigdon's letter "TO THE SISTERS OF THE CHURCH OF JESUS CHRIST OF LATTER DAY SAINTS," *Latter Day Saint's Messenger and Advocate* (Pittsburgh), Oct. 1845. Ann Eliza Young commented in her 1876 book that when Hyde returned from his mission "it was hinted to him that Smith had had [Nancy] sealed to himself in his absence, as a wife for eternity . . . that [Nancy] was his wife only for time" (Ann Eliza Young, *Wife Number 19; or, The Story of a Life in Bondage, Being a Complete Expose of Mormonism, and Revealing the Sorrows, Sacrifices and Sufferings of Women in Polygamy* [Hartford: Dustin, Gilman, 1876], 324-26).

Orson and Nancy Hyde continued to live together for a short time after arriving in the Salt Lake Valley, but after Brigham Young twitted Hyde with the intimacy between Joseph Smith and his wife, Orson separated from her. The couple divorced in 1870 (Quinn, "Latter-day Prayer Circles," 79-105).

39. Bennett, 245.

40. George W. Robinson to James Arlington Bennett, 27 July 1842, cited in Bennett, 245-47.

41. This description is from William H. Whitsett, "Sidney Rigdon—The Real Founder of Mormonism," 1885, 1233, Special Collections, J. Willard Marriott Library, University of Utah, Salt Lake City; hereafter Special Collections, U of U. John C. Bennett described Nancy as a "beautiful girl, of irreproachable fame, great moral excellence, and superior intellectual endowments" (Bennett, 241). Jessie Rigdon Secord wrote that even in her old age, Nancy Rigdon Ellis was "more than good looking, she was as beautiful as a Greek statue" (Secord to Arlene Hess, 19 May 1967, Hess Collection, Special Collections, Harold

B. Lee Library, Brigham Young University, Provo, Utah; hereafter Special Collections, BYU).

42. During an 1884 interview, when asked whether she had ever been sealed to Joseph Smith, Nancy Rigdon Ellis said no. Asked whether she understood sealing to mean "marriage and did it contemplate living together as husband and wife?" she replied, "I never so understood it." As an explanation for Joseph Smith's behavior she then added that "she thought Joseph Smith . . . quite a different man in spirit and manner the last year or two [of his life] than . . . from 1831 to 1842. . . . He seemed entirely different, but I never knew or even heard that he had more than one wife" (14 May 1884 interview with Elders William H. and E. L. Kelley, cited in Smith and Smith, 4:452-53).

43. J. Wickliffe Rigdon, "Life Story of Sidney Rigdon," 164. Wickliffe left at least two other accounts of the "Nancy Rigdon incident." He gave a lengthy interview which was printed in the 20 May 1900 *Salt Lake Tribune*. His 28 July 1905 statement, made while he was living in Salt Lake City, is in the LDS historical archives. In addition to the retrospective statements made by Wickliffe Rigdon, as well as the John C. Bennett and George W. Robinson accounts in Bennett's book, Oliver Olney, a close family friend of the Rigdons, wrote a contemporary account published in 1843. Olney's sketch noted:

> Nancy Rigdon had repeated calls to visit Nancy Hyde. When she did make a visit, Smith was there and "told her that he had the word of God for her, that God had given her to him for a wife." Miss Rigdon said to him, "you have a wife." "Well," said he, "you know the ancient order was, one man had many wives, that is again to be." Miss Rigdon was obstinate. He then got Mrs. H[y]de to come in, and made use of her persuasive arguments, that she was first unbelieving in the order, but had been better informed; although she had long been acquainted with M[iss] Rigdon, but her many arguments were of no account. Mr. Smith again used his influence by more rash means, that Miss Rigdon threatened to call for help, that he let her go, but soon a letter was conveyed to her, written by some one of the clan, that argued the doctrine of Polygamy (Olney, 16).

44. Wickliffe Rigdon, 28 July 1905 statement.

45. Scott G. Kenney, ed., *Wilford Woodruff's Journal–Typescript*, 9 vols. (Midvale, UT: Signature Books, 1983), 2:168.

46. *History of the Church*, 5:134-36. After showing the letter to her parents, Nancy then gave it to her suitor, Francis Higbee. Higbee passed it on to John C. Bennett who published it in his book. According to the Historian's Office Journal, on 6 November 1855, Thomas Bullock, a clerk in the Historian's Office, inserted the Nancy Rigdon letter into the history of the church then being prepared. Bullock incorrectly dated the letter 27 August 1842. Internal evidence shows that he used John C. Bennett's book for the copy. The letter was published in the *Deseret News*, 12 Dec. 1855.

47. Wickliffe Rigdon, 28 July 1905 statement.

48. Rigdon, "Life," 169.

49. *Latter Day Saints' Messenger and Advocate* (Pittsburgh), 15 Mar. 1845.

50. George W. Robinson to James Arlington Bennett, 27 July 1842, cited in Bennett, 246.

51. Rigdon, "Life," 166.

52. Robinson to James A. Bennett, 27 July 1842, cited in Bennett, 246. Orson Hyde later used this same justification in a venomous attack on the Rigdon family, particularly Nancy. "During my absence to Palestine," stated Hyde during an 1845 speech to the Nauvoo High Priest Quorum:

> the conduct of [Nancy Rigdon] became so notorious in this city, according to common rumor, she was regarded generally, little if any better than a public prostitute. Joseph Smith knowing the conduct she was guilty of, felt anxious to reprove and reclaim her if possible. He, accordingly, requested my wife to invite her down to her house. He wished to speak with her and show her the impropriety of being gallanted about by so many different men, many of whom were comparatively strangers to her. Her own parents could look upon it, and think that all was right; being blind to the faults of their daughter. . . . Miss Nancy, I presume, considered her dignity highly insulted at the plain and sharp reproofs she received from this servant of God. She ran home and told her father that Mr. Smith wanted her for a spiritual wife, and that he employed my wife to assist him in obtaining her. . . . Thus must an innocent and unsuspecting female suffer for putting down a hand to help, as it is verily believed, a poor miserable girl out of the very slough of prostitution (*Speech of Elder Orson Hyde, Delivered Before the High Priest's Quorum, in Nauvoo, April 27th, 1845, Upon the Course and Conduct of Mr. Sidney Rigdon, and Upon the Merits of His Claims to the Presidency of the Church of Jesus Christ of Latter-day Saints* [Liverpool: James and Woodburn, 1845], 27-28).

53. *Latter Day Saints' Messenger and Advocate* (Pittsburgh), 1 (15 Oct. 1844): 15.
54. Ibid., 1 (1 Jan. 1845): 75.
55. Rigdon, "Life," 167.
56. As far away as New York City, newspapers were reporting the rumor that in Nauvoo men and women "connected in promiscuous intercourse without regard to the holy bonds of matrimony" (see *New York Herald*, 16 May 1842).
57. Rigdon, "Life," 175.
58. *History of the Church*, 4:608.
59. Ibid., 5:6.
60. I was denied access to the original source of these references, "The Book of the Law of the Lord," which is in the custody of the First Presidency of the LDS church. This specific reference is cited in Dean C. Jessee, ed., *The Papers of Joseph Smith–Volume 2* (Salt Lake City, UT: Deseret Book Co., 1992), 2:382.
61. *History of the Church*, 5:6.
62. During the 15 March 1842 formal installation of the Nauvoo Lodge, Rigdon and Smith were made Masons at Sight, meaning they did not have to go through the usual preliminary steps for admission.
63. *History of the Church*, 5:46.
64. Rigdon to Smith, 1 July 1842, Joseph Smith Collection.
65. Robinson to John C. Bennett, 3 July 1842, cited in Bennett, 44-45.
66. Ibid. Respecting Smith's efforts to defame him, Robinson wrote: "This attack upon my character is in perfect accordance with other things which have shown themselves—that is when it is feared that a man has it in his power to make disclosures, his character is

assailed, to destroy the validity of his testimony, and save the guilty from reproach" (*Sangamo Journal*, 26 Aug. 1842).

67. An interesting example of Willard Richards taking a spiritual wife without permission or following the protocol of an officiator or third party witness is recorded in his 23 December 1845 diary. The entry reads: "[T]ook Alice L[onstrot]h by the [shorthand: "hand"] of our own free will and avow mutually [to] acknowledge each other husband & wife, in a covenant not to be broken in time or Eternity . . . as though the seal of the covenant had been placed upon us" (Willard Richards Collection).

68. T. B. H. Stenhouse, *Rocky Mountain Saints* (New York: D. Appleton, 1873), 198.

69. See Robert D. Hutchins, "Joseph Smith, III: Moderate Mormon," M.A. thesis, Brigham Young University, 1977, 33.

70. Robinson to John C. Bennett, 27 July 1842, cited in Bennett, 246-47.

71. For a more complete treatment of Sarah Pratt, see Richard S. Van Wagoner, "Sarah M. Pratt: The Shaping of an Apostate," *Dialogue: A Journal of Mormon Thought* 19 (Summer 1986): 69-99.

72. Manuscript History, 29 Aug. 1842.

73. This incongruity was discussed by Nancy Rigdon's son, S. M. Ellis, in a 17 November 1933 letter to L. J. Nuffer. "My grandfather knew of the secret conduct of the leaders of the church at that time," he wrote, "but for the welfare of the church he kept his mouth shut, the more he condemned the practice, the more bitter became the feeling against him with the result of which you know." Respecting the 1842 controversy that surrounded his mother he defended her by adding, "some one is wrong, BUT I KNOW MY MOTHER IS NOT. FOR SHE WAS THE PERSON MOST CONCERNED. . . . I would believe her, above any person living or dead. . . . SHE [WAS] NOT MISINFORMED OF THE CIRCUMSTANCES" (emphasis in original letter in Nuffer Collection).

74. On Mormon polyandry, see Van Wagoner, chap. 4.

75. Smith, after his rejection by Pratt, warned: "I hope you will not expose me, for if I suffer, all must suffer; so do not expose me . . . If you should tell, I will ruin your reputation" (Bennett, 228-31).

76. *Sangamo Journal*, 1 Aug. 1842.

77. *Wasp*, 27 Aug. 1842.

78. "Speech of Elder Orson Hyde," 27-28.

79. Van Wagoner, 35.

80. *History of the Church*, 5:389.

81. Ruth Alden Doan, *The Miller Heresy, Millennialism, and American Culture* (Philadelphia: Temple University Press, 1987), 1.

82. *Times and Seasons* 3 (15 Sept. 1842): 922. Bennett in his book gave his medical opinion of this near-death experience. He called it the "wild and incoherent sayings of Miss Eliza Rigdon, uttered during her recent severe sickness, when she was perfectly delirious,— (laboring under mental hallucination at the acme of consecutive exacerbations of high febrile and cerebral excitement, consequent upon an attack of *Pneumonia Typhoides*)" (Bennett, 340).

83. *History of the Church*, 5:123-24. The 21 Aug. 1842 source text for this *History of the Church* entry, the "Book of the Law of the Lord," shows that much of Rigdon's defense of the prophet was deleted from the published account. The original reference notes that

while Rigdon acknowledged that his daughter "had near denied the faith," he also "showed the folly of any person's attempting to overthrow or destroy Joseph Smith" (Jessee, 2:419-20).

84. Cited in *Sangamo Journal*, 16 Sept. 1842.

85. Olney added elsewhere: "I have been personally acquainted with her since she was a small child, and know that Miss Rigdon has sustained a good character at home and abroad. But what do we hear of her now, but as being of the blackest dye! Yes, she is defamed by all, both high and low, of the Latter Day Saints" (Oliver Olney, *The Absurdities of Mormonism Portrayed* [Hancock County, IL: n.p., 1843], 16).

86. Jackson, 13.

CHAPTER 22.

Dissembling the Truth

The History of Joseph Smith is now before the world, and we are satisfied that a history more correct in its details than this was never published.

—George A. Smith and Wilford Woodruff[1]

After the dust had settled over Joseph Smith's overtures to Nancy Rigdon, Smith was uncomfortable around the Rigdon family, viewing them with a keen sense of paranoia. Smith's imposing presence usually overshadowed disaffection, and the Rigdons' refusal to subordinate their interests to his angered him. He felt that his prophetic domain was compromised. Although the 1842-44 Smith-Rigdon relationship was not as acrimonious as depicted in official accounts, their mutual accommodation was an uneasy one. The unspoken truce was frequently disrupted by Smith's groundless charges that Rigdon, in league with John C. Bennett, was behind legal efforts to extradite Smith to Missouri. This apprehension was particularly evident in matters related to the Nauvoo Post Office. By 1841 Nauvoo had become the second largest city in Illinois with a population of nearly 7,000 citizens, many of them mail-hungry emigrants from Europe. The Rigdon family was kept busy and well-compensated by the large number of letters and newspapers that arrived at the office daily.

From the earliest Nauvoo settlement years, Smith was envious that George W. Robinson then Sidney Rigdon held the financially lucrative position of postmaster. In the midst of the Bennett controversy Smith initiated a campaign to attain the postmastership for himself. He may have also wanted to monitor mail from such apostates as John C. Bennett, Francis Higbee, and George W. Robinson. Because postal matters and the Rigdon family were outside of his control, Smith attempted to slander the Rigdons by asserting that the mails were regularly plundered and mishandled.

On 8 September 1842, while controversy over spiritual wifery raged, Smith dictated a letter to prominent New Yorker James A. Bennett (no relation to John C. Bennett). Read to the gathered Saints in Sunday meeting, the letter said:

> Our post office in this place is exceedingly corrupt. It is with great difficulty that we can get out letters to or from our friends. Our papers that we sent to our subscribers

are embezzled and burned, or wasted. We get no money from our subscribers . . . and I am sorry to say, that this robbing of the post office of money was carried on by John C. Bennett; and since he left here, it is carried on by the means of his confederates.[2]

Four days later Emma Smith, apparently at her husband's behest, sent a letter to Sidney Rigdon chastising him for what she saw as neglect in his postal duties. "I have noticed for some time back," the business-like letter began,

> there is not the care . . . in regard to the papers and letters belonging to Mr. Smith and the printing establishment that the nature of the case requires. . . . This is therefore to forbid your delivering either the letters or papers belonging to my husband or the printing office to any other person [other than William Clayton], untill further notice from Mr. Smith.
>
> And further, we have been credibly informed by different individuals, that persons unconnected with the Post Office are permitted, and have frequently been seen examining, over-hauling and handling both letters and papers belonging to Mr. Smith and opening and reading the papers to all which is entirely contrary to law and your obligations as Post Master; and I now enjoin upon you, to see that no such irregularity is permitted anymore; for you are aware of the consequences, and if it is continued we shall feel in duty bound to make complaint to the proper authorities, considering it absolutely and indispensably necessary for this peace and interests of the community at large, as well as my husband[']s public and private interests.[3]

Rigdon, surprised, wrote Emma the same day saying that when couriers from the printing office called at the post office for their mail, the newspapers were provided to them "in haste." If anyone was meddling with Smith's papers and mail, he replied, it was done without his knowledge. He then added that he himself received a large number of newspapers which "were the property of my family" and were intended for their personal reading.[4] Rigdon's response notwithstanding, the prophet continued accusing the Rigdon family of postal irregularities. The official *History of the Church* notes that on 8 November 1842 Smith called on Windsor P. Lyons and others "to make affidavits concerning the frauds and irregularities practiced in the post office in Nauvoo." Church leaders, at Smith's request, gathered signatures for a petition to U.S. senator Richard Young. The entreaty, according to Smith's account, urged the U.S. Postmaster General to "use his influence to have the present postmaster removed, and a new one appointed. I was recommended for the appointment."[5]

In a 26 November letter to Horace R. Hotchkiss, Smith's principal creditor, the prophet engaged in subterfuge:

> Few if any letters for me can get through the post office in this place, and more particularly letters containing money, and matters of much importance. I am satisfied that S[idney] Rigdon and others connected with him have been the means of doing incalculable injury, not only to myself, but to the citizens in general; and, sir, under such a state of things, you will have some idea of the difficulties I have to encounter,

and the censure I have to bear through the unjust conduct of that man and others, whom he permits to interfere with the post office business.[6]

In the meantime Rigdon's son-in-law, George W. Robinson, whose faith in Joseph Smith and Mormonism had been crushed by the prophet's duplicity over the Nancy Rigdon incident, went public defending Rigdon's administration of postal matters. Since the content of Nauvoo newspapers was controlled by Smith, Robinson made his case in Springfield's *Sangamo Journal*. To show "the malice which exists in the breast of Joseph Smith," Robinson sent along a 6 November 1842 letter he had received from the prophet. "Sir—I take this opportunity to give you a few items of my faith respecting yourself," began the searing communication:

> I believe you are a consummate scoundrel and that you embezzle my letters and steal my money that is sent to me by way of the post office, and that you are in *cahoots with others* in it—and I believe you are joined with thieves and robbers and are privately trying to do me all the injury you can, with some others which I shall not name now, and I give you this timely notice that I shall take every means to bring you to justice openly and boldly and publicly. P.S. I believe you are a whoremonger also, while you are crying out against others.

The prophet's letter as well as Robinson's same-day reply were published in the *Sangamo Journal* on 18 November. "Sir," he wrote, "I condescend to reply to your compliments of this morning, not however because I think you worthy of such *condensation*, but that I may perhaps through you make known my own faith concerning yourself":

> [D]o you imagine that an *idiot* could not see your *baseness* on this attempt to injure my feelings as well as my reputation? Is it not notorious that you have for nearly three years, used your power to the utmost to obtain the post office, and do not think, sir, that this attempt of which you speak, and of what you say you will do, will not be looked upon as tending to the same object? You say you will do the utmost in your power to expose me to the public. But sir, would you not first do well to remove the stigma on your own character, or employ some kind friend of yours, who can bear a scrutinizing eye without the *crimson blush of shame*? My conscience is void of offence against the laws of my country, or the insinuations of which you speak, notwithstanding your believe so's, your think so's, or your guess so's. I fear not *your* power, my dear sir; neither shall I shrink or be intimidated by you, nought of personal violence, save the assassin's steel, will harm a hair of my head, and for this I am duly prepared.
>
> With regard to my privately injuring you, I say bring forth your testimony, all I have said or done has been public, and you yourself have, or can see it, as well as others—and with regard to the balance of your calumny I have only to say, "Bah!" how can others believe that which *you yourself do not believe*? Yours with contempt.[7]

Robinson added a specific example of Smith's tactics. "In his letter to me," he began,

[Smith] does not name my associates in crime but unquestionably means Mr. Rigdon the present postmaster. Smith for a long time has tried his utmost to get the post office into his own hands, but having failed in every attempt, his last resort is to make the public believe that he has lost a monstrous amount of money and to this effect he had leveled his artillery against the *officers* of the place, hoping by that means to have them removed and himself fill the vacancy.

Despite such abuse, Rigdon not only remained in the church, he assisted Smith in evading extradition to Missouri. During the fall of 1842 and much of 1843, John C. Bennett worked openly to arrange Smith's extradition as an accessory in the attempted murder of former Missouri governor Lilburn Boggs.[8] Foremost among the prophet's defenders, Rigdon even handled much of Smith's legal correspondence.

In early October 1842 Rigdon and Elias Higbee were in Carthage, the Hancock County seat. In conversation with Judge Stephen A. Douglas, the two Mormons learned that Illinois Governor Thomas Carlin had issued a writ for Joseph Smith's arrest. Carlin thought Smith would go to Carthage to be acquitted before Judge Douglas, a known friend and associate of the prophet, but another officer of the state would be there to take custody of him. This plan was thwarted when Rigdon relayed the information to the prophet's secretary William Clayton.[9]

Rigdon also sent, on the prophet's behalf, a 17 October 1842 letter to Justin Butterfield, U.S. district attorney in Chicago, who rendered his opinion as to the "illegality of the requisition made by the Governor of Missouri upon the Governor of this State, for the surrender of Joseph Smith." Butterfield's belief was that the Illinois Supreme Court would discharge the prophet upon writ of *habeas corpus* in the case of the attempt on Governor Boggs's life, based on the fact that Smith had not fled from Missouri, nor was he in the state at the time of Boggs's shooting.[10]

A chronic complication in Rigdon's and Smith's love-hate relationship was the prophet's irrational fear that Rigdon, allied with Bennett, was out to get him. On 23 July 1842 the *Wasp*, a Nauvoo newspaper edited by William Smith, the prophet's firebrand younger brother, published a letter from Rigdon asserting: "As there seems to be some foolish notions that I have been engaged with J. C. Bennett, in the difficulties between him and some of the citizens of this place, I merely say in reply to such idle and vain reports that they are without foundation in truth."

A few weeks later further clarification was printed. On 1 September 1842 Robert D. Foster, while in New York, wrote a letter to the *Wasp* stating that Bennett, in a 31 August lecture, said he had just received a letter from Rigdon. Bennett alleged that Rigdon was "writing a book against Joseph, which would astound the world."[11] Rigdon responded angrily in the 21 September *Wasp* that Bennett's "statements are utterly false; I have never written a letter to [him] on any subject, nor received one from him, since he left Nauvoo; nor am I nor have I been writing a book on any subject. I have written to the New York Herald contradicting said report."

In early January, however, Rigdon did receive a message from Bennett. The 10 January 1843 letter, also addressed to Orson Pratt, incorrectly assumed that its recipients would sympathize with Bennett's plans to orchestrate the prophet's downfall:

> Dear Friends:—It is a long time since I have written you, and I should now much desire to see you; but I leave tonight for Missouri, to meet the messenger charged with the arrest of Joseph Smith, Hyrum Smith, Lyman Wight and others, for murder, burglary, treason, etc., etc., who will be demanded in a few days on new indictments, found by the grand Jury of a called court, on the original evidence and in relation to which a nolle prosequi was entered by the district attorney. New proceedings have been gotten up on the old charges and no habeus corpus can then save them. We shall try Smith on the Boggs case when we get him into Missouri. The war goes bravely on, and although Smith thinks he is now safe, the enemy is near, even at the door. He has awoke the wrong passenger. . . .
>
> P.S. Will Mr. Rigdon please hand this letter to Mr. Pratt after reading?[12]

After Rigdon read the letter he immediately handed it to Pratt, who then turned it over to Smith. The prophet, initially dismayed that Rigdon had given the letter first to Pratt, took the dispatch to John Taylor, editor of the *Times and Seasons*. Smith instructed Taylor to publish the letter along with a statement condemning Rigdon's actions. Taylor obediently prepared the following editorial:

> We are very sorry that our old and long esteemed friend, Mr. Rigdon, should be holding correspondence with such a notorious scoundrel as John C. Bennett; and more especially that he, of all others, should not acquaint President Joseph Smith with a circumstance of this kind, which threatened (in his opinion) to destroy him and other innocent men.
>
> Are we indeed forced from evidence to believe that Mr. Rigdon[,] who was charged with and imprisoned for the same crimes that those gentlemen mentioned in the letter ostensibly were, can countenance[,] cloak over, and virtually leave his companions in tribulation exposed to destruction, when he had it in his power to prevent it; and that he did believe that this was the case is evident from some remarks that he made to Mr Smith "that he would not take upon himself the responsibility of making it known," fearful of the consequences of exposing villainy and hiding himself under the iniquitous shade of their unhallowed protection. "How is the gold become dim? and the fine gold, how is it changed?"
>
> We are, however, happy to inform our readers that [John C. Bennett's] letter is all vain glorying and empty boast; it is a tissue of falsehoods intended to intimidate. Governor Ford informed Mr. Smith, when at Springfield, that such a requisition had been made from Missouri; but that he knew that a nolle prosequi had been entered and refused to issue a writ.[13]

Smith requested Taylor "to prefer charges against Sidney Rigdon before a court composed of twenty-four High Priests and three Bishops." When Taylor asked Smith who would testify against Rigdon, Smith said to collect what information he could, then "call upon him and Sister Emma who knew plenty to incriminate him."[14] Before Taylor could publish the editorial or initiate action against Rigdon, the prophet approached Rigdon and "charged him with being leagued with [his] enemies to destroy him." Rigdon, according to Taylor, responded: "I know it was wrong [not to give him the letter sooner]; but I darst not take upon myself the responsibility of making it known," apparently because of his position as postmaster.[15] Rigdon's explanation satisfied the prophet. When Taylor asked him if he should proceed with the trial and publish the editorial, Smith replied, "I think you had better not, we will save him if we can."[16]

Early on the morning of 11 February 1843, prior to meeting with the Nauvoo City Council where he appointed Rigdon as city attorney, newly-elected Mayor Joseph Smith decided to mend fences with his neighbor. According to his diary, he conversed with Rigdon who reportedly said that his family was "willing to be saved." "Good feelings prevailed," noted Smith, "and we have shaken hands together."[17] Wickliffe Rigdon adds interesting details: "Joseph Smith came to my fathers house a crying and wanted to shake hands with all the family and be good friends as they used to be he shook hands with all the family that was present."[18]

Despite the prophet's intent to make peace with Rigdon, behind his friend's back he still maneuvered to wrest away the postmastership. On 9 February 1843 Smith wrote Senator Richard M. Young soliciting his influence with the postmaster general to have Rigdon removed. The letter reads that the "citizens generally are suffering severely from the impositions and dishonest conduct of the postmaster and those connected with the post office in this city." Affidavits were enclosed, Smith wrote, showing "the people to be anxious for an immediate change." "It will be seen by the [accompanying] petition," added the prophet, "that I was nominated for the office. I can only say that, if I receive the appointment, I shall do my utmost to give general satisfaction."[19]

Although Rigdon was unaware of Smith's surreptitious grandstanding, he did learn of an additional petition in circulation to appoint William H. Rollison to the same post. On 13 February Rigdon showed Smith a "Copy [of a petition] to the Hon[orable] Mr. Bryant, 2[nd] Ass[istan]t [to the] P[ost] M[aster] General" supporting Rigdon and asked his friend to endorse him. That petition read:

> We, your petitioners, beg leave respectfully to submit that as an attempt is now, by certain individuals, being made to place the Post Office in this place into hands of William H. Rollison a stranger in our place, and one whose conduct since he came here, has been such as to forbid our having confidence in him, and we do hope and pray, both for our sakes, and that of the public, that he may not receive the appointment of Post Master in Nauvoo, Ill[.] but that the present Post Master may continue to hold the office.[20]

But the prophet would not help Rigdon retain his station. Near-phobic worries about John C. Bennett again preyed on his mind and on 27 March Smith dictated the following letter, quoted here in its entirety, to Rigdon:

Dear Sir:—It is with sensations of deep regret and poignant grief that I sit down to dictate a few lines to you, this morning, to let you know what my feelings are in relation to your-self, as it is again[s]t my principles to act the part of a hypocrite, or to dissemble in any wise whatever, with any man. I have tried for a long time to smother my feelings, and not let you know, that I thought, that you were secretly and underhandedly, doing all you could, to take the advantage and injure me: but, whether my feelings are right or wrong, remains for Eternity to reveal. I cannot any longer forbear throwing of[f] the mask, and let you know of the secret wranglings of my heart; that you may not be deceived, in relation to them, and [that you may] be prepared, Sir, to take whatever cou[r]se you see proper in the premises. I am Sir, honest, when I say that I believe, & am laboring under the fullest conviction that you are actually practicing deception and wickedness against me and the Church of Jesus Christ of Latter Day Saints, and that you are in connection with John C. Bennett and Geo W. Robinson in the whole of their abomin[a]ble practices, in seeking to destroy me and this people and that Jared Carter, is as deep in the mire, as you, [Sir], are in the mire, in your conspiracies and that you are in the exercise of a trait[o]rous spirit against our lives and interests, by combining with our Enemies and the murderous Missourians. My feelings, Sir, have been wrought upon to a very great extent, in relation to yourself, ever since soon after the first appearance of John C. Bennett in this place. There has been something dark & my[s]terious hovering over our business concerns that are not only palpable but altogether unaccountable in relation to the post office, and Sir from the very first of the pretentions of John C Bennet[t], to secure to me the Post Office, (which, by the bye, I have desired, if I could have justice done me in that department,) I have known, Sir, that it was a fraud practiced upon me, and of the secret plottigs & conniving between, him & yourself in relation to the matter the whole time, as well as many other things which I have kept locked up in my own bosom but I am constrained at this time, to make known my feelings to you. I do not write this with the intention of insulting you or of bearing down upon you or with a desire to take any advantage of you or with the intention of ever laying one straw in your way, detrimental to your character or influence, or to suffer anything whatever that has taken place, which is within my observation, or that [has] come to my knowledge to go abroad, betraying any confidence that has ever been placed in me but I do assure you most sincerely that what I have said I verily believe & this is the reason why I have said it, that you may know the real convictions of my heart, not because I have any malice or hatred, neither would I injure one hair of your head, and I will assure you that these convictions are attended with the deepest sorrow. I wish to God it were not so, & that I could get rid of the achings of my heart on that subject and I now notify you, that unless something should take place to restore my mind to its former confidence in you, by some acknowledgements on your part or some explanations, that shall do away my Jealousies, I must as a conscientious man, publish my withdrawal of my fellowship from you, to the Church, through the medium of the Times & Seasons, and demand of the conference a hearing concerning your case; that on conviction of justifiable grounds, they will demand your license. I could say much more but let the above suffice for the present.[21]

After Rigdon received the letter he replied immediately to the man who had been his close friend for more than a decade:

Dear Sir,—I received your letter by the hand of Dr. Richards, a few minutes since, the contents of which are surprising to me, though I am glad that you have let me know your feelings, so as to give me a chance to reply to them.

Why it is that you have the feelings which you seem to entertain, I know not; and what caused you to think that I had any connection with J. C. Bennett at any time is not within my power to say.

As to the Post Office, I never asked Bennett one word about it when I made application for it. If he ever wrote to the department at Washington anything about it, it was and is without my knowledge; for surely I know of no such thing being done at any time; neither did I know, at the time I applied for the office, that you intended to apply for it; nor did I know of it for some time afterwards. As far as the Post Office is concerned, these are the facts. I wrote myself to the department, offering myself as an applicant, and referred the department to several members of Congress to ascertain my character. This is all I ever did on the subject. I never wrote but one letter to the department on the subject; neither had I at the time any acquaintance of any amount with Bennett, nor for a very considerable time afterwards. He never was at our house [the post office] but very little, and then always on business, and always in a hurry, did his business, and went off immediately. I know not that Bennett ever knew that I had applied for the office; and I am quite satisfied he did not till some time after I had written to the department on the subject; and if he ever did anything about it, it was and is to this day without my having any knowledge of it.

As to the difficulties here, I never at any time gave Bennett any countenance in relation to it, and he knows it as well as I do, and feels it keenly. He has threatened me, severely, that he could do with me as he pleased, and that if I did not cease to aid you and quit trying to save "my Prophet" as he calls you, from the punishment of the law, he would turn against me; and while at St. Louis, on his way to Upper Missouri, he, in one of his speeches, made a violent attack on myself, all predicated on the fact that I would not aid him. Such are his feelings on the subject and his threatenings.

. . . Now, on the broad scale, I can assert in truth, that with myself and any other person on this globe there never was nor is there now existing anything privately or publicly to injure your character in any respect whatever; neither has any person spoken to me on any such subject. All that has ever been said by me has been said to your face, all of which you know as well as I.

As to your rights in the Post Office, you have just the same as any other man. In the new case which occurred yesterday, I have examined all the laws and rules in this office, and find but one section in relation to it, and that indirectly, but gives the postmaster no right to abate the postage, nor make any disposition of the letter or letters; but address the department, and they will give such instruction in the case as they may deem correct. I have written on the subject to the department.

I can conclude by only saying that I had hoped that all former difficulties had ceased for ever. On my part they were never mentioned to any person, nor a subject of discourse at any time nor in any place. I was tired hearing of them, and was in hopes that they slumbered for ever. While at La Harpe [with George W. Robinson] the subject was never once mentioned. . . . If being entirely silent on the subject at all times and in all places is an error, then I am guilty. If evading the subject at all times, whenever introduced by others, be a crime, then I am guilty; for such is my uniform custom.

If this letter is not satisfactory, let me know wherein; for it is peace I want. Respectfully, Sidney Rigdon. P.S. I do consider it a matter of just offence to me to hear about Bennett's assisting me to office. I shall have a lower opinion of myself than I now have when I think I need his assistance.[22]

The earnestness of Rigdon's letter evidently resolved the difficulties between the two men temporarily, for on 6 April 1843 they arrived together at church general conference arm in arm. When the prophet took the stand he presented the individual members of the First Presidency to the masses for their sustaining vote with this statement: "Are you satisfied with the first presidency, so far as I am concerned, or will you choose another?" First Brigham Young nominated Smith to continue as president of the church. Orson Hyde seconded. The congregational showing of hands was unanimous. Smith then presented Rigdon as his first counselor. Young nominated him to continue in his office. Hyde again seconded.[23] Rigdon then addressed the Saints:

The last conference I have had privilege of attending was at the Laying of the corner stone of this [temple]. I have had no health and been connected with circumstances the most forbidding which doubtless has produced some feeling. I have never had a doubt of the work. My feelings concerning Bennet[t] were always the same and [I] told my family to guard [against] that fellow, for some time he will make a rupture among this people. [I] had so little confidence [in him]. I always felt myself at his defiance.

. . . This is an increase of my health and strength and I desire to serve you in any way it is possible for me to do. If any one has any feelings [against me] I hope they will express them.

The vote was then put to the people and carried "almost unanimously," noted Smith in his diary.[24]

The following day, while the choir was singing, Smith leaned over and remarked to Rigdon, "This day is a millennium within these walls, for there is nothing but peace."[25] His statement seemed to reflect the blissful state of the relationship among the presidency as well.[26] Three weeks later the 1 May *Times and Seasons* began serializing Rigdon's autobiography which had been written several years earlier but not published.[27] Further indication of the amiable feelings between Rigdon and Smith is evidenced by a 9 May 1843 Mississippi River excursion with the Smith family and approximately 100 others. The steamship

Maid of Iowa embarked at 8 a.m. with the firing of a cannon from the Nauvoo dock. Aboard the paddle wheeler rode a "fine band of music," and "much good humor and hilarity" prevailed throughout the day. The excursionists journeyed to Burlington, Iowa, stopping at Fort Madison en route, and at Shokoquon on the return.[28]

By summer's end, however, after a season of continual legal harassment inspired behind-the-scenes by John C. Bennett, the prophet again turned on his counselor. On 13 June the Smith family left town to visit Emma's sister, Elizabeth Wasson, at Inlet Grove, Illinois, 200 miles northeast of Nauvoo. In mid-afternoon on 23 June Missouri sheriff Joseph H. Reynolds and Illinois constable Harmon T. Wilson arrived at the Wasson residence and arrested Smith.[29] Good fortune prevailed, and he managed with the help of friends to return to Nauvoo, where he obtained a 1 July writ of *habeas corpus* before the municipal court, thereby delivering him from the hands of the Missouri agent. Later that day the citizens of Nauvoo convened a mass meeting under the direction of Sidney Rigdon, where it was resolved that those who had assisted the prophet

> receive the warmest thanks of this meeting for the firm patriotism, bold and decided stand taken against lawless outrage, and the spirit of mobocracy, as manifested in the arrest or capture of General [of the Nauvoo Legion] Joseph Smith. . . . They have shown themselves republicans, patriots, and worthy citizens of this state, and have entitled themselves not only to the thanks of this meeting, but to that of all lovers of law and good order.[30]

One month later, based on a false report from Orson Hyde, the prophet publicly accused Rigdon of treason and responsibility for informing the Missouri agent of the Smith family's travel plans to Inlet Grove. Speaking at Elias Higbee's funeral on 13 August, Smith referred to a "certain man in this city who has made a covenant to betray and give me up to the Missourians." He then declared that based on testimony from gentlemen "whose names I do not wish to give," that man is "no other than Sidney Rigdon." In a foreboding manner Smith then announced to the audience: "I most solemnly proclaim the withdrawal of my fellowship from this man, on condition that the foregoing be true, and let the Saints proclaim it abroad, that he may no longer be acknowledged as my counselor; and all who feel to sanction my proceedings and views, will manifest it by uplifted hands." There followed a unanimous vote that Rigdon be "disfellowshipped, and his license demanded."[31] Another account of this meeting relates that Smith "showed that Sidney Rigdon had bound himself by an oath . . . to deliver J[oseph] into the hands of the Missourians." Smith then "in the name of the Lord withdrew the hand of fellowship from [Rigdon] and put it to the vote of the people. He was cut off by an unanimous vote and orders [were given] to demand his [ministerial] license."[32]

A careful reading of the record shows that Rigdon was innocent of the charges.

Smith's accusations were based on hearsay, and after Rigdon received a letter from Governor Thomas Carlin on 20 August denying Rigdon's involvement, Smith was forced to acknowledge this new piece of information. On 27 August, while addressing the gathered Saints, the prophet announced that "two weeks ago today something was said about Elder Sidney Rigdon, and a vote was taken to disfellowship him and to demand his license, on account of a report brought by Elder Hyde from Quincy."[33] He then read to the audience Carlin's 18 August letter to Rigdon:

> Dear Sir—Yours of the 15th inst. was received, but not in time to answer it by return mail. You say that a Mr. Orson Hyde, on board of the steam boat *Anawan*, a short time since, was told by an officer of the boat, that a Mr. Prentice, in the vicinity of Quincy, said that some person in high standing in the Church of Latter Day Saints in this place (Quincy) had an interview with [me], said, he would use all the influence that his circumstances would admit of to have Joseph Smith arrested and delivered into the hands of the Missourians.

Rigdon had explained to Carlin the common belief that he was the one who had covertly conversed with the governor. Carlin explained this away:

> Now sir, it gives me pleasure to be perfectly able to disabuse you. I have not seen you, to my recollection, nor had any correspondence with you, until the present since 1839, and in all the intercourse I have had with you; I have always looked upon you, as one of the most devoted followers of Joseph Smith, and one of the pillars of the church of the Latter Day Saints. I never sought through the aid of any person to entrap Joseph Smith. A faithful discharge of my official duties, was all that I attempted or desired.[34]

Smith remained distrustful, arguing that the governor's letter was "one of the most evasive things, and carries with it a design to hide the truth."[35] Rigdon, taking the stand in his own defense, turned to Smith and testified: "I never saw Governor Carlin but three times, and never exchanged a word with any man living on the subject. I ask pardon for having done anything which should give occasion to make you think so."[36]

The matter was put before the Saints who by acclamation decided to table the issue until October. The original version of Sidney's 7-8 October hearing, as recited in the *Times and Seasons*, was recast when reported in the *Deseret News* and later published in the *History of the Church*. This falsification conveyed an erroneous image of Rigdon that prevails in Mormon tradition to this day and warrants rectification. Hagiography being such a hallmark of Latter-day Saint history, this was particularly true in post-martyrdom Mormonism after the Quorum of the Twelve closed ranks, reserving the right to realign past realities. This labor to sanctify the Mormon experience resulted in distorted history heavily oriented toward justifying leaders. When "evil speaking of the Lord's anointed" was considered worse than lying, the truth suffered.

The official *History of the Church of Jesus Christ of Latter-day Saints* was published in book form under the direction of the First Presidency in 1902. The introductory assurance that "no historical or doctrinal statement has been changed"[37] is demonstrably wrong. Overshadowed by editorial censorship, hundreds of deletions, additions, and alterations, these seven volumes are not always reliable. The official history is a partisan chronology, a flawed legacy for rank-and-file believers. Not only does this history place polygamy and Brigham Young's ecclesiastical significance in the rosy glow of political acceptability, it smooths out Joseph Smith's rough-hewn edges, tidies up his more disreputable adventures, and deletes unfulfilled prophecies.[38] In the process of remaking Mormon history, a monumental disservice was done to Rigdon and others who challenged the Quorum of the Twelve's 1844 ascent to power.

The nineteenth-century propaganda mill was so adroit that few outside Brigham Young's inner circle were aware of the behind-the-scenes alterations so seamlessly stitched into church history. Charles Wesley Wandell, an assistant church historian, was aghast at these emendations. Commenting on the many changes made in the historical work as it was being serialized in the *Deseret News*, Wandell noted in his diary:

> I notice the interpolations because having been employed in the Historian's office at Nauvoo by Doctor Richards, and employed, too, in 1845, in compiling this very autobiography, I know that after Joseph's death his memoir was "doctored" to suit the new order of things, and this, too, by the direct order of Brigham Young to Doctor Richards and systematically by Richards.[39]

The Quorum of the Twelve, under Young's leadership, began altering the historical record shortly after Smith's death.[40] Contrary to the introduction's claim, Smith did not author the *History of the Church*. At the time of his 1844 death the narrative had been written up to 5 August 1838. By 4 February 1846, when the books were packed for the trek west, Willard Richards had completed the history to 1 March 1843. After Richards's death the account from 1 March 1843 to 8 August 1844 was finished under the direction of George A. Smith, the prophet's cousin. The full history was eventually concluded by Smith, Wilford Woodruff, and others in August 1856, seventeen years after it was undertaken.[41]

Viewed through the fragmented lens of time, one can only try to gain a clearer perspective of Sidney Rigdon's realities during that important three-day October 1843 general conference and airing of the charges against Smith's counselor. Bad weather on Friday, 6 October, postponed the convocation's opening. The first item of business the next day, according to the official record, was "The case and standing of Elder Sidney Rigdon, Counselor to the First President."[42] Rigdon, taking the stand in his own defense, briefly summarized the "subject of his situation and circumstances among the Saints." Smith then addressed the conference, stating his grievances against Rigdon as a counselor. Failing to mention the serious limitations imposed by Sidney's chronically poor health, Smith complained of his "not having received any material benefit from [Rigdon's] labors or counsels since their escape from Missouri."[43] He then invited members of the audience to voice any charges or complaints they wished to make. Several petty criticisms respecting Rigdon's management in the post office, having little relevance to his calling in the First Presidency, were expressed. Rigdon's supposed treachery in league with John C. Bennett was also brought up, along with the new charge of machination with Governor Thomas Carlin.

Smith then mentioned Rigdon's "detention of [legal] documents from Justin Butterfield." He referred to "indirect testimony from Missouri, through the mother of Orrin P. Rockwell, that said Rigdon and others had given information, by letter, of President Smith's visit to Dixon, advising them to proceed to that place and arrest him there."[44] The prophet declared that "in consequence of those, and other circumstances, and his unprofitableness to him as a counselor, he did not wish to retain him in that station, unless those difficulties could be removed; but desired his salvation, and expressed his willingness that he should retain a place among the Saints."

Rigdon stood again to defend himself, rebutting Smith's points one by one. The Butterfield letter was a personal communication to Rigdon, not to Smith. When Rigdon received it he was too ill to read it, unaware that its contents would benefit the prophet. Regarding Smith's capture near Dixon, Rigdon proclaimed that he had "never written to Missouri . . . and knew of no other person having done so." Furthermore, the only written communication he had received from Bennett, other than a business letter, was the 10 January 1843 letter to himself and Orson Pratt. Moreover, he had not written to Bennett on any matter.[45]

On Sunday at 10:00 a.m. Rigdon resumed his appeal, concluding with a moving plea to Smith "concerning their former friendship, associations and sufferings." He expressed his "willingness to resign" from the First Presidency, but tearfully said doing so would cause him "sorrowful and indescribable feelings." During this address, wrote one observer, "the sympathies of the congregation" were in Rigdon's favor.[46] Another account in the 18 November 1843 *Warsaw Message* reported that "Sidney Rigdon was brought up by the Prophet, and abused without measure," and that he had "cried for mercy like a whipped puppy."

The altered portion of the official record states that at this point the prophet arose and discussed Rigdon's "supposed treacherous correspondence with ex-Governor Carlin," and expressed an "entire lack of confidence in his integrity and steadfastness, judging from their past intercourse."[47] Hyrum Smith pled "with great earnestness and sympathy, to try Brother Sidney another year." Hyrum alluded to the "many trying scenes" their "aged companion and fellow-servant" had passed through, imploring, "I know that Brother Sidney has not done as he should, but let us forgive him once more, and try him again."[48] After Almon

Babbitt and William Law also spoke in Rigdon's behalf, the conference voted that "Elder Sidney Rigdon be permitted to retain his station as Counselor in the First Presidency."[49] According to the official account, an example of putting Brigham Young's words into Smith's mouth, the prophet then allegedly arose, shook himself, and said: "*I have thrown him off my shoulders, and you have again put him on me. You may carry him, but I will not.*"[50]

The contemporary transcript from the *Times and Seasons* presents a more moderate outcome, one more sympathetic to Rigdon, one lacking the final dramatic flourish on Smith's part:

> President Joseph Smith arose and satisfactorily explained to the congregation the supposed treacherous correspondence with Ex-Governor Carlin, which wholly removed suspicion from elder Sidney Rigdon, and from every other person. He expressed entire willingness to have elder Sidney Rigdon retain his station, provided he would magnify his office, and walk and conduct himself in all honesty, righteousness, and integrity; but signified his lack of confidence in his integrity and steadfastness, judging from their past intercourse.

Hyrum Smith then reminded his brother and fellow Saints of God's mercy, and the importance of their "exercising the same attribute towards their fellows; and especially towards their aged companion and fellow servant in the cause of truth and righteousness."[51]

Wickliffe Rigdon added that a few days later Smith came to the Rigdon home in tears and asked Sidney's "forgiveness for all he had said and done against him." Smith claimed "he wanted to settle all differences that had existed between them" that they might thereafter "live as Brothers of the church should live and be to each other the same old friends they had been in the past[.]" Sidney grasped Joseph by the hand, "and with tears in his eyes" avowed that "all matters of difference w[ere] settled." The prophet shook hands with family members, including Nancy, and he and Sidney "were good friends from that time."[52]

Members of the Quorum of the Twelve later united in a post-martyrdom effort to protect the practice of polygamy as well as to disregard Rigdon's succession claims. Thus the 8 October 1843 scenario was rewritten to portray Rigdon and Smith as irrevocably estranged. Orson Hyde, the quorum's *de facto* agent of disinformation, took particular pleasure in attacking Rigdon's reputation. Hyde later wrote, after the Saints voted to retain Rigdon in the First Presidency, that the prophet chastised the Twelve saying, "Why will you suffer the Church to put that old hypocrite upon my shoulders again, after I have thrown him down? But as you have neglected to help me put him down, you will have it to do yourselves when it will cost you more to do it than it would now."[53] Ebenezer Robinson, long-time church printer, presented a much more benevolent view of the prophet's 1844 assessment of his sporadic esteem for Rigdon. Called to accompany Rigdon to Pittsburgh in June 1844, Robinson was admonished by Smith to "stand by

[Elder Rigdon] under all circumstances, and uphold his hands on all occasions, and never forsake him . . . for he is a good man and I love him better than I ever loved him in all my life, for my heart is entwined around his with chords [sic] that can never be broken."[54]

Within days of Rigdon's mission to Pittsburgh, Smith was murdered, an act that forever after bestowed the halo of martyrdom. Of his deeds and good works, none possessed the power to nurture the spirit of Mormonism as much as the legacy of his bloody death. Ironically the tragedy, and the shift in power it engendered, buried Sidney Rigdon's body of accomplishment under the rubble and tangled history of the Quorum of the Twelve's rise to prominence.

Notes

Unless otherwise stated, all primary sources cited are located in the Historical Department of the Church of Jesus Christ of Latter-day Saints, Salt Lake City, Utah.

1. Statement upon completing the final segment of Joseph Smith, *History of the Church of Jesus Christ of Latter-day Saints*, B. H. Roberts, ed., 7 vols. (Salt Lake City: The Church of Jesus Christ of Latter-day Saints, 1902), 1:363; hereafter *History of the Church*. This work was serialized in the *Deseret News* and *Millennial Star* beginning in 1858 (*Deseret News* 7 [20 Jan. 1858]: 363).

2. *History of the Church*, 5:159. Although Smith mentioned no names, Rigdon and George W. Robinson interpreted this to mean them. See George W. Robinson to John C. Bennett, 16 Sept. 1842, in John C. Bennett, *History of the Saints* (Boston: Leland & Whiting, 1842), 248.

3. Emma Smith to Sidney Rigdon, 12 Sept. 1842, Joseph Smith Collection.

4. Rigdon's response is written on the bottom of Emma's 12 September letter to him.

5. *History of the Church*, 5:184.

6. Ibid., 196.

7. Emphasis in original. On 25 May 1844, as he was preparing to leave for his political mission to Pittsburgh, Sidney Rigdon resigned his position. Council of Fifty recorder Willard Richards, in a 26 May 1844 letter to Orson Hyde, wrote:

Sidney Rigdon, Esq., is about to resign the post office at Nauvoo, in favor of Gen. Joseph Smith, the founder of the city. He has the oldest petitions now on file in the general postoffice for that station, and has an undoubted claim over every other petitioner, by being the founder and supporter of the city, and by the voice of nineteen-twentieths of the people, and every sacred consideration; and it is the wish of the council [of Fifty] that you engage the Illinois delegation to use their influence to secure the office to General Smith without fail, and have them ready to act on the arrival of Mr. Rigdon's resignation, and before too, if expedient (*History of the Church*, 6:406).

8. The attempt on Boggs's life took place on the night of 6 May 1842. Orrin Porter Rockwell, one of Smith's closest friends, was arrested later that year and charged with the

attempted murder. Although neither the prophet nor Rockwell was convicted of the crime, Rockwell never denied shooting Boggs. General Patrick E. Conner reported that Rockwell told him, "I shot through the window and thought I had killed him, but I had only wounded him; I was damned sorry that I had not killed the son of a bitch" (Wilhelm W. Wyl [Wymetal], *Mormon Portraits, Joseph Smith the Prophet, His Family and His Friends* [Salt Lake City: Tribune Printing and Publishing Co., 1886], 255).

9. *History of the Church*, 5:168.

10. *Times and Seasons* 4 (15 Dec. 1842): 33-36.

11. Published in the *Wasp*, 24 Sept. 1842.

12. Journal History, 10 Jan. 1842, 3—a multi-volume daily history of the church compiled by official church historians; hereafter cited as Journal History. The 1842 date is erroneous and should read 10 January 1843.

13. Ibid., 3-5.

14. Ibid. Wilford Woodruff, who also worked in the *Times and Seasons* office, was present on this occasion. "In my hearing," he later wrote, Joseph Smith "requested one of the quorum of the Twelve to bring [Rigdon] up before the church that he might be dealt with according to the law of the church, that he might be cut off as a dead branch, and no longer encumber the tree, as there was sufficient testimony against him" (11 Oct. 1844 letter, printed in *Times and Seasons* 5 [1 Nov. 1844]: 698-700).

Rigdon, in the voice of revelation in 1868, said of Smith's unwarranted attacks:

When the first prophet and seer . . . got lifted up in the pride of his heart and had identified himself with the church of the Devil . . . he bent his whole fury on my serv[a]nt Sidney with all the influence that the position he had obtained gave him[.] He aroused every feeling of prejudice against my serv[a]nt Sidney that was possible for him to do[.] No fals[e]hood was too corrupt for him to fabricate and even to swear to in order to effect his object (1 July 1868 revelation, listed as Section 37 in Copying Book A, Stephen Post Collection, box 3, fd. 12).

15. Journal History, 10 Jan. 1843 [1842], 3.

16. Ibid., 5.

17. Scott Faulring, ed., *An American Prophet's Record: The Diaries and Journals of Joseph Smith* (Salt Lake City: Signature Books in association with Smith Research Associates, 1989), 302.

18. Evidently all Rigdon family members, except George W. and Athalia Robinson, who were living in La Harpe, were present (J. Wickliffe Rigdon statement of 28 July 1905).

19. *History of the Church*, 5:266-67.

20. Faulring, 304-305.

21. Dean Jessee, ed., *The Personal Writings of Joseph Smith* (Salt Lake City: Deseret Book Co., 1984), 555-56.

22. *History of the Church*, 5:315-16.

23. Andrew F. Ehat and Lyndon W. Cook, eds., *The Words of Joseph Smith: The Contemporary Accounts of the Nauvoo Discourses of the Prophet Joseph* (Provo, UT: Religious Studies Center, Brigham Young University, 1980), 174.

24. Faulring, 342-43. No discussion is made in the reference as to who did not sustain Rigdon.

25. Ibid., 353.

26. One probable exception to prevailing good feelings was a hoax evidently perpetrated on Rigdon by Smith. On 17 April Rigdon received a purported letter from Washington, D.C., informing him that the Nauvoo Post Office was abolished. Willard Richards's account reported that Rigdon "foolishly supposed it genuine, neglected his duty, and started for Carthage to learn more about it, but was met by Mr. Hamilton, an old mail contractor, who satisfied him it was a hoax, and he returned home and the mail arrived as usual to-day" (*History of the Church*, 5:368-69).

27. This serialization was continued in the *Times and Seasons* 4 (15 May 1843): 193-94; 4 (1 June 1843): 209-10; 4 (15 Aug. 1843): 289-90; and 4 (15 Sept. 1843): 320-21.

28. Journal History, under date; Faulring, 376.

29. The *Illinois State Register* (18 July 1843), cited in *History of the Church*, 5:513-15, speculates that Smith's arrest was a Whig conspiracy to compel the Democratic governor to issue a writ against Smith, pending the Congressional election. The Whigs theorized that this would create the necessity for hiring lawyer Cyrus Walker "to get [Smith] delivered out of the net of their own weaving, and thereby get the everlasting gratitude of the Mormons and their support for the Whig cause." Walker, shortly after his nomination as the Whig candidate for Congress, made a pilgrimage to Nauvoo to curry favor with the Mormons. He was disappointed, however, when it appeared that many Mormons supported the Democratic candidate.

Whatever the reason, John C. Bennett was behind it all, as explained in his 10 January 1843 letter to Rigdon and Pratt. The Missouri agent in Springfield showed to some a letter from Bennett "urging the importance of getting up an indictment immediately against Smith, for the five or six year old treason of which he was accused several years ago." In the letter Bennett reportedly told the Missourian:

> Go to the Judge, and never leave him until he appoints a special term of the court; never suffer the court to adjourn until an indictment is found against Smith for treason. When an indictment shall have been found, get a copy, and go immediately to the governor, and never leave him until you get a demand on the governor of Illinois for Smith's arrest; and then dispatch some active and vigilant person to Illinois for a warrant, and let him never leave the governor until he gets it; and then let him never come back to Missouri without Smith.

A special term of Daviess County, Missouri, circuit court was accordingly called. An indictment was found against Smith. A demand was then made and a writ issued by Governor Thomas Reynolds on 13 June 1843.

30. *Nauvoo Neighbor*, 19 July 1843.

31. Journal History, 13 Aug. 1843; Faulring, 406; *History of the Church*, 5:531-32.

32. Likely based on an entry in the "Book of the Law of the Lord," this reference is cited in Ehat and Cook, 243. William Clayton's 13 August 1843 diary entry noted that Smith "showed that Sidney Rigdon had bound himself by an oath to Governor Carlin to deliver Joseph into the hands of the Missourians if he could and finally in the name of the Lord withdrew the hand of fellowship from him and put it to the vote of the people. He was cut off by an unanimous vote and orders [issued] to demand his license" (in Ehat and Cook, 243).

33. *History of the Church*, 5:553. While the prophet initially suspected Rigdon of being a Missouri informant, he was not certain. For example, the 5 January 1844 reference in *History of the Church*, 6:170, shows Smith wondering: "can it be possible that the traitor whom Porter Rockwell reports to me as being in correspondence with my Missouri enemies, is one of my quorum? . . . Is it possible that Brother [William] Law or Brother [William] Marks is a traitor, and would deliver Brother Joseph into the hands of his enemies in Missouri?"

34. Ibid., 5:553-54.

35. Ibid.

36. Ibid., 556.

37. Ibid., 1:iv.

38. Four examples of failed prophecies from Joseph Smith's personal diary, which were never published in the *History of the Church* include:

> 1. His 20 January 1842 prediction, after Orson Hyde had told of the "excellent white wine he drank in the east [Palestine]," that "in the name of the Lord he would drink wine with him in that country" (Faulring, 294).

> 2. On that same occasion he prophesied that "from the 6th day of April next" he would accompany the Twelve on a "Mission through the United States and when we arrive at Maine we will take ship for England and go on to all countries where we are a mind for to go" (ibid., 294).

> 3. On 16 December 1843 in an address to the Nauvoo City Council Smith stated: "I prophecy by virtue of the Holy Priesthood vested in me in the name of Jesus Christ that if Congress will not hear our petition and grant us protection they shall be broken up as a government and God shall damn them. There shall nothing be left of them, not even a grease spot" (ibid., 432).

> 4. Finally, on 6 February 1844 "I prophesied [in the presence of the First Presidency and the Quorum of the Twelve] that 5 years would not roll round before the company would all be able to live without cooking" (ibid., 445).

39. Inez Smith, "Biography of Charles Wesley Wandell," *Journal of History* 3 (Jan. 1910): 455-63.

40. More than a dozen references to this may be found in the post-martyrdom record. For example, the 1 April 1845 citation records Brigham Young as saying: "I commenced revising the History of Joseph Smith at Brother Richard's office: Elder Heber C. Kimball and George A. Smith were with me" (*History of the Church*, 7:389; for other references regarding revisions, see ibid., 389-90, 408, 411, 414, 427-28, 514, 519, 520, 532, 533, 556).

That censorship of the official history came from Brigham Young is evidenced by an 11 July 1856 reference in Wilford Woodruff's diary. Woodruff, working in the church historian's office, questioned Young respecting a "p[ie]ce of History on Book E-1 page 1681-2 concerning Hyr[u]m leading this Church & tracing the [A]aronic Priesthood." Young advised, "it was not essential to be inserted in the History & had better be omitted." Woodruff then queried him about "Joseph[']s words on South Carolina" (see D&C 87;

130:12-13) which had recently been published in the *Deseret News*. Young said he "wished it not published" (Scott Kenney, ed., *Wilford Woodruff's Journal–Typescript*, 9 vols. [Midvale, UT: Signature Books, 1983], 3:429).

Years later Elder Charles W. Penrose, a member of the First Presidency, admitted that after Smith's death some things about the prophet were deleted from the official record "for prudential reasons" (Charles W. Pensose diary, 10 Jan. 1897, Utah Historical Society, Salt Lake City).

41. Dean C. Jessee, ed., "The Writing of Joseph Smith's History," *Brigham Young University Studies* 11 (Summer 1971): 466.

42. Journal History, 7 Oct. 1843.

43. Ibid., 8 Oct. 1843.

44. Ibid.

45. *History of the Church*, 6:47-48.

46. Ibid., 48.

47. Ibid., 48-49.

48. Jedediah M. Grant, *A Collection of Facts Relative to the Course Taken by Elder Sidney Rigdon in the States of Ohio, Missouri, Illinois and Pennsylvania* (Philadelphia: Brown, Bicking & Guilbert, 1844), 15.

49. *History of the Church*, 6:49.

50. Ibid.; emphasis in original. Also see same wording in Journal History, under date. Of course it is possible that compilers remembered details not originally recorded, and their memories were colored by later events, but the consistency of the alterations toward a clearly-defined goal makes the assumption of volition unavoidable.

51. *Times and Seasons* 4 (15 Oct. 1843): 330.

52. J. Wickliffe Rigdon, "Life Story of Sidney Rigdon," 178-79.

53. Orson Hyde, *Speech of Elder Orson Hyde, Delivered Before the High Priest's Quorum, in Nauvoo, April 27th, 1845, Upon the Course and Conduct of Mr. Sidney Rigdon, and Upon the Merits of His Claims to the Presidency of the Church of Jesus Christ of Latter-day Saints* (Liverpool: James and Woodburn, 1845), 51. Similar statements were made by Kimball (see *Times and Seasons* 5 [1 Oct. 1844]: 663), and Grant, 15.

54. *Latter Day Saints' Messenger and Advocate* (Pittsburgh) 4 (6 Dec. 1844).

CHAPTER 23.

The Prophet's Mantle

The brethren testify that brother Brigham Young is brother Joseph's legal successor.
You never heard me say so. I say that I am a good hand to keep the dogs and wolves
out of the flock.

—Brigham Young (1860)[1]

Eighteen hundred and forty-four was the defining year in Sidney Rigdon's eventful life. The new year found Nauvoo overcast with the same storm of enmity that had rained vengeance on the Saints in Missouri. Cordial Illinois citizens had come to detest what they viewed as Joseph Smith's ambition "to merge all religion, all law, and both moral and political justice, in the knavish pretension that he receives fresh from heaven divine instructions in all matters pertaining to these things."[2] In early January 1844 murmurs of mob action were voiced.[3] A month later a sizeable force of anti-Mormons convened at Carthage, the Hancock County seat, "to devise ways and means of expelling the Saints from the State."[4]

To try to control their destiny during this tempestuous period, Mormon leaders hedged their bets in every conceivable way. Convinced that conventional legal entreaties were futile, church leaders appealed to the citizenry of other states. Smith wrote to the "Green Mountain Boys" of Vermont, his native state. Rigdon addressed an eloquent appeal to the Pennsylvania Senate and House of Representatives. After a lengthy recital of Missouri tribulation he concluded: "Being refused redress by the authorities of Missouri, to whom shall your memorialist look? He answers, to the people of his native state, and through them to the general government."[5] James Arlington Bennett, prominent New Yorker and ally of the Mormons, had been trying for some time to convince church leaders to establish their own government, or essentially to create their own empire outside the boundaries of the United States. In April 1844 he wrote to church scribe Willard Richards that "millions would flock to an independent people. . . . [A] Patriarchal government with Joseph at the head would be just the thing."[6]

Stirred by these possibilities, colonization prospects in Oregon, Vancouver Island, Upper California, and Texas were ardently discussed during meetings of the Council of Fifty. This secret assembly, conceived by Smith in 1842 but not organized until March 1844, served as a forum for the church's political—and

330

especially colonizing—concerns.[7] The 1844 U.S. presidential race was seen as an opportunity to convince government leaders that Mormons were a viable political force. In a letter to Henry Clay the prophet flaunted his quiescent political potential by announcing he had 200,000 followers.[8]

In late 1843 Mormon leaders decided to inquire of the five candidates for the U.S. presidency "what their feelings were or what their course would be towards the Saints if they were elected."[9] Accordingly, letters were sent to Henry Clay, John C. Calhoun, Richard M. Johnson, Lewis Cass, and President Martin Van Buren. Only Clay and Calhoun responded, and neither was willing to commit to the special interests of the Saints. Outraged by what they viewed as disdain for Mormon civil rights, church leaders through the collective planning of the Council of Fifty opted to control their own destiny. Mormons had as much right as anyone to "make [a] political party to gain power to defend ourselves," Joseph Smith proclaimed, "we will whip the mob by getting up a President."[10]

On 29 January, during a local political caucus, Smith was nominated "to be a candidate for the next presidency." While addressing his supporters he urged, "Every man in the city who is able to speak in public throughout the land to electioneer and make stump speeches" in his behalf. Requesting that Rigdon go to Pennsylvania, the Prophet exhorted him and others to "Advocate the 'Mormon' religion, purity of elections, and call upon the people to stand by the law and put down mobocracy. . . . Tell the people we have had Whig and Democratic Presidents long enough; we want a President of the United States."[11] The political platform of the Mormon Reform Party was drawn up by W. W. Phelps, a seasoned if erratic newspaper editor.[12] Named *Joseph Smith's Views on the Powers and Policy of the Government of the United States*, the position paper reviewed the growth and development of the American government until it reached the "Acme of American glory, liberty, and prosperity" under the administration of Andrew Jackson, then began declining under the "withering touch of Martin Van Buren."[13] The platform advocated salary reform for Congressmen, rehabilitating convicts through public works, compensating owners for emancipated slaves, reducing taxes through increased government efficiency, establishing free trade and protecting international rights on the high seas, establishing a national bank with branches in every state and territory, increasing presidential power to intervene in civil disturbances within states, and annexing both Oregon and Texas.

The Mormon attempt to secure the presidential seat was not a half-hearted effort. Every aspect of the campaign was calculated and minutely planned. Hundreds of partisan missionaries were called by the Council of Fifty to preach the Mormon Reform Party as well as Mormonism. Special representatives were sent to Washington, D.C., to lobby Congressional leaders and power brokers. Copies of Smith's platform were mailed to the most influential men and principal newspapers across the nation.

On 4 March the Council of Fifty directed Willard Richards to write James Arlington Bennett requesting him to serve as vice president on the Mormon ticket. "General Smith is the greatest statesman of the 19th century," crowed Richards, and "[he] says if he must be President James Arlington Bennett must be Vice President."[14] But Bennett, an Irish citizen, was ineligible. Smith's second choice, Solomon Copeland of Tennessee, was not interested. On 6 May 1844, during a Council of Fifty meeting, Sidney Rigdon was selected to be Smith's running mate.[15] Inducted into the council on 19 March, Rigdon was enthusiastic about his investiture. Jedediah Grant wrote:

> After listening to the instructions and viewing the order of the council, and the manifestations of the power of God through Elder J[oseph] Smith, [Rigdon] leaped for joy, and walked the room as sprightly as a boy in his gayest frolics. Exclaiming, "Joseph! Joseph! Thou servant of the most High God, I will never leave nor forsake thee, for mine eyes now see what Kings and Prophets desired to see and hear." . . . Brother Joseph you have tried to shake me off for several years, but you cannot do it, I will hold on to the skirts of your garment, I am now determined never to let you go.[16]

Orson Hyde added that after being made aware of the council's agenda, Rigdon "began to speak, then to shout, then to dance, and threw his feet so high that he lost balance, and came well nigh falling over backwards upon the stove."[17]

Rigdon was enthralled to think that if the Mormon Reform political ticket succeeded in making a "majority of the voters converts to our faith and elected Joseph President . . . the dominion of the kingdom would be forever established in the United States. And if not successful, we could but fall back on Texas, and be a kingdom notwithstanding."[18] The contingency plan prepared for every eventuality, as evidenced by sending memorials to Congress and President Van Buren "for the privilege of raising 100,000 volunteers to protect" Texas and Oregon.[19]

During public appearances at the church's general conference on 6 and 7 April, Rigdon seemed the focus of attention despite the presence of Joseph Smith. Empowered by his new activities with the Council of Fifty, Rigdon took the stand in the grove near the temple and reflecting on his chronically poor health, he remarked: "It is with no ordinary degree of satisfaction I enjoy this privilege this morning; want of health and other circumstances have kept me in silence for nearly the last five years. . . . I am now come forth from a bed of sickness, and have enough of strength left to appear here for the first time in my true character."[20] He announced his text as "Behold the Church of Jesus Christ in the last days,"[21] and began a lengthy, detailed history of the organization. He took listeners back fourteen years to the time when the entire membership met in a small log cabin. He recalled being shut up in secret with the prophet in "an old smoky house" in Hiram, Ohio, where they had "nothing to eat but a little Jo[h]nny Cake & milk

& water."[22] Pondering those trying times, Rigdon recalled that although "I had little to eat, little to wear . . . yet it was the beginning of good days."[23]

He reminisced that he and Smith "talked[,] wept, & prayed & the Angels Administered unto us & the spirit of God was with us & the heavens opened unto us."[24] In his resounding tenor voice he testified that "Neither Could we disbelieve this to be the Church of God. We cannot disbelieve it for we see hear & feel. I have always known it to be. I Cannot see otherwise. Have I not seen God[']s glory by the visions of Heaven? Yea I have."[25] John Taylor, who followed Rigdon, commented that he seemed "animated . . . seemed to burn with zeal."[26] "We see in him," Taylor, a future president of the church, proclaimed, "a man of God who can contemplate the glories of heaven—the visions of eternity, and who yet looks forward to the opening glories which the great Eloheim has manifested to him pertaining to righteousness and peace—a man who now beholds the things roll on which he has long since beheld in prophetic vision."[27]

Rigdon's enthusiasm continued in his afternoon address, an oration brimming with subtle references to the Council of the Fifty. He was clearly championing the Mormon idea of government, manifest in the concept of the Kingdom of God, which he explained as having evolved from the earliest days of church history. "Mankind have labored under one universal mistake," he explained, and that was "that salvation was distinct from government." When God speaks of government, he added, "he means a government that shall rule our temporal & spiritual affairs."[28] "When God sets up his kingdom," he argued, "He will sustain it above all laws & kingdoms of the world & the world has no power over the kingdom of God." Declaring that he did not care anything about all the laws in the world, for "I will live above them," he concluded that although "God teaches his servants to respect kings Gov[ernors] Presidents, & men in authority . . . I have a right to proclaim myself a king and priest unto the most High God."[29] Referring to his vice-presidential campaign, he said, "I don[']t want any office in this government for I am determined to be a king in the kingdom of God."[30]

By now the hour was late and rain showers had begun. Rigdon dismissed the congregation until the following morning, saying he was still "full of preaching . . . I have not done half enough."[31] April 7 was a pleasant spring day. The sun was bright, wrote Wilford Woodruff, and the "air calm & serene." The largest crowd ever to gather in Nauvoo, "a vast multitude of about twenty thousand souls," assembled to hear the continuation of President Rigdon's discourse.[32] Congregational singing set the mood, after which Rigdon offered an affectionate appeal for the prayers of the Saints on behalf of the sick. After invocation, the prophet requested the police to maintain proper crowd control. Rigdon then took the stand and completed his powerful sermon on the "k[ingdom] of heaven [which] is actually a government."

Rigdon's impressive performance, which included allusions to "the mysteries," undoubtedly affected Joseph Smith's decision to preach the controversial two-hour King Follett funeral sermon that afternoon. Smith, following Rigdon's crowd-pleasing eloquence, told the funeral audience he intended to edify them "with simple truths from Heaven" rather than please their ears "with oratory [and] with much learning."[33] He then proceeded to deliver his best-known and perhaps best-loved discourse on the progression of humans and gods.

The following afternoon a large gathering of Elders assembled at the stand near the temple. In remarks deleted from the published record, Hyrum Smith, legal husband to Mary Fielding yet secretly also married to Mercy Fielding Thompson, Catherine Phillips, and Lydia Dibble Granger, spoke to the assembly for ninety minutes. He duplicitously assailed polygamy, stating he was decidedly "against it in every form." Rigdon, a life-long opponent of plural marriage, took the stand and sincerely, if naively, "concurred in Hyrum's remarks."[34]

Ten days after Hyrum and Sidney jointly denounced spiritual wifery, William Law, Rigdon's fellow counselor in the First Presidency, was excommunicated, along with his wife and four other people, for "unchristian like conduct" in opposing polygamy.[35] These anti-polygamy excommunicants branded Joseph Smith an adulterous prophet and established an opposition newspaper "through which we will herald [Smith's] [M]ormon ribaldry," wrote dissenter Francis Higbee, "and his unparalleled and unheard of attempts of seduction."[36] The prospectus for *The Nauvoo Expositor* was distributed to citizens on 10 May. Joseph Smith was so alarmed about the promised disclosures that he sent Rigdon as a special envoy on 13 May to "negotiate terms of peace" with William Law, leader of the separatists. Possibly as a reward for serving as messenger, Rigdon on 11 May was initiated into the Endowment Quorum, or Holy Order, which had been first instituted in the church on 4 May 1842 to introduce the Mormon temple ceremony and plural marriage to select Saints. W. W. Phelps nominated Rigdon for the quorum. Although Wilford Woodruff later said that Rigdon "came in without [the prophet's] wish or invitation, as he had no confidence in him,"[37] this seems improbable. Acceptance into the quorum, where one received the highest blessings of Mormon theology—the guarantee of eternal exaltation—required unanimous approval from all other initiates.[38] Furthermore, sending Rigdon to intercede with his colleague in the First Presidency is evidence that the prophet still had faith in his counselor.

According to Law, Rigdon informed the dissenting counselor that if they would "let all difficulties drop," church officials would restore him, his wife, and Dr. Robert Foster to their "standing in the church and to all their offices." But peace, Law declared, could only be achieved if Smith would "acknowledge publicly that he had taught and practised the doctrine of plurality of wives . . . and that he should own the whole system (revelation and all) to be from Hell."[39] Rigdon replied that he was not authorized "to go so far."

Other diplomatic measures failed as well. On 7 June the first issue of the *Expositor* came off the press. "We all verily believe, and many of us know of a surety, that the religion of the Latter Day Saints, as originally taught by Joseph Smith, is verily true," wrote the publishers. But "we are earnestly seeking to explode the vicious principles of Joseph Smith, and those who practice the same abominations and whoredoms," for, they claimed, "we verily know [they] are not accordant and consonant with the principles of Jesus Christ and the Apostles."[40] The essay discussed the "wretched and miserable condition of females in this place," and related the plight of some of them. New immigrant convert women, they claimed, were taken to secluded spots on arrival and forced to become Smith's "spiritual wives," their refusal resulting in "eternal damnation." The article maintained that "religious despotism" was "incompatible with free institutions." Additional disclosures in subsequent issues were promised.

The Nauvoo City Council convened to discuss the paper the next day. Mayor Smith declared, "The conduct of such men and such papers are calculated to destroy the peace of the city, and it is not safe that such things exist, on account of the mob spirit which they tend to produce."[41] Labeling the newspaper "libelous of the deepest dye . . . injurious as a vehicle of defamation,"[42] the prophet-mayor urged that it be declared a public nuisance and destroyed. The council concurred and a large group of citizens marched to the *Expositor* office, smashed the press, and scattered its type in the street. Francis Higbee had promised that if anyone "lay their hand upon it or break" the press, "they may date their downfall from that very hour."[43]

Within three weeks Smith, a victim of a process he set in motion in violating First Amendment rights, was arrested for his complicity in the destruction of the press and other matters.[44] He and his brother Hyrum were shot dead, and John Taylor and Willard Richards wounded, on 27 June by a rabble of freemasons while incarcerated, supposedly for their own protection, in the county jail at Carthage.[45]

Rigdon was not in Illinois at the time of the martyrdom. On 14 June he had sent a confidential letter (via his cousin Samuel James) to Illinois governor Thomas Ford declaring the *Expositor* "inflammatory and abusive to an extreme," though he stopped short of justifying its destruction. Fearing "a large assembly of persons assembled at Carthage making threats of violence," Rigdon advised the governor to disperse "all uncalled for assemblies, and let the laws have their regular course," not otherwise seeing the need for further "executive interference in this case." Requesting confidentiality, he added, "I wish not to take any part in the affair, or be known in it."[46] Four days later, on 18 June, the entire Rigdon family had departed on the steamer *Osprey* for Pittsburgh. But Sidney had not "apostatized and left Bro[ther] Joseph," as Brigham Young declared on 24 June 1868. Rather, he was sent there by the prophet for his personal safety to fulfill a prophecy of

Joseph Smith and to establish Pennsylvania residency to make him eligible for the vice-presidency.[47] On the day of the Rigdon family's departure, according to Wickliffe Rigdon, Joseph Smith and "many of the prominent members of the church came to the boat to bid them goodby[e]."[48]

Arriving in Pittsburgh on 27 June, the Rigdons, unaware of Joseph's and Hyrum's deaths, visited family members the following day, then located a rental house on 1 July. Five days later Sidney received the first news of the tragic deaths from a *Nauvoo Neighbor* brought to town by Jedediah Grant on his way to Philadelphia.[49] The next day Rigdon preached an elegiac Sunday sermon to a large audience on "Mr. Broadhurst's green." According to Orson Hyde, Rigdon "directed the whole tide and strength of his eloquence to extol and eulogize Joseph Smith."[50]

Rigdon also told Jedediah Grant that he felt prepared to claim "the Prophetic mantle" and that he would "now take his place, at the head of the church, in spite of men or devils, at the risk of his life."[51] Knowing that Grant planned to leave the following day for Philadelphia, Rigdon requested him to relay word to any of the Twelve he might meet, that it "was his wish and desire that they should come to Pittsburgh before going to Nauvoo, and hold a council."[52] Sidney also sent a letter to Brigham Young, in care of *The Prophet*, a Mormon newspaper in the East, suggesting a date to conference in Pittsburgh. But the Twelve, with succession aspirations of their own, disregarded Rigdon's wishes. Wilford Woodruff wrote from Boston to Brigham Young on 16 July urging quorum members in the East to convene in Massachussetts, suggesting they meet independent of Rigdon.[53] The Twelve then had Orson Hyde write Rigdon, informing him that they "thought it safer for them to return" through Buffalo and Chicago, requesting him to "meet them in Nauvoo, where they would council together."[54] Initially Rigdon had not planned to return to Nauvoo. According to his account, however, he heard the spectral voice of Joseph Smith directing him, "You must not stay, you must go."[55]

Despite frequent kidnapping and assassination attempts, Joseph Smith established no firm policies regarding presidential succession in the event of his death, throwing the prophetic transition into turmoil. He simply had not expected to die at thirty-eight. Never given to full disclosure to any man or woman, the prophet's public and private statements between 1834-44 suggested at least eight different methodologies for succession, each pointing to different successors with some validity.[56] Thus Rigdon found the Saints in a leadership quandary when he arrived in Nauvoo on Saturday, 3 August. Apostles Parley P. Pratt, Willard Richards, and George A. Smith invited him to meet with them at 8:00 a.m. the following day at John Taylor's home. The men waited an hour. Pratt, sent to find Rigdon, found him engaged with a lawyer, and by then it was too late for him to meet with the apostles as he had a speaking engagement at worship services. Taking as his text the scriptural concept "For my thoughts are not as your thoughts," Rigdon related to the audience a vision he received recently in Pittsburgh.

Declaring his manifestation as a "continuation of the same vision that he and Joseph had in Kirtland . . . concerning the different glories or mansions in the 'Father's House,'" Rigdon testified that the prophet "had ascended to heaven, and that he stood on the right hand of the Son of God, and that he had seen him there, clothed with all the power, glory, might, majesty, and dominion of the celestial kingdoms." He added that Joseph Smith still held "the keys of the kingdom . . . would continue to hold them to all eternity . . . and that no man could ever take his place, neither have power to build up the kingdom to any other creature or being but to Joseph Smith."[57]

Emphasizing his long-time role as "Spokesman to the Church," Rigdon reported the Lord's wish that "there must be a guardian appointed to build the Church up to Joseph."[58] He then explained that "he was the identical man that the ancient prophets had sung about, wrote and rejoiced over; and that he was sent to do the identical work that had been the theme of all the prophets in every preceding generation."[59] Declaring that the Lord's ways were not their ways, he veered into his favorite topic, the prophecies of Armageddon. The time was near at hand, he warned, when the Saints "would see one hundred tons of metal per second thrown at the enemies of God," and blood would flow as deep as "horses' bridles." With his usual extravagance he trumpeted:

> I am going to fight a real bloody battle with sword and with gun. . . . I will fight the battles of the Lord. I will also cross the Atlantic, encounter the queen's forces, and overcome them—plant the American standard on English ground, and then march to the palace of her majesty, and demand a portion of her riches and dominions, which if she refuse, I will take the little madam by the nose and lead her out, and she shall have no power to help herself. If I do not do this, the Lord never spake by mortal.[60]

During the afternoon meeting, while Charles C. Rich was speaking, Nauvoo Stake president William Marks, at Rigdon's request, interrupted to give public notice of a Thursday, 8 August, special assembly for the purpose of choosing a guardian of the church. Some suggested waiting until the full Quorum of the Twelve returned. But Rigdon said he was "some distance from his family," and wanted to "know if this people had any thing for him to do." If not, then he wanted to be on his way "for there was a people 1000's & 10,000's who would receive him[,] that he wanted to visit other branches around [but Nauvoo] first."[61] Many thought that Rigdon was pushing too fast. On Monday morning, 5 August, Parley P. Pratt, Willard Richards, John Taylor, George A. Smith, Amasa Lyman, and Bishop Newel K. Whitney called on Rigdon to ascertain his motives. He denied that he expected the people to choose a guardian on Thursday, saying he wished just a "prayer meeting, and interchange of thought and feeling [to] warm up each other's hearts."[62]

Later that evening five more members of the Twelve arrived in Nauvoo, bringing the number to nine. The next day a combined meeting of the Twelve, the Nauvoo High Council, and the High Priest's quorum was held in the second story of the new Seventies Hall. Brigham Young, who scheduled the meeting, called on Rigdon and requested that he make a statement to the church concerning his Pittsburgh revelation. Rigdon explained that the manifestation, while not an open vision, was presented to his mind. He was shown that the prophet sustained the same relationship to the church in death as he had in life. No man could be Joseph's successor, Rigdon said. The Kingdom must be "built up to Christ" through the dead prophet. Revelation was still required, and since Rigdon had been ordained as Smith's spokesman he was to continue to speak for him on this side of the veil "until Joseph Smith himself shall descend as a mighty angel, lay his hand on [my] head & ordain [me] & say, 'Come up & act for me.'" Concluding, he appended, "I have discharged my duty, & done what God commanded me. . . . The people could please themselves whether they accepted [me] or not."[63] Young then responded that he wished to hear the voice of the entire church in conference before a decision was made. He wryly commented that "he did not care who led the Church of God if God said so even if it was old 'Ann Lee' [the Shaker prophetess] but he must know that God said so."[64] Young added that he had "the keys and the means of knowing the mind of God on this subject."[65]

By rights of his 1841 ordination as "Prophet, Seer, and Revelator," Rigdon was entitled to visionary experiences. Yet critic Wilford Woodruff called Rigdon's disclosure "a kind of second [c]lass vision."[66] Young, inclined to sarcastic ridicule, called Sidney a fool to his face.[67] The "Lion of the Lord" did not suffer those he considered fools easily. Rigdon underestimated Young, soon to be one of the most powerful Americans of his generation. Rigdon was without question Young's oratorical superior, but Young, never a passive observer, was more clever, ambitious, and politically astute. Not content to let the mantle of leadership pass him by, he simply wrestled it away from Rigdon in mid-descent.

Young, like Rigdon, stunned by the news of Smith's murder, did not immediately conclude that the prophet's death placed the crown of leadership on the heads of the Twelve or on him. In fact, Young initially wondered if the prophet had taken the keys of authority with him. "I had no more idea of [the mantle] falling upon me than of the most unlikely thing in the world," he later told family members.[68] Equipped with a well-honed mind, Young became convinced en route to Nauvoo from Boston "by the visions of the Spirit," as he later told colleagues, that the Twelve constituted an interim church presidency from which a First Presidency eventually would arise.[69] Yet Young told no one of his intuition on this matter for three years. "I knew then what I now know concerning the organization of the church," he retrospectively proclaimed, but "I revealed it to no living being, until the pioneers to this valley were returning to Winter Quarters [Iowa]. Br[other]. Wilford Woodruff was the first man I ever spoke to about it."[70]

By 8 August 1844 the stage was set for the Rigdon-versus-Young morality play, an ecclesiastical contest, the winner of which would be the next Mormon caretaker. The happenings of this crucial day constitute Mormonism's most pivotal hour. By 10:00 a.m. more than 5,000 Saints had gathered at the grove east of the temple in response to William Marks's announcement. The minutes of this morning meeting, in stenographer Thomas Bullock's shorthand, have never been transcribed. By order of the current LDS Quorum of the Twelve Apostles they remain unavailable "for public scrutiny."[71] Nevertheless, several other accounts of the day's events survive.

As Rigdon began speaking, a strong headwind muted his voice, so he relocated to the leeward side and climbed on top of a wagon box. From that spot he addressed the Saints until 11:30 a.m. While some have painted Rigdon's discourse as uninspired, Orson Hyde, a long-time Rigdon critic, said he presented "his claims with all the eloquence and power that he was master of."

Despite assurances that the convocation was nothing more than a prayer meeting, Rigdon labored to gain a show of support from the throng of LDS faithful. Hyde reported that Rigdon was just "about to ask an expression of the people by vote; when lo! to his grief and mortification, [Brigham Young] stepped upon the stand . . . and with a word stayed all the proceedings of Mr. Rigdon."[72] Young, who later recalled the event in 1860, stated: "[W]hen I went to meet Sidney Rigdon on the meeting ground I went alone, and was ready alone to face and drive the dogs from the flock."[73]

Jacob Hamblin's diary for 8 August indicates that Young's stunning display of brinkmanship caused the audience to turn in their seats and face his commanding presence on the stand. "I will manage this voting for Elder Rigdon," he bellowed. "He does not preside here. This child (meaning himself) will manage this flock for a season."[74] He then wisely dismissed the meeting, allowing Rigdon's rhetoric to dissipate, and announced a special assembly for 2:00 p.m. Wilford Woodruff's diary records, "The[re] was a meeting appointed at the grove for the Church to come together for Prayers. But in consequence of some excitement among the People and a disposition by some spirits to try to divide the Church, it was thought best to attend to the business of the Church in the afternoon that was to be attended to on Tuesday."[75]

The afternoon meeting was organized in the manner of a solemn assembly with various priesthood leaders appropriately ordering their quorums. After prayer, Young stood before the people. It was a momentous occasion. For the first and only time in Mormon history, church leadership was about to be determined by the will of the people. Brother Brigham, who possessed a mean-weather-eye for prevailing winds from the masses, catered to the majority who had grown accustomed to being told what to do. While Rigdon, during his wild rhetoric of the previous week, had predicted a shift in Mormondom's leadership, Young perceived that the Saints "like children without a father, and sheep without a shepherd," mostly wanted comfort.[76] Lonely and bereaved, more than a third of the Mormon faithful were middle-class British immigrants, converted by Young and his fellow apostles. These new arrivals, conditioned from their earliest years, were used to working under direct guidance of a master's hand. Young saw their dependency, their inability to provide for their own emotional and economic sustenance. Accustomed to following directions from Joseph Smith, being told what to accept was a relief.

Fully confident, tossing off platitudes and pronouncements, Young's after-noon address on 8 August was a remarkable assertion of the Twelve's right to govern as well as his personal claim to be shepherd of the Mormon flock. "For the first time since [I] became a member of the church," Young began, "the Twelve Apostles of the Lamb, chosen by revelation, in this last dispensation of the gospel for the winding up scene, present themselves before the saints, to stand in their lot according to appointment."[77] After explaining "matters so satisfactorily that every saint could see that Elijah's mantle had truly fallen upon the 'Twelve,'" wrote a reporter in the 2 September 1844 *Times and Seasons*, Young, ever the masterful strategist, then asked, "I now want to ask each of you to tell me if you want to choose a guardian, a Prophet, evangelist or sumthing els[e] as your head to lead you. All that are in favor of it make it manifest by raising the right hand." No one did.[78]

Assuming a surrogate Mormon father role, Young responded, "I know your feelings—do you want me to tell your feelings?" Responding to murmurs and assenting nods, he continued:

> [H]ere [is] the 12 an independ[en]t body—who have the Keys of the K[ingdom] to all the whole world so help me God[, and] the[y] are, as the 1st pres[idenc]y of the church. . . . [Y]ou can[']t call a Prophet you can[t]t take El[der] Rig[don] or Amas[a] Lyman they must be ord[aine]d by the 12. . . . God will have nothing to do with you—you can[']t] put any one at the head of the 12.[79]

"Perhaps some think that our beloved brother Rigdon would not be honored, would not be looked to as a friend," Young added, "but if he does right, and remains faithful, he will not act against our counsel, nor we against his, but act together, and we shall be as one."[80] "Do you want a spokesman?" Young then asked. "Do you want the church properly organized, or do you want a spokesman to be chief cook and bottle washer?"

Discussing Rigdon's calling as spokesman to the prophet, Young agreed, "Very well, he was," but then quickly continued that "If he wants now to be a spokesman to the Prophet he must go to the other side of the vail for the Prophet is there, but Elder Rigdon is here. Why will Elder Rigdon be a fool? Who knows anything of the [fullness of the] priesthood, or of the organization of the kingdom of God [the Council of Fifty]? I am plain."[81] As the meeting progressed, the sentiment which had so recently changed in favor of the Twelve became palpable. When Amasa Lyman took the stand to speak, he placed himself in Young's corner. Shaken by the effect of Young's words upon the audience, the usually loquacious Rigdon declined to speak when afforded rebuttal opportunities. Considering Rigdon's rhetorical proclivities, his decision seems tantamount to conceding defeat. His face buried in his hands, Rigdon requested an old Missouri nemesis, W. W. Phelps, to champion his cause. The cagey editor, realizing Rigdon's cause was lost, delivered an ardent affirmation of the Twelve's position.

After Parley P. Pratt addressed the crowd, Young again took the stand. Attesting that if men "abide our Council they will go right into the K[ingdom] . . . [for] we have all the signs [and] the tokens to give to the Porter [and] he will let us in the qu[ay]," Young proposed a vote. "Do you want Bro. Rig[don] to stand forward as you[r] leader[,] your guide[,] your spokesman[?]"[82] Rigdon interrupted then, saying he "wanted him to bring up the other question first." So Young asked,

> [Does] this Ch[urch] want, [and is] their only desire to sust[ai]n the 12 as the 1st pres[idenc]y of this people[?] [H]ere [are] the A[postles], the Bible, the Book of Mormon, the doc[trine] [and] cov[enants] is here [and] here (head & heart) it is written on the tablet of my heart. . . . [I]f the Ch[urch] want the 12 to walk in to their call[in]g[,] if this is your mind[,] signify it by the uplifted hand.

The vote, according to Young, was unanimous, which he announced "supersedes the other question."[83]

Young then announced that "Rig[don] is . . . one with us—we want such men as Bro[ther] R[igdon.] [H]e has been sent away to build a K[ingdom;] let him keep the instruct[io]n [and] calling[,] let him raise up a k[ingdom] in Pittsburg [and] we will lift up his hand. I guess we[']ll have a printing office [and] gathering there." Wishing to support Rigdon in his calling as counselor, Young continued, "I feel to bring up Bro[ther] Rig[don.] [W]e are of one mind. . . . [W]ill this con[gregation] uphold him in the place . . . [and] let him be one with us [and] we with him?"[84] The voting was unanimous.

The leadership claim of the Twelve was beyond their February 1835 apostolic ordination, the March 1835 revelation that gave them authority equal to the First Presidency, and the July 1837 revelation that they shared the keys of the kingdom with the First Presidency. Their assertion was based entirely on Joseph Smith's commission to them and others of the "keys of the kingdom" during a spring 1844 meeting of the Council of Fifty, the organization Young referred to on 8 August saying, "if you let the 12 rem[ai]n the keys of the K[ingdom] are in them . . . we have an organ[izatio]n that you have not seen."[85]

Apostle Orson Hyde commented on this 26 March 1844 empowerment, commonly called Joseph Smith's "last charge," in an 1869 address:

In one particular place, in the presence of about sixty men, [Joseph Smith] said, "My work is about done; I am going to step aside awhile. I am going to rest from my labors; for I have borne the [burden] and heat of the day, and now I am going to step aside and rest a little. And I roll the [burden] off my shoulders on the shoulders of the Twelve Apostles. 'Now,' said he, 'round up your shoulders and bear off this kingdom.'" Has he ever said this to any one else? I do not know; I do not care. It is enough for me to know that he said it to the Quorum of the Twelve Apostles.[86]

Wilford Woodruff's account of this meeting quotes the prophet saying: "I tell you the burden of this kingdom now rests upon your shoulders; you have got to bear it off in all the world, and if you don't do it you will be damned."[87] The most explicit statement, however, came from Benjamin F. Johnson, the youngest council member. He wrote that the prophet

Stood before that association of his Select Friends including all the Twelve and with great Feeling & Animation he graphically Reviewed his Life of Pers[e]cution Labor & Sacr[ifice] For the church & Kingdom of God—Both-of-Which—he d[e]clared were now organized upon the earth. The burden of which had become too great for him longer to carry. That he was weary & Tired with the weight he So long had bourn and he then Said with great Veh[e]mence "And in the name of . . . the Lord I now Shake from my Shoulders the Responsibilaties of bearing off the Kingdom of God to all the world—and—here-& *now* I place that Responsibility with all the Keys Powrs & privilege pertaining there too upon the Shoulders of you the Twelve Apostles in Connection with this Council.[88]

The kingdom the prophet directed the Twelve to carry on their shoulders, however, was the political theocracy, the Kingdom of God, a shadow organization separate from the Church of Jesus Christ of Latter-day Saints. It was this organization, not the Quorum of the Twelve, that the prophet intended to help relieve the responsibilities of administering the temporal and secular affairs of the church.

While the Mormon vote on 8 August 1844 called for stability and ecclesiastical continuity, some have interpreted the assembly's actions as affirming Young's role as Smith's successor. That this was not intended is clarified in an epistle from the Twelve published in the 15 August 1844 *Times and Seasons*. The circular announced: "You are now without a prophet present with you in the flesh to guide you. . . . Let no man presume for a moment that [Joseph Smith's] place will be filled by another; for, remember he stands in his own place, and always will."[89] The 2 September *Times and Seasons* also editorialized: "Great excitement prevails throughout the world to know 'who shall be the successor of Joseph Smith.'" The paper then admonished, "be patient, *be patient* a little, till the proper time comes, and we will tell you all. 'Great wheels move slow.' At present, we can say that a special conference of the church was held in Nauvoo on the 8th ult., and it was carried *without a dissenting voice*, that the 'Twelve' should preside over the whole church, and when any alteration in the presidency shall be required, seasonable notice will be given."[90]

While no known contemporary record supports a supernatural occurrence the morning of 8 August when Brigham Young wrested away control of the meeting from Sidney Rigdon, over the years some have improvised a surrealistic view of the day. In LDS phraseology the alleged transcendental morning experience is known as the "Transfiguration of Brigham Young" or the "Mantle of the Prophet" incident.[91] "When Brigham Young arose and addressed the people," wrote future apostle George Q. Cannon two decades later:

> If Joseph had risen from the dead and again spoken in their hearing, the effect could not have been more startling than it was to many present at that meeting, it was the voice of Joseph himself; and not only was it the voice of Joseph which was heard, but it seemed in the eyes of the people as if it were the very person of Joseph which stood before them. A more wonderful and miraculous event than was wrought that day in the presence of that congregation, we never heard of. The Lord gave His people a testimony that left no room for doubt as to who was the man chosen to lead them.[92]

While accounts of this purported transformation were not written until the Utah period, retellings in a variety of forms exist in more than two dozen other sources.[93] Eliza Ann Perry Benson reminisced that the Saints arose "from their seats enmass" exclaiming "Joseph has come! He is here!"[94] While Eliza Ann Haven Westover, writing in 1918, remembered that "hundreds witnessed the [transfiguration], but not all that were there had that privilege."[95] Apostle Orson Hyde, foremost in exaggeration, did not even arrive in Nauvoo until 13 August,[96] yet he left two elaborate personal reminiscences of the "transfiguration." When Young began to speak that morning, Hyde recalled in 1869, "his words went through me like electricity." Hyde added for special emphasis, "it was not only the voice of Joseph Smith but there were the features, the gestures and even the stature of Joseph before us in the person of Brigham."[97] Eight years later, Hyde declared in general conference that as soon as Young opened his mouth "I heard the voice of Joseph through him."[98]

The best known account of the "transfiguration," thought by many to have been written in 1846, is George Laub's diary reference which reads: "Now when President Young arose to address the congregation his voice was the voice of Bro. Joseph and his face appeared as Josephs face & Should I not have seen his face but herd his voice I should have declared that it was Joseph." Unfortunately this small tan-colored leather diary, which has misled many scholars, is a copy of the original by Laub himself, with additions.[99]

When 8 August 1844 is stripped of emotional overlay, it was the force of Young's personality that swayed the crowd. George Miller, also present at the gathering, would later recall nothing supernatural. Young made a "long and loud harangue," Miller later wrote, for which I "could not see any point in the course of his remarks than to overturn Sidney Rigdon's pretensions."[100] Rigdon himself, in an 6 December 1870 letter to Brigham Young, accused him of duplicity:

> O vain man. . . . Did you suppose that your hypocritical and lying preten[s]e that the spirit of Joseph Smith had [e]ntered into you, was going to prevail with God and man. You knew you lied when you made that preten[s]e. Your ignorance was such that you did not know that there were those living who knew that there never was[,] is[,] nor will be[,] such a metamorphosis on this earth as you wickedly, heaven enduringly pretended had taken place with you.[101]

Apostles Brigham Young, Kimball, Richards, and Woodruff, all of whom made 8 August 1844 entries in their diaries, are silent as to any epiphany. Neither Nauvoo newspaper, the *Times and Seasons* nor the *Nauvoo Neighbor*, mentions such wonders. The assertive 1844 and 1845 accounts of Jedediah Grant and Orson Hyde, specifically written to refute Rigdon's succession claims, say nothing about a miraculous event, which, had it occurred, would have been their most compelling evidence.

Most convincing is the fact that on 8 August 1844 the congregation sustained a committee rather than an individual to run the church. They confirmed the collective Quorum of the Twelve as their presiding authority, not Brigham Young. Young's ascent to the presidency was no ceremonial stroll, as could be expected had the transfiguration been a reality. His emergence as the dominant, incontestible Mormon guiding force was not complete until late 1847, after the pioneer trek west. Even then there was some opposition to his singular leadership from within the Twelve itself. Particularly outspoken were Wilford Woodruff, Orson Pratt, and to a lesser degree Amasa Lyman. Woodruff went so far as to say that if three were taken out of the Twelve it would be like "severing the body in 2." If the Twelve surrendered its power "unto [three]," he added, "I sho[ul]d be totally opposed to it." Pratt's viewpoint was that the "head of the church consists of the Apostleship united together."[102]

The paramount question regarding the "transfiguration" is why so many otherwise honorable, pious people retrospectively remembered that they experienced something they probably did not. A rational and comprehensible explanation can perhaps be found in what psychologists call "scenario fulfillment," a phenomenon whereby one sees what one expects, especially retrospectively. Memory is more than direct recollection. It springs from tales harbored in the common fund which may then effect a re-shaping of a community's sense of itself. Joseph Smith had truly ushered in an age of miracles and wonder. Every streaking meteor in the heavens seemed to portend marvels for the Mormon masses. Viewed in the vague afterlight of the Utah period, the fact that Brigham Young had simply bested Sidney Rigdon, toe to toe, man to man, was not definitive enough to nurture and sustain the post-martyrdom Mormon psyche as a myth could. Thus nineteenth-century Latter-day Saints collectively and unwittingly began to interpret as miraculous what in 1844 had simply been a turf battle and a changing of the guard. That pious folklore lives on and on by the force of parrot-like iteration and re-iteration in present-day Mormondom.

Notes

Unless otherwise stated, all primary sources cited are located in the Historical Department of the Church of Jesus Christ of Latter-day Saints, Salt Lake City, Utah.

1. *Journal of Discourses*, 26 vols. (London: Latter-day Saints' Book Depot, 1854-86), 8 (3 June 1860):69; hereafter as *Journal of Discourses*.

2. Joseph Smith, *History of the Church of Jesus Christ of Latter-day Saints*, B. H. Roberts, ed., 7 vols. (Salt Lake City: The Church of Jesus Christ of Latter-day Saints, 1902), 6:4-8; hereafter *History of the Church*.

3. *Warsaw Signal*, 17 Jan. 1844.

4. *History of the Church*, 6:221.

5. A copy of the letter was published in *Times and Seasons* 5 (1 Feb. 1844): 418-23. On 6 June 1844, in a letter to correspondent Paul M. Closky, Rigdon explained that the Pennsylvania memorial was presented in the Senate by a Mr. Wilcox, and "after reading was referred to the Committee on the judiciary, since which I have heard nothing from it. . . . I presume, however, that it was passed over as easily as possible, so as not to [a]ffect the pending presidential election, which it might have done if the Legislature had done their duty" (*Nauvoo Neighbor*, 19 June 1844).

6. Bennett to Richards, 14 Apr. 1844, Joseph Smith Collection.

7. The Council of Ytfif (Fifty spelled backwards), as it was sometimes referred to in code, was also called the Special Council, General Council, or Council of the Kingdom. The full name, constitution, and parliamentary rules of order were given by revelation on 7 April 1842. The never-published disclosure read: "Verily thus saith the Lord, This is the name by which you shall be called, The Kingdom of God and His Laws, with the Keys and power thereof, and judgment in the hands of His servants, Ahman Christ."

During the two-year period between the 1842 revelation and the formation of this council in 1844, Smith introduced the ordinances whereby men were ordained kings and priests on earth (Joseph F. Smith Minutes of the Council of Fifty, 10 Apr. 1880, cited in Andrew F. Ehat, "Joseph Smith's Introduction of Temple Ordinances and the 1844 Mormon Succession Question," M.A. thesis, Brigham Young University, 1982, 254). For treatments of the Council of Fifty, see Klaus Hansen, *Quest for Empire: The Political Kingdom of God and the Council of Fifty in Mormon History* [2d ed. rev.] (Lincoln: University of Nebraska Press, 1974); and especially D. Michael Quinn, "Council of Fifty and Its Members, 1844-1845," *Brigham Young University Studies* 20 (Winter 1980): 163-96.

8. *Times and Seasons* 5 (1 June 1844): 547. The editor of the *New York Herald* wrote on 23 May 1844 that the Mormons "claim possession of from two hundred thousand to five hundred thousand votes in Nauvoo and throughout the Union." In actuality, Nauvoo never had more than 10,000 citizens (Leonard J. Arrington and Davis Bitton, *The Mormon Experience: A History of the Latter-day Saints* [Alfred A. Knopf: New York, 1979], 69).

9. Scott Faulring, ed., *An American Prophet's Record: The Diaries and Journals of Joseph*

Smith (Salt Lake City: Signature Books in association with Smith Research Associates, 1989), 425.

10. Ibid., 456.

11. Ibid., 443.

12. Various drafts of the platform can be seen in the W. W. Phelps Collection.

13. *History of the Church*, 6:197-209.

14. Ibid., 6:230-33.

15. Faulring, 477.

16. Jedediah M. Grant, *A Collection of Facts Relative to the Course Taken by Elder Sidney Rigdon in the States of Ohio, Missouri, Illinois and Pennsylvania* (Philadelphia: Brown, Bicking & Guilbert, 1844), 16.

17. Orson Hyde, *Speech of Elder Orson Hyde, Delivered Before the High Priest's Quorum, in Nauvoo, April 27th, 1845, Upon the Course and Conduct of Mr. Sidney Rigdon, and Upon the Merits of His Claims to the Presidency of the Church of Jesus Christ of Latter-day Saints* (Liverpool: James and Woodburn, 1845), 8-9.

18. *Correspondence of Bishop George Miller with the Northern Islander From His Acquaintance with Mormonism Up to Near the Close of His Life, 1855* (Burlington, WI: W. Watson, 1916), 20-21.

19. Faulring, 462.

20. Journal History, 6 Apr. 1844—a multi-volume daily history of the church compiled by official church historians; hereafter Journal History.

21. Thomas Bullock Minutes, 6 Apr. 1844, General Minutes Collection.

22. Scott G. Kenney, ed. *Wilford Woodruff's Journal, Typescript* [9 vols.] (Midvale, UT: Signature Books, 1983-85), 2:374-75.

23. Journal History, 6 Apr. 1844, 1.

24. Kenney, 2:374-75.

25. Ibid., 375.

26. Unknown scribe, minutes of 6 Apr. 1844, General Minutes Collection.

27. Journal History, 6 Apr. 1844, 2.

28. Unknown scribe, minutes of 6 Apr. 1844, General Minutes Collection.

29. Kenney, 2:378.

30. Ibid.

31. Ibid.

32. Ibid.

33. Conference Minutes, 6-7 Apr. 1844, General Minutes Collection.

34. The original account, from Joseph Smith's diary, is in Faulring, 468. The published version is from *History of the Church*, 6:321.

35. Faulring, 472.

36. May 1844 letter to Thomas Gregg, Mormon Manuscript Collection, Chicago Historical Society, Chicago, Illinois.

37. Ehat, 179.

38. Ibid., 86-89, 106.

39. William Law diary, under date, in Lyndon W. Cook, "William Law, Nauvoo Dissenter," *Brigham Young University Studies* 22 (Winter 1982): 68.

40. *Nauvoo Expositor*, vol. 1, no. 1.

41. *History of the Church*, 6:438.

42. Ibid., 466-67.

43. Faulring, 490.

44. The sanctity of an American free press was established as long ago as 1735 in the famous Zenger Trial. German immigrant John Peter Zenger settled in New York City and became a printer and publisher. In his newspaper, the *Weekly Journal*, Zenger carried articles criticizing the royal governor, William Cosby. Angered by these attacks, Cosby ordered Zenger's arrest. At his trial Zenger was defended by Andrew Hamilton of Philadelphia, one of the ablest lawyers of the day. Hamilton argued that as long as one told the truth, one had the right to expose and oppose unjust government. The jury verdict was "not guilty" and Zenger was freed. This case established the principle of freedom of the press, making it possible for newspapers to print truths openly critical of the government and its policies.

45. Josephine Rigdon Secord, the last surviving grandchild of Sidney Rigdon, made the following statement to Noel B. Croft on the afternoon of 23 August 1972: "Near the turn of the century my Aunt Athalia Robinson, wife of George W. Robinson, told me that the killing of Joseph Smith was the result of a complex political plot which included, among others, the Masons, John C. Bennett and George W. Robinson." She stated that Bennett as well as Robinson, who chaired the La Harpe precinct of the Hancock County anti-Mormon committee (see *History of the Church*, 6:462-66), intended to "control the church through Sidney Rigdon, whom they considered to be mentally unstable and that he could be easily controlled by them" (Noel B. Croft Collection).

Stories were told in Friendship, New York, respecting George W. Robinson's paranoid fear of Mormon reprisal for some unnamed deed. Rumor had it that he constructed a bullet proof room in his bank and had the lower windows of his home barred for protection against those seeking vengeance (see *The History of Friendship* [Friendship, NY: The Friendship Sesquentennial Corp., 1965], 29).

46. *History of the Church*, 6:469-70.

47. Young's false statement was made during Heber C. Kimball's funeral (Journal History, 24 June 1868). In Kirtland the prophet had pronounced that "my servant Sydney must go sooner or later to Pittsburg" (David Whitmer to Joseph Smith III, 9 Dec. 1886, cited in *Saints' Herald*, 5 Feb. 1887).

Joseph Smith's personal diary entry for 22 June 1844 notes that he had sent Rigdon from Nauvoo to keep him alive in case he was killed: "I have sent Br. R[igdon] away [and] I want to send Hiram away to save him [too], to avenge my Blood" (Joseph Smith diary, loose sheet under date, microfilm copy in Special Collections, Brigham Young University, Harold B. Lee Library, Provo, UT; hereafter BYU Library). I am indebted to D. Michael Quinn for drawing this unpublished reference to my attention.

48. J. Wickliffe Rigdon, "Life of Sidney Rigdon," 178-79.

49. Although Rigdon was shocked to learn of the prophet's death, in a 25 May 1873 letter to Charles F. Woodward, after his mind was addled by a series of strokes, he stated: "The Lord notified us that the church of Jesus Christ of Latter day saints were a going to be d[e]stroyed and for us to leave we did so and the Smiths were killed a few days after we started" (Rigdon Collection).

50. Hyde, 11.

51. Grant, 44-45.

52. Ibid., 17.

53. Woodruff to Young, 16 July 1844, in "Brigham Young Collection of Wilford Woodruff Correspondence, 1840-44," Brigham Young Collection.

54. Grant, 17.

55. This quotation is from either Willard Richards's or William Clayton's diary, both of which are presently unavailable to researchers. The citation is from Ehat, 197.

56. D. Michael Quinn, "The Mormon Succession Crisis of 1844," *Brigham Young University Studies* 16 (Winter 1976): 187-233.

57. Hyde, 12.

58. Ibid., 12.

59. Journal History, 4 Aug. 1844.

60. Hyde, 16.

61. Journal History, 4 Aug. 1844; Hyde, 40-41.

62. *History of the Church*, 7:226.

63. The original minutes of this 7 Aug. 1844 meeting, presently controlled by the Quorum of the Twelve, are "not available for public scrutiny" (F. Michael Watson, secretary to the First Presidency, to Richard S. Van Wagoner, 14 June 1993). The account of the meeting in William Clayton's diary (in possession of the First Presidency) is also unavailable. I therefore cite Ehat, 197-98.

64. Ann Lee Stanley (1736-84) claimed to be the female incarnation of Jesus and was leader of the United Society of Believers in Christ's Second Coming, the "Shaking Quakers."

65. Ehat, 198.

66. Kenney, 2:434.

67. Thomas Bullock's report of the special meeting, 8 Aug. 1844, General Minutes Collection.

68. Manuscript Minutes of Brigham Young sermon "on the occasion of a family meeting, held at his residence," 25 Dec. 1857, Brigham Young Collection.

69. Miscellaneous Minutes, 12 Feb. 1849, Brigham Young Collection.

70. Journal History, 7 Oct. 1860. Woodruff confirmed in his 12 Oct. 1847 diary:

> I had A question put to me by President Young what my opinion was concerning one of the Twelve Apostles being appointed as the President of the Church with his two Councellors. I answered that A quorum like the Twelve who had been appointed by revelation & confirmed by revelation from time to time I thought it would require A revelation to change the order of that Quorum (Kenney, 3:283).

Woodruff also recorded another of Young's references to this matter in his 28 July 1860 diary entry. Young said:

> When I met with the Saints in Nauvoo at the first meeting after Joseph[']s death in defending the true organization against Sidney Rigdon I had it in my mind all the time that there would have to be a Presidency of three Appointed but I knew the people Could not bear it at the time and on our return as the pioneers from the valley

I Broached the subject first to Brother Woodruff and afterwords to the rest of the Quorum. They received it & finally sustained it (Kenney, 5:478).

While the official reorganization of the First Presidency did not take place until 1847, it was a mere formality. The manuscript minutes of the 7 April 1845 general conference show that Young was unanimously voted on and sustained as "the President of the Quorum of the Twelve Apostles to this Church and nation, and all nations, and also as the President of the whole Church of Latter Day Saints."

71. F. Michael Watson, secretary to the First Presidency, to Richard S. Van Wagoner, 14 June 1993. Bullock's transcription of the afternoon meeting of 8 Aug. is available in the General Minutes Collection.

72. Hyde, 13.

73. Journal History, 6 Oct. 1860.

74. James A. Little, *Jacob Hamblin* (Salt Lake City: Deseret News, 1909), 20-21.

75. Kenney, 2:434-35.

76. Journal History, 8 Aug. 1844.

77. *Times and Seasons* 5 (2 Sept. 1844): 637. While my narration generally follows the 8 August 1844 Journal History account, which for the most part fleshes out Thomas Bullock's 8 August minutes (General Minutes Collection), other important references are Wilford Woodruff diary account (Kenney, 2:434-40); Brigham Young diary entry for 8 August 1844; William Clayton diary entry for 8 August 1844, cited in George D. Smith, ed., *An Intimate Chronicle: The Journals of William Clayton* (Salt Lake City: Signature Books in association with Smith Research Associates, 1991), 142 ; and *History of the Church*, 7:231-42.

78. Minutes, 8 Aug. 1844 (p.m.), General Minutes Collection.

79. Ibid.

80. Journal History, 8 Aug. 1844.

81. Ibid.

82. 8 Aug. 1844 minutes in Thomas Bullock's handwriting, General Minutes Collection.

83. Ibid. William C. Staines Journal, cited in *History of the Church*, 7:236, reported there were "a few dissenting voices." "History of William Adams, Wrote by himself January 1894," 15, adds that "out of that vast multitude about twenty voted for Rigdon to be Gardian" (Special Collections, Harold B. Lee Library, Brigham Young University, Provo, Utah; hereafter Special Collections, BYU).

84. 8 Aug. 1844 minutes in Thomas Bullock's handwriting, General Minutes Collection.

85. Ibid.

86. *Journal of Discourses* 13 (6 Oct. 1869): 180.

87. "Wilford Woodruff's Testimony On Priesthood and Presidency," delivered 23 Feb. 1892, cited in *Liahona: The Elders' Journal* 7 (16 Apr. 1910): 682.

88. Dean R. Zimmerman, *I Knew the Prophets, An Analysis of the Letter of Benjamin F. Johnson to George F. Gibbs, Reporting Doctrinal Views of Joseph Smith and Brigham Young* (Bountiful, UT: Horizon, 1976), 35.

89. *Times and Seasons* 5 (15 Aug. 1844): 618.

90. Ibid., 5 (2 Sept. 1844): 632.

91. This latter terminology likely evolved from a figurative or allegorical description such as the one in an anonymous letter published in the 15 October *Times and Seasons* (5:675). "Who can[']t see," began the communication, "that the mantle of the prophet has fallen on Pres. Young and the Twelve?" "The same spirit," continued the letter, "which inspired our beloved bro. Joseph Smith, now inspires Pres. Young."

92. Kate B. Carter, comp., *Heart Throbs of the West* (Salt Lake City: Daughters of Utah Pioneers, 1943), 4:420; see also Andrew Jenson, *The Historical Record* 1:789-91, and *Journal of Discourses* 23 (29 Oct. 1882): 358.

93. Caroline Barnes Crosby, "Retrospective Memoirs Written in 1851"; Homer Duncan Journal; Zadok Knapp Judd "Reminiscence Written at Age Seventy-five" (Utah Historical Society); Catharine Thomas Leishman Autobiography; George Morris Autobiography (Special Collections, BYU); John Riggs Murdock, in J. M. Tanner, *A Biographical Sketch of John Riggs Murdock* (Salt Lake City: Deseret News Press, 1909), 71; Zera Pulsipher, in Terry and Nora Lund, comps., *The Pulsipher Family History Book* (Salt Lake City: n.p., 1953), 10-24; William Lampard Watkins Autobiography; Samuel Amos Woolley Autobiography; Eliza Westover, "2 July 1916 Letter to Her Son"; Emily Smith Hoyt "Reminiscences and Diaries (1851-1893)"; Robert Taylor Burton "Statement of 28 July 1905"; Jacob Hamblin, in Pearson H. Corbett, *Jacob Hamblin: The Peacemaker* (Salt Lake City: Deseret Book Co., 1952), 22; "Wilford Woodruff's Testimony on Priesthood and Presidency—Delivered on 23 February 1892," in *Liahona The Elders' Journal* 7 (16 Apr. 1910): 683; "Wilford Woodruff Statement," in *Deseret News*, 15 Mar. 1892; Wilford Woodruff in *Journal of Discourses* 15 (8 Apr. 1872), 81; Journal History, 9 Oct. 1867; Benjamin F. Johnson, in Zimmerman, 17; Robert T. Taylor, in Janet Burton Seegmiller, *The Life Story of Robert Taylor Burton* (Salt Lake City: Robert Taylor Burton Family Organization, 1988), 49; William C. Staines, in *The Contributor* 12 (1891): 315; William Van Orden Carbine, in Kate B. Carter, comp., *Our Pioneer Heritage* (Salt Lake City: Daughters of Utah Pioneers, 1963), 6:203; Albert Clements, ibid., 12:219; William L. Watkins, ibid., 19:390-91; Talitha Cheney Autobiography, ibid., 15:118-19; Anson Call Autobiography and Journal; Ezra T. Benson, in John Henry Evans and Minnie Egan Anderson, *Ezra T. Benson: Pioneer, Statesman, Saint* (Salt Lake City: Deseret News Press, 1947), 88-89; "Typescript Account of Testimony of Bishop George Romney, by Mary R. Ross," and Emmeline B. Wells, "My Testimony," in Preston Nibley, comp., *Faith Promoting Stories* (Salt Lake City: Deseret Book Co., 1943), 137.

94. Donald Benson Alder and Elsie L. Alder, comps., *The Benson Family: The Ancestry and Descendants of Ezra T. Benson* (Salt Lake City: Ezra T. Benson Genealogical Society, Inc., 1979), 238.

95. Burton, 50.

96. See Wilford Woodruff diary under date; Kenney, 2:441.

97. *Journal of Discourses* 13 (6 Oct. 1869): 181.

98. Ibid. 19 (5 Apr. 1877): 58. In 1860 Hyde also embellished his recall of the 1847 organization of the First Presidency, saying he heard the voice of God declare: "Let my servant Brigham step forth and receive the full power of the presiding Priesthood in my Church and kingdom" (ibid. 8 [7 Oct. 1860]:234). Yet when President Wilford Woodruff was asked during an 1894 meeting of the First Presidency and Quorum of the Twelve if

he observed any of the special manifestations described by Hyde in connection with the 1847 organization, he said he did "not remember any particular manifestations at the time of the organization of the Presidency" (Abraham H. Cannon Journal, 30 Aug. 1894, Special Collections, BYU).

99. The tan-colored copy, incorrectly thought to be the original diary, was published in its entirety by Eugene England, ed., "George Laub's Nauvoo Journal," *Brigham Young University Studies* 18 (Winter 1977):151-78. Whereas the original maroon-colored diary is written in a variety of inks, as one would expect in a multi-year diary, the copy is written in only two inks (1-43, a dark ink; 44-139, a lighter ink). Extensive family genealogy is also included on the inside covers of the original diary. Not so with the copy. The lighter ink used in the copy is also evident after page 195 in the original. This reflects Laub's first entry in Utah. He did not arrive in Utah territory until 25 August 1852 (original, 266), and the copy was likely made after this date. The 25 August entry is a retrospective one, for he notes on 1 March 1857 "this day I commenced my daily Jurnel." Laub's insertion in the original (139, not 140 as England noted) "here ends the transfer of the first" is in the same light ink as the copy, leaving no doubt as to which is the original of the two.

Laub's treatment of Rigdon is considerably more negative in the copied diary, as well as more positive regarding Brigham Young, reflecting a retrospective change of heart. Also, at the exact spot where the "transfiguration" insertion is made in the copy, a + mark is made in the light-colored ink. The additional text in the copied version profoundly alters the sense of the original to reflect the retrospective image of the "transfiguration" that had become well-grounded in Utah folklore by the early 1850s. The original reads:

> Now after the Death of Jos & Hyrum[,] Rigdon came from Pittsburgh. (Because Jos. had sent him there to get him out of his way as Rigdon Desired to goe) to clame the presidency of the church to lead the church[.] But as the lord would have his servant Brigham Young the President of the Twelve to come just in time to tell the people who was the fals sheperd or who was the good shepard and Rigdon soon quaked and trembled and these things which he declared the day before to be revelations was then think [so's] and gess [so's] and hoap so and his words fell to the ground because they was Lies from the beginning to the End (original, 115).

100. "Correspondence of Bishop George Miller with *The Northern Islander* From his first acquaintance with Mormonism up to near the close of his life. Written by himself in the year 1855."

101. An undated copy is in the Stephen Post Collection, box 1, fd 1 (also listed as Section 61 in Copying Book A). The mailed letter to Young is in the Brigham Young Collection (box 42, fd 2, reel 73).

102. 5 Dec. 1847, Miscellaneous Minutes, Brigham Young Collection.

CHAPTER 24.

Excommunication

As regards the trial of Elder Rigdon at Nauvoo, it was a forced affair, got up by the twelve to get him out of their way, that they might . . . better arrogate to themselves higher authority . . . and also to prevent a complete exposé of the Spiritual-wife-system which they knew would deeply implicate themselves. The trial deserves no other name than that of a religious farce.

—Benjamin Winchester[1]

After Brigham Young's public subjugation of Sidney Rigdon on 8 August 1844, most Latter-day Saints accepted the Quorum of the Twelve as caretakers of the tradition and faith. While there were other lesser-known leadership aspirants in Nauvoo—namely James Strang, Lyman Wight, and James Emmett—they are today mere footnotes. Had Rigdon subordinated himself to the Twelve and subsequently migrated west with them, he likely would have been accommodated within the fold, much as eccentrics W. W. Phelps, Orson Pratt, and Amasa Lyman would be. Unlike these men, however, Rigdon refused to be at the beck and call of the Twelve. Moreover, his view of spiritual wifery as an abomination predisposed him against participation in a hierarchy hemmed in by polygamy, the defining characteristic of nineteenth-century Utah Mormonism.

Rigdon initially pretended to accept the decree of the special conference. But his true feelings soon surfaced through his private actions. For fourteen years he had been the apostles' ecclesiastical superior. He had counseled, cajoled, praised, and occasionally chastised them individually and as a group. Regardless of Joseph Smith's death, Rigdon was not about to serve in an inferior capacity under Brigham Young, Orson Hyde, Willard Richards, or any other member of the "spiritual wife fraternity," as he designated the Quorum of the Twelve. On the Sunday following 8 August, Rigdon, according to Jedediah Grant, "spoke a long time to the Saints, and blessed them in the name of the Lord." He then asked to "know the mind of the Church" regarding his returning to Pittsburgh, to which the Saints responded, "go in peace."[2] Brigham Young had also proclaimed: "[L]et [Sidney] raise up a k[ingdom] in Pittsburg [and] we will lift up his hand. I guess we[']ll have a printing office [and] gathering there."[3] Rigdon began gathering a group of adherents and close friends who "expressed a desire to go with me to Pittsburgh . . . where they could enjoy my society, as well as I theirs." They held several meetings in Nauvoo, Rigdon continued, "not in the least doubting our right to do so if we chose, but to our surprise a great excitement was got up." He asserted that Young, Hyde, Heber Kimball, Erastus Snow, and Parley and Orson Pratt made inflammatory speeches depicting him and his associates "as mobocrats, as murderers, as conspirators . . . and all this for the sin of desiring to go to Pennsylvania to live with our families."[4]

But there was more to the story than Rigdon admitted. A principal source of conflict between him and the Twelve, as they saw it, was his unauthorized administration of Endowment Quorum ordinations. Although Rigdon had received his Nauvoo endowment on 11 May 1844, Joseph Smith had apparently withheld anointing him to the fullness of the priesthood (called the second anointing) that would have made Rigdon a prophet, priest, king, and god in the flesh—probably because Smith could not win him over to polygamy. John Taylor's statement on 8 September that Rigdon "has been ordaining men to the offices of prophets, priests and kings; whereas he does not hold that [higher] office himself"[5] disclosed the official reason the Twelve wanted Rigdon out of the church.

Jedediah Grant reported that during a private meeting with a group of his followers on 12 August, Rigdon reflected on the 8 August conference, proclaiming himself to be "the stone that the Prophet Isaiah said the builders rejected." He also professed to have received the sealing keys of David, which gave him power to "shut and no man openeth, and to open and no man shutteth," along with the keys to ordain men "Prophets, Priests, and Kings." Waxing prophetic, Rigdon advised that the political Kingdom of God, as it advanced into the world, would meet with opposition, "making it necessary for them to raise an army to fight the battles of the great God." He ordained several persons to serve as commanders in the divine militia when it should be called to duty. Speaking against polygamy, or spiritual wifery, as nearly everyone in Nauvoo called it, he began to talk "of the existence of great iniquity in the church," Grant wrote, dropping "oblique hints" against Joseph and Hyrum Smith and the Twelve.[6]

On Sunday, 18 August, Young addressed a large congregation of the Saints at the grove near the temple. According to Wilford Woodruff, Young spoke of "the present excitement" surging through Nauvoo, "in consequence of unwise teaching by some that are trying to draw away a party after them." Despite Young's earlier approval of Rigdon's directing a gathering in Pittsburgh, he now spoke directly against him: "The report has gone forth," he recounted,

> that the Twelve has a secret understanding with those men who are going away to take a company with them, that they shall take all they can but the Twelve will blow it up in public but privately wish it to go on. But if it was the last words I had to say

before going into the Eternal world I would swear by the Holy Trinity that it was utterly fals[e] and not a word of truth in it.[7]

Meanwhile Rigdon, from his headquarters at the home of George W. and Athalia Robinson in nearby La Harpe, began to attract a sizeable following, perhaps as many as 300 or 400 adherents. The Twelve, wishing to bridge the schism, invited Rigdon and Nauvoo Stake President William Marks to meet with them on 29 August. Unwilling to be summoned by Young, Rigdon feigned illness and refused to attend. During the meeting Young stated to Marks "that in consequence of rumors & reports of the proceedings of him & E[lde]r Rigdon" he had called the group together to discuss the situation and see if a possible union could be managed. Marks, describing himself as "abused by the tongue of slander," explained that while the course the Twelve had pursued was "contrary to what he had expected . . . he did not intend to say any thing."[8]

Three days later on Sunday, 1 September, Rigdon preached his final sermon in Nauvoo. His discourse, according to most available accounts, was complicated, confusing, and rambling. Parley P. Pratt commented afterwards: "I thought we were concerned in building up [Nauvoo] and defending it." Yet all Rigdon spoke of was "Queen Victoria, battles . . . and talkings which were calculated to draw our minds away from those things wherein our eternal interest is at stake."[9] Others saw the speech as self-serving. Brigham Young's brother Joseph recalled that Rigdon mentioned a revelation he had received that proclaimed "he was to succeed Joseph and that the saints were to cease building up Nauvoo, and finishing the temple." The divine manifestation warned him that "the saints were to flee from their enemies and to scatter abroad, and get rich."[10] The imminent coming of Christ was to take place at Pittsburgh, "in the top of the Allegheny Mountains." The great battle of Gog and Magog was to be fought a few miles downstream from Pittsburgh on the banks of the Ohio River. Young added that Rigdon claimed he was to "lead the Queen of England over by the nose to join the saints, and help them fight their battles, etc. And also that God had given him great power, that he could [b]ind and it was bound, loose and it was loosed; he held the keys of David; and consequently could ordain men to be kings, and Priests to God."[11] Orson Hyde professed that the latter part of his discourse was so filled with "blood, war and conquest" that many listeners became concerned about his wild utterances.[12]

The following day, according to Hyde, during a meeting at the home of Nauvoo Stake high councilman Leonard Soby, Rigdon ordained several men "Prophets, Priests and Kings." He also apparently prophesied that the Nauvoo temple would never be built, that God had rejected the church because of the iniquity of the people, and that Nauvoo would soon be overthrown.[13] On 3 September Young and Hyde sought Rigdon out and, according to Young, took him by the hand, looked him in the eyes, and asked whether he had held a meeting the previous evening "where men were ordained to be prophets, priests and kings?" Rigdon, eyeing Soby, replied, "No, we had no meeting here; had we brother Soby?" Young pressed: "Did you have a meeting any where, brother Rigdon, in which men were ordained to be prophets, priests and kings?" Rigdon admitted there had been a meeting. "Elder Rigdon, did you ordain these men at that meeting last night?" Young asked. "Yes, I suppose I did," Rigdon replied. When Young asked by what authority he had ordained prophets, priests, and kings, Rigdon retorted, "Oh, I know about that!" Young then asked Rigdon: "Do you not think, really, that you hold keys and authority above any man, or set of men in this church, even the Twelve?" Rigdon replied, "Yes, I do." In response to Young's efforts to cross-examine further, Rigdon remonstrated, "Don't crowd upon my feelings too much; my feelings are tender, and I don't wish to be crowded."

Young proposed that he and others call on Rigdon later that evening for a continuation of the discussion. Rigdon readily agreed. Eight of the Twelve, together with Bishop Newel K. Whitney, met with Rigdon until 9 p.m. before adjourning to the nearby home of Willard Richards. "After mature deliberation," recorded Apostle George A. Smith, "[we] disfellowshipped him and sent Elders Parley P. Pratt, Orson Hyde and Amasa Lyman to demand his [ministerial] license."[14]

When the emissaries returned to Rigdon with their demand, he refused to comply. "I did not receive it from you," he informed them, "neither shall I give it up to you." Moreover, he continued, "I have sat and laughed in my sleeve at the proceedings of the Twelve this evening, for they have been fulfilling in this last act, the vision I had at Pittsburg[h]. I knew you would withdraw fellowship from me, I knew you would oppose me, in all my movements. It was all shown to me in the vision before I left Pittsburg[h]."[15] George A. Smith noted that Rigdon threatened to expose the Twelve's clandestine spiritual wifery by publishing "all he knew" against them. He further noted "he knew the Church had not Been Led By the Spirit of God for a Long time."[16]

Unable to tolerate Rigdon's unpredictable threats, the Twelve prepared to excommunicate him. The following day, 4 September, both the *Nauvoo Neighbor* and the *Times and Seasons* carried notices that Rigdon had been disfellowshipped and would be publicly tried for his membership the following Sunday, 8 September. Orson Hyde, who was prone to exaggerate, later wrote that during an early morning gathering of his followers on his day of hearing, Rigdon advised men to "arm themselves with deadly weapons and go upon the meeting ground, and there by force of arms, prevent the authorities of the Church from bringing him to trial." According to Hyde, cooler heads prevailed against such rash action.[17] Viewing the trial as a mockery of justice, Rigdon refused to attend.

Brigham Young began the six-hour inquisition by announcing that "all those who are for Joseph and Hyrum, the Book of Mormon, book of Doctrine and Covenants, the Temple and Joseph's measures, and for the Twelve" will be called on to "manifest their principles openly and boldly." Those with opposing views were to "enjoy the same liberty."[18] He then explained that Rigdon's case would be heard by the Nauvoo High Council, under the direction of Bishop Whitney, who would render judgment. Young made much of his personal feelings toward Rigdon: "I am willing that you should know that my feelings for Sidney Rigdon as a man, as a private citizen, are of the best kind. I have loved that man and always had the very best feelings for him. . . . But when it touches the salvation of the people, I am the man that walks to the line."[19]

Young then invited witnesses for the prosecution to present their testimony. All except W. W. Phelps and Newel K. Whitney were members of the Quorum of the Twelve. Their collective accusations meticulously stitched every seam, weaving Rigdon's smallest faults and past actions into a sinister shroud. A host of charges dating back to the days of Kirtland and Missouri were dredged up like fetid Mississippi River mud to besmirch Rigdon's reputation. Rigdon has not "conducted himself like a man of God . . . since he came here," Young charged. He is the "cause of our troubles in Missouri," Hyde added. He had "endeavor[ed] to palm upon the people, false revelations and lies in the name of the Lord," said Parley P. Pratt. He "correspond[ed] with John C. Bennet[t], and other mean, corrupt men," avowed Amasa Lyman. He "resist[ed] authority . . . try[ed] to subvert the order of God . . . a liar," said John Taylor. "His late revelations and his extraordinary ordination of prophets, priests and kings among the Gentiles [are] of the devil," proclaimed Phelps. And Kimball finished by arguing: "Brother Joseph shook him off . . . said he would carry him no more."[20]

After the Twelve had rhetorically pounded the absent defendant, Young summarized their testimony. Referring to Rigdon as "a black hearted wretch," he asked if anyone wished to produce testimony "in favor of the opposite side of the question." Only one fearless man braved the opposition. William Marks, who earlier had "made a solemn covenant with God, that if no other person stood by [Rigdon] he would,"[21] walked to the stand. Declaring "there has been a strong team against him . . . they all seem to speak against him," Marks declared his intent to "say something in his defence, for I have always been a friend to Elder Rigdon":

> In regard to his character there has been many things said which appear to be objectionable, but I can do some of them away. I hear objections to his authority, and to his conduct for four or five years past. There were charges brought before the conference, last fall, and one or two days spent in hearing of them, and it seemed to me, that every exertion was made that could be made, to criminate him and cut him off. There was time given to bring all the charges that could be got at, but there was not a single particle of the charges sustained. . . . Now I think if Brother Rigdon was restored at that time we ought not to go beyond the conference to fetch up charges today. . . . I have heard Brother Joseph say repeatedly since [last fall], that all things was right between them.[22]

Regarding church organization Marks said he "had always understood that the church would be imperfect without a quorum of three to stand as a first presidency," and despite a search of the scriptures he could not "find any law to say that this quorum should ever be dropped." Regarding the genealogy of Rigdon's authority, Marks related:

> I laid my hands on Brother Sidney with Brother Joseph and he ordained him to be a "prophet and a seer and revelator," and to be equal with him in holding the keys and authority of this kingdom.[23] I have known this for two years, and according to my understanding he has not lost it through transgression. I still feel that he is a member of the quorum of the first presidency, and I always expected that the quorum would be filled up the same as at the commencement. I always felt that there was a power and responsibility in that quorum which did not exist any where else.[24]

Citing several sections of the Doctrine and Covenants to buttress Rigdon's authority, Marks recapitulated:

> There [have been men] ordained prophets, priests and kings, but I have never heard of any one [else] being ordained a prophet seer and revelator. I think I am knowing to all the ordinations, but I don't know of a man who has been ordained to the office and calling Brother Sidney has; and if he is cut off, who will we have to obtain revelations? A man must be in possession of this power to be able to ordain a prophet, and a seer and a revelator. . . . I don['t] believe there are sufficient revelations given to lead this people, and I am fully of the belief that this people cannot build up the kingdom except it is done by revelation.[25]

Brigham Young then stood up, faulted Marks for attempting to "soft soap" the people, and bullied him with threats against his own church membership.[26] Rigdon is "going contrary to Joseph's instructions," Young insisted, and "he shall not lead the innocent to destruction . . . I say it in the name of Israel's God."[27]

The meeting had been long; the people were tired. At this point members of the audience raised a "call for the question." Young submitted the case to Bishop Whitney and the high council. Observing that Rigdon "was always either in the bottom of the cellar or up in the garret window," Whitney tagged him an "evil designing man . . . he has lied to carry out his theory."[28] After a rather weakly-worded motion passed, Hyde arose and said the proposition was not "explicit enough." Phelps proposed "that Elder Sidney Rigdon be cut off from the church, and delivered over to the buffetings of Satan until he repents." The vote of the high council was "unanimous in the affirmative." The congregation was then polled. The official account reported that the "vote was unanimous, excepting a few of Elder Rigdon's party, numbering about ten."[29] Those ten (actually more than twenty) were immediately "suspended until they can have a trial before the High Council."[30] That evening the dissenting faction composed a brief to show why they sustained Rigdon above the Twelve. Their two-column broadside, likely printed elsewhere as the Nauvoo press would have been closed to them, appeared in the 25 September *Warsaw Signal*:

> The melancholy catastrophe of the murder of Joseph Smith, the presiding President, and Hyrum his brother, resulted in leaving one individual only known to the church as pointed out by repeated revelations, as Prophet, Seer, and Revelator for the Church—viz. Sidney Rigdon. . . .
>
> We . . . declare our sincere conviction, that, in rejecting Sidney Rigdon, the Church of Jesus Christ of Latter Day Saints does no longer exist, except in connexion with him; and that God has given no authority for an organization of the church, differing from that contained in the Book of Doctrine and Covenants.[31]

An intriguing, though fraudulent, document supporting Rigdon's claim to the mantle of leadership was mentioned briefly on 8 September by Amasa Lyman. The previous Tuesday, 3 September, John C. Bennett had arrived in Nauvoo with a revelation claiming, according to Lyman, that "Elder Rigdon is to take the presidency, and [Bennett] is appointed to elder Rigdon's place."[32] Bennett's professed revelation, dated 7 April 1841, included a "To Whom it May Concern" statement at the bottom supposedly in Joseph Smith's handwriting:

> This is to certify that General John C. Bennett having promised me under a most solemn oath this day that he will faithfully preserve the within revelation, and hand it over to an authorized agent of the church should he survive me. I have communicated to him the full pattern, in whole, and in part . . . with the names of the men whom I desire to fill the alternate stations etc. . . etc. . . and he has sworn faithfully to confer all the degrees or enable some other person to so do, as I have shown him both the pattern and the names. It is my desire that the full organization should take place as soon after my decease as practicable.

After lauding Joseph Smith and his prophetic calling, the revelation attested: "the time will come, when he shall be gathered unto his fathers and another shall take his office." Rigdon would survive him, the document purported, and "shall be as Joseph unto my people . . . the imperial primate to all Israel and over all authorities & Eclesiastical powers and his counsellors shall be viceroys as in the reign of Joseph."

Regarding the rule of the Twelve, the revelation erred on the side of verbosity:

> Behold the great day of apostacy is at hand, and after the kingdom shall be set up there shall be great wickedness, such as never was before; and my people will reject their prophet, and refuse counsel, and they will set up strange Gods and follow rulers who will usurp authority for filthy lucres sake. And the apostacy shall be great and they shall be ruled by 12 horns pushing them to destruction; but the righteous shall be saved, for they shall follow the head, and the . . . horns shall be lopped off. . . .

The revelation contained an appropriate number of *beholds, hearkens,* and *thus saith the Lords.* But the use of florid words and phrases as *diadems, imperial primate, triumvirate*, and *Halcyon Order* identified it as the work of grandiloquent John C. Bennett.

Although Bennett's hoax was published in a special issue of the *Latter Day Saints' Messenger and Advocate* (Pittsburgh), and reprinted in *The Prophet* (New York) on 10 May 1845, Rigdon himself never used it to support his claims. In fact, when he wrote his lengthy 1856 treatise on his right to succession, mention of this alleged 1841 revelation was conspicuously absent.[33]

Rigdon left Nauvoo, never to return, aboard the paddle wheeler *Osprey* on 10 September. Several other prominent Mormons were also aboard, including Rigdon's nemesis Orson Hyde. During a two-day layover in St. Louis, while Rigdon waited to embark on the *Mayflower*, Hyde visited Rigdon, finding him ill "with the Diarhoe [having] vomited most of the night." During their lengthy conversation Hyde remarked that "as a friend . . . I indulged the hope that he would see the error into which he had fallen, and erelong retrace his steps." Fearing the disclosures Rigdon threatened, Hyde advised his former mentor, "be careful how you put pen to paper in this time of your excitement . . . wait a few months and then see how you will feel." Rigdon nevertheless responded that "his course was marked out before him and that he should pursue it." In the course of the visit Rigdon attested that he had "never felt happier." Hyde noted nonetheless that Rigdon's "happiness appeared to me like the blaze from shavings—lively and brilliant, but of short duration."[34]

As the remaining three decades of his life would prove, Rigdon was seldom content after 1844. Racked by poverty, poor health, and mental instability, he spent much of his dotage studying on his own cloud-encircled peak the ineffable secrets of God. But his soul's melody was the lamentation of a religious expatriate, continually pricked by a burning hatred for Brigham Young. Wickliffe Rigdon wrote that the 1844 rejection by the Twelve and their followers deeply hurt his father, who believed he had "done more to establish the Church" than anyone else and should have been rewarded with its leadership. Not only had he "spent the best years of his life in preaching the gospel," but he "had sacrificed fame and fortune to do it . . . [and could not] take a subordinate place under Young or any other man."[35]

Pragmatically speaking, Rigdon's limited administrative aptitude made him a seriously flawed standard bearer. Cast in the wrong role, as he was after Nauvoo, Rigdon was woefully inadequate as a leader. Willard Richards, possibly putting words in the prophet's mouth, attributed Smith as saying on 26 June 1844, the day before his death: "Poor Rigdon, I am glad he is gone to Pittsburg, out of the way; were he to preside, he would lead the Church to destruction in less than five years."[36] Conversely, Smith's younger brother William was cited in the 29 October 1845 *Warsaw Signal* as stating that the prophet predicted that if Brigham Young ever led the church "he would certainly lead it to destruction." Another corroborative source quotes Joseph as saying that "if Brigham Young were to lead the church, he would lead it to hell."[37]

Notwithstanding, Young, today an icon of classic magnitude, attained legendary status and wealth after leading the Saints to the Great Basin, proving himself beyond doubt to be the right man in the right place at the right time. "I do not think the Church made any mistake in placing the leadership on Brigham Young," wrote Rigdon's son Wickliffe at the turn of the twentieth century. "Sidney Rigdon had no executive ability, was broken down with sickness, and could not have taken charge of the Church at that time. . . . The task would have been too great for Father. I have no fault to find with the Church with doing what they did. It was the best thing they could have done under the circumstances."[38]

Notes

Unless otherwise stated, all primary sources cited are located in the Historical Department of the Church of Jesus Christ of Latter-day Saints, Salt Lake City, Utah.

1. Benjamin Winchester to John Hardy, 13 Nov. 1844, in *Latter Day Saints' Messenger and Advocate* (Pittsburgh) 1 (15 Feb. 1845): 128.
2. Jedediah M. Grant, *A Collection of Facts Relative to the Course Taken by Elder Sidney Rigdon in the States of Ohio, Missouri, Illinois and Pennsylvania* (Philadelphia: Brown, Bicking & Guilbert, 1844), 18.
3. 8 Aug. 1844 (p.m.) minutes in Thomas Bullock's handwriting, General Minutes Collection.
4. Sidney Rigdon, 12 Sept. 1844, letter to the *People's Organ* (St. Louis); cited in *Nauvoo Neighbor*, 2 Oct. 1844, 1.
5. *Times and Seasons* 5 (15 Sept. 1844): 61. George A. Smith, in a 25 Dec. 1874 sermon, also asserted that "Elder Sidney Rigdon had never received the Second Anointing, nor the keys pertaining to baptism for the dead" (*Millennial Star* 37 [2 Feb. 1875]:66).
6. Grant, 18.
7. Scott Kenney, ed. *Wilford Woodruff's Journal–Typescript*, 9 vols. (Midvale, UT: Signature Books, 1983), 3:442.
8. William Clayton journal, 29 Aug. 1844, cited in Andrew F. Ehat, "Joseph Smith's Introduction of Temple Ordinances and the 1844 Mormon Succession Question," M.A. thesis, Brigham Young University, 1982, 213.
9. *Times and Seasons* 5 (15 Sept. 1844): 652.
10. Illinois governor Thomas Ford also asserted in his writings that one of Rigdon's revelations exhorted rich Mormons at Nauvoo to follow him to Pittsburgh. This inflamed both the rich, who did not wish to leave their property, and the poor, who did not wish to be deserted by the wealthy, asserted Ford. "This was fatal to the ambition of Rigdon," Ford added, "and the Mormons tired of the despotism of a one-man government, were now willing to decide in favor of the apostles . . . with Brigham Young, a cunning but vulgar man, at their head" (Thomas Ford, *A History of Illinois* [Chicago: S. C. Griggs and Company, 1854], 58).

11. Joseph W. Young, "A History of the Persecution of the Church of Jesus Christ of Latter-day Saints Being Extracts From the Journal of Elder Joseph W. Young," 15.

12. Orson Hyde, *Speech of Elder Orson Hyde, Delivered Before the High Priests' Quorum, in Nauvoo, April 27th, 1845, Upon the Course and Conduct of Mr. Sidney Rigdon, and Upon the Merits of His Claims to the Presidency of the Church of Jesus Christ of Latter-day Saints* (Liverpool: James and Woodburn, 1845), 43.

13. Ibid., 17.

14. George A. Smith diary, 3 Sept. 1844.

15. *Times and Seasons* 5 (15 Sept. 1844): 650.

16. George A. Smith diary, 3 Sept. 1844. Hyde said that Rigdon later recanted his threat, saying "he was angry and did not mean to do as he said" (*Times and Seasons* 5 [15 Sept. 1844]: 651).

17. Hyde, 42.

18. *Times and Seasons* 5 (15 Sept. 1844): 648.

19. Ibid.

20. The full account of these accusations may be read in "Trial of Elder Rigdon," *Times and Seasons* 5 (15 Sept. 1844): 647-55; 660-67; 685-87. The original minutes of the 8 September 1844 trial of Sidney Rigdon, presently under control of the Quorum of the Twelve, are "not available for public scrutiny" (F. Michael Watson, secretary to the First Presidency, to Richard S. Van Wagoner, 14 June 1993).

21. Cited in Sidney Rigdon, "The Purposes of God," *Latter Day Saints' Messenger and Advocate* (Pittsburgh) 1 (15 Feb. 1845): 110-11.

22. *Times and Seasons* 5 (15 Sept. 1844): 665.

23. Marks later provided the precise wording: "I ordain you to be a prophet, seer, revelator, and translator, to be equal with me in holding the keys of this last kingdom, but not to excel: even so. Amen" (*Latter Day Saints' Messenger and Advocate* [Pittsburgh] 1 [1 Mar. 1845]: 129-30).

24. *Times and Seasons* 5 (15 Sept. 1844): 666.

25. Ibid.

26. During the October 1844 general conference Marks would be dropped as president of the Nauvoo stake because "he did not acknowledge the authority of the Twelve, but the authority of Elder Rigdon" (*History of the Church*, 7:296). In a 9 December 1844 letter, published in the *Times and Seasons* 5 (15 Dec. 1844): 742, Marks wrote:

> After mature and candid deliberation, I am fully and satisfactorily convinced that Mr. Sidney Rigdon's claims to the presidency of the church of Jesus Christ of Latter-day Saints, are not founded in truth. I have been deceived by his specious pretences, and now feel to warn every one over whom I may have any influence to beware of him, and his pretended visions and revelations. The Twelve are the proper persons to lead the church.

Marks, who later declared that the Twelve pressured him into signing the prepared document, never moved west to Utah. He ultimately became a founding leader of the Reorganized Church of Jesus Christ of Latter Day Saints.

27. Ibid.

28. Ibid., 686.

29. Ibid.

30. The list included Samuel James, Leonard Soby, J. B. Bosworth, George W. Crouse, Lewis James, George W. Robinson, Joseph H. Newton, Briggs Alden, Elijah Reed, John Evans, William Richards, George Soby, Samuel Bennett, John A. Forgues, G. Bentley, William Coltien, T. J. Lanyon, David Scott, Thomas Crompton, J. Hatch, and "many others," who were not specified.

31. LDS archives also has a copy of this broadside on file.

32. *Times and Seasons* 5 (15 Sept. 1844): 655.

33. Rigdon to Post, 22 Feb. 1856, Stephen Post Collection, box 1, fd. 3; hereafter Post Collection. The text of this document does not appear in any regular issue of the *Messenger and Advocate* (Pittsburgh). But Pratt, editor of *The Prophet* (New York City), on 10 May 1845, stated that he copied it from a *Messenger and Advocate* extra. On 1 February 1866 Stephen Post noted in his journal that Ebenezer Robinson said he had printed the revelation in Pittsburgh, but that Rigdon had no knowledge of the revelation until after his 8 September 1844 excommunication.

Commenting on the purported revelation in 1845 Rigdon said he knew "as much about it as Mr. Pratt":

> Dr. Bennett says it was by Joseph Smith deposited in his [Bennett's] hands to be disposed of as he did. This is what we know about it, Dr. Bennett sent the paper to another person's address, who has it now.—This is all we know about it, and Dr. Bennett has gone his own way, and attending to his own business, as far as we know; and we presume has as little idea of ever joining with the church of Christ, as he has with the Mormon church ("The Mormons," in *Messenger and Advocate* 1 [15 July 1845]: 266).

While it is mere conjecture, Bennett may have given the revelation to George W. Robinson, Rigdon's son-in-law, confirming Athalia Robinson's tale of a Bennett/Robinson conspiracy (Josephine Rigdon Secord statement to Noel B. Croft, 23 Aug. 1972, in Noel B. Croft Collection).

34. Orson Hyde to "Brethren," 12 Sept. 1844, Brigham Young Collection.

35. Karl Keller, ed., "'I Never Knew a Time When I Did Not Know Joseph Smith': A Son's Record of the Life and Testimony of Sidney Rigdon," *Dialogue: A Journal of Mormon Thought* 1 (Winter 1966): 39.

36. *History of the Church*, 6:593.

37. Jeremiah Root, "Experience and Testimony," *Autumn Leaves*, 10 (June 1897), 271.

38. Keller, 40. In a more lengthy treatment elsewhere, Wickliffe Rigdon, as a Mormon convert, wrote:

> Sidney Rigdon was not a leader of men having no talent in that direction he could talk[,] could interest an audience with his eloquence[,] but needed one to control and direct him & therefor[e] the Morm[o]n church at Nauvoo after the death of Joseph Smith made no mistake in placing Brigham Young at the head of the church he was the right man in the right place & Sidney Rigdon had been chosen to take that position the church would have tot[t]ered and fallen to the ground years ago. Brigham Young

was a born leader of men and it was by his efforts that the church was kept together[.] It required a man of great courage to lead the church . . . (J. Wickliffe Rigdon, "Life Story of Sidney Rigdon," 25).

Section 5.

Pennsylvania

CHAPTER 25.

Pittsburgh

Thirteen years ago, at a time when we were in [Pittsburgh] under circumstances calculated to render what we then were told doubtful, it was told to us, that we should live in this city, and do a certain work here pertaining to the kingdom of God; a work that must be done in this city and could be done no where else.

—Sidney Rigdon (1845)[1]

The excesses and eccentricities of Sidney Rigdon's post-Nauvoo ministry place him in a pantheon of baroque characters who enlivened the spectrum of Mormonism at the time. Rigdon was obsessed with religion; the flames of fanaticism smoldered like an unquenched fever. Ultimately his mania caused him to lose his equilibrium, his powers of sound reasoning, and almost all worldly possessions. Yet for most of the years between 1844 and his death three decades later, a rivulet of ardent followers ebbed and flowed in and out of Rigdon's life. Initially their numbers were impressive. But later, when Rigdon seemed to have lost his context in the "real world," his disciples dwindled to a few lost souls who accorded him and his theology their loyalty.

Bolstering his credibility as a prophet, seer, and revelator, Rigdon felt compelled to assemble his own competing organization after Brigham Young and the Quorum of the Twelve attained absolute jurisdiction over traditional Mormon power bases. Unlike typical visionaries, though, Rigdon no longer drew strength from the future, divining from tomorrow's promise a new order. Recasting his religious iron in Pittsburgh, he looked back to Kirtland, Ohio, when the old faith had been untainted by "strange doctrines which have crept in unawares." It was his intention "to contend for the same doctrines, order of church government and discipline, maintained . . . in Kirtland."[2]

His Pittsburgh newspaper, the *Latter Day Saints' Messenger and Advocate*, like the Mormon tabloids in Nauvoo, was hardly nonpartisan. The earliest issues contain letters from supporters disputing the Twelve's leadership claims, setting forth arguments supporting Rigdon. John A. Forgeus, later to serve as president of the Quorum of the Twelve in Rigdon's Church of Christ, cited a 19 January 1841 revelation: "And again, verily I say unto you, if my servant Sidney will serve me and be counselor unto my servant Joseph [Smith] . . . and if he will offer unto

me an acceptable offering, and acknowledgements, and remain with my people
. . . he shall lift up his voice again on the mountains, and be a spokesman before
my face" (D&C 124:103-104). Forgeus pointed out that Rigdon's ministry had
now commenced "among the mountains of Pennsylvania."[3]

Richard Savary, Benjamin Stafford, and Ebenezer Robinson, three of Rigdon's chief supporters, sent a 5 October 1844 circular "to the Saints throughout
the world," citing a substantial body of evidence from the Doctrine and Covenants
to legitimize Rigdon's claim as First President of the church. The trio expressed
disappointment "to see a people, who have taught these fourteen years that a
church without a prophet at its head, is not the church of God," proceed to "vote
deliberately, cooley, and dispassionately that they did not want a *guardian*, a
Prophet, or a SPOKESMAN to lead them." Rigdonites argued that the law of God
must be communicated through a prophet, and therefore through Rigdon, the
only still-living "prophet, seer, and revelator." Referring to Rigdon's three trials
"in Joseph's life time," the circular accurately pointed out that he was "always
proven innocent, never a charge sustained against him." They reminded the world
that he "enjoyed Joseph's confidence to the fullest extent, until the time of his
decease." They also documented that as late as November 1843 Smith "voluntarily
and of his own free will confered upon the head of Prest. Rigdon, all the
ordinations, gifts and blessings which had ever been placed upon him."[4]

Benjamin Winchester in a 15 October 1844 letter "To All the Members of
the Church of Jesus Christ of Latter Day Saints" further buttressed Rigdon's
claims: "It is abundantly evident to my mind that the [Q]uorum of the Twelve and
others have excited a certain portion of the Church to reject Elder Rigdon, (which
is a most horrid outrage upon the laws of the same,) from a fear he would bring
them to an account, or in other words, to justice for teaching and practicing the
doctrine of polygamy."[5] That charge was pursued on 12 October 1844 when a
conference of Rigdon's followers converged on Pittsburgh. Winchester stated that
the object of the meeting was "to distinctly ascertain the minds of the members of
the church in this place, relative to the heretical doctrines taught and practiced in
Nauvoo, by the quorum of the Twelve and some of their associates."

After the matter was discussed, several resolutions were sustained by the
congregation. The most crucial decree advocated that Rigdon should be "received
and sustained in the office of first president of the [church]." The Brighamite
Quorum of the Twelve and "their abettors" were disfellowshipped for rejecting
President Rigdon and "practising the doctrine of polygamy."[6]

The force behind Rigdon's year-long ministry in Pittsburgh was the *Messenger
and Advocate.* "We have held it as a maxim from early life," he editorialized in the
first issue,

> that there was a degree of courtesy and condescension, due from one member of
> society to another, from which men were not at liberty to depart, only when measures

of self-defence rendered it an imperious duty a man owed to himself. Men have their religious belief, which to themselves, if to none others, is sacred: they also have their feelings; both of which should be regarded, and treated in a manner becoming the true character of man.

. . . We have never, at any time, supported a system of religion which rendered necessary an attack on the character of any person to support it, nor never expect to.

. . . An appeal to the revelations of heaven, in all disputed points, is an end of all strife with us. To the law and to the testimony, and not men's characters, shall be our standing motto.[7]

His assertions notwithstanding, Rigdon's periodical, like the *Nauvoo Expositor*, aimed to expose spiritual wifery and related duplicity. Unknown to most Mormons today, a number of nineteenth-century sources provide evidence that within the month preceding Joseph Smith's death he realized that polygamy breached Nauvoo's safety and tried to disentangle himself from the practice. Even Brigham Young conceded in 1866 that "Joseph was worn out with it," adding, "I never knew that he denied the doctrine of polygamy . . . some said he did, but I do not believe he ever did."[8] Young's naivete may be the result of historical timing; when Smith broached the subject with Nauvoo Stake President William Marks, Young was in the eastern United States stumping for the Smith-Rigdon presidential ticket.

"We are a ruined people," Marks quoted Smith. "[T]his doctrine of polygamy, or Spiritual-wife System, that has been taught and practiced among us, will prove our destruction and overthrow. I have been deceived . . . it is wrong; it is a curse to mankind, and we shall have to leave the United States soon, unless it can be put down, and its practice stopped in the Church." Marks said Smith was determined to "have charges preferred against all who practice this doctrine" and instructed Marks, the presiding officer of the Nauvoo High Council, "to try them by the laws of the Church, and cut them off, if they will not repent, and cease the practice of this doctrine." The prophet was killed shortly after this conversation, and when Marks related Smith's comments to the returning apostles, all of whom by then were committed to plural marriage, his testimony "was pronounced false by the Twelve and disbelieved."[9]

On the public record, Smith and the Quorum of the Twelve denied polygamy. At the time of Smith's death, he and at least twenty-nine other known polygamous males in Nauvoo, including the Twelve, had married a total of 114 women. Many more would contract polygamous marriages before the main body of Saints trekked west.[10] These polygamists, an esoteric culture within a culture, engaged in an elaborate scheme of coordinated casuistry to protect themselves. Policies institutionalized by the prophet more than made room for imprecision in a world of pliant ethics, where lying was permitted if it served a higher purpose.[11]

Rigdon viewed spiritual wifery and the smokescreen that concealed it as reprehensible, less to do with God's work than the affairs of men. "It would seem almost impossible that there could be found a set of men and women, in this age of the world, with the revelations of God in their hands," he reasoned in a 15 October 1844 letter to James M. Greig, "who could invent and propogate doctrines so ruinous to society, so debasing and demoralizing as the doctrine of a man having a plurality of wives." Decrying the "transactions of the secret chambers," he divulged that "the Twelve and their adherents have endeavored to carry on this spiritual wife business in secret," adding that they "have gone to the most shameful and desperate lengths to keep it from the public. First, [by] insulting innocent females, and when they resented the insult . . . would assail their characters by lying." Venting his dismay at the deceptive practices of the purportedly pious, Rigdon asked: "How often have these men and their accomplices stood up before the congregation, and called God and all the holy Angels to witness, that there was no such doctrine taught in the church; and it has now come to light."[12]

Still the Twelve, privately teaching that plural marriage was the path to God's door, continued publicly to denounce Rigdon's accusations. "Wo to the man," the 15 November 1844 *Times and Seasons* warned, "who will thus willfully lie to injure an innocent people! The law of the land and the rules of the Church do not allow one man to have more than one wife alive at once." This retort, and others like it, assaulted Rigdon's easily aroused outrage. "Did the Lord ever tell any people," he asked in the 15 February 1845 issue of his *Messenger and Advocate*, "that sleeping with their neighbor's wives and daughters had any thing to do with preparing the way of the Savior's coming[?]" Yet, Rigdon pointed out, the "spiritual wife men" thought so.

"Nauvoo is a sink of corruption," he added in a 15 June 1845 editorial.

> Deception in its most forbidding forms, is resorted to by them, to make people think they are different from what they are in truth. They deny, or attempt to deny, the existence of the very doctrine on which they pretend that their exaltation depends. . . . A true saint would publish his faith to the world, though he would suffer death for it; and rejoice in the thought that he suffered death for Christ's sake. . . . Has it come to this, that men must lie, defame, and slander, in order to sustain the religion of Jesus Christ?[13]

Elsewhere Rigdon described how excommunication was used as a tool in Nauvoo to silence critics of spiritual wifery. "As soon as a member became dissatisfied with the doctrine of polygamy," he explained, "and was bold enough to call it incestuous or adulterous," he or she was "arraigned, charged," and "everyone who dared vote in favor of the person charged was threatened with immediate expulsion from the church." All were thus "compelled to obey the mandate of their masters." Rigdon claimed those who would not succumb were "excluded" and "their characters assailed."[14]

Polygamy, of course, did not emanate from the Quorum of Twelve Apostles. They merely promulgated what Smith had set in motion earlier. Therefore Rigdon could not assail plural marriage without also censuring its originator, the martyred prophet. But the key to power in post-martyrdom Mormonism, a key which the apostles quickly grasped, was to maintain and enhance an untarnished image of Smith. Rigdon had long since ceased worshipping at the shrine of Joseph Smith. Though he stated otherwise on numerous occasions, Rigdon came to believe, most likely after Smith's 1842 attempted seduction of Nancy Rigdon, that Joseph was a fallen prophet.

Rigdon's supporters wrote articles insisting that Smith had been "cut off by the Lord" as early as 1841, the year he appointed Rigdon as a prophet, seer, and revelator.[15] His backers reflected his own position, which for the most part he had kept to himself, "for Joseph's sake," as he later told Orson Hyde.[16] "This [plural marriage] system was introduced by the Smiths some time before their death," he wrote to James Greig in October 1844, "and was the thing which put them into the power of their enemies, and was the immediate cause of their death[s]." He had "warned Joseph Smith and his family," he explained, "of the ruin that was coming on them, and of the certain destruction which awaited them." But they did not listen to him, and now "have fallen into everlasting shame, and disgrace, until their very name is a reproach; and must remain so forever."[17]

"Oh, Joseph! Joseph! Joseph! Where art thou!" Rigdon rhapsodized in an 8 November 1844 sermon in Philadelphia. "Oh, Joseph! thou wicked servant, thou hast fallen because of thy transgression! Thou hadst the promise that thou shouldst live if thou wert faithful until the coming of the Saviour! Thou didst have the promise of translating more of the sacred Records! Oh Joseph! if thou hadst not sinned thou mightest have been here, to have thundered forth from Heaven's Eternal truth!"[18] Two months later Rigdon's newspaper attested that Smith had "departed from the living God . . . and like David and Solomon he contracted a whoring spirit, and . . . the Lord smote him for this thing—cut him off from the earth."[19]

Spiritual wifery was not Rigdon's only charge. Much later, writing to Stephen Post, he related that in Nauvoo Smith "got weary waiting on the Lord and said in his heart the Lord delayeth his coming and he went to eating and drinking with the drunken and abusing his fellow servants and the Lord cut him off[.]"[20] In a 9 May 1872 letter to Post, speaking of that "old rotten and cursed" Smith church, Rigdon wrote that Smith "corrupted [that] organization."[21] That October Rigdon penned a revelation to devotee Jesse Crosby. "After the Devil had overthrown my servant Joseph and got his soul turned to the corruptions of the world," Rigdon began in the voice of God,

> the devil used him for the purpose of leading all those who had been gathered to turn also from the service of the living God to serve the flesh: And after succeeding instead of the Zion of God there was a habitation of Devils.
> In consequence of this awful corruption . . . I the Lord abandoned him to his

enemies and they cut him off; for he had ceased to be my servant and the promise I
made to him as my servant lost its efficacy, for I had promised him the protection of
life in spite of all his enemies. . . . I the Lord caused this to be written as it is found
in the [B]ook of Mormon, based upon the fact that I knew he[,] Joseph Smith[,] would
turn from the truth & be cut off, and that all my people might know his being cut
off was proof[,] absolute that he was a high handed transgresser of a character so
heaven daring that he transfered his allegiance from the Lord to the devil so as to be
one of Satan's servants instead of the Lord[']s.[22]

Hatred of plural marriage burned in Rigdon's heart. Despite his life-long
aversion to polygamy, his detractors in the Brighamite (Utah Mormon), Strangite
(Michigan Mormon), and Reorganized Latter Day Saint (RLDS) movements tried
to undermine his credibility by linking him with the custom. "Beware of seducing
spirits, and doctrines of devils, as first introduced by John C. Bennet[t] under the
name of the 'Spiritual Wife' doctrine; and still agitated by the Pittsburg[h] Seer,"
wrote Apostle Parley P. Pratt, then the husband of six wives:

> It is but another name for whoredom, wicked and unlawful connexion, and every
> kind of confusion, corruption, and abomination.
> Should any elder or member, come unto you professing to hold to any such
> doctrine or practice, either secretly or publicly, you may be sure he is not of God; and
> it becomes your duty to reject him, and report him to the presidency of the church.
> . . . For know assuredly that no one has been authorized to teach, practice, or introduce
> any such doctrine in any of the branches of the church. Nor is there any such doctrine
> known, held, or practiced, as a principle of the Latter-day Saints.[23]

In a 21 October 1844 letter Apostle Orson Hyde, then husband of three
wives, wrote: "I will now venture a prediction, that since Nauvoo has thrown off
so much bile from its stomach [i.e., Rigdon] it will be more healthy, and less
complaints about spiritual wives, adultery, bogus making, &c. &c."[24] Apostle
John Taylor, editor of the *Times and Seasons* and husband of three wives, published
a hypocritical 15 November letter from "An Old Man of Israel" (Taylor's pen
name) which denounced the

> *sham* quotations of Sidney and his clique, from the Bible, Book of Mormon, and the
> Doctrine and Covenants, to skulk off, under the "dreadful splendor" of "spiritual
> wifery" . . . wo to the man or men who will thus wilfully lie to injure an innocent
> people! The law of the land and the rules of the church do not allow one man to have
> more than one wife alive at once, but if any man's wife die, he had a right to marry
> another, and to be sealed to both for eternity; to the living and the dead! There is no
> law of God or man against it! This is all the spiritual wife system that ever was tolerated
> in the church, and they know it.

Brigham Young on 21 January 1845 wrote eastern U.S. Mormon leader
Jedediah Grant, later of the First Presidency and a polygamist himself, that "If you
find any Elders that are confirming the Doctrine that Rigdon makes his Hobby

horse thinking to ride into power, cut off such Elders from the church—and send them immediately to Nauvoo, to give an account of themselves."[25]

Harvey Whitlock continued the fabricated assault on Rigdon's reputation long afterwards by testifying in 1858 that after Nauvoo Rigdon had engaged in an "arrangement for temporary swapping wives."[26] RLDS leader Isaac Sheen in 1864 commented erroneously that "Sidney is undoubtedly aware that if his elders 'discuss the doctrine of polygamy,' they will be put in remembrance of the detestable, adulterous system which he established in [Antrim Township] Pennsylvania about eighteen years ago."[27] Peter Hess, a Strangite, recounted in a 14 December 1846 letter to James Strang a secondhand story that during a September 1846 conference in Antrim Township "Mr. Rigdon had introduced a System of Wifery or the Battle Axe System or free or common intercourse with the women."[28]

But Ebenezer Robinson, by then a disenchanted counselor to Rigdon, when asked in 1886 if his former colleague had advocated polygamy while in Antrim, answered: "No, he did not. He was a firm believer in the divine authenticity of the Book of Mormon, which positively forbids it."[29] Furthermore, Rigdon claimed in a 4 March 1866 revelation: "I the Lord say unto my servant Stephen that the system of polygamy as had among a people who were called after my name was not of me. . . . I never gave to Joseph Smith nor any other man authority to introduce in my name that system as had among that people in any of its forms as a pretended spiritual relation or otherwise. . . . It is before me saith the Lord an abomination."[30] Unlike Joseph Smith, Brigham Young, and members of the Utah Quorum of the Twelve, no evidence exists of "another woman" in monogamist Sidney Rigdon's life. As Wickliffe Rigdon maintained, his father "took the ground no matter from what source it came whether from Prophet seer revelator or angels from heaven [that polygamy] was a false doctrine and should be rejected."[31]

In November 1844 Rigdon traveled further east. His agenda included Philadelphia, New York City, Boston, and in New Jersey, New Egypt and Woodstown. He arrived home in Pittsburgh at Christmas time, announcing in his newspaper that he had just returned from "a tour of upwards of two months in the eastern cities." The demands on my time "are so pressing," he claimed to the readership, "that we will have to place the paper in the hands of another editor [Samuel Bennett], for we cannot give the necessary attention to it." In his flamboyant, egotistical style, the Pittsburgh seer proclaimed: "Everything that we have undertaken, has prospered in our hands . . . far beyond our highest expectation, and we think, we may say without exaggeration, that our progress has so far been without parallel, in the history of any religious society in our country." Referring to the "large proportion of men of literature, tallents [sic] & intelligence" in the society, he concluded that "what crowns the whole is, that the Lord is with us, revealing his will to us, and what we lack in knowledge is abundantly supplied."[32]

Rigdon professed to have delivered at least one lecture per day to large audiences on the trip East. Two known accounts provide vivid characterizations of the preacher's lively manner. Jedediah M. Grant, a vitriolic Rigdon critic, wrote that when Sidney began his 8 November 1844 sermon in Philadelphia he "assumed a mild appearance." As the lecture picked up momentum, however, and the orator found his stride, he ranted and pounded the desk "with wild looks, and many vehement gestures." Then, lowering his voice dramatically, he commenced a commentary on the parables of Matthew 13, transforming them in his unique self-praising rhetoric. "When the wheat and tares grew together, the kingdom looked large," he said of 1844 Nauvoo Mormonism, but "after the wheat was gathered out it looked like a grain of mustard seed, very small indeed."

During a moment of vivid inner clarity he regretfully conveyed to his listeners "the most painful part yet." Reading from Matthew 24 he highlighted the Savior's reference to the "wicked servant at the time of his coming." This sinful domestic, lamented Rigdon, was Joseph Smith, "cut off in an hour when he looked not for it." Emoting "a half crying tone," he then groaned "Oh, Joseph! Joseph! Joseph! . . . thou wicked servant, thou hast fallen because of thy transgression! . . . I shall not see thee till I meet thee in the Eternal World!"[33]

While Rigdon was in New York City, a newsman sent to cover the famous Mormon religionist described the devout fifty-one-year-old crusader as

> a tall, stout, elderly, gentlemanly looking man apparently about sixty years of age, hollow mouthed, having lost his front teeth. His delivery is rather indistinct and low, and very rapid; at other times quite as loud, raising his voice to the highest pitch. He is evidently a person but of limited education . . . very disjoined in his manner, so as almost to defy knowing what particular object his subject had reference to. He used his left hand as if he was pumping violently, every now and then assisting with the right; and hitting the deck so violently with one or both as to make every thing on it spring upwards to a considerable height, and keeping those near him from napping if inclined.[34]

Rigdon and his Pittsburgh adherents received considerable press coverage, much of it sarcastic and disdainful. The 1 November 1844 *Times and Seasons* noted that Rigdon had resuscitated the *Latter-day Saints Messenger and Advocate* at Pittsburgh. "We understand that through this medium," John Taylor wrote, "the accessories to the murder of Joseph and Hyrum Smith, with *John C. Bennett* as the *ne plus ultra*, will form a union of all the excommunicated members from the Church of Jesus Christ of Latter-day Saints. —He that cannot endure a kingdom of glory, can go into one of darkness."

The *Pittsburgh Gazette*, in a favorable comment on Rigdon's movement, differentiated between "Nauvoo Mormonism" and "Pittsburgh Mormonism." The principal difference, the article avouched, is "that the Pittsburgh Mormons, to their credit be it spoken, repudiate and adjure the 'spiritual wife system,' the dogma that 'it is sometimes lawful to lie,' and assert the duty of obedience to the laws of the land."[35] That same newspaper a short time later sneered that Rigdon "has lately received so many new revelations that he bids fair to rival Joe Smith himself."[36] *The Connaut (Ohio) Reporter* on 26 June 1845 also mocked that the "new phase in fanaticism" was putting "forth remarkable super-natural revelation to astonish the ignorant and superstitious." The paper dismissed *The Messenger and Advocate* as "full of Rigdon's effusions."

No stranger to bad press, Rigdon announced in February 1845 that a general conference would be held in Pittsburgh on 6-7 April to effect "a full organization of the kingdom."[37] Elated at the prospects of finally establishing Zion, he waxed poetic:

A Song of Zion

The time is now coming the day is at hand
When Zion in strength and in beauty shall stand;
Awake from her slumbers, in glory arise,
And send her loud anthems to God in the skies. . . .
O Zion the glory, and praise of the earth;
Thy conquest is certain, from time of thy birth;
Though kingdoms and nations, in ruin are cast;
Thy strength and thy power, increase to the last.

Thy travail and sufferings shall not be in vain;
Thy children, in multitudes, lengthen thy train,
In numbers, like sand that's spread on the shore,
Thousands and thousands of millions, and more.

Thy peace like a river, in righteousness flow
Thy streams of salvation—all nations shall know;
The prince, and the peasant, the noble and mean;
Find salvation in thee forever, amen.[38]

On 12 February, "in good health and spirits," President Rigdon left Pittsburgh for Kirtland, Ohio, accompanied by Elder Bennett. They were beckoned to Rigdon's former home, "having received several pressing invitations from brethren and friends . . . to lay before them the peaceable things of the kingdom of God."[39] On the eve of 16 February he addressed a Sunday night "meeting at candle light" in the Kirtland temple which was attended, according to him, by nine hundred people. A full house was also present on Tuesday and Thursday of that week.

During his Thursday sermon he traced the history of Mormon polygamy, declaring that if the Smith brothers had not introduced the system into Nauvoo, "they might have been living men today."[40]

On Thursday ex-Mormon leaders William Law and William E. McLellin, currently residing in Hampton, Illinois, arrived unexpectedly in Kirtland.[41] "Brother Law addressed the congregation for some time," Rigdon reported, "setting forth what he knew about the people and the affairs of Nauvoo; some of which were new to us. He settled the question forever on the public mind, in relation to the spiritual wife system, and the abominations concerning it. As Joseph Smith and others had attempted to get him into it."[42]

Returning to Pittsburgh in late February, Rigdon spent early spring preparing for the upcoming conference. An avid vocalist, he had been working for some time on a new hymnal for his congregation, and on 1 March 1845 the *Messenger and Advocate* announced the near completion of *A Collection of Sacred Hymns. For the Church of Jesus Christ of Latter Day Saints.* Rigdon personally selected the 182 hymns. It sold for 37 1/2 cents a copy. "The following little volume of psalms, hymns, and spiritual songs," Rigdon noted in the preface,

> have been selected, in view of furnishing the saints of latter days, with a volume of such sacred poetry, as they could sing with the spirit. . . . Many of the hymns are original, and were never before published, and those which have been selected, are materially altered so as to render them more acceptable to the intelligent saint. Some are inserted without any alteration. It has been our principal object with the compiler, to select such compositions as contained subjects of praise. He has been careful to insert compositions which are rather subjects of praise than of prayer or of exhortation.

On Sunday, 6 April 1845, the fifteenth anniversary of Joseph Smith's original Church of Christ, Rigdon's Pittsburgh followers assembled at their 201 Liberty Street meeting place. President Rigdon preached that morning on priesthood, using as his text 1 Peter 2:9. Later that evening twenty-nine people were baptized. The following day, after reading aloud the first hymn in the new work, Rigdon led the congregation in song. He then "kneeled before God with the conference and addressed Him in solemnity, in tears, and in strong and fervent supplication, and dedicated himself and the conference to Almighty God." All who had been ordained under Rigdon's hands to be prophets, priests, and kings "unto God" were then asked to sit in front. Members of this "Grand Council" consisted of seventy-three men and boys, including Rigdon.[43] The prophet venerated the new quorum with the blessing: "I lay it upon you in the name of Jesus, that you shall be the kings over whom the Son of God shall reign as King of kings and Lord of lords. I lay it upon you to be crowned in the presence of God when Jesus shall come with all the hosts of heaven; when heaven and earth shall be redeemed."

After declaring the quorum "now full," Rigdon turned his attention to the congregation. "I now throw myself into your arms," he appealed. "What relation shall I sustain to this kingdom? What office shall I hold?" Joseph M. Cole then nominated Rigdon as "first president of this kingdom and church, and to stand as prophet, seer, revelator and translator, to this church and kingdom of Christ of the last days." The vote was carried without dissent.[44] William McLellin now stepped forward "in obedience to the word of the Lord to him in a vision," took Rigdon by the hand, and avowed "his determination to stand by him and his family in all righteousness before God until the time of the end." McLellin promised: "[T]his I do sir, in view of that relation which we as individuals shall sustain to each other in the last struggle; and the relation which we shall sustain to this kingdom at that hour; and the relation that we shall sustain to the heavens—to the Eternal God. I pray God, sir, to preserve you faithful in your office, till you meet the Son of God on mount Olivet, and the earth is redeemed."[45]

Carvel Rigdon then took his younger brother by the hand and recounted "the history of their youth, the scenes of early life, and their present union in the kingdom of heaven." This scene was so moving that "the whole house melted into tears." Carvel was followed by members of the Grand Council "one by one, their hearts overflowing with gratitude and thanksgiving to God," pledging to sustain and support President Rigdon in his calling. In the afternoon Rigdon nominated Samuel Bennett, Jeremiah Hatch, Jr., William E. McLellin, Joseph M. Cole, and George W. Robinson to "draft a preamble and resolutions expressive of the views and feelings of this kingdom, relative to the people of Nauvoo, and also an address to the people of these United States and the world, setting forth the iniquities of the people of Nauvoo, and the light in which we view them."[46]

During the morning session on 8 April Rigdon asked the congregation: "By what name shall this church be called?" It was moved and seconded that it be "The Church of Christ," the original 1830 name of the Mormon church. The following afternoon, after exercising what he knew of endowment ordinances, Rigdon disclosed:

> The spirit whispered to me this morning to set apart some brethren, and consecrate them to God, in a room in my own house, which I did . . . and after the washing and anointing, and the Patriarchal seal, as the Lord had directed me, we kneeled, and in solemn prayer we asked God to accept the work we had done; during the time of prayer there appeared over our heads, in the room, a ray of light forming a hollow square, inside of which, stood a company of heavenly messengers, each with a banner in his hand, with their eyes looking downward upon us, their countenances expressive of the deep interest they felt in what was then passing on the earth; there also appeared heavenly messengers on horseback with crowns upon their heads, and plumes floating in the air, dressed in glorious attire until, like Elisha, we cried in our hearts, "the chariots of Israel, and the horsemen thereof"; even my little son of fourteen years of age [Wickliffe] saw the vision, and gazed with great astonishment, saying, that he thought his imagination was running away with him, after which we arose and lifted our hands to heaven in holy convocation to God, at which time, it was shown an

angel in heaven registering the acceptance of our work, and the decree of the Great God, that the kingdom is ours, and we shall prevail; my anxieties therefore, in relation to our work in organizing the kingdom, and the acceptance of that organization, by our heavenly Father, is now forever at rest.[47]

On Thursday afternoon (12 May) additional washings and anointings took place, after which all quorums received their patriarchal seal, a general blessing from Rigdon. During the day an immense fire had spread through the city. In a prayer Rigdon asked God to "allay the violence of fire, that our whole city be not laid in ruins." During the prayer, observed the clerk, the "escort of heavenly messengers," which had periodically hovered about the place, was "seen leaving the room, the course of the wind was instantly changed, and the violence of the flames were stayed, and our city saved from an entire overthrow."[48] Nevertheless the inferno caused millions of dollars of damage and left thousands homeless before it abated. Some of Rigdon's followers held him responsible for not predicting the fire. One disciple confessed in a 30 April 1845 letter to the *Nauvoo Neighbor* that his confidence in Rigdon was "crippled by the event of the late fire." "Is it possible," he questioned, "that God would order his main spokesman on earth to locate himself and his followers in a city," only to "burn up that city . . . a week afterwards, and not tell his servant of it!" If Rigdon "knew the city was to be burnt, why . . . with all that he pretended to have, keep the word of God hid?" The answer seemed clear to the angry writer: because he "had no more to do with God, and coming events than Tom Thumb."

Rigdon did not see it that way. The morning after the fire, his focus was elsewhere. He informed his congregation that while they had covenanted with each other, it was now their duty to "bind the heavens by a covenant." Instructing them to stand "with uplifted hands to heaven, declaring in the presence of God, the holy messengers, and one another, . . . that if this Kingdom does not triumph and prevail, according to the promise made through the prophet Daniel, it shall not be your fault, thus binding the heavens for a fulfilment of the promises made, concerning it." The following day, during the conference's closing ceremonies, Rigdon affirmed that "the Kingdom and Church of Christ were now organized" and that God had "sanctioned all that had been done," and that this kingdom "should never fall, but should stand unbroken . . . unshaken." Conference was then adjourned until 6 April 1846.[49]

After the initial gathering to Pittsburgh of several hundred members, the Church of Christ grew spasmodically. From time to time, resolutions of allegiance would trickle in from distant areas, but the total number of Saints in Pittsburgh never exceeded four hundred. In June 1845, however, an optimistic Rigdon announced that a new age of promise had dawned:

The Nucleus, that the Lord showed us we should form in this city, has been organized, around which all the righteous of the earth, according to the promise, should centre, and our eyes are beholding the promise verified, the sound has gone forth, the righteous are gathering, and the saints are rejoicing, in the hope set before them, and though it has been but two months since the organizing of the kingdom, hundreds have entered in and are entering continually.[50]

In July he returned to Kirtland, preaching again in the temple, but to much smaller audiences. "The Old King has been here again," Reuben McBride reported to Brigham Young. But few came "out to hear him the most he had at anny [sic] time did not exceed 149 he was here two Sabbaths only preached caca. . . . [S]ome of his followers thought he would baptize a good many but he did not baptize one[;] his influence is on the wain here I as[s]ure you."[51]

Rigdon's Pittsburgh utopia was in fact disintegrating. By all measures it should have succeeded. Rigdon had considerable experience in church organization and numbered among his followers people of talent and wealth. But the idiosyncrasies of the Rigdonites in Pittsburgh, like the Brighamites in Nauvoo, precluded their nesting comfortably within the confines of general American society. Each community needed private space to try its own wings, and Zion proved will-o'-the-wispish for both peoples. The Quorum of Twelve/Council of Fifty ultimately established its theocratic kingdom in the Great Basin of the Rocky Mountains where Brigham Young ruled for three decades.[52] Rigdon's crusade for the golden land, his attempt to fashion a "New City of Jerusalem" in Pennsylvania's Cumberland Valley, failed as decidedly as had earlier efforts to establish Zion in Jackson County, Missouri, although for different reasons.

In early August 1845 Rigdon and William E. McLellin traveled by horseback along the Mercersburg-Greencastle turnpike to Antrim Township, Franklin County, Pennsylvania. Before them was the meandering Conococheague Creek with its willowed banks and sparkling waters wending east to the Potomac. Halting atop a stone bridge spanning the creek, about a mile and a quarter west of Greencastle, the men gazed north over Andrew G. McLanahan's 390-acre "Adventure Farm." Rigdon, according to a Franklin County history, proclaimed to McLellin: "This is the place the Lord has shown us in visions to be the site of the city of the new Jerusalem." The two, after dedicating the spot, lingered in the area for a few days gathering information on the district. By their "quaint manners and solemn converse," the local chronicle continued, they "won many friends in the neighborhood, and then departed as quietly and mysteriously as they had come."[53]

Rigdon returned to Pittsburgh, "in good health and spirits," from his mission "over the mountains to the interior and southern part of this State."[54] At some time during this early period his brother-in-law, Peter Boyer, apparently made a $1,500 deposit on McLanahan's farm against the asking price of $14,700.[55] A sardonic letter from Pittsburgh Mormon Amos Fielding to Brigham Young described his plans:

Mr. Rigdon is about to move on to the East, and there purchase lands and settle. He has a revelation to this effect that all his followers must sell all their goods and houses, and lands or the Lord will not bless them. . . . His main Revelation is this, that they must go eastward and purchase lands, and stay there till they shall be called upon by the rulers of this nation, who will have viewed their good works and conduct. Mr. Rigdon states that the war [of the Apocalypse] will commence in the West, and move eastward, and that they, the Rigdonites, will be prepared with power to join the great army, and so continue to move eastward till they shall arrive in England, where I suppose he intends fulfilling his prophecy: that is, making his hands serve instead of a handkerchief to Victoria's Nose![56]

During the Church of Christ's 1845 autumn conference in Philadelphia, the First Presidency appointed a five-man finance committee, headed by Peter Boyer, to procure the funds to purchase our "inheritance for the gathering of the saints."[57] On 3 April 1846, McLanahan was paid an additional $5,400. He gave a deed and took a judgment for the balance of money due—$8,700—payable 1 April 1847.[58] Principal benefactors Carvel Rigdon, Charles A. Beck, and Peter Boyer, prosperous farmers, pledged "their all," ultimately losing it, to the cause of the gathering.[59]

On 6 April 1846, while directing general conference, President Rigdon related a recent vision: "Thousands stood before him, and the Lord told him, that they were the honorable men of [Pittsburgh], and through them the means should come for the redemption of Zion." Attesting that "the devil had sought to overthrow this kingdom," Sidney was convinced that "there could be no doubt now in what relation we stand to the heavens, and by whose wisdom and power we are guided . . . the great God ha[s] clearly shown us that he was our guardian and protector. I feel as if we stand on 'terra firma.'"[60]

On the morning of 8 April Rigdon excused himself for arriving late by explaining that "it was through much affliction he was present . . . in consequence of the severe illness of his daughter Eliza." He had been up all night and felt she was now "lying upon the very verge of death." Although distraught, he was able to conduct some business matters, notably measures to secure the additional money needed to purchase the McLanahan farm. Did they wish this to be "the first and primary object of this church and kingdom until it is cleared from all incumbrances?" he asked. After an affirmative vote, he appointed a committee of five to "draft an instrument setting forth the best means to assess the liabilities of the church in the purchase of the land."

Between morning and afternoon sessions the delegation drafted a resolution, afterwards accepted as "the word of God" on the matter:

> Behold here is wisdom. Let a petition be presented to this conference, and also to all the brethren everywhere, praying for a liberal donation, that the promised possession may be obtained.
>
> Behold I have set my hand for the last time to gather my people, to do my work,

to bring to pass my act, my strange act in the eyes of this people. Therefore, let all the saints know assuredly that it is my will, that all that can be spared, from the widow's mite to him that has thousands, should be speedily given unto the Financial Committee for the redemption of Zion, and for a perpetual home for my saints, for I am God and beside me there is none else.

Rigdon then addressed the convocation in a "short but thrilling speech," no doubt influenced by the burdens resting on his mind. Despite the distress he was suffering, he rejoiced that

he was treading upon ground unexplored by man, for he had no predecessor, either in ancient or modern times. He had been assailed by malice, and the tongue of slander had poured its poisonous and vindictive tide upon his head. . . . His enemies had been aiming a death blow at the kingdom, but the Lord had stretched forth his hand in its deliverance from their reach, and covered its opposers with eternal shame. The beauty and order in the action of this kingdom could not fail to impress every heart with eternal conviction of its origin.

By the time the worried father "took his leave" from the stand, "every heart was filled with hallowed fire, every bosom swelled with emotions too deep for utterance, too thrilling for language to express." Conference then adjourned until 6 October 1845 when the Church of Christ would convene on the "Adventure farm, near Greencastle in the Cumberland [V]alley."[61]

Notes

Unless otherwise stated, all primary sources cited are located in the Historical Department of the Church of Jesus Christ of Latter-day Saints, Salt Lake City, Utah.

1. *Messenger and Advocate of the Church of Christ* 1 (15 June 1845): 235. Rigdon added that in May 1844, a month prior to Rigdon's leaving Nauvoo for Pittsburgh, and a month before Joseph Smith's assassination, Brigham Young remarked to him:

[W]hat a singular thing it was that the Lord should have revealed to us the fact of our returning to [Pittsburgh] to live, and afterwards to send us a direct different course, with no probability of the thing revealed ever being fulfilled; but, says he, the object the Lord had in doing so, was to prove you, and see whether you would be faithful and true to him in life or in death, and having found you faithful, he now sends you to do the work he revealed to you, you should do in your native land [Pennsylvania].

For a broad overview of Rigdon's post-Nauvoo life, see Thomas J. Gregory, "Sidney Rigdon: Post Nauvoo," *Brigham Young University Studies* 21 (Winter 1981): 51-67.

2. Sidney Rigdon in *Latter Day Saints' Messenger and Advocate* [Pittsburgh] 1 (15 Oct. 1844): 16.

3. John A. Forgeus to Samuel L. Forgeus, 22 Sept. 1844, in *Messenger and Advocate* 1 (15 Oct. 1844): 1. When asked why he did not go to the Rocky Mountains to fulfill

Smith's 1841 revelation that "he shall lift up his voice again on the mountains, and be a spokesman before my face," Rigdon said "the Lord had reference to the mountains in Pennsylvania, not the Rockies in the far west." He also argued that "all references in the Bible to the tops of the mountains and the Saints gathering to the mountains meant the Alleghenies in Pennsylvania" (E. Cecil McGavin, "Apostate Factions Following the Martyrdom of Joseph Smith," *Improvement Era*, 47 [Apr. 1944]: 205).

4. Cited in *Latter Day Saints' Messenger and Advocate* [Pittsburgh] 1 (2 Dec. 1844): 33-35.

5. Ibid. 1 (15 Oct. 1844): 14-15.

6. "Minutes of a Conference held in Pittsburgh, Oct. 12th 1844," in *Messenger and Advocate* 1 (15 Oct. 1844): 11-12.

7. Rigdon's *Messenger and Advocate*, a semi-monthly journal, became the *Messenger and Advocate, of the Church of Christ*, the new name of the church, with its 15 April 1845 issue. The March 1846 issue was the last published at Pittsburgh. The place of publication then became Greencastle, Pennsylvania. The move to the Cumberland Valley prevented the paper from being published in April and May. The first number at Greencastle appeared June 1846. It appeared monthly thereafter until the final issue of September 1846.

Although Rigdon served periodically as editor and contributed ponderous essays filled with biblical and historical allegories and complex scriptural comparisons and analyses, he was away preaching and traveling much of the time. His essays in volume 1 were titled: "The Purposes of God"; "The Present State of the World"; "The Law of God, and the Law of the Land"; "Future Events"; "Man"; "Prayer"; "Who Shall be the Greatest in the Kingdom of Heaven"; "The Plan of Salvation"; "Priesthood"; "Life and Death"; "The Calamities of the Last Days"; "Condemnation"; and "The Gospel."

In Rigdon's absence, editorial responsibilities fell on Samuel Bennett. Ebenezer Robinson was the firm's printer. Robinson had entered the printing business at Kirtland and was a founding publisher of the *Times and Seasons* in Nauvoo. After Rigdon's church collapsed in the fall of 1846, Robinson turned the press to secular uses, initiating a weekly newspaper at Greencastle, *The Conococheague Herald*, of which he printed thirteen issues in 1849 before selling out. The most complete copy of Rigdon's *Messenger and Advocate* is in the Coe Collection, Beinecke Rare Book and Manuscript Library, Yale University, New Haven, Connecticut.

8. Brigham Young, unpublished address, 8 Oct. 1866, Brigham Young Collection.

9. July 1853 letter to *Zion's Harbinger and Baneemy's Organ*. Rigdon also reported that Emma Smith said of her husband's involvement in polygamy "that he had brought the evil on himself, and that he had tried to escape the curse, but could not" (*Messenger and Advocate* 2 [Dec. 1845]: 402; see also Richard P. Howard, "The Nauvoo Heritage of the Reorganized Church," *Journal of Mormon History* 16 [1990]:41-49; and Linda King Newell and Valeen Tippetts Avery, *Mormon Enigma: Emma Hale Smith* [New York: Doubleday & Co., Inc., 1984], 179).

10. For a thorough treatment of plural marriage in Illinois, see George D. Smith, "Nauvoo Roots of Mormon Polygamy, 1841-46: A Preliminary Demographic Report," *Dialogue: A Journal of Mormon Thought* 27 (Spring 1994): 1-73.

11. See *Messenger and Advocate* (Pittsburgh) 1 (18 June 1845): 234.

12. Ibid. 1 (15 Oct. 1844): 13.

13. Ibid. 1 (15 June 1845): 233.

14. *Democratic Free Press* (Detroit), 25 Feb. 1845, clipping in Dale Morgan Collection, Utah State Historical Society, Salt Lake City. See also *Messenger and Advocate* (Pittsburgh) 1 (1 Jan. 1845): 88-89.

15. Ibid. 1 (15 Oct. 1844): 5; 1 (1 Nov. 1844): 11; 1 (16 Dec. 1844): 54; 1 (1 Feb. 1845): 105; Phineas H. Young et al. to "Beloved Brethren," 31 Dec. 1844, Brigham Young Collection.

16. Orson Hyde to Brigham Young, 16 Sept. 1844, Brigham Young Collection.

17. *Messenger and Advocate* (Pittsburgh) 1 (15 Oct. 1844): 13.

18. Jedediah M. Grant, *A Collection of Facts Relative to the Course Taken by Elder Sidney Rigdon in the States of Ohio, Missouri, Illinois and Pennsylvania* (Philadelphia: Brown, Bicking & Guilbert, 1844), 40-41. Rigdon informed the editor of *The Prophet*, a Mormon periodical in New York, that "there was a revelation given to Joseph Smith" "that he should live till his hair should become white, if he was faithful," and another one saying, "that if he was faithful he should live till the coming of Christ" (*The Prophet*, 16 Nov. 1844).

19. *Messenger and Advocate* (Pittsburgh) 1 (1 Jan. 1845): 75.

20. Rigdon to Post, undated letter, box 1, fd 15, Stephen Post Collection; hereafter Post Collection.

21. Rigdon to Post, 9 May 1872, box 2, fd 10, Post Collection.

22. Sec. 70 in Copying Book A, Stephen Post Collection, emphasis in original; see also undated Rigdon to Post letter, box 1, fd 2—part of letter missing.

David Whitmer's discussion "concerning prophets falling into error" reasoned that "Brother Joseph belonged to the class of men who could fall into error and blindness... [He] belonged to the weakest class—the class that were very liable to fall." Citing from a revelation to Smith, Whitmer noted that the directive warned: "because of transgression, IF THOU ART NOT AWARE, THOU WILT FALL" (emphasis in original). Respecting polygamy, which he also detested, Whitmer wrote:

> Brother Joseph must have set up his idol in his heart, or he would not have prayed to the Lord to know wherein David and Solomon were justified in polygamy, when God says in the Book of Mormon that they were *not* justified in it; that it was abominable before Him. David, Solomon, Saul, and many chosen men of God, afterwards drifted into error and lost the spirit of God, and why not Joseph Smith? Will you answer? Was not Joseph Smith a man subject to like passions? Had you been with him as much as I was, and knew him as I knew him, you would also know that he could fall into error and transgression: but with all his weaknesses, I always did love him. No man was ever perfect but Christ (David Whitmer, *An Address to All Believers in Christ By a Witness to the Divine Authenticity of the Book of Mormon* [Richmond, MO: David Whitmer, 1887]:35-43).

23. *Millennial Star*, 1 July 1845.

24. *Nauvoo Neighbor*, 4 Dec. 1844.

25. Young to Grant, 21 Jan. 1845, Brigham Young Collection. Young during remarks at a Zions Camp reunion on 10 October 1864 disparaged Rigdon by reporting the hearsay that he "stript himself naked, and stript his wife naked, and they marched through the

saints, naked, his apostles also, and the Seventies, Elders and the whole church went through the same disgusting performance" (Brigham Young Collection).

26. Journal History, 18 Apr. 1859—a multi-volume daily history of the church compiled by official church historians. Whitlock, who had been excommunicated in 1835 for adultery, afterwards was rebaptized but apostatized in 1838 during the Missouri troubles. An adherent of Rigdon's until 1846, Whitlock came to Utah in 1849, drifted to California, then came back to Utah where he was living in 1858 when he made the perjurous statement about Rigdon.

27. *True Latter Day Saints' Herald*, 15 Jan. 1864, 16.

28. Hess to Strang, 14 Dec. 1846, James J. Strang Collection, Yale University. Also see Benjamin Chapman to Strang, 24 Mar. 1846; Hazen Aldrich to Strang, [14] Apr. 1846; and James Smith to Strang, 16 May 1846, all in Strang Collection. Joseph Smith III, likely basing his statement on Sheen's earlier comments, in an 18 October 1899 letter to Joseph Davis wrote: "nearly all the factions into which the church broke had plural marriage in some form. . . . Sidney Rigdon had one form practiced by a few and that spasmodically as an outburst of religious fervor rather than as a settled practice" (Francis M. Lyman 1901-1903 Letterbook, 406).

29. Ebenezer Robinson to J. Fraise Richard of Chambersburg, Pennsylvania. The letter was subsequently printed in the *Franklin County School Annual and Program of the Seventy-sixth Annual Session of the Teachers Institute*, Chambersburg, Pennsylvania, 17-21 Nov. 1930, and cited in George L. Zundel, "Rigdon's Folly," *Improvement Era* 47 (Apr. 1944): 246-48.

30. Rigdon to Post, 27 Mar. 1866, Post Collection, box 1, fd. 12.

31. J. Wickliffe Rigdon, "Life Story," 184.

32. *Messenger and Advocate* (Pittsburgh) 1 (1 Jan. 1845): 90-91.

33. Grant, 40-41.

34. *New York Herald*, 18 Nov. 1844.

35. Cited in *The Connaut Reporter* (Ohio), 22 May 1845.

36. *Pittsburgh Gazette*, spring 1845; cited in *The Connaut Reporter* (Ohio), 15 May 1845.

37. *Messenger and Advocate* 1 (1 Feb. 1845): 111.

38. Ibid. 1 (15 Apr. 1845): 128.

39. Ibid. 1 (15 Feb. 1845): 123.

40. Ibid. 1 (15 Mar. 1845): 145.

41. McLellin, a former member of the Quorum of the Twelve, had written to Rigdon on 23 December 1844 expressing unshakable confidence in him: "the Lord has shown to me that by a union of President Law and yourself . . . that all the honest in heart among the Latter Day Saints and throughout the world will UNITE also, and form a company who will follow the saviour robed in white linen "clean and white" (*Messenger and Advocate* [Pittsburgh] 1 [1 Jan. 1845]: 92).

Having served as a secretary to the original Quorum of the Twelve, McLellin had in his possession records quoting Joseph Smith as saying "The Twelve are called to be a *traveling high council*, (not stationary) to preside over all the churches of the saints among the Gentiles, *where there is no presidency established*. They are to travel and preach among the Gentiles, until the Lord shall command them to go to the Jews. They are to hold the keys of this ministry—to unlock the door of the kingdom of heaven unto all nations, and preach the gospel unto every creature. —This is the virtue, power and authority of their apostleship."

McLellin further quoted Smith: "The twelve apostles have no right to go into *Zion, or any of its stakes*, where there is a regular high council established, and there undertake to regulate the matters pertaining thereto: but it is their duty to GO ABROAD and regulate and set in order all matters relative to the different branches of the church" (McLellin to Samuel Bennett, in *Messenger and Advocate* [Pittsburgh] 1 [15 Mar. 1845]): 150-51, emphasis in original).

42. Ibid. 1 (15 Mar. 1845): 145-46. A year later Rigdon, writing of a proposed merger between himself and Law, said that although their conversation was "a friendly one," it terminated in "convincing both parties that our religious views were so widely different that no union could exist, and we parted, agreeing to disagree, and so the matter ended" (ibid. 1 [15 July 1845]: 265).

43. The group, listed according to church position each member was called to at the same conference, included: Josiah Ells (apostle), Samuel James (counselor), Carvel Rigdon (patriarch), Richard Savary (standing high councilor), Ebenezer Robinson (counselor), Austin Cowles (presidency of High Priests' quorum), James Logan (standing high councilor), John A. Forgeus (standing high councilor), William Stanley (presidency of High Priests' quorum), Hyrum Kellogg (presidency of High Priests' quorum), Briggs Alden (presidency of Elders' quorum), Hugh Herringshaw (apostle), Timothy L. Baker (bishopric), John Duncan (presidency of Elders' quorum), William Richards (bishopric), Leonard Rich (president of Seventies), Lewis James (standing high councilor), Robert Kincaid (standing high councilor), Matthew Smith (standing high councilor), William Hutchings (president of Seventies), David L. Lathrop (apostle), Richard Croxall (bishopric), Jeremiah Hatch, Jr. (apostle), Thomas Lanyon (standing high councilor), Leonard Soby, James M. Greig (president of Seventies), E. R. Swackhammer (apostle), Charles A. Beck (standing high councilor), William White (presidency of Elders' quorum), John Frazier (standing high councilor), William Small (apostle), Peter Boyer (standing high councilor), Samuel Bennett (apostle), James Blakeslee (apostle), Fred Merriweather (president of Seventies), George T. Leach (president of Seventies), John Smith (standing high councilor), William E. McLellin (apostle), George W. Robinson (apostle), Sidney Rigdon (president), James Spratley (standing high councilor), Benjamin Winchester (apostle), John F. Olney (president of Seventies), Samuel G. Flagg, George M. Hinkle, Dennis Savary, Christian Seichrist, Jesse Morgan, James Twist, John W. Rigdon, Algernon S. Rigdon, Benjamin Stafford, Amos B. Tomlinson, Joseph Parsons, James Smith, George W. Cronse, Joseph M. Cole, James G. Divine, Jeremiah Cooper, William Brothers, Archibald Falconer, Joseph B. Bosworth, George Morey, John Evans, Joseph H. Newon, William D. Wharton, Jacob C. Lenks, John W. Latson, John Hardy, Edward B. Wingate, Abram Burtis, John Robinson, and Edward McClain. Ibid. 1 (15 Mar. 1845): 168.

Rigdon named Samuel James and Ebenezer Robinson as counselors and Carvel Rigdon as patriarch. He then organized a quorum of twelve apostles, seven presidents of Seventies, a standing high council, a presidency of the High Priests' quorum, a presidency of the Elders' quorum, a bishopric and presidency of the lesser priesthood, and a presidency over the Pittsburgh Stake.

44. Ibid.

45. "Minutes of a Conference of the Church of Christ, held in the City of Pittsburgh, commencing on the 6th and ending on the 11th of April, A.D. 1845," in *Messenger and Advocate* (Pittsburgh) 1 (15 Apr. 1845): 169.

46. Ibid. 1 (15 Mar. 1845): 168-69. The newspaper of this date also printed the "Preamble and resolutions of the Church of Christ":

> Whereas, In consequence of the rejection by that people, of what we undoubtedly deem to be the order of the church and kingdom of God, and introduction of doctrines and practices clearly inimical to the law of God, and altogether subversive of the laws of the land, abrogating the marriage contract, and substituting, under the professed sanction of heaven, a system of extreme licentiousness, uprooting every legal restraint. . . . Whereas, The better to conceal the justly odious system of polygamy—duplicity, hypocrisy, and falsehood, are inculcated as virtues—the most sacred obligations constantly violated, and families and individuals plunged into irevocable ruin and despair.

Following the preamble was the resolution to "hold no fellowship with the people calling themselves the Church of Jesus Christ of Latter Day Saints, and can have no communion with them, unless they repent and obey the principles of righteousness and truth."

47. *Messenger and Advocate* (Pittsburgh) 1 (1 May 1845): 185.

48. Ibid. 1 (1 May 1845): 186.

49. The full account of these proceedings is in the "Minutes of a Conference of the Church of Christ, held in the City of Pittsburgh, commencing on the 6th and ending on the 11th of April, A.D. 1845," in *Messenger and Advocate* 1 (15 Apr. 1845): 168-73; 1 (1 May 1845): 185-90. The 15 March date on the original is a typographical error.

50. *Messenger and Advocate* 1 (15 June 1845): 236.

51. McBride to Young, 28 July 1845, Brigham Young Collection.

52. While it is commonly believed among Mormons that Joseph Smith received a revelation that the Saints were to settle in the Rocky Mountains, this was a retrospective addition to the body of Mormon folklore on the subject after the Saints had settled in the Great Basin. On 25 April 1845, for example, Brigham Young, writing to Rhode Island governor James Fenner, unsuccessfully sought asylum for Mormons in that state, traditionally a bastion of religious freedom (Young to Fenner, in Douglas Wayne Larche, "The Mantle of the Prophet: A Rhetorical Analysis of the Quest for Mormon Post-Martyrdom Leadership, 1844-1860," Ph.D. diss., Indiana University, 1977, 58).

Young then addressed letters to governors of all states and territories of the union, asking them for asylum within their borders. Finding no takers he recalled plans to go to Vancouver Island. "[B]ut we had our eye on Mexico," he added, "and here we are located in the midst of what was then northern Mexico" (*Journal of Discourses* 11 [11 Dec. 1864]: 12). The plan seems to have been to continue farther west and south to "lower California." Responding to Sam Brannan on 6 June 1847, while nearing the Great Salt Lake Valley, Young wrote: "The camp will not go to the west coast or to your place [Yerba Buena] at present . . . we have not the means" (see Richard S. Van Wagoner and Steven C. Walker, *A Book of Mormons* [Salt Lake City: Signature Books, 1982], 21).

53. B. M. Nead, "The History of Mormonism with Particular Reference To the

Founding of the New Jerusalem In Franklin County," *Kittochtinny Historical Society Papers*, [9 vols.] (Chambersburgh, PA: Franklin Repository Press, 1923), 9:424. For McLellin's history on the dedication of the Antrim Township farm, see *Messenger and Advocate* (Pittsburgh) 2 (Mar. 1846): 464.

54. Ibid. 1 (15 Aug. 1845): 297. McLellin traveled east. Although a participant in the October 1845 conference in Philadelphia, he was suspended two months later from the Quorum of the Twelve by Rigdon, apparently for physically threatening Rigdon after being chastised (see "Extract from the minutes of a meeting of the grand council, held in Pittsburgh, Saturday evening, Dec. 13, 1845," in *Messenger and Advocate* 2 [Jan. 1846]: 426, and the 30 December 1845 minutes of the Grand Council reported in ibid., 427). On 6 April 1846 McLellin was replaced in the quorum by Algernon S. Rigdon, Sidney's seventeen-year-old son. On the same occasion fifteen-year-old Wickliffe Rigdon was appointed to fill a vacancy in the Grand Council.

55. Ibid. 1 (Nov. 1845): 398.

56. *New York Messenger* 2 (20 Sept. 1845): 92.

57. *Messenger and Advocate* (Greencastle) 2 (Nov. 1845): 399.

58. See "Deeds of Franklin County Pennsylvania, 1784-1963," 20:319-20, Family History Library, Church of Jesus Christ of Latter-day Saints, Salt Lake City, microfilm #42408, p. 66.

59. "Minutes of a conference of the Church and Kingdom of Christ, held in Pittsburgh, commencing on the 6th and ending on the 8th of April, 1846," in *Messenger and Advocate* (Greencastle) 2 (June 1846): 466.

60. Ibid.

61. Ibid. 2 (June 1846): 472. Although the exact date of Eliza Rigdon's death and her final resting place is unknown, she was dead by 13 May when her family left Pittsburgh for the Cumberland Valley. In a 5 June 1846 letter, George M. Hinkle provided a few details of Eliza's death to Ebenezer Robinson. Arriving in Pittsburgh in the last week of March 1846, Hinkle reported that on arrival at the Rigdon house, "I found this devout family somewhat indisposed, particularly his daughter Eliza, who has since closed her earthly career in the triumphs of faith, and has gone to rest in the paradise of God" (ibid., 2 [June 1846]: 477).

CHAPTER 26.

Antrim Township

Here then, is to be prepared a rest, a repose for the children of God; such a rest, as his people have never known, is in reserve for those who will forsake the tinsel and frippery of this world, and become the disciples of our Lord, and gather with his people to Zion. . . . Come then, ye honest, ere the gathering and destructive storm pours its fierce wrath upon you, and the hour of mercy be past speed to Zion.

—Sidney Rigdon, (1846)[1]

Situated in the rolling hills of south-central Pennsylvania, a few miles west of Gettysburg, lies the Cumberland Valley. Nestled in this 180-mile long vale, some twenty-five to forty miles in width, is an area that in 1846 was known as Little Cove Mountain or Antrim Township. Well watered by Conococheague Creek and Spring Brook, the locale boasted rich and fertile soil, an abundance of timber, and extensive limestone, clay, and sand deposits. Transportation to this Rigdonite Zion was also well established in 1846. Eleven miles to the north at Chambersburg lay the western terminus of the Philadelphia and Cumberland Valley Railroad. The Franklin Railroad branched southward, passed through Greencastle, then terminated in Hagerstown, Maryland, ten miles further south.

On 13 May 1846 the Rigdon family, consisting of Sidney and Phebe, their children Nancy (twenty-three),[2] Sarah (twenty-one), Algernon Sidney (seventeen),[3] Wickliffe (fifteen), Lacy Ann (thirteen), Phebe (ten), Hortense Antoinette (eight), and Ephraim (four), along with the Ebenezer Robinson family and others, left Pittsburgh and began the nearly 300-mile journey east to yet another "Land of their Inheritance."

Among the members of the Church of Christ who invested all their worldly wealth in Rigdon's visions of New Jerusalem and would soon lose it were 150-200 believers. These included professional men, mechanics, and farmers. Aside from Rigdon and Robinson, the company boasted Samuel James, William Richards, George M. Hinkle, Joseph H. Newton, Leonard Soby, Amos B. Tomlinson, Jeremiah Hatch, Jr., soon to marry Lacy Ann Rigdon, and Edward B. Wingate, who would marry Sarah Rigdon. Members set up housekeeping in various buildings on Adventure Farm and nearby Greencastle, where the Rigdons and

Robinsons temporarily situated themselves, renting the corner of Carlisle and Madison streets.[4] From this address the *Messenger and Advocate of the Church of Christ* was reestablished under Robinson.[5]

Regarding the events surrounding the church's removal to the Cumberland Valley, Robinson editorialized in June 1846:

> [W]e are here from the fact that our heavenly Father required our settling in this place at our hands; and had the requirement been made to have located in the frozen regions of the north, or the sunny climes of the south—in the pleasant and fertile valleys, or upon the sides of the mountains, it became not us to dictate, but to obey without a murmur or a word, consequently we are here, as "strangers in a strange land."[6]

True to the Mormon tradition of gathering for the Savior's advent, the prophet Sidney declared the "Word of the Lord" respecting Zion. "The door is now open for the gathering of my people," he pronounced, "and the less delay the better for them, verily, verily thus saith the Lord."[7] Under the prophet's guidance, according to editor Robinson, Adventure Farm was to "become the glory of the whole earth," a beautiful city with a magnificent temple, glassworks, cotton mills, and other public edifices.

One prominent man who called on Rigdon shortly after his arrival was Strangite George J. Adams, who had been appointed an apostolic emissary to Rigdon on 25 June 1846. James Strang had earlier written to Rigdon requesting that he serve as his counselor. But Rigdon either did not receive the letter, which had been written prior to 22 April 1846, or refused to answer.[8] The following month he rebuked Strang's missionaries, proclaiming that if they "preached for a thousand years the world would be no nearer the rest of God."[9] Returning to Strangite headquarters in Voree, Wisconsin, Adams reported that he "did not see" Rigdon in Greencastle and felt it "lost labor to pursue the matter further." When it was proposed that Rigdon be excommunicated, Strangite John C. Bennett declared that "he was a warm personal friend of President Rigdon and that he had ever held him in high estimation" and did not want to see harsh measures taken against him. He moved that Strang "enquire of the Lord in relation to the final disposition of President Rigdon's case."

Strang, during a general conference at Voree on 19 October 1846, declared "the answer of the Lord" respecting Rigdon:

> Behold verily my servant Sidney Rigdon rebelleth against me and hath rebelled against me for a long time and I was grieved with him yet I felt after him and had compassion on him and remembered his faith and his labors, and reproved him by my Spirit and by afflictions and by judgments but he would [heed] none of my reproofs. Satan troubleth him and he hath sought to establish his own works and not mine; for [S]atan inspireth him thereto and hath entered into him and giveth him thoughts and dreams and visions. Therefore he shall not stand in his presidency for I do take his office from him and give it unto one who will serve me.

Rigdon was then "replaced" in Strang's organization by George J. Adams.[10]

Rigdon stuck to his independence after 1844, refusing to serve as a subordinate to Brigham Young, James Strang, or any other religious leader. But his Zion in Cumberland Valley, like its Jackson County prototype, proved a delusion. The sect, with few financial resources, did nothing more than equip the farm's large barn as a meeting hall. Here the faithful as well as curious gathered to hear the famed prophet preach. Rigdon also evangelized in Greencastle and the nearby area now called Tomstown, and frequently visited a communistic group of German Seventh Day Baptists, located at Snow Hill in Quincy Township. He was reportedly charmed by their "devout conduct and more particularly by their spiritual music," but he converted no one. They were too "devout and well founded in their childlike faith in their beautiful mysticism to hearken to his strange doctrine," wrote a historian of the period.[11]

A more likely reason for Rigdon's failure was that he veered away from the ordinary world into temporary madness. His sermonizing during this period, according to son Wickliffe, "was at times so perfectly wild that [Sidney] could not control himself." Young Rigdon thought bereavement triggered the fanaticism. He explained that Eliza's death in Pittsburgh had so affected their father that he "never was the man he once was."[12] If pronouncing unfulfillable prophecies is symptomatic of mental instability, evidence of Rigdon's dementia can be seen in his September 1846 valedictory in the *Messenger and Advocate of the Church of Christ*. The decree was entitled "A Proclamation to the Kings, Princes, Rulers, & People, of all Nations, and to the Clergy and Laity of all Denominations being a Sketch of the World's History in Connection With the Economy of God." Pronouncing that his call was made by the "counsel of the same God who inspired the prophets and apostles of old," Rigdon, in thunderous Old Testament manner, prophesied impending doom:

> The time is at hand when all shall know, whether they believe us now or not, that what we have here written, is the truth of heaven; —for *this* generation shall not pass till all is fulfilled. Then as Noah did to the old world, so do we to the new world, and proclaim to all the inhabitants thereof, that this world is drawing near its close, the present order of things is shortly to pass away, and the Lord himself is about to take to himself his great power, and get to himself a great name. The Lamb that was slain, but is alive and liveth forevermore, is beginning to prepare for his second advent, not to be slain, but to put down all rule and all authority, but his own.[13]

Rigdon's New Jerusalem, like the proposed New Jerusalem in Jackson County, was taken to extremes. Enraged that his prophecies failed to engender a dramatic response, and disheartened by the scant showing of financial support from outside the enclave, Rigdon in a flare of temper, would withdraw from citizenship in the Adventure Farm. Unlike his experiences with hostile neighbors in Ohio, Missouri, and Illinois, the good people of Antrim Township indulged

Rigdon's rantings and viewed him as a colorful but ultimately benign crank. Robinson commented in a June 1846 editorial: "The citizens, so far as we have become acquainted, appear to be very generous, kind, and hospitable—willing that all people should enjoy their religious faith without molestation—and we find ourselves, (as in other places were our lot has been cast,) treated with that kindness and respect due one citizen from another."[14] The problem was that Rigdon had expected a spectacle, a phenomenon, rather than indifference.

But by year's end it was apparent that Rigdon's visions would prove to be nothing more than buoyant rhetoric, and financial disaster loomed on the horizon. William McLellin, who had lost faith before the move to Adventure Farm, wrote that by December 1846 Rigdon's fury had intensified. Raising an apocalyptic banner of doom, the prophet made a foray into Greencastle trying to provoke conflict so that "blood would cover the town."[15] He informed Greencastle citizens that "the conflict would rage till the streets were drenched with blood" and that there was not enough religion in the town "to save a nest of woodpeckers."[16]

In January 1847 the heavy hand of judgment fell on the Church of Christ in the form of impending foreclosure on the farm. Andrew Lanahan was awarded a $2,980 judgment against Peter Boyer, chair of the Rigdonite financial committee. Boyer, still living on his farm near Pittsburgh, either refused to or could not meet the obligation. In a last sad attempt to stave off the inevitable, Rigdon reportedly gathered his flock about him one wintry eve in early 1847 and petitioned for divine relief during an all-night prayer vigil. The small group of adherents, still loyal to their faltering prophet, knelt with him in the meadow behind the assembly hall from sunset until dawn, beseeching God for a hastening of the promised advent of the Messiah.[17] When the faithful realized their efforts were futile, there occurred "a general awakening and a serious backsliding from an absolute faith in the infallibility of their prophet." As one account described it: "That shivering company that repaired to their homes, when the light of morning came must indeed, have been a forlorn sight."[18]

Witnesses less cynical towards Rigdon saw it the same way. Abram Hatch, a printer's assistant in Robinson's office, recalling the initial "enthusiasm and faith of Sydney and his apostles," wrote that "Christ delayed his coming and Sydney Rigdon's church dissolved."[19] Wickliffe too reported that his father had expected to "receive an endowment from on high but failed to get it[.] His few followers became discouraged and did not believe their object would be accomplished and went away."[20]

Many of Rigdon's devotees had abandoned temporal concerns and ceased working because of the promised Advent. One account wrote that the Rigdonites

talked a great deal about what they intended doing—the streets and avenues they would lay out, the buildings, temple, mills, etc., that they would construct. But the most of them lived in idleness and all their plans came to naught. Their money was soon spent, many of them died,[21] others became discouraged and left.[22]

But the immediate reason for the Church of Christ's departure from Adventure Farm was eviction. The property was seized 7 April 1847 when the group was unable to make its final lump-sum payment to Andrew McLanahan.

Although detailed financial documents for the period are not available, Rigdon's followers lost at least $6,000. Evidently some, including Sidney's brother Carvel[23] and brother-in-law Peter Boyer, lost their mortgaged farms in the Library/Piney Fork area near Pittsburgh and began making threats in Rigdon's direction. When recalling the events of early 1847 a decade later, Rigdon, for whom a mystical explanation was always more satisfying, wrote that the Lord saved his life by plucking him "as a brand from the burning m[idst]."[24] "One exceedingly dark night," began his cryptic tale,

> a messenger stood before me, not on the earth but in the air who said some things which let me know that I must leave that place, but how to get away I knew not; but in the space of a few weeks I found by the workings of the spirit that I must leave without delay. But how to get away I knew not; I had no way but on foot. While I was pondering on this subject there came a strange woman there, some 50 years of age, saying the Lord had sent her there but she knew not what for. The day arrived that I must go. I mentioned in her presence that I wanted to leave but had no means to help myself; she turned and looked at [me] with an expression of countenance such as indicated surprise and exclaimed now I know what I was sent for, it was to enable you to get away; she put her hand into her pocket and took from thence a roll of bank bills and handed them to me saying now get ready and go home with me. I found the spirit pressing me to make no delay; accordingly I made all possible exertions; and that same day I found myself in possession of a car[r]iage and horses harnessed for the journey, and the messenger, [our driver] my eldest son, a lad of [18] years, and myself in it and all of us on the road, and after a journey of some 400 miles we reached her house.[25]

In an 1860 letter to Phineas Young, Rigdon added that the Lord had told him in 1847 that "He was going to take me away to a home he had provided for me that I knew not of."[26] That home was located on a farm near Cuba, New York, where Rigdon had never been. The mysterious woman who told him "go buy a carriage and horses and go home with me" was probably his daughter Athalia Robinson, who since 1844 had been living with her husband on Jackson Hill, Allegheny County, New York, where the Rigdon family was soon situated.[27]

Rigdon's uncharacteristically brief farewell message to bystanders in Antrim Township was: "If any ask to know where I am gone, tell them I am gone to Hell on a thousand years' mission."[28] While his personal prospects turned out better than his forecast, Rigdon's sudden departure was the final blow to the hopes and prospects of the Church of Christ.[29] Jeremiah Hatch, Jr., and Ed Wingate,

Rigdon's future sons-in-law, were still in the Cumberland Valley in mid-July putting up hay. In a letter to a nephew, Hatch wrote that "on the sixth of August the [Adventure] farm will be sold unless payment is made before that time, & in all human probability this will not be the case. Sidney Rigdon is still in N. York where he will remain in case the farm be not redeemed & to which place the family will go in that event."[30] The foreclosed farm was sold at a sheriff's sale auction. Andrew McLanahan was the successful bidder, and Adventure Farm, the New Jerusalem that never was, "dropped back," as one observer noted, "to an ordinary farm."[31]

The Rigdonites took little with them when they abandoned their settlement for they had virtually nothing of value left. Among the accumulated debris in their temple barn was a large array of printed sheets, unfolded and unbound, from their hymnal. Scavengers reportedly gathered the papers and sold them to drygoods and grocery stores in Greencastle, where merchants used them for wrapping paper.

One Cumberland Valley woman collected loose pages and made them into a small book, a cherished relic lost when the Confederate Army raided the area in 1863. In 1915 the unnamed woman recalled for a historian one of the hymns she had memorized. It seems a fitting eulogy to the saga of Rigdon's Antrim Township ministry:

> *Now we'll sing with one accord*
> *For a Prophet of the Lord,*
> *Bringing forth his precious word*
> *Cheers the Saints as anciently.*
>
> *When the world in darkness lay*
> *Lo! He sought the better way,*
> *"Go, and prune my vineyard, Son."*
>
> *And an Angel surely, then*
> *For a blessing unto men,*
> *Brought the Priesthood back again*
> *In its ancient purity.*
>
> *Even Joseph he inspires*
> *Yes, his heart he truly fires,*
> *With the light that he desires*
> *For the work of righteousness.*
>
> *And the Book of Mormon, true*
> *With its covenants ever new,*

For the Gentile and the Jew,
He translated sacredly.

The Commandments of the Church
Which Saints will always search
(Where the joys of Heaven perch)
Came through him from Jesus Christ.

Precious are his years to come
When the righteous gather home
For the Great Millennium
Where he'll rest in blessedness.

Prudent in this world of woes
He will triumph o'er his foes
While the realm of Zion grows,
Purer for Eternity.[32]

Notes

Unless otherwise stated, all primary sources cited are located in the Historical Department of the Church of Jesus Christ of Latter-day Saints, Salt Lake City, Utah.

1. *Messenger and Advocate of the Church of Christ* (Greencastle) 2 (Aug. 1846): 565.

2. On 13 September 1846 Nancy married Robert Ellis, a member of Rigdon's Grand Council, in Pittsburgh. The Ellises spent the remainder of their lives in Pittsburgh.

3. Commonly known as Sid.

4. James Smith to James Strang, 16 May 1846, item 22a, Strang Papers, Beinecke Rare Book and Manuscript Library, Yale University, New Haven, Connecticut; hereafter Yale Library.

5. Beginning with the first issue of volume 2, Ebenezer Robinson is listed as editor and proprietor of the newspaper, a position he maintained until the final number was published in September 1846. On 19 September 1849, two years after the Church of Christ collapsed, Robinson and J. Kilbourn began publishing another newspaper, *The Conococheague Herald* (thirteen numbers in all). According to its prospectus the paper occupied a "neutral or independent ground in politics and religion; advocating the particular claims of no party or sect but will be at liberty to speak of passing events as they transpire without reference to either."

Remaining in Greencastle until 1855, Robinson also compiled and published a children's book and several editions of a small work entitled *Legal Forms For The Transaction Of Business and a Set of Tax and Interest Tables together with a Short System of Bookkeeping,* of which 40,000 copies were sold. For a history of Robinson's publishing ventures in

Greencastle, see "Echo-Pilot Made Bow As Conococheague Herald," *The Echo-Pilot*, 22 Sept. 1949.

6. *Messenger and Advocate of the Church of Christ* (Greencastle) 2 (June 1846): 473.

7. Ibid. 2 (June 1846): 478.

8. James Strang to James Smith, 22 Apr. 1846, item 22, Strang Papers, Yale Library.

9. James Smith to James Strang, 16 May 1846, item 22, Strang Papers, Yale Library.

10. See Warren Post Diary, 25 June 1846, 64-65, Warren Post Collection, film 298 #8, Brigham Young University Family History Library, Provo, Utah.

11. B. M. Nead, "The History of Mormonism with Particular Reference to the Founding of the New Jerusalem in Franklin County," in *Kittochtinny Historical Society Papers* [9 vols.] (Chambersburgh, PA: Franklin Repository Press, 1923), 9:424. See also Jacob H. Stoner, *Historical Papers–Franklin County and the Cumberland Valley Pennsylvania* (Chambersburgh, PA: Craft Press, Inc., 1947), 264.

12. Karl Keller, ed. "I Never Knew a Time When I Did Not Know Joseph Smith: A Son's Record of the Life and Testimony of Sidney Rigdon," *Dialogue: A Journal of Mormon Thought* 1 (Winter 1966): 15-42, cited 40.

13. *Messenger and Advocate of the Church of Christ* (Greencastle) 2 (Sept. 1846): 523-36.

14. Ibid. 2 (June 1846): 473.

15. William McLellin, *The Ensign of Liberty of the Church of Christ* (Kirtland, OH), Apr. 1847, 19.

16. *Kittochtinny Historical Society Papers*, 9:351-52. When the Confederate army invaded the north, Greencastle was the first village taken. The entire area was ravaged by soldiers as General Robert E. Lee's army passed through Greencastle on its way to Gettysburg. In Greencastle a monument marks the spot where the first southern soldier fell on northern soil, but the streets have never "run with blood." See also George L. Zundel, "Rigdon's Folly," *Improvement Era* 47 (Apr. 1944): 204, 245-48.

17. Peter Hess to James Strang, 14 Dec. 1846, item 45, Strang Papers, Yale Library; Joseph H. Newton to Stephen Post, 29 Aug. 1864, Stephen Post Collection, hereafter Post Collection; Frederick B. Blair, comp., *The Memoirs of W. W. Blair* (Lamoni, IA: Herald Publishing House, 1908), 133; Thomas Gregory, "Sidney Rigdon: Post Nauvoo," *Brigham Young University Studies* 21 (Winter 1981): 252-54.

18. Nead, 423.

19. Abram Hatch, "Autobiography," 4.

20. J. Wickliffe Rigdon, "Life Story of Sidney Rigdon," 184. 21. The Rigdonite dead were buried on top of a local prominence known as "Mormon Roller Hill." The graves were marked by blazed trees rather than gravestones (see Zundel, 245).

22. *The News-Chronicle* (Shippensburg, PA), 10 Aug. 1934, cited in Journal History, 10 Aug. 1934–a multi-volume daily history of the church compiled by official church historians.

23. Thirty-one years later, on 26 March 1878, Phebe Rigdon, writing to Stephen Post, noted that Carvel's wife "was a great enem[y] to the truth" (Post Collection, box 5, fd. 9).

24. Rigdon to Stephen Post, 23 Jan. 1856, Post Collection.

25. Ibid.

26. Rigdon to Phineas Young, 1 May 1860, Phineas Young Collection.

27. Sometime in the fall of 1844, after Joseph Smith's martyrdom, George W.

Robinson traded a farm in Nauvoo for one belonging to Mr. and Mrs. George Paddison on Jackson Hill, near Cuba, Allegheny County, New York (untitled Rigdon family manuscript in Arlene Hess Collection, mss. 1281, box 1, fd. 3, Special Collections Brigham Young University, Harold B. Lee Library).

28. Journal History, 14 Nov. 1849, 4.

29. Ebenezer Robinson, in a 24 April 1886 letter to J. Fraise Richard, Jr., detailed what he knew of the whereabouts of all former leaders of Rigdon's Church of Christ in Cumberland Valley. The letter was subsequently printed in the *Franklin County School Annual and Program of the Seventy-sixth Annual Session of the Teachers' Institute*, Chambersburg, Pennsylvania, 17-21 Nov. 1930, and is cited in its entirety in Zundel, 246-48.

30. Jeremiah Hatch, Jr., to Abram Hatch, 11 July 1847, Abram Hatch Papers.

31. *Kittochtinny Society Papers*, 9:353.

32. Nead, 419-22.

Section 6.

New York

CHAPTER 27.

Exiled in Friendship

And now saith the Lord out of all those who were called from the nations one only
was found who could accomplish the work of separation and that one was my serv[a]nt
Sidney Rigdon[.] . . . I the Lord took him into exile and there alone I called upon him
to perfect the work of separation which only could be done by becoming acquainted
with the true character of Zion as well as that of the church of the devil . . . which
required a long period of many years.

—Revelation to Sidney Rigdon (1868)[1]

The Rigdons' rescue from the failed Cumberland Valley utopia was not unconditional. Upon the family's arrival at George W. Robinson's Jackson Hill farm near Cuba, New York, Robinson admonished his father-in-law that before he would "take him in and give him a morsel of bread," Sidney must promise "never [to] open his mouth about religion again."[2] Wickliffe Rigdon, frequently lamenting his father's religious excesses, added that after the collapse of the Adventure Farm experiment family members would not allow his father to accept preaching engagements. "He seemed sane upon every other subject except religion," young Rigdon later wrote. "When he got on that subject, he seemed to lose himself and his family would not permit him to talk on that subject, especially with strangers."[3] In an earlier account Wickliffe wrote that when his father arrived in New York he received "many requests" to preach and declined all invitations but one: addressing "the residen[ts] of Jackson H[i]ll at a school house in the district." On the evening of the lecture the place was filled to capacity "with people who came out of curiosity." At the conclusion of the old preacher's sermon, according to Wickliffe, the congregation was convinced that "he could preach no matter what else could be said against him."[4]

Cuba, during the two years the Rigdons lived there, was a bustling hamlet of more than two thousand New Yorkers.[5] Work on the nearby Genesee Valley Canal and the Erie Railroad had commenced during the early 1840s; both projects would be completed in 1851. The large number of workmen and artisans created a thriving market for produce and dairy products. "Money was reasonably plenty," wrote a historian of the era, "and it was a time of quite general prosperity."[6]

Rigdon, now fifty-seven, along with twenty-one-year-old son Sidney Jr. and nineteen-year-old Wickliffe, is listed in the 1850 Cuba census as a farmer, apparently running the Jackson Hill farm.[7] George and Athalia Robinson had moved in 1847 into nearby Friendship where Robinson, capitalizing on the area's booming trade opportunities, established a mercantile.[8] Robinson sold the Jackson Hill farm in late 1850, after which the Rigdons relocated to the Robinsons' spacious mercantile home at the intersection of Friendship's Main and Water streets.[9] Robinson was rapidly becoming one of the town's most prosperous men. The Friendship census of 26 July 1860 lists the forty-four-year-old former Mormon as a banker with real estate ownings of $18,000 and personal assets of $65,000. "General Robinson," as he was known locally, was also Worshipful Master of the local freemason fraternity, Allegheny Lodge No. 225. He, Rigdon, Jeremiah Hatch, Ed Wingate, and five others had chartered the lodge on 18 June 1851.[10]

While Rigdon maintained cordial relations with his sons-in-law Hatch and Wingate, ties to Robinson were permanently severed in the early 1850s. This forced Sidney and Phebe to move into Ed and Sarah Wingate's home on upper Depot Street.[11] Although the record of the fray between Rigdon and Robinson is incomplete, the conflict evidently erupted over the sale of the Jackson Hill farm, property Rigdon had come to view as his own. Twenty-five years later, in a 24 February 1875 revelation to his followers, Rigdon wrote:

> My serv[a]nt Sidney whose surname is Rigdon, labored before me the Lord his god while villa[i]ns were stealing his property and ceased not until they had left him without house or home having stolen all he had. . . . The two scoundrels who did this work was George W. Robinson . . . [and] John Olney. . . . I the Lord will say that no two men were more corrupt and heaven denying since the days of Cain than they are.[12]

Rigdon, who would live in abject poverty the last twenty-five years of his life, owned no property after Nauvoo except the family cemetery plot in Friendship. On 8 December 1853 he and a group of others formed the "Friendship Rural Cemetery Association." Rigdon's interest in the burial ground was personal. Fifteen-year-old Hortense Antoinette (Nettie) Rigdon, who had died that year on 6 September of unknown causes, was buried there. Ultimately she would be joined by Sidney, Phebe, and four other Rigdon children.[13]

Try as he might, Rigdon could not rise above impoverishment in Friendship. Listed as a farmhand in the 1860 census, he engaged in seasonal agricultural work and labored for a time in the area's lumber industry. Writing to old friend Lyman Wight, then a religious expatriate in Texas, Rigdon told him he was "hired by a company of shingle makers as their packer and thus I live." Rigdon's principal interest in writing Wight was to determine if news of the discovery of a "rich gold region . . . in your state" was reliable. If so, Rigdon wrote, he intended to "change my mode of living from a shingle packer to a gold digger."[14] It is uncertain whether Wight responded, but Rigdon never panned for gold in Texas. His only known income for the remainder of his life, other than gratuities from followers, was a meager stipend for his occasional delivery of history and geology lectures on the lyceum circuit. These speeches were likely arranged by son-in-law Jeremiah Hatch, Jr., who had married Lacy Ann Rigdon in 1846. Hatch was principal from 1849-54 of the Friendship Academy where Rigdon delivered most of the lectures.[15]

Rigdon's interest in geology—"the history of the world," as he called it—may have been inspired by his well-educated son-in-law, an 1840 graduate of Vermont's Middlebury College. A former student of the Friendship Academy described principal Hatch as "a fine scholar and natural orator" and noted that it was "while listening to his eloquent lectures on geology at Friendship I was first awakened to a love of that science."[16] Writing to a nephew in 1857, Hatch said of his father-in-law: "The old man has been very quiet for years, & talks publicly upon nothing except the science of geology for which he has formed a great attachment— he has lectured some on that subject, but has said nothing on religion, since leaving Pennsylvania."[17]

While Rigdon did not live as a recluse in Friendship, he was forbiddingly private, a thwarted prophet enduring a peculiar sense of exile. Described later in one his revelations, the prophet's banishment was "such as no other man was required to [e]ndure that ever stood before me that I the Lord might prove him before the angels, and that he might learn obedience from the things which he suffered and thereby perfect his ministry for the great work where unto he had been called."[18] Rigdon involved himself in personal theological studies for most of the 1850s and early 1860s. To prevent family friction he kept most of his activities from everyone except his wife. In his own words, he was taught "in a prophetic school[,] one that the Lord instituted for myself specially and over which he presided."[19] Wickliffe wrote that during this period his father "had but few acquaintances." While he occasionally attended various churches, he "seemed to wish to be left alone to commune with his thoughts and for a day or so would hardly speak to anyone . . . oblivious to all going on around him."[20]

One window into Rigdon's life during this period is his 1 May 1860 letter to Phineas Young, Brigham's brother. Discussing in detail his divine calling to prepare for the coming of the Savior and Elijah, as prophesied by Joseph Smith in December 1830 (D&C 35:4), Rigdon noted that fulfillment of this prediction necessitated separating himself from the body of the church. He explained that God's purposes behind his "course of instruction" during his exile were three-fold: "First to have expounded by the Spirit all the prophecies extant that are in possession[.] Second to receive through the Spirit a correct history of the world from the creation to the end thereof[.] Thirdly to be taught how to lay revelations before the Lord and read them in his presence." Rigdon refused all correspondence, "retiring into as perfect obscurity as we could." He read the Book of Mormon ten times, after which he intellectually held "its contents in possession."

Next, he wrote Young, he began studying the "prophecy of Isaiah," during which he received a revelation "which continued for a considerable time probably half a day during which we got a great many principles pertaining to intelligent existence and their modes of action."

Rigdon then initiated a fervent study of geology, after which he began writing a physical history of the world. "For month after month we continued our work," he explained to Young,

> but despite our secrecy it got noised through the village that we were writing some thing and curiosity was all awake to know what. The principal of the academy [Prosper Miller] being a man of great learning asked to hear us read a portion of what we had been writing we consented and read to him for an hour or more[.] He was struck with the extraordinary character of that method of teaching the history of the world[.] He mentioned the fact to two learned preachers in the place they also asked the priviledge of hearing portions of the manuscript we gratified them a consultation was held among them and a request was presented to us to arrange the manuscript in the form of public lectures and have them delivered in the chapel of the academy to anyone who might choose to hear. . . . The effect was astonishing; my name and fame spread far and wide and we were adjudged to be the greatest historian that now lives[.][21]

In a less self-congratulatory letter to Stephen Post, Rigdon provided a truer assessment of his endeavors: "I was called upon by the citizens of a village about 30 miles from here," he wrote, "to deliver a course [of six] lectures on the science of geology on the last week of June. . . . There are others who have notified me that they will want a course in few weeks and I have agreed to go[.] How much business I will get in that line I do not know but those who have heard think I will be kept constantly going after the season gets favorable."[22] Rigdon never again mentions the topic in his letters to Stephen Post. Accounts of the Friendship Academy extol Jeremiah Hatch's lectures on geology, but Rigdon's name is never mentioned.

By the late 1850s Rigdon, fresh out of followers, seemed to have burned out. Aside from his devoted wife Phebe, no other man or woman evidenced interest in his mission to redeem Zion. Solitary zeal was a devastating sentence to be imposed on so vocal a prophet. That hush was broken on 23 January 1856, however, when Rigdon walked to the Friendship post office to receive a letter from Stephen Post, a one-time Latter-day Saint who until recently had been a Strangite. Post, then living in Centerville, Pennsylvania, was like Rigdon a fervent seeker of the redemption of Zion. "I am looking for the consolation of Israel," Post had earlier written to his brother, and "long for the time to come when Zion shall arise & put on her beautiful garments & become the joy of the whole earth."[23]

Post, who had investigated and rejected other emerging Mormon splinter groups, wrote Rigdon seeking information on his ministry. Rankled over the invasion of his privacy, Rigdon brusquely responded that although he had no personal interest in Post's letter, "yet common courtesy requires that I should answer it." He then proceeded with a verbose discussion of his "calling before the Lord" to prepare the way for the coming of Elijah and the Messiah, as promised in Doctrine and Covenants 35:4. Ever since "the Lord took me away from Nauvoo," Rigdon revealed, it has taken all my "time and abilities" to gain the knowledge "necessary to qualify me for that work." To prevent Joseph Smith from becoming a "fals[e] prophet," Rigdon explained that he, the spokesman, had to suffer exile from society and made "mighty in expounding all scriptures" that he might know "the *certainty of all things pertaining to the things of his kingdom on earth.*"

It was no "ordinary undertaking to get so enlightened," Rigdon boasted, "my whole soul has been engaged in solving the mysteries of revelation" for the past eight years. He concluded with a cryptic disclosure that "there were another people [later revealed as Mennonites] to whom the word of the Lord must be sent before it went to the Lamanites." He asked Post not to share his letter with others as "I have no interest in giving my history to the world either past or prophetic."[24]

Rigdon and Post, two yoked visionaries, while seeing each other face-to-face only once, would correspond with each other for twenty years.[25] In a revelation to Post on 17 March 1856 Rigdon wrote:

> And now I the Lord . . . call [thee] to a great work in assisting my servant Sidney Rigdon in preparing the way before me, and Elijah which should come, and I say unto thee, as my servant Sidney Rigdon assisted my servant Joseph Smith with all his might mind and strength . . . I [have] called thee to assist my servant Sidney Rigdon. . . . Thine eyes shall see mine elect gathered and Zion redeemed, and thou shall shout Hosannahs in the midst of my people while Babylon shall shake and tremble, and the inhabitants thereof shall quake with fear, and howl, and weep, and mourn for anguish of soul, even so, amen.[26]

Post accepted his calling. A month later the prophet directed his assistant to convene a general conference for scattered Mormons at Kirtland in October and to issue a pamphlet setting forth his views on the LDS leadership succession issue. For unknown reasons, possibly lack of funds, neither of these missions was accomplished. In a 27 September 1856 letter Rigdon requested Post's help in publishing "a treatise on the destiny of the world with the future events which will lead to that result, as revealed in the revelations of heaven." Ever the doomsday prophet, Rigdon warned Post that "the whole world is approaching a certain crisis, terrific in its character." To alert the populace to this coming cataclysm, Rigdon proposed that the treatise be written in sermon form based on Revelation 19:20: "And the beast was taken, and with him the false prophet that wrought miracles before him, with which he deceived them that had received the mark of the beast, and them that worshipped his image. These both were cast alive into a lake of fire burning with brimstone."

In what was to become a life-long symbiotic relationship, Rigdon made the first of many requests to Post for financial support. Exulting that while he had the intelligence to write the treatise, "I lack the means, the money I have not." If someone were willing to "supply me with $25," the entrepreneurial prophet added, "I could get it on paper." "Can you aid me or can you not[?]" the old visionary asked. "If not [I] must wait till the Lord raises up one who can."[27] Post, with help from a follower Ebenezer Barnum, obtained the $25 and forwarded it to Rigdon on 17 December 1856. "I will have the contemplated work on paper as soon as possible," the grateful prophet wrote three days later. "It will be a work of much labor," he noted, which would "require great Biblical research and care in the compilation." Lest anyone doubt his abilities, Rigdon added that the completed work would "be a powerful auxillary in directing the attention of all who believe to the true character of the work of the Lord."[28]

By late February 1857 Rigdon had completed the manuscript, which he pointed out to Post was a "constitution or basis" for his calling to prepare the "way before the Lord." "The whole platform was given to me by revelation," he wrote; "the spirit held me bound and if I were going wrong I would be stopped and counseled[.] I was made to cease at one time for a whole week till the spirit had given such light and instruction as enabled me to proceed correctly[.] It is badly written but I think you can decipher it."[29] Although Post received the mailed document, it was never published, most likely because the $25 Post raised to enable Rigdon to write the treatise was all he could raise. The rambling, prosaic dissertation was not a tide destined to raise many ships.

Undaunted, Post maintained faith in Rigdon's calling. "I have much consolation," Post wrote of Rigdon in his 1858 diary, "looking with him for the redemption of Zion, the overthrow of Babylon and the bringing in of the millennial glory."[30] On 11 March 1859 Post wrote of a day-long revelatory trance during which he saw the glory of the afterlife and "other spiritual wonders." In the evening, emerging from his catalepsy, Post recorded, "the Spirit said to me, 'I have ordained a lamp for mine anointed.'"[31] Subsequent events in Post's life indicate he understood he was being called to serve as the "lamp" for Sidney Rigdon, the Lord's "anointed."

In early 1859 Post began pressuring Rigdon to visit Centerville and preach. Rigdon responded on 20 March that he would be unable to travel to Pennsylvania because of the illness of a married daughter. At year's end, however, he made the journey, much to the chagrin of his son Wickliffe, then studying law in Albany. On 3 December 1859 young Rigdon wrote to Post:

I understand my father Sidney Rigdon is at Centerville preaching Mormonism & that you and some others induced him to come there & preach[.] What I wish to say to you is this: My father is in no condition to preach to any people[,] he is a Maniac on religion & you did very wrong to influence him to leave his home & he must & shall return home & that immediately & I trust sir you will use your influence to induce him to do so[.] The idea of trying to build up a church of Mormons in that country is . . . nonsense[,] yes[,] worse than nonsense & am surprised to hear that there is a man this side of Salt Lake that would wish to do so.

I appeal to you as a man & hope you will dismiss him at once & send him home[.] There is no good [that can] come of his preaching[.] It will if persisted in put you all to shame & disgrace[.] I speak from experience.

Let me hope sir that my wishes in this matter may be complied with if they are not I will try & see if there is not some way to put a stop to it as far as my father is concerned at least.[32]

For a time Post backed off from his relationship with Rigdon. There was no known exchange of letters between them during 1860. In 1861, however, during the Civil War, a Philadelphia merchant Joseph Newton, former Rigdon adherent in Nauvoo, Pittsburgh, and Cumberland Valley, began corresponding with his erstwhile mentor. Newton, like Rigdon, and most Utah Mormons of the period, believed that the Civil War commenced the final war that was to be "poured out upon all nations," a battle that would not end until "the coming of the Son of Man." The basis of their belief was an 1832 prophecy of Joseph Smith (D&C 87:1), later reaffirmed in 1843 (D&C 130:12).[33]

Aside from mutual agreement about the war, little evolved from the Newton/Rigdon relationship until 1862, when several people approached Newton requesting baptism. The enthusiastic zealot wrote Rigdon, seeking his blessing. Although unimpressed at first, Rigdon came to view Newton's Philadelphia success as a divine manifestation that the "[F]ather has indeed commenced his work for the deliverence of Zion."[34]

Further manifestations were forthcoming. In an October 1862 letter to Post, Rigdon wrote that, overwrought with anxiety about the Civil War, he prayed an entire day "in behalf of Zion[,] praying that the Lord in his mercy would found her in strength and deliver her from the d[e]structions and blood which have and are spreading over the land." While he was praying the audible voice of the Lord spoke three brief sentences to him: "This house is holy. Zion is here. I have purified it by fire."[35] This epiphany further convinced Rigdon, as he later stated, that "the Lord is now moving in view of bringing Zion into remem[brance] in order to establish her in accordance with his promise."[36] Compounding apocalyptic war-time delirium, Rigdon was shocked by the tragic news of Captain Jeremiah Hatch's death from typhoid pneumonia on 21 December 1862 while stationed at Suffolk, Virginia.[37]

The following summer, while guns thundered and thousands of Americans died on the bloody fields and hills of Gettysburg, Rigdon traveled to Philadelphia to meet Joseph Newton and his small group of believers. Post, in an 1872 treatise championing Rigdon's ministry, wrote that like John the Baptist, the word of the Lord came to Rigdon in exile in the "wilderness of the people," saying, "Arise and go to Philadelphia . . . that the work of the Father might commence in preparing the way for the fulfilling of his covenants to the house of Israel."[38] In Philadelphia Rigdon, Newton, and others established The Church of Jesus Christ of the Children of Zion. According to Rigdon the appellation came from the parable of "the woman and the unjust judge" as expounded in Doctrine and Covenants 101:81-85. While the organization occurred in June 1863, Post later noted that "we hold our natal day on the 4th of July."[39]

Shortly after returning to Friendship Rigdon wrote Post describing events that had taken place in Philadelphia:

> As the cause of Zion is the only subject of any importance to us I would say a few things in relation to it. As far as I can understand the manifestations of the spirit there is a ray of hope springing up in my heart that the Lord is now moving in view of bringing Zion into rememb[rance] in order to establish her in accordance with his promise. I think I can see the shadow of that great event throwing itself before. In so saying I think I am not mistaken.

Rigdon had decided where the new gathering was to take place but did not want to make it known until later, after the area—in Iowa—had been scouted. "We have settled upon the place where Zion is to be established," he wrote, "and we wait on the Lord to prepare the way for our going thither."[40] Two months later Rigdon wrote Post that:

> The Lord commenced his work in Philadelphia in a way that I could not tell what he was going to do but as it progressed and as it now exists he has let us all see what he was doing. He was bringing together those, however far apart, who had been calling upon him for the deliver[a]nce of Zion and forming a provisional government with which to move the cause of Zion. He has called on five persons with whom he has formed this government and by who he will move the cause of Zion namely the three persons whose names are appended to the appeal yourself and myself.

He then told Post "not to preach the gospel to the world but [e]ntirely with that old church . . . whether they are walking alone or not you will cover the [e]ntire ground from Pittsburgh to the Lakes and as far west as that people are scattered." The commission, which excluded Utah Mormons, advised him to tell the elect that as soon as possible they were "to dispose of their affairs and go west of the Mississippi quietly as other citizens go" and to settle in either Iowa or Nebraska until they were "called for."[41]

During his three-week stay in Philadelphia Rigdon convinced well-to-do Joseph Newton to publish his treatise *An Appeal to the Latter-Day Saints*, an assault on the claims of Joseph Smith III, who three years earlier had become the founding president of the Reorganized Church of Jesus Christ of Latter Day Saints. On 10 September 1863 Rigdon commanded Post to see Joseph III and "to warn him of the judgments of God" which awaited him unless he ceased "his abominations before the Lord." Instead of traveling to see young Joseph, however, Post went to Pittsburgh where members of Rigdon's former congregation, now leaning towards Smith's claims, still resided. Using An Appeal to the Latter-Day Saints as a proselyting tool, Post attempted to win people back to Rigdon. Josiah Ells, a prominent former Rigdonite in Pittsburgh and Cumberland Valley, formulated a rebuttal to Rigdon's pamphlet. His reply, a lengthy analysis of Rigdon's doctrinal arguments and erratic behavior, was published in a two-part feature in the 15 January and 1 February 1864 issues of the True Latter Day Saints' Herald, the official organ of the RLDS church.

After debating Rigdon's claims to leadership with Ells on 10 November, Post quickly drafted a letter to young Smith. His discursive 11 November 1863 essay was published in early 1864 in a pamphlet entitled Zion's Messenger.[42] For reasons that are unclear, Phebe Rigdon, now taking an active part in her seventy-one-year-old husband's ministry, opposed Post's endeavors. Responding in his wife's behalf, Rigdon wrote a very unusual letter on 10 March 1864 which detailed

> The word of the Lord which came to Phebe his prophetess saying to his servent Stephen[:] Beware[,] beware of pride saith the Lord in writing for thou art in danger of falling under condemnation by reason of it[.] Do all things that thou doest in relation to Zion in great meekness and humility before me.
>
> I send you this as delivered to me by her whom the Lord has chosen and ordained to warn the sons of Zion when they are in danger.[43]

Following the pattern that had been established by Joseph Smith from the earliest days of the church, Rigdon insisted on financial support from his adherents. "Father Rigdon," as the Children of Zion affectionately called him, spelled out his pecuniary expectations in an October 1863 revelation entitled "The Word of the Lord Concerning Zion":

> I have through much tribulation and sore scourging, placed in the heart of my servant Sidney as in an earthen vessel the light that shall shine forth for the redemption of Zion. And I have called on my servant Stephen [Post] to go forth and cause that light to shine forth among the people: First upon those who are called by my name, and then Lo & behold! To others as the wisdom of your redeemer may direct. . . . And I appoint you my servant Joseph [Newton] to be head of the financial concerns of Zion. And as such the promin[e]nt duty in your calling is to see that the vessel where I the Lord have placed the light for salvation of Zion, is supplied with oil, that the light may shine in its strength. It is therefore required of you that you should see that the temporal wants and necessities of my servant Sidney are supplied.[44]

All the while Rigdon feverishly worked the mails to effect a new gathering of the Children of Zion in the East, his two sons, oblivious to their father's surreptitious religious activities, were seeking their fortune in the Brighamite stronghold in the West. Thirty-five-year-old Sidney, a former railroad agent, left behind his wife Anna and their two sons, Walter (7) and Georges (4). Wickliffe, a thirty-three-year-old lawyer who had married late in life, left behind his pregnant wife Sophia Jane and their year-old daughter Genevieve Aurelia.[45] The Rigdon boys found work in Idaho Territory mines. Wickliffe became ill and spent the winter of 1863-64 in Salt Lake City. When Brigham Young heard that Sidney's boys were in town he sent for them. "He seemed glad to see us," wrote Wickliffe. During the course of their conversation Young asked the brothers if they thought Sidney and Phebe, both in their seventies, would come to Utah if he sent for them. The Mormon leader suggested sending a mule train after them in the spring which "would bring them across the plains in a carriage in comfort." Willing to let bygones be bygones, Young promised to "take care of them during life." Wickliffe said he would write, but "did not think they could come." In "about 35 days," young Rigdon noted, "an answer came declining the offer."[46]

Wickliffe's account is retrospective, written forty years later. Two 1864 letters from Sidney himself, who had drunk too deeply of the cup of bitterness ever to forget its taste, provide considerably more information on the absorbing situation. On 1 March 1864 he wrote to Stephen Post: "I have had another pressing invitation from Brigham [and] Heber [C. Kimball] to go to Utah[.] I have answer[ed] their communication and will wait the result."[47] A 23 March letter from Rigdon to Joseph Newton spelled out Rigdon's written conditions to Young, Kimball, Daniel H. Wells, and "others of the leaders of the People of Utah." "I can entertain no proposition to the effect of their requests," Rigdon wrote,

> unless they will call a general conference, and in that conference every Branch of the[ir] church shall be represented, and they shall there take a note declaring that every thing they had said and published designed to injure myself and family, they should there and then declare to be false and without foundation in truth, and they should also at the same conference, proclaim ourselves [meaning Rigdon] as the Head of that people, resigning every power up into our hands.[48]

While Young's response is unknown, he sensed something deeply amiss in his old adversary. During a 7 October 1866 general conference address in Salt Lake City, Young said of Rigdon, "What has he come to? He sits in the midst of the woods East mumbling to himself; but scarcely able to speak an intelligent word; he is almost a lunatic."[49] While Young's assessment of Rigdon was self-serving, it was not too far off the mark. The last decade of Rigdon's life is a cheerless and tragic commentary on the regression of what had once been one of the finest minds in Mormondom.

Notes

Unless otherwise stated, all primary sources cited are located in the Historical Department of the Church of Jesus Christ of Latter-day Saints, Salt Lake City, Utah.

1. 1 July 1868 revelation signed by Sidney Rigdon and listed as section 37 in Copying Book A, Stephen Post Collection, mss. 1304, box 1, fd. 16; hereafter Post Collection.

2. Journal History, 6 Apr. 1848, 4–a multi-volume daily history of the church compiled by official church historians.

3. Karl Keller, ed., "'I Never Knew a Time When I Did Not Know Joseph Smith': A Son's Record of the Life and Testimony of Sidney Rigdon," *Dialogue: A Journal of Mormon Thought* 1 (Winter 1966): 40.

4. J. Wickliffe Rigdon, "Life Story of Sidney Rigdon," 185. While Wickliffe could not recall the full sermon, he remembered that it touched on "when Pharoh got to the bottom of the Pit he looked and saw all the Kings of the Earth there and was comforted" (ibid.).

5. The 1850 population was 2,243 as cited in *History of Allegheny County N.Y.–with Illustrations Descriptive of Scenery, Private Residences, Public Buildings, Fine Blocks, and Important Manufactories, from Original Sketches by Artists of the Highest Ability; and Portraits of Old Pioneers and Prominent Residents* (New York City: F. W. Beers & Co., 1879), n.p.

6. John S. Minard, *Allegheny County and Its People–A Centennial Memorial–History of Allegheny County, New York* (Alfred, NY: W. A. Fergusson & Co., 1896), 101-102.

7. See 2 Oct. 1850 Cuba, New York, census, 238 (LDS Family History Library, Salt Lake City).

8. Several entries in an 1847 ledger of the F. L. S. & Company (412, 501, and 594) show Robinson trading in Friendship (untitled and unannotated manuscript #1281, in Arlene Hess Collection, box 1, fd. 3, Special Collections, Harold B. Lee Library, Brigham Young University; hereafter Hess Collection).

9. Sidney is also listed as a patron of the F. L. S. & Company store in November 1850 (Hess Collection, box 1, fd. 1). The Robinson home, still standing in Friendship today, for many years also housed the First National Bank of Friendship, of which Robinson was president. Later, when he built his new home and bank on the corner of Main and Depot Streets, Robinson gave his former home to his sister-in-law Lacy Ann Hatch, widow of Jeremiah Hatch. Since then the place has been known as "the Hatch House."

Friendship's population during Rigdon's residency was as follows: 1850–1,675; 1855–1,838; 1860–1,889; 1865–1,725; 1870–1,528; 1875–1,871 (*History of Allegheny County N.Y.*, 276).

10. See Minard, 717. Also see *The History of Friendship* (Friendship, NY: Friendship Sesquicentennial Corp., 1965), 31. Wickliffe Rigdon wrote that his father was a "Verry dedicated Mason and was a regular atendant at the Masonic Lodge of [Friendship] and was frequently called upon to speak on public occasions of that order[.] . . . [He] was also an [O]dd [F]ellow and used to meet with them frequently" (Rigdon, 187).

11. See 26 July 1860 Friendship, New York, census, 619 (LDS Family History Library). Sidney, Phebe, and Phebe Jr. had moved into the Wingate home prior to 2 June 1859 (see Jeremiah Hatch to Abram Hatch, 2 June 1859, Hatch Family Papers). The other Rigdon children are listed in the 1860 census as still living in the Robinson home.

12. Undated letter from Sidney Rigdon to Stephen Post, Post Collection, box 1, fd. 1. The first part of the letter is missing but is complete in Copying Book B, Post Collection, where it is listed as section 92. Ex-Mormon John F. Olney, George W. Robinson's brother-in-law, became like Robinson a prominent Friendship citizen.

13. Hess Collection, box 1, fd. 3. Sidney and Phebe, Athalia Robinson, Sarah

Wingate, Lacy Ann Hatch, Phebe D. Spears, and Nettie are buried in Friendship's Maple Grove Cemetery.

14. Rigdon to Wight, 22 May 1853, Lyman Wight Letterbook, Library and Archives, Reorganized Church of Jesus Christ of Latter Day Saints, Independence, Missouri (hereafter RLDS archives).

15. The Friendship Academy, organized 5 February 1848, opened on 1 December 1848 after public subscription raised $3,000. Situated on Main Street property donated by Roswell Spears, the large three-story building contained five recitation rooms, a library, a large auditorium which could seat a thousand, and a chapel where Rigdon delivered his lectures on geology. The academy was destroyed by fire in 1893 (*History of Allegheny County*, 288-89).

16. William H. Pitt, cited in Minard, 713. In 1855 Hatch was appointed a Genesse Canal collector and moved to Oramel, New York. He eventually formed the law firm of Laning, Hatch & Lanina. From 1858 to 1862 he was in partnership with Samuel Hayden. In 1862, during the Civil War, he was prominent in raising and organizing the 130th N.Y. (1st N.Y. Dragoons). Captain Hatch died of typhoid pneumonia in December 1862.

17. Jeremiah Hatch, Jr., to Abram Hatch, 3 Aug. 1857, Hatch Family Papers. By then Abram was in Lehi, Utah, while Jeremiah was in Oramel, Allegheny County, New York.

18. See undated Rigdon to Post revelation, Post Collection, box 1, fd. 1; first part of letter is missing, but is included in its entirety in section 92, Copying Book B, Post Collection. For additional detail on this "law of exile," see Sidney Rigdon to Lyman Wight, 22 May 1853, Lyman Wight Letterbook, RLDS archives.

19. Sidney Rigdon to Stephen Post, 7 Dec. 1856, Post Collection, box 1, fd. 3.

20. Rigdon, 186.

21. Rigdon to Young, 1 May 1860, Phineas Young Collection.

22. Rigdon to Post, 19 July 1857, Post Collection, box 1, fd. 4.

23. Stephen Post to Warren Post, 3 Oct. 1851, Warren Post Collection, Family History Library, Harold B. Lee Library, Brigham Young University, Provo, Utah; hereafter BYU Library.

24. Rigdon to Post, 23 Jan. 1856, Post Collection, box 1, fd. 3; emphasis in original.

25. Following Post's 1879 death his family preserved the more than two hundred letters Rigdon wrote to him during this period, along with numerous revelations copied into bound volumes (arranged in sections like the Doctrine and Covenants), certificates and receipts, sermons, and the twelve-volume Post diary. In 1971 Mormons Terry K. Van Duren and David E. Rowe made contact with Post's grandson, Edward O. Post, keeper of the Stephen Post materials, who was living in Winnipeg, Manitoba, Canada. The LDS historical department obtained possession of the items that year. After cataloging, the Post Collection was made available to researchers (see "Register of the Stephen Post Papers," and Max J. Evans, "The Stephen Post Collection," *Brigham Young University Studies* 14 [Autumn 1973]: 100-103).

26. Rigdon to Post, 17 Mar. 1856, Post Collection, box 3, fd. 12. A decade later Rigdon wrote that he was with Joseph Smith when the prophet was told by God that he was "not the one the Lord had chosen through whom the way was to be prepared for the coming of Christ and Elijah." After this divine edict, Smith expressed to Rigdon his "deep sorrow of heart at the Lord's having chosen another instead of himself." Rigdon added

that while the Lord had given Joseph "the keys of the mysteries of the things which had been sealed," notwithstanding, "I was to prepare the way before him and Elijah." Further explaining his and Smith's roles, Rigdon added that "the question with regard to the transgression of JS is here for ever put at rest. He was to hold the keys of revelation for the church till Christ came *if he did not transgress*; nothing but that could deprive him of it. Behold he is gone and Christ has not come, and another has taken his place as revelator" (Rigdon to Post, 1 June 1866, Post Collection, box 1, fd. 2; emphasis in original).

27. Rigdon to Post, 27 Sept. 1856, Post Collection, box 1, fd. 3.

28. Rigdon to Post, 20 Dec. 1856, Post Collection, box 1, fd. 3.

29. Rigdon to Post, 26 Feb. 1857, Post Collection, box 1, fd. 4.

30. Stephen Post Diary, Aug.-Sept. 1858, Post Collection.

31. Ibid., under date.

32. Wickliffe Rigdon to Stephen Post, Post Collection, box 1, fd. 7. Regarding Sidney's religious aspirations, his son-in-law Jeremiah Hatch, Jr., wrote his nephew Abram Hatch on 2 June 1859: "The old man is a Mormon still. . . . Mr. Rigdon has been very quiet for more than 10 years. I have not spoken to him about religious matters for that long period till a few weeks ago. . . . He still thinks God will do something with him. I expressed my surprise & left him" (Hatch family papers, under date).

33. The most vivid account of this perspective of the war, from a Utah Mormon, is found in the Wilford Woodruff diaries for 1860-64 (Scott G. Kenney, ed. *Wilford Woodruff's Journal- Typescript*, 9 vols. (Midvale, UT: Signature Books, 1983-85). See also Susan Staker, *Waiting for World's End: The Diaries of Wilford Woodruff* (Salt Lake City: Signature Books, 1993).

34. Rigdon to Post, 26 Sept. 1863, Post Collection, box 5, fd. 7.

35. Rigdon to Post, Oct. 1862, Post Collection, box 2, fd. 3.

36. Rigdon to Post, 6 July 1863, Post Collection, box 1, fd. 8.

37. Of the eighty-one Friendship men who served in the war, including Lieutenant Ephraim Rigdon, Jeremiah Hatch, Jr., was the first to die. He enlisted on 10 July 1862, and one month later was commissioned captain of the 130th Regiment of the 1st N.Y. Dragoons. His body came home for burial on 27 December 1862 (see "News Items, Friendship Register," respecting Lacy Ann Rigdon Hatch, Hess Collection).

38. Stephen Post, *A Treatise on the Melchisedek Priesthood, and The Callings of God* (Council Bluffs, IA: Nonpareil Printing Co., 1872), 11.

39. Undated newspaper clipping in Post Collection, box 3, fd. 10.

40. Rigdon to Post, 6 July 1863, Post Collection, box 5, fd. 7.

41. Rigdon to Post, 26 Sept. 1863, Post Collection, box 5, fd. 7.

42. Stephen Post and William Hamilton, *Zion's Messenger* (Erie, PA: Sterrett & Gara, 1864).

43. Rigdon to Post, Post Collection, box 1, fd. 9; also listed as section 13 in Copying Book A—dated 10 Mar. 1864, box 3, fd. 12.

44. Post Collection, section 3 in Copying Book A, box 3, fd. 12.

45. For genealogical data on the brothers, see 1860 Friendship, New York, census, 634, and *The Utah Genealogical and Historical Magazine* 27 (Salt Lake City: Genealogical Society of Utah, 1936), 162.

46. Keller, 41. At least four years earlier rumors circulated that Rigdon was coming

west. In his 1 July 1860 diary, John D. Lee noted reports that said: "Sidney Rigdon had boldly acknowledged that he was in an error, & Testified that Brigham was a Prophet of God & the true Shepherd of Iseral & that Polygamy was from Heaven, & those that fought against it fought against the Buckler of Jehovah &c., & that he was on his way to the vally & Br[i]gham had sent a Team to help him from the [Bluffs]" (Robert Glass Cleland and Juanita Brooks, eds., *The Mormon Chronicle: The Diaries of John D. Lee–1848-1876* [San Marino, CA: Huntington Library, 1955], 261).

47. Rigdon to Post, Post Collection, box 1, fd. 9.

48. Joseph H. Newton to Stephen Post, Post Collection, box 1, fd. 9.

49. *The Essential Brigham Young* (Salt Lake City: Signature Books, 1992), 146.

CHAPTER 28.

Children of Zion

I the Lord their God chose my serv[a]nt Sidney to be the head of Zion even before he was born and he was mine from his mothers womb[.] I the Lord his God watched over him from his crad[le] to the present moment. The int[e]grity of his heart I knew. The honesty of his soul was always before my eyes long before I sent him the fulness of my gospel for him only did I chose among the sons of men whose intention of soul and purposes of heart were such as to warrant the Lord your God in choosing him for this high and Holy calling[.] I the Lord made him mighty in the earth among the great ones thereof from the beginning even in his youthful days I made him one to be wondered at. As he advanced in life I made him a terror to those who opposed him untill his name became famous in the midst of the great ones of the earth.

—Revelation to Sidney Rigdon (1866)[1]

Wickliffe Rigdon, who in 1904 at age seventy-four became a Mormon, frequently expressed qualms about his father's religious career. During his 1863-64 stay in Utah young Rigdon was not impressed by Mormonism. "I saw a great many things among the members that seemed so different from what they were," he later wrote:

> They would swear, use tobacco, were vulgar in habits, drank whiskey and g[o]t drunk. They did not preach the gospel when they went to church. They would tell about drawing wood, how to raise wheat and corn, and not a word said about the gospel. [They] came to meetings in everyday clothes and did not seem to care anything about religion. Mormonism seemed a humbug and I said when I got home I would find out from my father how the Book of Mormon came into existence. I made up my mind he should tell me all he knew.[2]

Shortly after Wickliffe reached Friendship in the fall of 1865 he asked his father about Mormonism. After relating the conditions he had found in Utah, Wickliffe said: "You are an old man and you will soon pass away and I wish to know if Joseph Smith in your intimacy with him for fourteen years had not said something to you that led you to believe he obtained that book in some other way than what he had told you." Sidney paused, gazed at his son momentarily, then slowly raised his arm to the square. "With a tear glistening in his eyes," he stated with great solemnity, "My son I can state as before high heaven that what I have told you about the origin of that book is true":

> [A]ll I ever knew . . . was what Parley P. Pratt[,] Oliver Cowdery[,] Joseph Smith[,] and the witnesses who claimed they saw the plates have told me and in all of my intimacy with Joseph Smith he never told me but the one story and that was he found it [e]ngraved upon gold plates in a hill near Palmyra N.Y. and that an angel had appeared to him and directed him where to find it and I have never to you or any one else told but the one story.[3]

Sidney's life for better or for worse was bound to the Book of Mormon and millenarian zeal. But particularly through his autumn years in New York, his life, as Wickliffe stated, was "full of trouble and sorrow." Young Rigdon observed that his father had "spent the best years of his manhood for the benefit and prosperity of the Morm[o]n church and in his old age he was repudiated by the church he had labored so hard to establish and as he believed without a just cause." He felt that for the services he had rendered to the church he was entitled "to some promotion."[4]

No doubt Wickliffe told his father how wealthy Brigham Young had become since settling in Utah.[5] That fact must have rankled the penniless prophet, who correctly viewed his contributions to early Mormonism as more significant than Young's. Seeking compensation for his efforts during the last decade of his life, Rigdon struggled to sustain a personal retirement from the meager resources of a few hundred adherents. While a more affluent lifestyle eluded Rigdon in Friendship, his yearning for veneration became the foremost aspiration of his declining years. Numerous pronouncements demonstrated his desire not only for financial remuneration, but for recognition for personal sacrifices and the role he had once played in Mormonism. In a 25 January 1864 revelation explicating his background to devotee Dr. Abraham Bartis, Rigdon waxed eloquent:

> I have put at the head of Zion my servant Sidney Rigdon as the organ through which I shall speak to you in all matters pertaining to Zion, and none other shall you receive; for him only have I proven before my face, by tribulations and afflictions, buffetings & scourgings. For Satan stood before me and claimed the right to scourge him in a similar way as he did Job, believing that he could overthrow him. . . . And I the Lord say to you that no man that ever stood before me had a greater trial of his faith than this was. No, Noah, Daniel nor Job, Abraham, Moses nor Samuel.

As a reward for the Rigdons' sacrifices, the revelation made clear that they were to be compensated. God required the Children of Zion "to relieve the temporal necessities of the priesthood through which their salvation comes. . . . I the Lord have seen [Sidney and Phebe] toiling with their hands day and night to purchase a scanty subsistence for many years, until they have passed the age of man."[6]

The prophet expected money not only for himself but for his impoverished daughter Nancy, mother of seven, then married to Civil War veteran Robert Ellis and living in Pittsburgh.[7] In late 1864 Sidney wrote Joseph Newton, financial officer of his church, and explained that "the fountains of revelation had closed for the present in consequence of a new trouble brought upon him by the Devil to hinder the progress of Zion." He recounted how Ellis, an alcoholic, had "become very disipated, d[e]stroying all he had, and leaving his family d[e]stitute, and [had] gone back to his father for assist[a]nce and protection." To meet this "extra expense" Rigdon requested additional money from the hard-pressed Newton.[8]

One month later, 5 November 1864, financial worries were deepening. Rigdon informed spokesman Stephen Post that "the management of the temporal matters [does] not belong to me but to you as the Lord has said that I shall have no power in temporal things." He added that recently while engaged in study his wife warned him "you are expecting your mind beyond what it is ab[le] to bear surrounded and pressed as you are with worldly cares." Fearing the effect of such behavior on his health, she cautioned, "you will faint and your mind break . . . you must wait till . . . your mind [is] [e]ntirely relieved from worldly cares and then the great mysteries of time will be revealed."[9]

However diligently Post, Newton, and others worked to succor the Rigdons, it was never enough. Rigdon—in the name of God—cajoled, urged, and threatened adherents to fulfill their duties towards him. In a 1 April 1866 revelation to new converts Ebenezer and Loran Page, Rigdon sketched surrealistic images of himself: "Verily, verily saith the Lord Jehovah of Zion there is one standing before me to whose faith[,] diligence[,] patience[,] [e]ndurance[,] and undying devotion to the cause of Zion every soul that ever will be in Zion is indebted for their salvation." Like a biblical prophet, he persisted: "[W]ith strong crying tears and supplications ceased not day nor night for many long years to humble himself and seek the salvation of Zion." Rigdon's struggle was "such as no other man ever had." In the process "his heart was cleansed and purified every whit . . . and Verily I the Lord say unto you that in him there is no sin before me neither can he sin for he is altogether born of God." Furthermore, when "God made covenant with Abraham that he would gather his seed in the last days and establish them forever in their own land it was made in view of him who is the head of Zion on earth [i.e., Rigdon]."[10]

Six months later in another revelation on this same subject, Father Rigdon continued plucking at the heart strings of his followers:

> I the Lord let Satan drag [Sidney and Phebe] through the furnace of affliction [to] overwhelm them in sorrow and grief such as few have ever endured before the Lord our God. . . . The tears that they shed are bottled up in heaven and their groans of affliction are written on the records on high. They ceased not day nor night to implore the abid[a]nce of the Holy Spirit even when at labor and toil to procure enough to

sustain life. . . . There were no sufferings no reproach, no privations no shame no disgrace no revilings no temporal necessities could change the purposes of their hearts yet they brought *all* they had and laid it down at the foot of the cross.

Lest Rigdon's disciples miss the point, the revelation stressed: "And now verily saith the Lord the Children of Zion owes a debt of gratitude to them that they never can pay for through [them] their salvation has come. . . . Will not therefore the Children of Zion smooth down the path of life in old age?" Rigdon saw nothing rhetorical in the questions. "I the Lord require this at your hand," the disclosure demanded, "that the priesthood [Sidney and Phebe] be delivered from cares and anxieties [that they] may attend constantly to the work unto which they are called otherwise the Children of Zion will stand condemned before me."[11]

Citations for valor in battling with the devil were bestowed on Rigdon in an April 1867 pronouncement which the prophet sent to Post to be read to the Children of Zion:

Now I the Lord declare unto Zion a great mystery if they will receive it behold the great battle that was fought with the devil for the salvation of Zion was fought between the devil and the Man child [i.e., Rigdon] which John saw in his vision, the woman brought forth who was caught up to heaven (symbolically) till the time should come for his appearance . . . [T]he conflict lasted 20 years before the devil would yield. But he found after an entire trial of his strength that he against whom he was contending was as mighty in war as he was great in council; . . . the devil found him defended by the shield of faith, with the girdle of truth about his loins, the sword of the spirit in his hand, & his feet shod with the preparation of the gospel, and he found that fighting against him was of no use, and he yielded.[12]

An October 1868 revelation declared the redemption of Zion indisputably linked to satisfying the Rigdons' temporal needs. After addressing the impropriety of a prophet "[e]mployed in temporal concerns and hav[ing] to devote his time to the obtaining of the necessary supplies for the support of himself and family," the revelation praised the distinctiveness of Rigdon's singular life. "Let it then be known in all the land and be proclaimed in the ears of all who seek salvation," the reveltion read, "that salvation cometh only through the ministration of my serv[a]nt Sidney Rigdon for he alone maintained his integrity in the day when Satan overwhelmed the first church with his corruption and took it to himself." Moved to indignation on the Rigdons' behalf, the Lord threatened: "If his wants are not supplied to the fulness I the Lord will not bless the children of Zion."[13]

By 1871 seventy-eight-year-old Rigdon had come to view himself without peer in the annals of humankind. "There was but one man in the world who could endure the scourging which he has suffered without failing," the aging prophet proclaimed in God's voice to backer Jessie Crosby. He and Phebe were "as much the Father and Mother of Zion as was Abraham the father of his family or the father of the faithful."[14] In a 24 February 1875 revelation, after a series of strokes,

Rigdon still sang his own accolades in God's voice. "During this course of trial," God said, Rigdon had "learned things concerning man and woman such as no other person on this earth knows, or can know only through him."[15]

Although Rigdon remained in Friendship the remainder of his life, directing his organization through the mails, he instructed followers on 26 June 1864 to gather to Iowa, the newly designated place of refuge, "to escape from the desolations of [B]abylon which [are] about to fall on the heads of those who dwell in the Eastern lands":

> For I the Lord have decreed a consumption on all the region of this country laying between what you call the Atlantic on the east and the Mississipi on the west and between the gulf of Mexico on the south and the great lakes on the north as it named among you. . . . And I would farther say to you my serv[a]nts that it will be to your advantage when you [go] to such a home that you go as far west as the place known as Council Bluffs in Iowa.[16]

The ruling priesthood of the Children of Zion—Joseph Newton, Stephen Post, William Stanley, and Abraham Burtis—were warned to make their residences in the center of the state, near each other, after disposing of their property "to the best advantage you all can." Others were instructed to settle farther west, approximately 200-300 hundred miles apart, to "avoid Missouri and Kansas, those two states of blood." They were to prepare themselves for the time when the Lord would call them up "to take possession of their inheritance by blood," a day Rigdon predicted was nine years away. "The great matter for us," the revelation concluded, "is to get the priesthood [i.e., Rigdon] settled, there will be a day not far distant when thousands will be glad to go where they will find the way hedged."[17]

Rigdon had appointed William Stanley as church purchasing agent to buy land and property in Iowa, but Stanley apparently lost interest. Joseph Newton wrote Stephen Post on 11 August 1864 that the prophet had appointed him (Newton) instead. Newton told Post that he had "received within the previous two weeks, five or six letters from Father Rigdon urging [him] to make preparations to leave Babylon."[18]

By April 1865 both Post and Newton had located in Attica, Marion County, Iowa, a small hamlet in the Des Moines Valley.[19] With an annual precipitation of thirty-three inches and a growing season of 170 days,[20] Attica was a superb farming and ranching locale. An 1865 description of the area praised the "beautifully undulating, high, and gently rolling" prairies interspersed with "groves of linn, elm, and burr oak timber." The soil, a "rich, black sandy loam" from two to six feet deep, was "well adapted to the production of cereals," which brought "a good price, owing to the great demand for flour in the northern part of Missouri." Wheat and oats did well, the promotion noted, as did "Irish and sweet potatoes . . . Indian corn [and] . . . sorghum." Marion County was touted as "one of the best counties in the State for stock, particularly cattle and hogs." Water "of the best quality can be had in any part of the county by digging to the depth of eighteen or twenty feet."[21]

Initially Rigdon planned to relocate to Attica, which by 1870 had a population of 1,332.[22] In a 1 September 1864 letter to Counselor Post, the prophet warned him that he was "appointed the head of a great mission" to prepare living quarters for the Rigdons. If he should fail, "it would be fatal to you." Post was advised that

> you must provide for my own use a comfortable house and a place where I can attend to the duties of my calling. The Lord would frown on me should I attempt to do such a thing myself, and he would shake the operative priesthood to the centre, if not to hurl them down to stand before him no more forever. . . . [I]t is required of me to stay where I am till all things are prepared before me, and here I must and will stay till that is done.

Rigdon announced that he should be made a "father to Zion . . . to be known and reverenced." Then, like a distant echo from Missouri, he interjected the "Law of Zion," which demanded that "those who do not reverence the Father . . . be cut off from the midst of the children of Zion, and in my due time, [they] shall be trampled under foot of men as the salt that has lost its savor." The prophet appended a postscript that at the exact moment he was writing to Post "*all the heavens are rejoicing[–]Abraham[,] Isaac & Jacob are shouting praises to God on high* that there is a man found on earth to be a second father to Israel, through whom all the promises and covenants obtained for their children can now be fulfilled." Rigdon closed his letter melodramatically: "[M]y heart melts within me. I feel ashamed to lift my eyes towards heaven, my spirit tells me I am a poor sinful worm of the dust, O my God help me."[23]

By 6 October 1864 Post and William Stanley, who by now was recommitted to the project, had purchased three homes in Attica, including one for the Rigdons. But Joseph Newton, still in Philadelphia, and Abraham Burtis, in New Egypt, New Jersey, were not producing sufficient income to lure the prophet and his wife to give up their quarters in the Wingate home in Friendship.[24] In late 1864 Rigdon sent an eighteen-page revelation to Newton chastising the Children of Zion. Newton, not wanting to recopy the entire document, apprised Post of the "most remarkable revelation ever given to man," as he called it. Newton recorded the conclusion:

> Behold saith the Lord, Satan is trying to overthrow the children of Zion . . . I the Lord have gotten for the place of my habitation a goodly land, yea, a delightsome place, and my serv[a]nt Stephen has gotten possession of it–But Zion is not there, neither can it ever be there, till my holy priesthood [meaning Rigdon], to which I have given Zion is taken there, and established according to what I have said. . . . I the Lord have made my holy priesthood to the children of Zion, what the Ark of the Covenant was to the Children of Israel, and their salvation depends on having it with them[.]

Newton advised Post that he had done his best to "supply the wants of the messenger, or Prophet and leader of the Children of Zion." For two years Newton had done his utmost to assist the Rigdons, but he had impoverished himself in the process. "It seems that Satan is determined to starve out the old Prophet," Newton wrote, "and in order to do it he is sweeping away what little I had. All my brethren seem to think that I must do it all myself, not a living soul seems to be disposed to help me in this work of loving kindness and charity." I now "ask coun[sel] of you, as the second operative priesthood," Newton concluded, "what I shall do in this trying emergency."[25]

Relatively nothing could be done. The flock had been fleeced. But having exhausted his arsenal of threats, Rigdon now turned to bribes. A 12 January 1865 revelation announced that all

> who now come forward and cast in their means power and influence to effect the establishment of the priesthood [meaning Rigdon] on the land which has been appointed for that purpose, shall be called the sons of God pre-eminently above all others and when they have accomplished this work, you my servants Sidney [Rigdon] & Joseph [Newton], shall bless them in my name, and in my name ordain them to the holy priesthood of prophet priest and king to take their places in the Celestial council of the ancient of days, that they and their work may be had in remembrance before the Lord forever and ever.[26]

Yet another revelation threatened the group that unless they properly provided for their prophet he would be conveyed to a people who would respect him—the Utah Saints:

> And now I the Lord say unto you if the Children of Zion do not come forward and raise you up out of your afflictions and bear your burdens I the Lord say unto you I will take you away as I live saith the Lord to a people thousands of whom are desiring with all their hearts to have you in their midst,—I do not speak this of their leaders and those who have usurped authority over them, but of the thousands of others, and I the Lord have gotten to me a priesthood so shall Zion come forth out of that old Church.[27]

In July 1865 Rigdon wrote to Post that he had recently received a revelation attesting that "Satan had made an attack on Zion for the purpose of its d[e]struction." Although the prophet's letter on this subject is muddled, he believed his life was endangered by the RLDS faction under Joseph Smith III's leadership. "The scheme is now plainly manifesting itself even unto intended murder," the prophet wrote, "this [e]ntire device is arranged through the organization [Satan] has effected through young Joseph Smith. . . . Should I be placed in a situation [in Attica]," Rigdon warned Post, "where my life will face a prey you will share the same fate."[28]

The apprehension of danger dispelled any intention on Rigdon's part to relocate to Attica. Until 1870, however, when he began expounding the dominion of Canada as the place of refuge, he continually prodded Post and others to gather the Children of Zion to Iowa. From 1864 to 1869 Post, the "Head of the Evangelical order of the Priesthood,"[29] occasionally traveled about Iowa and Illinois preaching and baptizing. As many as 200, mostly former Mormons, became convinced that Rigdon's ministry was heaven-inspired as a result of Post's efforts.[30]

In the fall of 1865, as the Civil War came to an end, the prophet, fearing imminent fulfillment of Joseph Smith's 1832 prophecy that "war will be poured out upon all nations . . . until the consumption decreed hath made a full end of all nations,"[31] issued a special revelation to Post and Newton. His decree ordered them into immediate missionary work to ensure that "there may be a people prepared to receive my saints in the day when destruction & desolation shall come on the gentiles to the very uttermost."[32] Two months later Post and Solomon Tripp visited Joseph Smith III in Nauvoo. Post introduced himself as a representative of "one who had been a friend of his father's and had suffered with him also for this work." Joseph answered that "he did not wish to hear any call himself a friend of his father who slandered him." Smith, an articulate attorney, impugned Rigdon's claims by debating their legality with Post, and the two men separated in anger.[33]

For the first decade of his ministry, Post had been instructed to proselyte only believers in the Book of Mormon. On 2 March 1866, however, Joseph Newton sent a communication to Post, "My Dear Bro And fellow laborer in the preparation of the glorious Coming of the son of God," informing him of an "important document from Father Sidney." The new revelation instructed the two men that the gospel from this time forth must "commence to be preached to the gentiles, as well as to the freedman, or man of color, for this cause the Lord had liberated them by the late war."[34]

Post was divinely appointed to be "Spokesman in Zion" in a subsequent 27 March 1866 revelation.[35] In Stephen Post, Rigdon found not only a spokesman but someone tolerant of his eccentricity. Despite Wickliffe Rigdon's 1859 warning that "My father . . . is a Maniac on religion,"[36] Post maintained a belief in Rigdon's prophetic integrity until his own death three years after Rigdon's.[37]

In the spring of 1867 prominent Utah Mormon Abram Hatch, nephew of Rigdon's deceased son-in-law, Jeremiah Hatch, Jr., visited Rigdon in the Wingate home at Friendship and described the seventy-four-year-old prophet as a "grand looking old man, large and portly," who impressed him with his "intellectual importance." After listening to Rigdon's testimonial of the Book of Mormon and his tirade against Brigham Young, Hatch concluded that Rigdon was "an intellectual giant of a certain type . . . a man of extraordinary spiritual aspirations."[38] Former Pittsburgh Rigdonite, A. W. Cowles, on assignment for *Moore's Rural New Yorker* in 1869, left a similarly sympathetic and little known portrait of Rigdon in his later years. Cowles wrote that the "venerable old man of nearly eighty years" was endowed with a "snowy beard and a keen eye." "His health seems good," the writer continued, and "his mind clear and vigorous." While the former Mormon acknowledged that Rigdon possessed "a quick, excitable manner, and a fondness for strong, emphatic expressions," Cowles considered them "relics of his old fanaticism."

Rigdon asserted to Cowles that Joseph Smith was "tempted by the devil to vanity and self-confidence" until he "became corrupt in morals and an apostate from the truth which had been revealed to him." Rigdon settled into narrating his own early history "with entire freedom, and with an old man's pardonable pride in the early proofs of remarkable talents and extraordinary successes." Cowles closed his account of the interview by observing that Rigdon, with a grand sweep of his hand, proclaimed: "Yes, if I were only young again I could sweep away all your religions from under the whole heaven!"[39] The gesture and grandiloquence was vintage Rigdon. In this uncanny moment of self-characterization, he sketched his self-portrait in living words, his life-long medium of choice.

Notes

Unless otherwise stated, all primary sources cited are located in the Historical Department of the Church of Jesus Christ of Latter-day Saints, Salt Lake City, Utah.

1. Sidney Rigdon to Stephen Post, 1 Dec. 1866, listed as section 26 in Copying Book A, Stephen Post Collection, mss. 1304, box 3, fd. 12; hereafter Post Collection.

2. Karl Keller, ed., "'I Never Knew a Time When I Did Not Know Joseph Smith': A Son's Record of the Life and Testimony of Sidney Rigdon," *Dialogue: A Journal of Mormon Thought* 1 (Winter 1966): 41.

3. J. Wickliffe Rigdon, "Life Story of Sidney Rigdon," 191-93; also see Wickliffe's slightly different account in *Latter-day Saints' Millennial Star* 66 (13 Oct. 1904): 643.

4. Rigdon, 198-99.

5. Brigham Young in his first public discourse after the Quorum of the Twelve was sustained on 8 August 1844 declared: "I want my support and living by the church hereafter, so that I can give my whole time to the business of the church" (Joseph Smith, *History of the Church of Jesus Christ of Latter-day Saints*, B. H. Roberts, ed., 7 vols. [Salt Lake City: The Church of Jesus Christ of Latter-day Saints, 1902], 7:257; hereafter *History of the Church*). By the time of his 1877 death Young was one of Utah territory's richest men. A lawsuit, brought against his estate by the church, was necessary to separate commingled personal wealth from church funds (see Leonard J. Arrington, *Brigham Young: American Moses* [New York: Alfred A. Knopf, 1985], 422-30).

6. Section 4 in Copying Book A, Post Collection, box 3, fd. 12. Regarding the sacrifices of the entire Rigdon family, a 1 July 1868 revelation noted that even the children "from early life have had to share with him the persecutions and violence hurled against him so that they have never known what it was to enjoy the common privileges of life." Proclaiming

the family as "victims of the Devil," the pronouncement added that during the "time of their greatest affliction" Sidney and Phebe had dedicated their children to God, "because the persecutions lay so heavily" on them, and requested him to "take them and dispose of them" (Post Collection, box 1, fd. 16).

7. Ellis served as a private in the 101st New York, an infantry regiment (see Samuel M. Evans, comp., *Allegheny County, Pennsylvania in the War for the Suppression of the Rebellion–1861-1865* [Pittsburgh: Board of Managers, Soldiers and Sailors Memorial Hall, 1924], n.p.).

8. Joseph H. Newton to Stephen Post, 6 Oct. 1864, Post Collection, box 1, fd. 10. On 1 June 1866 Nancy, who had given birth to twins the previous year, lost a four-year-old son. Rigdon wrote to Post: "The case of Nancy is in the hands of the Lord for him to do as his wisdom directs and neither you nor myself can do any thing on the premises" (Post Collection, box 1, fd. 12).

Robert and Nancy Ellis, who married on 13 September 1846, parented nine children: Margaret Allen Ellis Forrest (1847-1928), Phoebe Eliza Brooks Ellis Chalmers (1849-1923), Elva Viola Ellis (1851-1928), Frank Glenthorn Ellis (1855-81), Robert Sidney Ellis (1857-1927), Samuel Marshall Ellis (1858-1937), Charles Colvin Ellis (1862-66), and twins John Clarke (1865-1934) and Sarah Wingate (1865-1916). Nancy R. Ellis died in Pittsburgh on 1 November 1887 (see Robert and Nancy Ellis Family Group Sheet, Lloyd J. Neuffer Collection).

Early in his career, Robert Ellis was a stage actor. His niece, Jessie R. Secord, wrote that Ellis "was a man of much talent, who if he had let drink alone might have gone far in the theatrical mold." He later became a successful Pittsburgh printer and remarried after Nancy's death (Secord to Arlene Hess, 19 May 1967, Arlene Hess Collection, Special Collections, Harold B. Lee Library, Brigham Young University, Provo, Utah; hereafter Hess Collection).

9. Rigdon to Post, 5 Nov. 1864, Post Collection, box 1, fd. 12.

10. Rigdon to Joseph Newton, 1 Apr. 1866, Post Collection. "Our guide in all matters pertaining to Zion"—in essence, Rigdon's thesis on Zion—was given in a 1 May 1867 letter to Stephen Post. Explaining that at the time he "separated from the people of the old church"

> The devil had got the word of the Lord corrupted[,] darkened[,] and covered with rub[b]ish. . . . Zion was not on the earth and there was but one way in which it ever could get into the world[.] Some body [meaning himself] had to fight the great battle of redeeming the word of the Lord from under his power and influence or else Zion could never be in the world.
>
>   . . . All the judgements pronounced against the wicked in connection with the redemption of Zion and salvation of Israel shall take place in connection with our work in redeeming the world whether it be thunderings or lightenings earth-quakes or convulsions of the world blood or fire or pillars of smoke. If the Son is darkened the moon turn to blood or the stars of he[a]ven fall all will be reason of our moving Zion on to her glory of the mountains [where we will] meet with blood and blood flow from the fountains of the waters [but] they will come because Zion is in the world moving to her triumph. If sword famine and pestilence lay waste the earth it will be by reason of the existence of Zion. If the rich men the noble men every poor man

bond and free call upon the mountains to fall on them and hide them from the face of him who sitteth upon the throne and from the wealth of the Lamb it will because "Zion" is pressing forward to perfection. Let the heavens then shake and the earth roll to and fro like a drunken man. Let the wicked fear quake and tremble. Let their knees smite together and their faces gather blackness and their loins be pained. But let the children of Zion pray without ceasing read continually study devotedly that they may store up a rich treasury of the words of eternal life in their hearts that they may be full of intelligence and mighty to proclaim the word of eternal life and all will be well with them Forever and Ever (Post Collection, box 1, fd. 14).

11. Post Collection, section 26 in Copying Book A, box 1, fd. 12.

12. Post Collection, box 5, fd. 17.

13. Oct. 1868 revelation, Post Collection, section 45 in Copying Book A, box 1, fd. 17. One month later in a November 1868 revelation to newly appointed Bishop Israel Huffaker, Rigdon complained that he "has nothing of this world's goods left nor has he a shelter he can call his own. . . . What sayest thou my servent Israel to these things[.] Hast thou not an heart to feel hast thou not a conscience to require duty surely thou hast?" Huffaker was then admonished: "you will see that my serv[a]nt Sidney and mine hand-maiden Phoebe be your special charge. . . . See to it then that the voice of necessity does not from henceforth come up into the ears of the Lord your god from that place" (Post Collection, box 1, fd. 17; also listed as section 46 in Copying Book A, box 3, fd. 12).

14. The revelation is signed by both Sidney and the prophetess Phebe, Post Collection, box 1, fd. 2.

15. 24 Feb. 1875 revelation in Post Collection, listed as section 92 in Copying Book B, box 3, fd. 13.

16. 26 June 1864 revelation in Post Collection, listed as section 7 in Copying Book A, box 1, fd. 19.

17. Rigdon to Joseph Newton, 19 July 1864, Post Collection, box 1, fd. 9; also listed as section 7 in Copying Book A, box 3, fd. 12.

18. Newton to Post, Post Collection, box 1, fd. 10; also in section 10 in Copying Book A, box 3, fd. 12.

19. Attica, situated in the northern part of Indiana Township, was laid out by Stanford Doud, county surveyor, on 16 May 1847 for James Barker and Nathaniel and Rhoda Cockelreas. Until 1852 the town's name was Barkersville. But after Barker committed adultery, the designation was changed to Attica (John W. Wright and W. A. Young, *History of Marion County Iowa and Its People* [S. J. Clarke Publishing Co., 1915], 159).

20. John Clements, *Iowa Facts* (Dallas: Clements Research, Inc., 1988), 193.

21. James T. Hair, ed. and comp., *Iowa State Gazetteer* (Chicago: Bailey & Hair, 1865), 277-79.

22. An 1881 description of the town, shortly after the Rigdonites left, notes three general stores, two drugstores, a cobbler, a harness shop, two blacksmith shops, a wagon shop, a gristmill and a sawmill, two potteries, a sorghum mill, two physicians, two ministers, a hotel, a post office, and one school (*The History of Marion County* [Des Moines, IA: Birdsall, Williams & Co., 1881], 782-83).

23. Section 18 in Copying Book A, Post Collection, box 1, fd. 10.

24. In a 27 January 1865 letter to Stephen Post, Joseph Newton noted that Burtis had told him that since they had presented the "old prophet with a House," he (Burtis) "thought it was his duty to take Father Sidney to Attica . . . he wanted to buy a farm there and he would try and sell his property with the view to do it." Newton commented that "he has a good deal of valuable property, and I pray that he will do as he promises but I fear that his [meaning Burtis] love of money will hinder him" (Post Collection, box 1, fd. 10).

25. Joseph Newton to Stephen Post, 16 Dec. 1864, Post Collection, box 3, fd. 4. By the end of 1866 Newton, like Rigdon, had become a charity case. Writing to Elders Mitchell, Forgues, and Perrini, the formerly prosperous merchant pled:

> You brethren are doubtless aware, that for nearly four years, I have poured out my money and that by commandment of the Lord in assisting & moving the cause of Zion onward. . . . But now all is gone & I know not how to live through the winter; I need coal wood flour and the common necessaries of life; there is nothing that I can do, to realize one cent; and I have not strength to work at days labor; and if I had I could not do it. I have no time, for I am writing all my time to brethren in every part of the country. Men every where are writing to me for information. It is said in the parable that a merchant man sold all he had to purchase a field containing a pearl of salvation; but this was not done for our salvation only; but yours also, as well as the whole world. . . . In the day of Zion's infancy, weakness & poverty I stood alone in supporting the father of Zion, and done it willingly & cheerfully to the best of my ability, and now I appeal to my brethren to take this burden from my shoulders and comfort the old man's heart.—otherwise, I fear the fountain of revelation will be closed; and if such should be the case, wo be to the children of Zion. . . . I will now purpose a covenant that I will make with you, namely that if you assist me in getting a living . . . then I will take it upon myself to copy & send you many sublime revelations, which are on record, and all others as they may come hereafter. The history of the priesthood by Father Sidney alone would be worth more than all you do for me; this history fills sheets of cap paper (Post Collection, box 5, fd. 8).

26. 12 Jan. 1865 revelation in Post Collection, listed as section 20 in Copying Book A, box 3, fd. 12.

27. No date on this "Extract of Revelation" in the Post Collection, box 5, fd. 17, but it is filed between a 12 Jan. 1865 and Apr. 1867 entry.

28. Rigdon to Post, 1 July 1865, Post Collection, box 5, fd. 8.

29. 18 Oct. 1867 revelation listed in Post Collection as section 31 in Copying Book A, box 1, fd. 14.

30. The number of Post's baptisms, tallied from Post's journals and Children of Zion branch records, is cited in Carol Freeman Braby, "Rigdonites in Manitoba, 1874-1884," *John Whitmer Historical Association Journal* 11 (1991): 74.

31. "The prophecy on the Civil War," as it is best known, is recorded in LDS D&C 87.

32. 16 Oct. 1865 revelation listed in the Post Collection as section 21 in Copying Book A, box 3, fd. 2.

33. See Journal of Stephen Post, entries for 17, 21, and 23 Dec. 1865, Post Collection, box 6, fd. 4.

34. Post Collection, box 2, fd. 12.

35. Ibid.

36. Wickliffe Rigdon to Post, 3 Dec. 1859, Post Collection, box 1, fd. 7.

37. Keller, 40.

38. Orson F. Whitney, *History of Utah* (Salt Lake City: George Q. Cannon & Sons Co., 1904), 4:167.

39. Sidney Rigdon in A. W. Cowles, "The Mormons: Pen and Pencil Sketches, Illustrating their Early History," *Moore's Rural New Yorker*, 23 Jan. 1869, 61, Special Collections, Harold B. Lee Library, Brigham Young University, Provo, Utah.

CHAPTER 29.

Elect Sisterhood

*Let no man therefore exercise authority over a woman, & let not a woman act unseemly
to a man, let the man treat the woman as a companion and the woman in like manner
treat the man. If a man thinks he sees error in a woman, let him correct that error by
admonitioning with prayer & supplication and let his admonition be given in a meek
and humble spirit & let the woman do likewise. Instead of Authority let there be prayer
to obtain the right spirit by which admonition can be given to profit with all . . . . Let
each one[,] both man and woman[,] strive for peace[,] that within the courts of Zion
harmony and love may dwell and not confusion and disorder.*

—Sidney Rigdon, 1866[1]

A side from his obsession with Zion, the most intriguing element of Sidney
Rigdon's post-1845 religious career was his bestowal of priesthood on
women. The concept of a female priesthood did not originate with Rigdon. In an
1868 statement he asserted that Joseph Smith brought "to light the glorious and
queenly female priesthood." He claimed "Emma [Smith] was the one to whom
the female priesthood was first given."[2] Thus Rigdon's action was based on
Smith's precedent.

On 30 March 1842, two weeks after organizing the Female Relief Society of
Nauvoo, Joseph Smith announced to the women that the "Society should move
according to the ancient Priesthood" and that he was "going to make of this Society
a kingdom of priests as in Enoch's day—as in Paul's day."[3] One month later, in a
28 April 1842 lecture, the prophet again addressed this issue. According to his
personal account, he "gave a lecture on the pries[t]hood sh[o]wing how the Sisters
would come in possession of the privileges & blessings & gifts of the priesthood
& that the signs should follow them, such as healing the sick[,] casting out devils
&c. & that they might attain unto these blessings."[4]

The Endowment Quorum or Holy Order was the vehicle through which
Smith conferred priesthood on women. On 28 September 1843, in an upper room
of his home, the Nauvoo Mansion, the prophet set in motion the promised
"kingdom of priests" by administering the washing, anointing, and priesthood
endowment to Emma. At this same meeting the Smiths became the first couple

to receive the "second anointing" or "fullness of the priesthood" wherein each was "anointed & ordained to the highest & holiest order of the priesthood"—to become gods in this life.[5]

Following Smith's example, Rigdon twenty years later ordained his wife Phebe to the priesthood, thereafter referring to her as "the prophetess." The precise date of this bestowal, likely late 1863 or early 1864, is not known. The earliest existing reference is a 25 January 1864 revelation directed to Abraham Bartis. The pronouncement praised her as "having more faith than any other living woman." Speaking jointly of Phebe and her husband, the communication added: "I thus place at the head of Zion a perfect priesthood . . . let not Zion arrogate to themselves the right or power to deal with them [meaning the Rigdons] for I alone have the charge of them."[6]

Sidney himself revealed in October 1864 the circumstances surrounding Phebe's ordination. "At a time years gone," he spoke as God's mouthpiece, "when alone and in exile, and thick darkness shrouded [the Rigdons] in their temporal necessities[,] pressing them heavily, I the Lord said to my Servant Sidney, take my handmaiden Phebe alone and ordain her to the prophetic office before me. . . . I the Lord was present and sanctified the ordination as is this day manifest to all Zion."[7] The earliest known evidence of Phebe exercising her prophetic calling is her 10 March 1864 revelation warning Stephen Post of pride.[8]

In compensation for Phebe's long travail and poverty, Sidney worked incessantly during the final decade of his life to highlight her accomplishments. His accolades were effusive and diverse, but none depicted his true feelings better than a 23 October 1871 tribute, advanced in God's name:

> But what shall I say of and to my hand maiden Phebe, the light of the world, the Lord's lamp in Zion, the first born daughter of the holy Priesthood who alone first taught the true knowledge of the righteousness of Zion[?] . . . [T]here is no glory in heaven too great for her to possess. . . . She is the first born of woman there were none like her before her day and there will be none after equal to her.[9]

Although none were ordained by him personally, because he never visited Attica, several other women were inducted into the Rigdonite "elect sisterhood" or "Holy Order of the female department."[10] The first was Sarah Newton who still lived in Philadelphia at the time. In an October 1864 letter to her husband Joseph, a member of the ruling operative priesthood, Rigdon instructed him to ordain "mine handmaiden Sarah before me to the office of a prophetess in Zion, to send forth when I the Lord require the voice of blessing, and of warning to the priesthood of Zion and through them to all the children of Zion."[11]

Father Rigdon, in a revelation directed to Sarah Newton, then pronounced what must have been surprising news to the happily married woman:

> I the Lord dissolved all old covenants by which thou wast bound that thou mightest

be wholly mine, for I the Lord thy God art thy husband, to the exclusion of all others, that thou mightest do my will, and stand before me thyself, that I the Lord might organi[z]e a quorum of female prophets for the benefit of Zion. . . . It is my will, saith the Lord, that the quorum, should be free from all earthly authorities, that I the Lord might be their ruler without men or the sons of men having any claim to them by virtue of any gentile covenant.

Newton's startling revelation furthermore explained that:

My servant John [the Revelator] saw in his great vision . . . a woman clothed upon with the sun, the moon under her feet, and a crown of 12 stars on her head. Thus signifying that all the authorities of Zion should give heed to her voice. The quorum of female prophets which I the Lord am preparing, was what the woman in the vision represented. John saw the woman that she brought into the world a man child who was caught up into heaven . . . this man child was to rule the world with a rod of iron, or the word of God. Verily saith the Lord this man child is Zion which is now preparing for his rule in his strength.

The revelation to Newton specified equality between the sexes: "Behold saith the Lord this order is in accordance with the faith and prayers of your father Adam before me for he has the same respect for his daughters that he had for his sons, and it was his prayer that when the celestial order of the ancient of days was established that his daughters should have a voice in that council."[12]

Phebe Rigdon and Sarah Newton were soon advanced from the quorum of prophetesses to the operative or ruling priesthood. Thus the First Presidency of the Children of Zion was established, consisting of the Rigdons, the Newtons, and Stephen Post, whose wife Jane was not baptized until 30 April 1865. In a February 1867 directive entitled "The Word of the Lord to the quorum of the First Presidency of his Kingdom as called and organized for the fulfillment of the covenants made to the House of Israel," the Children of Zion were instructed that these five members of the First Presidency were chosen before the world began. "I the Lord," began the revelation, "having called and chosen you out of all the world to order an age and establish my kingdom for the salvation of Israel," had done so "according to the coven[a]nt made with their Fathers[.]"[13]

A significant difference between the manner in which Rigdon and Joseph Smith bestowed priesthood on women was that at least ten Rigdonite women—including Sarah Newton, Jane Post, Susannah Myers, Mary Hughes, Hannah Jones, Nancy Jacques, Louisa Sellers, Arrabella Allen, Mary Metcalf, and Rachel Clark—were ordained elders as well as prophetesses. Smith never ordained women to specific priesthood offices.

Although no evidence indicates that Sidney ordained Phebe to any position other than prophetess, the Children of Zion revered her as the elect lady. From 1865 through 1871 Phebe's principal contribution to the organization, aside from exhorting and blessing, was a series of written lessons on the Book of Mormon.

Each completed guide was mailed to either Sarah Newton or Jane Post in Attica for copying and distribution. These handwritten Book of Mormon lessons[14] are an engrossing look at the simple faith and piety of the woman who shared Sidney's life for more than half a century. In a preface to lesson 1 the prophetess wrote that she had "received from the Lord the duty of our calling," which was to

> bless the priesthoods and the children of Zion . . . to this end it is our duty to read and study the Book of Mormon continually that we may understand the doctrine, principles, requirements and feelings of soul and heart that is here required for us to perform and possess in order that all may receive the blessings of heaven. It is required of us that we should see that the Book of Mormon is had in remembrance amongst the priesthoods and children of Zion.[15]

The lessons express childlike beliefs and illustrate uncomplicated axioms. A sample from Phebe's first lesson teaches:

> It is our duty to commence at the first of the book when Lehi took his journey into the wilderness, how Nephi obtained the plates from Laban. That it was in keeping the commandments of God. So it was in every thing they did they were prospered when they obeyed the commandments of God. So it will be with us all if we pay strict attention in keeping the commandments of God, he will prosper us. It is all laid down in the book of Mormon how to proceed in every thing we do. We can follow them until they came to the great waters and Nephi was directed to build a ship he was told how to proceed but his brethren rebelled. . . . Nephi went on with the ship and built it according to the directions of the Lord. And so it will be in building up Zion.[16]

The prophetess, concluding this first exercise, admonished Sarah Newton that "if there are any contentions or confusion with the Children of God, it is your duty to require of every one to search their own hearts before the Lord to know if there is any evil in them, for it is the will of the Lord that the female priesthood should be to the children of Zion as a refiners fire and as fullers soap."[17]

Initially Sarah, Phebe's surrogate in Attica, was held in high esteem by the Rigdons. When a Quorum of the Twelve was to be established among the Children of Zion, Rigdon wrote that "The Lord . . . visited sister S[arah] by a Holy and Heavenly messenger and gave her power to choose the 12."[18] The prophet added that while Sarah was under the ministrations of this spiritual entity, whom he identified as Obadiah, she saw the visages of the "men chosen to stand in the holy priesthood of the 12 before the world was."[19]

The church was enthralled by this opening of heaven's doors. The occasion was augmented by a special February 1868 revelation declaring: "I the Lord appoint unto you the 4th day of July 1868 . . . as the day when you shall appear before me the Lord your God in a Holy Convocation to ordain and organize the quorum of 12 according to the pattern you have received." The conference was to be held at Attica. The directions included this instruction to Joseph Newton:

[T]ake my serv[a]nt Stephen [Post] and let him be washed in clean water before me saith the Lord and then let him anoint him with the "Holy Oil" of consecration. . . . After the anointing let my servent Joseph and mine Handmaiden Sarah lay their hands upon his head and ordain him to the Holy calling of Prophet Priest and King before me saith the Lord and then let my Handmaiden Sarah bless him in my name according to the power of her Holy calling Thus putting the quorum of the first Presidency in perfect order before the Lord their god[.]

In turn, the consecrated presidency was to administer to the Twelve that "this quorum of 12 that I the Lord have chosen as of the whole world should be the mightiest quorum of 12 that were ever on the earth."[20]

Rigdon, though he made no plans to attend the Holy Convocation, was enthusiastic about the event. "Among all the days of my existence," he wrote Post in April 1868, "I have never contemplated one with such awful solemnity as we do this approaching 4th of July." He compared the day's religious import to the birth of a new nation "whose destiny it will be to take the place . . . first given to another nation and another people whom the Lord is about to displace and bear it off. . . . We wait in solemn and almost breathless anticipation for the transpiring of the events of that day[,] *events* rendered awfully impressive by the influences of the Spirit of Holiness."[21]

The actual fireworks of that day, however, fizzled like a wet match. Although invitations had been mailed to the Twelve to appear for presentation to Sister Newton, apparently only John Forgues attended.[22] Post wrote Rigdon on 7 July expressing discouragement at the poor turnout. Writing Post on 13 July the prophet rationalized:

I had reason to suspect that you would be disappointed not that I doubted the correctness of Sister's vision but it is one thing to get these manifestations and another to place them. . . . [W]hat Sister N[ewton] saw are all true beyond all doubt but instead of being fulfilled at the time you supposed they will be fulfilled in the course of the apostolic ministry from time to time.[23]

Sarah Newton's prestige in the Children of Zion increased dramatically after a 1 June 1868 revelation on her behalf heralded:

I the Lord now require of you that you should separate unto me out of the daughters of my people an elect sisterhood one out of each branch of Zion. . . . Those who are distinguished for their love of the truth, and their devotedness to the cause of righteousness to be set apart to minister before the Lord in the holy things pertaining to Zion.

Newton was further advised to call a holy convocation in Attica on 4 January 1869 and to ordain the selected women. "In accomplishing this work," the revelation added, "you can call upon those who are spiritual to assist until the work is accomplished."[24] Further instructions specified that in local matters, "where ever there is a male authority there must be a[n] [equivalent] female." These female authorities were not mere tokens. The female priesthood "has all the authority and power of the male if an elder, to baptize[,] lay on hands for the gift of the Holy Ghost[,] administer the sacrament[,] and preach and teach . . . this is a pattern for all."[25]

When Rigdon received word that manifestations of spiritual gifts, baptisms, washings, anointings, and the ordination of Jane Post as presiding elder of the Attica branch had occurred during the January gathering, he was ecstatic. "The fact that the Lord has placed the seal of his approbation upon his Holy order of elect sisters," Rigdon wrote to Post on 18 January 1869, "has placed in Zion a perpetual miracle before the eyes of all his children so that all may know and all may see that Zion is at last come into the world."[26] To Joseph Newton in January 1869 the prophet pronounced the elect sisterhood a "perfect success . . . a source of as much satisfaction as the heart is capable of." Respecting Sarah Newton Rigdon declared that she stood "forth in bold relief a witness for both myself and the Lord as the one which . . . has reached the highest position ever ordained of God for '*woman*' we mean to stand at the head of an elect sisterhood chosen of God before the foundation of the world."

After a self-congratulating outburst, the prophet announced that among the "principal ones" who offered the "perfect sacrifice were two females and the Lord has set them at the head of Zion . . . and . . . gives them a position that makes the male priesthood bow to their mandates." Wondering why this was so, Rigdon concluded that the women

> had power to offer a greater sacrifice than man could offer and hence their position. The glory of this female priesthood is only dawning and to where it will go time will only disclose. . . . Here stands that which made the greatest of all the apostles gaze with wonder and astonishment[,] females clothed with the power of the greatest of all priesthoods.

Rigdon was thrilled about the female priesthood, exclaiming: "While we write this our heart raises its ejaculations to God and the Lamb with Hallelujah. . . . [T]hou hast given us the victory over earth and hell and let thy glorious Queenly priesthood stand in Zion and in the midst of her children as an everlasting monument that we thy servants hath done all things right."[27] By early 1869 Rigdon was teaching that "all must see that Zion is moving under the ruling of the *Female* and not the male priesthood." With the clearly understood exception of himself, he condemned by contrast the male priesthood which "had come to a dead stand when the Female priesthood came before the Lord and *moved* the cause of Zion. . . . The female priesthood is the ruling power within the operative Quorum."[28]

Ultimately, controversies over Spiritualism, then sweeping the country, led to both Sarah's and her husband's falling from grace. The Newtons and several others were forced from the Attica group over a contention centering on a young woman in the branch named Evva Force Adams, Post's niece. In early 1868 Evva prayed to God to show her an apparition of heaven and hell. According to Post, once she entered the visionary state she "went into the spirit and sang beautifully to her brethren & sisters."[29] Joseph and Sarah Newton were critical of the woman, seeing her behavior as dangerously near Spiritualism. Furthermore, the Newtons as members of the First Presidency feared that the young mystic was usurping their power. And Evva, married to Post's nephew James Adams, had sullied her reputation by attempting to abort her baby, douching with a mixture of charcoal and whiskey. Then fearing that as a result the baby would be born black, she prayed to God bemoaning her misdeeds and beseeching His grace. At this point, according to at least two women in the Attica branch, an angel "ap[p]eard to her and showed [the unborn baby] to her and it was whit[e] and then she began to sing for joy and she sings yet."[30]

Post supported his disreputable kin, announcing to the Children of Zion that she "sang the truth as far as I knew."[31] He also wrote Rigdon, describing Evva's supernatural manifestation without reference to the attempted abortion. The prophet in a letter to Post confirmed "the visions of God . . . [and Evva's] gift."[32] One month later Evva's husband told Post that an angel of the Lord had appeared to his wife admonishing her to warn the Children of Zion that they "are in darkness & should keep the commandments of the Lord & love one another."[33] Rigdon affirmed that the angel was "the martyr Stephen," again supporting Evva's claims.[34]

"That our sister was under a spiritual power that was not of man all must agree," Rigdon wrote to his saints on 1 April 1869. "Some spiritual influence had full control of her." The question is "from whence came that spirit?" The Newtons argued that her source was the Devil because "she under the influence of that inspiring power spoke against [Sarah Newton who] had been previously ordained of the Lord." But Rigdon argued that the Newtons "violated most barefacedly the law of the Quorum of [the] first presidency *That* requires that nothing could be done unless it was agreed to by all the Quorum." By unilaterally censoring Evva Adams, the Newtons abandoned "the spirit of Holiness" to become "a prey to the Devil."[35]

All the Rigdons knew of Evva's situation came from Post's communiques. Thus it was not surprising that on 7 March 1869 the Rigdons directed a revelation to the Children of Zion which said in part: "I the Lord your God gave my handmaiden Evva the vision through which her eyes were opened to see things which to the natural eye are invisible that all of the children of Zion might know that Zion is mine saith the Lord your God." Rigdon then admonished those who had been critical that "if you do not go and make an humble confession, and ask her forgiveness, I the Lord will not bless you."[36] Once Rigdon had committed himself, he was too imperious to reverse himself when Margaret Hamilton and S.

Alden wrote to inform him of Evva's abortion attempt. The prophet wrote to Jane Post on 23 July 1870 that "the contents of this letter are so absolutely at vari[a]nce with letters which we have received from others on the subject" that "if the things said in this letter are true then we have been awfully misinformed."[37]

Anxiety over the incident caused Rigdon to suffer a stroke. Writing to Post on 21 October 1870, he explained that

the Devil crowded on us with all the power he had obtained in addition to his natural power from those calling themselves the children of Zion by all kinds of letter writing coming from every quarter like a flood. . . . [T]his mass coming on us like a wave of the ocean crushed [me] under its weight an [I] fell shocked by a paralysis to all appearances unto death[.] The limbs were rigid as pillars of marble[.] The eyes were motionless[.] The countenance as ghastly as the impress of death in its most ghastly form[.] The tongue paralyzed in this condition. We lay one day our family waiting to see the last but second day we revived and the third day we got up and have continued so since[.] There have been none of those dehabilitments as useless arm or leg or any other local part of the body seriously impaired.[38]

After recovering sufficiently, Rigdon broached the same subject with Post again: "For some length of time we have been crowded with letters from various persons . . . the most of which were for unworthy persons." Referring to two "vulgar letters" from Sisters Hamilton and Alden he declared "their testimony unbelievable." Attacking the character of the two women, both wives of stalwart Attica men, the naive prophet sputtered:

Their letters spoke a language not to be mistaken—we mean indirectly—that they in their girlhood were any thing but chaste[.] One who is enlightened by the spirit of truth could see that the spirit that indited these letters could not enter the heart of a female only through unlawful intercourse with men and that such must have been the case with them. . . . We write this as a measure of self defense to let debauched females know that they must find some other receptacle for their fulsome abominations than us.[39]

This as well as other whimsical reactions to problems within the fold alienated virtually all Rigdon's followers except Post and a loyal few others. The prophet's eccentricity drove away the devoted Newtons, Hamiltons, and Aldens, and even John A. Forgues, president of the Quorum of the Twelve, a steadfast Rigdon disciple since Nauvoo. Forgues, who had been forced into poverty attempting to provide for the Rigdons, wrote seeking financial assistance from the meager church coffers. His pleas met condemnation and abuse. "Br[other] Forgues has got into a habit of writing that can not be admited any longer," Rigdon wrote to Post in October 1868, "his everlasting murmurings are disgusting and unbearable[.] The Children of Zion did not make him poor . . . he did it himself. . . . He must bear the burden of his own folly."[40]

On 1 December 1868 Forgues, then living in Little Sioux, Iowa, sent a copy of a 25 October 1868 Rigdon letter to both Newton and Post. "If there is a christlike spirit in it then I am a stranger to the spirit of truth," Forgues admitted. The document, aside from chastizing Forgues, is an essay on Rigdon's personal views towards poverty, which he viewed as a kind of schoolmaster:

> When under circumstances of poverty as great as yours, for you have nothing strange to tell me, when you told me about poverty. The consolation & the only consolation I see was this. "If you will be very humble & very meek before me you shall overcome." The Lord gave me this in a time of trouble such as you know nothing of, for in addition to great poverty, persecution raged against me, as hot & furious as "Hell," And that was the word of deliverance marked out for me.
>
> There is but one view I can take in relation to your poverty, you were not reduced to it by serving the Lord. . . . Inasmuch as you used your money when you had it, not only for the everlasting overthrow of Zion but for the personal & individual destruction of myself so that the loss of your property & your deep poverty are to me and could not be otherwise than be a source of gratification.
>
> It is of little consequence how poor we are that is a matter with the Lord & to him & not to me letter your complaints, you cannot be poorer than were the prophets who have gone before us nor Lazarus, but these things did not hinder them from obtaining the end of their faith (the salvation of their souls)[.] If we keep this as our "load star" & make the entire object of our faith we will see that poverty however inconvenient, has not power to prevent our reaching eternal life.

"Now you have it," Forgues added in a post script to Newton and Post, "the charge of using my money for the everlasting overthrow of Zion & for his personal & individual destruction, is *false* & the spirit of God never dictated it. . . . [T]o rejoice in my poverty is so monstrous that I detest it with all my heart."[41]
Rigdon's next response to the destitute man was to call him on a mission to St. Louis. When the infirm and impoverished Forgues explained the impossibility of fulfilling such an assignment under his present conditions, Rigdon fumed:

> Behold saith the Lord I know man and all that is in him and need that no man teach me[.] What man can do and what he can not do I the Lord know[.] The circumstances of all are present before me[.] Therefore when I the Lord call any person to do a work before me it is I alone who know that person's abilities to do that work and when any person assumes to himself or herself the right to judge of that person's abilities such person is a transgresser before me the Lord.

Unless Forgues repented, he was to be judged "before the presidency of my Zion."[42]
When Post informed Forgues of the prophet's invective, Forgues replied to the spokesman, "I will not bow to the tyranical edicts of S[idney] R[igdon] any sooner than I would to another man." Complaining that his contributions to the church now left him in rags, "without means to help myself or family; thrice worse crippled with rheumatism," Forgues added that while he still believed

Rigdon held "the Keys of the Kingdom," he could see "as plain as can be that his present course will [fail] as did his Pittsburg & Cumberland Valley projects." In a personal warning note to Post, Forgues advised: "You may believe as you please but unless you interfere & stop his wild tyranical course you will see sorrow & trouble."[43]

Rigdon wanted charges preferred against his Quorum of the Twelve president for "insult and missrepresentation of the Father in Zion."[44] Bishop Israel Huffaker wrote Forgues instructing him to stop preaching and administering in the Children of Zion church until "these things are settled." An enraged Forgues retorted:

> I have since 1844 seen so much transgression & usurpation of power in opposition to the "written law" that I am not disposed to trifle with or trifle with others. . . . I have been slandered abused & attempts have been made to oppress me, until I am tired of it, and when I bow my neck to the yoke of tyranical oppression it will be when I have no power to resist it, or tongue to speak. I have labored for 3 years with my might, spent my money, land[,] cattle[,] Cows[,] Hogs[,] waggons & farming utensils, am now not only in debt but in rags—destitute of the neccessaries of life, my wife sick & crippled with Rheumatism—my daughter unable to do any thing, my son has been sick confined to the house and for more than 2 months and I doubt whether he ever will be well again, and I am an invalid with Rheumatism and unable to work and my present poverty *is* because I have desired and labored for the promotion of Zion while others labored for money for themselves & their children.[45]

Rigdon exhibited little emotion over the loss of the Newtons and Forgues. When Stephen and Jane Post expressed sorrow over the egress of the much beloved leaders, the prophet was derisive:

> I am at a loss to see why you and sister P[ost] should have any grievous feeling about [the Newtons]. Their fall is your exaltation if you stand steadfast in the truth[.] They have shown that they were in their hearts not of the children of Zion but fals[e] hearted Babylonians who pretended to enter Zion not to serve god but to serve their own ambitious desires and the Lord searched them out most effectually and put them away and caused them to depart as he has other ambitious rebels.[46]

Even after the Newtons and Forgues were excommunicated, Father Rigdon continued his tirades against them. When Newton prophesied that Rigdon would go to hell, the prophet responded: "Poor miserable wretch he need not trouble himself about our going there for he will be in '*Hell*' before the Lord will open the way for *our* going there." Lest any of the Children of Zion commiserate, Rigdon instructed them through Post that "Newton and Forgues are to us as though they had never been. If they write answer them not[.] Treat any and every thing they can do with silent indifference[.] We would recommend to you if Forgues writes to you just put it into another envelope and send it back to him unread and there let him stay."[47]

When Post helped the needy Forgues, Rigdon ranted that he had transgressed:

"Learn O man to be a man of god in deed instead of taking the damnable trash of the gentiles. . . . What the gentiles call benevolence and charity is a damning sin in the sight of the eternal High Council."[48] Explaining away his earlier assertion that the Newtons had been chosen before the world began, Rigdon claimed the Lord knew beforehand that they were "basely corrupt and most scandalously hypocritical" and were put in "high places in his church" to "expose the fiendish corruption and damning hypocrisy of their hearts." His pummeling went further: "Of all the unfortunate wretches that ever lived on this earth since the days of Cain[,] J[oseph] H. N[ewton] and J[ohn] A. F[orgues] are certainly among the most corrupt and for the stupidity of their ignorance it never was surpassed . . . "[49]

By the late 1860s the Rigdonite organization was unable to fend off forays of RLDS missionaries. In 1867 two Reorganized emissaries, William W. Blair and Ebenezer Robinson, Rigdon's former counselor in Pittsburgh and Cumberland Valley, arrived in Philadelphia to proselyte a group of Rigdonites, many of whom had lost faith in their prophet. The two men ultimately baptized ten of the Children of Zion.[50] Blair, an eloquent speaker, also published four fluent attacks on Rigdon in the RLDS newspaper.[51]

Rigdon did not mince words regarding the movement. "I have had very little to say" about the organization, he commented in March 1868, because "it is so grossly and stupidly contemptable that common sense feels itself insulted by having to look at it." He insisted that in order for the Lord to establish a church, apostles, prophets, revelators, and "gifts and miracles" were necessary. "What has these stupid creatures got," he said of RLDS leaders. "If stupidity can beat that you will have to go to hell to find [it]."[52] Rigdon's principal criticism of young Joseph III was that he did not bestow the priesthood on women. "When did the Lord ever before select authorities out of the whole world to be ordained before him by inspiring a woman from on High for this purpose through the ministrations of an Holy Angel[?]" he asked. "No where and at no time[.] This great thing is peculiar to ourselves. . . . Such are the facts pertaining to this greatest and most glorious of all events that ever transpired on this earth."[53]

By late 1870 the Attica branch had dwindled to fourteen members.[54] When Post held a 12-13 November 1870 convocation in Council Bluffs, Iowa, the minutes listed just twenty-six "names of those who desire to serve god in the Church of Jesus Christ of Children of Zion."[55] Most of these would soon lose faith, when once again Rigdon heard a clarion call to flee into the wilderness on another mission impossible.

Notes

Unless otherwise stated, all primary sources cited are located in the Historical Department of the Church of Jesus Christ of Latter-day Saints, Salt Lake City, Utah.

1. Rigdon to Post, 1 Dec. 1866, listed in Stephen Post Collection as section 26 in Copying Book A, box 1, fd. 14, hereafter Post Collection.

In Mormonism's early years Rigdon and Emma maintained a cordial relationship. As discussed earlier, they had differences in Nauvoo but reconciled prior to Joseph's death. When Sidney was leaving Nauvoo in September 1844, Emma evidently offered him the original manuscript of the Inspired Version, the biblical revision Smith and Rigdon had jointly worked on early in their careers. Sidney also claimed Emma told him in 1844 she intended to follow him to Pittsburgh (see Orson Hyde to "Dear Brethren," 12 Sept. 1844, Brigham Young Collection, box 39, fd. 18).

By 1857, however, Rigdon had altered his assessment of Emma and called her a "[perfect] she devil" (Rigdon to Post, 6 Mar. 1857, Post Collection, box 1, fd. 4). Writing to Post in 1864, Sidney hammered on Emma even though he once proclaimed her a good friend. His paranoid belief of late was that Emma, now affiliated with her sons in the RLDS movement, had attempted to destroy his influence back in Nauvoo by "kindling her envy into fury" and throwing "her spirit into her husband," which spread a "spirit of malice, of slander, [and] of l[y]ing" throughout the church (Post Collection, listed as section 4 in Copying Book A, box 3, fd. 12).

Sidney did acknowledge in 1866 that Joseph Smith ordained his wife to the priesthood "and in connection with the ordination was the duty of expounding the scriptures and to exhort the church." Emma did not, Rigdon accused, "discharge the duties of this high calling" and is "doomed to the perdition of ungodly men for where Christ is she never can come" (Rigdon to Post, 25 Jan. 1864, Post Collection, box 1, fd. 15).

2. Undated 1868 letter from Rigdon to Post, Post Collection.

3. "Minutes of the Female Relief Society of Nauvoo," 30 Mar. 1842. When these minutes were published in the *History of the Church*, leaders omitted Smith's first use of the word "Society" and changed the second "Society" to "Church," so that the prophet's meaning was entirely altered (see Joseph Smith, *History of the Church of Jesus Christ of Latter-day Saints*, B. H. Roberts, ed., 7 vols. [Salt Lake City: The Church of Jesus Christ of Latter-day Saints, 1902], 4:570; hereafter *History of the Church*).

Phebe Rigdon and Athalia Robinson, charter members of the Nauvoo Relief Society, were deliberately deleted when the list was eventually published.

4. Book of the Law of the Lord, 28 Apr. 1842, cited in Dean C. Jessee, ed., *The Papers of Joseph Smith*, 2 vols. (Salt Lake City: Deseret Book Co., 1992), 2:378-79. The prophet's reference to "gifts of the priesthood" was omitted when published in *History of the Church*, 4:603.

5. "Meetings of anointed Quorum—Journalizings," 28 Sept. 1843, Joseph Smith papers, Special Collections, Harold B. Lee Library, Brigham Young University, Provo, Utah; hereafter BYU Library. My understanding on this matter was enhanced by D. Michael Quinn, "Mormon Women Have Had the Priesthood Since 1843," in Maxine Hanks, ed., *Women and Authority: Re-emerging Mormon Feminism* (Salt Lake City: Signature Books, 1992), 365-409.

6. Rigdon to Bartis, listed in Post Collection as section 4 in Copying Book A, box 3, fd. 12.

7. Listed in Post Collection as section 17 in Copying Book A, box 3, fd. 12. In a 5

February 1870 letter to Post, Rigdon said that before the Lord endowed Phebe for this work,

> He put her through trials conflicts and scourgings such as no other woman on this earth knows anything about until he had d[e]stroyed every feeling of unchastened ambition in her heart until she mourned before the Lord in the agony of her soul until every feeling of her mind sank into hopelessness and she was sinking in d[e]spair on her own account mourning that she was a wretch unworthy of any favor of heaven.
>
> But in the midst of this horror of soul the Lord spake to me and bade me say to her that her life should be precious in his sight and he would preserve it for future work. I told her as I was directed. She lifted her heart and thanked god (Post Collection, box 2, fd. 3).

8. Rigdon to Post, 10 Mar. 1864, Post Collection, box 1, fd. 9.

9. Rigdon to Post, 23 Oct. 1871, Post Collection, box 2, fd. 8; listed as section 63 in Copying Book A.

10. Rigdon "to the children of Zion," 18 Jan. 1869, Post Collection, box 2, fd. 1.

11. Listed in Post Collection as Section 16 in Copying book A, box 3, fd. 12.

12. Listed in Post Collection as Section 15 in Copying Book A, box 3, fd. 12.

13. Post Collection, Feb. 1867. The envelope containing this revelation included another one as well, which reads in part: "[T]hese are the same persons seen by Obadiah in his great vision . . . namely my serv[a]nt Sidney Rigdon and mine handmaiden Phebe Rigdon my serv[a]nt Joseph H. Newton and mine handmaiden Sarah Newton and my serv[a]nt Stephen Post" (also listed in Post Collection as section 27 in Copying Book A, box 3, fd. 12).

One month later in another revelation Rigdon proclaimed that after the Lord had struggled with Satan for thirty-five years he brought "out of the midst of his fire smoke and darkness" five persons whom Satan could "not corrupt neither turn their hearts away from the word of the truth of salvation and hence the Lord obtained a first presidency d[e]spite all the devil could do after giving him full liberty to do his utmost" (Post Collection, 1 Mar. 1867, box 1, fd. 13).

14. Ibid., box 5, fd. 14.

15. Ibid., box 5, fd. 8.

16. In a 9 August 1870 letter to Stephen Post, Rigdon described how Phebe prepared the lessons:

> You will see her every spare minute she has with her book in her hand and her paper pen and ink beside her noting every important thing the spirit directs her to note[.] [A]fter the family have gone to bed she with her candle will read for an hour or more[.] In the morning when she rises the first spare minute will find her with book in hand before the Lord and thus she continues day and night before the Lord[.] She takes the books Bible, Mormon and D & C at the beginning and goes through them in order and when she goes through she goes back and goes it again and thus she devotes her life day and night (Post Collection, box 2, fd. 5).

17. Ibid.

18. Rigdon to Post, 7 Mar. 1868, Post Collection, box 1, fd. 15.

19. 15 Mar. 1868 revelation, Post Collection, box 1, fd. 15.

20. Post Collection, box 1, fd. 16; also listed as section 32 in Copying Book A.

21. Post Collection, box 1, fd. 15.

22. Post Diary, Jan. 1868, Post Collection, box 6, fd. 5.

23. Post Collection, box 1, fd. 16.

24. Ibid., listed as section 35 in Copying Book A, box 3, fd. 12.

25. Rigdon to Post, Jan. 1869, Post Collection, box 2, fd. 1

26. Ibid., 18 Jan. 1869, box 2, fd. 1.

27. Ibid., box 5, fd. 8.

28. Rigdon letter "To the presidency," 15 Feb. 1869, Post Collection, box 5, fd. 8; emphasis in original.

29. Stephen Post Diary, 26 Feb. 1869, Post Collection, box 6, fd. 1.

30. See Margaret Hamilton to Rigdon, 17 July 1870, and S. Alden to Rigdon, 5 Aug. 1870, Post Collection, box 2, fd. 5.

31. Post Diary, 26 Feb. 1869, Post Collection, box 6, fd. 1.

32. Ibid., box 6, fd. 5.

33. Ibid., 20 Mar. 1869, box 6, fd. 5.

34. Rigdon to Post, Feb. 1869, Post Collection, box 2, fd. 1.

35. Rigdon circular "To the children of Zion," 1 Apr. 1869, Post Collection, box 2, fd. 2.

36. 7 Mar. 1869 revelation, signed by both Rigdons, and listed in the Post Collection as section 51 in Copying Book A, box 3, fd. 12.

37. Rigdon to Jane Post, 23 July 1870, Post Collection, box 2, fd. 5.

38. Rigdon to Post, 21 Oct. 1870, Post Collection, box 2, fd. 6.

39. Rigdon to Post, 31 Oct. 1871, Post Collection, box 2, fd. 6..

40. Rigdon to Post, Oct. 1868, Post Collection, box 1, fd. 17.

41. Forgues to Newton and Post, 1 Dec. 1868, Post Collection, box 1, fd. 17.

42. Feb. 1869 revelation, Post Collection, box 2, fd. 1.

43. Forgues to Post, 2 May 1869, Post Collection, box 2, fd. 2.

44. See Rigdon to Post, 5 May 1869, Post Collection, box 2, fd. 2.

45. Forgues to Huffaker, 11 May 1869, Post Collection, box 1, fd. 14.

46. Rigdon to Post, 21 May 1869, Post Collection, box 1 fd. 14.

47. Rigdon to Post, 4 July 1869, Post Collection, box 2, fd. 2.

48. Rigdon to Post, 14 Sept. 1873, Post Collection, box 2, fd. 11.

49. Rigdon to Post, 10 July 1869, Post Collection, box 2, fd. 3.

50. Frederick B. Blair, comp., *The Memoirs of W. W. Blair* (Lamoni, IA: Herald Publishing House, 1908), 83, 132-33.

51. *True LDS Herald*, 15 Apr., 15 May 1868, 100-102, 113-17, 129-32, 145-47.

52. Rigdon to Post, 7 Mar. 1868, Post Collection, box 1, fd. 15.

53. Ibid.

54. 10 Nov. 1870 roster of Attica Branch is listed in Post Collection, box 5, fd. 10.

55. "Minutes of 13 November 1870 conference held by the Children of Zion near Council Bluffs," Post Collection, box 2, fd. 6.

CHAPTER 30.

The Final Quest

I the Lord will give to [Sidney Rigdon] . . . length of days and power, and glory until the whole work of God is completed; and then shall he be crowned with glory such as neither men nor angels ever saw before.

. . . The names of Noah, Daniel and Job, of Moses, Elias and Samuel, of Abraham, Isaac, Jacob & Joseph shall [pale] into insignificance before me. On earth his power shall be supreme nothing but what shall move at the sound of his voice. The mountains shall shake, the hills shall tremble, the vallies shall rise and sink at his command. All things that God has made things animate or inanimate, men or beast shall hear and obey. The heavens shall shake by the blast of his nostrils and the stars of heaven shall obey his command. His voice shall be my voice on the earth says the everlasting God. . . . All nations under heaven shall hear the voice of this priesthood and tremble before it. Again saith the Lord to those who have [i]nquired of me, at first until it is required to move, [Zion's] feet shall be planted in the country known among you as Canada.

—Sidney Rigdon (1873)[1]

Rigdon's cerebral hemorrhages in 1870 and 1872 were followed by a quick succession of seven apoplectic incursions resulting in his death in 1876. Shortly after recovering from the initial stroke, and possibly because of its aftershocks, Ridgon grew wholly obsessed with the conviction that the United States was on the eve of destruction and that the Children of Zion should flee elsewhere to find safe haven.

Exercising his prophetic prerogative on 6 December 1870, Rigdon wrote an astounding warning to "The people at Utah who have professed to receive the Book of Mormon and to receive the word of the Lord in these last times":

We[,] in the name of Jesus Christ, by the authority of the Eternal Father, and in accordance with all the powers and principalities above[,] doom you to an absolute and everlasting d[e]struction. You shall be cut off by the hand of wicked men. Your land shall be to you a desolation and your city shall be smitten with d[e]struction. . . . In the hour of your calamities, you shall voice for help but none will pity; you shall ask for mercy but none will hear. You shall be as the salt that has lost its savor fit only

440

to be cast out and trodden under foot of man. . . . [We have the] awful duty of notifying you of the ruin to which you are doomed, and the wasting and desolation which are rolling upon you, and the blood and horrors through which your calamities will be perfected.

Training his apocalyptic rhetoric on his archenemy Brigham Young, Rigdon discharged a full salvo. "O vain man," he bombasted, "Did you suppose that your hypocritical and lying pretence that the spirit of Joseph Smith had [e]ntered into you, was going to prevail with God and man. You knew you lied when you made that pretence. . . . The days of your wicked corrupt and senseless career is shortly to close with the [e]ntire overthro[w] of you and all that you have and are."[2]

Wickliffe Rigdon, then living in Pleasant Hill, Missouri, and unaware of his father's latest behind-the-scenes religious affectations, once again sought Brigham Young's assistance in relocating the Rigdons to Utah. In a 27 June 1871 letter to the Mormon leader, Wickliffe, then a practicing attorney, did not apologize for his family's long-standing antagonism towards Young's prophetic mandate. "But one thing is certain," he conceded, "you have been prospered when all other factions of the church have gone down or been blotted out of existence[. T]his fact leads me to believe that you are occupying the position it was designed you should occupy."

Referring to Young's 1863 request that Sidney call on him, Wickliffe revealed, "My Father I know has a secret wish to visit the church which in his manhood he helped to establish & in his old age he has not forgotten." Wickliffe urged the reunion, pleading that his father might "again mingle with those with [whom] he labored in former years that his heart might again be made to rejoice." He promised Young that if he "would place in my hands the necessary means to bring him there[,] if I would be able to gain his consent to go[,] I will do all in my power to bring about the desired visit."

In a secretary's handwritten memo at the bottom of Wickliffe's letter is Young's response: "If his father is disposed to come here and you will bring him to this city we will refund you the money."[3] During a 26 August 1871 assembly of the School of the Prophets in Salt Lake City, Young reaffirmed his willingness that they should come, "provided they could be brought without too much expense."[4] Upon receiving Young's 28 July 1871 affirmative response Wickliffe informed his father. On 18 August he read a favorable reply from Sidney providing that he first settle some business matters. Wickliffe informed Young the following day of his father's reaction, explaining that the offer to reimburse him for travel expenses would not do since "the means for the purpose are not within my control & consequently would be impossible for me to advance." He added that his father would not travel without Phebe and that another female would be needed to attend her. Since Sidney insisted that Wickliffe also accompany him, Rigdon found that "means necessary for such a journey would amount to more than a poor lawyer like myself could command who had not been blessed with much of this world[']s goods & who has been unfortunate enough to have his dish upside down whenever it has rained porridge."

The audacious barrister appealed directly to Young's wealth: "But Sir[,] to a rich man like yourself[,] who control[s] the finances of a whole country & who is the owner of a Rail Road[,] the means necessary & passes over the road could be easily obtained & without any inconvenience whatever. . . . [I]n conclusion let me say it remains with you to say whether my Father visits Utah or not[,] of course if he goes it is with the understanding that the party shall have the means of returning when desired."[5] But only days after Sidney had consented in principle to the trip west, he vacillated, reversing his position, and wrote to Post on 22 August 1871:

> What has come over B Young[?] [H]e has sent to us to know if we would go to Utah providing the people there would furnish the means to pay all expen[ses.] He says there will be a seat secured in a first class palace car if we will only agree to go there[,] that the [e]ntire community [is] unite[d] in the manifestations of deep desire for us to go there[.] . . I do not believe in the religion of the people of Utah neither do I believe that the priesthood is there in any of its departments[.] What can they want with me[?]
>
> We have declined going[,] though at first we did think we would like the ride[,] but more mature reflection has caused us to determine otherwise. For us to go there and unite with that people all is so absurd that we must[,] yea we will not do it.[6]

For all the fervor in the refusal, Rigdon reversed himself again. On 3 September 1871, twenty-seven years after Young orchestrated Rigdon's excommunication, the Friendship prophet wrote his nemesis directly, spelling out the imperatives for his visiting Utah. In what is probably one of the strangest letters the Lion House ever received Rigdon admonished:

> [B]y the authority and power of the Holy Priesthood we say in order that you of Utah can have [my] counsel and be delivered from a scene of blood which might appall the heart of a savage for unless you do so you will see it and wait and howl in [that] hour like damned spirits when there will be no eye to pity nor arm to save[,] you will send here free of expen[s]e to us the sum of one hundred thousand dollars ($100,000) in gold and silver which you can do by express and unless you do this all correspondence must close here and no more of it exist forever.[7]

Young was ill when Rigdon's letter was read to him. Rolling over in bed, Brigham drawled out, tongue-in-cheek: "I wonder if Sidney wouldn't take one hundred thousand dollars in greenbacks?" Young's castigation ended all talk of a face-to-face reunion between the two old adversaries.[8]

Rigdon, now more convinced than ever that Utah's destruction loomed, aimed a 9 October 1871 directive at Stephen Post ordering the Children of Zion into readiness. "The time has now come," he wrote. "Organize yourselves as speedily as possible[,] call your solemn assemblies and let all the priesthoods take their places both male and female." The "judgments of god which are now coming on to Utah . . . shall continue till the world is overthrown." There was no mistaking. "[O]n us," wrote Rigdon, "the end of the world has come.[9] In letters written on 12 and 17 October the prophet detailed ghastly particulars of the impending calamities awaiting Utah, including tempests, fires, and earthquakes.[10]

Meanwhile the Rigdonite community in Attica, riddled with dissension, was disintegrating. Robert Bohn wrote Rigdon on 5 January 1872 that during his recent visit to Attica "I saw a spirit of conten[t]ion. Some for Joseph [Newton]. Some for Stephen [Post]. . . . It looks to me that Zion in Attica is not working."[11] David L. Rees, William Hamilton, and Ebenezer Page, three other adherents, recounted a similar tale on 10 January, complaining that Post, instead of "building Zion . . . handles the word of the Lord for his own exaltation and Bablyonish customs [to] build up [a] Kingdom of his own."[12] Rigdon forwarded the letters to Post, advising that he would not receive communications from anyone except his spokesman. "In this case," he concluded tersely, "I consider there is nothing else called for[.] The consecrated Priesthoods of Zion could not give even a passing notice to such corrupt and fiendish stupidity."[13]

In late November 1872 the prophet suffered another stroke so severe that newspapers around the country carried notice of his death. Writing to Post on 14 January 1873 Rigdon resolved: "Seeing there ha[s] been a good deal said in the public papers and otherwise relating to our death . . . [I thought] it but proper to let you know the whole case and what gave rise to the report that we were dead." He told Post that two months earlier, at about 1:00 a.m. Phebe awoke to find her husband "helpless and powerless in the bed." For three days and nights he hovered near death, and two attending doctors pronounced "the case fatal without a remedy." On the third night, however, those gathered about his bed "saw signs of returning reason with a renew[a]l of life." The opinion of the physicians, according to Rigdon, was that his recovery was "unparalleled in the history of the disease . . . they supposed that restoration was out of the question."[14] What may have seemed miraculous to bystanders was viewed by Sidney and Phebe as the fulfillment of God's word that his prophet would not yet die.

Rigdon never anticipated his own demise, not in 1872, not in 1876. His disregard of death was based on faith in a divine promise of rejuvenation, confirmed to him on two separate occasions. Rigdon explained the history of this assurance of immortality to Post:

Through the first patriarch of the church I the Lord said to my servant Sidney Rigdon that he should renew his age and become a young man. This patriarch was Joseph Smith Senr. Then several years afterwards I the Lord renewed this promise to my servant "Sidney Rigdon" by my servant Carvel Rigdon another patriarch. Let the Lord here say he approved of both of these patriarchs and they are both, while I cause this to be written, rejoicing among the redeemed in paradise. This greatest of all promises that I the Lord ever made to man I caused to be confirmed by the first female prophetess, namely my hand maiden Phebe Rigdon that I the Lord appointed in my church.

The revelation explained that the nature of the promise given to Rigdon was not unheard of in ancient days "for as the tree had no limits fixed to their life so should it be with the Lord's elect or priesthood."[15] In the earliest reference to this promise, at age seventy-eight, Rigdon conveyed the prophetess Phebe's intuition that "nothing can prevail against [the Rigdons] to hinder them from doing the work [to] which they are ordained. Old age with its infirmities shall give place to the vigor of early maturity; so for the days of a tree so shall be their days, and they (mine elect) shall long enjoy the work of their hands."[16]

"As to the paralysis," Rigdon wrote after his 1872 stroke, "I know not that I am effected by it at all . . . if I were afflicted by it in any degree my hand would tremble but as it does not I conclude that it has not left any of the results of its effect behind it."[17] But Rigdon may have been downplaying the effects of his apoplexia to deter Post from usurping his position. God had not called Post "to watch over the revelator," Rigdon warned him in a 25 May 1873 letter, "you have not such overseeing power and an attempt on your part to assume that to yourself will be a damming sin."[18] The probability that Rigdon suffered significant physical impairment was admitted in a 25 May letter to Charles F. Woodard in which he described himself as "fourscore years old and seriously afflicted by paralysis."[19] The disability was confirmed by the prophetess Phebe, who wrote Post that prior to Sidney's death he had "been very weak and feeble for six or seven years . . . had been like a child he could do but little for himself."[20]

Whatever the extent of his handicap, Rigdon viewed the impediment as only a temporary barrier to his plans for relocating Zion to western Canada. He likely borrowed guidance from an 1843 prophecy Joseph Smith had issued to a small group gathered in the basement of the unfinished Nauvoo temple:

> England or the nation of Great Brittain [sic] would be the last nation to go to p[ie]ces. She would be instrumental in aiding to crush other nations even this nation of the United States & she would only be over thrown by the 10 tribes from the North. She would never persecute the saints as a nation. She would gather tog[e]ther great treasures of God & yet we should seek refuge in her dominion.[21]

Rigdon's interest in Canada, aside from early missionary junkets there, was first made known in a 25 November 1868 revelation calling evangelists to "preach the gospel to the colony of colored people in the country which is called among you Canada west."[22] On 31 December 1869 Post was specifically informed that "It is required by me saith the Lord that my servant Stephen shall see that the mission to the coloured colony in Canada is executed to perfection, that is to success."[23] Though Post immediately embarked on the mission, no converts were gained from the group of free blacks. While in Chatham (now Ontario), Post received an intriguing lesson on Book of Mormon geography from Father Rigdon. Post had evidently asked his mentor where the ancient Nephites made their first landing. Telling his counselor to consult a map, Rigdon admonished, "[L]ook on it at a point on the west side of the Mississippi opposite Alton in Ill[inois] which is in Northern Missouri and then look to a point on the Beam west in the neighborhood of Sitka [now Alaska] and then trace a track from one of these points to the other keeping below in the waters north and the waters south till you reach Peace River there you find the pass through the mountains through which they went and you have their course."[24]

Notwithstanding such geographical detail in this case, Rigdon's references to the new Zion were initially vague. The exact spot was not pinpointed until after the area under consideration was reconnoitered. On 4 November 1872 the prophet wrote Post, again in Chatham, that he was to appoint a "commission of the authorities there" to search for a place which "the Lord will shew them." Rigdon directed that the place be "as near the shore of Lake Superior as can be found and also on some river."[25]

After scouts Jesse Crosby and George W. Robinson (not Rigdon's son-in-law) reported back to him, Rigdon was more confident. "The Lord is going to remove [Zion,]" he confirmed. "This is eternally settled[.] I have waited till this fact is settled to a certainty."[26] Each of Rigdon's letters over the ensuing months provided minutia about the eschatological implications of the relocation. While the Children of Zion would be safe under the protective umbrella of the Dominion, those living in the United States "shall be drinking their own blood as the old prophetic word has told us."[27]

In a broad reference to the earlier failed Mormon utopian experiments which he called "Zion in embryo," the prophet announced that at last Zion had found "a place for the soles of her feet . . . something which has been denied her in this the land of our nativity." Declaring that the audible voice of God had pronounced his earlier ideas "too limited," Rigdon asserted that the grant for Zion "covers the whole country from the sea east to the sea west and from the Lakes to the Nephites" known as Eskimos.[28] Here is where "Zion is to become terrible," he continued in the Lord's voice, and where our "enemies are to be vanquished."[29]

In a lengthy letter, Rigdon stressed the importance of the undertaking. "The writer of this spent upwards of 40 years before the Lord," he boasted,

> regarding not the follies of men, neither their notions nor opinions, their love nor their hatred, their good will nor their condemnation: but untiring and unceasing he continued before the Lord, till the Lord has notified him to begin to prepare for the gathering of Israel, at an age like that of Moses 80 years. . . . There is but one people in the world from the midst of whom Zion can come forth[.] It is alone in the British possessions of this country where Zion can be established[.] No where else on the earth are Nephites found[.] Here also are Lamanites and here also is the colony of

Blacks. Here then is a platform for gathering Israel that can be found no where else in the world. . . . Sell all the property you have there . . . and go your way as soon as you can.

The prophetess, as capable of ignoring past utopian failures as her husband, added a postscript: "We have waited for many years to see this day." Although "old and feeble and not able to do much," they had the Lord's promise to renew "his aged servant to strength and vigor again to go forth to gather Israel."[30]

The prophet's vision became increasingly focused. He announced that Zion "shall be on the waters of the largest stream which flows from the south" into Lake Winnipeg.[31] Post was to start northward on 1 June 1874 to explore that Red River Valley of southern Manitoba.[32] In late August he crossed the border near Fort Pembina, Dakota Territory. His diary entry reflects: "I went over to a new town two and one-half miles from Pembina named Emerson. Staid here. I had a vision of a township there. There was a land office from which I got much information from the agent named George Newcomb."[33]

When Post wrote Rigdon about the new land he had explored the prophet was jubilant. Post had settled the "most important question there ever was in existence pertaining to Zion." Convinced that this was the place, the locale for the gathering of the Lord's people, Rigdon announced that the Children of Zion must "go to become citizens of that country and cease to be citizens of the government of the United States."[34] Rigdon warned that it was "not necessary to crowd into [the Red River Valley] like Nauvoo,"[35] but he need not have worried. Records of the period confirm that only eleven families, representing approximately thirty men, women, and children, heeded his mandate to emigrate.[36]

When it became evident that the world would not end after 1873, the prophet amended his basis for sending Post and the others into the northern wilderness. "From the days of Joseph Smith," he now submitted, "a great question was sprung on the children of Zion." Smith had told the Saints if they could not redeem Jackson County through non-violent means, bloodshed would be required. "This could not be done until the saints had become a great army," Rigdon explained, thus raising the issue of "where would the children of Zion get a place where they could thus be multiplied."[37]

The answer was, of course, Canada. But where were God's soldiers to come from in such sparse areas? "The Lord . . . promised me many years ago as early as 1844," Rigdon explained to Post, "that he would provide for me a great people. . . . [B]ut who they were and from whence they were coming I knew not." The source of those reinforcements was now clear—"the veil is lifted off of the mystery and the people[,] without our search[,] are coming as moved by a divine impulse."[38] These people were coming "from a far country" and would "not [be] prejudiced against my people" but would "hear and obey" "when my voice is spoken unto them in their own language." The people of mystery were Mennonites, the persecuted Swiss, Dutch, German, and Russian emigrants who, as Rigdon had read, were settling the great plains of Canada where they remain today in large numbers.[39]

In August 1875 Post returned to Canada and applied for a homestead. He spent the winter in Emerson building a log cabin and cultivating the land to establish homestead rights. On 6 September 1875 Rigdon mailed Post a revelation announcing that

> The Lord . . . had promised "*to us*" as well as to others that he would give us a "*New Name*" (Isaiah 62nd chapter and 3 verse). . . . [He] says the name of Mormon shall no longer be known among us but puts upon us himself the name of the people whom he has sent to meet us from a strange land. "*From hence saith the Lord the God of Zion my people shall cease to call themselves Mormons, but shall be called Mennonites for the mouth of the Lord has spoken.*"[40]

There is no indication that the Children of Zion fully heeded this edict. They did not have time. Four months later Rigdon informed them that henceforth, "The people of the Lord will then neither be the Church of Christ nor Zion by denomination but will be the Kingdom of '*heaven*' into the likeness of which it is a going to be assimilated."[41]

That anyone remained in the fold of the Children of Zion at this point is surprising. As their increasingly confused prophet continued dictating their lives in his helter-skelter style, most abandoned him. Yet Post, the last of the last, in an October 1875 letter to his wife, still in Attica, wrote:

> In writing to you from [Emerson] I ask myself the question why I have come to this far off Northern Country. And as I reflect upon it I have to say for my salvation and glory in Christ[']s kingdom. . . . We have left the United States because the word of the Lord points out plainly that Christ[']s kingdom never will be established under that government. . . . The Lord will not come & go with his people until they are pure and sanctified before him.[42]

The Post family and some twenty others eventually gathered in Manitoba. The Rigdons, content to govern by mail, had no intention of journeying to Zion. The prophet had made that clear, conveying "it is not my will that he should go there at present . . . if my serv[a]nt Sidney should be there the Devil would stir up a furious persecution on him . . . that would finish the work of redeeming Zion. . . . Therefore I the Lord your god have kept him and must keep him away until the storm is passed."[43]

An important Rigdonite who did not trek to Manitoba was Israel Huffaker, First Bishop in Zion, then living in Dover, Illinois. In a 5 February 1872 revelation Huffaker was warned to "make sale of all of the property you can not take with you and pass over the Mississippi as early as you can." The Lord told the bishop in no uncertain terms that the United States was soon to be destroyed. "My sword is bathed in heaven for your destruction and everlasting overthrow and none can save you," he was warned. "Destruction shall come on you . . . blood shall follow you until you are utterly wasted. Therefore my servant Israel save your family from destruction, and your house from desolation."[44]

When Huffaker refused to sell his property and donate all to the church, Rigdon ordered him to tithe instead. And "In case you do not get tithing enough to supply at any time the needs of him whom is at your head," Rigdon hedged, "you must borrow, for his needs must be supplied or Zion must fail."[45] But Rigdon's financial woes continued, and in June he pleaded with Post: "Brother I write this note in necessity or I should not write at present[.] We are in straightened circumstances[,] our means of living are exhausted[.] [H]elp d[ea]r Brother if you can."[46]

In October, Huffaker, who had lost his hearing through illness, made no effort to move west. Rigdon warned that God was angry for showing "more regard for the things of the world than for the duties of his holy calling." Since the salvation of the Huffaker family came through the sacrifices of the Rigdons, an angry God blustered, "I the Lord require that you shall see that [Sidney and Phebe] are crowned with blessing at your hand, and that not sparingly but bountifully."[47] Huffaker was finally bullied into covenanting that "for each dollar that all the rest of the saints would give for the sustaining of the department of the revelation [meaning the Rigdons] he would give one himself."[48] In early 1876 the bishop received an $8 donation, which he matched with a like amount, and forwarded to Father Rigdon. Instead of expressing gratitude, the irate prophet exploded:

> Your $16 has been received[.] I am required of the Lord to say to you that your whole transaction in this case is an abomination in his sight. . . . Did you think that you were dispensing penury to a begger when you sent your $16[?] . . . My anger [a]rose and beware lest it kindles into indignation and you fall among the dammed to rise no more; for if you fall from where you now stand you sink to *hell*.

The Lord, suddenly obsessed with paltry matters, issued Huffaker a new law "concerning my Holy priesthood" upon which "depends your salvation." The bishop was commanded to pay Rigdon "$50 every three months." "I know that you can do it," the Lord continued, and "on it hangs the issues of your life and death."[49] Huffaker was aghast. Seeking sympathy from Post, he concluded his letter with the pertinent question, "how can we recon[c]ile these things with the word of god."[50] Informed of Huffaker's impertinence, the prophet in God's name ordered the convening of a "court of death." Huffaker was to be tried by five high priests, with Post serving as "judge and organizer of this court of the kingdom." He is "worthy of death," Rigdon ranted, "and let the court so decide and the Lord will see to the rest."[51]

Two months later, however, on 27 May 1876, prior to any action against Huffaker, Rigdon collapsed at his residence, the Edward and Sarah Wingate home on Depot Street. The 1 June *Friendship Register* noted that "at the present writing [he is] in very critical condition." Phebe wrote to Post on 15 June informing him of the "calamity that has befallen my husband." She explained he had been sitting in a chair and as he stood up "fell down on his back, he is not able to move himself." Two "strong men" were required to lift him in and out of bed. She added:

> He appears to be paralyzed, he has no use of his hips to move or take a step I do not know what will be the result. I cannot let myself think for a moment that our Heavenly Father is going to take him away at this time. I think of all the promises that has been given to him. If you have faith I pray you will all raise your hearts to the Lord for his recovery. I am alone in the faith[;] the only one to say a word to is my husband. He is not able to converse much at present. O may your faith be strong that you may call upon him for the recovery of his servant.[52]

The 18 June *Friendship Register* bid the "dangerously ill" Rigdon well: "That he may speedily recover is the wish of his numerous friends. His friendly grasp of the hand and cheering words are greatly missed." But the apoplexy worsened through successive strokes. By mid-July all hope for recovery had been "given up by his friends and relations," the 13 July 1876 *Friendship Register* noted. Phebe later wrote that during the six weeks preceding his demise on 14 July her husband "was deranged . . . he complained of his head a dull heavy feeling . . . lay on his back all the time." Though she "held onto the [rejuvenation] promises all most to the last of his life," she too finally lost hope. "I feel myself alone we lived together fifty six years," the grieving widow wrote, "but he is gone [and] I feel his loss greatly."[53]

Rigdon's little-noticed obituary in the 18 July *Friendship Register* chronicled his religious activities, concluding with a summary befitting the life of a man few local citizens knew or understood:

> Since his excision from the ruling body of the church, at Nauvoo, he has been living in our village, in the main very quiet, repelling rather than courting the curiosity which his prominence in one of the most extraordinary social phenomena of times, drew upon him. He has often been interviewed by those intent upon clearing up some of the mysteries and delusions that attended the origin of Mormonism, but invariably without success.
>
> On these occasions he would defend the Mormon account of the origin [of] the Book of Mormon, and also the chief doctrines of the early Mormon church, and in many ways exhibit sympathetic interest in its prosperity. His mind had a natural religious bias; and his conclusions respecting Bible doctrines, subject to diverse interpretations, were conservative. In his prime he took an active part in the theological controversies that raged so fiercely in this and western states and was then and always familiar with the Bible, and had in him the material for a useful minister of any denomination, yet for many years past he held himself aloof from the church affairs in this vicinity, and his whole conduct held naturally to the inference that his religious

ambitions were buried at the time he was superseded by Young, or perhaps at the time when the polygamous doctrines of Joseph Smith were promulgated.

. . . Mr. Rigdon leaves a wife, five daughters and three sons, who are almost all near-by residents, and highly respected. His funeral was attended by many of our citizens and by the Masonic fraternity of which he was long an active member. For five years past the infirmaties of old age weighed heavily upon his frame, but his mental vigor remained substantially unimpaired. He became entirely helpless, and death came to him as a happy relief.[54]

Wickliffe, in an unpublished tribute, contributed a portrait of his father as "a man who had his fa[u]lts[,] he was subject to like passions as other men[,] yet he was a man who I believe always intended to do right even if he did sometimes miss his way."[55] The prophet, whose involvement with the Children of Zion was unknown to his family except Phebe, was given a masonic funeral by Friendship's Allegheny Lodge No. 225. "Tears of sorrow were shed over his grave by his family and . . . friends," remarked Wickliffe. Ultimately "he and his wife who had shared his joys and sorrows sleep side by side in the little cemetery in Maple Grove where loving hands . . . laid them to rest beneath the sod."[56]

Notes

Unless otherwise stated, all primary sources cited are located in the Historical Department of the Church of Jesus Christ of Latter-day Saints, Salt Lake City, Utah.

1. Sidney Rigdon to Stephen and Jane Post, 5 Dec. 1873, Stephen Post Collection, box 2, fd. 12, also listed as section 84 in Copying Book B, box 3, fd. 13 (hereafter Post Collection).

2. Rigdon, as was his custom, made two copies of this letter. An undated one is in the Post Collection, box 1, fd. 1, also listed as section 61 in Copying Book A. The other, in the Brigham Young Collection, box 42, fd. 2, reel, 75, is dated 6 Dec. 1870.

3. J. Wickliffe Rigdon to Brigham Young, 27 June 1871, Brigham Young Collection, box 34, fd. 4, reel 64.

4. Journal History, 26 Aug. 1871—a multi-volume daily history of the church compiled by official church historians..

5. J. Wickliffe Rigdon to Brigham Young, 19 Aug. 1871, Brigham Young Collection, box 34, fd. 4, reel 64.

6. Rigdon to Post, 22 Aug. 1871, Post Collection, box 2, fd. 8.

7. Rigdon to Young, 3 Sept. 1871, Brigham Young Collection, box 42, fd. 2, reel 75.

8. W. Wyl, *Mormon Portraits or The Truth About The Mormon Leaders From 1830-1886* (Salt Lake City: Tribune Printing and Publishing Co., 1886), 124.

9. Rigdon to Post, 9 Oct. 1871, Post Collection; listed as section 62 in Copying Book A, box 3, fd. 12.

10. Rigdon to Post, 12 and 17 Oct. 1871, Post Collection, box 2, fd. 8.

11. Bohn to Rigdon, 5 Jan. 1872, Post Collection, box 2, fd. 9.

12. Rees, Hamilton, Page to Rigdon, 10 Jan. 1872, Post Collection, box 2, fd. 9.

13. Rigdon to Post, 26 Jan. 1872, Post Collection, box 2, fd. 9.

14. Rigdon to Post, 14 Jan. 1873, Post Collection, box 2, fd. 11.

15. Rigdon to Post, 1 Nov. 1875, listed as section 96 in Copying Book B, box 3, fd. 13.

16. Rigdon to Post, 23 Oct. 1871, Post Collection, box 2, fd. 8; listed as section 63 in Copying Book A, box 3, fd. 12.

17. Rigdon to Post, 3 May 1873, Post Collection, box 2, fd. 11.

18. Rigdon to Post, 25 May 1873, Post Collection, box 2, fd. 11.

19. Rigdon to Woodard, 25 May 1873, Rigdon Collection.

20. Phebe Rigdon to Stephen Post, 20 July 1876; listed in Post Collection as section 100 in Copying Book B, box 3, fd. 3.

21. See Charles Ora Card Diary entry for 21 Jan. 1887.

22. 25 Nov. 1868 revelation listed as section 48 in Copying Book A, box 1, fd. 17.

23. Listed in Post Collection as section 57 in Copying Book A, box 2, fd. 6.

24. Rigdon to Post, 21 May 1870, Post Collection, box 2, fd. 3.

25. Rigdon to Post, 4 Nov. 1872, Post Collection, box 2, fd. 10.

26. Rigdon to Post, 22 Sept. 1873; listed as section 76 in Copying Book A, box 2, fd. 6.

27. Rigdon to Post, 4 Oct. 1873; listed in Post Collection as section 79 in Copying Book B, box 3, fd. 13.

28. This allusion to Nephites as Eskimos was first made in a February 1870 communique "To the first presidency and the children of Zion":

> I the Lord your god maketh known unto you a great mystery which men seeth but understandeth not. . . . It is for the revealer of secrets to throw light into the midst of this darkness[.] You read in the book of Mormon that Lehi gave a promise to his son Joseph that his seed should not be "*destroyed*." . . . [B]y virtue of this promise a remmnant of this seed was preserved, at the time of the d[e]struction of the Nephites and their descendents remain to this day; a people whose history is hid from all the world and always was[.] . . . Now behold and be amazed saith the Lord your god for I the Lord reveal the great fact unto you. . . . there are . . . Nephite children of the pure blood to this day[.] By the gentiles they are known by the name of Esquimeaus (Post Collection, box 3, fd. 1; also listed as section 58 in Copying Book A, box 3, fd. 12).

29. Rigdon to Post, 9 Oct. 1873, Post Collection, box 2, fd. 12; also listed as section 80 in Copying Book B, box 3, fd. 13.

30. Rigdon to Post, 3 Nov. 1873, Post Collection, box 2, fd. 12; also listed as section 82 in Copying Book B, box 3, fd. 13.

31. Rigdon to Post, 11 Dec. 1873, Post Collection, box 2, fd. 12.

32. After the Canadian government reached an agreement with the Hudson's Bay Company, allowing the Northwest provinces to enter the Dominion, original French-Canadian settlers worried that their land titles would not be recognized. Led by Louis Riel, a Metis (mixed French and Indian), insurgents staged an unsuccessful revolt in 1869 to establish a provisional government at Winnipeg. Several Red River Expeditionary Forces

primarily composed of volunteer soldiers were sent to pacify the Metis. Many of the soldiers, paid in land bounty certificates, chose to homestead in southern Manitoba. Post noted in his diary that "the area was a wild country with soldiers, half-breeds and Indians" (Post Diary, entries for Sept. and Oct. 1874, Post Collection, box 6, fd. 6).

33. Ibid. When Post filed his claim, more than 6 million acres were available for homesteading in Manitoba. Any adult could purchase one section (640 acres) for one dollar per acre. After erecting a residence and tilling the land for three years, the homesteader could then apply for a patent and receive title to the land provided he was a subject of the British Crown by birth or naturalization (Canada, Minister of Agriculture [Thomas Spence], *Manitoba and the North-West of the Dominion*, 1874, 37-39, cited in Carol Freeman Braby, "Rigdonites in Manitoba, 1874-1884," *John Whitmer Historical Association Journal* 11 [1991]: 76).

34. Rigdon to Post, 23 Sept. 1874, Post Collection, box 3, fd. 13; also listed as section 89 in Copying Book B.

35. Rigdon to Post, 26 Dec. 1874, Post Collection, box 2, fd. 14.

36. The 1876 records of the "Branch of Zions Church at Manitoba Canada" list twenty members. See Post Collection, box 5, fd. 10. Also see unpublished diary of A. J. Hinkle, 1879-83, cited in Braby, 77.

37. Rigdon to Post, 23 Sept. 1874, Post Collection, box 2, fd. 14; also listed as section 89 in Copying Book B, box 3, fd. 13.

38. Rigdon to Post, 12 Apr. 1875, Post Collection, box 3, fd. 11.

39. Undated Rigdon to Post revelation (first part of letter missing), Post Collection, box 1, fd. 1; dated 24 Feb. 1875 and listed as section 92 in Copying Book B, box 3, fd. 1.

40. Rigdon to Post, 6 Sept. 1875, Post Collection, box 5, fd. 9; emphasis in original.

41. Rigdon to Post, 23 Jan. 1876, Post Collection, box 3, fd. 3.

42. Stephen Post to Jane Post, Oct. 1875, Post Collection, box 3, fd. 2.

43. Rigdon to Post, 23 Oct. 1871, Post Collection, box 2, fd. 8; also listed as section 63 in Copying Book A, box 3, fd. 12.

44. Rigdon to Huffaker, 5 Feb. 1872, Post Collection; also listed as section 65 in Copying Book A, box 3, fd. 12.

45. Rigdon to Post, 26 Dec. 1873, Post Collection, listed as section 85 in Copying Book B, box 2, fd. 12.

46. Rigdon to Post, 4 June 1874, Post Collection, box 2, fd. 13.

47. Rigdon to Huffaker, 10 Oct. 1874, Post Collection, box 3, fd. 11.

48. 18 October 1875 revelation signed by both Jane Post and Phebe Rigdon, listed in Post Collection as section 94 in Copying Book B, box 3, fd. 13.

49. 7 Jan. 1876 revelation listed in Post Collection as section 97 in Copying Book B, box 3, fd. 3.

50. Huffaker to Post, 26 Feb. 1876, Post Collection, box 3, fd. 3.

51. Rigdon to Post, 20 Mar. 1876, Post Collection, listed as section 98 in Copying Book B, box 3, fd. 3.

52. Phebe Rigdon to Post, 15 June 1876, Post Collection, listed as section 100 in Copying Book B, box 3, fd. 13.

53. Phebe Rigdon to Stephen Post, 20 July 1876, Post Collection, box 3, fd. 3.

54. All citations from the *Friendship Register* are located in the Arlene Hess Papers, Special Collections, BYU Library.

55. Rigdon, "Life Story of Sidney Rigdon," 199.

56. Ibid., 200.

Epilogue

When a superior intellect and a psychopathic temperament coalesce . . . in the same individual, we have the best possible condition for the kind of effective genius that gets into the biographical dictionaries. Such men do not remain mere critics and understanders with their intellect. Their ideas possess them, they inflict them, for better or worse, upon their companions or their age.

—William James (1902)[1]

Phebe Rigdon and Stephen Post continued to communicate by mail after Sidney's death. But the prophetess ceased referring to herself as such and performed no leadership role other than an occasional blessing. Although Post continued to shepherd the small group of Rigdonites on the cold plains of Manitoba, he was lost without Father Rigdon's guidance. "You seem to take the death of S. R. pretty hard," wrote his nephew James Adams, still living in Attica on 3 September 1876:

> Well I can[']t blame you for you have been led by him for a long time[.] [F]irst to sacrifice a good comfortable home in P[ennsylvania] to come to Iowa . . . till the final move to Jackson Co., but this was a mistake. North of the state[s was then] the place for you & there you are now. . . . What does the rev[elation] amount to [in which Rigdon] claimed to have his age renewed (or the promise) for the gathering of the House of Israel . . . it amounts to just what the rest of his revelations does[.] Just the imaginations of a man[']s mind. . . . Uncle it is all bosh and there is no use of your trying to make me believe any thing else. I believe in the principles of the B[ook of] M[ormon] but further than that I cannot go[.] if S. R. had lived and come and joined with his people[,] showed by his works that he was what he professed to be I would [have] been up there if I would have had to walk[.] I may come yet but not on the account of religion. . . . I don't lay anything to your charge in regard to this[.] I believe you are innocent of all for you actually believed S. R. would have his age renewed & thousand of other things that he had said of himself & wife.[2]

On 28 June 1879, after attending a Sunday meeting, Post confided in his diary: "All professed to have lost faith in the moving of Zion to Canada and recriminated on the presidency as the cause of the present state of things here, finding fault with some of the revelations."[3] Unable to appease his people, six months later, on 18 December, a dejected Post, who had been ill for two months, joined his prophet in death. A. J. Hinkle, son of prominent Missouri Mormon

454

George Hinkle, succeeded Post as presiding elder in Emerson. But in early June 1880 Hinkle wrote Joseph Smith III, president of the Reorganized Church of Jesus Christ of Latter Day Saints:

> I have been advocating your organization to this people. Some are not favorable to it, though others are. For my part, I want to work while the Lord is working. There are twelve members here belonging to Sidney's organization; and there are outsiders favorable to the gospel. . . . If it could be that an Elder could be sent here, the chances are favorable to build a branch here.[4]

But during a reorganization of the Canadian Rigdonites on 15 February 1882 Hinkle was replaced with Post's widow and negotiations with RLDS headquarters lapsed. James L. Adams, who had since come to Manitoba, noted that high priest Jesse Crosby made "some very pointed remarks on the present condition of Zion" and then "appointed Sister Jane Post to stand at the head of the branch in her office" so that the church could be carried on "under the instruction of the female priesthood." After comments from both Crosby and Adams the small branch of a dozen or so members voted to sustain her.[5]

On 19 August 1882 RLDS missionaries William H. Kelley and George A. Blakeslee, responding belatedly to Hinkle's request, arrived in Manitoba. "Today finds me at Bro. A. J. Hinkle's residence," Kelley wrote his brother. "We held a meeting yesterday with about a dozen in attendance. They are the followers of Stephen Post. They came up here on a wild goose chase and now see their foolish move. They would like to get back to Iowa if they could dispose of what they have got."[6] The RLDS elders also met with Mother Post, who "claimed to be President of the Church and successor of Sidney after his death," Kelley wrote. Although she and her small knot of adherents treated both evangelists kindly, they were not "impressed just now to give up their old views, the notion of S[tephen] Post. Hence, went events without much hope of success."[7] However, ten people in the Hinkle faction were baptized by Elder Blakeslee in the Roseau River on 27 August 1882. By 1884 most had returned to the United States or merged into the general populace of Manitoba. The followers of Jane Post disbanded after her death.

Phebe Rigdon, eighty-six at her death, lived a decade longer than her husband. "I have a good home & live with my daughter [Sarah,] her husband [Ed Wingate] is one of the best of men," she wrote Stephen Post three months after Sidney's death.[8] Within ten months, however, both Sarah Rigdon Wingate and Lacy Rigdon Hatch were dead. "I feel their loss greatly," Phebe wrote Post on 13 August 1877; "I must try to be reconciled to the will of my heavenly father[,] it is all most to[o] much for me to bare."[9]

After Sarah's death Phebe continued to live with Wingate. "I live with my son-in-law[,] he is one of the kindest of men," she wrote. "I expect to live with him as long as I live."[10] But on 24 March 1881, the Wingate home on Depot Street was incinerated during a fire which destroyed a large portion of town. Phebe moved into the home of her daughter Phebe and son-in-law Samuel Spears.[11] The older Phebe died at age eighty-six on 27 February 1886 in this Friendship home that still stands on Main Street. Her funeral services were held in the home the following day.[12]

Prior to Phebe's death, according to some family members, she burned all Sidney's private papers. Granddaughter Jessie Rigdon Secord related in 1967: "I was told that [grandfather] made grandmother promise that upon his death everything he had ever written would be destroyed so a short time after, on the absence of the family, she burned all the records, and the brilliant sermons and orations lay in a heap of ashes."[13] Grandson Edward Hatch, a New York Supreme Court justice, stated in 1896 that "during the last six or seven years of his life" his grandfather "wrote a great deal, daily using from seven to nine pages of foolscap paper; but as to the subject matter no one knew anything, as at his death all the manuscripts were burned, the family not considering them of any real worth; today they regret their haste in thus destroying."[14]

Except Phebe Rigdon, none of Sidney's family members were privy to his Children of Zion following. It is unlikely Phebe destroyed these important documents. Post received a copy of essentially everything Rigdon wrote during the last twenty years of his life, as Phebe confirmed when she wrote Post on 8 June 1878 informing him that she had found a "writing on the priesthood" while rummaging through some papers. "I expect you have [a copy]," she added, I know "he allways sent them to you."[15] The manuscript Phebe found was probably the same one Sidney told a correspondent he had "written . . . while in my 80th year."[16] On 25 October 1871 he had written Post:

> By much labor and exertion I have succeeded in getting put on paper the word of the Lord to enable you to process understanding in the organization of Zion. This is the first time the father has caused his system of truth to be placed in full before his saints and made his Zion a school where all the children of Zion can and must learn or else not be the children of Zion at all.[17]

Unknown to Phebe, Sidney on earlier occasions as well had instructed Post to publish the work under his name rather than Rigdon's. Accordingly *A Treatise on the Melchizedek Priesthood, and the Callings of God* appeared in Council Bluffs, Iowa, in 1872.[18] A year later, fearing his name would be linked to the publication, Rigdon warned Post in a revelation:

> I want to say to you that it is the gravest violation of the laws of the Holy priesthood for you ever to mention your having received a paper reflecting on the Holy priesthood[.] If you get such you will cast it behind your back[.] Never mention it again that you had ever heard any thing but cast it into the fire.[19]

That kind of idiosyncratic behavior was the measure of Rigdon's life, especially as he aged. Stressful circumstances exacerbated his symptoms of chronic manic-depressive illness. Nevertheless, true mystics have always walked perilously close to the abyss of madness. In his classic treatise on the subject, *The Varieties of Religious Experience*, William James concluded that "As a matter of fact a religious life, exclusively pursued, does tend to make the person exceptional and eccentric." Moreover, "religious geniuses" like Rigdon

> Often . . . have led a discordant inner life, and had melancholy during a part of their career. They have known no measure, been liable to obsessions and fixed ideas; and frequently they have fallen into trances, heard voices, seen visions, and presented all sorts of peculiarities which are ordinarily classed as pathological. Often, moreover, these pathological features in their career have helped to give them their religious authority and influence.[20]

Perhaps Rigdon erred most seriously in outliving Joseph Smith, in having functioned as the prophet's right arm too effectively, in wanting too much to carry Smith's prophetic legacy forward. After Nauvoo, Rigdon's contemporaries peered down their collective noses at him, considered him a has-been, a fraud, and a lunatic. Dauntless, he nevertheless took most of his dreams, unrealized visions, and prophecies to the grave. Rigdon was not unique in such prophetic unfulfill-ment. Failed prophecies appear in the pronouncements of virtually all nineteenth-century millenialists. In presenting their colorful history to the world, twentieth-century Mormons overlook or are unaware of the fact that many of the divine predictions of Joseph Smith, Brigham Young, Parley P. Pratt, Wilford Woodruff, and other church leaders did not materialize.[21]

Dim as the past may seem, its ambiguity is deepened by our inability to confront it. In nineteenth-century Mormon understanding, a prophet was one defined by his ability to see beyond the finite, who uttered holy scripture, thundered oracular, unpopular words of warning. Oracles were measured by how fully their predictive statements came to be. If an oracle were truly inspired of God he was precisely accurate, there could be no margin of error or God would have ceased to be omnipotent. Viewed from twentieth-century perspective this rigid literalism of our forbearers' belief system seems quaint. Failed prophecy, in Sidney Rigdon's case as well as in others, is proof that visionaries err. In proclaiming to reveal God's truths, they often expressed unfulfilled longings of their own psyche.

Social scientist Mircea Eliade has noted there is little possibility of under-standing another's mental universe without in some measure taking it seriously.[22] Rigdon's eccentricities make it difficult to accord him such respect despite his undeniable contributions to Mormonism. In the final analysis, Rigdon manifested a pathological kind of religiosity. Madmen claiming to speak for God can infect others with their madness. Rigdon strove to be an exemplar to the world, and more than a century after his death that is ironically what he had become: his unfortunate, cautionary life warns of the perils of religious excess. It warns all of us that we must ultimately think for ourselves rather than surrender decision-making to others, especially to those who dictate what God would have us do.

Notes

Unless otherwise stated, all primary sources cited are located in the Historical Department of the Church of Jesus Christ of Latter-day Saints, Salt Lake City, Utah.

1. William James, *The Varieties of Religious Experience: A Study in Human Nature* (New York: Longmans, Green, and Co., 1902), 23-24.

2. Adams to Post, 3 Sept. 1876, Stephen Post Collection, box 3, fd. 3; hereafter Post Collection. A year later, after reading of Brigham Young's death, Adams again wrote his uncle: "I sent you our last week's *[Times]* to let you see how things were progressing in the States & esp[ecially] the death of Brigham Young. Now what does that prophecy of S. R. amount to about his downfall[?] [H]e is dead but he died a natural death. But previous to his death regulated all his affairs in good shape his church is increasing all the time" (Adams to Post, 9 Sept. 1877, Post Collection, box 3, fd. 6).

3. Stephen Post Diary, Jan.-Dec. 1879, under date, Post Collection, box 6, fd. 6.

4. A. J. Hinkle to Joseph Smith III, *Saints' Herald* 27 (15 July 1880): 222.

5. Church Records of the Church of Jesus Christ of the Children of Zion, 15 Feb. 1882, cited in Carol Freeman Braby, "Rigdonites in Manitoba, 1874-1884," *John Whitmer Historical Association Journal* 11 (1991): 43.

6. William H. Kelley to E. L. Kelley, 21 Aug. 1882, William H. Kelley Papers, archives, Reorganized Church of Jesus Christ of Latter Day Saints, Independence, Missouri (hereafter RLDS archives).

7. William H. Kelly Journal, 26 Aug. 1882, RLDS archives.

8. Phebe Rigdon to Post, 7 Oct. 1876, Post Collection, box 3, fd. 3.

9. Rigdon to Post, 13 Aug. 1877, Post Collection, box 3, fd. 6.

10. Rigdon to Post, 13 Aug. 1877, Post Collection. In various sources Winget is listed as a lumberman, clothier, and bookbinder, but eventually became business manager of the Friendship Sash and Blind Factory, the town's most important industry. Described as a "huge jolly red-head [whom] the sun always seemed to shine on," Winget was often called a "one man chamber of commerce." He died in 1887 (see various references in Arlene Hess Collection, Special Collections, Harold B. Lee Library, Brigham Young University, Provo, Utah, and *Friendship Register*, 31 Mar. 1881).

11. Phebe Jr., as she was often called, was remembered in Friendship as a bitter woman who married at thirty-six. Her husband Samuel E. Spears was never an ambitious man. He inherited money and when short simply got more from his sister and daughters. He was the son of Roswell Spears—famous for his axes and edged tools. Phebe and Spears had two children, Evelyn and Maudex (see various references in Hess Collection).

12. *Friendship Register*, 5 Mar. 1886.

13. Jessie R. Secord to Arlene Hess, 27 Feb. 1967, Hess Collection.

14. Arthur F. Barnes interview with Edward Hatch in 27 May 1896, *Deseret Evening News*.

15. Rigdon to Post, 8 June 1878, Post Collection, box 3, fd. 7.

16. Rigdon to Charles F. Woodard, 25 May 1873, Rigdon Collection (original in New York Public Library).

17. Rigdon to Post, 25 Oct. 1871, Post Collection, box 2, fd. 8.

18. Two copies of this publication are found in the Post Collection, box 4, fd. 6.

19. Rigdon to Post, 9 Oct. 1873, listed as section 80 in Copying Book B, box 2, fd. 12.

20. James, 6-7.

21. Prophets from Joseph Smith through Wilford Woodruff, as indicated throughout chapter 12 of this work, declared on numerous occasions in the name of the Lord that the Saints would redeem Zion (Jackson County) "in this generation," meaning those who were alive in 1832. This promise was one of nineteenth-century Mormonism's holiest grails. Additionally, Joseph Smith, aside from predicting Zion's redemption by 11 Sept. 1836 (Joseph Smith, *History of the Church of Jesus Christ of Latter-day Saints*, B. H. Roberts, ed., 7 vols. [Salt Lake City: The Church of Jesus Christ of Latter-day Saints, 1902], 2:145; hereafter *History of the Church)*, prophesied that the world would end in 1891 (*History of the Church*, 2:182).

Although the prophet's well-known 25 December 1832 "Revelation and Prophecy on War" was correct in foreseeing that the war would begin "at the rebellion of South Carolina," the most important event predicted in that renowned revelation did not occur. The Civil War did not engulf "all nations" in war as portended (D&C 87:1-3).

Brigham Young, who preferred to see himself as a "Yankee guesser" rather than a clairvoyant, seldom prophesied. But he did predict in 1856 that "I say as the Lord lives, we are bound to become a sovereign State in the Union, or *an independent nation by ourselves.* I am still, and still will be Governor of this Territory to the constant chagrin of my enemies; and twenty-six years shall not pass away before the Elders of this Church will be as much thought of as kings on their thrones" (*Deseret News*, 1 Sept. 1856). Parley P. Pratt in an 1838 prophecy to La Roy Sunderland proclaimed that "there will not be an unbelieving Gentile upon this continent 50 years hence; and if they are not greatly scourged, and in a great measure overthrown, within five or ten years from this date, then the Book of Mormon will have proved itself false" (Parley P. Pratt, *Mormonism Unveiled: Zion's Watchman Unmasked* [New York: O. Pratt, E. Fordham, 1838], 15). In a remarkable pronouncement he entitled "One Hundred Years, Hence. 1945," Pratt later predicted that by then a great earthquake would have "leveled the mountains over the whole earth." In digging for the foundation of "our new Temple in the 124th city of Joseph . . . near where the City of New York once stood," a box was seen in a vision and found to be filled with relics. A silver Liberty fifty-cent piece with an eagle on one side and a seated woman on the other indicated that "the government had fallen from the *splendor* of an eagle to the pleasure of women." After returning from a "pleasure ride" in the chariot of Jesus Christ, Pratt saw a table set for 300,000 saints, where *Jesus Christ* sat at the head. After the feast Pratt stepped into the "news room" and the first article to attract his attention was "the minutes of the General Conference held in Zion (Jackson County) on the 14th day of the first month, A.D. 1945, when it was motioned by Joseph Smith, and seconded by John the Revelator, that *forty-eight* new cities be laid out and builded" (*Nauvoo Neighbor*, 10 Sept. 1845).

Wilford Woodruff, the church's fourth president, in perhaps one of the most imprudent of all Mormon prophecies, pronounced in 1868 to Saints gathered in Logan,

Utah, that in 1898 Cache Valley would be filled with "Cities & magnificent Palaces & Towers occupied by one Million of the Saints." Woodruff prophesied that Apostle Ezra T. Benson would go thirty years later with "President Young [and] others to Jackson Co. Mo. to Build the great Temple & the New Jerrusalem." The America of his vision had "been broken to peaces," Woodruff continued, "the City of New York [destroyed] by the Sea . . . Albany was utterly Destroyed by fire. . . . Boston was sunk with an Earthquake. . . . Chicago was struck with lightning burned with fire & Brimstone for their Abomina-tions. . . . Millions of the People of the United States & other Nations of the Earth were destroyed with their Cities By the Great Judgments of God Because of their great sins & wickedness in the sight of Heaven & Earth. . . . The United States became so weakened & Broaken to peaces that they Called upon Brigham Young to take the Presidency of the United States to save the Constitution & the remnant of the Nation from utter destruction." At the end of Woodruff's predictions, Brigham Young announced that the "remarks were given By Revelation" (Scott G. Kenney, ed. *Wilford Woodruff's Journal–Typescript,* 9 vols. [Midvale, UT: Signature Books, 1983-85] 5:421); for an interpretation of Woodruff's prophecies, see Susan Staker, *Waiting for World's End: The Diaries of Wilford Woodruff* (Salt Lake City: Signature Books, 1993).

22. Mircea Eliade, *The Sacred and the Profane: The Nature of Religion,* trans. Willard R. Trask (New York: Harper, 1961), 165.

Appendices

1. SIDNEY RIGDON ON THE SEALED PORTION OF THE GOLD PLATES

One of Sidney Rigdon's most interesting explications is on the contents of the sealed portion of the "gold plates" of the Book of Mormon which Joseph Smith was not allowed to translate. Rigdon included his exegesis in a 1 September 1868 letter "To the First Presidency of Zion" (original in Stephen Post Collection, box 1, fd. 16, also sec. 42, Copying Book A, box 3, fd. 12; archives, Historical Department of the Church of Jesus Christ of Latter-day Saints, Salt Lake City, Utah).

Inasmuch as I the Lord desire to have peace and unity among the children of Zion[,] I will, as far as wisdom in me requires, give to my people an understanding of the character of the things which are engraven on the sealed plates.

Let the children of Zion therefore know that the record spoken of differs from the book of Mormon in its being historical instead of doctrinal[.] The [B]ook of Mormon teaches . . . the requirements of the Lord pertaining to perfection with the laws of obedience and all things pertaining to the gospel[.] As also to show unto the saints the proper applications of the prophecies of the former prophets to themselves and how to understand them as pertaining to their own salvation.

But the untranslated record deals [with] the history of Zion . . . as it existed from the commencement under the administration of Joseph Smith and gives not only the history of Zion but of Joseph Smith also under whose administration it first made its appearance shewing how it was that "*He*" was called to that work giving the history of his corrupting his way before the Lord and using the grace of god bestowed on him to gratifiy la[s]civious desires and the prostitution of it to carnal and sensual purposes and gratifications[.] It gives his history untill he was rejected and cut off from before the Lord and it continues his history to his final doom being cast out with the hypocrits into outer darkness where there is weeping and wailing and gnashing of teeth.

These plates also give a history of Joseph in Egypt being lifted up in the pride of his heart and his having desired to use the power he had to obtain worldly fame and to be thought great amongst men[,] and to gratify this ambition sought to glorify his name "*Joseph*" and knowing that from his loins was to come the priesthood that should gather Israel in the last days he desired of the Lord that the name of the servant revelator might be Joseph "and" by reason of this covenent Joseph Smith was called.

In addition to this saith the Lord those plates give the history of the family to which Joseph Smith belongeth giving an account of their being lifted up in the pride of their hearts and in consequence of that fell into the condemnations of the Devil and were rejected of god; and He the god of Zion swore in his wrath that they nor any of their descendents should ever have power or authority in Zion forever and ever.

And now saith the Lord can not the children of Zion understand the reason why no part of this accord could be made known untill an other revelator stood before the Lord through whom it could come and had there not another revelator rose up before the Lord no part of it could ever have come to light; for it was not possible for any man to have brought to light his own fate as it is written in that record.

The sealed plates saith the Lord also follows the corrupted church through the period of its existence giving the names of the 12 [apostles] who succeeded the Smith family in the rule of that people untill they, like the Smith family, were cut down and cast into the fire from whence there is no return.

Again saith the Lord, after giving the history of the first organization till it disappeared from the earth the record gives the history of the coming forth of Zion out of the ruins of the corrupted church giving the names of those through whom it came both men and women including the 12 through whose faith and mighty works Zion shall be pushed to her triumph. . . . The vision of Obadiah is of that number which is recorded on the sealed plates in fact. There are also of the prophecies of the former prophets such as Isaiah Jeremiah Ezekiel Daniel and other[s] of the prophets transferred onto the sealed plates [and] were connected with the plates from whence the book of Mormon was translated such as relate to the affairs of the authorities of Zion as redeemed from the corruptions of the old church and delivered directly to the children of Zion and none other separating those prophecies from all others so that Zion might have her own appointed to herself.

But behold and Lo! saith the Lord the rise and progress of Zion to her perfection are a practical translation of the sealed plates so that Zion as she passes along practically translates the sealed plates.

2. BOOK OF MORMON AUTHORSHIP

LDS Seventies president Brigham H. Roberts (1855-1933) believed that

Joseph Smith, severely underestimated by his critics, needed no assistance from Solomon Spalding or Sidney Rigdon had he himself authored the Book of Mormon. According to Roberts, Smith was "superior in talents . . . [and] in literary power of expression" to either of them. Commenting on the more than 3,000 corrections made in the Book of Mormon since 1830, Roberts added that if Rigdon, a known grammarian, had authored the work, "it would not have been so full of petty errors in grammar and the faulty use of words as is found in the first edition of the Book of Mormon. . . . They are ingrained in it; they are constitutional faults."[1]

The conjecture that Smith alone wrote the Book of Mormon, and that its purpose was to explain the origin of Native Americans, has gained recent attention. The Book of Mormon seems to distill what authors as early as the sixteenth century had been saying about American Indians, that they were of the House of Israel. Numerous books and articles were published on the topic prior to the Book of Mormon. A listing of the most significant works includes James Adair's *History of the American Indians* (1775), Elias Boudinot's *A Star in the West; or, a Humble Attempt to Discover the Long Lost Ten Tribes of Israel* (1816), Caleb Atwater's "Description of the Antiquities Discovered in the State of Ohio and Other Western States," in *Archaeologia Americana* (1820), Ethan Smith's *View of the Hebrews* (1823; 1825), and Josiah Priest's *The Wonders of Nature and Providence, Displayed* (1825).[2]

Some theorists are satisfied that the *Palmyra Register* and *Wayne Sentinel*, local newspapers available to Smith, published sufficient information about American antiquities to provide a foundation in understanding the controversy. B. H. Roberts postulated that even non-readers were privy through hearing such subjects discussed at gathering places of common people: "the village store, the wheel-wright's shop, the town meeting, and post office, the social meetings of the community, the gathering and dispersing throngs in attendance upon church services—in all such places the people hear and absorb knowledge of such subjects as are of general interest, until there is formed what I have referred to as 'common knowledge' of things."[3]

The prevailing theory among current secular historians, however, is that Ethan Smith's *View of the Hebrews*, first published seven years before the Book of Mormon, was probably a principal source—perhaps second only to the Bible—from which Smith and Cowdery, not Rigdon, formulated the Book of Mormon narrative. The similarities between the two works seem to be too substantial to be mere coincidence. The major thesis of each is to explain the origin of the American Indian. Chapters in each relate the destruction of Jerusalem and the scattering of Israel, then predict a regathering in the promised land. Vast portions of the Book of Isaiah are quoted extensively in each work (the Book of Mormon incorporates eighteen chapters nearly verbatim). Both discuss polygamy, seers and prophets, and the use of breastplates and Urim and Thummim. In each account, sacred records, handed down from generation to generation, are buried in a hill, then discovered years later. The characters inscribed on the gold plates of the Book of Mormon were reportedly "Reformed Egyptian" whereas *View of the Hebrews* discusses evidence of "Egyptian Hieroglyphics."

Perhaps the most important parallel is that both Ethan Smith's and Joseph Smith's works detail in similar fashion two classes of people in ancient America, one barbarous and the other civilized. Ethan Smith wrote that

> It is highly probably that the more civilized part of the tribes of Israel after they settled in America became wholly separated from the hunting and savage tribes of their brethren; that the latter lost the knowledge of their having descended from the same family with themselves; that the more civilized part continued for many centuries, that tremendeous wars were frequent between them and their savage brethren until the former became extinct. (!)
>
> This hypothesis accounts for the ancient works, forts, mounds, and vast enclosures as well as tokens of a good degree of civil government which are manifestly very ancient and for centuries before Columbus discovered America.[4]

Both authors identify American Indians as the "stick of Joseph or Ephraim" (the northern Ten Tribes of Israel) that are expected to be reunited with the "stick of Judah" (the Jews of the southern kingdom of Judah). Furthermore, each work defines the mission of the American (gentile) nation in the last days as a calling to gather these native American remnants of the House of Israel, convert them to Christianity, and bring them to the "place of the Lord of Hosts, the Mt. Zion."[5]

After years of intensive investigation into the Book of Mormon, particularly the possibility that much of the framework to *View of the Hebrews* can be seen in the Book of Mormon, B. H. Roberts in a 24 October 1927 letter asked, "Did Ethan Smith's *View of the Hebrews*, published . . . years before Joseph Smith's Book of Mormon, supply the Structural Outline and some of the Subject Matter of the Alleged Nephite Record?" After noting eighteen remarkable parallels between the two works, he commented that many others were just as "striking."[6] One of the principal conclusions of Roberts's work "Studies of the Book of Mormon" was that "it is more than likely that the Smith family possessed a copy of this book by Ethan Smith, that either by reading it, or hearing it read, and its contents frequently discussed, Joseph Smith became acquainted with its contents. . . . I say this with great confidence."[7]

Several theories suggest how the Smith family may have come in contact with the *View of the Hebrews*. Josiah Priest's *The Wonders of Nature and Providence, Displayed* (1825) contained extensive quotations from Ethan Smith's work. This book was available in the local Manchester Rental Library when Joseph Smith lived in the village.[8] Furthermore, Ethan Smith, possibly on a promotional tour for his book, was known to have visited Palmyra in late 1826 or early 1827. The

Wayne Sentinel on 31 December 1826 and 5 January 1827 posted his name for letters remaining in the Palmyra Post Office.

B. H. Roberts noted that when Ethan Smith wrote the work he was living in the next county, just fifty miles from where the Smiths had earlier lived in Sharon, Windsor County, Vermont.[9] Even if "the Smiths never owned the book, never read it, or saw it," Roberts speculated, "its contents—the materials of which it was composed—would be, under all the circumstances, matter of 'common knowledge' throughout the whole region where the Smiths lived from the birth of Joseph Smith in 1805, to the publication of the Book of Mormon in 1829-30."[10]

Roberts's investigations and conclusions, because of their controversial nature, were kept from the public eye until their publication in 1985, more than fifty years after Roberts's death. Since then additional research has provided a more complete understanding of the long-suspected relationship between the Book of Mormon and *View of the Hebrews*. Ethan Smith, born in 1762 in Belchertown, Massachusetts, like Solomon Spalding was a graduate of Dartmouth College. Their education at the New Hampshire school overlapped for the year 1786-87.[11] Ethan Smith's grandson recalled that "Solomon Spaulding was a warm admirer of Dr. Smith and when a young man studied under his tuition . . . and became interested in his theories regarding the settlement of America."[12] While none of Spalding's writings were published during his life, Ethan Smith was among the luminaries of New England literati.[13] *View of the Hebrews*, his best-known work, was published in Poultney, Vermont, where Oliver Cowdery, principal scribe during production of the Book of Mormon, also resided from 1803 to 1825.

At the time Ethan Smith was writing his volume, he was minister of Poultney's Congregational church where he served from 21 November 1821 until December 1826. Cowdery's stepmother and three of his sisters were members of the congregation, according to Poultney church records.[14] Presumably Oliver Cowdery, a school teacher and highly literate for his day, would have been familiar with his family minister's book. The first edition, which was advertised in the *Northern Spectator*, the local newspaper, quickly sold out.

Although it is speculative, young Cowdery may have been even employed by Smith & Shute, the Poultney firm that printed *View of the Hebrews*. The editor of the *Ashtabula* (Ohio) *Journal*, on 4 December 1830, commented that he knew Cowdery seven or eight years earlier, "when he was a dabbler in the art of Printing, and principally occupied in writing and printing pamphlets, with which as a pedestrian ped[d]ler, he visited the towns and villages of eastern N[ew] York, and Canada." Although the newspaper editor does not name any of the works Cowdery sold, it is possible he was a traveling agent for Smith & Shute and had copies of the 1823 edition of *View of the Hebrews* nestled in his knapsack when he visited his relatives the Smiths. This may explain why Joseph Smith's mother Lucy reported that in the fall of 1823, four years before her son began his work on the Book of Mormon, Joseph Jr. provided his family with

> some of the most amusing recitals that could be imagined. He would describe the ancient inhabitants of this continent, their dress, mode of traveling, and the animals upon which they rode; their cities, their buildings, with every particular; their mode of warfare; and also their religious worship. This he would do with as much ease, seemingly, as if he had spent his whole life among them.[15]

That Cowdery was unfamiliar with Ethan Smith or *View of the Hebrews* seems improbable. Precisely how this presumed acquaintance with Native American ethnological and theological speculation of the day impacted the Book of Mormon text is, of course, the subject of continuing examination.

Notes

1. Brigham H. Roberts, "The Origin of the Book of Mormon," *American Historical Magazine* 4 (Mar. 1909): 179-81, 196. In the original 1830 edition of the Book of Mormon Joseph Smith was designated "Author" on both the "Title Page" and "The Testimony of Eight Witnesses." These statements were later changed to read "Translator" in subsequent printings.

2. The most comprehensive summary of this topic is Dan Vogel, *Indian Origins and the Book of Mormon: Religious Solutions from Columbus to Joseph Smith* (Salt Lake City: Signature Books, 1986).

3. Brigham D. Madsen, ed., *B. H. Roberts's Studies of the Book of Mormon* (Urbana: University of Illinois Press, 1985), 153-54.

4. Ibid., 332. An excellent treatment of this subject is George D. Smith, "Joseph Smith and the Book of Mormon," *Free Inquiry* 4 (Winter 1983/84): 21-31.

5. Madsen, 323-44.

6. Ibid., 58-60. In 1923, B. H. Roberts warned LDS church president Heber J. Grant: "Maintenance of the truth of the Book of Mormon is absolutely essential to the integrity of the whole Mormon movement, for it is inconceivable the Book of Mormon should be untrue in its origin and character and the Church of Jesus Christ of Latter-day Saints to be a true church" (cover letter submitted with Roberts's published paper "A Book of Mormon Study," to the First Presidency, 15 Mar. 1923, in George D. Smith, "Defending the Keystone: Book of Mormon Difficulties," *Sunstone* 4 [May-June, 1981]: 45).

7. Madsen, 155.

8. David Persuitte, *Joseph Smith and the Origins of The Book of Mormon* (Jefferson, NC: McFarland & Co., 1991), 123.

9. Madsen, 155.

10. Ibid.

11. George T. Chapman, *Sketches of the Alumni of Dartmouth College* (Cambridge, MA: n.p., 1867), 39; Howe, 279; L. A. Smith, *Annals of the American Pulpit II*, ed. Wm. B. (Sprague, NY: n.p., 1866), 297.

12. Cleveland *Plain Dealer*, 24 Apr. 1887. Both Ethan Smith and Solomon Spalding

likely attended classes taught by fellow Congregationalist John Smith, professor of religion and languages at Dartmouth. William D. Morain, in his unpublished manuscript "The Sword of Laban: Joseph Smith, Jr., and the Unconscious," presents compelling evidence that in John Smith's extant lecture notes for his "Natural Philosophy" class he frequently lectured on possible origins of the American Indian.

13. A number of his sermons was printed during his lifetime. He also authored or edited several books, including A *Dissertation on the Prophecies relative to Anti-Christ and the Last Times* and *Memoirs of Mrs. Abigail Bailey* (Madsen, 27).

14. These significant records, discovered and photographed by David Persuitte in 1977, were in possession of the Poultney Historical Society. The originals have since been stolen (Persuitte, 7-8n270).

15. Preston Nibley, ed., *History of Joseph Smith by His Mother Lucy Mack Smith* (Salt Lake City: Bookcraft, 1958), 83.

3. SIDNEY RIGDON'S MARCH 1836 SERMON

On 24 August 1876, one month after Rigdon's death, the Pittsburgh Telegraph published an anonymous letter recounting an extraordinary mid-March 1836 sermon delivered by Rigdon at Meadville, Pennsylvania. In a 26 November 1881 letter to James T. Cobb, Robert Paterson, then the editor of Pittsburgh's Presbyterian Banner, identified the author of the letter as John Murdock (original in Mormon Collection, Chicago Historical Society). The letter to the editor reads:

I observed that several papers besides the TELEGRAPH notice the late Sydney Rigdon. Rigdon was a curious genius, more knave than fool. I will never forget the first and only time that I was ever in his company. A friend had purchased a farm upon Sugar Creek, Crawford county, who wished me to go up to Meadville for him, and have the title examined, and if all right, to make the first payment upon it. This was about the middle of March, 1836. While in Meadville flaming posters were placed all over the town stating that at a certain hour, at the Court House, Sydney Rigdon would deliver a discourse upon Mormonism and how Joe Smith became the Mormon prophet. Upon arriving at the Court House, I found myself somewhat late, as Mr. Rigdon was upon his feet and speaking. The audience was large, and he was telling it a wonderful rigmarole of an eagle arising in the East and flying to the West, and of the [rod] of Ephraim breaking the staff of Jacob, &c., when the people got restless and broke in with, "Mr. Rigdon, we want to hear all about the Mormon bible, and where Joe Smith got it."

This call brought Sydney to a stand still, when he said: "Well, I will tell you all about it. Joe Smith some few years previous was a poor boy who, to earn a living, herded cattle in Ontario county, New York. He was a good boy, and one day while herding cattle he fell into a trance, when the angel Gabriel appeared to him and told him that he was the chosen of God, appointed to be His prophet to reveal mysteries to the world that had been kept hidden to the present time, and for him to go to a particular spot, which he designated and dig, that he would there find a revelation from God, which he was to proclaim to the world. Joe, when he awoke, was so forcibly impressed with the heavenly vision that he started off directly for a mattock and shovel, and went to work at the place. After getting down about waist deep Joe came to a nice square stone box. The four sides and bottom were each eighteen inches square. The top was wider, projecting an inch or so over the sides, so as to throw off water. In the center was a large iron ring into which a man could comfortably put his hand. After clearing out all the earth from around it, Joe lay hold of the ring to pull it out and get it up; but there was no moving to it. Joe tugged and tugged and tugged (his exact words) but move it wouldn't. When he raised himself up out of the hole and threw himself down upon his face to wonder over its stubbornness, the fact came to his remembrance that the angel told him that he was to take up the box when he was exactly twenty-one years of age, and that that day he was only twenty. So Joe turned to and filled up the hole and carried back his shovel and hoe and waited another year with great patience, until the eventful hour arrived when he returned in full faith that he was now to receive a crown of rejoicing. The earth was again taken out of the hole, the box cleared off, and he again laid hold of the ring, when (with a graceful wave of his right hand, making a circle in the air, bringing it down past his face to his left side), it just came up like that.

When the box was once safe upon deck every one then was anxious to hear what was in it, when we were told that it contained fourteen gold plates, covered with mysterious characters, together with the sword of Gideon and the spectacles of Samuel the prophet! Joe, he said, was a very illiterate man, was unable either to read or write; but when he put on his nose the prophet's spectacles, and took the gold plates one by one, letter by letter and word by word presented themselves, and with the aid of an amanuensus the Bible that he held in his hand was [a] literal translation of the writing upon the gold plates.

As a good many were putting questions to Sydney, the Writer's question to him was, "Had he seen the contents of the mysterious box, and what kind of a sword was it that could be packed away in an eighteen inch box?" But Sydney had seen nothing. "But here," he said, turning to the back of the Bible, "are the sworn statements of those who have seen it." To the question, "What eventually became of the box?" we were told that Joe, after having had the mysteries that he was to proclaim translated into English, packed away everything again in the box and put it back where he got it.

As the programme stated that Sydney, like the Apostles of old, was to address us "in tongues," at this stage of the proceedings a sharp, little man to my right, in spectacles, who, I was afterwards told, was a Professor in Allegheny College, said, "Mr Rigdon, I believe you to be a good German and Greek scholar, and after you have spoken to us in those languages, I want you to speak to us in five or six other languages, giving a list of them." This proposition was a stumper which closed up poor Sydney, who, after looking all around him, declared us to be such a set of unbelievers that he wouldn't open his mouth to us again that day, and he sat down with his head upon his breast. Then a lawyer to my left, said to be called Potter, put his hand in his coat tail pocket and brought out a handful of shelled corn, which he flung all around Sydney's head and shoulders, but Sydney neither looked up nor moved. An old gentleman with a small Bible in his hand, called Col. Cochran, here arose, and after a word to the audience, pitched into Sydney. "To think," he said, "that a man who had once been a minister of God joining with an imposter to delude the simple and weakminded that he might be a big and looked up to man among them, is horrible!"

Sydney bore a long, excoriating address without ever looking up or speaking. I left him surrounded by a volunteer guard, who promised to see him off without letting him be mobbed. As Brigham Young has had a great many "latter day revelations," I thought that I would give you Joseph Smith's first one, as told by Sydney Rigdon.

4. THE SIDNEY RIGDON FAMILY IN NAUVOO

No contemporary account portrays the Sidney Rigdon family in richer detail than the 5 March 1843 letter of Charlotte Haven, later published in The Overland Monthly *(San Francisco) 16 (July-Dec. 1890). Describing her visit to the Rigdons' Nauvoo home, which also served as the post office, Haven wrote:*

We enter a side door leading into the kitchen, and in a corner near the door is a wide shelf or table, on which against the wall is a sort of cupboard with pigeon-holes or boxes—this is the post-office. In this room, with the great cooking stove at one end, the family eat and sit. Mrs. R[igdon] when I go for the mail always invites me to stop and rest, which after a cold, long walk I am glad to do, thus opening an acquaintance with Elder Sidney Rigdon, the most learned man among the Latter Day Saints. He is past fifty and is somewhat bald and his dark hair slightly gray. He has an intelligent countenance, a courteous manner, and speaks grammatically. He talks very pleasantly about his travels in this country and Europe, but is very reticent about his religion. I have heard it stated that he was Smith's chief aid in getting up the Book of Mormon and creed. He is so far above

Smith in intellect; education, and secretiveness, that there is scarcely a doubt that he is at the head in compiling it. I looked over his library—on some book-shelves in the kitchen. It was a very good student's collection,—Hebrew, Greek, and Latin lexicons and readers, stray volumes of Shakespeare, Scott, Irving's works, and a number of other valuable books. He studied for the ministry in his youth, then was employed in a newspaper office. His wife is always busy with domestic labor. They have five daughters.

The only party I have attended in this Holy City was at their house. Here is a copy of the invitation. You will observe the date was a year ago. However, we concluded it was a slight mistake, as the Judge received an invitation somehow with this year's date.

> NAUVOO Feb 20 1842
>> The company of Mr Mrs and Miss Haven is Solicited to attend a party at the house of Mr Rigdon on Thursday the 24 inst at three oclock P M
>> Sarah Rigdon
>> Eliza Rigdon

The judge called me, and we trudged off. We were met at the P.O. door by Miss Sarah; her mother, who was paring potatoes near the stove, came forward, the venerable Elder stood behind the cook stove (which was in full operation) dressed in his Sunday best suit, the highest and stiffest shirt collar, and a white neckerchief with ends flowing over his shoulders.

. . . Leaving my escort in the kitchen, I was ushered into the next room—where lo! there was a large quilting frame, around which sat eight of the belles of Nauvoo, to each of whom I was introduced, then a seat was assigned me near the head of the frame, and equipped with needle, thread, and thimble, I quilted with the rest. But not a word was said, and fearing my presence had checked hilarity, I offered a few kindly remarks, only to be answered with "Yes, Marm," or "No, Marm." It was quite embarrassing, when my next neighbor timidly whispered, "We talk in the evening."

So I was stilled and put all my energy on the quilt, which was finished and taken out of the frame by six o'clock. The door to the kitchen or living room was then thrown open and we were ushered in. The scene, how changed! Through the whole length of the room from the post-office to the stove, a table extended, loaded with a substantial supper, turkey, chicken, beef, vegetables, pies, cake, etc. To this we did silence justice.

Leaving the family to clear away, we young people returned to the other room and placed ourselves like wall-flowers. Gentlemen soon came in in groups, and when all were assembled, Mr. Rigdon came in, shook hands with the gentlemen, then placed himself in the middle of the room, and taking a gentleman by his side, commenced introductions, "Mr. Monroe,—Miss Burnett, my daughter, Miss

Marks, Miss Ives, my daughter, Miss Ivens, Miss Bemis, my daughter from La Harpe, Miss Haven, my daughter."

Mr. Monroe retires and another gentleman is called up and the ceremony repeated, until all the strangers had been introduced. Then Mr. R. says, "Is there any other gentleman who has not been introduced?" when a Mr. Ives came forward and pointing with his finger, "I have not been introduced to that lady (Miss Haven) and that (Miss Bemis)."

This ceremony over, all seemed more joyous; songs were sung, concluding with the two little girls singing several verses of the Battle of Michigan, deaconed out to them line by line by their elder sister, Miss Nancy. Then followed an original dance *without music*, commencing with marching and ending with *kissing!* Merry games were then introduced, The Miller, Grab, etc., not at all of an intellectual order; so I suggested Fox and Geese, which was in vogue with us ten years ago. It took well. Brother says he called at the office during the evening, and the Elder was urging his wife to look in upon the young people. He heard him say that he had been half over the world but never had seen anything equal to this in enjoyment. At nine o'clock we went out to a second edition of supper, and then the games were renewed with vigor. We left about ten. The Miss Rigdons, who called on us the next day, said the party did not break up till twelve.

5. "SIDNEY ON THE BRAIN"

Although Joseph and Emma Smith's youngest son, David Hyrum (born after his father's death), never met Sidney Rigdon, he wrote the following satirical ditty sometime in the mid-1860s after the Reorganized Church of Jesus Christ of Latter Day Saints was founded. This original is housed in the Wilford Wood Collection, Bountiful, Utah (courtesy Buddy Youngreen).

SIDNEY ON THE BRAIN

Of all the sickness I have seen,
To plague mankind with torment mean,
The latest thing that has come out,
Is what I now will sing about.
The very worst malady could befall
A saint to give them pain,
This very bad malady we might call,
The Sidney on the brain.

The way this evil first begins,
Is talking of the Prophets sins,
And telling how he went astray,
From out the long and narrow way.
Then give the covenants a little twist,
To make the matter plain;
For this the funniest symptom is,
Of Sidney on the brain.

And then again, they try to show,
That Joseph is a boy you know,
And knows not what he is about,
Lo, is not fit to lead us out.
Unto his promises give no heed,
Why you can see it plain,
For are not we all of Joseph's seed.
With Sidney on the brain.

Sometimes they try to tell us of
The Lord and Jesus Christ above
And Holy Ghost the wondrous three.
The great and mighty trinity,
That we had a trinity here below
Why don't you see it plain,
Since two are lying in the grave we now
Have Sidney on the brain.

The next good thing they treat us to,
A revelation fresh and new,
Which tells of Sidney this strange thing
That he of Zion is the King.
Is it not written that upon that land
No King but Christ shall reign
But try to swallow for your pipes expand
If Sidney's on the brain.

The remedy I now will tell,
Ap[p]ly it, it will answer well,
Turn right about upon your track,
Shake mister Sidney from your back.
And then you will imitate Joseph Smith

And make the matter plain.
Or kick the bucket and perish with,
Your Sidney on the brain.

6. SIDNEY RIGDON AND THE BICKERTONITES

Sidney Rigdon's Church of Jesus Christ of the Children of Zion disintegrated within a decade after his death. And both the Church of Jesus Christ of Latter-day Saints and the Reorganized Church of Jesus Christ of Latter Day Saints ultimately relegated him to footnote status when their official histories were written. But the Church of Jesus Christ, a small sect organized in 1862 by William Bickerton, still venerates Rigdon.

Bickerton, an 1845 convert to Sidney Rigdon's Church of Christ, found himself adrift after Rigdon's failures in Pittsburgh and the Cumberland Valley. For a brief period in the early 1850s Bickerton affiliated with a branch of the Utah Mormons at West Elizabeth, Pennsylvania, although he personally declared that "his testimony . . . is that the blessings he received came thr[o]u[gh] obedience to the restored Gospel in 1845 with Rigdon's people."[1]

After the Utah church publicly announced its long-term practice of polygamy in 1852, Bickerton left that organization. In 1854 he held a successful conference in West Elizabeth at which several persons were baptized. By 1858 he had attained a following of nearly 100 persons and had organized them into branches in Wheeling, West Virginia; Pine Run, Allegheny; and Greenock, Pennsylvania.

In an 1859 conference Bickerton was acknowledged as a prophet by his followers. Two years later he was sustained a "Prophet and President of the Church" with counselors Charles Brown and George Barnes. During a July 1862 conference at Greenock twelve apostles and a number of evangelists were ordained. The church was also officially organized during this conference although not legally incorporated until 10 June 1865.

The church, which maintains its world headquarters today at Monongahela, Pennsylvania, at last report numbered 10,000 members. The current First Presidency is Dominic Thomas, Paul Palmieri, and Robert Watson. The church is organized into seven districts in the U.S. and has missions in Canada, Mexico, Guatemala, Kenya, Ghana, Nigeria, India, England, Italy, Holland , and Germany.

Note

1. Charles Ashton, Alma B. Cadman, William H. Cadman, *A Brief History of the Origin of the Church of Jesus Christ with Headquarters at Monongahela, Pennsylvania* (Monongahela, PA: The Ladies Uplift Circle, 1947), 4.

Index